THE
MINISTER'S MANUAL

SEVENTY-EIGHTH ANNUAL ISSUE

THE MINISTER'S MANUAL 2003

Edited by

JAMES W. COX

JOSSEY-BASS
A Wiley Company
www.josseybass.com

Editors of THE MINISTER'S MANUAL
G. B. F. Hallock, D.D., 1926–1958
M. K. W. Heicher, Ph.D., 1943–1968
Charles L. Wallis, M.A., M.Div., 1969–1983
James W. Cox, M.Div., Ph.D.

Translations of the Bible referred to and quoted from in this book may be indicated by their standard abbreviations, such as NRSV (New Revised Standard Version) and NIV (New International Version). In addition, some contributors have made their own translations and others have used a mixed text.

Jossey-Bass is a registered trademark of John Wiley & Sons, Inc.

Jossey-Bass books and products are available through most bookstores. To contact Jossey-Bass directly, call (888) 378-2537, fax to (800) 605-2665, or visit our website at www.josseybass.com.

Substantial discounts on bulk quantities of Jossey-Bass books are available to corporations, professional associations, and other organizations. For details and discount information, contact the special sales department at Jossey-Bass.

We at Jossey-Bass strive to use the most environmentally sensitive paper stocks available to us. Our publications are printed on acid-free recycled stock whenever possible, and our paper always meets or exceeds minimum GPO and EPA requirements.

Jossey-Bass also publishes its books in a variety of electronic formats. Some content that appears in print may not be available in electronic books.

Library of Congress Cataloging Card Number

25-21658
ISSN 0738-5323
ISBN 0-7879-6099-3

FIRST EDITION
HB Printing
10 9 8 7 6 5 4 3 2 1

CONTENTS

PREFACE

The Minister's Manual 2003 presents sermonic contributions from a wide range of preachers, teachers, and writers. They come from many geographical, denominational, and theological backgrounds. I am convinced that although they do not always agree on every issue, they speak responsibly and their thoughts deserve careful consideration. They share our common faith and enrich our personal understanding and devotion. Nevertheless, they speak for themselves, and their views do not necessarily represent those of the publisher, the editor, or the Southern Baptist Theological Seminary.

I owe thanks to Carol M. Norén, professor of homiletics at North Park Theological Seminary, Chicago. She has made valuable contributions of her own to *The Minister's Manual* over the past few years and has enlisted a number of other contributors of unusual merit.

I am grateful to the seminary, where I have taught since 1959, for providing valuable secretarial assistance in producing the manuscript. I wish to thank especially Linda Durkin and Roberta Knudson for their faithful and efficient assistance. I also wish to thank the authors and publishers from whose works I have quoted. It is hoped that the rights and wishes of no one have been overlooked. Again, I am deeply grateful.

James W. Cox
The Southern Baptist Theological Seminary

SECTION I

GENERAL AIDS AND RESOURCES

CIVIL YEAR CALENDARS FOR 2003 AND 2004

2003

January	February	March	April
S M T W T F S	S M T W T F S	S M T W T F S	S M T W T F S
1 2 3 4	1	1	1 2 3 4 5
5 6 7 8 9 10 11	2 3 4 5 6 7 8	2 3 4 5 6 7 8	6 7 8 9 10 11 12
12 13 14 15 16 17 18	9 10 11 12 13 14 15	9 10 11 12 13 14 15	13 14 15 16 17 18 19
19 20 21 22 23 24 25	16 17 18 19 20 21 22	16 17 18 19 20 21 22	20 21 22 23 24 25 26
26 27 28 29 30 31	23 24 25 26 27 28	23 24 25 26 27 28 29	27 28 29 30
		30 31	

May	June	July	August
S M T W T F S	S M T W T F S	S M T W T F S	S M T W T F S
1 2 3	1 2 3 4 5 6 7	1 2 3 4 5	1 2
4 5 6 7 8 9 10	8 9 10 11 12 13 14	6 7 8 9 10 11 12	3 4 5 6 7 8 9
11 12 13 14 15 16 17	15 16 17 18 19 20 21	13 14 15 16 17 18 19	10 11 12 13 14 15 16
18 19 20 21 22 23 24	22 23 24 25 26 27 28	20 21 22 23 24 25 26	17 18 19 20 21 22 23
25 26 27 28 29 30 31	29 30	27 28 29 30 31	24 25 26 27 28 29 30
			31

September	October	November	December
S M T W T F S	S M T W T F S	S M T W T F S	S M T W T F S
1 2 3 4 5 6	1 2 3 4	1	1 2 3 4 5 6
7 8 9 10 11 12 13	5 6 7 8 9 10 11	2 3 4 5 6 7 8	7 8 9 10 11 12 13
14 15 16 17 18 19 20	12 13 14 15 16 17 18	9 10 11 12 13 14 15	14 15 16 17 18 19 20
21 22 23 24 25 26 27	19 20 21 22 23 24 25	16 17 18 19 20 21 22	21 22 23 24 25 26 27
28 29 30	26 27 28 29 30 31	23 24 25 26 27 28 29	28 29 30 31
		30	

2004

January	February	March	April
S M T W T F S	S M T W T F S	S M T W T F S	S M T W T F S
1 2 3	1 2 3 4 5 6 7	1 2 3 4 5 6	1 2 3
4 5 6 7 8 9 10	8 9 10 11 12 13 14	7 8 9 10 11 12 13	4 5 6 7 8 9 10
11 12 13 14 15 16 17	15 16 17 18 19 20 21	14 15 16 17 18 19 20	11 12 13 14 15 16 17
18 19 20 21 22 23 24	22 23 24 25 26 27 28	21 22 23 24 25 26 27	18 19 20 21 22 23 24
25 26 27 28 29 30 31	29	28 29 30 31	25 26 27 28 29 30

May	June	July	August
S M T W T F S	S M T W T F S	S M T W T F S	S M T W T F S
1	1 2 3 4 5	1 2 3	1 2 3 4 5 6 7
2 3 4 5 6 7 8	6 7 8 9 10 11 12	4 5 6 7 8 9 10	8 9 10 11 12 13 14
9 10 11 12 13 14 15	13 14 15 16 17 18 19	11 12 13 14 15 16 17	15 16 17 18 19 20 21
16 17 18 19 20 21 22	20 21 22 23 24 25 26	18 19 20 21 22 23 24	22 23 24 25 26 27 28
23 24 25 26 27 28 29	27 28 29 30	25 26 27 28 29 30 31	29 30 31
30 31			

September	October	November	December
S M T W T F S	S M T W T F S	S M T W T F S	S M T W T F S
1 2 3 4	1 2	1 2 3 4 5 6	1 2 3 4
5 6 7 8 9 10 11	3 4 5 6 7 8 9	7 8 9 10 11 12 13	5 6 7 8 9 10 11
12 13 14 15 16 17 18	10 11 12 13 14 15 16	14 15 16 17 18 19 20	12 13 14 15 16 17 18
19 20 21 22 23 24 25	17 18 19 20 21 22 23	21 22 23 24 25 26 27	19 20 21 22 23 24 25
26 27 28 29 30	24 25 26 27 28 29 30	28 29 30	26 27 28 29 30 31
	31		

Church and Civic Calendar for 2003

January

1	New Year's Day
5	Twelfth Night
6	Epiphany
10	League of Nations anniversary
13	Baptism of the Lord
17	St. Anthony's Day
20	Martin Luther King Jr.'s birthday, observed
25	Conversion of St. Paul

February

1	National Freedom Day
2	Presentation of Jesus in the Temple
9	Race Relations Sunday
12	Lincoln's Birthday
14	St. Valentine's Day
17	Presidents' Day
22	Washington's Birthday
24	St. Matthias, Apostle

March

4	Shrove Tuesday
5	Ash Wednesday
9	First Sunday in Lent
16	Second Sunday in Lent
17	St. Patrick's Day
18	Purim
23	Third Sunday in Lent
25	The Annunciation
30	Fourth Sunday in Lent

April

6	Fifth Sunday in Lent
13	Passion Sunday
	Palm Sunday
13–19	Holy Week
17	Maundy Thursday
18	Good Friday
20	Easter
25	St. Mark, Evangelist
27	Law Sunday

May

1	May Day
	Law Day
	Loyalty Day
	St. Philip and St. James, Apostles
1–5	Cinco de Mayo Celebration
4–11	National Family Week
11	Mother's Day
26	Memorial Day, observed
29	Ascension Day

June

6	Shavuot
9	Pentecost
	Children's Sunday
11	St. Barnabas, Apostle
15	Trinity Sunday
	Father's Day
22	Corpus Christi
24	St. John the Baptist
29	St. Peter and St. Paul, Apostles

July

1	Canada Day
4	Independence Day
22	St. Mary Magdalene
25	St. James, the Elder, Apostle

August

4	Civic Holiday (Canada)
14	Atlantic Charter Day
15	Mary, Mother of Jesus
24	St. Bartholomew, Apostle
26	Women's Equality Day

September

1	Labor Day
21	St. Matthew, Evangelist and Apostle
27	Rosh Hashanah (Jewish New Year)
29	St. Michael and All Angels

October

5	World Communion Sunday
6	Yom Kippur
11	First Day of Sukkoth
13	Columbus Day, observed
18	St. Luke, Evangelist
23	St. James, Brother of Jesus
24	United Nations Day
31	Reformation Day
	National UNICEF Day

November

1	All Saints' Day
2	All Souls' Day
9	Stewardship Day
11	Veterans Day
	Armistice Day
	Remembrance Day (Canada)
16	Bible Sunday

27	Thanksgiving Day
30	First Sunday of Advent
	St. Andrew, Apostle

December

7	Second Sunday of Advent
14	Third Sunday of Advent
15	Bill of Rights Day
20	First Day of Hanukkah
21	Fourth Sunday of Advent
25	Christmas
26	Boxing Day (Canada)
	St. Stephen, Deacon and Martyr
27	St. John, Evangelist and Apostle
28	The Holy Innocents, Martyrs
31	New Year's Eve
	Watch Night

The Revised Common Lectionary for 2003

The following Scripture lessons are commended for use by various Protestant churches and the Roman Catholic Church and include first, second, and Gospel readings, and Psalms, according to cycle B from January 5 to November 23 and according to cycle C from November 30 to December 28.[1]

Jan. 5: Jer. 31:7–14; Ps. 147:12–20; Eph. 1:3–14; John 1:(1–9) 10–18

Epiphany Season

Jan. 6: Isa. 60:1–6; Ps. 72:1–7, 10–14; Eph. 3:1–12; Matt. 2:1–12
Jan. 12: Gen. 1:1–5; Ps. 29; Acts 19:1–7; Mark 1:4–11
Jan. 19: 1 Sam. 3:1–10 (11–20); Ps. 139:1–6, 13–18; 1 Cor. 6:12–20; John 1:43–51
Jan. 26: Jonah 3:1–5, 10; Ps. 62:5–12; 1 Cor. 7:29–31; Mark 1:14–20
Feb. 2: Deut. 18:15–20; Ps. 111; 1 Cor. 8:1–13; Mark 1:21–28
Feb. 9: Isa. 40:21–31; Ps. 147:1–11, 20c; 1 Cor. 9:16–23; Mark 1:29–39
Feb. 16: 2 Kings 5:1–14; Ps. 30; 1 Cor. 9:24–27; Mark 1:40–45
Feb. 23: Isa. 43:18–25; Ps. 41; 2 Cor. 1:18–22; Mark 2:1–12
Mar. 2: 2 Kings 2:1–12; Ps. 50:1–6; 2 Cor. 4:3–6; Mark 9:2–9

Lenten Season

Mar. 5 (Ash Wednesday): Joel 2:1–2, 12–17; Ps. 51:1–17; 2 Cor. 5:20b–6:10; Matt. 6:1–6, 16–21

---

[1]Copyright 1992, Consultation on Common Texts

Mar. 9 (Lent 1): Gen. 9:8–17; Ps. 25:1–10; 1 Pet. 3:18–22; Mark 1:9–15

Mar. 16: Gen. 17:1–7, 15–16; Ps. 22:23–31; Rom. 4:13–25; Mark 8:31–38

Mar. 23: Exod. 20:1–17; Ps. 19; 1 Cor. 1:18–25; John 2:13–22

Mar. 30: Num. 21:4–9; Ps. 107:1–3, 17–22; Eph. 2:1–10; John 3:14–21

Apr. 6: Jer. 31:31–34; Ps. 51:1–12; Heb. 5:5–10; John 12:20–23

Holy Week

Apr. 13 (Passion/Palm Sunday): Liturgy of the Palms: Mark 11:1–11; Ps. 118:1–2, 19–29; Liturgy of the Passion: Isa. 50:4–9a; Ps. 31:9–16; Phil. 2:5–11; Mark 14:1–15:47

Easter Season

Apr. 14 (Monday): Isa. 42:1–9; Ps. 36:5–11; Heb. 9:11–15; John 12:1–11

Apr. 15 (Tuesday): Isa. 49:1–7; Ps. 71:1–14; 1 Cor. 1:18–31; John 12:20–36

Apr. 16 (Wednesday): Isa. 50:4–9a; Ps. 70; Heb. 12:1–3; John 13:21–32

Apr. 17 (Holy Thursday): Exod. 12:1–4 (5–10), 11–14; Ps. 116:1–2, 12–19; 1 Cor. 11:23–26; John 13:1–7, 31b–35

Apr. 18 (Good Friday): Isa. 52:13–53:12; Ps. 22; Heb. 10:16–25; John 18:1–19:42

Apr. 19 (Holy Saturday): Job 14:1–14; Ps. 31:1–4, 15–16; 1 Pet. 4:1–8; Matt. 27:57–66

Apr. 19 (Easter Vigil): Gen. 1:1–2:4a; Ps. 136:1–9, 23–26; Gen. 7:1–5, 11–18; 8:6–18; 9:8–13; Ps. 46; Gen. 22:1–18; Ps. 16; Exod. 14:10–31; 15:20–21; Exod. 15:1b–13, 17–18 (resp.); Isa. 55:1–11; Isa.12:2–6 (resp.); Prov. 8:1–8, 19–21; 9:4b–6 (alt.); Ps. 19; Ezek. 36:24–28; Ps. 42–43; Ezek. 37:1–14; Ps. 143; Zeph. 3:14–20; Ps. 98; Rom. 6:3–11; Ps. 114; Mark 16:1–8

Apr. 20 (Easter): Acts 10:34–43; Ps. 118:1–2, 14–24; 1 Cor. 15:1–11; John 20:1–18

Apr. 27: Acts 4:32–35; Ps. 133; 1 John 1:1–2:2; John 20:19–31

May 4: Acts 3:12–19; Ps. 4; 1 John 3:1–7; Luke 24:36b–48

May 11: Acts 4:5–12; Ps. 23; 1 John 3:16–24; John 10:11–18

May 18: Acts 8:26–40; Ps. 22:25–31; 1 John 4:7–21; John 15:1–8

May 25: Acts 10:44–48; Ps. 98; 1 John 5:1–6; John 15:9–17

June 1: Acts 1:15–17, 21–26; Ps. 1; 1 John 5:9–13; John 17:6–19; Ps. 47; Eph. 1:15–23; Luke 24:44–53

Season of Pentecost

June 8 (Pentecost): Ezek. 37:1–14 or Acts 2:1–21; Ps. 104:24–34, 35b; Rom. 8:22–27; John 15:26–27; 16:4b–15

June 15 (Trinity): Isa. 6:1–8; Ps. 29; Rom. 8:12–17; John 3:1–17

June 22: 1 Sam. 17:(1a, 4–11, 19–23) 32–49; Ps. 9:9–20, 133; 2 Cor. 6:1–13; Mark 4:35–41

June 29: 2 Sam. 1:1, 17–27; Ps. 130; 2 Cor. 8:7–15; Mark 5:21–43

July 6: 2 Sam. 5:1–5, 9–10; Ps. 48; 2 Cor. 12:2–10; Mark 6:1–13

July 13: 2 Sam. 6:1–5, 12b–19; Ps. 24; Eph. 1:3–14; Mark 6:14–29

July 20: 2 Sam. 7:1–14a; Ps. 89:20–37; Eph. 2:11–22; Mark 6:30–34, 53–56

July 27: 2 Sam. 11:1–15; Ps. 14; Eph. 3:14–21; John 6:1–21

Aug. 3: 2 Sam. 11: 26–12:13a; Ps. 51:1–12; Eph. 4:1–16; John 6:24–35

Aug. 10: 2 Sam. 18:5–9, 15, 31–33; Ps. 130; Eph. 4:25–5:2; John 6:35, 41–51

Aug. 17: 1 Kings 2:10–12; 3:3–14; Ps. 111; Eph. 5:15–20; John 6:51–58

Aug. 24: 1 Kings 8:(1, 6, 10–11) 22–30, 41–43; Ps. 84; Eph. 6:10–20; John 6:56–69

Aug. 31: Song of Solomon 2:8–13; Ps. 45:1–2, 6–9; James 1:17–27; Mark 7:1–8, 14–15, 21–23

Sept. 7: Prov. 22:1–2, 8–9, 22–23; Ps. 125; James 2:1–10 (11–13), 14–17; Mark 7:24–37

Sept. 14: Prov. 1:20–33; Ps. 19; James 3:1–12; Mark 8:27–38

Sept. 21: Prov. 31:10–31; Ps. 1; James 3:13–4:3, 7–8a; Mark 9:30–37

Sept. 28: Esther 7:1–6, 9–10; 9:20–22; Ps. 124; James 5:13–20; Mark 9:38–50

Oct. 5: Job 1:1; 2:1–10; Ps. 26; Heb. 1:1–4; 2:5–12; Mark 10:2–16

Oct. 12: Job 23:1–9, 16–17; Ps. 22:1–15; Heb. 4:12–16; Mark 10:17–31

Oct. 19: Job 38:1–7 (34–41); Ps. 104:1–9, 24, 35c; Heb. 5:1–10; Mark 10:35–45

Oct. 26: Job 42:1–6, 10–17; Ps. 34:1–8 (19–22); Heb. 7:23–28; Mark 10:46–52

Nov. 2: Ruth 1:1–18; Ps. 146; Heb. 9:11–14; Mark 12:28–34

Nov. 9: Ruth 3:1–5; 4:13–17; Ps. 127; Heb. 9:24–28; Mark 12:38–44

Nov. 16: 1 Sam. 1:4–20; Ps. 16; Heb. 10:11–14 (15–18), 19–25, Mark 13:1–8

Nov. 23 (Christ the King): 2 Sam. 23:1–7; Ps. 132:1–12 (13–18); Rev. 1:4b–8; John 18:33–37

Advent and Christmas Season

Nov. 30 (Advent): Jer. 33:14–16; Ps. 25:1–10; 1 Thess. 3:9–13; Luke 21:25–36

Dec. 7: Mal. 3:1–4; Luke 1:68–79; 3:1–6; Phil. 1:3–11

Dec. 14: Zeph. 3:14–20; Isa. 12:2–6; Phil. 4:4–7; Luke 3:7–18

Dec. 21: Mic. 5:2–5a; Luke 1:39–55; Heb. 10:5–10

Dec. 25 (Christmas Day): Isa. 9:2–7; Ps. 96; Titus 2:11–14; Luke 2:1–14 (15–20) or Isa. 62:6–12; Ps. 97; Titus 3:4–7; Luke 2:(1–7) 8–20 or Isa. 52:7–10; Ps. 98; Heb. 1:1–4 (5–12); John 1:1–14

Dec. 28: 1 Sam. 2:18–20, 26; Ps. 148; Col. 3:12–17; Luke 2:41–52

Four-Year Church Calendar

	2003	2004	2005	2006
Ash Wednesday	March 5	February 25	February 9	March 1
Palm Sunday	April 13	April 4	March 20	April 9
Good Friday	April 18	April 9	March 25	April 14
Easter	April 20	April 11	March 27	April 16
Ascension Day	May 29	May 20	May 5	May 25
Pentecost	June 8	May 30	May 15	June 4
Trinity Sunday	June 15	June 6	May 22	June 11
Thanksgiving	November 27	November 25	November 24	November 23
Advent Sunday	November 30	November 28	November 27	December 3

Forty-Year Easter Calendar

2003 April 20	2007 April 8	2011 April 24	2015 April 5
2004 April 11	2008 March 23	2012 April 8	2016 March 27
2005 March 27	2009 April 12	2013 March 31	2017 April 16
2006 April 16	2010 April 4	2014 April 20	2018 April 1

2019 April 21	2025 April 20	2031 April 13	2037 April 5
2020 April 12	2026 April 5	2032 March 28	2038 April 25
2021 April 4	2027 March 28	2033 April 17	2039 April 10
2022 April 17	2028 April 16	2034 April 9	2040 April 1
2023 April 9	2029 April 1	2035 March 25	2041 April 2
2024 March 31	2030 April 21	2036 April 13	2042 April 6

Traditional Wedding Anniversary Identifications

1 Paper	7 Wool	13 Lace	35 Coral
2 Cotton	8 Bronze	14 Ivory	40 Ruby
3 Leather	9 Pottery	15 Crystal	45 Sapphire
4 Linen	10 Tim	20 China	50 Gold
5 Wood	11 Steel	25 Silver	55 Emerald
6 Iron	12 Silk	30 Pearl	60 Diamond

Colors Appropriate for Days and Seasons

White. Symbolizes purity, perfection, and joy and identifies festivals marking events in the life of Jesus, except Good Friday: Christmas, Epiphany, Easter, Eastertide, Ascension Day; also Trinity Sunday, All Saints' Day, weddings, funerals. Gold may also be used.

Red. Symbolizes the Holy Spirit, martyrdom, and the love of God: Good Friday, Pentecost, and Sundays following.

Violet. Symbolizes penitence: Advent, Lent.

Green. Symbolizes mission to the world, hope, regeneration, nurture, and growth: Epiphany season, Kingdomtide, Rural Life Sunday, Labor Sunday, Thanksgiving Sunday.

Blue. Advent, in some churches.

Flowers in Season Appropriate for Church Use

January: carnation or snowdrop	July: larkspur or water lily
February: violet or primrose	August: gladiolus or poppy
March: jonquil or daffodil	September: aster or morning star
April: lily, sweet pea, or daisy	October: calendula or cosmos
May: lily of the valley or hawthorn	November: chrysanthemum
June: rose or honeysuckle	December: narcissus, holly, or poinsettia

Quotable Quotations

1. We can offer up much in the large, but to make sacrifices in little things is what we are seldom equal to.—Johann Wolfgang Von Goethe
2. Whoever marries the spirit of this age will find himself a widower in the next. —W. R. Inge
3. The best practical advice I can give to the present generation is to practice the virtue which the Christians call love.—Bertrand Russell
4. Alms are but the vehicles of prayer.—John Dryden

5. Never work before breakfast; if you have to work before breakfast, eat your breakfast first.—Josh Billings

6. Bigotry tries to keep truth safe in its hand with a grip that kills it.—Rabindranath Tagore

7. The slanderous tongue kills three: the slandered, the slanderer, and him who listens to the slander.—The Talmud

8. One thing stirs me when I look back at my youthful days: the fact that so many people gave me something or were something to me without knowing it.—Albert Schweitzer

9. Holiness consists of doing the will of God with a smile.—Mother Teresa of Calcutta

10. The created world is but a small parenthesis in eternity.—Sir Thomas Browne

11. There was a time when a fool and his money were soon parted, but now it happens to everybody.—Adlai Stevenson

12. I wish you could convince yourself that God is often nearer to us, and more effectually present with us, in sickness than in health.—Brother Lawrence, *The Practice of the Presence of God*

13. The innkeeper loves the drunkard, but not for a son-in-law.—Jewish proverb

14. The vocation of every man and woman is to serve other people.—Les Tolstoy

15. It is better to be hated for what you are than loved for what you are not.—André Gide

16. Bad men excuse their faults; good men will leave them.—Ben Johnson

17. If every gnat that flies were an archangel, all that could but tell me that there is a God, and the poorest worm that creeps tells me that.—John Donne

18. Every man should keep a fair-sized cemetery in which to bury the faults of his friends.—Henry Ward Beecher

19. If we had no faults, we should not take so much pleasure in noting those of others. —La Rochefoucauld

20. I have no pleasure in any man who despises music. It is no invention of ours; it is the gift of God. I place it next to theology.—Martin Luther

21. A religion without mystery must be a religion without God.—Jeremy Taylor

22. In time of desolation one should never make a change, but stand firm in the resolutions and decisions that guided him the day before the desolation.—St. Ignatius of Loyola

23. The true test of sincere love is not positive emotions and good intentions, but tangible actions.—John MacArthur

24. Nothing is more unpleasant than a virtuous person with a mean mind.—Walter Bagehot

25. Miracles are God's signature, appended to his masterpiece of creation.—Ronald Knox

26. Home is the place where, when you have to go there, they have to take you in.— Robert Frost

27. An infatuated young man sought counsel at the bazaar of an ancient and prayed the ancient to tell him how he might learn of his fair lady's faults. "Go forth among her women friends," spake the venerable one, "and praise her in their hearing."— George Jean Nathan

28. I don't believe in heroes, heroic deeds are chance. The hero is the person who has the courage to make a good thing of his whole life.—Georges Simenon
29. A religion that is small enough for our understanding is not great enough for our need.—A. J. Balfour
30. A great man stands on God. A small man stands on a great man.—Ralph Waldo Emerson
31. There is not enough darkness in all the world to put out the light of even one small candle.—Robert Alden
32. Through faith man experiences the meaning of the world; through action he is to give to it a meaning.—Leo Baeck
33. A human act once set in motion flows on forever to the great account.—George Meredith
34. Life, we learn too late, is in the living, in the tissue of every day and hour.—Stephen Leacock
35. It is not the sins that damn but the sin into which sins settle down.—P. T. Forsyth
36. We have fewer friends than we imagine, but more than we know.—Hugo Von Hofmannsthal
37. Nervous breakdowns are hereditary. We get them from our children.—Graffito
38. What the mother sings to the cradle goes all the way down to the coffin.—Henry Ward Beecher
39. Moderation is the silken string running through the pearl chain of all virtues.—Thomas Fuller
40. I would rather live in a world where my life is surrounded by mystery than to live in a world so small that my mind could comprehend it.—Harry Emerson Fosdick
41. No one can make you feel inferior without your consent.—Eleanor Roosevelt
42. There is nothing that makes us love a man so much as praying for him.—William Law
43. If the world is really the medium of God's personal action, miracle is wholly normal.—D. Elton Trueblood
44. The universe begins to look more like a great thought than like a great machine.—Sir James Jeans
45. The elect are whosoever will, and the nonelect, whosoever won't.—Henry Ward Beecher
46. Men never do evil so completely and cheerfully as when they do it from religious conviction.—Blaise Pascal
47. Many a man in love with a dimple makes the mistake of marrying the whole girl.—Stephen Leacock
48. I've developed a new philosophy—I only dread one day at a time.—Charles M. Schulz
49. One is never so easily fooled as when one thinks one is fooling others.—La Rochefoucauld
50. The only known cure for fear is faith.—William S. Sadler
51. There are people who are always anticipating trouble, and in this way they manage to enjoy many sorrows that never really happen to them.—Josh Billings

52. Irreligion, when it is radical and complete, involves disbelief in life itself—its spiritual source, its ultimate meaning, its undergirding purpose, its eternal value.—Harry Emerson Fosdick

Questions of Life and Religion

1. How is baptism related to our faith?
2. Does suffering bring God's love into question?
3. When, if ever, is it right to be angry?
4. Does obedience guarantee abundant life?
5. What is Jesus' remedy for anxiety?
6. How are belief and faith different?
7. What can we do for people going through a time of bereavement?
8. In what sense is the Bible the Word of God?
9. Can we be certain about our salvation and standing with God?
10. How is character formed?
11. How can adults be good models for children?
12. How are works of charity related to the Christian life?
13. What factors figure into the choices we make?
14. Does any individual have to be bad?
15. What is the Church?
16. Are citizenship and discipleship ever in conflict?
17. Is humor a valuable ingredient in Christian living?
18. How relevant are the Ten Commandments for life today?
19. How does regular participation in Communion contribute to the spiritual life?
20. When and how should we confess our sins?
21. Is there a best way to resolve conflict?
22. Can conscience be badly trained?
23. How can we learn self-control?
24. What are the sources of courage?
25. How does the Cross figure into our Christian experience and way of life?
26. Does the Christian faith change the way we think of death?
27. What should one do in dealing with depression or despair?
28. Is doubt sometimes a part of a true believer's experience?
29. What responsibility do we have for protecting the environment?
30. How far can we trust the opinions of the "experts" who predict the future?
31. What is our duty in forgiving one another?
32. In what sense are we "free" in Christ?
33. Are all believers to be ministers?
34. How can we discern God's will?
35. In what ways do the four Gospels differ from one another?
36. Is there a special call to pastoral ministry?
37. Of what does greatness consist?
38. What does one do when feeling guilt?
39. How can one break a bad habit?

40. Is true happiness attainable?
41. What is the role of prayer in healing?
42. How can we describe heaven?
43. What is the role of the Holy Spirit in the believer's life?
44. Why is hope highly rated, along with faith and love?
45. Can we overdo the virtue of humility?
46. What is hypocrisy?
47. When can we commit idolatry?
48. Is it possible in our actions and behavior to do what Jesus did?
49. How far should we reach out to embrace people who are different from us?
50. How can we explain and overcome envy and jealousy?
51. Can we discover true joy in the midst of difficulties?
52. How are we justified in the sight of God?

Biblical Benedictions and Blessings

The Lord watch between me and thee when we are absent from one another.—Gen. 31:49

The Lord our God be with us, as he was with our fathers; let him not leave us nor forsake us; that he may incline our hearts unto him, to walk in all his ways and to keep his commandments and his statutes and his judgments, which he commanded our fathers.—1 Kings 8:57–58

Let the words of my mouth and the meditation of my heart be acceptable in thy sight, O Lord, my strength and my redeemer.—Ps. 19:14

Now the God of patience and consolation grant you to be like-minded one toward another according to Christ Jesus; that ye may with one mind and one mouth glorify God, even the Father of our Lord Jesus Christ. Now the God of hope fill you with all joy and peace in believing, that ye may abound in hope, through the power of the Holy Ghost. Now the God of peace be with you.—Rom. 15:5–6, 13, 33

Now to him that is of power to establish you according to my Gospel and the teaching of Jesus Christ, according to the revelation of the mystery, which was kept secret since the world began but now is manifest, and by the Scriptures of the prophets, according to the commandments of the everlasting God, made known to all nations for the glory through Jesus Christ forever.—Rom. 16:25–27

Grace be unto you, and peace, from God our Father, and from the Lord Jesus Christ.—1 Cor. 1:3

The grace of the Lord Jesus Christ and the love of God and the communion of the Holy Ghost be with you all.—2 Cor. 13:14

Peace be to the brethren, and love with faith, from God the Father and the Lord Jesus Christ. Grace be with all them that love our Lord Jesus Christ in sincerity.—Eph. 6:23–24

And the peace of God, which passeth all understanding, shall keep your hearts and minds through Christ Jesus. Finally, brethren, whatsoever things are true, whatsoever things are honest, whatsoever things are just, whatsoever things are pure, whatsoever things are lovely, whatsoever things are of good report; if there be any virtue, and if there be any praise, think on these things. Those things which ye have both learned and received, and heard and seen in me, do; and the God of peace shall be with you.—Phil. 4:7–9

Wherefore also we pray always for you, that our God would count you worthy of this calling and fulfill all the good pleasure of this goodness, and the work of faith with power; that the name of our Lord Jesus Christ may be glorified in you, and ye in him, according to the grace of our God and the Lord Jesus Christ.—2 Thess. 1:11–12

Now the Lord of peace himself give you peace always by all means. The Lord be with you all. The grace of our Lord Jesus Christ be with you all.—2 Thess. 3:16–18

Grace, mercy, and peace, from God our Father and Jesus Christ our Lord.—1 Tim. 1:2

Now the God of peace, that brought again from the dead our Lord Jesus, that great shepherd of the sheep, through the blood of the everlasting covenant, make you perfect in every good work to do his will, working in you that which is well-pleasing in his sight, through Jesus Christ, to whom be glory for ever and ever.—Heb. 13:20–21

The God of all grace, who hath called us unto his eternal glory by Christ Jesus, after that ye have suffered a while, make you perfect, establish, strengthen, settle you. To him be glory and dominion for ever and ever. Greet ye one another with a kiss of charity. Peace be with you all that are in Christ Jesus.—1 Pet. 3:10–14

Grace be with you, mercy, and peace from God the Father, and from the Lord Jesus Christ, the Son of the Father, in truth and love.—2 John 3

Now unto him that is able to keep you from falling, and to present you faultless before the presence of his glory with exceeding joy, to the only wise God our Savior, be glory and majesty, dominion and power, both now and ever.—Jude 24:25

Grace be unto you, and peace, from him which was, and which is to come; and from the seven Spirits which are before his throne; and from Jesus Christ, who is the faithful witness, and the first begotten of the dead, and the prince of the kings of the earth. Unto him that loved us, and washed us from our sins in his own blood, and hath made us kings and priests unto God and his Father, to him be glory and dominion for ever and ever.—Rev. 1:4–6

SECTION II

SERMONS AND HOMILETIC AND WORSHIP AIDS FOR FIFTY-TWO SUNDAYS

SUNDAY, JANUARY 5, 2003
Lectionary Message

Topic: The Genius of Christianity
TEXT: John 1:(1–9) 10–18
Other Readings: Jer. 31:7–14; Ps. 147:12–20; Eph. 1:3–14

I. What is the genius or the essence that separates Christianity from other religions? Some would say it is love—that the God of the universe is love. They would be wrong—for many if not most religions teach that God is love and that people are to love one another. No, it is not love.

Some would say that it is that God is one—"radical monotheism" is how the theologians put it. That is not the genius of Christianity. Our mother religion, Judaism, and our aunt religion, Islam, both affirm God as one.

The same is true for joy, for peace, for living a life of sacrifice and commitment to God. When we study the eleven major religions, there are similarities in their emphases. Christianity differs from them in one key aspect, which is both its genius and its greatest scandal. The genius of Christianity is the Incarnation—that God came to Earth in the form of one Jesus of Nazareth. That the essence of divinity was "in-fleshed" in this human body, and only in this human body is a teaching that no other religion possesses. This belief is seen as incredible by some and impossible by others. However, with this belief Christianity rises or falls.

John's Gospel begins not with the manger but with this truth. He takes the central Greek concept—the Logos—and uses it to describe who Jesus Christ is. The scandal comes in the fourteenth verse: "The Word (Logos) became flesh and lived among us." With that one verse John established a radical separation between Christianity and all other religions. For most religions, the impossibility of the Incarnation precluded such nonsense. For others, incarnation happened repeatedly. The great Buddha was incarnated fifty-four times before he achieved nirvana. (That's nothing compared to the average eight and a half million times for most people!) Christianity said no to repeated incarnations. The Incarnation happened only once—in the person of Jesus the Christ, the unique Son of God.

Christianity has defended the Incarnation since its earliest days. Why? Let's face it: the Incarnation is not the easiest teaching to accept. Rather than defend its possibility, lets look at the implications for our lives in accepting the Incarnation.

II. *This life matters.* Other religions try to help us escape from this life, but not Christianity. Yes, this body will one day die and be left to decay—but this body is more than a shell. This body is who I am—my self-understanding is wrapped up in this body. Spirit and soul are inseparable from the body while on the Earth. This body matters. Ask any family member who has just lost a loved one if that body is only a shell. A mother whose fifteen-year-old daughter had been killed in an automobile accident screamed at her minister when he tried to tell her that the body was only a shell. "I'll let you know when that body becomes just a shell. Until then, that body is still my daughter."

Too often we encounter statements such as, "The purpose of life is to be saved so we can go to heaven when we die." This is so wrong. This life is holy, created by God and filled with value, purpose, and meaning. Eternal life is not some entity that begins when I die, but is purposeful life in the present. This life is what God is about. God created this life, created humankind in God's image—and said that it is good. Then God came to Earth in human form and once more said that this life is good.

Most religions of the world teach an escapism, that this life is only a phase and that the goal of life is to escape the flesh and be returned to the great spirit or soul of the universe. Christianity is a materialistic religion; it teaches that the divine has indwelled this life and therefore this life is of vital importance. Our living, our breathing, our laughing and crying, our joys and our sorrows, our ups and our downs—are all part of the stuff that is real life. Christianity teaches that what happens to us, how we live, how we treat one another, how we treat this planet and this universe are all sacred acts, because they deal with the sacred—this life. What we do, what we become, and how we live is sacred to God and should be sacred to us.

III. *People matter.* People matter because flesh was created in the image of God and was indwelled by the very being of God. People matter because the nature of God is love and relationship—a love and desire for relationship that brought Jesus to Earth. Relationships matter—they reflect the nature of God as relationship. Love matters—for the nature of God is love. People matter—for in them we express our love and live in relationship.

If people matter, then all people matter. Young people and old people, fat people and skinny people, people who are book smart and people who are street smart, athletically gifted people and athletically challenged people—all people matter. When God chose to identify with us, God came as the lowliest of the low: all people matter.

IV. *Individuals matter.* How does John put it? "To all who believed he gave the power to become the children of God." Christianity is social in that we do not live our faith absent from a community of faith. Christianity is personal in that each of us is required to make our own decision regarding Jesus the Christ.

If individuals matter, then each of us matters to God. A woman research technician on the staff of a certain hospital was asked by a surgeon to call on a young man who had undergone surgery that had caused him to lose all function below his chest. He was depressed and wished to die. In addition, he had developed severe gangrenous peritonitis, and the accompanying odor was horrendous. When the technician entered the room, the odor was so staggering that she gagged, backed out of the room, and ran into the doctor. "Have you seen my young man?" he asked. "I tried, but I couldn't breathe," she replied. The doctor grabbed her arm and firmly but gently guided her back to the room. "I know it smells bad, but there is a heartbroken and dying young man. Go to him and find the man inside that stink."

Is not the Incarnation God's definitive statement of identification and intimacy with God's creation, even when we stink? Life matters. People matter. Individuals matter.—Robert U. Ferguson Jr.

ILLUSTRATION

FAULTLESS.   I heard the story of an old Italian artist who had lost some of his skill. One evening he sat discouraged before a painting he had just completed. He noticed that he had lost some of his touch. The canvas didn't burst with life as his previous work had once done. As he went to bed, his son heard him say, "I have failed, I have failed."

Later that evening, his son, also an artist, came to examine his father's work, and he, too, noticed that it did not reflect his father's usual work. Taking the palette and brush, he worked far into the night, adding a little touch here, a smudge there, a little color here, a bit of depth, a shadow or two, some highlights. The son worked until he knew that the work would fulfill his father's vision.

Morning came, and the father descended into the studio. He stood before the perfect canvas and in utter delight exclaimed, "Why, I have wrought better than I knew!"

We, too, like this painting, fall short of the Father's glory. Scripture tells us, "All have sinned and fall short of the glory of God" (Rom. 3:23). And although we may try through good works, church attendance, or charitable deeds, it is impossible to restore ourselves.

But the Son, Jesus, came and gave His life on the cross so that He could restore us. If we give Him the canvas of our lives, He will begin the restoration process. He will touch up here and there, add a bit of depth, some color and highlights, and even a shadow or two. Each canvas will receive His personal attention, His unique strokes, His finishing touches. He will work until the canvas reflects the Father's glory. Then, when it is complete, the Scriptures tell us that He will present us faultless before His Father in heaven (see Jude 1:24). On that day, we, too, because of Jesus, will be able to exclaim with utter joy, "Oh, I did better than I thought!"—Gigi Graham Tchividjian with Ruth Bell Graham[1]

SERMON SUGGESTIONS

Topic: The Attitude of Faith
TEXT: Hab. 2:1
(1) Commit your problem to God. (2) Expect an answer from God. (3) Watch and wait for the answer.—D. Martyn Lloyd-Jones

Topic: Wise Men Rejoice
TEXT: Matt. 2:1–12
(1) Because of God's plan. (2) Because of sharing in God's plan.

CONGREGATIONAL MUSIC

1. "My Song Is Love Unknown," Samuel Crossman (1664)
   RHOSYMEDRE, John D. Edwards (1838)
   This venerable hymn magnifying the inscrutable love of God would be particularly appropriate when sung in connection with the Gospel lesson, especially the words: "He came to his own, but his own received him not" (John 1:11).

---

[1]*A Quiet Knowing* (Nashville: W Publishing Group, Thomas Nelson, Inc., 2001), pp. 172–174.

2. "To God Be the Glory," Fanny J. Crosby (1875)

TO GOD BE THE GLORY, William H. Doane (1875)

The thrice-repeated refrain of the Epistle reading (Eph. 1:3–14), "to the praise of His glory," is echoed in this classic gospel song by the "Queen of Gospel Song Writers," Fanny Crosby. Its refrain could be used as an antiphon sung each time this phrase appears in the Scripture reading.

3. "My Tribute" (To God Be the Glory), Andrae Crouch (1971)

MY TRIBUTE, Andrae Crouch (1981)

This is a shorter expression of the same theme as Crosby's song and could be sung in the same way as suggested above.

4. "I Am the Lord Your God," Helen Ott (1985)

RUSSIA, Alexey Lvov (1833)

This free paraphrase of Jeremiah 31 could be sung in connection with the Old Testament reading. Stanza 2 of the hymn, about God's in-gathering of all peoples from all parts of the Earth, relates specifically to the selected verses (7–14) in the lectionary.

5. "Now Praise the Lord," Fred R. Anderson (1986)

ST. ANNE, William Croft (1708)

A modern version of Psalm 147, "Now Praise the Lord," sung to the familiar ST. ANNE tune, could well be used in lieu of the psalm reading.—Hugh T. McElrath

WORSHIP AIDS

CALL TO WORSHIP.   "Praise the Lord! How good it is to sing praises to our God; for he is gracious, and a song of praise is fitting" (Ps. 147:1).

INVOCATION.   Gracious Lord, your power is beyond our imagining, but your love is our daily experience amid all circumstances. So, we praise you in faith, knowing in our hearts your constant kindness.

OFFERTORY SENTENCE.   "Sing to the Lord with thanksgiving. He covers the heavens with clouds, prepares rain for the earth, makes grass grow on the hills. He gives to the animals their food, and to the young ravens when they cry" (Ps. 147:7a, 8–9).

OFFERTORY PRAYER.   Lord, you provide for the animals and birds and give us our daily bread. As you have blessed all of us, we yearn to be a source of blessing to one another, sharing especially the bread of everlasting life through the offerings we now bring.

PRAYER.   Eternal God, in the stillness of this moment, in the quiet recesses of our heart and the inner reaches of our mind, inspire us with a vision of thy Kingdom. Grant that we may with singleness of purpose and constancy of commitment pursue the dream beyond all earthly prizes, follow the path of the wounded feet of our Lord, seek first of all thy Kingdom and thy righteousness, serve thee with unfettered feet, and follow always with the glad freedom of faith and grace.

Grant to us now openness of mind in order that we might perceive thy truth more clearly, openness of heart that we might love thee more profoundly, openness of hand and life that we might serve thee more devotedly.—Paul D. Simmons

SERMON
Topic: The Paradox of Anxiety
TEXT: 2 Cor. 11:28

For most of us, anxiety is a problem. In fact, without grossly exaggerating, it could be called *the* problem—private enemy number one. It is the enemy of health, happiness, harmony, and achievement. It is directly or indirectly responsible for many illnesses, both of the body and of the mind.

We go to enormous lengths to conquer anxiety. An every-growing library of books are being written on the subject, and they rapidly become best-sellers. Magazine articles galore deal with it. And how many sermons are preached on aspects of anxiety and worry!

What we need to grasp is that anxiety is not simply a problem to be solved; it is also a paradox to be accepted. What is a paradox? My dictionary says that it is "a statement that seems to be contradictory, unbelievable, or absurd, but that actually may be true." Life is full of paradoxes. So is religion. And anxiety is paradoxical.

Take these two statements of Paul. First, "There is the daily pressure upon me of my anxiety for all the Churches." Here is a man consumed with anxiety for the churches he established under God. These churches were his daily burden. You can easily imagine how he felt.

Second, turn the pages of the New Testament and you will find this very same man writing, "Have no anxiety about anything." Was he a blatant humbug? Was he guilty of preaching but not practicing? No! This is a paradox of anxiety. We must understand that, this side of eternity, it is never possible to overcome it entirely.

Let us look closely at this paradox of anxiety, and work out some of its implications.

I. On the one hand, *anxiety is a sign of maturity.* In a world like this, only the immature and shallow are careless.

(a) Take the commands of God. Anxiously we must ask, Are we obeying them? Men and women who break these commands with impunity, who talk of God only with a sophisticated sneer, who never lie awake at night and fret over their sins, are wise indeed—if there is no God. But there is a God—so that's another story!

(b) Take the responsibilities of citizenship. Anxiously we must ask, Are we accepting them? The more we love our country, the more concerned we should be about its direction, moral tone, government, and laws.

(c) Take the duties of churchmanship. Anxiously we must ask, Are we fulfilling them? To join a church is to accept the duties of membership. It is to be concerned about the welfare of Christ's body, to be personally responsible for its worship, work, and witness, its spiritual impact and financial stability.

(d) Take the needs of people. Anxiously we must ask, Are we serving them? We must feel them, assume them as our own burdens. Parents must be anxious about the welfare of their growing children. Children must be anxious about their aging parents. The affluent must be anxious about the poor, the hungry, the hopeless. The healthy must be anxious about the sick.

Here is legitimate anxiety. It is certainly basic Christianity. The commands of God—Are we obeying them? The responsibilities of citizenship—Are we accepting them? The duties of churchmanship—Are we fulfilling them? The needs of people—Are we serving them? The answers we give to these questions will be the measure of our maturity, the clue to our discipleship.

II. Turn now to the other side of the paradox of anxiety. It is this: *anxiety is a sin of unbelief.* I know that sounds severe. We are more inclined to speak of our worrying nature as an amiable weakness. The severity, however, carries the authority of Jesus. In the section of the Sermon on the Mount dealing with anxiety, he made it clear that worry is really practical atheism. It is sheer faithlessness, an absolute distrust of God. If you trust, you do not worry. If you worry, you do not trust. Paul was echoing his Master's words when he wrote, "Have no anxiety about anything." It is a sin, a sin of unbelief.

Why is it a sin, and why do we succumb to it? Sinful anxiety is rooted in self-interest, self-pity, self-centeredness. So many chronic worriers are wrapped up in themselves, are fretful and fearful about themselves, are living in a narrow world bounded north, south, east, and west by themselves.

Consider carefully what Jesus had to say about anxiety as a sin, and what Paul had to say, and you will find a practical strategy for overcoming it. It can be summed up in four words:

(a) *Bury!* Conduct a joyful funeral service, as a friend of mine puts it, and bury a lot of the past that haunts and harasses us. Bury your sins, if they have been repented of and forgiven. Reject the mistaken virtue we seem to feel in continually punishing ourselves by resurrecting their memory.

(b) *Simplify!* This was Thoreau's famous exhortation—"Simplify, simplify!" He was echoing Socrates, who said, "How many things I can do without!" Much of our modern anxiety springs from our passion to acquire things, material things—money, possessions. This is a point Jesus made forcefully in his teaching.

(c) *Pray!* "But in everything by prayer and supplication, with thanksgiving, let your requests be made known to God." This is not trite, cheap advice. It is profound when you really explore its depths. Pray in detail—for our God is a father who takes a father's interest in the detail of his children's lives. If anything is big enough to worry about, it is big enough to pray about. Pray with thanksgiving—for gratitude, an awareness of our blessings and assets, simply cannot exist side by side with anxiety. Pray and work—do anything within your power to correct the situation that worries you, and by action seek to achieve the answer to your own prayers.

(d) *Trust!* The positive alternative to anxiety is faith. That is why anxiety is a sin of unbelief. "Why are you anxious?" Jesus asked, "O men of little faith." Our basic need is security, and real security cannot be found in ourselves or in any facet of a world that is passing away. It can be found only in God, who has been made known to us in Jesus Christ, and whose everlasting arms are always underneath us.—John N. Gladstone[2]

SUNDAY, JANUARY 12, 2003
Lectionary Message

Topic: Home for Christmas?
Text: Mark 1:4–11
Other Readings: Gen. 1:1–5; Ps. 29; Acts 19:1–7

I. *Are you going home for Christmas?* has been a frequent question in recent days. There came a time when we had to leave home, when we had to take those steps out the door—both

---

[2]*All Saints and All Sorts* (Huntsport, Nova Scotia: Lancelot Press, 1982), pp. 94–102.

emotionally and physically—and make our way in the world. Yet we never tire of going home. Have we noticed how many persons, when they retire, move back to where they grew up, even though they have not lived there for years and years? There is something about our need for a place to call home that is universal and unending.

We may be home physically, but are we home spiritually? Most of us left our spiritual home years ago. We may have been wanderers looking to see what the world is about. We may have been pilgrims, seeking the city of God. We may have been rebels, leaving God and all that were taught. Whatever our reasons, most of us have left our spiritual home at one time or another. We know what it is like to be in exile, to be where it is always "three-o-clock in the morning." We know what it is like to awaken with the eerie feeling of unease or the sour sense of malaise and know that we are not home. The longing for home takes many different manifestations, but they all have one common thread: it aches in the pit of our stomach like nothing we have ever known.

II. *What does exile look like?* Exile is a land that has many names: self-pity, arrogance, greed, anger, resentment, bitterness, sadness, grief, emptiness, doubt, meaninglessness, and many others. We find ourselves in exile, estranged from the love of God, whenever we walk away from our worship and love of God. Exile is where we go whenever we no longer feel and trust the love of God. Exile is where, like Jonah, we sit under the dried-up vine and argue with God. Exile is where, like Ebenezer Scrooge, we grab all we can for ourselves and ignore the needs and wants of others. Exile can be in a far country or in the community where we grew up. It can be far away from a community of faith or in a sanctuary in the middle of worship. You can be here this morning and be home—or you can be here and in exile.

Exile is determined by our relationship with Christ. If we are in love with Christ so that our lives are lived in obedience to him, then we are home no matter where we may go. However, if we are distanced from Christ, if we are separated from the love of Christ by some event, some action, some deed, some thought or feeling, then we are in exile even in the house of God. Exile is where we lose our joy, our hope, and our love for our Lord and life. Has life become routine, following the same pattern every day with no breath of fresh wind blowing through your spirit? When joy is missing, you can be sure that you are in exile, separated from the joy of Christ that is so life-giving.

III. *How do we leave exile and come home to Christ?* Can we just pack up our spiritual bags and go home? Yes, but we must go with the spirit of repentance. John the Baptizer called the people to repentance—and they did not like that any more than we do today. Let's talk about love, the manger, Baby Jesus and the shepherds. Let's talk about the Magi, Mary and Joseph, and an innkeeper who gave the best he had. Let's not talk of sin and repentance at Christmastime. Yet without repentance we will stay in exile. Mark says, Get ready for God to come and make his home here. Repent! The way home is the way of repentance, the path of acknowledging that we are far less than we should be—even on our best days—and who has that many best days?

Repentance is often confused with remorse and regret, and though these may accompany repentance, they are not the same. Remorse is emotional grief over our actions, and regret is wishing that we had not done them—or that we had not been caught. Repentance is turning around in our beliefs and our actions, committing not only to think differently but to act differently as well. Repentance is not falling to our knees when confronted with our greed and selfishness. Repentance is giving up that which has become so near and dear that it is our god. Repentance is more than saying, "I am wrong." Repentance seeks to restore and renew, to live differently because of our sin.

The crucial question is this: Will we believe in the reality of God's call to come home through Jesus Christ, or will we believe in the reality of our enslavers? Will we trust the love of God to provide the home we need or will we listen to the slave masters of society who led us into exile in the first place? Will we listen to those who would trade the wonder of our humanity for something called "net worth," or to the Lord who loves the "least of these?"

IV. *When we return home to Christ everything changes*—especially the celebration of Christmas! We are freed from preoccupation with what others think of us, from the frenzied and frantic focus on having the right gifts, from the compulsion to ensure that our home is ready for *Southern Living,* and we are empowered to focus on relationships and service to others.

When we come home to Christ, we realize again—for the first time—that we are loved not because we are beautiful, smart, wealthy, or good, but because we are God's. Will we come home? Christ waits for us to come home.—Robert U. Ferguson Jr.

ILLUSTRATION

TURNING OFF THE TEARS.   "All night long I flood my bed with weeping and drench my couch with tears" (Ps. 6:6). What does it mean to live in complete dependence on God? It often seems that such dependence only follows brokenness. Most followers of Jesus will tell you that there has been a time, or there have been times, when they felt totally broken—void of the ability to do anything further on their own. Perhaps you have been there. Perhaps you are there right now. Perhaps your circumstances or personal sins are so overwhelming that you can't even pretend to make another move on your own. You are totally broken, totally dependent on God.

What does that mean?

The totally broken person is totally humble. Her first request to God isn't for help, it's for mercy. "O Lord, do not rebuke me in your anger or discipline me in your wrath. Be merciful to me, Lord, for I am faint" (Ps. 6:1-2). She knows she doesn't deserve the help she is requesting. There is absolutely zero sense of entitlement.

From this humbleness, the totally broken person has a clear view of her condition. Her bones are in "agony" (v. 2), her soul is in "anguish" (v. 3). She is "worn out" (v. 6) and "weak with sorrow" (v. 7).

But in humbleness, the totally broken person can embrace the hope that is found only in a loving God. In prayer and confession, the totally broken person gives the circumstances and the sin to the Lord and immediately finds comfort. Evil loses its grip. Depression dissipates. Tears dry up. Strength and power, gifts from God, return. "Away from me, all you who do evil, for the LORD has heard my weeping. The Lord has heard my cry for mercy; the Lord accepts my prayer" (vv. 8-9).

In your lowest moments, how long do you wallow in self-pity, waiting for an entitlement before you finally admit your brokenness and turn it over to God?—Stephen R. Graves[3]

---

[3]*Focus* (Nashville: W Publishing Group, Thomas Nelson, Inc., 2001), p. 31.

SERMON SUGGESTIONS

Topic: The Best Friend

TEXT: John 11:1–6, 19–44

(1) Jesus is a loving friend (vv. 3–5). (2) Jesus is an understanding friend (vv. 21–36). (3) Jesus is a mighty friend (vv. 37–44).—James Braga

Topic: One Greater Than John

TEXT: Luke 3:15–17, 21–22

(1) Greater in his task. (2) Greater in his source of power. (3) Greater in his identity.

CONGREGATIONAL MUSIC

1. "Give Glory to God, All You Heavenly Creatures," Ps. 29; vers. Calvin Seerveld (1983)
   ARLES, Charles H. Gabriel (1912)

   This free paraphrase could be sung in alternation with the parallel parts of the psalm that are read, as follows: read verses 1–2, sing stanza 1; read verses 3–4, sing stanza 2; read verses 5–6, sing stanza 3; read verses 7–9, sing stanza 4; read verses 9–10, sing stanza 5. For variety and contrast, some stanzas of the hymn could be sung antiphonally, alternating men's and women's voices.

2. "When Jesus Came to Jordan," Fred Pratt Green (1973)
   COMPLAINER, William Walker (1835)

   This hymn, set to a typical shape-note tune, would be appropriate as either introduction or response to the Gospel lesson on the ministry of John the Baptist and the baptism of Jesus (Mark 1:4–11).

3. "God, Who Made the Earth and Heaven," Reginald Heber (1827), William Mercer (1864)
   AR HYD Y NOS, trad. Welsh melody (c. 1784)

   This well-known hymn could be sung in connection with this Sunday's Old Testament reading about God's creation of light (Gen. 1:1–5). The fifth and sixth phrases of each stanza could be sung by the choir, with the congregation singing the other six phrases.

4. "Holy Spirit, Ever Dwelling," Timothy Rees (1922)
   IN BABILONE, trad. Dutch melody (eighteenth century)

   This hymn would be meaningful sung in relation to both the Old Testament lesson and the Epistle reading, where the focus is on the Holy Spirit's moving on the face of the waters (Gen. 1:2) and descending on the converts of the apostle Paul (Acts 1:6).—Hugh T. McElrath

WORSHIP AIDS

CALL TO WORSHIP.   "The Lord sits enthroned as King forever. May the Lord give strength to his people! May the Lord bless his people with peace" (Ps. 29:10b–11).

INVOCATION.   O God, when storms of all kinds are raging, comfort us with your presence. Today, strengthen us with assurance that you are enthroned above all earthly changes and challenges and that your love is as real and true as ever.

OFFERTORY SENTENCE.   As Jesus passed along the Sea of Galilee, he saw Simon and his brother Andrew casting a net into the sea—for they were fishermen. And Jesus said to them, "Follow me and I will make you fish for people" (Mark 1:16–17 NRSV).

OFFERTORY PRAYER.   Our Father, we thank you for placing us in the fishing business—following Jesus in bringing people to you. Use these offerings, we pray, to further the outreach of your love to the ends of the Earth.

PRAYER.   Eternal God, our Father, we draw near once more in awe and reverence to worship thee. Often have we besought thee to fall upon us like showers of rain. Today we beseech thee that we may retreat into the secret places of our own hearts and find thee rising there like a spring, close at hand, cleansing and refreshing. Thou art the source of every secret aspiration, thou art in everything that lifts and liberates our souls, and as thus we come to thee in worship, we pray for genuineness and sincerity. Lead from the unreal to the real.

Lead us away from the unreality of this world we live in, from the tinsel of the things we touch, from its shallowness and superficiality, from all that is cheap, showy, and ostentatious in ourselves and in our fellows. Make us genuine today.

Let our faith be real. We do not ask thee to give us faith. Thou seest how much of it we have, with what carelessness and credulity we bestow it on many passing whims. Lift up our faith, we beseech thee, that it may turn toward the Eternal. Set it on things above, where Christ is. Help us to believe, this day, in the Highest.

Let our love turn toward the real, we beseech thee. We do not pray to thee that we might have love. Thou seest that as the skies are made for winds to blow in, so our hearts are made for love. Thou seest with what carelessness our affection turns every which way and attaches itself to all manner of things. Help us this day to love the Highest when we see it.

Turn our hopes, we beseech thee, to aims that are real. Thou knowest the expectations that throng our hearts this day, the hopes that walk up and down the avenues and alleyways of our souls. Set our hopes on things that are genuine and right. Help us to serve with our hope and devotion the will of God in our generation before we fall on sleep.—Harry Emerson Fosdick

SERMON
Topic: When Our Ideals Betray Us
TEXT: Isa. 6:1–8

For the preacher, Isaiah 6:1–8 is a classic. It would be difficult to find a more practical passage to illustrate the dynamic of our religion and its life-transforming power in hostile circumstances. Here is a message that speaks to our condition, its power of inspiration giving to every man a challenge and a hope. It is our finest interpretation of worship. It tells of the making of a prophet and becomes a thrilling story of how a man found his life's vocation. It confronts us in our personal experience of disillusionment with a dramatic testimony of the power of God to transform the bitter into the better. It thrills us with the thought that we have a religion in which things happen. Isaiah's dramatic experience illumines the dramatic quality of our faith, where victory is wrested precariously from adverse circumstance, and the darkness of disillusionment is shattered by the light of the presence of the Living God. To people whose religion has become a routine observance, Isaiah's vision of God presents a new and startling view of religion as a life-transforming spiritual adventure.

"In the year that King Uzziah died"—how easy it is to miss the excitement of these words! This is not simply a dating of Isaiah's vision of God; it is the story of a shocking disillusionment and an amazing experience of emerging from darkness into the light. For King Uzziah was everyone's hero; his glorious reign of fifty-two years was second only to Solomon's in splendor and blessing to the nation. But he died a leper. The shock waves swept through the land, for leprosy was seen as God's judgment on sin. The young Isaiah was disenchanted and disillusioned, and went into the temple for solace of spirit. It was there that he saw the Lord! When he lost his human hero, he found the Divine Hero. "In the year that King Uzziah died I saw the Lord . . . and his train filled the temple" (Isa. 6:1). The hour of despair became the hour of blessing!

Isaiah had discovered a mighty truth: there is only one hero, and that is God! To be sure, Uzziah seemed to be a wonderful hero. Crowned king at the age of sixteen, he reigned for fifty-two years, bringing strength and glory to Judah. A religious man, "he set himself to seek God . . . and as long as he sought the Lord, God made him prosper" (2 Chron. 26:5). He won victories over hostile neighbors—the Philistines, the Ammonites, and others. He fortified Jerusalem with towers, and also built towers in the wilderness, for "he loved the soil" and had large herds, vineyards, and fertile farms. His army was the pride of the nation. "And his fame spread far, for he was marvelously helped, till he was strong" (2 Chron. 26:15).

Then catastrophe came, for he was betrayed by his own success. "But when he was strong, he grew proud, to his destruction." His pride became the presumption that destroys the spirit of reverence and humility in the presence of the Holy God. A glorious reign came to a ghastly end—the mighty king was brought to an inglorious death—"and behold, he was leprous!" (2 Chron. 26:20).

Isaiah's hero-worship shattered, he entered the temple, there to have such a vision of the God whose strength and character never fail as to make him one of the supreme prophets of all time.

This tells us we need not despair if we find our human heroes failing us, for we have a Divine hero who never fails. When our ideals betray us and our human needs and aspirations come to naught, then faith can take command; and when we have our vision of God, we know that failure is not final, that God's grace is greater than any calamity, that what happens to us is not so important as what happens in us.

Now you may think that if a man looks up to God in faith, then he will be happy and at rest. Not so. When we look up to God we are ashamed of ourselves. Like Isaiah's, our cry is one of anguish: "Woe is me! For I am lost. For I am a man of unclean lips" (Isa. 6:5). This is the challenging nature of true religion. Just at the moment that we see the Lord, we also see ourselves, and in the light of God's presence our sinfulness and selfishness give us an overwhelming sense of unworthiness. We feel the shame and moral embarrassment of personal encounter with one whom we are unfit to meet. Yet there is hope.

For God's purposes are positive, not negative. He seeks to save us, not crush us. He seeks the real person, made in the image of God, intended for a true and wonderful life. So God offers forgiveness. He cleanses and heals. He raises us up from abasement and self-doubt to fresh confidence and courage. He restores our soul. So Isaiah was given the gift of cleansing and forgiveness. One of the seraphims took a coal from the altar, flew to Isaiah, touched his lips, and said the words of renewal and absolution: "Your guilt is taken away, and your sin is forgiven" (Isa. 6:7).

Many people dislike this form of words, yet how needed they are! We need to face candidly and humbly our need for forgiveness and gratefully accept God's gracious and forgiving mercy. We may prefer to talk about unfortunate circumstance, hampering heredity, difficult environment. An author asks, "Whatever became of sin?" We need the honesty to confess our sins and the penitence to accept our forgiveness in order to move on, unburdened and free, in our life's work. The deepest meaning of our Christian fellowship is here: we are a fellowship of the forgiven—persons who have confessed their sin and found their joy and peace in God's forgiveness and their cleansing from sin.

When Isaiah was forgiven and cleansed of his sin, was he then at rest? No, he was not. Nor will we be until we place our new life in the hands of God. For there is a mighty work to be done on planet Earth, and God challenges us to use our redeemed lives to serve and to help make God's will and spirit effective in our world of need. When we are aglow with the vision of God, ashamed of our sins and happy in our experience of forgiveness, this is not the end. It is the beginning. Now we are sensitive to God's call. We are sensitive to the needs of the world. We are sensitive to God's grace, eager to give blessings to all men. Because we know whose we are, we know who we are. We are persons poised for action, ready to live!

It was when Isaiah found personal cleansing that he became sensitive to the call of God. He heard God speaking words, not of specific command but of earnest desire: "Whom shall I send, and who will go for us?" (Isa. 6:8). God is always saying this, but we do not hear him. To hear God's call we must be within calling distance. It is only when we look up to him in faith and find our selfishness and stubbornness and sin cleansed away that we are able to hear what God is saying. Suddenly we understand that God is seeking colleagues to help in his unceasing work of love among men. What an amazing thought—that God seeks us to be his colleagues! What a dignity it gives to our lives! Isaiah hears God's call and he cannot be at rest until he responds. Eagerly he gives himself: "Here am I! Send me."

Now that Isaiah had looked to God in faith, had found his sins forgiven, and had given himself in total dedication to God, surely the end of the story was happy success? Not so. It was as if God had called him to an impossible task, asking him to preach to an impossible people. He had to go and tell the message of God to a people who would not hear or heed the message. He had to work without the balm of success. No wonder he cried, "How long, O Lord," for this was a hard commission. Nor was the answer reassuring: "Until cities lie waste without inhabitant . . . and the land is utterly desolate . . . and the Lord removes men far away." Hard would be the task, and he would be denied the superficial pleasure of success. Yet it was God's task, and his will is our glory. So God gave the vision of the remnant to be saved. In spite of the tragedy of a people who would not listen to God or heed his will, God's purposes went marching on. "The remnant" meant the ongoing of God's truth, and out of it a savior in the fullness of time.

So Isaiah found that there is no darkness in our human experience from which we cannot emerge into the light. The grace of God lifts us from disillusionment and despair into his victorious world, where our life is lit by hope and the joy of his presence. With God we can never fail; without him we can never succeed. The darkness of Earth simply accentuates the light of God's love, which gives glory to His people in all the vicissitudes of this our life.— Lowel M. Atkinson[4]

---

[4]*Apples of Gold* (Lima, Ohio: Fairway Press, 1986), pp. 178–181.

SUNDAY, JANUARY 19, 2003
Lectionary Message

Topic: Against All Odds

TEXT: John 1:43–51

Other Readings: 1 Sam. 3:1–10 (11–20); Ps. 139:1–6, 13–18; 1 Cor. 6:12–20

I. A man was invited to play Augusta National. This was his lifelong dream. Now he had a different dilemma: who to bring? Rather than alienate his friends, he held a lottery at his club, and three friends were selected to accompany him. They arrived on the given day, were assigned to a caddy, and began to play. They came to hole fifteen, a par five that is reachable in two good shots. The problem is that there is a lake in front of the hole, so if you hit short you will go into the water. This man hit the drive of his life, and found himself with a decision: "Do I hit a three wood and risk going into the water or do I lay up with an iron and play it safe?" He went back and forth: five iron or three wood? five iron or three wood? He selected the iron when his caddy interrupted: "May I ask you a question?" "Certainly." "How many times in this life do you think you will play this hole? Go for it!" He realized that this was the only time he would ever play Augusta National. He took the wood and decided to go for it.

II. Allow me to be your caddy this morning and ask you a question: How many times will you get to live this life? Why not live it to the fullest? Why are we always playing life so safe, laying up when we should be going for it? The presence of so much boredom in our world is the result of refusing to take risks and not having any purpose outside of our own meager existence. This is the very opposite of our risk-taking God.

- God took a risk in creating human beings as free moral creatures.
- God took a risk in making covenants with Abraham, Isaac, and Jacob, bringing in the possibility that these people would dishonor God with their lives—which happened.
- God took a risk in using Moses, a fugitive from justice, to liberate his people.
- God took a risk in calling Mary to bear his Son, Jesus the Messiah.
- God took the ultimate risk in coming as Jesus, knowing that in coming as a human being he could be rejected and murdered—which happened.
- God took a risk in entrusting the good news of Jesus Christ to humankind, knowing that we could distort it and use it for our own purposes—which happened.

III. God has always been in the risk-taking business. If we are to be God's people then we must be about risk-taking as well. I am not talking about jumping out of airplanes with a backpack or off bridges tied to a bungee cord; or about taking all one's savings and buying junk bonds, or quitting one's job and moving to the Bahamas. Faith as risk-taking involves seeing what needs to be done in this world and getting involved in it—for Christ's sake. When we are not living life with risk, we are confining ourselves in a prison of our own making—and prisons are rarely productive for human growth. God created us to grow, mentally, emotionally, and physically through a life that takes us to the edge.

Our text speaks of the calling of Philip and Nathaniel. Jesus calls Philip, and he immediately responds by finding Nathaniel and bringing him to Jesus. Philip believed immediately; Nathaniel was a bit more skeptical. However, both took a risk in following Jesus. Both were betting that Jesus was who they thought he was—the Messiah.

Serving our Lord is not always a matter of life nice and easy. There are defining moments, those times in our lives when we are faced with momentous decisions. Such moments are not always recognizable as such—they are not necessarily the moments we think of. They are not necessarily the big economic decisions, but they are the decisions that keep us awake at night, the ones that hinge on our values and beliefs, that reveal our true character.

IV. Jesus took risks all the time. Calling disciples was a risk. When others focused on the faults of people, Jesus looked for what was good and brought it out. When others focused on saying no to the wrong things, Jesus dared to say yes to the right things. In doing so, he empowered all around him to be liberated from the cultural prisons in which they found themselves and to live life positively, not negatively.

What about us? Are we living life to its fullest or are we being cautious and careful? After Warren Buffet was told that he was the second richest man on Earth he was asked, "What do you want to be next?" He replied, "The oldest." If we are not careful, we will focus so much on "not dying" that we will miss the opportunity to live. Harry Emerson Fosdick once said, *To have everything to live with and nothing to live for is the greatest tragedy there is.* When we live life in "safe mode," we miss so much of what life is about.—Robert U. Ferguson Jr.

ILLUSTRATION

LIFE IS TO GIVE.   We can never tell what effect our words or unexpected acts of kindness will have on another person. It might be difficult to see Christ "in the least of these," especially if that person is as unkempt-looking as Jean Valjean or has injured or threatened us. But this story of the bishop's kindness and Luke's story about Jesus and the thief on the cross remind us that when we become channels of God's grace, nothing is impossible. Like the crucified thief, the seemingly depraved Jean Valjean received grace at the time of his greatest need, thanks to an elderly clergyman who valued a human life far more than he did silver dinnerware.

The bishop took a risk. Some might call him foolish, perhaps even aiding and abetting a known criminal. However, the bishop, like the Lord whom he emulated, saw in the wretched man brought back by the police not a depraved criminal but a child of God. That child of God he thought well worth taking a chance on, even to the point of telling a lie for him and seemingly throwing away his best silver pieces. What a difference such love can make in the recipient's life!—Edward McNulty[5]

SERMON SUGGESTIONS

Topic: What Is Worship?
To worship is (1) to quicken the conscience by the holiness of God, (2) to feed the mind with the truth of God, (3) to purge the imagination by the beauty of God, (4) to open the heart to the love of God, (5) to devote the will to the purpose of God.—William Temple

---

[5]*Praying the Movies* (Louisville: Geneva Press, 2001), p. 3

Topic: Conflicting Reaction to Our Good Deeds

TEXT: Mark 14:3–9

(1) People's criticism of those deeds. (2) Christ's acceptance of those deeds.

CONGREGATIONAL MUSIC

1. "Lord, Speak to Me, That I May Speak," Frances R. Havergal (1872)
   CANONBURY, Robert Schumann (1839)

   Echoing the words of the young Samuel in the Temple, "Speak, Lord, for your servant hears" (1 Sam. 3:9), this hymn of obedience and commitment could be sung as a response to the Old Testament lesson.

2. "Lord, You Have Searched Me," Ps. 139; vers. Psalter (1912)
   FEDERAL STREET, Henry K. Oliver (1832)

   The singing of this Bible song, a free rendering in meter of Psalm 139, could well take the place of the Psalter reading.

3. "Built on the Rock," Nikolai F. S. Grundtvig (1837)
   KIRKEN DEN ER ET, Ludwig N. Lindeman (1840)

   The singing of this hymn would be an appropriate response to the Epistle lesson. Among its several themes is that of God's Spirit dwelling in our bodies (stanza 2).

4. "Jesus Calls Us, O'er the Tumult," Cecil F. Alexander (1852)
   GALILEE, William H. Jude (1874)

   Use this hymn to introduce or respond to the reading of the Gospel lesson, which pertains to Jesus' calling of Philip and Nathaniel to discipleship (John 1:43–51).—Hugh T. McElrath

WORSHIP AIDS

CALL TO WORSHIP.   "O Lord, you have searched me and known me. You know when I sit down and when I rise up; you discern my thoughts from far away. You search out my path and my lying down, and are acquainted with all my ways" (Ps. 139:1–3).

INVOCATION.   There is no getting away from you, O God, and in our heart of hearts we wish to be close to you. May what we learn and say and do here now bring us closer to you, with confession of our sins and the assurance that we are forgiven through Jesus Christ our Lord and boldly able to tell others of your goodness and grace.

OFFERTORY SENTENCE.   "The next day Jesus decided to go to Galilee. He found Philip and said to him, 'Follow me'" (John 1:43).

OFFERTORY PRAYER.   The more we follow the Christ who gave his all for us, the more we want to give of ourselves and our material possessions to help others to know him and serve him. Use these offerings, we pray, to strengthen and prepare your people for your service and to bring others to know your redeeming love.

PRAYER.   Father, we pray for our enemies. Be gracious to them, bless them, accept them. We pray for the enemies of the Church, the enemies of faith and of your crucified Son. Peace be with them! Be gracious to those who despise us and persecute us. Take fear and hate from our hearts. We pray for the enemies of our country and its political order. Peace be with them!

Graciously accept the people who find us unendurable, and awaken love for them in our hearts. Give peace in the midst of conflict. Give love where people hate each other. May your Kingdom come and the law of retaliation pass away. May your suffering transform us from enemies to friends, who can rejoice in one another in your peace.—Jürgen Moltmann

SERMON
Topic: God—Just but Loving
TEXT: Various

I. *God is just.* I once had a good friend who was a Jewish rabbi. One day I asked him, "What is the essence of Judaism?" He thought for a moment and replied, "Ethical monotheism. God is not only one; he is also ethical. He is just and requires justice of those who believe in him."

(a) In addition to the word *just* there are two other words that speak of God's ethical nature—*holy* and *righteous.*

God is holy. It must be quickly said that before the term *holy* had ethical meaning, it was heavily theological. Holiness is the distinctive thing about God. It is that which, more than all other things, makes him God. He is the Other. He is God and not man.

Men, women, and things are not holy within themselves. They become holy because they are dedicated to God. The Israeli people were holy, not because of any virtue, goodness, or gift within them, but because God had chosen them to be his people.

Yet the term *holy* was ethicized. That this could happen tells a lot about Judaism and Christianity. It indicates the heavy stress both religions put on morality, and how the theological and ethical are bound together. The theological and ethical belong together the way the back and palm of my hand are bound together.

When we say that God is holy in an ethical sense, we say that he is just and righteous. These three words form a trilogy.

God is just. "The works of his hands are faithful and just, all his precepts are trustworthy" (Ps. 111:7; see also Ps. 145:7; Dan. 4:37).

When we say that God is just, we mean that he is faithful, trustworthy, and responsible. He wants life ordered with equity and fairness. He becomes angry when the strong take advantage of the weak and the rich exploit the poor.

God is righteous. "Thou hast fulfilled thy promise, for thou art righteous" (Neh. 9:8). Although God's righteousness and justice mean essentially the same thing, he is spoken of as being righteous much more frequently than as being just (see Ps. 7:9; Jer. 9:24). The reason is likely that righteousness expresses relationship better than justice does.

(b) God exercises his just nature in judgment. God is judge. He is judge of people, nations, and the world. "Shall not the Judge of all the Earth do right?" Abraham asked (Gen. 18:25).

There is a consistent picture of God's judgment running through the Bible. His judgment is impartial, falling on all alike. Israel, being the special people of God, felt that we would show partiality to them, but he didn't. Amos tells of God's judgment upon the surrounding nations, but God did not spare Israel. "You only have I known of all the families of the Earth," said God. "Therefore I will punish you for all your iniquities" (Amos 3:2).

There is nothing capricious, whimsical, or arbitrary about God's judgment. It is in keeping with who he is. His judgment flows from his righteous nature.

Again, the working of moral law and God's personal wrath are involved in his judgment.

God has built moral law into the structure of the universe, into the very warp and woof of it. While the moral laws have a kind of hiddenness that the physical laws do not, they are rock-ribbed, formidable, and powerful. Individuals as well as nations who willfully ignore and violate these laws can be destroyed by them.

When men, in their arrogance, flout moral laws that are God's ethical nature built into the universe—when people are heartless and ruthless, when the weak are trampled beneath the feet of the powerful, when men and women are shoved and pushed about as if they were things—God becomes angry. The fact that God is wrathful in judgment does not indicate weakness. It is a sign of strength.

Further, there is love and mercy in God's judgment. His justice is a seeing justice; it is not blind. His justice is a feeling justice; it has heart in it.

The end of God's justice is salvation. His acts of judgment may be deeds of salvation (see Ps. 36:6; Isa. 45:21b).

God is like a surgeon who says, "You have a bad leg. It will have to come off, and it will be painful. But I shall amputate it so that you can live and be healthy."

God's judgment can be very severe, like a surgeon's knife, but it cuts to save. It can be as devastating as the hot, scorching winds that sweep over us from the desert, but those winds are followed by refreshing showers.

(c) God demands justice of those who believe in him. Not only is God just, but he also calls us to be just and righteous (interchangeable terms).

The righteous person God calls each of us to be is a two-directional person who is right with God and right with his neighbor. Therefore, justice or righteousness is relational in nature.

The righteous person is in right relations with his or her brother or sister. Such a person is socially oriented. He seeks to preserve the place and wholeness of the community, meeting the demands of communal living. He establishes peace.

God seeks righteous men and a just society. Justice gives stability to the community, and righteousness wins the approval of God.

Amos lived during a time when immorality and religion both flourished. Injustice and religious piety walked side by side without disturbing each other. Many of the people left their ill-gotten gain at the altar as tithes and offerings to God. They thought they could buy off God. But Amos told them that no matter how huge their crowds, big their offerings, or moving their liturgy, or how justly they sang their hymns, God would not accept their worship (Amos 5:23–24).

Micah's message was essentially the same (Mic. 6:8).

(d) Let us look at righteousness that is of faith. Paul strongly emphasized this. It makes a lot of sense if righteousness is, as I have claimed, essentially a relational term. By faith in Christ our lives are set right with God, and that relationship works itself out horizontally in faithful and loving relationships with our neighbors.

Paul spoke of "the righteousness of God through faith in Jesus Christ for all who believe" (Rom. 3:22). Or again, "For we hold that a man is justified by faith apart from works of law" (v. 28). Righteousness, then, is not so much keeping laws and rules, which is legalism, as it is a relationship made possible by faith in Christ.

This was not something new to Paul, or to the New Testament. The Old Testament spoke of a righteousness that is of faith (see the story of Abraham, Gen. 15:1–6).

II. *God is love.* We have heard people say that the God of the Old Testament is a God of justice, while the God of the New Testament is a God of love. That is highly inaccurate. The God of the Old Testament is also a God of love, and the God of the New Testament is also a God of justice, although the love of God is accented in the New Testament. We make a serious mistake when we break the continuity between the Old and New Testaments. The God of the Old Testament is also the God of the New. Yet this is not to deny the uniqueness of the New Testament. It is indeed unique. The love of God is historicized and personalized in Jesus of Nazareth as nowhere else. The best of the Old Testament is fulfilled in him, and God is present redemptively in Jesus as in nobody else.

There are few attempts to define God in the Bible. It is almost as if it says, "God is too wonderful to be expressed in our human definitions of him." But there are three attempts at this in the New Testament and we are surprised by their simplicity: "God is spirit" (John 4:24), "God is light" (1 John 1:5), and "God is love" (4:16). Three short words in each definition. Imagine it!

The greatest of these is "God is love." It is the most personal and comes closest to the heart of who God is.

God has caught up his whole creation in his great arms of love: "For God so loved the world that he gave his only Son, that whoever believes in him should not perish but have eternal life" (John 3:16). In spite of the brokenness, rebellion, and sin of his world, he cannot give it up.

We have seen God's love best in the face of his Son, Jesus Christ. God's love is embodied in Jesus.

What kind of love is this we have seen in Jesus? The New Testament calls it *agape* love. It is a nonmanipulative, nonutilitarian, nonpossessive love. *Agape* does not depend in any sense on the object, but solely on the giver. It loves not only the healthy, beautiful, good, and virtuous, it loves the sick, broken, marred, and sinful. It loves those who do not love themselves, whom the world does not love, and those who do not love God. It loves the discards and the rejects of our world. There is no depth into which it will not descend to lift up the fallen, no distance it will not go to find the lost, and no pain it will not bear to heal the brokenness of our world.

It is God's love, *agape,* that came to us and our world in Jesus Christ. That makes our gospel exceedingly good news.

Karl Barth once said, "My experience has been that if I simply try to say, to repeat, what the Bible says about God, the people understand. Many clergymen fail to do this. We must simply accept the fact that human beings are loved by God, even in their faults and hostilities. We must tell man that he is 'a loved one.'"

I have talked about the justice and love of God. They are inseparably bound up together in his life. His justice is in his love, and his love is in his justice. His justice keeps his love from being too soft and sentimental, and his love keeps his justice from being too harsh and impersonal.—Chevis F. Horne[6]

---

[6]*Preaching the Great Themes of the Bible* (Nashville: Broadman Press, 1986), pp. 65–75.

SUNDAY, JANUARY 26, 2003
Lectionary Message

Topic: The Called Ones

TEXT: Mark 1:14–20

Other Readings: Jonah 3:1–5, 10; Ps. 62:5–12; 1 Cor. 7:29–31

I. It's a bare facts story, to be sure. Jesus has emerged from the desert and his engagement with Satan and is now proclaiming the good news that the Kingdom of God is at hand. While walking beside the Sea of Galilee, he sees Simon and Andrew fishing with nets. Jesus looks at the two and calls them to follow him, promising to make them fishers of something far more important: persons who have been lost and estranged from God. Miraculously, Simon and Andrew drop their nets and follow him. No questions—just dropped everything and followed. Farther down the beach James and John are mending their nets with their father Zebedee and their hired help. The call comes and they respond, as did the others—drop everything and follow.

Amazingly, none of these four men ask any questions. They do not inquire about pay, fringe benefits, time off, or even their position in the Kingdom of God—though they will get to that question later. They do not ask Jesus who he is, what he is about, and where he is going. Had they already heard about Jesus from others? Had they been at his baptism by John the Baptizer? Had they heard Jesus preach in the preceding days and sensed something different about this man?

II. Whatever the case, we do know this: we know what it is like to be called by God, do we not? The very fact that one is interested in the things of Christ indicates that the Holy Spirit has issued the call to follow Christ. Most if not all of us can recall that time when we responded to the call of Christ—when the message went forth in the power of the Spirit and it was, in the words of the spiritual, "not our brother or our sister, but me, O Lord, standing in the need of prayer." That particular day the call had our name on it, and we responded.

III. Calls come in different forms and for different reasons, but they share one common element: they come from the heart of Christ and are an expression of the unrelenting grace of God. The call of salvation, to follow and accept Christ as Lord and Savior, is foundational. Without this call there will be no others. Grace means that God calls us, not that we call God. As an act of grace, God seeks us in his love to bring us home. Too often I hear the statement, "When I get my life together, then I will turn to God." That's not the way it works. Jesus called Simon and Andrew, James and John, warts and all, to follow him. Simon, with his raging temper and blustery personality, responded to the call. James and John—spoiled momma's boys, temperamental, ambitious, and jealous of others—came with all this baggage.

IV. The next call is the call to Christian ministry, to utilize our spiritual gifts in the community of faith. On our spiritual pilgrimage we realize that God did not call us just to "save us," but that we might be empowered and gifted through the Spirit in sharing the gospel of Jesus the Christ.

What is it about being called that so captivates us on the one hand and scares us to death on the other? We yearn to be called by someone or something greater than ourselves, for which we can spend our lives, but too often we back away from the call. Why do we respond in this fashion? We are deathly afraid of giving up control—of saying "yes" and not knowing what we have just agreed to do. We humans are into control, are we not? We control in different ways. Some of us are graspers, hanging onto every bit of power and material goods our grubby little fingers can touch. Others are manipulators, working behind the scenes to get our way, even when we smile and seem so innocent on the surface. Others are dictators, barking commands and taking charge no matter what the situation. Each and every one of us has our own methods of trying to control the situations and relationships in our lives. This is why the call is so threatening to us: it comes from beyond us, demands our total allegiance, and is beyond the scope of our control.

Adam and Eve, in the Garden of Eden, had life perfectly in balance, until they decided they wanted to control their own destiny. Abraham was faithful in following God, until he tried to control matters and take them into his own hands. Twice he passed off his wife Sarah as his sister, and he used Hagar to produce Ishmael to be his heir, because God had not come through. The rich young ruler came to Jesus and wanted to be his disciple, but he would not give up the money that gave him power and control. Until we are willing to give up control of our lives to our Lord Jesus Christ, we have not taken the basic step of discipleship.

V. What does it mean to respond to the call of Christ? Following Christ means attachment to the person of Jesus the Christ. When Jesus called these men, he said, "Come and follow me." Discipleship is attaching ourselves to the person of Jesus completely and totally. When Simon and Andrew responded to Jesus, they left their nets behind. To follow Jesus is to put aside all other attachments as secondary and to live for him, in him, and through him. This is not some nebulous theological principle or esoteric idea; this is Jesus of Nazareth, the only begotten Son of the Father, who walked on this Earth as a flesh and blood human being.—Robert U. Ferguson Jr.

ILLUSTRATION

FOLLOW ME.   The main point of denying ourselves is to help us follow wherever Christ leads us. This is really the hard part, because our egos want to determine our direction, and they certainly do not want to follow God's direction. In order to follow the way of Christ, we have to be willing to pay attention to the world around us so we can listen for how Christ calls us. For each of us the call is unique and particular, so we have to be not only willing and able to listen, but also courageous enough to follow.

The biggest problem most people have is not necessarily in their desire to follow Christ, but in understanding how to listen for God's voice in their lives. Most people do not realize that divine directives are woven throughout their lives. They keep waiting for God to speak to them through an audible voice or via a dramatic sign. The reality is that God speaks most often in a subtle voice that uses symbols, events, relationships, the language of the heart, past experiences, and future possibilities. It is as though we keep staring at God's lips, waiting for God to speak in English, while God is communicating to us in sign language or writing down messages to us. We get so focused on expecting God to speak in a certain way that we ignore the full scope of the ways God speaks. We expect God to speak in one voice, and instead God is speaking in a thousand other voices.—N. Graham Standish[7]

---

[7]*Paradoxes for Living* (Louisville: Westminster John Knox Press, 2001), pp. 35–36

SERMON SUGGESTIONS

Topic: The Rich Christians

TEXT: 1 Cor. 4–9

(1) The source of the riches. (2) The nature of the riches. (3) The purpose of the riches.
—Robert U. Ferguson

Topic: Jesus Declares His Mission

TEXT: Luke 4:14–17

(1) In a fitting context. (2) With a pointed message. (3) At the appropriate time.

CONGREGATIONAL MUSIC

1. "Dear Lord and Father of Mankind," John G. Whittier (1872)

    REST, Frederick C. Maker (1887)

    The second stanza of this classic hymn pertains directly to the calling of the disciples by Jesus as recorded in this day's Gospel reading (Mark 1:14–20).
2. "Abide with Me, Fast Falls the Even Tide," Henry F. Lyte (1847)

    EVENTIDE, William H. Monk (1887)

    "The time is short; the form of this world is passing away" (1 Cor. 7:29–31). This venerable hymn can be a reassuring response to this warning of the apostle Paul. In particular, stanza 2 addresses the truth of the constancy of our Lord in contrast to the change and decay of this world.
3. "My Soul Finds Rest in God Alone," Ps. 62; vers. David J. Diephouse (1986)

    BETHLEHEM, Gottfried W. Finkin (1842)

    This paraphrase of Psalm 62 furnishes an appropriate response to the Psalter reading. Antiphonal singing between choir and congregation of each stanza would be suitable and meaningful.
4. "God Moves in a Mysterious Way," William Cowper (1774)

    DUNDEE, Scottish Psalter, (1615)

    God's dealings with Jonah and the inhabitants of Ninevah show forth his mercy, love, and forgiveness. These are celebrated in this classic hymn, which could appropriately accompany the Old Testament reading.—Hugh T. McElrath

WORSHIP AIDS

CALL TO WORSHIP.   "Trust in him at all times, O people; pour out your heart before him; God is a refuge for us" (Ps. 62:8).

INVOCATION.   You are our last resort, O God, it is true, but grant through your grace and our faithful worship that we put you first in our thoughts and deeds. Let this service of worship give us new perspectives and priorities, we pray.

OFFERTORY SENTENCE.   "For the present form of this world is passing away" (1 Cor. 7:31b).

OFFERTORY PRAYER.   Our Father, we pray that as many things in which we have invested confidence are passing away and failing us, we may place greater trust in you and the eternal verities. Take these offerings of material substance and endue them with permanence as they undergird your purposes and bless those who need your Kingdom that cannot be shaken.

PRAYER.   Dear Father, how we need to be here today, to abide in your presence, to be refreshed in our spirits, to be challenged in our minds through the thinking of sacred thoughts, and to be fortified for living. We are weak in every area of life. We struggle with temptation and cannot resist its power. We fight with recurring sins and cannot defeat them. We fail in relationships and cannot repair them. We miss the wonder of daily living because of our self-determination, and we cannot recapture the glory of life. We stand in need of strength from beyond ourselves to resist temptation's power. We long for victory over our sins, which only you can provide. We truly seek avenues along which to travel to restore broken relationships. We plead for humility, that we might forget self-determination and find your will for us in all things. We need this hour, Father, for we need to return to the source of all love and power and guidance and forgiveness.

We need to discover the presence of your Holy Spirit anew, that wonderful presence that when adhered to guards out pathways, fortifies our souls, increases our faith, and justifies our trust. We need here this morning to cease our resistance to the in-dwelling of your Spirit, that we might rise above so much that keeps us from attaining the stature of the very glory of Christ. We need this hour because we need the in-breaking of the presence and power of the Holy Spirit.

We need this hour that we might intercede for others around us in the world. From our reasonable health and good fortune, we ask for help for those who know illness of great gravity and poverty of various degrees. We ask that power for living be granted to those who face drastic circumstances of health and sorrow. We ask for courage for the fainthearted and friendship for the lonely. We ask for release from hard pain and a way out for those who have come to a dead-end street.

So, Father, we need this hour, for we cannot manage without meeting you and tasting regularly of your grace given through our Lord Christ, in whose name we pray.—Henry Fields

SERMON
Topic: Life-Giving Streams
TEXT: Isa. 43:2–7; Luke 3:15–17, 21–22

In the Scriptures today the image of water is very evident, as is the image of fire. In these Scriptures, both fire and water have both positive and negative images associated with them.

The prophet Isaiah was a creative writer. He wrote with clarity and imagination, with poetic beauty. In the passage we read earlier this morning are seven verses of a poem that is much larger. The poem actually starts in chapter 42, beginning at verse 19. The first part of the poem speaks about the people of Israel and their life in the past and the present. It speaks of their life as being a life under judgment, because they have been an unfaithful people. So the image is one of negativity. It is harsh, because life was harsh for those folks.

In chapter 43, verse 1, there is a turn, and God says, "I will redeem you." The image is positive and looks to the future, with hope because of the redemption of God. God will be present with the people. God will be in their lives, and they will experience the grace of God. So their future is a future of openness, hope, possibility, and positiveness.

Isaiah used both water and fire to symbolize the dangers of life. He wrote about these dangers in the section we read. When the presence of God comes into our life, it doesn't do away with all the dangers of life. It doesn't protect us, but it does say that God will be with us in those dangers, in the fiery times, in the rushing times. With God present with us in those times we can see our way through. That is the word of Isaiah—using a negative image for water and fire, but saying that even in those negative, dangerous, terrible times of life, God will be there with us. The wording is so wonderful: "You are precious in my sight." "I love you," God says. "You do not need to be afraid, because I will be with you in those times."

Then, moving to the passage in the New Testament, we see positive images of water and fire. John the Baptizer said, "I will baptize you with water." That is a positive image. The water of John's baptism was water of forgiveness for sin. The water of our baptism is the baptism of sin. The water is a symbol of the grace of God washing over us, renewing us, refreshing us, energizing us, and reminding us that God's forgiveness is always with us. God forgives us not only for things that we have done in our past, and for things that we are doing right now, but God also forgives us for those things we might do in the future. So there is a timeless quality about God's grace. God's grace is bigger than time and stretches throughout time.

We call baptism a "covenant." It is a sacrament, a sacred act, but we call it a covenant because it is a promise. A promise is not only something for the past but also something for the future—a promise without any time constraints.

John the Baptizer went on. He said, "There is one coming who will baptize you with the Holy Spirit and with fire." We don't have any record in Scripture of Jesus doing any baptizing. We don't know whether he did or not. It just isn't recorded in Scripture. Perhaps what John was doing was giving us an image for Jesus' entire ministry, for his teaching and his preaching and his healing. Everything was an immersing of people in the Holy Spirit.

The image of fire is a common one for Luke. Remember what Luke wrote in the Book of Acts about the event on the Day of Pentecost? He used the image of fire. "The Spirit rested upon the people as tongues of fire," he said. Almost always when fire is used positively in Scripture it is the image of a refining agent. Refiners use fire with metal, burning out the impurities, the dross, so that what remains is stronger and more useful. The same is true for our lives. When the Holy Spirit comes into us, it gets rid of impurities, it gets rid of that which weakens us, so that we are better and stronger people, more faithful—people who can live the righteous life by the power of God's grace.

So in Isaiah we have the promise that God will be with us. We see the fulfillment of that promise in the person of Jesus and the gift of the Spirit in baptism. In Isaiah we have a negative image of fire and water, and in the Gospel of Luke we have a positive image of fire and water. We are talking about the presence of God in our lives in both situations.

I have been asked on several occasions about these questions that are asked as part of the baptismal covenant: Baptism is so full of joy; how can you ask such negative questions? How can the questions concentrate on what is evil in the world? Baptism is about reality, that's why. There is a lot of negativeness in the world. There is a lot of evil in the world. There is a lot of pain and suffering in the world. So the first question is, "Do you renounce the spiritual forces of wickedness, reject the evil powers of this world, and repent of your sin?" It goes from cosmic to global to personal, saying there is a lot that works against God. Where are you going to stand in that reality?

I have had people say to me, "My faith just doesn't mean much for me" or "My baptism didn't mean anything for me." Friends, the reason I think faith and baptism sometimes don't mean anything for us is we don't take the questions seriously. We don't recognize that we have to make decisions. The grace of God is abundant and without end, but we have to choose to receive it. So the second question is, "Will you accept the freedom and power that God gives you? Do you recognize the evil, now will you accept the grace?"

The third question is, "Do you confess Jesus as your Lord? Do you believe in his grace and will you be faithful? Will you live that grace? Will you let it empower you and direct you and energize you?"

The grace of God is without measure. It is abundant. It washes over all of us throughout all time. It is a life-giving stream. But we have to choose to stand in that stream. We have to choose to drink of that stream. We have to choose to live by that stream, or it just washes over us and passes us by.

The waters of baptism are without boundaries. That's the nature of God's grace. The prophet Amos in the Old Testament says, when you experience that grace, then "let justice roll down like waters, and righteousness like an ever-flowing stream." We merge our faithfulness with the grace of God, and that is truly a life-giving stream—not only for us but also for all whom we meet.—Jim Standiford

SUNDAY, FEBRUARY 2, 2003
Lectionary Message

Topic: Show and Tell
TEXT: Mark 1:21–28
Other Readings: Deut. 18:15–20; Ps. 111; 1 Cor. 8:1–13

"Show and Tell" was a regular event when I was in elementary school. The teacher set aside a block of time for students to show something interesting brought from home and talk about it—whether the item was a bird's nest, a souvenir from a trip, or a special birthday gift. Show and Tell gave us experience in public speaking, but it also implicitly taught us the connection between seeing-experiencing and hearing. When I had something for Show and Tell, I was eager to share it, because the object signified something important to me. Others in the class were just as enthusiastic when it was their turn.

I. *What the gospel shows and tells.* Today's reading from the Gospel of Mark—and indeed, the entire chapter—is full of show and tell. Jesus was beginning his public ministry at a synagogue in Galilee. Verses 1–28 depict Jesus speaking four times. First, he said, "The time is fulfilled, and the Kingdom of God is at hand; repent, and believe in the gospel." His next words were to Simon and Andrew: "Follow me and I will make you fishers of people." Third, he taught those gathered for worship, and people were amazed at the authority with which he explained the Word of God to them. Finally, he rebuked the unclean spirit that was tormenting a man in the synagogue, declaring, "Be silent, and come out of him!" Not only did his words tell who he was, but his actions showed it—inviting others into relationship with him, glorifying God, and healing the afflicted.

Other characters in the text show and tell the reader who Jesus is. Mark begins the book by proclaiming, "the gospel of Jesus Christ, the Son of God." John the Baptist describes Jesus as one who is "mightier than I, the thong of whose sandals I am not worthy to stoop down and untie," who will "baptize with the Holy Spirit." The Spirit is shown descending like a dove at Jesus' baptism, and a voice from heaven announces, "Thou art my beloved Son; with thee I am well pleased." The unclean spirit confesses that Jesus is "the Holy One of God," and the crowd at the synagogue marvels at Jesus' miraculous power as well as his words. The mood of the narrative is one of urgency, as though Mark is eager to show and tell "immediately" (a favorite adverb in this Gospel) who Jesus Christ is.

II. *The season is one of show and tell.* During the weeks after Christmas, the church continues to focus on the meaning of the Incarnation: God's love made visible in the birth of Jesus Christ. The name for the season is "Epiphany," which means manifestation or showing forth. What is more, today itself is a special one for most of the Western Church. On February 2, Christians commemorate the purification of Mary, the mother of Jesus, and the presentation of Christ in the Temple (Luke 2:22–39). This, too, was a show and tell event. Mary is shown to have been a devout and holy mother, obedient to the customs Jews followed to show honor to God. Mary and Joseph showed the infant Jesus to Simeon and Anna. Simeon confessed, "Mine eyes have seen thy salvation which thou hast prepared in the presence of all people, a light for revelation to the Gentiles, and for glory to thy people Israel." Anna, in turn, was also shown that Jesus was the awaited Messiah, and it says she gave thanks to God and spoke of him to all who were looking for the redemption of Jerusalem.

In addition to commemorating the Presentation and the Purification, many Christians also know this day as Candlemas, a day when candles are blessed and dedicated for use in the church that year. Perhaps one reason this day was chosen was because of Simeon's reference to Jesus as "a light for revelation to the Gentiles." We certainly know Jesus as the Light of the World, "a light that shines in the darkness, and the darkness has not overcome it" (John 1:5). Light reveals what might otherwise be hidden from our sight. It shows us the truth. John the Baptist, the first in Mark's Gospel to *tell* about Jesus and *show* reverence to him, has been described as "not the light, but [one who] came to bear witness to the light" (John 1:8).

III. *God invites us to show and tell.* Our text demonstrates that no one who encountered Jesus was unaffected. There was always a reaction: honor, confession of Jesus' identity, wonder, and so on. Lives were changed, and people *showed* it both by their reaction and by *telling* others. We do not have Jesus in the flesh among us, so we encounter him by faith rather than by sight. And if he has transformed our lives, we should let it show! The Lord, who invited Simon and Andrew to become "fishers of men" and who commissioned his followers to "go and make disciples of all nations," includes us in the ongoing work of redemption. The Light of the World bids us to "let your light so shine before others, that they may see your good works and give glory to your Father who is in heaven." It is our calling. It is our privilege. And if we love Jesus, it is our joy to show and tell others about him.—Carol M. Norén

ILLUSTRATIONS

ASPIRATION.   An old gospel song expresses well a Christian's aspiration to show and tell others who Jesus is:

> Let the beauty of Jesus be seen in me.
> All his wonderful passion and purity.
> O, Thou Spirit divine, all my nature refine

Till the beauty of Jesus be seen in me.
Let the fruit of the Spirit be seen in me;
Grant me grace all sufficient that I may be
True and faithful each day, every step of the way,
Pointing souls to the Savior on Calvary.[1]

THE REAL CELEBRITY.   Where I live it is the custom in some restaurants for the owners to display photographs of various famous people who have eaten there. The celebrities are never pictured alone, however; the restaurant owner is always in the picture, grinning widely and posed to suggest close friendship with the celebrity. The cumulative effect, however, is that the restaurant owner is more important than the people who have dined there. After all, the owner is depicted over and over, in every photograph.

If it were possible to photograph your or my relationship with Christ, what would the world see? Would Jesus be at the center of every picture, and would the photos suggest the richness and depths of his nature? Or would viewers see us mugging for the camera, taking center stage, eclipsing rather than revealing the one who honors us with his presence?—Carol M. Norén

SERMON SUGGESTIONS

Topic: Receiving and Giving
TEXT: Mic. 6:1–8
(1) What God has done for us. (2) What God requires of us.

Topic: God's Foolishness
TEXT: 1 Cor. 1:18–31
(1) In the means of salvation that he chose. (2) In the people he accepts for salvation.

CONGREGATIONAL MUSIC

1. "God Has Spoken by His Prophets," George W. Briggs (1952)
   ODE TO JOY, Ludwig van Beethoven (1824)
   This fine hymn would fit well with the Old Testament reading about God's raising up prophets to speak forth God's commands.
2. "Silence, Frenzied, Unclean Spirit," Thomas H. Troeger (1984)
   EBENEZER, Thomas J. Williams (1890)
   Based directly on the incident recorded in today's Gospel lesson (Mark 1:21–28), this contemporary hymn offers a meaningful, prayerful response for worshippers seeking healing in mind and heart.
3. "I Would Be True," Howard Arnold Walter (1906)
   PEEK, Joseph Yates Peek (1909)

---

[1]Albert Orsborn, "Let the Beauty of Jesus," in N. A. Woychuk (ed.), *Making Melody* (St. Louis: Bible Memory Association, 1949), no. 119.

This early twentieth-century hymn, sung congregationally or by a youth choir, would be appropriate as a response to the Epistle reading (1 Cor. 8:1–13) on the theme of positively influencing those who may be weaker.

4. "God's Holy Ways Are Just and True," Ps. 111; para. Barbara Woolett (c.1984)
 LASST UNS ERFREUEN, Geistliche Kirchengesang (1623)

This free, Christianized paraphrase of Psalm 111 would be effective sung immediately after the Psalter reading for this day.—Hugh T. McElrath

WORSHIP AIDS

CALL TO WORSHIP.   "Shout praises to the Lord! With all my heart I will thank the Lord when his people meet. The Lord has done many wonderful things! Everyone who is pleased with God's marvelous deeds will keep them in mind" (Ps. 111:1–2 CEV).

INVOCATION.   How can we keep from shouting our praises to you, O Lord, for you have been good to us beyond all our deserving. Help us to meditate on all the marvelous things you are doing even now among us as we worship, we trust, in Spirit and in truth.

OFFERTORY SENTENCE.   "For us there is one God, the Father, from whom are all things and for whom we exist, and on Lord, Jesus Christ, through whom are all things and through whom we exist" (1 Cor. 8:6 NRSV).

OFFERTORY PRAYER.   All things belong to you, O God, yet we presume to bring an offering to you of the very things you have provided. Use these expressions of our faith and love, we pray, that others too may know of your Fatherly love, especially the gift of your Son, our Lord Jesus Christ.

PRAYER.   Our heavenly Father, we praise you for your infinite wisdom, while we stand in awe of the mystery of your ways. Again and again, in the history of the world and in our personal and private stories, you have proven that your way is best. Still, we often reluctantly conclude and confess that you have been at work in all things to accomplish your good and gracious purpose.

We thank you for the wisdom of the cross, by which you have purchased our salvation and in which you freely give us all things. We thank you for the wisdom of our own crosses, which we often fail to understand and even rebel against. Yet grant to us the grace not to crucify Christ afresh to ourselves by any reckless thought of your power to overrule our sins. And grant to us the grace not to add to the burden of the crosses that others must bear in their brave and costly discipleship.

SERMON
Topic: How to Ask for Help, How to Give It
TEXT: James 2:14–17; 3:13

This sermon is based on two fundamental assumptions: we all have problems, and from time to time we could all use—or offer—a little help for dealing with those problems.

Neither of these is easy for most of us: to struggle through life's difficult times and to ask for help in our struggles, or to give help. The fact is, lots of us feel helpless around people who are having a hard time. Helpless and guilty. Whatever we say seems weak and stiff, empty and meaningless. Whatever we try to do doesn't seem to make the slightest dent in their need.

We're left wondering, How can we help? What can we do? And if it were us, how would we ask for help? How would we ever muster the courage to let others know that we need them? That's what this sermon is about. Let's get started.

I. *How do we go about asking for help?* Let's face it: asking doesn't come easily for most of us. If, however, you know that you need help, here are some principles for asking for it.

(a) *Ask.* No one can read your mind. And even though God can, he still expects you to verbalize your need. It's an adult game, you know. Children don't play it. They're much too open and direct. They say how they feel. They tell you what they want.

But how many times have you heard some adult say, "Well, if you really loved me, I wouldn't have to ask!" Well, it's not true! It really is possible that someone could love you and still not know what you want or need—still have no idea what it would take to make you happy.

What happens in the game we play is that when someone doesn't respond exactly the way or at precisely the time we thought they should—even though we never told them what we expected—deep resentments begin to build up.

(b) *Start with God.* The reason is simple. The apostle Peter writes, "Cast all your anxiety on him because he cares for you" (1 Pet. 5:7). Isn't that enough of a reason to start with God? When you have a problem, don't you want to share it with someone you trust, someone who has your best interests at heart, someone who cares for and loves you, who understands you, and who always knows just the right thing to say? Of course you do. Then who meets all those qualifications better than God does?

Immediately upon recognizing that you have a problem, take it to the Lord, before it becomes too complicated and tangled—even before you discuss it with anyone else. Don't wait! Ask for his wisdom in dealing with the situation early on.

(c) *Be liberal with your requests for prayer, but discerning with your specific pleas for help.* In other words, be careful about broadcasting the details of your problems to the whole world. It's perfectly all right to ask all your friends and acquaintances—even your Sunday school class or church—to pray for you. However, be very discreet about how much of your personal life you share with more than a few people. Those closest to you—those you know best—may not always be able to help you. Be prayerfully discerning about those with whom you share your deepest needs.

(d) *Seek only Godly counsel.* The Scripture states, "Oh, the joys of those who do not follow the advice of the wicked . . . but they delight in doing everything the Lord wants" (Ps. 1:1). I cannot tell you how strongly I believe this, but I do believe that Christians have a responsibility to seek out, listen to, and do their best to consider prayerfully only the advice and counsel of other spiritually mature Christians.

We live among people and are surrounded by perspectives and worldviews that have no relationship whatsoever—no respect, connection, or interest—in God. To follow the advice and counsel of persons who hold those philosophies and to come under the influence of such worldly and nonspiritual teachings is nothing more than to deliberately separate ourselves from God. Seek and accept counsel and advice only from those who recognize God as the source and destiny of the soul.

(e) *Be realistic in your expectations.* No one can "fix" your problem for you. Only you and God can do that. Let people do what they can, even if it's not everything you thought it would be. If you refuse what they offer, or begrudge it as insufficient, you may be refusing, or begrudging, a gift sent by God.

II. *Some pointers on how to give help.*

(a) *Be a person of prayer.* Pray, but not just in the moment of crisis. Be one whose life is devoted to nurturing a relationship with God and lifting others up to him in concern and out of love.

(b) *Be a person of integrity and confidentiality.* The writer of Proverbs warns that "a gossip betrays a confidence, but a trustworthy person keeps a secret" (11:13).

(c) *Be a helpful, sensitive, loving person—one who is full of grace.* Understand that the reason most people show up at church after a lengthy period of absence and inactivity is because they're going through a difficult time. Often they're in the throes of a crisis and are just turning to—or perhaps returning to—God and his church—to whom they've always been told they could turn for help. Be glad when you see someone after a long absence, and in your private and personal prayer time, lift up those for whom you've neglected to pray for some time.

(d) *Defer judgment.* It's difficult sometimes to listen to people's stories without judging them. Your friends need you to care, not to criticize, to confront them with the truth, not to condemn them because of their failures. No one likes to be on the receiving end of a lecture, but everyone longs to be loved—genuinely, sincerely, deeply loved—especially if they've been unlovely and unlovable.

(e) *Listen.* When friends ask for help, usually they just want someone to listen. Ninety-nine percent of the time they don't want advice—at least at first. There's no shortage of people willing to talk and to give advice; but a person who's quiet and who tries to understand will be the one who will be able to help the most.

(f) *Avoid simple solutions.* The Bible reminds us that in the Christian's life, things are seldom what they seem. Whatever problem a friend is dealing with, however, it is always appropriate to pray. You will find that people discover a real peace when you pray with them. Such a partnership can also serve as a model to help them restore, renew, or reclaim their own conversational life with God.

(g) *Be discreet.* The Bible directs God's people to avoid all appearances of evil (1 Thess. 5:22) and never to place ourselves in a situation where Satan can gain an advantage over us (James 4:7; 1 Pet. 5:8–9). It is therefore always best to let men help men and women help women. There is a special kind of intimacy that occurs in helping relationships, and if it's not properly and maturely handled, it can lead to sin.

(h) *Know your limits—and that God has none!* If you're committed to helping others, it won't be long until you're faced with an "impossible" situation. You'll stand beside some friend who's facing a crisis like none you've ever seen before. You won't be able to understand how they got there and you won't be able to see any way out. But that's not the time to give up. Instead, that's the time to confess your limitations, your weaknesses, your frailties, and your own inabilities. It's the time to take your friend to God—the one with whom you know nothing is impossible.

Lead them to the Father, about whom Jesus said, "Come unto me all you who are weary and burdened, and I will give you rest" (Matt. 11:28). With God there is healing and wholeness and hope! What more could you possibly need?—Gary C. Redding

SUNDAY, FEBRUARY 9, 2003

Lectionary Message

Topic: Not *Quite* All Things

TEXT: 1 Cor. 9:16–23

Other Readings: Isa. 40:21–31; Ps. 147:1–11, 20c; Mark 1:29–39

A denomination in North America was publishing its first new hymnal in many years. As part of the advance publicity, the hymnal was featured in the denomination's magazine, along with a color photograph of the book. The photographer or editor was someone with a sense of humor, as evidenced by the name on the cover of the "personalized" hymnal: Hilda Dyon. It was an apt pun, for many worshipers have such strong feelings about church music—that it *is,* metaphorically, a "hill to die on." They will do battle for a music-worship style that is to their liking. Devout Christians argue bitterly about the type of music used in worship, labeling their opponents' preferences as boring, stuck in the past, no different from rock music, lacking any sense of reverence, unappealing to Generation X, simplistic, and so on.

I. *Questions that makes us nervous.* Music is not the only hot-button issue in the Church. Roman Catholics debate the issues of an all-male priesthood and the requirement of celibacy. Given the general decline in religious vocations (except in Third World countries), many call for their church to change its policies. Evangelical denominations and independent churches continue to struggle with the changing role of women in the church and society. My own denomination, like many others, argues about homosexuality—both the ordination of self-avowed, practicing homosexuals, and the call for clergy to officiate at same-sex-union services. As a newspaper reporter said to me, "Well, if there are gay couples in the church and in the neighborhood around the church, and it really means a lot to them to get married, shouldn't a minister meet that need? Isn't the church supposed to minister to people's needs?" Every "hill to die on" I have mentioned raises a question suggested by today's Epistle reading: If Paul was willing to "become all things to all people, that he might by all means save some," what things should *we* become? What needs to change, and what should emphatically *not* change?

II. *Answers that make us nervous.* Without minimizing the significance of all the issues just named, it does seem to me we put the cart before the horse when our primary attention is on the *"hills"* rather than the *"die on."* Or to put it another way, we lose sight of what is most important when we give our energy to negotiating what ground may be yielded instead of on the faith that guides our negotiating. The driving force behind Paul's exhortation to the Church at Corinth was his passion for the gospel. As he says in verse 18, "What then is my reward? Just this: that in my preaching I may make the gospel free of charge, not making full use of my right in the gospel." For Paul, making Christ known as Savior and Lord was more important than how he dressed, what he ate, local customs, personal preferences, or assuming his rights as an apostle. He could speak the dialect of his listeners, using the indigenous imagery of "an unknown god" to present the gospel in Athens (Acts 17:22–33) or appealing to the faith of Abraham to explain justification to the Judaizers in Galatia. It was not "market analysis" he used to accommodate local beliefs and customs, for the only faith Paul proclaimed was in Christ crucified and risen—a gospel that he realized would win some but not all. So zealous was Paul for bringing sinners into a reconciling relationship with God through Christ that he was a slave for the cause—that is, he was loving and self-giving to the point of death. This is a far cry from the self-preservation or perpetuation that motivates some congregations to "become all things to all people."

III. *Questions to ask about "becoming all things."* If we wish to be ambassadors for Christ, as Paul was, and faithful witnesses in a contentious and narcissistic society, our decision making will be informed by a set of values our listeners probably won't perceive—and even if they do, they may not understand. When faced with controversial questions of his day, such as whether to eat food sacrificed to idols or whether to conform to certain Mosaic laws, Paul's bottom line was, Does this proclaim the gospel of Jesus Christ and glorify him? Is it confirmed by God's Word? Will it strengthen Christian faith? If we can answer affirmatively, we too may become "all things to all people"—all things that truly point people to God.—Carol M. Norén

ILLUSTRATIONS

THE CHAMELEON.   When a person is described as a "chameleon" it is generally not meant as a compliment. It suggests that the person is duplicitous—willing to change appearance or viewpoints in order to blend into his or her surroundings. And yet, while a chameleon does change colors, it is never anything but a chameleon. It breathes and eats and acts true to its nature. As Christians we can learn something from chameleons. We can show that we take our surroundings seriously, and harmonize with the cultural context. But at the same time, our nature as children of God through Jesus Christ must remain the same. That identity, rather than our surroundings, will determine the way we speak and live.—Carol M. Norén

FAITHFUL WITNESS.   In *The Nun's Story,* Kathryn Hulme described a wealth and variety of personalities manifested in the convent, in spite of the relative anonymity created by wearing the habit. She mentioned a sister whom the other nuns referred to as a "Living Rule." It was believed that if the written rule of the order was ever lost or destroyed, it could be reconstituted by studying the Living Rule. Her life so embodied the rules and beliefs of the order that other nuns could learn what they needed to know by observing her. So it should be with disciples who live outside the cloister. We are not identical to one another, nor are we called to be. But faithful witness means the world should be able to see the same Christ, our "Living Rule," in our words and actions.—Carol M. Norén

SERMON SUGGESTIONS

Topic: Self-Denial That Accomplishes Something
TEXT: Isa. 58:3–9a
(1) Self-denial is an honorable and effective way to spiritual health. (2) Self-denial of a kind may be a substitute for a more important religious duty. (3) A lifestyle of total discipline not only does the will of God but also brings rewards.

Topic: God's Saving Truth
TEXT: 1 Cor. 2:1–11
(1) It bursts the bounds of human experience. (2) It transcends the subtleties of human philosophies. (3) Its power lies in the weakness of the cross.

CONGREGATIONAL MUSIC

1. "Be Strong in the Lord," Linda Lee Johnson (1979)

   FETTKE, Tom Fettke (1979)

   This contemporary Scripture song makes reference to the metaphor of mounting up as eagles (Isa. 40:31). Consequently, it could quite naturally be sung after the reading of the Old Testament lesson.

2. "Your Hands, O Lord, in Days of Old," Edward H. Plumptre (1866)

   ST. MICHAEL'S, W. Gawler's Hymns and Psalms (1789)

   This thoughtful nineteenth-century hymn has the same theme as the Gospel lesson (Mark 1:29–39) focusing on the healing ministry of Jesus and would be appropriately sung thereafter.

3. "May the Mind of Christ My Savior," Kate B. Wilkerson (1925)

   ST. LEONARDS, A. Cyril Barham-Gould (1925)

   This simple hymn of commitment, which magnifies Christ and not self in seeking to win others, would be an effective response to the reading of the Epistle lesson (1 Cor. 9:16–23).

4. "O Praise the Lord, for It Is God," Ps. 147:1–13; vers. Psalter (1912)

   MINERVA, John H. Stockton (1874)

   This rather extended metrical version of the first part of Psalm 147 could be sung in lieu of the reading of the Psalter lesson. Alternate singing line by line between choir and congregation would be effective.—Hugh T. McElrath

WORSHIP AIDS

CALL TO WORSHIP.   "Praise the Lord! How good it is to sing praises to our God; for he is gracious, and a song of praise is fitting" (Ps. 147:1).

INVOCATION.   O Lord, our Lord, give us eyes to see and hearts to appreciate the wonder of your grace. You have entered our lives through many doors, and we have been made aware of your concern for us and for your entire creation. Now may our songs and hymns and listening ears be glorifying to you.

OFFERTORY SENTENCE.   "So, then, each of us will be accountable to God" (Rom. 14:12).

OFFERTORY PRAYER.   Not only our money, O God, but all that we have and are is a gift from you. Help us to find the joy of sharing our blessings with others through our Christian stewardship, in anticipation of our Lord's approval, saying, "Well done, good and faithful servants."

PRAYER.   Accept, O Lord, our thanks and praise for all that you have done for us. We thank you for the splendor of the whole creation, for the beauty of this world, for the wonder of life, and for the mystery of love.

We thank you for the blessing of family and friends, and for the loving care that surrounds us on every side.

We thank you for setting us at tasks which demand our best efforts, and for leading us to accomplishments which satisfy and delight us.

We thank you also for those disappointments and failures that lead us to acknowledge our dependence on you alone.

Above all, we thank you for your Son Jesus Christ; for the truth of his Word and the example of his life; for his steadfast obedience, by which he overcame temptation; for his dying, through which he overcame death; and for his rising to life again, in which we are raised to the life of your Kingdom.

Grant us the gift of your Spirit, that we may know him and make him known; and through him, at all times and in all places, may give thanks to you in all things.—*The Book of Common Prayer*

SERMON
Topic: This Is the Day
TEXT: Ps. 118:24

The world is filled with people who wake up in the morning dreading the day. They may not actually dread it, but they do not look forward to it, they take no delight in it, and they secretly wish it were over before it has begun.

It is the experience of all religious people, I think, and especially Christians, that such a negative response to life does not really come from any external condition that cannot be changed. Rather, it comes from an internal religious attitude, which can be changed.

It is fair to say, I am sure, that all of us wake up some days dreading the day that is to come, and some of us find that it has become a chronic habit. Therefore, it is part of our religious duty and obligation to see if we can alter our religious attitude toward life so that we will meet the day that God gives us with gladness. One of the psalmists helps us in the affirmation he makes, which has been repeated so many times through the centuries. "This is the day the Lord has made; we will rejoice and be glad in it."

I. One of the first things the psalmist's words suggest is that there is no time like the present. "*This* is the day." Yesterday is gone and it cannot be recalled. Tomorrow is not yet here and it cannot be anticipated; neither can its way toward us be hastened by any daydreaming in which we may indulge. But today is here, with all its infinite possibilities.

Some people live in the past, wrapping themselves up in memories they have enjoyed so that the day through which they live never brushes them. You know the type of person who looks back on his college days with so much delight and thinks so well of the relationships he had then that he never seems to make any adult, mature relationships as life goes on from year to year. Other people miss the day by living in the past because they worry about mistakes they have made and they see the consequences of those mistakes accumulate and pile up until they feel themselves under a mountain of regrets and remorse.

Other people live in the future. Their minds are set on some distant time that may someday exist. They may see the future with anxiety or they may see it with a certain kind of anticipation, but however they see it, they concentrate so entirely upon it that they miss the day that now passes.

This is not so with Jesus, our Lord and Master. Certainly no one ever appreciated the past any more than he did. He drew on the reserves of the past constantly. He was always turning back to the spiritual insights of his forefathers and drawing from them the strength and inspiration to live his own life. And certainly he did not ignore the future. His prayer was, "Thy Kingdom come"—in the future, in its fullness. But certainly we cannot observe the life of Jesus carefully and not recognize that while he appreciated the past and looked to the future, he lived in the present. *This* day was for him the important day. Listen to his prayer:

"Give us *this* day our daily bread." Not enough bread for the years to come, but for this day. And when people were anxious about the future, he pointedly put to them in very brief terms, "Sufficient unto the day is the evil thereof."

We have to do some readjusting of our religious attitudes, and the first thing to do is to say over and over again to ourselves, *There is no time like the present.* If you have made mistakes, do what you can *today* to correct them. If you are not prepared for the future, do what you reasonably can *today* to make those preparations, and then let the past go, let the future take care of itself, and live today. Enjoy it. That is what God wants you to do—not to endure it. Enjoy it as a gift filled with manifold blessings. That is the first thing.

II. Another thing these words suggest—and this you will perhaps not be quite so ready to receive—is that there is no such thing as good days and bad days, for they are all God's days. "This is the day which the Lord hath made." You did not make it. This is not your day, even though sometimes you presume to think of it in such terms. It is his day. He made it and filled it with all its divine possibilities. And if that is true, it is true as a corollary that there is no such thing as good days and bad days.

While we are not saying that everything that comes to us in life comes directly from God— it does not always; it sometimes comes from our stupidity and folly and the sin of our fellow men—nevertheless, the day comes from God, and in that sense it is good, and in that sense every thing that happens to us in the day has its divine possibilities, because God is in it. There are people in life who consciously cultivate an attitude that habitually accepts whatever comes as having divine possibilities.

Dread not the day, for it is indeed God's day, and if as you meet it you see dark shadows casting themselves across the day, say to yourself, "The shadows, too, are in God's hands, and even though this day be a grim one, I am approaching it as one who expects the possibility, at least, that it may be a great one because it is God's day, not my day."

III. This sentence from the psalmist leads us to one final thought: A man can be better than he feels. Notice the English grammar of the last line. "This is the day which the Lord hath made. We *will* rejoice and be glad in it."

If the sentence read, "We *shall* be glad in it," it would mean that just as a matter of course we shall be glad. But we *will* be glad means that we are deliberately going to be glad, we are determined to rejoice. We may not feel like it at all, but we are going to do it because we have a share in the control of our emotions and we are not entirely the victim of the way we feel at the moment.

You can do it by making simple affirmations that at first may come only from the lips, but if you try you will be surprised to find how they do get down there and do change your feelings. For instance, you can get up in the morning and say to yourself, This is the day which the Lord hath made; I will rejoice and be glad in it—regardless. You can find other affirmations that give the same implication in their message to your emotions. One of the ones I say over and over again is, "O be joyful in the Lord all ye lands. Serve the Lord with gladness and come before his presence with song."

As you make these affirmations and these suggestions that go out as messages to your feelings, you realize that you are no longer the victim of your feelings and you are better than you feel. Take, then, these suggestions as they apply to your own lives, and begin experimentally tomorrow morning not to dread the day. It is God's day, and miraculous to say, you can be better than you feel.—Theodore Parker Ferris

SUNDAY, FEBRUARY 16, 2003
Lectionary Message

Topic: God's Power, Our Response

TEXT: 2 Kings 5:1–14

Other Readings: Ps. 30; 1 Cor. 9:24–27; Mark 1:40–45

The adult Sunday School class was having an animated, almost heated discussion. The subject was a staff member at this mainline church who had been suffering from cancer for several years. Dorothy had undergone many experimental and unpleasant treatments, seemingly to no avail. A recent set of tests revealed two new tumors along her spine. About the same time, she began participating in a nondenominational women's Bible study and prayer group. The leader of the group suggested that the members lay hands on Dorothy and pray for healing, and they did so. And now the latest tests showed that the two new tumors had disappeared.

"God doesn't work that way today!" exclaimed Barbara. "That was just for Bible times." George needled her, saying, "Gee, can you find a text to support that idea?" Haley said, "I'm just glad Dorothy is better. I don't care if it was prayer, or crystals, or coincidence—whatever works." Joanne wondered why God hadn't healed *her* mother. And Carl remarked, "What's the matter? You seem more upset by the possibility that God hears and answers prayer than the possibility that he doesn't." Needless to say, there was no resolution to this argument in one class session. But Dorothy and her family rejoiced in what God had done.

I. *God can heal and save.* Like the Sunday School class, Naaman and his contemporaries had definite and conflicting ideas about healing. Naaman's wife's servant girl claimed that the prophet Elisha could heal Naaman of his leprosy. The king of Syria evidently believed that kings had more power than prophets did, so he sent a letter and a bribe to the king of Israel—as though healing could be bought. Naaman himself expected that Elisha would wave his hand over him, invoke the name of his God, and instantaneously cure him of his leprosy. And the king of Israel was far more concerned about the political ramifications of it all than he was about God's power to heal.

The Lord can and does heal; both the Old Testament and the Gospel readings for today bear witness to that. In Mark 1:40–45, Jesus healed the leper immediately, as soon as the leper knelt and said, "If you will, you can make me clean." The process described in 2 Kings 5 is less straightforward; Naaman was required to wash in the Jordan seven times. The divine power to save is manifested in an endless variety of ways throughout the Bible: parting the Red Sea so the children of Israel could escape to safety, delivering Daniel from the lion's den and the three young men from the fiery furnace, bringing wholeness to a woman who merely touched the hem of Jesus' garment, and so on. All these acts of God were not retold in order to claim particular virtue for those healed or saved, but to bear witness to God's sovereignty and good purpose. Genesis 18:14 asks the rhetorical question, "Is anything too hard for the Lord?" and people of faith know the answer.

II. *God is not bound to our expectations.* Naaman was angry, because God's prophet Elisha did not heal him in the way he expected. Jonah was peeved when God's power to save extended not only to him but also to other sinners living in Nineveh. Mary and Martha expressed despair that Jesus had not come immediately when their brother Lazarus was dying. The Pharisees were dismayed that our Redeemer healed on the Sabbath. And we, too, are prone to become discouraged, fearful, or impatient when God acts in ways we did not expect.

Sometimes, as with Naaman, limited understanding is our problem. Naaman apparently knew little about the God of Israel; in verse 11 he refers to "the Lord *his* [Elisha's] God." Unfamiliar with the faith and tradition of the Covenant people, he was unaware of the significance of being asked to wash seven times in the Jordan. Seven was the number of completion and perfection. The Jordan was the site of many miracles in Bible history. Naaman was being asked to align himself symbolically with the people of faith. But because of his ignorance, he resisted Elisha's instructions. Other times we are like the Pharisees, hindered by the presuppositions and prejudice we have about divine action. The Pharisees knew what the Scriptures said, but seemed to suppose that God was bound by the text, rather than that the written word bore witness to God's freedom and sovereignty. We may also bring to our prayers the cultural prejudices of a post-Enlightenment or postmodern mind-set.

III. *Obedience and praise open our eyes to God's power.* Naaman experienced the healing power of God once he did what God's prophet commanded. "His flesh was restored like the flesh of a little child, and he was clean," according to verse 14. He praised God before Elisha and a great company of witnesses, and vowed to worship the Lord of Israel. The mourners with Mary and Martha followed Jesus' order to roll away the stone from the tomb of Lazarus. Only then could they witness the power of God manifested. In both cases, a request was not answered in the time or in the manner expected.

God's power is still available in our world. Do we invite it to work in our lives? Do we believe our Lord's purpose is ever directed to his children's good? Let our prayer be, "For all that has been: thanks. For all that is to be: yes. For all that you are: glory!"—Carol M. Norén

ILLUSTRATION

MENDING A DAMAGED FAITH.   It was painful for me to write this book and tell the many stories in its pages, but it would have been much more painful for me not to write this book at all. God gave me an enduring love for the Church more than twenty-five years ago within a small Bible study group I attended in college. It is this love for the Church that compels me to challenge the Church to hear and attend to the cries of its own wounded. Paradoxically, the testimonies of the dechurched may provide a key to the ongoing transformation of the Church into the image of Christ.

I long for the day when the Church is known within the world more for its honesty than for its hallelujah's, more for its courage than for its cacophony of voices, more for its sensitivities than for its structures. I love the Church, and I wrestle with it. I love the Lord, and I wrestle with my faith as well. In that visceral relationship between loving and wrestling, I find strength, hope, and life that cannot be extinguished.—Mary Tuomi Hammond[2]

SERMON SUGGESTIONS

Topic: The Right Way

Text: Deut. 30:15–20

1) To love God continuously. (2) To obey God when moral choices appear. (3) To cling to God in times of desperation.

---

[2]*The Church and the Dechurched* (St. Louis: Chalice Press, 2001), p. 189.

Topic: The Secret of Success in Christian Service

TEXT: 1 Cor. 3:1–9

(1) We are workers together under God. Different workers with different roles can be equally important. (2) In the last analysis, our best work amounts to nothing apart from the blessing of God, who makes our work truly succeed. (3) Therefore, there is no room for jealousy and strife in the Christian community, since it is "only God who gives the growth."

CONGREGATIONAL MUSIC

1. "Praise to the Lord, the Almighty," Joachim Neander (1680); trans. Catherine Winkworth (1863)

    LOBE DEN HERREN, Stralsund Gesangbuch (1665)

    A fine hymn for the beginning of worship, "Praise to the Lord" relates also to the healing themes in the Old Testament lesson (2 Kings 5:1–14) and the Gospel reading (Mark 1:40–45).
2. "Jesus' Hands Were Kind Hands," Margaret Cropper (c. 1926)

    AU CLAIR DE LA LUNE, trad. French melody

    This lovely little hymn could be sung by a children's choir in connection with the healing of the leper in the Gospel reading (Mark 1:40–45).
3. "Fight the Good Fight with All Your Might," John S. B. Monsell (1863)

    PENTECOST, William Boyd (1864)

    This classic nineteenth-century hymn could be sung as a response to the Epistle reading (1 Cor. 9:24–27) in which the apostle speaks of the discipline of the Christian life in athletic terms.
4. "Come Sing to God," Ps. 30; vers. Fred R. Anderson (1986)

    ELLACOMBE, Gesangbuch der H.W.K. Hofkapelle (1784)

    A free modern paraphrase of Psalm 30, "Come Sing to God" could be sung at the opening of worship or at the place of the Psalter reading.—Hugh T. McElrath

WORSHIP AIDS

CALL TO WORSHIP.   "Sing praises to the Lord, O you his faithful ones, and give thanks to his holy name. For his anger is but for a moment; his favor is for a lifetime. Weeping may linger for the night, but joy comes with the morning" (Ps. 30:4–5).

INVOCATION.   O God, you are forever loving us in spite of the things we do that we should not do, and in spite of the things we fail to do that we ought to do. How we must often grieve your heart, yet you patiently work with us to bring us back to duty and obedience, and withal to the joy that faithfully serving you restores to our life and witness.

OFFERTORY SENTENCE.   "The Earth is the Lord's and all that is in it, the world and those who live in it" (Ps. 24:1).

OFFERTORY PRAYER.   Lord, the Earth is yours and we are yours. Thank you for the partnership you have given us in the use and distribution of your good gifts that you have bestowed upon us. Bless this time of our returning to you a portion of what we have received from you, and may the use of these offerings glorify your name.

PRAYER.   Our Father, we know that you love us. No gift of yours could be greater than the gift of your Son, the revelation of your love and the means of our salvation. Yet some of us come before you perplexed. We have prayed for one thing and received another, or nothing at all. We have expected abundant life, yet life has become for us pinched and frustrated. Nevertheless, you have promised your help to those who cry to you. Grant that we may not look so longingly at doors closed that we cannot see other doors opening before us. Give us the grace to accept, if it is your will, some lesser good that we may discover at last to be what is best of all. Let us not be afraid to struggle with you in our disappointments, assured that you sometimes inspire us to pray bold, believing prayers that may seem to be defiant even of you. Yet may we always be prepared to say, "Not my will, but yours be done."

SERMON
Topic: The Business of Temptation
TEXT: Luke 4:1–13

A lot of it is about establishing credentials. The voice of God may have just declared Jesus to be his Son and told everyone to listen to him; but the Children of Israel have had a long history with God and they know some of the things that the chosen of God have gone through to validate their positions. So this story of Jesus being led into the wilderness for a period of forty days in which he will engage in some very powerful wrestling with the powers of evil has as one of its missions the linking of Jesus with the past prophets of God.

Moses and the children of Israel were rambling around in the wilderness, and Moses was invited up into the presence of God and spent forty days and forty nights up on Mt. Sinai in negotiations with God. After the great battle with the gods of Baal, Elijah fled for forty days into the wilderness to wrestle with his feelings of isolation and abandonment, to be ministered to by God and to hear the still, small voice of assurance. King David was hunted and pursued by King Saul and spent years hiding in the wilderness and caves to avoid Saul's jealousy. Jesus' visit to the wilderness has a great number of precedents that confirm that Jesus was called by God to a special work.

The anointed of God have consistently been called to a period of testing in the wilderness over the same kind of issues—trust and obey—to do it God's way, to hunger for bread, to go where they're led. Remember how critical the question and the hunger for bread became for Moses and the children of Israel? How God answered with manna? Remember how often the children of Israel became disgusted with the way and the direction in which Moses was taking them, and talked about going home? Remember how even after bread had been supplied they became rebellious again when they became thirsty? Certainly, in the wilderness Moses had to wrestle with the demands of physical needs, with trusting God's way of doing things, and with the question of the nature of the covenant people of God.

As we have come to expect, God's chosen goes into the wilderness for a time of testing, and we are assured that if Jesus is tempted and tested, all human beings are tempted and tested. If God's Son is not exempted, none are exempted. Like Adam and Eve, Jesus encountered Satan, and Satan wanted to engage Jesus in a few friendly theological discussions.

Sometimes the rest of us are tempted to believe that good people never suffer temptations. The saints don't understand the pressures and the pains and the attractions of some of our sins. But temptation comes only in the form of encouraging us to do what is within our own powers, to do what just may be possible. The greater the gifts, the greater the temptations. We are usually tempted to try to step up, to exceed our ability. What we know we cannot do or what we know we can easily do seldom tempts us. ACC basketball analysts will say over and over again this week, he is trying to do too much. He is trying to make things happen. He needs to wait and let the game come to him. Temptation comes when we are urged to stretch beyond our abilities.

So Satan came and began this little discussion. "If you are the Son of God. . . ." Now, there are some people for whom just the mention of that word, *Satan*, makes this story into a kind of fairy tale. The whole image of a personal devil strikes many as superstition and unreal. Pitchforks, tails, and horns might make Elizabeth Hurley a little more interesting to some, but the whole notion of that kind of personal temptation turns the discussion of evil into a Flip Wilson comedy routine. The reality of evil is, however, the only Christian doctrine that can be scientifically verified. Just look at the murder rate in this country and the number of people in prison. Nobody can see the bruises, cuts, and swollen faces of little children battered by child abuse and not see evil.

The image of Satan is the best way that human beings have found to be able to express the truths about evil without having to write a book each time the subject comes up. The reality of Satan affirms the reality of evil, and the power and potential of evil. There is a devil because there is evil, and it has a power that seeks to get a grip on human lives and to influence the direction of society. We speak of a personal devil, Satan, because it affirms that evil is personal. Evil comes into existence as individual people make choices between options and some options are not good for them at the time. Evil is created by personal choices that affect individual lives as well as all of society. Evil is always just a distortion and misuse of a good. So it is never possible to say that something like beer is always evil. It is the misuse and destructive use of a good process of fermentation that results in evil. And Satan always comes to us looking good. So much of the attraction of evil is that at the time it looks so good. I remember once hearing a psychologist say that no one intentionally chooses to do evil. They first convince themselves that it is a good and necessary thing to do, then they choose it. "I have to go see my grandmother. She is sick and in the hospital and may be dying and I just have to go see her; but I don't have any gas, so I will fill up the car and drive off without paying because I have to see my grandmother." Evil presents itself as a good, and Satan is one of the ways we remind ourselves that evil is always the enemy. Evil is always the enemy of God.

"If you are the Son of God, turn these stones into bread." Satan doesn't try to justify that suggestion. We can hear the arguments for it on so many different levels. Jesus has been in the wilderness forty days and nights. He is hungry. Certainly the Son of God needs to keep up his strength. He needs to take care of himself. Turn these stones to bread for yourself. Charity begins at home. Use your powers to take care of yourself.

"If you are the Son of God, turn these stones into bread." That could be your mission. Go about the countryside turning the stones into bread and providing a balanced, basic diet for all of the citizens of Israel. There are so many hungry in the world, certainly a program like Bread for the World would be a wonderful use of God's gifts.

"If you are the Son of God, turn these stones into bread." Let that suggest that you use your powers to take care of the basic human physical needs: food, shelter, clothing, health, and sanitation. If you care for these people, help them obtain the healthy and prosperous life. Maslow has provided evidence to suggest that until you have satisfied the lower needs, people have no interest in the higher needs. "If you are the Son of God, turn these stones to bread." Provide for the needy the physical and material things of life.

Jesus provides us with the question by which we try to find our way out of these temptations as they come to us. "Man does not live by bread alone." Jesus demonstrates that in the face of such temptations we are to ask ourselves what other needs and realities there are and what other possible actions might be taken. Giving bread is fantastic, but is that all that needs to be done? Are there ways by which other needs might also be met? Is there more that might be offered?

Barry Saunders of the *News and Observer* writes about Willie Gary, a Shaw graduate and a lawyer, who is now the CEO of Major Broadcasting Cable Network of Atlanta. Gary is attempting to bring clean, family values to television, "stuff you can watch with your kids." Gary is contrasted with Bob Johnson, who is CEO of Black Entertainment Television, which has made millions airing vile, sexual explicit programming that Johnson won't even let his own children watch. Barry Saunders says that for two decades Bob Johnson has been bombarding viewers with the electronic equivalent of crack.

Barry says that whenever he has criticized Bob Johnson in the past, Barry himself is subjected to all kinds of attacks from his black readers because Bob Johnson is a black entrepreneur who has been giving people jobs, and "the dude's getting paid." As if that justifies whatever he does. Jesus says, "Man does not live by bread alone." The fact that the dude's getting paid and paying others is not the only factor in deciding if Black Entertainment Television is a worthy enterprise.

We are expected to seek more than just the obvious and the simple and the quick. We are not to settle just for the good without asking what is the best.

Satan then took Jesus up to the Temple tower and showed him all the power, wealth, fame, and prestige of the world in a twinkling of an eye. A friend of mine at Yale Divinity School suggested that that was Satan's great mistake. Everybody becomes suspicious when the salesman pulls out the product, shows it to you quickly, and then puts it away. We all begin to think that maybe there is not as much to it; maybe it is all appearance and no substance; maybe it can stand to have its tires kicked and its doors slammed. Satan flip-charted all the power, fame, and wealth of the world before Jesus and told him it could all be his if Jesus would simply worship Satan. Satan offered to help Jesus accomplish what he had come for—to become ruler of all creation, to be lifted up as Lord of heaven and Earth, and to have every tongue confess that Jesus is Lord and every knee bow before the throne of glory. Satan was willing to give it to Jesus then, without the fight, without the pain, without the cross, if Jesus would simply bow. We know these suggestions as the temptation to achieve the right ends by the wrong methods, the right results with the inappropriate means, the final results by techniques that are incompatible with the end that is desired; as the temptation to achieve the Kingdom of God's grace by the right-handed power of might and intimidation. So many times in so many other places, I have watched as Christian groups have achieved their end of large and happy groups by means of parties, trips, and social prestige that are ultimately in conflict with the egalitarian love of the gospel. All of this is yours if you will now simply bow down and worship me. Jesus affirms that when you worship God's ends, you live by God's means, and only him shall you worship. In the Kingdom of God, the means are the ends.

Of course, if we accept the means and the ends, we are not freed from the temptation to try to do something that will make it happen a little faster, to force it to be done now, to put God in the position of needing to come through for the sake of his own consistency, to act so that he must keep his own promise. We are not freed from the temptation to recklessly build bombs of massive destruction because we believe that God has promised never again to destroy the world. If you are the Son of God, jump off this tower and make God keep his promise not to let you get hurt.

Throw yourself off the wall. Force God to act more swiftly. Put God to the test. Call on his promises. Jesus says that we shall not tempt or test the Lord God. Certainly it is an answer that forces us to explore more deeply our own motives for the testing. Why do we want to jump off the cliff? The young prophet Isaiah came to King Ahaz when Israel was heavily under siege by the armies of the Syrians. Isaiah assured King Ahaz that God would take care of Israel. King Ahaz was still frightened and considering surrender when Isaiah said to him, well, just ask the Lord to give you a sign. It can be anything you want, from heaven or hell. Just ask for some sign to prove to you my word about God's protection. And King Ahaz said exactly this: "I will not ask for a sign. I refuse to put the Lord to the test." Rather than applauding that answer, Isaiah got so peeved: "Listen you wimp, it is bad enough for you to wear out the patience of your people by your fear and apprehension, but do you have to be such a pain in the neck to God? Well listen, God is going to give you a sign whether you want it or not. A young woman who is now pregnant will have a son, and you will name him Immanuel." God wanted Ahaz to test him, and Ahaz refused.

As every preacher knows at stewardship time, there are these words in Malachi that Jesus knew in which God spoke to his people: "Bring the full amount of your tithes to the Temple so that there will be plenty of food there. Put me to the test and you will see that I will open the windows of heaven and pour out on you in abundance all kinds of good things." God challenged his own people to put him to the test. Jesus said, you shall not tempt the Lord God. Not for your own satisfaction, not just to cover up a doubt in your own heart, not to try to prove the existence of God to someone else.

Jesus encountered temptations. We encounter temptations. Everything Jesus refused to do at that time he in fact did at some time in the Scriptures. He did turn the stones into bread in the feeding of the five thousand. He did throw himself off into the void on the cross, trusting that God would not abandon or forsake him. He did become the Lord of heaven and Earth and was seated at the right hand of God, from whence he shall come to judge the living and the dead. Even for Jesus it was not the actions that were evil, but the when and the why and the wherefore. What are the other criteria by which this action has to be judged? Humanitarian aid is good, but is that all we are going to do? Are the means and the ends cut from the same cloth? We must be fussy about the means because there is only one way by which a kingdom of grace can be created, and that is by means of grace. What is the motive for your prayer? Why do you want God to respond to your test? Whose agenda will the testing validate?

And Satan went away until a more appropriate time.—Rick Brand

SUNDAY, FEBRUARY 23, 2003

Lectionary Message

Topic: Ever See Anything Like This?

TEXT: Mark 2:1–12

Other Readings: Isa. 43:18–25; Ps. 41; 2 Cor. 1:18–22

I. It is said that in 25 percent of all the autopsies performed on men over age 65 in the United States, prostate cancer is discovered in men who did not die of the disease. If the men had not died when they did, the undetected prostate cancer could have proven fatal. In warfare, in sickness, and in much of the rest of life, the most dangerous enemies are those we cannot see, because they catch us unaware.

There are two "enemies" afflicting the man whose friends lowered him through the roof to see Jesus. One enemy was the paralysis, which was evident to all who saw him on his pallet. The other, unseen enemy was sin. And unlike paralysis, sin holds every person present in the grip of death.

This sinister analysis of the miracle in Mark 2:1–12 is different from the way the lesson is taught to us in Sunday school. I can remember hearing this story for the first time and then building a flat-roofed house out of Popsicle sticks with the other children in the class. We sang songs about the kind friends who brought the paralyzed man to see Jesus the Healer. We were encouraged to do for others as the friends of the sick man did for him, that is, to bring our friends to Sunday school. Our point of identification with the text—though we didn't use such sophisticated language—was the onlookers or the good people who helped someone in need. It was a comfortable message. It also meant we never bothered much with the question of sin.

II. *Why we ignore the unseen enemy.* It is not so surprising that the primary focus of our interpretations is on the healing from the visible affliction—paralysis—rather than from the less obvious affliction—sin. The relationship between sin and sickness has always troubled followers of Jesus. The word *salvation* has the same root as the word *healing,* and just as we make a logical association between salvation and health, we make a similar connection between *needing* salvation and forgiveness and *needing* health and healing. Sometimes making that association is an error. When our Redeemer healed the man born blind (John 9), the first thing the disciples asked was, "Rabbi, who sinned—this man or his parents—that he was born blind?" They assumed that illness was a punishment for sin. Jesus' response indicated that blindness was not the result of sin. But in the healing of the paralytic, our Lord seems to encourage thinking of sin and sickness in the same frame of reference. That makes many Christians uneasy.

A second possible reason for avoiding mention of the "unseen enemy" is that an element is missing from this healing story that appears in other miracles in Mark's Gospel (1:40; 5:23; 5:34). There is no mention of the connection between *faith* and healing. This is an instance in which Jesus does not say, "Your faith has made you well." Because Christians believe that faith in Jesus Christ is necessary for the forgiveness of sin, and because faith is often mentioned in connection with healing, the healing of the paralytic poses something of a problem for us, so we avoid what we cannot see.

III. *Everyone there needed deliverance from the unseen enemy.* What sets this healing apart from those that occur earlier in Mark's Gospel is what aroused the wrath of the scribes who witnessed the miracle. Jesus' words pointed to the unseen affliction—sin. It was the first time Jesus exercised his divine power to forgive sin—an affliction that plagued everyone present at the scene. In this sense, this tale resembles the famous story of the woman taken in adultery, recorded in John 8. The crowd was ready to stone the woman for what she had done, but Jesus said, "Let the one who is without sin cast the first stone." He extended forgiveness to the woman, but his words and actions indicted the onlookers. In the same way, his pronouncement in Mark 2:1–12 convicts everyone present and simultaneously offers hope of forgiveness. The reaction from the crowd in verse 12 is testimony: "We never saw anything like this!" They had seen healings; they hadn't seen Jesus claim his rightful, divine power to forgive sin. The healing, then, is a sign or confirmation of the power to forgive, rather than an end in itself.

If we were honest with ourselves, where would you and I be standing in that crowded house in Capernaum? Would we be with the scribes, resistant to acknowledge either our need of forgiveness or our Lord's authority to give it? Or would we number ourselves with the paralytic and the crowd, amazed and thankful that such grace has been manifested before our eyes? What do we choose to see in this story? Only when we welcome Jesus as "God alone" (v. 7) do we see his salvation and health graciously offered to us.—Carol M. Norén

ILLUSTRATIONS

UNRECOGNIZED NEED.   A tragedy that seems to occur every time we have an unusually hot summer is the death of one or more athletes due to heat stroke. The shock of these deaths is greater because we assume that these people, usually football players practicing for the upcoming season, are in top physical condition. It is true that they are stronger and bigger than most of us. But it doesn't mean they can afford to disregard their bodies' needs. In one such recent death, the player showed warning signs of heat stroke, and coaches and teammates urged him to rest and take care of himself. But he refused help, continued to work out, and collapsed and died a short time later.

We might say that the Pharisees of Jesus' day were "spiritual athletes." They spent more time studying the Word and engaging in religious practices than the average person did. They were often admired as good examples. But all their own efforts could not cancel out their need for the grace made incarnate in Jesus Christ. Without his forgiveness and help, their extraordinary efforts toward holiness were for nought.—Carol M. Norén

THE REAL FOCUS.   One tantalizing aspect of the Gospels is that we are often not told much about the people whose lives were touched by Jesus. Have you ever wondered about the paralytic whose friends lowered him through the roof of that house in Capernaum? Were they friends of the man, or did he pay them to take him to Jesus? We don't know. Was he frightened or embarrassed as he was lowered from the roof? We don't know. Where did he go and what did he do after he was healed and forgiven? We don't know. As much as I'd like to have this additional information, perhaps the Gospel writers were wise not to supply it. After all, it nudges me away from preoccupation with the recipient of the miracle (and the possibility of narcissistic identification with that character). Instead, it urges me to focus on the Healer: who Jesus is, what he has done, and why that matters for all people.—Carol M. Norén

SERMON SUGGESTIONS

Topic: The Victories of Faith

TEXT: Gen. 37–50

The life of Joseph embodied a series of notable triumphs: (1) his victory over the temptation to despondency and despair, (2) his triumph over the temptation to impurity, (3) his victory over the temptation to abuse power and to live a life of self-indulgence and ease.—Charles R. Erdman

Topic: God Loves You

TEXT: John 3:14–21

(1) He gave his Son for you. (2) He offers you life in his Son. (3) He delivers you from judgment through faith in his Son.

CONGREGATIONAL MUSIC

1. "If You Will Trust in God to Guide You," Georg Nuemark (1641); trans. C. Winkworth (1863)

     WER NUR LIEBEN GOTT, Georg Nuemark (1657)

     A worshiping group would find the singing of this hymn meaningful following the reading of the Epistle lesson (2 Cor. 1:18–22), with its positive affirmation of God's goodness in his promises.
2. "Creating God, Your Fingers Trace," Jeffrey Rowthorn (1974)

     KEDRON, attr. Elkanah Kelsay Dare (1799)

     This contemporary Trinitarian hymn could be used effectively at the opening of worship. It would also relate appropriately (stanza 3) to the healing ministry of Jesus, as evidenced in the Gospel reading (Mark 2:1–12).
3. "How Blest Are They Who Thoughtfully," Ps. 41; vers. Bert Polman (1985)

     GREELEY, Roy Hopp (1984)

     A modern paraphrase of Psalm 41, this hymn could be sung either congregationally or chorally at the time of the Psalter reading.
4. "Great Is Thy Faithfulness," Thomas O. Chisholm (1923)

     FAITHFULNESS, William M. Runyan (1923)

     This vibrant song of faith could be used in connection with the Old Testament reading, with its stress on the new thing God is doing.—Hugh T. McElrath

WORSHIP AIDS

CALL TO WORSHIP.   "Blessed be the Lord, the God of Israel, from everlasting to everlasting. Amen and Amen" (Ps. 41:13).

INVOCATION.   Almighty God, you are and have always been the faithful deliverer of your people in the earthshaking events of human history. Come to us now in those lesser events of our personal lives and lead us to victory and joy. Toward those ends, let this time of worship deepen our reliance upon you, who can do "exceedingly abundantly above all that we ask or think."

OFFERTORY SENTENCE.   "For every wild animal of the forest is mine, the cattle on a thousand hills" (Ps. 50:10).

OFFERTORY PRAYER.   All things belong to you, O Lord; yet we have a role in the drama of your mighty works as we bring our little gifts for your use in the work of your Kingdom. We thank you that you have made us partners in your wonderful work.

PRAYER.   O Lord, you have proven your care for us again and again. You have spared our lives in hours of grave danger and in times of illness. You have comforted us in our suffering and in out sorrow.

Today we come to this place of worship with many needs. The whole range of human experience has affected us in one way or another. If we ever feel untouched, it is only for a moment.

Life has borne down so hard upon some of us that we sometimes doubt you. Do you care if we perish? Is there no relief forthcoming? Are your hands tied by the laws you have established? All these questions lurk in our inner shadows.

Help us, O Lord, to be honest with you and to put to you our hard questions. But give us the patience to live with the questions, either until the answers come or until a chastened faith allows us no longer to demand an answer.

SERMON
Topic: The Stone That the Builders Rejected
TEXT: Mark 12:1–12

We are still trying to understand the event on April 20, 1999, in Littleton, Colorado, when two angry young men armed with assault rifles and pipe bombs took the lives of fifteen people, including themselves, at Columbine High School. Charles Andrew Williams killed two and wounded thirteen other students in a suburban high school in San Diego County, California. During the same week, CNN noted sixteen incidents in California alone in which students were detained for making threats or carrying weapons, and thirteen incidents in schools from Seattle to Savannah. We are caught up in an atmosphere of self-doubt and fear. The media get blamed for exploiting the sensation and detailing events for copy-cats, and we get caught up in the blame game. Although experts say that the schools are safer than most other places in our communities, this is not about statistics.

Dr. Michael Sise, a trauma physician at the hospital where most of the San Diego victims were treated, was asked for an opinion. Sise observed a combination of a culture of violence and access to weapons by troubled teens leading to deadly consequences. Jim Copple, a former high school principal with the National Crime Prevention Council, observed, "Kids are sending warning signs, telling people that they are going to do something. . . . Parents and teachers need to key in on those types of clues."

We are beginning to see patterns. The troubled kids who explode with violence are almost always described as outcasts and loners. Someone told me last week, "That could have been me." In spite of the goodwill and good work of great teachers and administrators, the social ecology of a school is a place where kids have always been graded, classified, and labeled. The peer pressure of the social anthill in most high schools can be difficult at best and cruel at worst. Kids are often pitted against one another and get classified as winners and losers. High school is a place where kids are graded, and sometimes degraded, especially by peers. All of us have to deal with the rat race all our lives, and adults are little better prepared to deal with rejection than kids are. Maybe that is a key. We need to pay more attention to processing rejection in life.

As we approach the cross, we are reminded of the description of the "suffering servant" in Isaiah 53:3; this description was remembered in the face of Jesus: an appearance problem, "despised and rejected," acquainted with infirmity, "and we held him of no account." Does this sound something like the profile of the disturbed student who explodes with violence in our schools?

I. We live in a culture of violence. TV, arsenals of available weapons, and the Internet have been targeted as "the problem." However, kids were reflecting a troubled world long before the second half of the last century. Many of our external problems are reflections of the disease of the spirit that has infected humankind as long as recorded history can remember. The sin of the world is manifest in a culture of violence.

The parable of Jesus is really an allegory. Although the story seems to address a general audience, it is designed as an exposé of the religious leadership. The chief priests and the scribes had demanded from Jesus a permission slip from the proper authority for his ministry and teaching. Fred Craddock observed that the religious bosses were standing at the edge of the crowd "overhearing" the message. There was no mistaking the identity of the characters in the story. Isaiah 5 pictures Israel as the vineyard of the Lord rejected by God for yielding wild grapes. The story of Jesus starts out with Isaiah's vineyard, but turns in a different direction a bit closer to home. A man cultivated a vineyard and leased it to tenants. When he attempted to collect his share of the harvest, the tenants reacted with violence, beating and sometimes killing the messengers, reminding the listeners of the violent reaction of Israel to the prophets of God. In a final act of desperation, "He had still one other, a beloved son." The tenants decided that this was their chance to end the matter: Do away with the son and dispose of the heir. They killed the son and threw him out of the vineyard—an obvious reference to the execution about to take place in Jerusalem.

The story was presented in a culture of violence that could have been on the evening news. Joachim Jeremias said it pictured the attitude of Galilean peasants aroused by the Zealot movement toward foreign landlords. The Romans used crosses. The Zealots used guerilla tactics to kill the foreign invaders, but they would never have seen their violence as directed against God.

The violent culture represented in the death of Jesus still presents a problem. A half-century ago Theodore Clark wrote *Saved by His Life* as a protest to the "bloody" religion of the cross. The blood atonement still presents a problem for sensitive souls. The cross was probably more of a problem for early Christians than it is for us. Whatever else the cross reveals, it certainly exposes the culture of violence then and now.

II. We need a culture of redemption. Sometimes rejection by the world is a revelation of the greater purpose and bigger picture that God has for us. A. M. Hunter saw this as a parable for the church—describing the turn of God's favor from the Jews to the Gentiles, casting out the tenants and giving the vineyard to "others." This interpretation may be accurate, but it needs to be exposed as anti-Semitism that perpetuates the violence done to Jesus.

James Stewart detected the note of redemption. He called the parable "Loves Last Appeal," suggesting that Jesus was trying to reach the leaders of his people, to stop the violence before it happened. The central paradox of the gospel is found on the cross—the victim became victor. The one despised and rejected was the center of God's forgiving grace. The Son, who was killed and cast out, was raised from the dead to reign with the Father eternal. "The stone which the builders rejected has become the cornerstone."

The violence of the cross can never be vindicated. Violence begets violence, and normally falls back on the people who promote it. Grace begets grace, and leads to redemption of the lost and the rejected children of our world. Follow Jesus to the cross and you will see one who entered a culture of violence to break the mold and interrupt the chain reaction.—Larry Dipboye

SUNDAY, MARCH 2, 2003
Lectionary Message

Topic: The Sufficiency of God
TEXT: 2 Cor. 4:3–6
Other Readings: 2 Kings 2:1–12; Ps. 50:1–6; Mark 9:2–9

Paul declared that by himself he was not sufficient to think anything of himself, but his sufficiency was from God.

I. *Sufficient for ministry.*

(a) There is no such thing as *self*-righteousness. Anyone who today mentions Christ and the way of salvation to a nonbelieving friend is instantly accused of being self-righteous. Paul knew that there were imitators of disciples who sought to discredit him and his ministry and who accused him of self-aggrandizement, of seeking letters of commendation to take from Corinth to gain recognition in other places. They accused him of commending himself in order to gain the respect of the people of Corinth.

(b) Paul rejected that idea. He declared that the only epistle he needed was written on his heart by the faithful believers in Corinth. He said that God had caused him to triumph in Christ and made him a sweet savor of Christ in those who were saved (2:15). His epistle was written not with ink, nor on tables of stone, but in the Spirit of the living God, on tables of human hearts. He had no need to blow his own horn, because wherever the Corinthian believers were, Paul's ministry was authenticated by their faith and their lives—open epistles of God, known and read by all men.

(c) If God is to have sufficient witness in the world, it must come forth from the lives of those who believe in him through Jesus Christ. By the Spirit of God, Paul had been a sufficient minister of grace to those he visited, who in turn had become his epistle. The basic necessity of life is faith in the living God. Any confession must, of course, be based on the real possession of new life in Christ, and if it is there, it must come out—it cannot be kept secret, because all of an individual's life is an expression of the core of his convictions. It is an epistle, known and read by all men, as Christ was God's expression of love for the world. And the Spirit of God is sufficient for our ministry today.

II. *Sufficient for service.*

(a) A ministry that, in the sufficiency of God, is able to write the truths of redemption on human hearts is also able to make every believer into a dedicated servant. At the end of this passage, Paul gives the credit to God, who made him an able servant of the Spirit. The Greek word used here is *diakonous*, referring to those who willingly give thought, effort, and love to the work of spiritual service—teaching, preaching, healing (heart as well as body), building, feeding, clothing, and comforting those whom they seek out for God.

(b) The New Covenant is a way of life based on trust. It is well known that documents consisting of words are subject to interpretation. Laws can be made to suit various purposes. The "letter" of the law is often a killer. There is the story of an employer who decided to fire nine of his agents. For eight of them he had employment contracts several pages long and he was able in each contract to find sufficient means of termination without penalty. For the ninth agent, who had been out of town when he was hired, the employer had only a telegram in which he had defined the job, the terms, and the pay. He could not legally break the telegram contract.

(c) When the Spirit is absent, the "letter" is insufficient as the basis of an agreement. When one reads the Bible apart from the Spirit of God who inspired it, one can find ways to question, doubt, and deny its truthfulness, as many unbelieving detractors have done through the years. That is why God did as all successful communicators do—he suited the medium to the message. He had a message of life, of life to last for eternity, and he chose the medium that can convey such a message—the human hearts of ministering believers. He sent his Word, in the person of his Son, to write his epistle from his heart on all human hearts by his Spirit.

Our sufficiency for life eternal and our adequacy for a life of ministry are indeed of God, because in ourselves we are not sufficient.—John R. Rodman

ILLUSTRATION

CARRIERS OF OTHERWISE.   The whole collage of *otherwise* defies the way the world is, and sets the watching, listening community into a dangerous, alternative life, an alternative not even visible as long as we stay with the settled story line of the kings.

When we hear the recital of Elijah, we are supposed to name the names of the *carriers of otherwise* who are closer at hand, who keep reflowing the juices of possibility. We have names in common and we each have our own inventory:

- Clarence Jordan, who defied racism in America
- Mother Teresa, who defied poverty for the sake of life
- Nelson Mandela, who did not grow weary or cynical
- Eugene Debs, who insisted that public power must serve real people
- Martin Luther King Jr., who dreamed beyond hate and lingers even now with power
- Frederick Douglass, W.E.B. DuBois, and Malcolm X, none of whom could make a difference but did, and were commonly thought to be both "troubler" and "enemy"

The phrasing conjures and makes available all these who thought otherwise and who, like Elisha in the train of Elijah, noticed the mountains covered with friendly horses and friendly chariots and friendly resources that the king could neither discern nor control (2 Kings 6:14–17).—Walter Brueggemann[1]

---

[1]*Testimony to Otherwise* (St. Louis: Chalice Press, 2001), p. 39.

SERMON SUGGESTIONS

Topic: Obedience—Path to Discipleship

TEXT: Rom. 6:12–23

(1) Obstacles to obedience (v. 12). (2) Obedience, the crucial test of discipleship (vv. 15–16). (3) Obedience, the path of life (v. 19).—C. Neil Strait

Topic: Jesus' Prayer for His Own—God Keep You

TEXT: John 17:11–19

(1) The need for protection. (2) The means of protection. (3) The purpose of protection.

CONGREGATIONAL MUSIC

1. "O Bless the Lord, My Soul," James Montgomery (1825)
   ST. THOMAS, Aaron Williams (1770)
   James Montgomery, probably the greatest of lay hymnists, created this free paraphrase of parts of Psalm 103 for the purpose of public worship. No better hymn could be found to open this day's worship or introduce the reading of the psalm.
2. "He Sat to Watch O'er Customs Paid," William Bright (1866)
   BRESLAU, Lochamer Gesangbuch (c. 1450)
   This hymn describes the calling by Jesus of Levi (Matthew), the tax collector, and points to the lesson to be learned from this calling. It could naturally be sung in connection with the reading of the Gospel lesson (Mark 2:13–22).
3. "Love Divine, All Loves Excelling," Charles Wesley (1747)
   BEECHER, John Zundel (1870)
   Charles Wesley's masterful hymn on the divine love could be sung after the Old Testament reading (Hos. 2:14–20), in which Hosea's pursuit of a faithless wife serves as a metaphor for God's merciful, patient love for an unfaithful Israel.
4. "Lord, I Want to Be a Christian," African American spiritual
   I WANT TO BE A CHRISTIAN, African American spiritual
   This appealing spiritual poignantly expresses aspirations for having a right heart toward God and others. It could be sung in connection with the Epistle lesson (2 Cor. 3:1–6), in which the apostle Paul speaks of the New Covenant being written on the tablets of the heart rather than in stone.—Hugh T. McElrath

WORSHIP AIDS

CALL TO WORSHIP.   "Bless the Lord, O my soul, and all that is within me, bless his holy name. Bless the Lord, O my soul, and do not forget all his benefits" (Ps. 103:1–2).

INVOCATION.   We are called, O Lord, to bless you for who you are and for what you do for us. May we never forget which is more important, but may we always remember that every good and perfect gift comes from you. For the blessing of this time of worship we thank you.

OFFERTORY SENTENCE.   "The silver is mine, and the gold is mine, says the Lord of hosts" (Hag. 2:8).

OFFERTORY PRAYER.   Make us faithful, our Father, in our use of all that ultimately belongs to you. Because of what you have put in our hands, our lives are enriched personally and the outreach of the gospel is extended to the ends of the Earth. We thank you for making us partners in all your works of love and grace.

PRAYER.   Lord, who in love comes to every sinner, we are grateful that you are our Savior. In all you said and did while walking the Earth, through your death and Resurrection and through the witness of the Church through the ages, we are made aware of your voice calling us to you. How can we ever forget that when we were despised and fallen, you brought forgiveness and restoration; when we were broken and burdened, you brought healing and strength; when we were homeless, you gave us a dwelling place for our very souls; when our hearts have overflowed with sorrow, you have brought to us such comfort that we have needed no other. How many times have you answered the cry of our troubled hearts!

Dwell among us this morning, we pray. Reveal to us the things that are faithful to you day by day. Inspire us to encourage those who daily live with pain and struggle, which is not the common lot of most of us. Enable us to be good examples of Christ's love and action to those among whom we walk, that folks lost along the way may find the road that leads home.

Now we ask that a word be fitly spoken that will lift some soul to a new knowledge of Christ, a word that will encourage a struggler along the way, a word that will enlighten someone walking in the darkness apart from the Lord. Make this an hour to be remembered as we continue our worship in your presence, we pray in Jesus' name.—Henry Fields

SERMON
Topic: On Being a Genuine Christian
TEXT: Matt. 6:16–18

Hypocrisy in any realm of life—and it is a human failing by no means confined to religion—is ugly, repellent, and very subtle. It is important to understand clearly the real nature of religious hypocrisy. It is not failing to live up to the creed you profess. We all fail to do this. The gospel is bigger, far bigger, than any one of us. Hypocrisy is *pretending* to live up to a creed and not *trying* to do so. It is playacting, wearing a mask of religiosity to cover a fundamental lack of integrity. It is keeping up a form of religion but having nothing to do with it as a force.

No one who reads the New Testament can doubt that hypocrisy was an abomination in the sight of Jesus. He lashed out against it with scathing invective. Take the section of the Sermon on the Mount in which he discusses the three major duties of a conventionally religious man—almsgiving, fasting, and prayer.

I. *Genuine Christianity expresses itself in a disciplined life.* Pious Jews fasted on Mondays and Thursdays as a sign of penitence. Jesus did not condemn that. Indeed, his approval of it is obviously implied by the words, "But when you fast. . . ." His condemnation was directed at the abuse of fasting, the turning of a legitimate duty to God into an empty, theatrical gesture devoid of all spiritual meaning.

Our concern as Christians, whatever our particular brand of churchmanship, should be with the principle behind the practice of fasting—personal discipline in the interests of vital religion.

The religion that takes discipline lightly is worse than useless—it is blasphemous. Discipline is the prelude to discovery, liberty, and victory on every level of existence. The soldier, the author, the musician, the scientist, and the preacher can achieve success only by renunciation, by intense and unrelaxing concentration, by self-denial, by cultivating the capacity to take pains.

It is true that Christianity does condemn self-indulgence and extravagance—indulgence is destructive to the health of the body and the soul, and extravagance mocks the desperate poverty of others who are just as precious in the sight of God.

The ultimatum of Christ is unambiguous: "If any will come after me, let him deny himself and take up his cross and follow me." Paul saw himself as a spiritual athlete striving for self-mastery, refusing to pamper or pollute his body. "Every athlete," he wrote, "practices restraint all around." Jeremy Taylor put it magnificently in this prayer: "Let my body be the servant of my spirit, and both body and spirit, servants of Jesus."

II. *Genuine Christianity also expresses itself in a natural manner.* The motive of the hypocrite was the praise of men, not the glory of God. The dismal appearance, the disfigured face smeared with ashes, the absurdly unnatural manner were all directed to that trivial, unwholesome end. "Be disciplined," says Jesus in effect, "but be natural. If you are real about your religion, you will be concerned only with your status in the sight of God."

We are far too worried about our image in the eyes of the world, far too self-consciously religious. So our manner becomes stilted, forced, unnatural—and hypocritical. Ministers of religion are particularly exposed to this danger. Rightly expected to be professional in the performance of our duties, we can easily lapse into religious professionalism—a very different thing.

When our religion is utterly real, our manner is completely natural. It is free from pious affection, indifferent to the kind of impression we may be making, forgetful of self. We are not tempted to waste valuable time and energy morbidly conducting our own public opinion poll. Our one objective is to please God and glorify his name.

III. *Genuine Christianity expresses itself in a radiant spirit.* "Do not look dismal like the hypocrites," says Jesus. The depth of a man's devotion is not measured by the length of his face. Hypocrisy is a terrible kill-joy. It has no sense of humor, no capacity to relax and laugh, no desire to enjoy God or man. It is ponderous, intense, and exceedingly grim.

The hypocrite has enough religion to make himself miserable: the whole sordid game introduces a new tension into his personality, creating an inevitable unhappiness. It is better by far to be a thoroughgoing pagan. Genuine religion is radiant religion. It shines and sparkles, it lifts and liberates, it soars above all circumstances and laughs in the face of death itself.

J. C. Pollock makes it clear that D. L. Moody, the great evangelist, stood in this tradition of radiant religion. He quotes a journalist who covered one of Moody's tours and afterwards said, "D. L. Moody with all his real piety is sometimes *unbearably funny.*"

The authentic Christian knows how to take life seriously without taking it solemnly. To be sure, we are called to wrestle with "the giant agony of the world," to confront the sin and suffering of humanity with the stark realism of the cross. It is hard to be a Christian, and Christ places on our shoulders burdens from which we may well shrink. But we are also called to enjoy God as we glorify him.

What is the secret of this radiance, this joy of the Christian? It is the joy of salvation—

the exhilaration of being ransomed, healed, restored, forgiven. It is the joy of security—the assurance that nothing in life or death can separate us from the love of God. It is the joy of service—of giving ourselves to others in a meaningful, useful way. It is the joy of sacrifice—of feeling the weight of the cross and yet seeing beyond it to the light that streams from an empty tomb in an Eastern garden.

The spirit of genuine Christianity is a spirit of joy, a radiant spirit that goes on shining in the most chaotic times, and through the darkest nights.—John N. Gladstone[2]

SUNDAY, MARCH 9, 2003
Lectionary Message

Topic: The Powers Subject to Christ

TEXT: 1 Pet. 3:18–22

Other Readings: Gen. 9:8–17; Ps. 25:1–10; Mark 1:9–15

None of the powers at large in the world can win the struggle for the lives of people against the power of Jesus Christ. As Peter declares, Jesus is in heaven, "at the right hand of God," and angels, authorities, and powers have been made subject unto him.

I. *The power to defeat the power of sin.*

(a) The doctrine of substitutionary atonement declared by Peter is the basis for our receiving the Spirit of God as our power for daily living. Jesus suffered and died once for our sins. There is no need for any other to die for sins again. There is no necessity for repeated sacrifice of animals or humans, or for the scapegoat, to carry away our sins. Jesus has done it, in his suffering and death. Our Day of Atonement is not an annual observance on the tenth day of the seventh month every year. It has taken place on Calvary once and for all.

Christ's death was the death of the Just for the unjust. He was righteous from his birth through all his days, and the only one who could ever satisfy the law of his Father for the whole world of sinners, the only one who could enter the Holy of Holies of eternal righteousness for the salvation of mankind.

Before acquiring the benefit of Christ's suffering and death, a person must conscientiously include himself or herself in the company of the "unjust," recognizing his or her need of, and qualification for, the atonement Christ earned for us.

(b) The power of Christ is the power of his Spirit, by which he was "quickened," brought forth to life, and raised to heaven after communing with his disciples. It may be difficult for some people to realize a spiritual element in life, but whatever we call it, it is the part of our consciousness that by innate feeling keeps us in touch with those we love, that responds to their needs, that sorrows when hearing of sadness in their lives, that grieves when hearing of other lives destroyed by catastrophe. It is also what brings us peace and contentment in the sound of beautiful music, makes us smile and gives us energy when we see glorious displays of nature, and makes us disturbed and restlessly concerned when we have violated a rule or done something mean or cruel.

---

[2]*A Magnificent Faith* (Hantsport, Nova Scotia: Lancelot Press, 1979), pp. 50–56.

Christ's power is a spiritual power, able to transfer power to those who give their lives to him. It could bring him forth from the grave because it was the original source of the creative power of the universe.

II. *The power to free even today's prisoners.*

(a) In its early days the Church had, and perhaps still has today, difficulty answering the question about where Jesus was and what he did between the Crucifixion and the Resurrection. Peter answered that question by telling us that the Spirit led Jesus to the place of the dead, where Jesus preached and ministered to the spirits imprisoned in death. This answer supports the statement in the Apostles' Creed, "He descended into hell." There he assured them of God's eternal love.

(b) Peter also described the departed spirits as those who were disobedient, pushing God's patience and long-suffering beyond the limit, while Noah was preparing the ark.

The sins of these erring souls tested God to the limit and beyond; then he purged the filth of the world by the great flood so that only eight souls—Noah and his wife, his three sons and their wives—were saved through the water.

(c) The flood-judgment is a symbol of what will happen to the world at God's final judgment. Peter compared the salvation of the eight people through water to the washing of regeneration we exemplify in baptism, which does not just clean the body but also yields a fresh beginning through the Holy Spirit, wherein the soul makes a conscientious pledge to follow Christ, renouncing the ways that had soiled the spirit. The Epistle of Titus (1:15) reminds us of the complete devastation of an impure spirit.

III. *The power of a reconstructed life.*

(a) The spirits of many people today are certainly in prisons, many of their own making by the adoption of false goals based on erroneous and delusive principles. Disappointment and frustration are constant companions of these spirits.

(b) If angels and authorities and powers are made subject unto Christ by the power of his spirit, why not bring the present life of our own spirits under his control? There are challenges before us and around us—people are in desperate need, not only of food, clothing, and shelter, but also of direction, energy, spiritual strength, and power to overcome the evils in their lives and in their communities.

(c) The development of spiritual strength is the gift of Christ. Others have recommended personal strength by development of personal gifts and talents, and surely if every one in the world could and would take responsibility for himself or herself, then there would be no need for others to be concerned about anyone but themselves. John Stuart Mill, the philosopher of utilitarianism, recommended just that—the opposite of Christian mission dedication:

I have never . . . belonged to the benevolentiary, soup-kitchen school. Though I hold the good of the species . . . to be the ultimate end . . . believe with the fullest belief that this end can in no other way be forwarded but by . . . each taking for his exclusive aim the development of what is best in himself.[3]

---

[3]Richard Kenin and Justin Wintle, *Dictionary of Biographical Quotation* (New York: Knopf, 1978), p. 534.

Jesus, of course, saw things from quite a different viewpoint, placing his people in a world with great needs for compassion and generosity toward the poor and the ill. In other words, his people should belong to the "benevolentiary, soup-kitchen school."

Søren Kierkegaard places our responsibilities in a more accurate light:

> Oh, then let us by this most horrible thing, which once took place (and that it happened only once is not to the world's credit, but rather that the crucified one is eternally and essentially different from every other man), let us learn wisdom in the lesser relationships. . . . Let us rightly consider that a generation is not . . . superior because it understands that a previous generation acted wrongly, if in the present moment they themselves do not understand how to discriminate between the momentary and the eternal aspect of the thing at hand.[4]

Our call to live in the power of Christ is a call to recognize the "eternal aspect" in all our contacts and opportunities.—John R. Rodman

ILLUSTRATION

OUR PLACE.   Atlanta, which began as a rough-and-ready railroad town and was originally named Terminus, is now a megacity without equal in the southeastern United States. It is said that the Atlanta metropolitan area has experienced the most dramatic expansion of real estate development in the shortest span of time of any metropolis in history. The consequences of this growth have been dramatic. The economy is booming. Unemployment is at its lowest level in thirty years. Opportunity and prosperity abound for many. But the consequences are not all positive. The "rising tide lifts all boats" approach to economic development has not worked for many. Homelessness, inadequate housing, low wages, and hunger are everyday realities for them. The income gap between the rich and the poor continues to widen. Streets, boulevards, and interstate highways are clogged with traffic. Air and water pollution are at crisis levels.

Because our city's population has become strikingly diverse in terms of ethnic identity and religious identity, no longer can homogeneity of perspective or background be assumed. As in many other regions of the United States, however, the role of religion is becoming increasingly confined to the private spheres of life and is commonly considered to be irrelevant to the issues that affect public life. The secular values of individualism, consumerism, and success are now the values that prevail.

Race continues to be the predominant factor in determining many of the patterns of community life and practice.

Economic disparities loom equally as large. Two important questions arise for final consideration:

> How can the affluent and the relatively affluent receive the gift of God's future if
> their hands are full of the fruits of their own success and their minds are full of their
> own plans?

---

[4]*Purity of Heart Is to Will One Thing* (New York: HarperCollins, 1956), p. 139.

How can those who have been left out of prosperity—or who are struggling not to be—receive the gift of God's future if despair has depleted their capacity for hope?—Joanna Adams[5]

SERMON SUGGESTIONS

Topic: A Sure Refuge

TEXT: Ps. 61:2–3

(1) When we should pray: "When my heart is overwhelmed." (2) How we should pray: Earnestly—"I will *cry* unto thee." (3) Where we should pray: "From the ends of the Earth." (4) For what we should pray: "Lead me to the rock." (5) Why we should pray: "For thou hast been a shelter."—A. F. Barfield

Topic: Come, Holy Spirit, Come!

TEXT: John 16:5–15

(1) "Convince us of our sin." (2) "Then lead to Jesus' blood." (3) "And to our wondering view reveal the mercies of our God."

CONGREGATIONAL MUSIC

1. "God of Creation, All-Powerful," Margaret Clarkson (1987)

    SLANE, trad. Irish melody

    This contemporary hymn, with its emphasis on the "Covenant God" (stanza 5) and its focus on the Old Testament reading about God's covenant with Noah (Gen. 9:8–17), would be useful for the opening of worship having.

2. "O God Love, O God (King) of Peace," Henry W. Baker (1860)

    QUEBEC, Henry Baker (1854)

    In the Psalter reading for this day, the psalmist prays, "Remember not the sins of my youth, . . . according to thy steadfast love, remember me" (Ps. 25:7). This fine nineteenth-century hymn, especially in stanza 2, echoes this thought and makes it more universal. Accordingly, it could be sung as a response to the Psalter lesson.

3. "When Jesus Came to Jordan," Fred Pratt Green (1973)

    DE EERSTEN ZIJN DE LAASTEN, Frederick A. Mehrtens (1975)

    The singing of this twentieth-century hymn would be particularly appropriate as a response to the Gospel lesson (Mark 1:9–15) about the baptism and temptation of Jesus.

4. "My Song Is Love Unknown," Samuel Crossman (1664)

    LOVE UNKNOWN, John Ireland (1918)

    This seventeenth-century hymn gathers in its stanzas the essence of the apostle Paul's teaching in 1 Peter 3:18 about the death of Christ, which brought humankind to God, making them alive in the Spirit. The length of the hymn makes it appropriate to alternate between singing and quoting the seven stanzas.—Hugh T. McElrath

---

[5]*Hope for the World,* ed. by Walter Brueggemann (Louisville: Westminster John Knox Press, 2001), pp. 28–29.

WORSHIP AIDS

CALL TO WORSHIP.   "Make me to know your ways, O Lord; teach me your paths. Lead me in your truth, and teach me, for you are the God of my salvation" (Ps. 25:4–5a).

INVOCATION.   Take our minds, our hearts, and our wills down those rewarding paths of worship, O Lord, that we may learn more of your ways, of your love, and of our need to respond to the truth that you will reveal to us. Bless all who worship, as we open ourselves to what we see and hear in your house today.

OFFERTORY SENTENCE.   "But strive first for the Kingdom of God and his righteousness, and all these things will be given to you as well" (Matt. 6:33).

OFFERTORY PRAYER.   Gracious Lord, your Word assures us of your care for us when we put first things first, even when times are hard. As we seek your Kingdom as our priority and receive your countless blessings, even of material things, may we always remember that we are fortunate stewards, and that it is still more blessed to give than to receive.

PRAYER.   Almighty God, thou who hast exalted thy Son Jesus Christ to the highest heaven, to bear the name that is above every name, we worship thee. We would bow to thy power, thy wisdom, and thy righteousness. We would yield our hearts to thy love. Yet all do not reverence thee, all do not love thee. We pray for those who set their human strength supported by military might against thy almightiness, those who set their human understanding against thy omniscience, those who set their selfish schemes against thy concern for all people. We pray for those who hear only a cold, stony silence coming from what they think is an unfeeling cosmos.

Send fear into the hearts of the rulers of the Earth, lest some rash act of theirs betray thy care of all the Earth. Send faith into the heart of each of us, that we may be confident of thy final victory over all thy foes, and that we may be assured of thy help as we seek thy will and way.

SERMON

Topic: Ashes to Ashes
Text: Isa. 58:1–10

Ashes and dust appear to be the basic stuff of which almost everything is made—including people. Either by fire or through the slow process of natural decomposition, all things seem to be going toward dust and ashes. Dust and ashes are biblical symbols of human mortality. Wearing sackcloth, sitting in dust or ashes or casting the dust over one's head, and fasting were ways of expressing grief, or acts of solemn repentance, and expressions of sorrow for sin in biblical times. Thus, Job sat in ashes in grief over the loss of his children, his wealth, his health, and his personal significance. And we begin Lent with ashes.

I. *Disconnected ritual does not qualify as worship.* In the Bible, worship involves both feasting and fasting. Feasting is celebration of the joy and goodness of God. Fasting is a reminder of the sin and pain of our existence. Baptists have always been better at feasting than at fasting, and we have found comfort in the prophet's commentary on empty ritual. We are a practical people who find more meaning in feeding the hungry than in acting out hunger through a fast. In 1992, I was forced to do without food for five days. My liquid diet was void of all calories, and the stuff they called broth was barely more than tap water. At first, I did not really care. I was too sick. After a few days, I began to feel better and hungrier, but the test went on. One morning I removed the cover from my breakfast tray and could not believe my eyes. There were scrambled eggs, sausage, biscuits, butter, jelly, coffee, milk, and juice. Before I could get my jaw back in place and my fork in gear, the nurse ran in and snatched the tray away with the feeble explanation that it was a mistake. I am still holding a grudge against Dr. Dew. There was no religious experience here. Actually no religious meaning was intended. This fast was totally involuntary. Can you imagine fasting on purpose?

We sometimes forget that Jesus began his ministry in the stark wilderness of temptation. Like a child under the bed, Jesus got in touch with himself and drew the boundaries on his mission out of the deep well of the Scriptures. He made a solemn commitment to a truth we often forget: we do not live by bread alone. When the tempter called attention to stones that looked like bread and suggested that Jesus might consider easing the pain of his fast, Jesus declared that he was more than dust. That is the point of fasting: self-imposed hunger, and getting in touch with the Earth. They are reminders of our roots. We are *physical* selves in need of daily food and drink, but we are far more than bodies in need of food. We are souls in need of the bread of life, food for the spirit.

Wednesday we touched the ashes. The tradition is ancient. For more than nine centuries, Christians have begun the journey toward the cross on Ash Wednesday. Touching the ashes puts you in touch with your own mortality. "Ashes to ashes" is a familiar phrase from the *Book of Common Prayer* pronounced over the grave of loved ones in the final rites of committal. To say the least, it is sobering and humbling to remember that you are dust. The universe existed without me for untold billions of years before my birth, and I can assume that it will go on for untold billions of years after my death. I really should not get too attached to my physical importance here, and perhaps I ought to be as concerned to feed the soul as I am to feed the body. Time is short. If I am going to make a difference here, I need to get busy.

II. *Acts of worship lead to acts of compassion.* The Jews had returned from exile and were answering the call to rebuild the Temple, but religion is more than buildings and institutional forms. There is a bridge between what we *confess* and *commit* in worship before God and what we *are* and *do* in the world.

Mark Buchanan makes a strong argument for fasting in this age of consumption: "More and more people are food gluttons and biblical anorexics." Fasting, deliberately denying oneself, is not exactly foreign to the gospel of Christ. As an act of self-discipline, an expression of sorrow, and an act of worship, fasting is practiced throughout the Bible; and it is assumed, not argued, by Jesus. In the Sermon on the Mount he says, "when you fast," not "if you fast."

Buchanan tells about a friend who organized a dinner in his church to raise money for famine relief in the Sudan. About eighty people came. The room had tables that seated from six to fifteen people. The people were allowed to take seats at random. The small tables were served a lavish dinner, and the room was filled with its aroma. At the middle-size tables the food was dumped into bowls. It was messy and bland. The guests had to fend for themselves. Two of the largest tables were served nothing but buckets of warm water, slightly colored, with a wooden ladle to drink from. It did not take long for the people to catch on to the way the world works. If indeed "all men are created equal," it is a condition only of creation and not of the reality of this world, and we have never known another day of equality.

Hal Warlick remembers a conversation with Billy Graham about the unresolved dimension of his ministry—the austerity of poverty and hunger in the world. In India the people do not respond to success, but they understand deprivation and austerity. James said it: "Faith without works is dead." We need both. Giving up a meal does something to you. Giving a meal to a hungry neighbor changes the world.—Larry Dipboye

SUNDAY, MARCH 16, 2003
Lectionary Message

Topic: On Condition of Faith

TEXT: Rom. 4:13–25, esp. 4:24

Other Readings: Gen. 17:1–7, 15–16; Ps. 22:23–31; Mark 8:31–38

There are two stalwart champions of redeeming faith: Abraham, on the forefront, pioneering absolute faith as a means of justification and victory; and Paul, on the side near us, in the stream of divine revelation, upholding justification by faith, the saving support of those who follow Christ.

Why did Paul hark back to Abraham, a precursor of the faithful in the family of God? He did it because he admired Abraham, because Abraham "wavered not through unbelief, but waxed strong through faith, giving glory to God." Abraham relied on God's promises as absolutely dependable. Abraham's faith was tested, not by any troubles he encountered but by God's promises—and he did not waver in the face of impossibility.

I. *Faith is essential to life.*

(a) Nothing can break the spirits of people—not sin, not hardships, not crime or wickedness, not hypocrisy or deception, not cruelty or pain—as long as they believe God's promises, as Abraham did: that he will prepare a place for us and make sure we reach it, saving our souls by his grace.

(b) God has given us, in the lives of Abraham and the prophets, and in Jesus Christ, enough promises to establish our eternal security and our present spiritual comfort—even to have hope when hope is senseless—as long as we believe those promises. What we need is more faith to believe the promises he has already made, faith to walk out on the invisible highway, across the depths of human challenge and temporary despair.

(c) We have often been warned in God's book of the deceptive nature of material goods, even of money in the bank. We have experienced the chimera of "possessions," the evanescence of ownership. Our real treasure consists not of the things we can count but of the God on whom we can count.

(d) In the first chapter of Romans, Paul tells us, "The just shall live by faith." Stop and think about how much of your present life you accept on faith—your family background, father and mother and grandparents, their love—all accepted by faith. The food you bring home from the grocery, the water you drink, the fiduciary money you take for your work or the fiducial marks of your surveyor. Even the most dependable scientific discoveries and principles are accepted by most of us entirely on faith in someone else's work. For the scientist, faith in his substances and materials, in his measures and scales, and in the records of previous workers is the first requirement. Science would be as dead without faith as religion would be. One excellent preacher has written, "What anyone believes is of infinitely more value than what he knows."

II. *The faith we have builds our lives.*

(a) The first meaning of the example of Abraham is that there is no limit to what God can do in our lives, even when we are at "the end of our rope." His promises are the knot we grasp in order to hang on.

(b) The imputation of righteousness to Abraham based on his faith is an example of how faith can cause righteousness to be imputed—that is, counted as wiping out the bankruptcy in our accounts—for our sakes. Every person who believes in Christ must feel that he or she has no future, no hope of strength, except through his or her fervent, constant faith in God, who promises each person a forthcoming realization of the ultimate aim of life.

(c) The outcomes of a life of faith are often beyond expectation. L. T. Lawrence has written of a humble itinerant minister of the Wesleyan Church in England who was often discouraged. His work was hard, his compensation was meager, and he was tempted many times to give up. Three daughters grew to womanhood in his home. In time all three were married. One became the mother of Burne-Jones, the celebrated artist; one was the mother of Stanley Baldwin, the prime minister; the other was the mother of Rudyard Kipling.

III. *The life of faith is a life of loving expression.*

(a) Let us write the doctrine of our faith experimentally, from our lives. The very concepts on which our actions are based are read by others as our declarations of faith. Our actions must support that we believe in God—the God of Abraham—and in Christ, who "was delivered for our offenses and was raised again for our justification."

(b) It is also by our love, our unfounded interest in and care even for those we do not know, that our faith shows forth. Robert Wodrow was the compiler and author of historical narratives of Scottish religious life in the seventeenth century. He wrote in *Analecta,* volume 1, page 362 (his dialectic spellings are preserved), "Mr. Robert Blair said, speaking of the union betwixt Christ and believers, that 'The two graces that made it up, upon our part, were faith and love'; and compared these two to the gleu and wooping of a club [a golf club, the head glued on, then bound by cord]! Faith is like the glue, because it's the uniting grace (this blessed union being made up by the Spirit upon his part, and faith upon ours); and love is like the wooping, because, after this union is made up, it is love that keeps it firm and fixed."

(c) So it is on condition of faith that righteousness is imputed to us by "him that raised up Jesus our Lord from the dead."—John R. Rodman

ILLUSTRATION

A REVOLUTIONARY RELATIONSHIP.   To live in loving relationship with God means to have a radical, revolutionary relationship of stewardship with our bodies, minds, and spirits. God created us for ultimate intimacy, out of love, to think, to grow, to learn, to be, to share. Speaking biblically, in the first creation story God speaks, something exists, and God calls that thing good. On the sixth day, God speaks human beings into existence and calls us good. Our minds, bodies, spirits, thoughts, sensuality, and sexuality have all been pronounced good by God. To function as a steward, in a balanced, loving capacity, requires that we know who we are. We are sacred beings, and we live in a sacred world. Health, spirituality, and ecology must be priorities. As ethical praxis, stewardship of bodies, minds, and spirits means a daily, living commitment to a healthy lifestyle. We need to understand how to use our bodies; how to strengthen our minds; how to gird up our spirits; how to eat, exercise, think, pray, meditate, and discern; how to choose not to violate or be violated. Stewardship requires that we set boundaries as we put God first, ourselves second, all others third.—Cheryl Kirk-Duggan[6]

SERMON SUGGESTIONS

Topic: Facing Our Skeptical Moods

TEXT: Ps. 39:1–13

(1) Verses 1–3: the keynote here is *repression*. (2) Verses 4–6: the keynote here is *resolution*. (3) Verses 7–9: the keynote here is *realization*—realizing the one thing needful. (4) Verses 10–13: the keynote here is *recapturing*—recapturing the pilgrim spirit.—James S. Stewart

Topic: Getting Up Out of the Dumps

TEXT: Pss. 42, 43

(1) Memory is a way out of the dumps. (2) Faith is a way. (3) Light and truth are ways.— Craig Skinner

CONGREGATIONAL MUSIC

1. "The God of Abraham Praise," Thomas Olivers (c. 1770)
   LEONI, Synagogue melody; arr. Meyer Lyon (c. 1770)
   The Old Testament lesson about the covenanting of God's dealings with Abraham can be highlighted by this ancient Hebrew doxology. It would serve admirably for the beginning of musical worship.
2. "Amid the Throng of Worshipers," Ps. 22:22–31; vers. *Psalter* (1912)
   FOREST GREEN, trad. Eng. melody; arr. R. V. Williams
   This modern paraphrase of the Psalter selection for this day's reading could be sung antiphonally between choir and congregation in place of the reading of the psalm.
3. "Jesus Comes with All His Grace," Charles Wesley (1749)
   WUERTTEMBERG, *Hundert Arien* Dresden (1694)
   Charles Wesley's little-known hymn magnifies the salvation wrought for all the "seed of Abraham." It constitutes a natural response to the Epistle reading (Rom. 4:13–25) in which, in brilliant discourse, the apostle Paul asserts that Abraham and all his descendants are justified by faith.
4. "Take Up Your Cross, the Savior Said," Charles W. Everest (1833)
   GERMANY, W. Gardiner's *Sacred Melodies* (1815)
   This fine American classic hymn can be sung as a natural accompaniment to the Gospel lesson (Mark 8:31–38) about Jesus' teachings on self-denial and cross-bearing.—Hugh T. McElrath

WORSHIP AIDS

CALL TO WORSHIP.   "I will tell of your name to my brothers and sisters; in the midst of the congregation I will praise you" (Ps. 22:22 NRSV).

---

[6]*Misbegotten Anguish* (St. Louis: Chalice Press, 2001), p. 217.

INVOCATION.   Duty calls us to worship you, O Lord, but praise wells up in our hearts that is beyond and above all duty. Let every word we say and all music from instruments or lips glorify you.

OFFERTORY SENTENCE.   "But the one who did not know and did what deserved a beating will receive a light beating. From everyone to whom much has been given, much will be required; and from the one to whom much has been entrusted, even more will be demanded" (Luke 12:48).

OFFERTORY PRAYER.   Lord, you have endowed us with both goods and grace, and it is now our privilege once again to place in your compassionate hands our offerings that can bring blessing to us and immeasurable benefit to the work of your Kingdom.

PRAYER.   We come to this place of worship, Father, with many different needs and various feelings. Some come burdened with sorrow. Some come frustrated with jobs. Some come fearful of tomorrow and its promise. Some come sunk in the pits of self-disdain. Some come burdened with guilts that weigh heavily on their souls. Some come caught in the vise of repeated sin. Some come this morning longing for love. Others are here seeking companionship in their loneliness. Young people come longing for some word to direct them in their future adventures. Older folks come seeking rest from their labors. The cheerful are here beside the sad. The optimists sit with the pessimists. The hopeful are found in the company of the ones who have lost hope. What a diverse group we are! Yet how alike we are, too. For we know that only you can meet our deepest need and hear our most muffled cry. So we ask that your presence invade us and your Spirit fill us as we gather in this place. Hush our babbling cries, still our busy lives, and in these moments let each of us find our needs met so we can go forth to declare the wondrous things we have discovered in the Lord. Then will others know that there is a God in our land, a God of love and power and presence and salvation.

We have come, Father. That is a beginning for many of us. Do such mighty works among us that we will come again and again to abide in your presence and drink from your cup of wholeness, we pray in Christ's name.—Henry Fields

SERMON
Topic: Challenge and Hope
TEXT: Various

The Lenten season confronts us with the challenge to seek afresh the moral meaning of life. It is a time for honest self-appraisal in the light given by God. At once we realize that our need is great. St. Paul speaks for all of us. "For I do not do the good I want, but the evil I do not want is what I do" (Rom. 7:19). The Bible calls us to moral and spiritual self-discipline, to purposeful training, to look toward a glorious goal and strive for it. "All athletes exercise self-control in all things. They do it to receive a perishable wreath, but we are imperishable" (1 Cor. 9:25).

The problem of meaning is the major problem we face. Modern man is all dressed up with nowhere to go. The Bible challenge is to look to God for that leading and light that give life direction and meaning. This obstacle course that we call life need not daunt us with its difficulties. If we believe that God is in everything, then the obstacles become opportunities, our problems and difficulties become something to grow on. We need our needs. They turn us Godward. They open our eyes to the grace God is eager to give. What a candid picture of life St. Paul gives: "As servants of God we commend ourselves in every way: through great endurance, in afflictions, hardships, calamities, beatings, imprisonments, tumults, labors, watching, hunger"—in short, through all the problems and difficulties men face. Yet in the presence of the Living God, who is in all things, we witness "by purity, knowledge, forbearance, and kindness the Holy Spirit, genuine love, truthful speech, and the power of God; with the weapons of righteousness for the right hand and for the left; in honor and dishonor, in ill repute and good repute" (2 Cor. 6:4–8). The outward appearance may be fearful, but the inner reality of the God-guided life is glorious. The Christian can praise God no matter what happens, abounding in thanksgiving. "We are treated as imposters, and yet are true; as unknown, and yet are well known; as dying, and yet, behold, we live; as punished, and yet we are not killed; as sorrowful, yet we are always rejoicing; as poor, yet we make many rich; as having nothing, yet we possess everything." No matter how puzzling the paradoxes of life, the presence of God in all these things gives life needed point and purpose, a glorious meaning by which we can live.

For with the Lenten challenge comes the Lenten hope. God's purpose is not to plunge us into despair, but to quicken us to new life by his love. For the Lord will not cast us off forever, but though he cause grief he will have compassion according to the abundance of his steadfast love; for he does not willingly afflict or grieve the sons of men (Lam. 3:31–33).

When the people of Israel cried out, "Our transgressions and our sins are upon us, and we waste away because of them; how then can we live?" God commissioned Ezekiel, "Say to them, 'As I live, says the Lord God, I have no pleasure in the death of the wicked, but that the wicked turn from his way and live'" (Ezek. 33:10–11). Our hope is in the character of God, not in the character of circumstances. His love freely offered is the hope the Heavenly Father gives his children. How beautifully Lamentations (3:22–23) portrays this hope:

> The steadfast love of the Lord never ceases,
> his mercies never come to an end;
> They are new every morning.

The mercies of God constitute our hope. By faith we take our life stance on the God-lighted side of our problems. When the outlook is bad, we trust the uplook. The believer is not spared problems, but the problems are wrapped around promises. The adventure of life is seeking out the golden heart of meaning in every experience, painful or pleasant. At the center of every problem is the promise of the mercies of God. We can look out on each new day through windows of surprise, for the mercies of God are new every morning, and we confront the day's experiences with eager expectancy, knowing we shall find God there. In our quest for successful living, of this we can be sure: with him we cannot fail, without him we cannot succeed!

The glorious rhythm of promise and fulfillment thrills us as we turn to the Bible readings in the Lectionary. "What God promised to the fathers, this he has fulfilled to their children by raising Jesus." The dependable character of God inspires our faith and loyal devotion.

It is the fact of Easter that provides the foundation of our faith. God has not forsaken his Son, despite the shattering tragedy of the Crucifixion. The death of Christ is the door of hope that opens onto a newness of life never before known. "If Christ has not been raised, your faith is futile . . . but in fact Christ has been raised from the dead, the first fruits of those who have fallen asleep. . . . For as in Adam all die, so also in Christ shall all be made alive" (1 Cor. 15:17, 20, 22). God's purpose shines through the ministry of Christ. Through him we see the Father, and we rejoice in our God whose nature and name are love. The love of God is the answer to our quest for meaning. In his love we find power to cope, and joy in work. St. Paul concludes the great chapter on the Resurrection with this practical and heartening assurance: "Therefore, my beloved brethren, be steadfast, immovable, always abounding in the work of the Lord, knowing that in the Lord your labor is not in vain" (1 Cor. 15:58).

The Easter fact is the guarantee of eternal life for mortal men, "that as Christ was raised from the dead by the glory of the Father, we too might walk in newness of life" (Rom. 6:4). The purpose of God is life for his children—victorious life, with grace to overcome and "glory begun below." The readings in St. Paul echo with shouts of joy. "Who shall deliver me from this body of death? Thanks be to God through Jesus Christ our Lord" (Rom. 7:25).

> O death, where is thy victory?
> O death, where is thy sting?

"But thanks be to God, who gives us the victory through our Lord Jesus Christ" (1 Cor. 15:55, 67).

When St. Paul proclaimed the Resurrection to the congregation at Antioch, he cried, "But God raised him from the dead . . . and we bring you the good news" (Acts 13:30, 32). In a world of bad news, God gives us good news that transforms our experience and makes us forever new to life. "If any man be in Christ Jesus he is a new creature; old things are passed away. Behold, all things are become new" (2 Cor. 5:17). What a glorious promise of fulfillment! Our greatest problem is to find freedom from the old world of selfishness where our cosmos is all ego, that we may enter God's glorious new world of meaning and hope and exhilarating spiritual freedom. The new life we so deeply need comes to us as God's gift of love through the Lord Jesus Christ. "If any man be in Christ" is the answer to our problem. It is when we know whose we are that we know who we are!—Lowell M. Atkinson[7]

SUNDAY, MARCH 23, 2003

Lectionary Message

Topic: The Foolishness of Preaching Christ

TEXT: 1 Cor. 1:18–25

Other Readings: Exod. 20:1–17; Ps. 19; John 2:13–22

Why don't Christians wear gold replicas of a stable manger on chains around their necks? Why not decorate our churches and homes year-round with mangers? Why, in the face of the wonder of the holy birth of the Son of God, do we use the cross as our ubiquitous symbol of Christian faith?

---

[7]*Apples of Gold* (Lima, Ohio: Fairway Press, 1986), pp. 53–56.

Because the cross on which Christ died is the essence of our faith, a foolishness to those who are lost, but the power of God to those who are being saved. The Church may look forward with hope and joy to the shining light in the clouds announcing the Second Coming of Christ, but not without first looking back at the place of his death, where once and for all he gave his life for our redemption from sin.

At the heart of the disagreements and divisions of the Presbyterian and other great churches is not the question of sexual orientation or of political organization and power. It is the question of orthodoxy, of the centrality of the redemptive love of Christ as the motive and unifying force of all believers. When we can agree on that, we can agree.

Paul refers in our text to the Jews. Do we have any "Jews" among us? There are those who dwell on historical correctness and outward conformity as the seal of perfection—but love is lost! Paul asks, "Where are the wise? Where is the scribe? Where is the disputer of this world?" He later declares, "but we preach Christ crucified, unto the Jews a stumbling block, and unto the Greeks foolishness, but unto them which are called, both Jews and Greeks, Christ the power of God and the wisdom of God."

Perhaps by "the wise" Paul is referring to the Greek philosophers, whose works the Corinthians must have known well. Perhaps by "the scribe" he is referring to the Hebrew scholar. And the "disputer of this world" could represent the divider of words, the sophisticated rhetorician, the sophist, who conducted arguments in the stoa about what language meant. But they are all, in asserting worldly wisdom over God's truth, made foolish and purposeless in the face of the cross of Christ.

The point Paul is making is that any intellectual search for wisdom, for the understanding of human motives or behavior, is doomed to failure, or at best to an orderly life of self-disciplined thinking, because the human mind cannot by itself grasp, in its searching, the infinite wisdom and love of God, revealed in the cross of Jesus Christ. No one can read the Epistles containing Paul's thought on the current problems of his readers without recognizing that, rather than deriding thought and intelligence or the application of human logic, he brought the full force of a trained and capable intellect into the application of the gospel to human lives. But in all instances his wisdom is "the power of God, and the wisdom of God."

Of course the wisdom of God must manifest itself so that the individual is transformed in the purpose and function of all the major elements of a person—the cognitive, affective, and psychomotor elements. In many instances, these parts may be in contention or stress among themselves—a person may learn a fact (cognitive) that denies the validity of a feeling he has (affective) and thus causes him to behave (psychomotor) in an unpredictable manner, occasionally to the disruption of family or organizational structures.

The transformed believer has strong ties to God through the love of Christ on the cross, and his whole being is affected by the fact of his salvation so that his emotions come under the control of that love, along with his actions toward others. While industrial and economic society attempts to control the work and the contributions of employees, the ones most treasured as employees are the ones who see their work as the fulfillment of larger objectives in their own lives, and as also fitting the needs of society. There is the fulfillment of God's purpose as well when the wisdom of the cross creates in a person an understanding that constructively develops his emotional stability and directs his total behavior toward the fruits of the Spirit he possesses in Christ.

Think for a moment about the world that human wisdom had prepared for the time of

Christ. There were crimes untold, slavery, lust, and wickedness we cannot imagine even today. Corruption was everywhere. Exploitation of men and animals was aimed at serving greed and selfishness. No wonder Paul said, "The world by wisdom knew not God." Nations of people worshiped the carvings of animals and people they made from sticks and stones, not knowing how to represent God. It was only through the preaching of Christ crucified that the Jews' stumbling block became a stepping-stone, and the Greeks' "foolishness" the source and presence of the power and wisdom of God.

If the civilization of the world had been on the road to improvement, to peaceful justice for all persons, to an understanding of the worth of human life and its protection, to whole-world fairness and justice—in short, if the world had been on the way toward perfection for every creature—God would have blessed every part of it, for it and all its people would have known the wisdom of God. Instead, God was forced to declare the wisdom of the wise as fit for destruction, and the understanding of the prudent as equal to zero. So much for signs and wisdom.

We are being given notice that we must pay attention—for our lives and for eternity—to God's promise through the foolishness of preaching to save those who believe.—John R. Rodman

ILLUSTRATIONS

A ROAD TO CHRIST.   It was a favorite dictum of the preachers of a bygone day that, just as from every village in Britain there is a road that by linking you to other roads will bring you to London at last, so from every text in the Bible, even the remotest and least likely, there is a road to Christ. Possibly there were occasions when strange turns of exegesis and dubious allegorizings were pressed into service for the making of that road; but the instinct was entirely sound that declared that no preaching that fails to exalt Christ is worthy to be called Christian preaching. This is our great master theme. In the expressive, forthright language of John Donne, "All knowledge that begins not and ends not with His glory is but a giddy, but a vertiginous circle, but an elaborate and exquisite ignorance."—James S. Stewart

THE NECESSITY OF PREACHING REPENTANCE.   Even the most cursory study of the preaching in Acts shows that the gospel according to the apostles was a clarion call to repentance. At Pentecost, Peter concluded his sermon—a clear lordship message—with this: "Therefore let all the house of Israel know for certain that God has made Him both Lord and Christ—this Jesus whom you crucified" (Acts 2:36). The message penetrated his listeners' hearts, and they asked Peter what response was expected of them. Peter said plainly, "Repent, and let each of you be baptized in the name of Jesus Christ for the forgiveness of your sins" (v. 38).

Note that he made no mention of faith. That was implied in the call to repentance. Peter was not making baptism a condition of their salvation; he simply outlined the first step of obedience that should follow their repentance (compare Acts 10:43–48). Peter's audience, familiar with the ministry of John the Baptist, understood baptism as an external corroboration of sincere repentance (compare Matt. 3:5–8). Peter was not asking them to perform a meritorious act, and the whole of biblical teaching makes that clear.

But the message he gave them that day was a straightforward command to repent. As the context of Acts 2 shows, the people who heard Peter understood that he was demanding unconditional surrender to the Lord Jesus Christ.—John McArthur[8]

SERMON SUGGESTIONS

Topic: The Biblical Revelation

TEXT: 2 Pet. 1:21

(1) The Bible is a unique book. (2) The Bible is a powerful book (Heb. 4:12). (3) The Bible is a living book. The word in Hebrews 4:12 translated in the King James Version as "quick" literally means "living." (4) The Bible is a divine book (2 Tim. 3:16).—Richard Bennett Sims

Topic: Christ's Legacy to an Ailing World

TEXT: John 14:27

What this peace is not: (a) mere animal contentment, (b) mere stagnation. (2) What this peace is: (a) a thing that comes from a sense of values, (b) the peace of right action, (c) the peace that springs from a certain relationship: "Thou wilt keep him in perfect peace whose heart is stayed on thee."—Frederick K. Stamm

CONGREGATIONAL MUSIC

1. "Nature with Open Volume Stands," Isaac Watts (1707)

   GERMANY, W. Gardiner's *Sacred Melodies* (1815)

   This magnificent hymn by the greatest of all hymn writers in the English language is suitable for the opening of worship. It relates particularly to the opening thoughts of Psalm 19 as well as to the Corinthian passage in the Epistle lesson (1 Cor. 1:18–25).

2. "My Soul, Recall with Reverent Wonder," Exod. 20:1–17; vers. Dewey Westra (1942)

   LES COMMANDMENTS, *Genevan Psalter* (1547)

   The singing of this metrical version of the Ten Commandments could well replace the reading of the Old Testament lesson. It would be best to alternate singing and speaking the nine stanzas of the hymn in order not to consume an inordinate amount of time while not omitting any of the commandments.

3. "The Old Rugged Cross," George Bennard (1913)

   OLD RUGGED CROSS, George Bennard (1913)

   This well-loved gospel hymn, particularly in its second stanza, relates to the truth of the Epistle lesson, which asserts that the preaching of the cross is foolishness to the world, but for those who are redeemed, it is the power and the wisdom of God. If all stanzas are sung, it might be a hedge against falling into extreme sentimentality to delay the singing of the refrain until the very end.

4. "The Spacious Firmament on High," Ps. 19:1–16; vers. Joseph Addison (1712)

   CREATION, Franz Joseph Haydn (1798)

   Well known because of its famous tune from Haydn's oratorio *The Creation,* this free paraphrase of Psalm 19 would make a glorious beginning for public worship. Its first stanza could be sung by a large choir before inviting congregational participation in the remainder of the hymn.—Hugh T. McElrath

---

[8]*The Gospel According to the Apostles* (Nashville: W Publishing Group, 1993, 2000), p. 83.

WORSHIP AIDS

CALL TO WORSHIP.   "The law of the Lord is perfect, reviving the soul; the decrees of the Lord are sure, making wise the simple; the precepts of the Lord are right, rejoicing the heart; the commandment of the Lord is clear, enlightening the eyes" (Ps. 19:7–8).

INVOCATION.   Gracious and forgiving God, you have given us your commandments for our good and we thank you for these priceless teachings. We ask you now to grant us the wisdom to appropriate, appreciate, and live by them to your glory and the rejoicing of our hearts.

OFFERTORY SENTENCE.   "Moreover, it is required of stewards that they be found trust-worthy" (1 Cor. 4:2).

OFFERTORY PRAYER.   Our Father, we are assured that you will never fail or forsake us. Give us strength in our time of weakness, so we do not fail you in the stewardship of all we are and have.

PRAYER.   Lord, you have been our dwelling place age after age. Before the mountains were born, before the Earth or the world came to birth, you were God from all eternity and forever. Times and seasons, days and years, peoples and nations have come and gone "to the praise of your glory," and in you we "live and move and have our being." You have created us, preserved us, brought us to this very day. You have instructed us in wisdom, chastened us in love, borne with us in patience and compassion. For who you are, and for what you have done for us and meant to us across the years, we thank you. We thank you for each other: family, friends, colleagues. We thank you for the ministry of the Church in the world, and we pray that as you have called us and prepared us to take part in it, you will guide and guard us in our work. Keep us from any wrong that distorts the mind, from any willful desire that twists life away from your purpose. Deliver us from cherished hatred and thoughtless contempt, from pride of place and from envy. Bring us in every moment of decision to set before you the choices we would make, submitting our knowledge to your wisdom, and yielding all that we are to the service of what you would have us be. The future rests with you, O God. Grant that we may delight in it and not grieve it. As you anointed your Son to preach good news to the poor, to proclaim release to the captives and recovery of sight to the blind, to set at liberty those who are oppressed, and so to proclaim the acceptable year of the Lord, make us bold to preach, to proclaim that same word; and do not let us think, even for a moment, that you will be pleased with some other word, some easier word. Keep us from wishful thinking. Keep us from the vain thought that you will find any year acceptable other than that one in which the kingdoms of this world become the Kingdom of our Lord and of his Christ. That he may reign in us, in the Church, and in the world, who reigns with you eternally, we beseech you for the presence and power of your Spirit. O blessed disturber of our peace, come! O Holy Spirit, come! And grant us always to know your peace, through obedience to the word and will of him who sends you. This we ask not in fear of consequences of our disobedience, but in hope of knowing and finding ways to express that perfect love which casts out fear; even the love of Christ Jesus, God's Son, our Savior.—Charles L. Bartow, paraphrased from a prayer by Paul Scherer

SERMON
Topic: Faith
TEXT: 1 John 5:1, 4

Paul says in Ephesians 2:8, "By grace are ye saved through faith." We are not saved by works. We are not saved by the merits of others. We are saved only by the grace of God. We are saved by the energy and life of God that flows in us; we are saved by grace through faith, the instrument through which this life of God enters us. Faith is cardinal and basic in the Christian religion.

Faith is vital because it is an experience with God. Success rather than failure in the Christian world is due more to faith in God than to anything else. There is a proverb among us that says, "The hammer that shatters glass forges steel." The same hammers of circumstance, environment, difficulties, tragedy, sorrow, and providence that will crush one man into pieces will make another into a character of beauty, strength, and effectiveness. The difference is faith.

The faith that overcomes this world is faith in God. It is not faith in things. Faith in things, faith in our fellow Christians, and faith in ourselves are the outcroppings of faith in God. It is faith in God that enables us to overcome this world.

Nowhere does God admonish believers to have faith in prayer. Faith in God is what God calls us to. If we have faith in God, in the integrity of God, in the goodness of God, and in the wisdom of God, if we send up a dozen petitions that God in his wisdom does not see fit to answer, it will not shake our faith in him. Our faith is not in petition. It is not in prayer. It is not in things. It is not in Christians. It is not even in the Church. Our faith is in God. Surely we trust our Christian brothers, but the faith that overcomes the world is faith in Christ.

The victory that overcomes the world is a faith that dares. This faith characterized the Old Testament followers of the Lord. It characterized the New Testament believers, and characterizes all believers up to the present.

Truth characterized the ministry of the early disciples and of the apostle Paul when he went into Asia Minor, preaching to those who were confused and bewildered with false philosophies. He preached the simple gospel to them. He met opposition, but he also had victory. At Lystra they stoned him almost to death. Then they dragged him outside the city and left him for dead. Then in the night, when the cold breezes blew into his face and he came back to consciousness, Paul got up and returned to his task, not counting the cost.

Most of us have no scars; we are well cared for, well fed, and well financed. We are so diplomatic that we are loved by everybody. The tendency today is to get along with our world, and we go along with it to an extent, but there must be a line of cleavage. We must use all the common sense that God has given us. We must outmaneuver diplomatically the godlessness and the evil around us, but not to the extent of compromising the gospel. Our faith is a faith that dares. Where is our daring? It goes with a faith that is in God. The faith that overcomes is the faith that dares.

The faith that overcomes this world is a directional force. All around us are great reservoirs of spiritual power. In the days of Benjamin Franklin, God was trying to speak to the scientists in the voice of thunder, to say to them, "There are invisible forces of power around us with which you can revolutionize the wheels of industry." And one day Franklin flew his famous kite, discovered electricity, and revolutionized the wheels of industry.

All around us are great, invisible worlds of spiritual power. There will be a few that will dare to venture into that frontier and come back with the indefinable something that makes the difference.

How can God deliver us? Do not forget that when God made this universe, he made it out of nothing. Give God great cities and all the countryside filled with ignorant people, sin-cursed and enslaved, and observe the results. Add to all this a thin line of human faith and watch God translate the confusion into hospitals, seminaries, colleges, institutions, and saved people marching like armies on the empires of ignorance. Watch the light of God crush the darkness all around it. This is because of faith.—C. E. Autrey[9]

SUNDAY, MARCH 30, 2003
Lectionary Message

Topic: Living Again for God
TEXT: Eph. 2:1–10
Other Readings: Num. 21:4–9; Ps. 107:1–3, 17–22; John 3:14–21

The passage that forms the text for this sermon has been a very popular basis for preaching. Many outstanding preachers have chosen this text not only once but several times. It is easy to see why: because it promises the greatest miracle imaginable; it settles the central problem of human life (how to reconcile sinful man with holy God); it offers hope to people in all kinds of hopeless situations; it establishes the true relationship between faith and "works" in the Christian life. For these reasons, it could easily become the life-text for anyone desiring a successful life and a place in eternity with God.

I. *Our condition by nature.* Throughout the Epistle to the Ephesians, Paul refers to "you" and "us." He begins addressing the Christians at Ephesus, describing their present situation in Christ, and very soon broadens his statements to include all believers, referring to "us." Whether Jews or Greeks, he says, "We all had our conversation in times past in the lusts of our flesh . . . and were by nature the children of wrath." He means that all people are objects of the anger of God in the beginning of our very nature.

He describes the condition that afflicts all of us as death. He means that without faith in Christ active within us we are not alive. Our bodies, we know, are subject to death any time, for we are just a heartbeat away from it at any moment of our lives. It is hard to realize that we are really dead without Christ. Even though one may have a beautiful face, a strong body, and an active and retentive mind, he or she is dead until Christ takes over and restores life.

The evil desires of the natural human life are symbols of death, for all are deadly. An innocent, beautiful person who does not know Christ is just as dead as the lifeless corpse on the slab in a morgue. Some show more active signs of it than others, being farther along on a path of destruction by reason of extreme indulgence in corrupting activities and habits. Some have pushed mistreatment of their ideals and their strengths to the limit, challenging death itself with careless abandon.

The Bible is clear in its message throughout its pages, "The soul that sinneth, it shall die" (Ezek. 18:4). "All we like sheep have gone astray, we have turned every one to his own way;

---

[9]*Southwestern Sermons*, ed. by H. C. Brown Jr. (Nashville: Broadman Press, 1960), pp. 1–6.

and the Lord hath laid on him the iniquity of us all" (Isa. 53:6). "If thou doest not well, sin lieth at the door" (Gen. 4:7). "Every man shall be put to death for his own sin" (Deut. 24:16). We must be quick to proclaim that not all of us have lived out in practice the full nature of sin that is in us. There are many who have been well brought up, who have good social graces and a benevolent outlook on their associates, who are honest and truthful to a large degree, who are law-abiding and charitable. These people may even be so well liked and so successful that they themselves may come to think they do not need a savior. But still it is necessary to point out that "without faith it is impossible to please God" (Heb. 11:6). The force of our natural being is such that it makes us inadequate to achieve the righteousness which is of God by faith.

II. *Our restoration to life in Christ.* Where can we turn or what can we do to escape from our natural condition before God? There is nothing we can do except ask God to help us. Paul declares the help that can save us. "But God, who is rich in mercy, for his great love wherewith he loved us, even when we were dead in sins, hath quickened us together with Christ (by grace ye are saved)." Christ, as shown by his saving of Lazarus, can quicken again to life even the longest and most noticeably dead, no matter how far gone because of sin.

The riches of God, shown to us in the mercy he gives us, are purely riches of grace. We can hardly appreciate what grace implies or to what extent it goes to redeem us. Grace is defined in many terms. It is, first and foremost, unmerited. We have no claim of innocence, either of intention or deed, on which to base such a salvation. Our only claim is the promise of God and the death of his Son. Paul goes on to say that it is not of works, meaning that no manner of life or work of goodness can qualify a person for this gift of faith in grace. He who shows grace is the ruler and the judge.

In my early high school days I was employed by the father of a good friend who owned the biggest drugstore in the suburb where I lived. I did all sorts of jobs, from taking deliveries, waiting on soda-fountain customers, and cooking chocolate syrup, to filling capsules of his special cold medicine. Then I was entrusted with the job of stocking the shelves, marking prices on containers and putting them in the proper place, according to the FIFO rule (first in, first out). Once, while shelving some one-inch glass globes of expensive imported perfume, I lost my grip. One bottle shattered. At the time I had no hope of paying for that bottle of perfume in less than a year of work. When I showed it to him, the druggist told me not to worry, just to be more careful. I was so thankful that I cried. He let me continue to work, till I became a cashier and a salesperson. Can you imagine my loyalty from then on?

When Paul says (v. 5), "By grace you have been saved," we may misunderstand the perfect tense of the verb. Of course, it means that the work of Christ and the gift of God are perfect in completeness and effectiveness and were finished at a specific time in the past. What about their application to us? "You have been saved," yes, but not to the extent that you may become arrogant about it, forgetting the debt you owe, and assuming that everything you do henceforth is holy and blameless. In fact, the outcome of our saving faith may be to make us more conscious than ever of needing to incorporate saving faith into our lives.

III. *Saved unto good works.* Since we are no longer prisoners of death and are restored to life, we have lives to live as Christian believers. Paul goes on to say that we are God's workmanship, "created in Christ Jesus unto good works." Whereas the past works and good deeds we have done could not outweigh, in the balance, our sins springing from a sinful nature, now, redeemed by grace, we may do works that will count for good. One believer in the past century stated, "I will henceforth live as a man ought to live who has been redeemed at such a price." There are moments of appreciation marked by feelings of profound regret. John Wesley wrote, "We find a taint of . . . unbelief . . . so that we are now more ashamed of our best duties than formerly of our worst sins . . . and for these also we should be guilty before God, were it not for the blood of the covenant."[10]

In the new life of grace and salvation, we ought to practice two kinds of works—those of ensuring our growth in faith and the fellowship of other believers, and those of service in Christ's name for needy persons of all kinds. We must say to ourselves, as Paul advises Timothy, "Study to show yourself approved unto God, a workman who need not be ashamed, rightly dividing the word of truth" (2 Timothy 2:15). Then we must ask ourselves in regard to our communities and concerning the poor and the homeless, the sick and the imprisoned, "What would Jesus do?" When in all conscience we answer that question and follow its implications, we may live in fullness of faith.—John R. Rodman

ILLUSTRATIONS

CLOSED DOORS.   Dr. Bruce Waltke, one of my mentors in the Hebrew language at seminary, used to say, "The longer I live and the closer I walk with Christ, the more I believe He does not take the time to explain why. So we trust him through our lives without expecting the 'why?' to be answered."

I find a similar kind of comfort in the third chapter of Revelation. This chapter not only has something to say about who's in charge of the closed door, it also puts the responsibility where it belongs: squarely on the Lord.—Charles R. Swindoll[11]

THE POTTER.   I've watched a few potters at work, and it's a funny thing. I have seen them suddenly mash the clay down and start over again. Each time they do this, the clay comes out looking entirely different. And with gifted potters, they can start over and over—each time it's better and better.

He is the potter, we are the clay. He is the one who gives the commands, we are the ones who obey. He never has to explain himself, he never has to ask permission. Nor does he predict ahead of time that we're just about to encounter a closed door. He is shaping us into the image of his Son, regardless of the pain and heartache that may require. Those lessons are learned a little easier when we remember that we are not in charge. He is.—Charles R. Swindoll[12]

SERMON SUGGESTIONS

Topic: Retreat Impossible

TEXT: Judges 11:35a

We should not make an evil vow to God. If we have made such a vow, it would add to the evil to keep it. Good vows to God must be kept. (1) We have opened our mouths to the Lord by the several ways in which we have professed our faith. (2) We cannot go back because of

---

[10]"The Scripture Way of Salvation," in Blackwood, *The Protestant Pulpit* (New York: Abingdon-Cokesbury Press, 1947), p. 28.
[11]*The Mystery of God's Will* (Nashville: W Publishing Group, 1999), p. 146.
[12]*The Mystery of God's Will*, p. 147.

the nature of our salvation, the penalties incurred in disobedience, and the loving constraints of joy and grace.—Adapted from C. H. Spurgeon

Topic: God's Laws Are for Our Good
TEXT: Mark 2:23–28
(1) They focus on human need. (2) They point to Christ.

CONGREGATIONAL MUSIC
1. "O Bless the Lord, My Soul!" Isaac Watts (1719)
   FESTAL SONG, William H. Walter (1894)
   A good opening for musical worship is this free paraphrase of Psalm 103 by the great hymnist Isaac Watts. Its sixth stanza, with its reference to Moses, gives it a natural relationship to the Old Testament reading (Num. 21:4–9).
2. "Thanks Be to God Our Savior," Ps. 107; vers. David J. Diephouse (1985)
   GENEVAN 107, *Genevan Psalter* (1551)
   Stanzas 1, 3, and 4 of this modern metrical paraphrase of Psalm 107 relate to the selected passages in today's Psalter reading. Alternate reading of the psalm and singing of the paraphrase could follow this plan: verses 1–3, stanza 1; verses 17–19, stanza 3; verses 20–22, stanza 4.
3. "Not What These Hands Have Done," Horatius Bonar (1861)
   ST. ANDREW, Joseph Barnby (1866)
   An expansion of the truth of Ephesians 2:8, this fine expression of Christ's saving work could be sung as a response to the Epistle lesson (Eph. 2:1–10).
4. "To God Be the Glory," Fanny J. Crosby (1875)
   TO GOD BE THE GLORY, William H. Doane (1866)
   One of Fanny Crosby's finest, this gospel hymn gathers up the theme of John 3:16. Because of its length, all stanzas of the song could be sung before singing the refrain as a meaningful climax.—Hugh T. McElrath

WORSHIP AIDS
CALL TO WORSHIP.   "O give thanks to the Lord, for he is good; for his steadfast love endures forever. Let the redeemed of the Lord say so" (Ps. 107:1–2a NRSV).

INVOCATION.   We are here today, O Lord, because you have stood by us and walked with us through all difficulties. Let our worship today express our gratitude in all we say and do.

OFFERTORY SENTENCE.   "Like good stewards of the manifold grace of God, serve one another with whatever gift each of you has received" (1 Pet. 4:10 NRSV).

OFFERTORY PRAYER.   You have given us many good things for our own use and joy, O God. Now grant that we may see how we can share these gracious gifts in our offerings of time, of money, and of deeds for the good of others.

PRAYER.   Almighty and everlasting God, we thank thee though thou dost inhabit eternity and dwell in light unapproachable, yet thou dost visit our tragic Earth with the touch of thy triumph. Thou givest hope to the oppressed, pardon to sinners, friendship to the lonely, strength to the weak, and a place in thy Kingdom to little children. How could we fail to give thee thanks?

Many of us have found thy salvation at the very moment when all seemed lost, when nothing went right, when our guilt rose like a mountain before us, when no one seemed to care, when fear and trembling had us in its grip. And now, realizing that there are multitudes at this very moment who find themselves where we suffered in our desperation, we pray that the sunlight of thy grace and truth may break into their darkness, so that they too may have reason for thanksgiving and rejoicing.

Renew our rejoicing today. We confess that the way of thy Kingdom is not always easy. We feel keenly the pain of our disappointments, the humiliation of our lapses from fidelity, the isolation that ethical commitment often brings, and the anguish of hopes unrealized, plans gone awry, and uncertainty ahead. Help us, like children in the carefree abandon of the moment, to know once more the joy of they salvation. May our stony hearts cry out in praise, because we realize even this day that the King of our salvation is among us.

SERMON
Topic: The Years of the Locusts
TEXT: Joel 2:21–25

I had a friend who became a Christian after his eightieth birthday. Every time I went to see him, his conversation included a wistful reference to the lost years of his life. They were years without joy, peace, and service to Christ. They were years that the locusts had eaten.

The little book of Joel was written in the midst of national turmoil. The prophet, about whom we know precious little, had a burning conviction that the natural catastrophes that had settled upon land and people were but the heavy hand of God's judgment. The prophet saw the legend *Ichabod*—"the glory is departed"—writ large across the face of the nation. One half of the seventy-three verses in the book are devoted to this message of doom. But in the midst of his writings, the mood of the prophet shifts. He is gripped in a kind of prophetic ecstasy and sees the possibility of restoration for his little nation. It is in this happier frame that Joel gives us the beautiful and meaningful promise of our text: "I will restore the years that the locusts have eaten" (2:25).

Embraced in this engaging little metaphor are great Bible truths that may be expressed in three simple sentences:

God's eye is on the sparrow.
God's hand is in the storm.
God's grace covers our sin.

I. *God's eye is on the sparrow.* This word of Joel was prompted by a memorable disaster of nature. Judah was devastated by an invasion of locusts.

Here was distress enough to paralyze the whole of life. The markets and shops in the villages of the countryside were idle. The shelves were empty. Food was scarce. The cattle were dying for want of pasture and water. The ground was stripped bare. Organized society had collapsed. Temple services were suspended. Life was on its simplest, most primitive level.

It is fairly easy to believe in God's goodness when things are going well for us. We settle into a comfortable routine and observe that God "helps those who help themselves while idlers come to grief." But then life gets unstrung, gives us the back of the hand, and faith is hard to come by. It is not difficult to understand the mood of Job's wife, who counseled, "Curse God and die."

You have to think about it a while before it dawns on you that even this reaction has behind it a religious assumption. The assumption is that God is good and God knows.

One of the sweetest word pictures Jesus ever painted of the Heavenly Father is this: "Are not two sparrows sold for a farthing? And one of them shall not fall on the ground without your Father. Fear ye not therefore, ye are of more value than many sparrows" (Matt. 10:29, 31).

But there remain the locusts, and we must look elsewhere for an explanation.

II. *God's hand is in the storm.* This brings us to our second truth. It springs directly from the first, and both are the conclusions of faith.

In a dramatic innovation, Joel sees the locusts descending out of the north as an army of the Lord. They come rank upon rank, company upon company, devouring and destroying as they come. Walls do not stop them; they simply eat their way through them. Houses do not stop them; they simply march up and over them. Well disciplined, they tramp through the land, leaving it barren and desolate.

Joel contends that they march at the command of the Lord!

Here is an insight we must not miss. Joel saw that this natural disaster was the hand of the Lord. God had not abandoned Judah, nor had God forgotten Judah. Rather, God was deeply concerned and irrevocably committed to Judah and Jerusalem. The fierce countenance of nature was the evidence. The disaster was not evidence that they were orphaned in the universe; it was proof that they were God's very own.

Joel's word to us who face the darkness of an unknown future is that God's stars glimmer in the darkness for those who look with eyes of faith.

That was Joel's breathtaking contention. The storm was not an occasion for bitterness and cynicism. It was God's way of breaking up fallow ground.

III. *God's grace covers our sin.* We move, then, with the irresistible logic of the prophet, to his conclusion. Since God's eye is on the sparrow and God's hand is in the storm, there is hope. This is the way the prophet expressed that hope: "Rend your heart, and not your garments, . . . and I will restore to you the years the locust hath eaten" (2:13, 25).

In the face of the locusts, Joel called for repentance. Only by repentance could Judah see God in the locusts. Should Judah repent, the scourge would be lifted, and the Lord God would restore all the years the locusts had eaten.

The good tidings at which Joel hinted and the gospel that the apostle preached is this: When you make that surrender, God gives you of his own Spirit, so that you may go forth clothed in God's strength. You do not see a miracle, you are a miracle. And God himself restores to you all that the locusts of those lost years have eaten.—Ralph L. Murray[13]

---

[13]*Plumblines and Fruit Baskets* (Nashville: Broadman Press, 1966), pp. 75–81.

SUNDAY, APRIL 6, 2003
Lectionary Message

Topic: The New Covenant

TEXT: Jer. 31:31–34

Other Readings: Ps. 51:1–12; John 12:20–23; Heb. 5:5–10

The Bible speaks a great deal about covenants. A covenant is an agreement that individuals make with one another and, in the Bible, with God. The covenant is one of the great teachings of the Bible. References to covenants between God and humanity appear 286 times. From Genesis to Revelation, the Bible refers to a covenant that has been made between God and humankind. God selected the nation Israel as God's bride. "You are my chosen betrothed," God said to Israel. God entered into a covenant with the people.

But the covenant required Israel to be faithful. God made a covenant with Abraham (Gen. 17). Later we read about the covenant relationship that God made with Moses on Mt. Sinai (Ex. 20). Prophets such as Hosea, Amos, Micah, and others referred to Israel's covenant relationship with God. These prophets spoke boldly about Israel's unfaithfulness to that covenant and about how God continuously called them back into the love relationship.

In our text today, the prophet Jeremiah proclaimed that there would be a new covenant one day. This covenant he envisioned would not be centered on the human condition but would be written within the heart. Since Israel had been unable to keep the old covenant, God would bring about the consummation of the new covenant.

I. *Jeremiah offered a new prospective.* Jeremiah seemed to be standing on top of a mountain and looking down in one direction to the past and to God's covenant with Moses, which was written on stone. But Israel, since the time of Moses, had failed to live according to the covenant. Even the reforms under Josiah had finally failed (11:1–23). Then Jeremiah looked in the direction of the future and saw that a new covenant would arise out of this broken relationship.

(a) Some have called Jeremiah's concept of the new covenant "the Gospel before the Gospel." His concept is without question the high point of his teaching. It is one of the most profound and stimulating passages in the Old Testament. Some have surmised that this concept of the new covenant is one of the earliest, and closest to the New Testament understanding of faith commitment.

(b) Jeremiah was bold to declare that the new covenant would be brought about by God's action. God is sovereign and would initiate the changes within the hearts of persons. God's covenant would be radically new and God would be the Lord of the covenant. "I will be their God, and they will be my people" (v. 33).

(c) Jeremiah viewed Israel as God's elect people (33:24; 12:7–9) but he was deeply concerned that the people had turned their backs on Yahweh and had broken their covenant and gone after false gods. Many of his oracles and images depict the disloyalty of Israel. Because Israel had gone the way of the harlot (3:1), Yahweh declared war on Israel (4:5–8). Her only hope was to repent (25:1–14), but she had set her face in a direction from which she seemed unwilling to turn (2:2–4).

II. *The new covenant contains a future dimension.* "Behold, the days are coming" (v. 33).

(a) The new covenant would involve the creation of a new person through new divine action. God would pour God's will into the heart of persons and would be willing to forgive and forget their sins (v. 34). The revelation of God's direction for God's people would be seen as God "wrote God's own laws" on the heart—the inner conscience of men and women. This new covenant would denote the end of the way God had dealt with God's people in the past. A new day had arrived and it was God who took the initiative.

(b) Jeremiah sounded five notes about the new covenant:

(1) *The covenant would be an inward experience.* The prophet was speaking not about material blessings, such as plentiful harvests, but about peace with men and beasts. There would be a changed nature so that persons would of themselves know and do right.

(2) *There would be fellowship with God.* Jeremiah was speaking out of his own experience because he believed that he belonged to God and that God belonged to him.

(3) *Persons would experience a sense of immediacy with God.* Prophets, priests, and other intermediaries would no longer be required. Jeremiah had lived alone with God, and the way would soon come that all persons could commune directly with God.

(4) *The new covenant would be universal.* All would know God. The new covenant would take effect for all, without exception. It would be made with the House of Israel, yet for each person there would be a personal, sovereign experience, independent of rank and office; the common person having it as well as the prophet.

(5) *God would give full and final pardon.* The sin that had been written "with the pen of iron with the point of a diamond" upon the hearts and altars would be wiped clean forever. Life would be a fresh page on which better things could be written in a wonderful new day. Sacrifices would be needed no longer—at least this was implied, though Jeremiah said nothing about it. A fresh era in humanity's thinking about God would come.

III. *The new covenant prediction was fulfilled in the life, death, and Resurrection of Jesus Christ.* Because Israel was unable to keep the old covenant, God brought about the consummation of the new covenant.

(a) The old covenant was based on righteous living, but Jesus Christ has ushered in a new testament, a new covenant. The old covenant was based on law. The new covenant is based on love. The old covenant was based on the requirement of keeping rules and on a person's loyalty to God. The new covenant is based on the grace of God. No matter how hard human beings try, men and women cannot keep the strict laws of the old covenant as they seek to worship God. Through his death and Resurrection, Jesus Christ has sealed the new covenant (Matt. 26:28). We cannot remove our own sins, but the Lamb of God takes them away for us.

(b) Every time we observe the Lord's Supper we proclaim the newness, comprehensiveness, forgiveness, and depth of God's grace and love, which are revealed in the new covenant. "This cup is the covenant in my blood, which is shed for many" (see Luke 22:7–20).

(c) Jeremiah promised a new covenant. Jesus Christ has ushered in this new covenant. Remember that Christ is present with us in a covenant relationship as the Risen and living Lord. Let us celebrate his risen presence at the communion table and in our daily life.—William Powell Tuck

ILLUSTRATIONS

THE CELESTIAL ESCORT.   Our moods shift, but God's mood doesn't. Our minds may change, but God's mind doesn't. Our devotion may falter, but God's never does. Even if we are faithless, he is faithful, for he cannot betray himself (2 Tim. 2:13). He is a sure God. And because he is a sure God, we can state confidently, "Surely goodness and mercy shall follow me all the days of my life."

And what follows the word *surely?* "Goodness and mercy." If the Lord is the shepherd who leads the flock, goodness and mercy are the two sheepdogs who lead the flock. Goodness *and* mercy. Not goodness alone, for we are sinners in need of mercy. Not mercy alone, for we are fragile, in need of goodness. We need them both. As one man wrote, "Goodness to supply every want. Mercy to forgive every sin." Goodness to provide. Mercy to pardon.

Goodness and mercy—the celestial escorts of God's flock. If that duo doesn't reinforce your faith, try this phrase: "all the days of my life."

What a huge statement. Look at the size of it! Goodness and mercy follow the child of God each and every day! Think of the days that lie ahead. What do you see? Days at home with only toddlers? God will be at your side. Days in a dead-end job? He will walk you through. Days of loneliness? He will take your hand. Surely goodness and mercy shall follow me, not some of, not most of, not almost all, but all the days of my life.—Max Lucado[1]

NEW COVENANT.   We can see why the New Testament—and "testament" is simply the Latin word for "covenant"—claims that this hope of Jeremiah's has been fulfilled in Jesus. In him we see the unbridgeable bridged. In him we see a human life that in all its glory and true humanity gives the obedience that Israel was never able to give. But if we look at Christians, at the new people of God, at the Church, what are we to say? If Jeremiah were in our midst today, might he not still be looking forward to a new covenant, for precisely the same reasons that led him to talk about the need for one in his own day? Is there any evidence that we in the Church today are any more obedient to God than Jeremiah was, or that the people in his own day were? Perhaps instead of talking glibly, as we Christians sometimes do, about the new covenant, we ought to take a long hard look at ourselves . . . and wonder.—Robert Davidson[2]

SERMON SUGGESTIONS

Topic: What Is Worship?
To worship is (1) to quicken the conscience by the holiness of God, (2) to feed the mind with the truth of God, (3) to purge the imagination by the beauty of God, (4) to open the heart to the love of God, (5) to devote the will to the purpose of God.—William Temple

Topic: Conflicting Reactions to Our Good Deeds
TEXT: Mark 14:3–9
(1) People's criticism of those deeds. (2) Christ's acceptance of those deeds.

CONGREGATIONAL MUSIC
1. "O for a Heart to Praise My God," Charles Wesley (1742)
   RICHMOND, Thomas Haweis (1792)

---

[1]*Traveling Light* (Nashville: W Publishing Group, 2001), pp. 144–145.
[2]*Jeremiah Vol. 2, and Lamentations,* Daily Study Bible Series (Philadelphia: Westminster Press, 1985), p. 90.

This classic Wesleyan hymn would be an appropriate response to the Psalter lesson (Ps. 51:1–12).

2. "Fairest Lord Jesus," Anon, *Gesangbuch,* Münster (1677)

   CRUSADER'S HYMN, Silesian Folk Song (1842)

   This venerable hymn that exalts and glorifies Christ relates to both the Epistle lesson (Heb. 5:5–10) and the Gospel reading (John 12:20–23). It could effectively precede or follow either of these readings.

3. "Standing on the Promises," R. Kelso Carter (1886)

   PROMISES, R. Kelso Carter (1896)

   God's new covenant with Israel (Jer. 31:31–34) was a promise written in their hearts, signifying God's eternal reliability. Singing worshipers can express their faith in God's covenantal promises with this nineteenth-century gospel hymn. To impart its true meaning, the congregation should sing this song not glibly but rather in a way that stresses God's constant faithfulness.

4. "Lord Jesus, Think on Me," Synesius of Cyrene (c. 410); trans. A. W. Chatfield (1876)

   DAMON, William Damon's *Psalms* (1579)

   An ancient hymn that voices universal need, "Lord Jesus, Think on Me" echoes David's prayer for mercy and purity of heart. It could be sung in connection with the Prophecy reading (Jer. 31:31–34), which focuses on God's merciful forgiveness, or with the Psalter reading (Ps. 51:1–12), which expresses David's—and therefore the singers'—penitence.—Hugh T. McElrath

WORSHIP AIDS

CALL TO WORSHIP.   "O Lord, open thou my lips; and my mouth shall shew forth thy praise. The sacrifices of God are a broken spirit: a broken and contrite heart, O God, thou wilt not despise" (Ps. 51:15, 17).

INVOCATION.   We confess our sins to you, O God, for we, many of us, at this very moment, have hearts that are broken and contrite. Forgive us, we pray, that our worship will be acceptable to you and that we can truly praise you.

OFFERTORY SENTENCE.   "As Jesus sat near the temple treasury, he watched the people as they dropped in their money. Many rich men dropped in a lot of money" (Mark 12:41 TEV).

OFFERTORY PRAYER.   You know our hearts, O God, and the spirit in which we bring our offerings. Teach us how to do what we do with willing hearts, remembering our Savior and his great gift of himself for us.

PRAYER.   Almighty and everlasting God, we thank thee that though thou dost inhabit eternity and dwell in light unapproachable, yet thou dost visit our tragic Earth with the touch of thy triumph. Thou givest hope to the oppressed, pardon to sinners, friendship to the lonely, strength to the weak, and a place in thy Kingdom to little children. How could we fail to give thee thanks?

Many of us have found thy salvation at the very moment when all seemed lost, when nothing went right, when our guilt rose like a mountain before us, when no one seemed to care, when fear and trembling had us in its grip. And now, realizing that there are multitudes at this very moment who find themselves where we suffered in our desperation, we pray that the sunlight of thy grace and truth may break into their darkness, so that they too may have reason for thanksgiving and rejoicing.

Renew our rejoicing today. We confess that the way of thy Kingdom is not always easy. We feel keenly the pain of our disappointments, the humiliation of our lapses from fidelity, the isolation that ethical commitment often brings, and the anguish of hopes realized, plans gone awry, and uncertainty ahead. Help us, like children in the carefree abandon of the moment, to know once more the joy of thy salvation. May our stony hearts cry out in praise, because we realize even this day that the king of our salvation is among us.

SERMON
Topic: Love Is the Only Good
TEXT: 1 Cor. 13:1–3

When we look into that inner world where our balances are struck, that inner world from whence comes the issue of our own lives, this Scripture reminds us that love is the only good.

The Corinthian Christians prided themselves on their spiritual and humanitarian achievements. They had struck for themselves a style of life that was both distinguished and satisfying. But the Corinthian community was also fractured with strife, tension, rivalries, and alienation. Your good, the apostle wrote in effect, is no good. Love is the only good.

It will be easier for us to understand just what the apostle said if we do these things: First, we will identify the goals for which the Corinthians were straining every nerve. Then, we will ponder Paul's incisive analysis of the one vital missing element. Finally, we will come back to the theme of the passage: Love is the only good.

I. *Goals of no value.* Just take a good look at the goals these Corinthians held for themselves.

Some wanted to become spellbinding orators. As Phillips puts it in his translation *Letter to Young Churches,* they wanted to "stir men like a fanfare of trumpets or the clashing of cymbals." Isn't that a graphic picture?

Others had a dream for themselves that embraced an intellectual bent. They aspired to the skills of contemplation and explanation. They wanted to understand all the mysteries of human existence; to be able to explain such things as evil, death, and the instinctual dream of immortality. They aspired to become oracles of wisdom, opening to men new vistas of understanding of themselves and their world. These were planners, the gifted organizers of Corinth, and their dreams and planning centered around Christian activities. Had they lived in our century, they would have been in some denominational center, dreaming up clever ways of motivating people to achieve impossible goals of Christian enlistment and training. They were religious activists with faith strong enough to move mountains.

Another group cited were less flamboyant than these others. They were the ascetics, who schemed to find better ways of economizing on their own needs so they might help others. They were the ultimate ascetics who "gave all their goods to feed the poor."

A final group—like the young American soldier of Vietnam—held that the highest good was to give your life for some cause. They were "willing to give their bodies to be burned"— the ultimate altruism.

Now, simply to look at these goals, all cast in superlative molds and for religious use, is to be impressed by their laudability. Could you compile a more commendable set of goals for human endeavor?

Yet Paul puts them in a column, adds them all up, and draws down a cipher. He says they are nothing, goals of no value? Why?

II. *One thing missing.* All these commendable efforts add up to nothing because love is not behind them. And if love is not in what we do, and aspire to do, all our effort comes to naught.

But what is love?

C. S. Lewis helps us distinguish between four kinds of love, all involved in fact or in possibility, in human experience. The first is *affection,* a love of familiar and homely objects and persons; the second is *friendship,* a love that is selective and reciprocating; then comes *eros,* that special state of those who are "in love"; and finally, *charity,* which Lewis identifies as the divine energy that brought man and his world into being and that offers man the means of redemption through Jesus, the Son of God.

Lewis helpfully points out the difference between natural loves and divine love. He distinguishes the two with the terms *need-love* (natural) and *gift-love* (divine). The kind of love designated by the term *gift-love* is rooted in the historical life, death, and Resurrection of Jesus. It rises above all other loves—even the natural capacity for love that God has built into our natures. The special quality of this gift-love is found in the fact that God in Christ loved us when nothing in us warranted such love. This is gift-love, the old-fashioned word for which is *grace.*

A line of a popular song goes, "What the world needs now is love, sweet love." The Scripture before us agrees with that, but with this distinction: the love that the world needs finds its measure and expression first in the person hanging on Golgotha's tree.

The cross refracts a new truth about God for men: God is love. The love revealed by the cross is the kind of love the world needs. It is the kind of love that can baptize our accomplishments, however meager or grand, and make them instruments of redemption and care. And the finest accomplishments, without this kind of love, are nothing.

That was what was missing in the achievements of the Corinthians.

III. *Love is the only good.* If the finest action, done without love is nothing, then love is the one thing that makes the difference. Love, then, is the only good.

It is "good" to have a nice career or a well-paying job; to have a modern home, replete with all the up-to-date conveniences (which are always getting out of working order); to have a late-model car, preferably two; to have leisure and the money to do something exciting and different with it; to give a college education to the children—and you add your own items. When you have it all abstracted, put a label on it: "The Good Life—American Style."

And then back off and take a look at this so-called good life: What are its components? What is at the bottom of it all? Is it love? Or covetousness? Or greed? Or that good capitalistic word *profit?*

Somerset Maugham, the British novelist, once wrote a sentence that needs to be inscribed on the lintels of every church in the land: "The great tragedy of life is not that people perish, but that they cease to love." For what good are all our impressive achievements if through failures of love we destroy ourselves and the world God gave us to live in?

The apostle—the man who wrote these lines—had walked both sides of the street. He knew what it was to be an achiever without love. He had an impressive list of accomplishments, garnered with ruthless efficiency and driven by fierce ambition. But he also knew how charred and empty such a life was.

On the other hand, Paul knew what it was to turn his back on everything the world of his day called "good," letting love shape his lifestyle and his day-to-day involvements. And out of this experience he wrote these lines of our Scripture—1 Corinthians 13:1–3.—Ralph L. Murray[3]

SUNDAY, APRIL 13, 2003
Lectionary Message

Topic: The Silence of God
TEXT: Mark 14:1–15:47
Other Readings: Liturgy of the Palms: Mark 11:1–11; Ps. 118:1–2, 19–29; Liturgy of the Passion: Isa. 50:4–9a; Ps. 31:9–16; Phil. 2:5–11

Many voices are raised today, asking, "Why is God so silent in the face of so much suffering and pain?" One place where God seemed the most silent was at the cross of his own Son, Jesus Christ. Jesus himself cried, "Eloi, Eloi lama sabachthani." "My God, my God, why have you forsaken me?" The words, "My God, why?" have echoed down through the centuries. "God, why?" Why was God so silent at Jesus' cross? Only Mark and Matthew recorded these words from the cross. Luke and John recorded other words that were not contained in the other two Gospels. "Why have you forsaken me?"

I. *What provoked this outcry?*

(a) Was it a cry of *doubting?* Hanging on the cross, did Jesus ask himself, "Have I misunderstood my calling? Have I been wrong about the mission of the Messiah?" Did this cry raise large question about the purpose of his life? Being crucified like a common criminal forced him to rethink his mission. Were the mocking tongues right? Had he wasted his life?

(b) Was it a cry of *depression?* Here, nailed to the cross, he was isolated and rejected by his friends. Some members of his own family called him insane. Broken and misunderstood, his spirits sank into deep depression. He saw his dream to bring in the Kingdom of God aborted.

(c) Was it a cry of *desertion?* All had forsaken him. Where was Peter at the cross? Where was Matthew? And Zacchaeus? Where was the centurion whom he had helped? Where was the once blind Bartimaeus? Where were the crowds of people who had pressed around him? Where were they now? Here he was—deserted, isolated, and alone.

(d) Was is a cry of *dereliction?* Did God abandon him at the cross, as some theologians have suggested? Was it a cry of absolute isolation? Did God turn his back on his Son? A derelict ship is one that is abandoned by men and even rats. Did Jesus raise his cry against an empty sky? Was he in the depths of despair? Did the cross thrust him into the "dark night of the soul"? Was that the cause behind his cry?

---

[3]*Christ and the City* (Nashville: Broadman Press, 1970), pp. 87–96.

(e) But could the cry of Jesus have been one primarily of *identification?* Here at the cross God was uniquely in Christ. At the cross we see God identifying with man/woman in their suffering. God was nowhere more present than at the cross. At the cross Jesus completely identified with our humanity as he suffered the consequences of humanity's sin.

II. Those around the cross misunderstood Jesus' cry and thought he was calling for Elijah. Muttered through painful lips, "Eloi" might be mistaken for the prophet's name.

(a) But insight into his cry might be found in realizing that the words, "My God, My God, why hast thou forsaken me," are likely a quotation from Psalm 22. The last few lines are a cry of hope and assurance (Ps. 22:23–24, 27, 31).

(b) The final words on the cross were not "I am forsaken"—a cry of despair—but a great shout of victory, "It is finished!" *Forsaken* was not the last word. There was a cry of identification, which ended in a triumphant assurance of the presence of God.

III. At the cross of Christ you and I discover that God gives us the same kind of answer in his silence that he gave his Son at Golgotha.

(a) Have you ever thought about how much silence surrounded the life of Jesus? When he was born, only a small number of people, a few shepherds and several wise men, knew of his birth. In one of our Christmas hymns we sing about this mystery: "How silently, how silently the gift is given." The Scriptures focus on only one episode in his childhood—when he was twelve years old in the Temple at Jerusalem. What happened during that other period of his childhood? How silent the biblical writers were! There is nothing but silence about his young manhood until he began his ministry at thirty years of age. Most of his life is unknown to us. The Scriptures are silent.

Do you remember the story about the Syrophoenician woman who came to Jesus and asked him to heal her child, and Jesus did not answer her a word? He was silent. When he stood before the high priest, Herod, and before Pilate, he was silent. When he prayed in the Garden of Gethsemane, "My God, let this cup pass from me," he received only silence from God. When he hung on the cross and cried out, "My God, my God, why have you forsaken me?" there again was only silence.

(b) What does all this silence teach us? Maybe it reveals that God does not explain to us the mystery of suffering and pain. Rather than an explanation, God gives us a presence. The answer is found in our awareness that God is in both good and evil. The book of Job struggles with the dilemma of suffering. Job discovered that there is no easy answer to the enigma of suffering. He was unwilling to attribute all suffering to the punishment of sin. The biblical writers affirmed that God is not only in the beautiful dimensions of life but also in the ugly and difficult. They affirmed God's presence in the flood as well as in a flower. God is present in the storm as well as in the sunshine, in plenty but also in famine, in defeat as well as in victory. All of life is under the sovereignty of God. Nothing separates us from his presence.

God does not answer all of our questions. God gives us God's presence. God gives God's self to us in the midst of our struggles. Sometimes God's presence is discovered not in the noise around us but in silence. At the cross, God's great redemption is accomplished in that silent act of suffering. In the midst of our own pains, struggles, and difficulties we discover that we are not left to bear them alone; God is present. An ancient Christian writer, Ignatius, once wrote, "God effects more by his silence than others do with all their talking."

As you and I reflect on the cross, let us remember that God gives us not an explanation to the problem of evil, suffering, and pain but a presence. God has not forsaken us; God is always present. In the most silent moments of your life's deepest pain, you are not alone, but the God who was in Christ on the cross is present also with you.—William Powell Tuck

ILLUSTRATIONS

THE CHALLENGE.   The story is told of a beginning teacher in Illinois who loved her first-year experience as a teacher, but because the principal had not visited her classroom to evaluate her teaching skills, she assumed that her contract would not be renewed for an additional year.

At the end of the school year, she packed up her personal material and prepared to say goodbye to students and colleagues. The principal saw her, smiled, and said, "We have enjoyed having you here this year and look forward to having you teach with us again next year!" The woman was astonished and replied, "Well, I haven't received a contract to teach next year, so I just assumed you thought I had done a poor job and didn't want me back."

The principal assured her, saying, "We really want you back. Your students scored higher on their achievement tests than any of our other students in the last ten years. You've got to come back next year." Deflecting the compliment, the teacher said, "It's easy to teach when you have such a great group of kids as I had. They were sharp, interested, motivated, and all of them have IQs of 150, 152, 153, and even higher."

The principal asked how she knew that the students possessed such high IQ scores. She cited the materials he had given her at the beginning of the school year, which contained a sheet of paper with the students' names and IQ scores on it. The principal smiled at her and said, "Those were their locker numbers."

There is an important lesson in this story: because she believed that the students had high IQ scores, the teacher treated them and taught them as though they were highly intelligent, creative, and motivated young people. Her attitude demanded high-level, quality work. She had great expectations and backed them up with a belief that the students would rise to the academic challenge and accomplish their work.—Victor M. Parachim[4]

THE USE OF SUFFERING.   In *The Trial of God*, Elie Wiesel wrote that he witnessed three rabbis who decided one winter to indict God for allowing children to be massacred. "When the trial was over and God was found guilty, the rabbis realized that it was time for prayers, so they bowed their heads to pray." In the face of the horror of horrors, the rabbis still felt the need to stay in contact with God. They struggled with the problems created when one chooses between God's macho power and God's power of compassion.

When we decide to let go of the idea that God is all-powerful, omnipotent in the worldly sense of power, we are free to love a God worthy of loving. Once that leap of faith grasps us, we are on our way to a little understanding of suffering. As Soelle claims, "The Christian faith relates to suffering not merely as remover or consoler. It offers no *'supernatural remedy for suffering,'* but strives for supernatural use of it."[5]—Loren Broadus[6]

---

[4]*Healing Grief* (St. Louis: Chalice Press, 2001), pp. 27–28.
[5]Dorothee Soelle, *Suffering* (Minneapolis: Fortress Press, 1984), p. 155.
[6]*Responses to Suffering* (St. Louis: Chalice Press, 2001), p. 91.

SERMON SUGGESTIONS

Topic: He Dies, He Must Die

TEXT: Luke 24:26

(1) Could anyone but a crucified Savior reveal our sins? (2) Could anyone but a crucified Savior save us from our sins? (3) Could anyone but a crucified Savior meet us in our agony?— W. E. Sangster

Topic: How Jesus Came to Jerusalem

TEXT: Luke 19:29–40

(1) He entered confidently. (2) He entered humbly. (3) He entered in the name of God. (4) He entered to the sound of rejoicing.

CONGREGATIONAL MUSIC

1. "Ride On! Ride On in Majesty!" Henry Hart Milman (1827)

   THE KING'S MAJESTY, Graham George (1939)

   One of the classic traditional hymns for Palm Sunday, "Ride On! Ride On in Majesty!" captures the spirit of Jesus' triumphal entry into Jerusalem and draws the worshiping congregation into the solemn but festive scene. Its use as a processional hymn for this day is naturally suggested.

2. "Open Now the Gates of Beauty," Benjamin Schmolck (1732); trans. C. Winkworth (1863)

   UNSER HERRSCHER, Joachim Neander (1680)

   This fine chorale relates particularly to the Psalter lesson (Ps. 118:12, 19–29) and would be particularly appropriate for the opening of worship.

3. "All Praise to Christ," E. Bland Tucker (1938)

   ENGELBERG, Charles V. Standford (1904)

   A great hymn based on the Epistle reading (Phil. 2:5–11), "All Praise to Christ!" is recognized as one of the finest expressions to come out of twentieth-century America. It would be appropriate as a praise hymn at the beginning of worship.

4. "In You, Lord, I Have Put My Trust," Adam Reissner (1533); trans. C. Winkworth (1863)

   IN DICH HAB GEHOFFET, Sunderreiter's *Himmlische Harfen* (1573)

   The general spirit of Psalm 31 is reflected in this chorale from the sixteenth century. Two stanzas could be sung before the Psalter reading, and two after.

5. "To Mock Your Reign, O Dearest Lord," Fred Pratt Green (1972)

   KINGSFOLD, Eng. melody; arr. R. V. Williams

   This contemporary expression by the greatest Methodist hymnist since Charles Wesley is appropriate for use on Passion Sunday. Though it does not relate precisely to any of the readings appointed for this day, it would be appropriate to sing it with any of them.

6. "Ah, Holy Jesus," Johann Heermann (1630); trans. R. S. Bridges (1899)

   HERZLIEBSTER JESU, Johann Crüger (1640)

   No Holy Week season should pass without the use of this poignant Passion hymn. It would be suitably sung in connection with any of the Passion Sunday readings.—Hugh T. McElrath

WORSHIP AIDS

CALL TO WORSHIP.   "O Give thanks unto the Lord; for he is good: because his mercy endureth for ever" (Ps. 118:1).

INVOCATION.   Today, O God, as we remember the cross of our Lord Jesus Christ, grant that we may get a renewed vision of what it means to take up our own cross and follow him in today's world.

Bless and strengthen all who walk the blood-sprinkled way with their Lord, and may they share the joy that was set before him.

OFFERTORY SENTENCE.   "The children of Israel brought a willing offering unto the Lord, every man and woman, whose hearts made them willing to bring forth all manner of work that the Lord had commanded to be made by the hand of Moses" (Exod. 35:29).

OFFERTORY PRAYER.   O God, we are all together in your wonderful work among us and throughout the world, and we are in a long line of men and women who have offered themselves, their service, and their witness for your cause. May the spirit of their sacrifice inspire what we do as we bring our offerings today and as we follow your commands in the days ahead.

PRAYER.   Almighty God, creator of Earth and heaven, who in creation breathed into us the breath of earthly life, who in the cross breathed into us the breath of eternal life, we worship and praise you this blessed day of Holy Passion.

> Eternal God,
> Lord of all seasons, Lord of Holy Week,
> Lord of all places, Lord of Jerusalem,
> Lord of all persons, Lord of our Lord, Jesus Christ,
> Lord of all grace and mercy, Lord of the cross,
> We worship and praise you this beautiful spring morning, and prepare our lives for the continued journey to the cross.

Sovereign God of time and events, Palm Sunday, like our lives, is a blending of triumph and tragedy, of glory and sorrow, of courage and fear, of knowing and not knowing.

Bless and strengthen us, each one, as we lean into the mystery of your suffering love, your purity of heart, your strength of obedience, your cross and crown.

Understanding and forgiving Father, the cross lays bare and exposes our sin. We choke on cheap excuses. The cross clashes with our values and our way of doing things. We still believe in clubs and swords and strength through might, in being first, and in saving our lives. Lead us to the foot of the cross this Holy Week. Let us see how wrong we are and how costly our sin is, and allow us to repent and confess our sin and receive your pardon

While at the cross, let us embrace the suffering Savior. As we see his sacred head wounded, in response let our every thought be an act of love for you. As we view his nail-torn feet, in response let our gentle steps be an act of love for you. As we remember his scarred hands, in response let the reach and touch of our hands be an act of love for you. And as we see his side run through by a sword, in response let our every breath and every beat of our hearts, be used as an act of love for you.

O God in Christ, as we worship and live this Holy Week, let us walk, O Master, with and close to you.—William J. Johnson

SERMON
Topic: Who Was on Trial?
TEXT: John 18:13–14, 19–24, 28–19:16

On that infamous day, Jesus was on trial before the courts of humanity, but in reality those involved in the human trials were on trial before the judgment seats of history and eternity. This message examines the former in light of the latter.

I. *The Jewish trial* (John 18:13–14, 19–24). Apparently Judas fulfilled his agreement to betray Jesus sooner than he had expected. It was sometime after midnight. The members of the Sanhedrin were asleep. Some time was necessary to assemble them. In the meantime, Jesus was taken before Annas, a former high priest and the father-in-law of Caiaphas, the present high priest. Though Annas had been removed from office by the Romans, he still had great influence with them. Any charge against Jesus by Annas would have great influence with Pilate.

So, having arrested Jesus, the temple police "led him away to Annas first" (v. 13). But apparently Annas failed to get any charge against Jesus (vv. 19–23).

Indeed, Jesus had done nothing to deserve being on trial in the first place. All he had done was to expose the sins of the people and especially those of the Jewish leaders.

By this time, the Sanhedrin had assembled. So Annas sent Jesus "unto Caiaphas, the high priest" (v. 24). It was during Jesus' appearance before that body that Peter denied him three times (vv. 16–18, 25–27).

The other Gospels report the Jewish trial, except for the brief episode before Annas, but John merely mentions that Jesus was brought before the Sanhedrin and that this body took him to appear before Pilate, the Roman Procurator. The other Gospels show that the proceedings before that body were little more than a kangaroo court. It was illegal in every respect. The one on trial was abused. The trial was held at night. False witnesses who did not agree with one another were used. Under oath, Jesus was forced to incriminate Himself. In the voting procedures of the Sanhedrin, in order that the votes of the younger members not be influenced by the others, the younger members voted before the older ones did. In Jesus' case, Caiaphas himself was the first to vote that Jesus should die (Matt. 26:65–66). Jewish law forbade convicting and sentencing to death on the same day. So, after convicting Jesus in a night meeting, the court adjourned, then met again after daylight to pronounce sentence formally (Matt. 27:1). But according to Jewish time it was still the same day. The entire procedure was "Get the trial over so we can hang him."

We follow such proceedings with disgust. But how many of us arbitrarily reject Jesus on the same or less evidence? Is it because we do not want to change our lifestyles? Why not look ahead and see where your present way of life is leading you?

II. *The Roman trial* (John 18:28–19:16). The Roman government vested in the Sanhedrin civil and religious authority. But it reserved for itself authority to impose the death penalty. So even though the Jews and Pilate despised each other, the Sanhedrin had to take Jesus to him for imposing and carrying out the death penalty. John gave a fuller account of the trials before Pilate, adding details omitted by the other Gospels.

Since it was the time of the Passover, members of the Sanhedrin refused to enter the dwelling of a Gentile lest they be defiled. Pilate therefore came out to them, but Jesus was taken into the palace.

In verses 29–31 we see the antagonism between the Jews and Pilate. In response to his inquiry as to their accusation against Jesus, they said, "If he were not a malefactor, we would not have delivered him up unto thee." To them, Pilate's query was an insult that questioned their authority. Thinking the matter had to do with religion, Pilate told them to handle the matter. And though it rankled them to admit it, the Sanhedrin reminded Pilate that only he could sentence a man to death. They had not brought Jesus to Pilate for trial, but merely to get Pilate to sentence Jesus to death. John noted that this fulfilled Jesus' prediction that he would be crucified. Had the Jews put him to death it would have been by stoning.

So Pilate entered the palace to question Jesus (vv. 33–38). According to Luke 23:2, the Jews had accused Jesus of claiming to be a king and, therefore, Caesar's rival. This was the only charge that interested Pilate. But after a preliminary examination in which Jesus said that his was a kingdom of truth, Pilate saw that Jesus posed no threat to Caesar. So he went out and told the Jews that he found no fault or crime in Jesus worthy of death (John 18:38). It was at this point that he sent Jesus to Herod Antipas (Luke 23:6–12).

Soon Jesus was back before Pilate. Knowing that Jesus was innocent, Pilate resorted to a custom of releasing a prisoner chosen by the people. At that time he held a notorious prisoner name Barabbas. Mark 15:7 describes Barabbas as an insurrectionist, robber, and murderer. He had probably presented himself as a false messiah.

Failing at this point, Pilate again attempted to spare Jesus by appealing to the Jews' sense of mercy (John 19:1–5). After scourging Jesus, the soldiers mocked him by dressing him as a king. They made a crown of thorns that pierced his brow. Then, bringing Jesus forth to be viewed by the crowd, Pilate uttered his famous words, *Ecce homo,* meaning "Behold the man" (v. 5). But still the crowd shouted, "Crucify him, crucify him" (v. 6). When asked if Pilate should crucify their king, the chief priest said, "We have no king but Caesar (v. 15). Thus they totally rejected Jesus. Furthermore, they said that if Pilate released Jesus, he was not Caesar's friend. This was a veiled threat to report to Caesar Pilate's many cruel and unlawful deeds. So the procurator gave in. He sentenced Jesus to be crucified—after declaring him innocent! The vaunted Roman justice trailed in the dust that day.

Symbolically, Pilate washed his hands of guilt (Matt. 27:24), saying, "I am innocent of the blood of this just person: see ye to it." The Jewish people replied, "His blood be on us, and on our children" (v. 25).

But the guilt does not stop there. In crucifixion it was customary to place above the victim's head a board on which was written the crime for which that person was crucified. "Pilate wrote a title, and put it on the cross . . . Jesus of Nazareth the King of the Jews" (John 19:19). So Jesus died as a king.

Only John noted that the sign was written in Hebrew, Greek, and Latin (v. 20). Hebrew, or Aramaic, was the language of Palestine, Greek was practically a universal language, and Latin was the official language of the empire. But John was a mystic, and often we must look beneath the surface to discover his meaning.

G. Campbell Morgan noted that Hebrew was the language of religion, Greek was the language of culture, and Latin was the language of government. He noted that these three streams of life flowed together at Calvary. Institutional religion rejected Jesus, pagan culture ignored him, and institutional government crucified him. Yes, we were all there when they crucified the Lord.

During the Vietnam War I read the following story. In the South Pacific there were two

American soldiers. One was a Jew, the other was of Italian descent. The Italian insisted on calling the Jew a Christ killer. When the chaplain heard about it, he called the Italian boy in for a conference. He suggested that they review some Bible history. Said he, "The Jewish Sanhedrin declared Jesus guilty of a capital offense, did it not?" to which the young man said yes. "But it was Pilate, the Roman procurator, who sentenced Jesus to death, was it not?" Again the young man answered yes. "Now," said the chaplain, "the Romans were from Italy, were they not?" "Yes," replied the soldier. "So they were Italians, were they not?" "Yes." "And you are of Italian descent, are you not?" "Yes."

The chaplain concluded, "So it seems to me that this Jewish boy is no more a Christ killer because of what his ancestors did than you are a Christ killer because of what your ancestors did." The young man had to agree.

Yes, we were all there when they crucified our Lord! That brings us to our question: Who was on trial?—Herschel H. Hobbs[7]

SUNDAY, APRIL 20, 2003
Lectionary Message

Topic: A Case for Resurrection (Easter Sunday)
Text: 1 Cor. 15:1–11
Other Readings: Ps. 118:1–2, 14–24; John 20:1–18; Acts 10:34–43

I. *The early Christian tradition.*

(a) Paul began with a ringing declaration: "I am not giving you Corinthians something that is just *my* words. This message is not original with me, I am telling you what you have already received." This declaration was based on the oral tradition and sketchy notes that some of the disciples probably made. Paul did not originate the tradition but handed on to them what was considered the early creed of the Church—Christ crucified, dead, buried, and risen again.

(b) Paul also noted that what he proclaimed to the Corinthians was according to the Scriptures. Although it is difficult to know exactly which Scriptures the early Church saw as predictions that Jesus would rise again, several could have been in their minds, such as Isaiah 53:1–12, Psalm 2:1, Psalm 16:8–11, Psalm 110:1, Psalm 118:22, Hosea 6:2, Jonah 1:17, and others.

II. *Theories denying the Resurrection.*

(a) The earliest theory that tried to disprove the Resurrection of Jesus was proposed by the Jewish chief priests, who claimed that the disciples of Jesus had stolen his body (Matt. 28:11–15).

(b) Others have conjectured that Jesus merely swooned on the cross and did not really die. This theory claims that Jesus fell into a coma at the end of the sixth hour and was revived later after he was taken down from the cross and placed in the tomb.

(c) Still others have suggested that the women who came to anoint Jesus' body on Easter morning came to the wrong tomb and found it empty. Did Peter and John also go to the

---

[7]*Basic Bible Sermons on John* (Nashville: Broadman Press, 1990), pp. 103–111.

wrong tomb? Whose grave clothing was found in the empty tomb? The soldiers and the priests both claimed that the stone had been rolled away from the grave where Jesus had been buried.

(d) Another attempt to disprove the resurrection has been the theory that the emotional strain of the death of Jesus and the disciples' strong desire to believe that he would live again caused them to hallucinate. If any of these theories were accepted, the Christian religion would be founded on a delusion.

III. *The Resurrection appearances of Jesus.* Paul claimed that the Church is not a memorial society but is built on the Resurrection of Christ. The Resurrection is the solid foundation of the Christian Church. In his Corinthian letter Paul listed six Resurrection appearances of Christ. Only ten or eleven are recorded in the Gospels, Acts, and Paul's letters. Paul affirmed that he first appeared to Peter, then to the twelve, to more than five hundred persons at one time, to James, to all the apostles with Thomas present, and finally he appeared to Paul himself.

(a) The Gospels state that Jesus first appeared to three women, among them Mary (Mark 16:9; Matt. 28:1–10; John 20:11–18). Paul may not have included women on his list because people might have discounted the experiences of women.

(b) The second recorded appearance of Christ occurred on Easter afternoon as two disciples of Jesus were on their way to Emmaus (Mark 16:113; Luke 24:13–35).

(c) He appeared also to the disciples by the Sea of Tiberius (John 21:7–14), on a mountain in Galilee (Matt. 28:16–20), and on Mt. Olivet just before his Ascension (Luke 24:50).

(d) In the Book of Acts, Luke states that Jesus "presented himself alive after his passion by many proofs, appearing to them during forty days, and speaking of the Kingdom of God" (Acts 1:3).

IV. *What if there was no Resurrection?*

(a) Paul argued first that if the disciples had not believed that Christ was raised, their preaching would have been in vain. The Resurrection of Christ was the foundation on which the disciples had based their preaching. It had been the transforming factor in the faith of the early disciples. If Christ had not been raised, their preaching would have been based on a lie, and they would have had no right to preach such a delusion. But Christ was raised from the dead, Paul exclaimed, and the disciples' preaching bore testimony to that reality.

(b) Continuing his argument, Paul declared that if Christ had not been raised, then our faith is in vain. If we do not believe that Jesus has been raised from the grave, our faith is empty, futile, and hopeless. Instead of standing on a rock, we are positioned on quicksand. There is no solid foundation. Without the Resurrection, everything in our belief tumbles; but Christ was raised; therefore our trust is assured.

(c) Paul went even further: "If Christ has not been raised, then we misrepresent God." In their preaching, Paul and the other Christians had declared that God was like Jesus—caring, loving, suffering, redemptive, and sacrificial. The Resurrection was seen as an act of God, vindicating the life and ministry of Jesus. If God did not raise Jesus Christ from the grave, then the early Church misrepresented God and lied about God's actions.

(d) If Christ was not raised, Paul continued to argue, we are still in our sins. Paul and others had preached that the death of Christ on the cross brings redemption, ransom, and forgiveness. The death of Christ would have been futile without the Resurrection. If Christ was not raised, we are still burdened with our sins.

(e) "If Christ has not been raised," Paul continued, "then those who have died have died hopeless and without any possibility of life after death." If Christ has not been raised, there is no hope for any of us. Our hope in life after death is based on the assurance of his Resurrection. This is the great affirmation of the Christian faith: because Christ lives, we too shall live.

On Easter Sunday morning two thousand years later, we join the voices of millions of other Christians and exclaim, "Hallelujah. Christ is risen!" With Paul we affirm that the Resurrection of Christ is the foundation of the Christian Church. It was one thing—the only thing—that could have turned the defeated, despairing disciples into crusading evangelists for the gospel of Christ.—William Powell Tuck

ILLUSTRATIONS

THE CROSS.   Following the death of Victor Hugo, the noted French author, there was a riot, and the French people secularized the Pantheon. They pulled the gilded cross down because they wanted to remove all evidence of Christianity from the building. A Christian orator stood up and tried to stop them from pulling the cross down. "You think you can take away the cross from the Pantheon," he cried. "We have taken it away," they shouted. "We've torn it down." "You'll never take away the cross from the Pantheon," the Christian orator shouted. "It is taken away, and down with the church," they yelled. After the shouting died down, he stated quietly, "You cannot take away the cross from the Pantheon, for the Pantheon is built in the form of a cross, and when you have taken away the cross, there will be no Pantheon anymore."—William Powell Tuck

THE CENTRAL TRUTH.   C. H. Dodd, one of the great New Testament scholars, spoke to a large throng of people who had gathered in Westminster Abbey on March 15, 1961, on the 350th anniversary of the publication of the authorized version of the Bible, what you and I call the King James Version. At that celebration, the New English Bible was presented as a fresh translation. C. H. Dodd, the general director of the new translation, spoke about the meticulous work of the host of scholars, but he also reminded the congregation that day that the supreme fact to which the first Christians gave witness was not the cross but the Resurrection. The Resurrection is the central truth of the Christian faith. Without the Resurrection, the cross has no meaning.—William Powell Tuck

SERMON SUGGESTIONS

Topic: Jesus Lives!
TEXT: Matt. 28:1–20
(1) A fountain of joy for you this Easter morn. (2) A source of strength for you for your entire life. (3) A stream of grace for you in the Holy Communion. (4) A wellspring of hope for you in the face of death.—R.C.H. Lenski

Topic: At Early Dawn
TEXT: Luke 24:1–10
(1) A visit and a disappointment. (2) A vision and a recollection. (3) Return and recital.

CONGREGATIONAL MUSIC

1. "Good Christians All, Rejoice," Cyril A. Alington (1925)

   GELOBT SEI GOTT, Melchoir Vulpius (1609)

   Here is a modern Easter carol written specifically to this ancient but vibrant chorale tune. A strong Easter text with a climaxing "Alleluia" refrain, this hymn could function as a ringing call to worship.

2. "This Is the Day," Ps. 118:24; para. Les Garrett (1967)

   THE LORD'S DAY, Les Garrett (1967)

   The theme of this contemporary Scriptural song—"the day of the Lord"—quotes directly Psalm 118:24 and thus could be sung as a response to the Psalter reading. The plan of this song envisages antiphonal treatment. The singing group can respond to each phrase sung by a soloist (cantor), with all coming together on the last phrase. The second stanza, of course, refers specifically to the Resurrection.

3. "Come, Let Us with Our Lord Arise," Charles Wesley (1763)

   SUSSEX CAROL, trad. Eng. carol; harm. R. V. Williams (1919)

   The singing of this fine Wesleyan hymn would be effective preparation for the reading of the Scriptures appointed for this Easter Sunday, especially John 20:1–18. Its carol tune should be sung lightly and with joyful spirit.

4. "Alleluia, Alleluia! Give Thanks" Donald Fishel (1971)

   ALLELUIA NO. 1, Donald Fishel (1971)

   Another contemporary expression that captures the excitement and joyful praise of the Resurrection is this song with its folklike tune. It would be appropriate to sing it at any point in the Easter service.—Hugh T. McElrath

WORSHIP AIDS

CALL TO WORSHIP.   "The stone which the builders refused is become the headstone of the corner. This is the Lord's doing; it is marvelous in our eyes" (Ps. 118:22–23).

INNVOCATION.   You have triumphed over your enemies, O God, for Christ has risen and holds out the cup of salvation to all who will receive it, even to those who crucified him. In the strength of that love, may we give ourselves to work and pray for those for whom Jesus prayed, "Father, forgive them, for they know not what they do."

OFFERTORY SENTENCE.   "If it is to encourage others, we should do so. Whoever shares with others should do it generously; whoever has authority should work hard; whoever shows kindness to others should do it cheerfully" (Rom. 12:8 TEV).

OFFERTORY PRAYER.   We are always learning how to do better what we do in your service, O God. As we bring our offerings, teach us how to give with willing and generous hearts and discover the joy of our stewardship.

PRAYER.   Dear God, forgive our lack of courage in the midst of serious crises, our carelessness with holy things, our apathy in the face of Kingdom needs, and our reluctance to follow the lead of your Spirit.

Grant that in our worship we bring our hearts to give you a steadfast love, our minds and thoughts to bless your name, our spirits as the reflection of your power within us, and our strength to pursue your purposes in the world.

Teach us to bring our best gifts to the altar of our worship: our bodies as temples of your Spirit, and our gifts to bring healing, wholeness, hope, and food to the needy of the world.

We ask in Christ's name, but for all our sakes.—Paul D. Simmons

SERMON
Topic: Christianity as It Really Is
TEXT: Col. 1:6 (TEV)

There is in the world a vast amount of Christianity as it really isn't! The words *Christian* and *Christianity* are constantly in the headlines of the media, and they are ascribed to people and to actions as far from New Testament Christianity as the East is from the West. In Northern Ireland, Catholics and Protestants hate and kill in the name of Christ and the Church—or so it appears. In Lebanon, it is Moslem and Christian locked in an endless fratricidal war. We know this is not Christianity, but what a terrible travesty it all is, and what a formidable barrier to an unbelieving world. Can you look at this dreadful carnage and say with Paul, "The gospel keeps bringing blessings"? Christianity as it isn't keeps bringing division, sectarianism, murder, war, and rumors of wars. Christianity as it really is! The Good News of God the Father, the Son, and the Holy Spirit—God in Christ reconciling the world to himself.

I. *Christianity is a personal religion.* There is nothing so fundamental as this. It begins at the center, not at the circumference. First and foremost, Christianity is a vital, personal relationship to Jesus Christ. It is not belief in a philosophy or way of life. It is not the acceptance of a moral code. It is not attendance at or attachment to an organization. It is trust in a personal God through an experience of a personal Savior. As Paul says here to the Colossian Christians, "We have heard of your faith in Christ Jesus." There is no Christianity without that faith.

A lady came to me and said, "What really does all this talk about being a 'born-again' Christian mean?" I don't normally use the phrase *born-again Christian* about myself, but I cherish what it means. We are not born Christians. It is a common mistake to suppose that we are. The fact is that we are all born into the providential care of God the Father, and we are all born potential Christians. But Jesus did not come and live and die and rise again merely to improve us; he came to transform us. His purpose was far more radical than getting us to add a few virtues to our lives or subtract a few vices or multiply a few efforts to be good and kind. Nothing less than a new beginning, a new birth, a new and intimate relationship to God through Christ will suffice.

It is Jesus Christ's idea. "You must be born again," he says in John, chapter 3. And he said it to a decent, devout, scholarly pillar of the establishment. We could accept his words more easily if they had been spoken to a cheat like Zacchaeus, a traitor like Judas, a tyrant like Herod. But they were spoken to a model of morality like Nicodemus! We must be born again. That is not a judgment pronounced but a declaration and an invitation extended. We may be born again!

There is no single or stereotyped way in which this new birth happens. It may be dramatic—a critical response after a long, agonizing search—or it may be a simple decision to accept Christ, be baptized, and join a church. It is a miracle nevertheless. "The wind blows where it will, and you hear the sound of it," said Jesus, "but you do not know whence it comes or where it goes: so it is with everyone who is born of the spirit." Always it is a personal response to a personal Savior. Christianity as it really is begins there.

II. *Christianity is a social religion.* This is not contradictory, but complementary to the first point. We become related to Christ singly, but we cannot live in Christ solitarily. John Wesley had a profoundly personal experience of conversion, but this did not prevent him from saying, "Christianity is essentially a social religion. To turn it into a solitary religion is to destroy it." In the Scripture before us the apostle writes, "We have heard of your faith in Christ Jesus, and of your love for all God's people."

This is so because God's purpose in Christ is to create a new humanity, a redeemed community living in fellowship with one another and with himself. Therefore, to be in Christ is the same as to be in the Church, the Body of Christ. We express this social aspect of our faith by uniting with a local church—the visible, concrete embodiment of the invisible, universal Church.

Christianity involves sharing a common social life in the church, loving all God's people, and sharing the responsibilities and joys of that life together. Two rules suggest themselves on this point.

(a) *We must respect the temperaments of others.* We hold in common a basic faith in Jesus Christ as the Son of God and the Savior. But we all have our own histories—our family histories, our ethnic histories, our emotional, educational, and personal histories. Each of us in the church starts from a different vantage point.

We should rejoice in this rich variety, these differing temperaments, and never suspect the sincerity or reality of one another.

(b) *We must respect the convictions of others.* We do not all interpret Scripture in the same way. No one Christian or denomination can grasp the gospel in all its fullness.

III. *Christianity is a practical religion.* At its best, Christianity has never been just a whiff of holy chloroform, a pious dabbling in symbols, sacraments and sermons, while an unredeemed world rushes madly to hell. Faith and works, meditation and action, communion with God and concern for humankind have always gone together. Jesus said, "Not everyone who says to me 'Lord, Lord,' shall enter the Kingdom of heaven, but he who does the will of my Father in heaven."

It is not a question of either personal religion or social action. It is a question of both/and. God has joined the two together, and we dare not put them asunder.

Christianity is frankly and unashamedly otherworldly. There is no need to be apologetic about that. It brings the horizons of eternity to our little life span—the gospel of the Resurrection, the promise of a richer, fuller life beyond death.

Christianity is also frankly and practically this-worldly. It is concerned with the here and now, with this life, this body, the physical and material needs of men and women.

IV. *Christianity is a universal religion.* "Spreading through the whole world," says the apostle, Christianity is a world religion. The gospel is addressed to all people—red and yellow, black and white, communist and capitalist. And a universal religion is a missionary religion. We preach Jesus as Lord—not one among many saviors but one Lord in a galaxy of gods. We crown him Lord of all!

We are therefore committed to patient dialogue with non-Christian religions and to exploring their insights and searching after God. But we proclaim the uniqueness of Christ, and we obey his commands to teach and make disciples of all nations. This is our duty. It is emphatically not an open question.

So we are missionary products. We owe an incalculable debt to those who have seen Christ as the light of the world and the Lord of all.—John N. Gladstone[8]

SUNDAY, APRIL 27, 2003
Lectionary Message

Topic: Doubting Thomas
TEXT: John 20:19–31
Other Readings: Ps. 133; Acts 4:32–35; 1 John 1:1–2:2

The disciple Thomas is a patron saint for many of us. He has often been called "doubting Thomas."

I. *Why was Thomas absent when Jesus appeared to the disciples?*

(a) We are not sure why Thomas was absent. It seems unlikely that he had gone back to his job at that time. The other disciples had not gone back to their jobs of fishing or other work they had done before they met Jesus.

(b) Maybe Thomas was like others today when they experience a tough blow in life or encounter some tragedy, difficulty, or sorrow. They withdraw from the fellowship and isolate themselves from their church community.

(c) Maybe Thomas was just a victim of his moods. He seemed to be a bit of a moody person. He was low, and when the other disciples met he simply didn't feel like going. So he didn't go. He didn't realize that religion is not based on one's feelings. Whatever his reason, Thomas was not present.

II. *Our text reveals that Thomas accepted a secondhand faith.* Thomas said, "Unless I can see the prints of the nails in his hands and the place where his side was pierced, I will not believe." He would not accept the testimony of the others.

(a) Their words just seemed like idle tales to him. He wouldn't accept the words of the other ten disciples, who said they had seen Jesus. Their experience was not sufficient for him. His faith was not going to be based on someone else's words. He was a realist. He demanded proof.

(b) Thomas was the disciple who always asked questions. In the upper room Jesus told his disciples, "I am going to prepare a place for you. I shall come and receive you to myself so that where I am you may be also; and my way is known to you" (John 14:3–5). Thomas said, "Wait a minute, Lord. Tell us how we can know this?" I don't believe that Thomas was the only disciple present who had that question, but Thomas was the only one who asked it.

(c) Thomas's questions did not mean that he was a man without courage. When Jesus received word that Lazarus had died, he indicated that he was going to return to Bethany. All of the disciples knew of the danger. However, it was Thomas who said, "Well, let us go to Bethany with Jesus and die with him." He was courageous. He was willing to stand with his Lord, even to lay down his life.

---

[8]*Living with Style* (Burlington, Ontario: Welch, 1986), pp. 37–44.

(d) I don't think that questions and doubts are wrong. It is a shame that we make people feel guilty because they have any kind of skepticism, questions, or doubts. Some of the greatest advances, discoveries, and new insights in the world have come about because people have been willing to raise questions and express their doubts about what somebody else has said or done.

(e) Some of the deepest faith has come about through the struggles persons have had with the questions and doubts that Abraham, Moses, Elijah, Jeremiah, Job, and many of the psalmists raised to God. "There is more faith in honest doubt, believe me, than in half the creeds," wrote Tennyson.

III. *The text reveals that Thomas's skepticism changed to adoration.*

(a) Jesus did not condemn Thomas because he had doubts. We don't hear the other disciples saying to Thomas either, "Just listen to Jesus. Quit asking questions." Christian growth often develops out of the pilgrimage of the questions we ask about the faith.

(b) Thomas was with the disciples in the upper room the second time they met together. Thomas set up high expectations about what he wanted to see before he would believe in the Resurrection. He said, "Unless I touch the nailprints, I won't believe."

When Jesus stood in their midst, he repeated to Thomas almost the very words that Thomas had asked for proof. But there is no evidence that Thomas actually touched Jesus. He stopped short of what he said he would require. He fell down at Jesus' feet and cried, "My Lord and my God." Jesus' appearance in the upper room took place to satisfy the questioning spirit of Thomas. There is no evidence that Jesus appeared this time for anybody else but Thomas.

(c) The one who had been the worst skeptic made the most profound confession of faith recorded in the Gospels: "My Lord and my God." That was a remarkable confession for a Jewish man. But this confession is what the whole Gospel of John was moving toward. In the prologue to the Gospel, John wrote, "In the beginning was the Word and the Word was with God, and the Word was God" (John 1:1).

(d) Thomas confessed that Jesus Christ had revealed the very nature of God. He acknowledged that Christ was both Lord and God. The Word about which John wrote was identified with Jesus of Nazareth. His Gospel "had been written," John said, "that you might believe that Jesus is the Christ, the Son of God" (John 20:31).

IV. *Our text reveals a new beatitude, which Jesus pronounces for future generations.*

(a) When Thomas made this confession of faith, Jesus did not say, "Blessed are you, Thomas, for such faith." Instead Jesus declared, "Blessed are those who have not seen and yet have believed." Why? Jesus wanted you and me and other future generations to know that even without physical sight or physical touching, you and I can also experience the reality of his presence. We might not know Jesus in a physical sense, as Thomas and the other disciples did, but deep within our spiritual being the presence of Christ can still be a reality to us.

(b) Jesus' tangible presence to the early disciples was also a sign to us. We draw on their testimony, but through the generations individuals have sensed intuitively the power and presence of the living Christ. We have "known" him and experienced him without tangible signs. This vision is based not on our senses but on a direct inward perception of the unseen reality of a living Lord.—William Powell Tuck

ILLUSTRATIONS

A CHANGED LIFE.   In Aberdeen, Scotland, a noted preacher named Brownlow North was preaching in one of the churches in the city. Right before he was to go into the pulpit he was handed a letter. The letter was from a man in the city who recounted a shameful incident in North's past and told him if he dared to go into the pulpit that day, the man would rise in the congregation and tell everybody what North had done.

Brownlow North had lived a wild life as a young man before he became a Christian. He walked into the pulpit and read the letter to the congregation. He told them that what this man had said was true, but he also told them about the good news of Jesus Christ that changed his life. He spoke of Christ's forgiveness and how his past was put behind him and he was able to begin a new life. He used his own failure to point other persons toward Christ.—William Powell Tuck

OUR OWN LIGHT.   When Horace Bushnell was a teacher at Yale, the campus was experiencing a religious awakening. For some reason Bushnell could not commit his life to what was happening. He had grown up as a committed Christian but his Christian ideals had slipped away from him. He was not even sure he believed in God anymore. He realized that he was influencing some of the students on campus who were not participating in the religious revival. He began to ask himself, "What can I still believe? I believe," he said, "that there is a difference between right and wrong." He felt that if God existed he would be on the side of what is right, so he decided to put his life on the side of what is right. He made his first step by acknowledging that he believed something. His belief in the difference between right and wrong was the first step that gradually began to move him back into a deeper awareness of God. Later he became one of the most noted professors and ministers in our country. He made his journey back by walking in the light that he had.—William Powell Tuck

SERMON SUGGESTIONS

Topic: Barnabas—"Son of Encouragement"

TEXT: Selections from Acts

What sets persons like Barnabas apart from the rest of us? Vision, the ability to see what is hidden from the rest of us. (1) He sees a gift to give where others see a profit to keep (4:36–38). (2) He sees the future saint where others see the former sinner (9:26–27a). (3) He sees grace for all where others see grace for the elect (11:23). (4) He sees the potential for steadfastness where others see the reputation of irresolution (15:37–40).—James M. King

Topic: God's Persistent Quest

TEXT: Luke 15:1–10

(1) Commences in a sense of loss. (2) Continues despite all discouragements. (3) Concludes with fulfillment and rejoicing.

CONGREGATIONAL MUSIC

1. "Christ Is Risen," Nicholas Martinez (1960); trans. Fred Kaan (1972)
   ARGENTINA, Pablo Sosa (1980)

At this Easter season, this modern Easter carol from Latin America would be effective for the opening of worship. Its message relates to the testimony of the early Church to the Resurrection of Christ (Acts 4:32–35).

2. "Behold the Goodness of the Lord," Ps. 133; vers. Fred R. Anderson (1986)

   CRIMOND, Jessie S. Irvine (1872)

   This metrical paraphrase could effectively be sung alternately with the reading of the Psalter lesson in the following manner: read verse 1, sing stanza 1; read verse 2, sing stanza 2; read verse 3, sing stanza 3.

3. "Trust and Obey," John H. Sammis (1887)

   TRUST AND OBEY, Daniel B. Towner (1887)

   The Epistle lesson (1 John 1–2:2) centers on the theme of walking in the light, which is the main thrust of the first line of this familiar gospel song. It also relates to the Gospel reading (John 20:19–31).

4. "We Walk by Faith and Not by Sight," Henry Alford (1844)

   GRAFENBERG, Johann Crüger (1647)

   This good hymn would be suitable and appropriate as a response to the Gospel lesson about "doubting Thomas."—Hugh T. McElrath

WORSHIP AIDS

CALL TO WORSHIP.   "Behold, how good and how pleasant it is for brethren to dwell together in unity" (Ps. 133:1).

INNVOCATION.   Our heavenly Father, with gratitude for the gift of family in Jesus Christ, our older brother, we celebrate our special kinship with one another. In all that we do in this service of worship today, strengthen the tie that binds our hearts in Christian love.

OFFERTORY SENTENCE.   "If you are eager to give, God will accept your gift on the basis of what you have to give, not on what you don't have" (2 Cor. 8:12 TEV).

OFFERTORY PRAYER.   Lord, we would bring our offerings with willing hearts. Open our eyes wide enough to see clearly the needs to be supplied by what we can give, and deepen our love for you and for those in need so we can know the joy of a cheerful giver.

PRAYER.   God of the ages, our God, great are the works of your hands and of your heart. As we meditate on what you have done and what you are, we are filled with wonder and awe. As we reflect on what we have done and what we are, we have to confess that because of our own self-will we have not allowed you to do in and through us all that you desire to see in our lives, and our shortcoming is ever before us. Forgive us, O God; deepen our desire to glorify you in every aspect of our lives. May your name be hallowed within our family relationships, at our work, in our recreation, among our friends, in the community of believers, and in our private thoughts. Lift us above our frequent discouragement and occasional despair by a renewed and renewing sense of your purpose working out in history despite all hindrances and apparent failures.

SERMON
Topic: How to Face Failure
TEXT: John 21:1–6

Failure is life's greatest common denominator. All persons fail one or more times in the ventures of life. Some fail to keep promises they have made to themselves. Others fail to keep promises they have made to God. A number of persons fail family, friends, and loved ones.

Failure is no respecter of persons. Babies learning to walk fail and fall many times before learning the art and skill of walking. Elderly persons work, pay taxes, rear families, and upon retiring face pension and security checks that are eaten up by inflation.

All persons experience failure. People fail in marriage and in rearing their children. Students fail in education, business men and women fail to make adequate profits. Failure is a universal companion.

Nations fail to win wars. Politicians fail to win elections. Saints sometimes fail to win each moral struggle; and sinners seldom win a spiritual victory.

How do people face their failures? Some blame others for their failures. A few carry the burden of guilt and punish themselves for their failures. There are those who curse God and the Church because of their failures. There are those who fail to win fairly. There are those who face the possibility of continuous failure by exercising unfair and dishonest methods. Well, we know how some face failure. How should people face failure?

How should Christians face failure? Our text answers this question. John 21:3 says, "Simon Peter saith unto them, I go a-fishing. They say unto him, We also go with thee. They went forth, and entered into a ship immediately; and that night they caught nothing." This verse describes their failure. Verses 4–6 have an important lesson for you and me. These verses teach us that Jesus has an important message for those who fail. Listen to the message: "But when the morning was now come, Jesus stood on the shore; but the disciples knew not that it was Jesus. Then Jesus saith unto them, Children, have ye any meat? They answered him, No. And he said, Cast the net on the right side of the ship, and ye shall find. They cast, therefore, and now they were not able to draw it in for the multitude of fishes."

Let us study these verses. Let us examine in these verses the message Jesus has for those who have failed.

I. *No failure is final until we quit.* They had fished all night as failures. Yet in the morning they obeyed Jesus' voice and continued fishing.

A young man of twenty-two failed in business. A drunken partner destroyed the business. At thirty-nine, some seventeen years later, he paid off his debt. The only woman he truly loved died. At forty he ran for political office and won, but two years later he was kicked out of office. Some twelve years later he became President Abraham Lincoln.

He started out as a powerful baseball pitcher. In his second year as pitcher his arm failed him. He picked up a baseball bat and hit 714 home runs over the balance of his career. His name was George Herman ("Babe") Ruth.

He failed in Boston as a Latin teacher. Learning that Jesus had a message for those who failed, he became the author of the Christmas carol "O Little Town of Bethlehem." He served the famous Trinity Church of Boston as pastor. His name was Phillips Brooks.

No failure is final until we quit. Keep trying!

II. *Failure haunts all of us.* It dogs our tracks. But remember that success is closer than we think. For Jesus' disciples, success was only a boat's width away. Jesus said to them, "Cast the net on the right side of the ship." We may be closer to success than we think. Thomas Edison, after many failures, gave us the electric light bulb. He failed eighty-one times. He found light in the eighty-second experiment. A friend asked him if he became discouraged. Edison answered, "I always believed success would come on my next try."

III. *How should Christians face failure?* Christians need to face failure by remembering (1) no failure is final until we quit, (2) success is much closer than we realize, and (3) failure may be necessary to sensitize us to the will of God.

In verse 3, "Simon Peter saith unto them, I go a-fishing. They say unto him, We also go with thee." By themselves they thought they were adequate as fishermen. Their own skill, their own knowledge, their own experiences seemed adequate as they started out on a fishing project. After they failed by using their own education and experience, they were ready to accept Jesus' offer to help. Failures make us sensitive to God's will. Failures drive us to faith in God. Failures force us to look for help from above ourselves.—J. Alfred Smith Sr.[1]

SUNDAY, MAY 4, 2003
Lectionary Message

Topic: The Effective Rebuke
TEXT: Acts 3:12–19 NRSV
Other Readings: Ps. 4; 1 John 3:1–7; Luke 24:36b–48

Pick up a business book, look at a parenting article, check out the latest wisdom on developing good people skills. Each will offer some advice about giving criticism and handling necessary rebukes. You'll read something along the lines of "Most corrections and rebukes produce defensiveness and surface change. Few bring effective, long-lasting, real-life change." And they are probably right.

Think about it. How do you want someone to give you painful information? How do you want someone to tell you that you are very much mistaken in the conclusions you have drawn? When you have done something that has caused great harm to another person, how would you like to be told about it? Whom do you want to tell you? And with what kind of attitude?

When looking at this passage, we see what looks like a stinging rebuke given by Peter to a group of Israelites gathered around him in response to something they had just seen. He immediately told them that they were mistaken in their conclusions. Mincing no words, he reminded them, quite clearly, that they had handed over Jesus, the servant of God, to Pilate. He said, "You rejected the Holy and Righteous One and asked to have a murderer given to you, and you killed the Author of Life, whom God raised from the dead."

Conventional wisdom tells us to use lots of "I" when giving rebukes and to avoid using "you." But this whole speech is littered with "you": "Why do you wonder at this?" "Why do

---

[1]*The Overflowing Heart* (Nashville: Broadman Press, 1987), pp. 58–60.

you stare at this?" ". . . whom you handed over." "But you rejected. . . ." "You killed the Author of Life."

These are tough words. Most of us, upon hearing such harsh words coming our way, would immediately raise our defensive shields and stop listening. Indeed, some members of the group must have become angry, for we find out later on that Peter, as well as John, who was with him, did get arrested that day. But about five thousand people heard that message and responded when Peter said, "Repent, therefore, and turn to God so that your sins may be wiped out."

Why did these people hear and respond to these words? What was it about Peter that made this message so compelling to them? So believable?

Let me suggest a couple of things. To understand the first suggestion, we need to turn to the beginning of this passage and understand what happened that had drawn the people around Peter and John in the first place.

I. *Peter's belief.* The two of them were on their way to the Temple to pray. Very simply, they were practicing the disciplines of their faith, seeking to know God better. When they got near the Temple, a beggar, described as one "lame from birth," asked for money. In today's terms, we'd label this individual a "street person," out to grub a living from the occasional generosity of those passing by.

Peter didn't give the beggar any money. He didn't have any to give. But he gave what he did have: the power in the name of Jesus. Peter reached out his hand, raised up this man, one who had never before in his life taken a step, and the two of them, accompanied by John, walked joyfully into the Temple, praising God.

Everyone who frequented the Temple knew of the lame man—he had been brought there daily to beg. So when he walked into the Temple, fully healed, the crowds were shocked. This is what brought them to Peter and John in wonderment.

The first thing that made Peter's message so compelling is this: Peter believed, and his behavior was consistent with what he believed. He believed that God had the power to heal, so he offered healing. Peter didn't say he believed one thing then do another. He didn't say, "Hey, buddy, I believe God can heal you. Hope you can find God and get well someday." Instead, he said, "In the name of Jesus Christ of Nazareth, stand up and walk."

Pretty bold, isn't it? To actually live what one believes. To say, "God loves me," and then live as one who is fully loved. To say, "My sins are forgiven," and then embrace the freedom from shame and guilt, as one does who has been fully forgiven. To know "God is powerful," and then to offer that power to someone else.

II. *Peter's brokenness.* Even so, I would suggest that bold belief alone would not be enough for the crowds to hear and respond to Peter's rebuke. If Peter had given them his belief and boldness from a position of superiority, of condescension, of arrogance, those defensive shields would have remained in place. There is a second factor.

Peter, instead, spoke from his own brokenness—for he knew that he, too, had participated in the death of Jesus. Three times he had betrayed his Savior on the night before the Crucifixion. Three times he denied even knowing who Jesus was. Three times he lied about being a follower of Jesus. Peter knew the experience of wallowing in sin and guilt. He had lived in the awfulness of separation from the Holy and Righteous One. The people to whom he was speaking in the Temple that day had acted in ignorance. Peter couldn't claim that for himself. He had acted in full knowledge that this one was the Messiah. And he still turned his back on Jesus.

In verse 19, Peter invited these listeners to repentance: "Repent, therefore, and turn to God so that your sins may be wiped out." Peter gave this powerful rebuke with no intent to shame, to discourage, to declare his own superiority. He delivered it because he knew the power of repentance, the full changing of the mind and the soul that opens the door to the outpouring of grace and forgiveness. Peter was able to make that invitation because he had discovered that forgiveness was possible even to one who had discovered Jesus at his Lord's greatest hour of need. Peter spoke out of his lived-out belief, and his lived-out brokenness. If forgiveness was available to Peter, then it is available to anyone.

That includes you. And that includes me. Let us repent together and find forgiveness. Thanks be to God.—Christy Thomas

ILLUSTRATIONS

BEGGAR'S BLESSING.   A few weeks ago, I spent several days in Miami, seeking to find some rest and refreshment for my soul. Early each morning, I rose and took a long walk on the beach, watching the sun come up, and being reminded of the power of God to bring about such daily beauty and hope.

On my walks I also noticed a number of people sleeping on the beach in those dawn hours. Street people, bums, the unemployed. Dregs of society. I had been warned by a resident in the area to take care during those early morning walks and to avoid isolated areas or areas with a lot of vegetation, for there had been reports of harm coming to individuals there. So I gave those unwashed ones a wide berth, being watchful to protect myself.

One morning after my walk I headed to a nearby shop to pick up a morning newspaper. The streets were still nearly deserted. I passed by one of those unwashed ones and heard him say, "Do you have any spare change so I could get a cup of coffee?" I passed by and said nothing, my fear silencing me.

But as I bought my paper, I knew I needed to give him some money. So I walked back to him. As I approached he looked up but did not speak. He had already tried once and apparently did not intend to try again. I simply handed him enough money for breakfast, asked for God's blessing, and walked on.

Later I kept asking myself, "What if I had pronounced him healed in the name of Jesus? Would he have thought I was crazy? Would he have responded?" I'll never know. I missed the opportunity to speak boldly of my belief that God does indeed heal our souls. I wish I had been as faithful as Peter. Who knows who may miss hearing the good news of forgiveness because I would not speak out of what I believe?—Christy Thomas

TOUGH LOVE.   It was Tuesday of Holy Week and the service was about to begin. The church phone rang. Michelle, the caller, said that the church had helped her before and that she had to have $40 by 9:00 P.M. that evening or she and her daughter would be thrown out of the motel where they were staying, having gone there for a safe place after her husband had threatened her.

Lauri, a friend of mine and a woman with no fear, took the call and asked if I could help. I serve as a volunteer with the local domestic violence agency and have had training in intervention procedures. I agreed and requested some cash from church funds set aside for such needs, and we headed out for the motel.

After paying her bill and getting Michelle and her daughter dinner, I told her that I would be back at 10 A.M. the next morning to take her to the shelter where she could get some counseling and a place to live for a few weeks in order to make some decisions about her life. I requested that she have her things packed and be ready. Lauri couldn't go with me, but she volunteered her husband, Art, and his pickup truck for the task.

Art and I found Michelle the next morning at 10 still in bed, with nothing ready to go. We both had only short windows of time in which to perform this task, so we began putting her things in bags. Michelle stayed in bed and started to watch TV.

At that point, I turned to Michelle and said, "Michelle, these are your things and this is your life. If you want help, get out of the bed and start packing. When you get to the shelter, you will have to get up early, bathe yourself and your daughter [it had clearly been some time since either of them had bathed], participate in housework, and make decisions for yourself. If you don't want to do this, tell me now and Art and I will leave. It is not our job to pack your things."

Michelle, clearly startled, got up and began to pack. A few minutes later, we dropped her off at the shelter and made sure she had a room and was started on the procedures. I went home deeply troubled. Had I been too rough? How many of my middle-class values, such as cleanliness, order, and personal hygiene, was I projecting on her? Had I spoken too much out of my frustration and too little out of compassion? Yet Art told me how very much he appreciated my firmness with her. He sensed she had milked the system before and was set to do it again.

A couple of months later, Michelle called the church. She said, "There was a lady there who came out and talked tough to me. I want to thank her. I'm now in my own apartment; I've got a job and things are looking up. Please let her know what has happened."

Yes, indeed, there is such a thing as an effective rebuke. An honest word on a receptive heart can change eternity.—Christy Thomas

SERMON SUGGESTIONS

Topic: The Cry for Bread
TEXT: Ex. 16:2–15
(1) The need for bread is crucial. God did not ignore it. Jesus taught us to pray for it. We may be God's miracle to answer that cry. (2) Jesus Christ is the bread of life, the answer of God to the world's most crucial need (John 6:31–40). For the distribution of the bread that we as Christians have, in the long range, is an even more urgent responsibility.

Topic: The Mystery of God's Mercy
TEXT: Rom. 11:13–16, 29–32
(1) Because of the disobedience of Israel, the Gentiles are blessed. (2) Because of the obedience of the Gentiles, the Jews are blessed. (3) The final truth is that all have been disobedient and all need God's mercy.

CONGREGATIONAL MUSIC
1. "Jesus, Thy Boundless Love to Me," Paul Gerhardt (1563); trans. John Wesley (1739)
   ST. CATHERINE, Henri F. Hemy (1864)
   This 16th-century hymn, which magnifies the love of God who laid down his life for humankind, could be meaningfully used in connection with the Epistle lesson (1 John 3:1–7).

2. "My Song Is Love Unknown," Samuel Crossman (1664)

RHOSYMEDRE, John D. Edwards (1838)

This poignant hymn, sung reverently, would be an appropriate response to the reading in Acts (3:12–19), which sets forth the apostle Peter's address on the Christian message.

3. "Lord, You Give the Great Commission," Jeffery Rowthorn (1978)

ABBOT'S LEIGH, Cyril V. Taylor (1941)

It would be meaningful to sing this contemporary hymn, which focuses on the commissioning words of our Lord, in connection with the Gospel lesson (Luke 24:36–48).

4. "Lord of All Hopefulness," Jan Struther (1931)

SLANE, trad. Irish melody (c. 1780)

This joyful song would be an effective accompaniment to the Psalter reading (Ps. 4:7).—Hugh T. McElrath

WORSHIP AIDS

CALL TO WORSHIP. "There be many that say, Who will shew us any good? Lord, lift thou up the light of thy countenance upon us" (Ps. 4:6).

INVOCATION. "O Lord, dispel the darkness that surrounds many in our world, some of them perhaps among us who have met to worship. Let your word and bold decisions of faith shine upon us and put gladness in our hearts.

OFFERTORY SENTENCE. "Give unto the Lord the glory due unto his name: bring an offering, and come into his courts" (Ps. 96:8).

OFFERTORY PRAYER. O God, you are worthy of our praise in whatever way we can give it. As a token of our esteem we present these offerings, knowing that they may be the means by which others who do not know you can learn to praise you for your gift of salvation and eternal life.

PRAYER. We thank thee, O God, that we are not as other men are—*underfed*. The fruits of the fields are ours and the harvest truly plenteous. Our barns are glutted with the bounties of thy hand. Hunger keeps its distance and starvation to us is a stranger. While our Christian brethren faint and die, and malnutrition takes its toll, gluttony is our temptation. Forgive us, O God.

We thank thee, O God, that we are not as other men are—*empty of hand*. Things clutter up our lives. The hand cannot hold the abundance of things that are ours. Possessions choke our souls and rot our spirits. While our Christian brethren across the world suffer lack of worldly goods, we cast away our overflow. Forgive us, O God.

We thank thee, O God, that we are not as other men are—*ill-clothed*. The latest fashions are ours and we cling to the style of the moment. Our garments overflow our closets. Forgive us, O God.

We thank thee, O God, that we are not as other men are—*ill-housed*. Our roofs protect us from the cruel hand of nature. The walls of our abodes retain the warmth that cheers our souls and comforts our bodies. We defy the elements. Help us to remember our brothers who live in caves and whose weary feet know no resting place. Protect them, O God, from the natural world, which would destroy them.

Forbid that this service be a mockery unto thee, that we pray and praise thee with our lips while our hearts are far from thee—far distant because we are smug and complacent about Christians who accept the Christ as we.—Fred E. Luchs

SERMON
Topic: The Brother of a Prodigal
TEXT: Luke 15:25–32

In Arthur Miller's play *Death of a Salesman* the central character is a salesman in his early sixties named Willy Loman. Willy has worked hard but has never really made it big. As a matter of fact, not long before retirement Willy is having a hard time paying his bills. The son of the man Willy has worked for more than thirty years is now in charge of the company. The new boss has made Willy travel more and has taken him off his base salary, making him work strictly on commissions. Willy is almost at the breaking point. He sees and talks to persons from his past. One person is his older brother, Ben, who recently died. At the age of seventeen Ben had set out for Alaska to find their father, who had left them years before. Ben wanted Willy to go with him, but Willy stayed at home. Quite by accident Ben got on a ship that went to Africa. After discovering diamonds, he had a fortune four years later.

Now Willy wishes more than ever that he had gone with Ben and thereby shared in the diamond fortune. Ben had left home, but he had done so well. When Ben appears on stage, Willy longs to talk with him, the way he never could with his father. He asks Ben to stay for a few days. But Ben is in a hurry to return to Africa and too busy to talk. He rushes off, and Willy goes on with the empty feeling that he has stayed at home, worked hard all his life, and now has no appreciation, understanding, or anything to show for his life's work. Willy was so very unhappy with his life.

I. We have examined closely the prodigal son, and many of you may have thought from past impressions that the parable was basically concluded when the younger son came home. Not so! When we finish viewing the life of the prodigal, we have not completed the parable Jesus told. There is another dramatic picture. This one is of the prodigal's brother. It seems that Jesus was careful to include this part of the parable, for it is easy to condemn the obvious social sins, to look down on the young and reckless, and to belittle those who waste their possessions. So often we cannot see the equally deadly sins in our lives and the lives of those who live close by us.

The younger brother typified the publicans and sinners of Jesus' day, those who had basically abandoned the accepted religious practices. The elder brother, however, is representative of the self-righteous religious leaders. The scribes and Pharisees stayed in their places of responsibility; they were outwardly faithful in their service but were inwardly filled with hate, greed, and contempt for God and his creation.

How Jesus upset the apple cart of sins and virtues! But even though he did so, we have often fallen into the same kind of false values that place the emphases in the wrong places. Even if a man has insight, knowledge, faith, and human kindness, and has not love, he has accomplished nothing! Jesus never approved of the sins of indulgence in fleshy pleasures, yet he treated all sinners with pity. He was much more harsh and impatient with his judgment of those God had called to be his chosen people, his spiritual leaders, his blessed people who would bless others. These religious people had continued to carry out their religious functions. They had remained at home, done their duty, and been near the Father; but they were filled with jealousy, anger, pride, and indifference toward others. They were almost completely out of touch with God. They failed to carry out God's desire for them.

I urge you to stand before the mirror of this Scripture to see if your life is reflected there. Most of us have convinced ourselves that we are not similar to the prodigal. But let us open our lives for the examination of sin in a somewhat different form and appearance. There were two sons in the parable—a prodigal who left home and a respectable, hardworking, religious person who stayed at home. These two sons are representative of the two kinds of people we find everywhere. There are the self-centered, arrogant types who are always climbing, ignoring God's teaching, and stepping thoughtlessly on others. And there are the elder brothers, the contemporary Pharisees of today. They appear to do all of the right things, but they do them for the wrong reasons! The pharisaical elder brothers are just as selfish and egotistical as the reckless prodigals. All of their religiosity, righteousness, and discipline are premeditated with the intent of gaining recognition for themselves and what they want in life. The elder brothers stay at home and are physically near the father, but emotionally they have gone into a far country just as the young prodigals have! Rather than taking the risk of going away from the father, the elder brothers play it safe and stay home. All the while they are cunningly plotting how they can use their father and get even more for themselves.

The book *The Prodigal Heart* illustrates that a man may be extravagant and wasteful in his heart, just as he can be in his body. From Jesus' parable it seems we can conclude that the younger son was prodigal in body. He went to a far country and recklessly wasted his possessions and his body, yet his heart never completely left home. But the elder brother was prodigal at heart—he was never really loyal to his father, even though he stayed at home. His heart was centered on the wealth and the land he would accumulate and what he would do to live it up when his father died. The elder brother was at home in the body alone. His heart was reckless and wasteful, for he never really accepted or returned his father's love. Both sons went away from their father. Both sons were self-centered and greedy. One was more open about it and went away. The other was secretive and stayed in his father's shadow. Only the younger brother decided to return to his father and enjoy his love once more. The elder brother chose to remain outside in the cold.

II. What was wrong with this elder brother that continues to plague many religious people today?

(a) It is apparent that this brother was *ungrateful*. He was not thankful for his father's companionship and assistance over the years. He actually longed to be rid of him so he might have his idea of a good time. He did not appreciate that his father had provided him with food, clothing, a nice house to live in, and a successful family business to work in and eventually inherit.

(b) The elder brother's ungratefulness was surpassed by *self-righteousness*. He not only called himself a hardworking servant of his father, but he also said he had never disobeyed any of his father's commandments! There is not much room for improvement in a man who feels he has arrived with all the virtues and answers. The religion he professed, like that of the Pharisees, was one of legalism—not so much a legalism of positive action but one of observing many "thou shalt nots." There was no life or spirit in his religion, in which he kept the law. In this perverted religious practice, he had his name on the roll of the Temple. He was respected by everyone in the community, but he had never been converted to God's way of thinking.

(c) This elder brother had another problem. He was *loveless.* What he had been hiding for years surfaced when his brother came home to royal treatment. Although he had been a hard-working man, he had never loved his father or brother nearly as much as he loved himself. In fact, he may have never loved them at all! He was so wrapped up in himself, his own greed and thoughts, that he had no time or place for his own family.

When there is no love, a person may cover up his self-righteous ingratitude with piety.

III. The disarming aspect of this parable is that many prodigals are condemned while many elder brothers wind up being praised and imitated by others! If we are not careful, our church can be filled with and dominated by such attitudes that will cause us to become self-centered and prodigals at heart. It was true with the scribes and Pharisees in Jesus' day. And if we feel we are immune to such attitudes, then we have already acquired a great deal of this self-righteousness!

The point Jesus made in his parable is that God loves both types of sons. The same father who ran down the road to greet the prodigal when he was barely visible on the horizon was the same father who rushed out of the celebration to urge the elder brother to come on in. He assured him that he did not have to be perfect or better than everyone else to be loved. He told his son that he loved him and that his son had by inheritance what he was tying so hard to earn. He urged him for one time in his life to relax and accept what was offered him, to come into the homecoming party and rejoice!

The parable stops here. We do not have the ending, because both the religious people of Jesus' day and the religious people of today have to write their own ending. Can you see yourself? Are you willing to arise and come to the Father who has already given us his love and blessing? Are you willing to accept and share God's love?—Robert W. Bailey[2]

SUNDAY, MAY 11, 2003
Lectionary Message
Topic: The Shepherd's Life Is Offered for the Sheep
TEXT: John 10:11–18
Other Readings: Acts 4:5–12; Ps. 23; 1 John 3:16–24

I. One of the most familiar and beloved biblical illustrations that portray our relationship to God is that of the shepherd with the sheep. In those memorable and comfortable words of the twenty-third Psalm, the psalmist declares, "The Lord is my shepherd, I shall not want." Yahweh is depicted as the Good Shepherd who cares for faithful, trusting, sheeplike believers. Whether the believer is city born or country bred, the image of the Good Shepherd is a favorite. The psalm spoke reassuringly to us when we were little children, and its words may well be the last words we hear whispered in our ears as Jesus carries us to our eternal home.

---

[2]*Award Winning Sermons*, Vol 2, ed. by James C. Barry (Nashville: Broadman Press, 1978), pp. 1–7, 116.

In the earliest Christian art, the Good Shepherd was painted on the walls of the catacombs, and in hymns, ancient and modern, the praise of the Shepherd has echoed down the corridors of time.

Jesus draws on the psalm's imagery in his words, "I am the Good Shepherd. The Good Shepherd lays down his life for the sheep." Jesus' listeners understood well that a shepherd's first concern is the well-being of the flock. The faithful shepherd will guide the sheep to nourishing food and refreshing water. When a wolf lurks in the shadows and stalks its prey, the shepherd will guard the sheep, personally risking life and limb.

It has been traditional in the liturgical churches to lift up the image of Jesus as Good Shepherd during Eastertide. The glory of Easter is reflected in our faith and conviction that the crucified and Risen Lord lives—lives not only to prepare a place for us but also to walk with us always. In his risen life, Jesus leads and guides us, bears us up in his mighty arms, and holds us close to his loving heart, just as the kind shepherd embraces the small, helpless lamb.

II. But Jesus is not the Good Shepherd simply because he is loving, caring, and gentle. If one interviewed shepherds tending the flocks of Palestine, including the Bedouins of today outside of Jerusalem, there would be many who would match this description. According to John the Evangelist, Jesus is the Good Shepherd because he laid down his life for his sheep. In total freedom and love, Jesus, our Good Shepherd cements our relationship with him by offering up his own life in the face of the evil enemy that stalks the flock of God.

Why has the Church remembered the Good Shepherd during these Sundays of Easter? Christians have just renewed their faith in the mystery of salvation. We have been witnesses once again to Jesus' supreme act of self-giving. We have remembered the events of Holy Week. We have received again the pledge and promise that Jesus meant what he said—he would lay down his life for the sheep. Because Jesus Christ has been raised from the dead, living in the glory of the Resurrection, his promise to shepherd us and guide us is certain. It is this promise to which we cling in life and in death.

III. A very close bond ties us to our Lord. Jesus knows his flock well as he leads and guides us. The intimacy that exists between Jesus and us reflects the same intimacy that exists between Jesus and his Father. Nothing, therefore, not even death, will ever separate those who love and know Jesus from his gracious shepherding care.

Ah, yes, the image of Christ as our Good Shepherd is soothing. But do we really like being described as sheep? Any farmer will tell you that sheep are neither smart nor independent. When I served two congregations in rural East Chain, Minnesota, I remember the day that a flock of sheep escaped from the Larson farm. Following their leader, the entire flock moved as one—out of the fences, down into the drainage ditch, then up to the highway, where speeding trucks threatened to run them down. The flock followed the lead animal, no matter where he led them. Their brains seemed programmed to "follow the crowd; let others do the thinking."

But these are no less human traits. Many women and men wander aimlessly, without direction or goals, wondering what will happen next and following the crowd. It is no wonder that popular celebrities, fads, and philosophies have such an easy time corralling human flocks. There are many dangers in this world—wolves in sheep's clothing, tempting us to follow as we struggle to avoid falling over the edge of despair, hopelessness, pain, and death. There are many rocks and brambles waiting to ensnare us, and too many hirelings who would abandon us. Experts teach new ways to build self-esteem, invest for early retirement, and make personal relationships more fulfilling. Many leaders offer advice about dying or how to prepare for it. Death is never far away. The one mark that clearly sets Jesus apart from other shepherds, hirelings, and religious leaders is his willingness to lay down his life. It is not because self-sacrifice is unique to Jesus—additional persons have given their lives for others—but because Jesus alone rescues his sheep from death and raises them to new life.

IV. The Good Shepherd, the appointed Messiah of God, alone can defeat the death of us all. He does so by laying down his life for us and by his Resurrection. But it isn't enough simply to rest in the good news that Christ is our shepherd. Because of this pledge, we need to remember those sheep who are still absent from Christ's fold and consider how we also are called to be shepherds, gathering and leading those who need to find their way home to God. Trusting the promise of Christ's love and care, we cannot forget the commission that each of us received in baptism. This commission confers upon each one of us the status and vocation of a shepherd in a world that is filled with lost and hungry sheep who need to find the security and comfort of God's loving arms. We rejoice and know the comfort of Christ's rod and staff, and we can bring that same comfort to others.

V. By his one cosmic act in history, Jesus Christ, the Good Shepherd, ended the reign of death forever. He who bought us with his own blood and leads us through all circumstances and trials of life is our friend. Christ knows us and calls us to follow him forward through the fields of this life with their pleasant grass, rocky hills, and steep cliffs. This Good Shepherd will lead us and guide us to "dwell in the house of the Lord, forever." Amen.—Dennis K. Hagstrom

ILLUSTRATIONS

SUBMISSION TO TYRANNY.   Writing in *The Christian Century,* Walter Wink said, "There is a downside to all the talk in Psalm 23 and John 10 about being God's sheep. . . . I am wary of these texts. Christians have been instilled with a sheepish docility that has played into the hands of the powers for centuries. Obedience has been made the highest Christian virtue. . . . As a result, Christians have colluded in their own injury. They have accepted without resistance totalitarian rulers. They have been submissive in the face of tyrannous hierarchies in church and state, corporations and schools. Women have submitted to battering, economic exploitation, and wage inequality. Men have been led off to war like sheep, flocking to their doom without resistance. . . ."—Dennis K. Hagstrom

CALLED TO BE SHEPHERDS.   The *Lutheran Book for Worship* and the *Book of Common Worship* (Presbyterian) offer this prayer for the day for the fourth Sunday after Easter: "God of all power, you called from death our Lord Jesus, the great shepherd of the sheep. Send us as shepherds to rescue the lost, to heal the injured, and to feed one another with knowledge and understanding; through your Son, Jesus Christ our Lord, who lives and reigns with you and the Holy Spirit, one God, now and forever." This prayer assumes two things: Jesus is proclaimed as the Risen Lord, the Good Shepherd who is the leader and guide of God's people. Also, we too are called to be shepherds, we are to be aware of those sheep who are not yet part of the fold, and we are reminded how we are called out to bring them in and share with them the loving shelter of Jesus' embrace. We can try to live out the model of Jesus' self-giving love as God gives us the power and strength.—Dennis K. Hagstrom

THE REAL SHEPHERD.   Recalling his experience as a wartime army chaplain, Arthur Gossip wrote somewhere about the heavenly experience of renewal that had come to his battle-weary company in France, of being withdrawn from the woesome desolation of the front, where there was neither blade of grass nor any tree and the scarred earth showing nothing but miles and miles of shell holes. And how like heaven it was to go back to rest where the grass grew green and burgeoning spring was in every hedgerow, and "one's dry soul lay greedily soaking in the sheer beauty of it all." But then the word came that they were needed back at the front, back at the old place of horror and death, because there was grave danger of an enemy breakthrough. Trying to come to terms with the hard necessity of military life, the chaplain had gone for a walk, had turned down a little lane with a little brook, and a meadow carpeted in tender green and dappled with golden flowers. Then, totally unexpectedly, there came through a gap in the hedge a shepherd tending his flock of two-dozen sheep. And Gossip says, "He was not driving them in our rough way with barking dogs. But he went first, and they were following him, and if one loitered, he called it by name, and it came running to him. So they moved on, down the lane, and up a little hill, up to the row and over it, and so out of my life." Gossip stood transfixed like David the Shepherd King, realizing that God was his divine shepherd, leading and guiding no matter what dangers lay ahead.—Dennis K. Hagstrom

SERMON SUGGESTIONS

Topic: Truth and Consequences

TEXT: Acts 2:42–47

(1) *The truth:* the apostles' teaching, new fellowship in Christ, the Lord's Supper, private and public prayer, the solid facts and disciplines of Christian faith and life. (2) *The consequences:* signs of God at work, a special warmth of feeling for one another, a generous response to human need, attendance at public worship, the winning of people to Christ and the Church.

Topic: Honorable Suffering

TEXT: 1 Pet. 2:19–2

(1) Suffering is not honorable if it is the fruit of wrongdoing. (2) Suffering is an honor borne in obedience to Christ and for him. (3) Christian suffering has a redemptive quality that benefits even the oppressor.

CONGREGATIONAL MUSIC

1. "The King of Love My Shepherd Is," Henry W. Baker (1868)
   ST. COLUMBA, Irish melody (c. 1873)
   This Christianized paraphrase of Psalm 2 can, of course, take the place of the Psalter reading. Quite effective would be the alternate singing and reading of the five stanzas.
2. "Father Eternal, Ruler of Creation," Laurence Housman (1919)
   LANGHAM, Gregory Shaw (1921)
   The focus in the Epistle lesson (1 John 3:16–24) on love of humankind as proof of love of God finds forceful expression in this twentieth-century hymn with its prayful refrain, "Thy Kingdom come, O Lord, Thy will be done." This petition stands in stark contrast to the confession of national pride, greed, and lack of love that results in sinful strife and confusion.

3. "Savior, Like a Shepherd Lead Us," attr. Dorothy A. Thrupp (1836)

    BRADBURY, William B. Bradbury (1859)

    Relating to both the Shepherd Psalm and the Gospel reading (John 10:11–18), this children's hymn has universal appeal. Antiphonal singing of its stanzas line-by-line would be effective.

4. "Christ Is Made the Sure Foundation," Latin (17th century); trans. J. M. Neale (1851)

    WESTMINSTER ABBEY, Henry Purcell (c. 1680)

    In its first line, this noble Latin hymn reflects the truths of Acts 4:11–12 about Christ as the "head of the corner." It would be appropriately sung for the opening of worship and particularly for processional use.—Hugh T. McElrath

WORSHIP AIDS

CALL TO WORSHIP.   "He leadeth me in the paths of righteousness for his name's sake" (Ps. 23:3b).

INVOCATION.   O Lord, grant us the wisdom to understand that the paths of righteousness— the right paths—are for our well-being, while we glorify you in following these paths. Lead us now, we pray, as we seek to walk in your ways with joy and love.

OFFERTORY SENTENCE.   "Honor the Lord with thy substance, and with the first fruits of all thine increase" (Prov. 3:9).

OFFERTORY PRAYER.   Help us, O God, to think of you and thank you whenever we are blessed with material goods. And show us how we may honor you with timely offerings from your providential generosity.

PRAYER.   Creator of all that is, was, and shall be, we marvel that you have so created us in your image that we are not left to the loneliness of our fortitude but communicate and relate to you as a child to his or her parent. With what love you love us, that this should be our privilege of all creatures of the created order. Whatever our language, you hear us. There is a "deep speaking unto deep" that undergirds the elusive and broken words we attempt to form with our lips.

From the beginning you have been speaking a life-giving Word. Your Word was so spoken through the affairs of the people Israel as to reveal your being and purpose to all humankind. Their pilgrimage from slavery through the trials of the wilderness to the Promised Land haunts the human race as the likely pilgrimage of every person. Even more presently, your Word is here in the flesh and blood of Jesus and dwells among us in the meaning of his life, ministry, passion, and living again. May the indwelling gift of your Spirit to illumine and energize call to mind your Word from the beginning and quicken our minds and hearts and wills that we may do your will in the flesh and blood of our time and space.

May we so hunger and thirst for your Word that for us it becomes the bread of life and the well of living water, springing up into everlasting life. For your Word of grace mediated through forgiveness that make all things new, we pray, not only for our personal relationships but for the healing of the nations. Deliver us from those who would provoke rather than reconcile—who incite fear rather than inspire brotherhood and sisterhood—who are motivated by political ambition rather than the desire to serve.

For the president of these United States and all those who share in the governance of this country and of other nations and in the United Nations, we pray for an earnest seeking for truth that makes for justice, for the order that makes for peace, for the compassion that leads to life.

Where there is any brokenness among us—in health, in sorrow, in love, in disappointment, in failure—we pray for the ministry of your Word of grace that alone makes us whole. We pray through him who is your Word from the beginning, is now, and ever shall be.—John Thompson

SERMON
Topic: A New Look at Home Sweet Home
TEXT: Deut. 6:1-9

I. *The biblical and biological basis of the home.* Many anthropologists and sociologists begin their studies of the family by saying that the family's roots are purely biological. They insist that two facts made necessary the institution of the family. First, we as sexual beings need each other. Second, the young offspring of human beings have long periods of helplessness when they are totally dependent on their parents.

Christians do not deny these basic biological facts, but they see much more involved in the beginning of the family. The Bible asserts that the family and the home originated in the mind of God. They were his creation, his design, and his plan. The Genesis story shows that the home did not just evolve as a biological convenience, but rather came from the eternal plan of God.

When Jesus was asked about marriage and the family, he went back to the creation story and repeated it. He would never have made this passage the basis of his teachings about God, the home, and the family if it were not factual and accurate.

Hazen Warner has written a small, fascinating book called *The Bible and the Family.* He points out that many of the common biblical metaphors and figures of speech were taken from the context of our family life. These terms were used to picture man's relationship to God as well as God's relationship to man. Jesus taught his disciples to pray to God as a "Father." In the Scriptures, believers are called the "children of God." When Jesus talked about the necessity of conversion, he described the experience with the words "new birth." Paul used the metaphor of husband and wife in picturing the relationship of Christ and the Church. "Heavenly," the most beautiful term, was used by Jesus when referring to heaven. He said, "In my Father's house there are many mansions [or rooms or dwelling places]" (John 14:2). Our Lord used the picture of a comfortable, earthly home to give us a preview of our long awaited home.

The home came not from the mind of man but from the heart and plan of God. Never can we underestimate the home's importance. It came before the Church and was the first of all institutions that came from the creative touch of God.

II. *The spiritual and psychological basis of the home.* The Bible establishes the home as the basic unit of society. Psychologists agree on one thing—that the home has tremendous influence in shaping the personality. The first few years of a child's life are the most important in determining habits of behavior as well as depth of character.

There are three basic things a child may get from his parents and his home:

(a) *A picture of himself.* For months prior to birth, the mother furnishes a safe environment for the unborn child. Then the shock experience, known as birth, hits. At this time the child is separated from the mother and in a real sense becomes "a living soul." However, as a real person he hardly exists; in fact, he is a person only in potential. He is dependent on his parents, his home, his environment to make him into a real person. The people around the child tell him who he is, what he can do, and what is expected of him.

The home furnishes the child his self-image. This is the most important piece of personality equipment a human being possesses. The family can give the child love, security, and a sense of confidence. Unless a person is taught that he is worth something to himself, he won't feel that he is worth much to God and others.

A successful young pastor confided to some preacher friends, "I run scared all the time. I feel as if I cannot do anything successfully." Some could not understand why this popular, handsome, well-educated young man felt this way. Those who knew his background understood his problem.

He had grown up in a family overshadowed by a very beautiful older sister. The parents continually belittled him as a child until his self-image was ruined. It is difficult for a minister, counselor, or teacher to restore the self-image when parents have seriously damaged the individual in the home. Remember that the child gets his image of himself, his potential, his personal worth largely from the home, and that this comes early in life.

(b) *A picture of life.* Dr. John Drakeford described the home as being the "laboratory of life." It is in the early years that a youngster learns the realities of life. The child is a great experimenter in that he soon learns that doing right produces happiness while doing wrong produces unhappiness. All this training comes about through the exercise of discipline.

(c) *A picture of God.* The home opens the great window of life through which we get our basic view of heavenly things. If the home does not furnish a climate of love, mercy, grace, and concern, the child's concept of God may be blighted. What he sees and hears from his parents will make a difference. We are responsible to God, not only for our actions and thinking, but also for every word and deed in the home that may determine the thought processes of our children, God's gift to us.

Our image of our heavenly Father may come from our impressions of our own father and our feelings about him. It is altogether possible that our feelings toward our earthly father may be transferred to our relationship with our heavenly father.

Now, if all we have said is true, isn't it about time we put everything else in second place and make our homes and families the most important things in the entire world? If our homes are this important, shouldn't Christ have priority in all we do? Will you let him come into your heart and home today?—W. LeRay Fowler[3]

---

[3]*Award Winning Sermons*, Vol. 4, edited by James C. Barry (Nashville: Broadman Press, 1980), pp. 82–87.

SUNDAY, MAY 18, 2003

Lectionary Message

Topic: God Is Love, and Those Who Abide in Love Abide in God

TEXT: 1 John 4:7–21

Other Readings: Acts 8:26–40; Ps. 22:25–31; John 15:1–8

You and I today live in a world permeated with damaged relationships, in which genuine love is conspicuously absent. Marriages flounder and fail. Parents and adult children remain enmeshed in hurtful, destructive relating patterns. Business partnerships are sometimes strained to the breaking point. Even churches and church leaders find themselves in conflicts that threaten the foundational purpose for which God created the Church in the first place.

People's private lives and relationships *do* have an impact on the public and on the institutional—for good or for harm. Far too often today young adults enter their professions and new relationships carrying with them significant handicaps because of earlier life experiences of unlove, unacceptance, unforgiveness. These experiences are passed on to future relationships, as well as negatively affecting effectiveness in professional or work contexts.

I. *The way of love.* Is there any way out of damaging patterns and cycles that are marked by the absence of love? Is there a way toward wholeness and unity that can restore and reintegrate broken lives? In his first letter, the apostle John gave a picture of *what*, or *who*, is the way to restoration and healing. It is the way of love—love that is a reflection of the character and nature of our Trinitarian God, who is love.

(a) *Modeled by the Trinity.* Before humankind ever was—before the foundation of the world—there were Father, Son, and Spirit living in love and unity and community with one another—giving and receiving love, each seeking to glorify the others. "Father, glorify me in your own presence with the glory I had with you before the world began . . . because you loved me before the foundation of the world . . . so that the love with which you loved me may be in them, and I in them" (John 17: 5, 24, 26). It is the relationship within the Trinity that is the foundation and model of the love John stresses in this first Epistle.

(b) *Love for others linked to love for God.* Notice that the writer assumes that loving, harmonious relationships with others are inextricably tied to our knowing and loving God. "Whoever does not love does not know God, for God is love." The writers of the Scriptures did not permit us to think that relations with others are somehow in a separate category from right relationships with God. "As long as I attend church and pray and give charitably, it doesn't matter that I harbor bitterness or unforgiveness or an unloving grudge against my brother, or in-law, or coworker." *Not so!!* It does matter. Cornelius Van Til is quoted by one of his students as having said that all truth is nothing but the externalization of the personality of the Trinity. What characterizes that personality? "God is love," not "God is loving." Love is the very nature and personality of God—such that only those who abide in that love abide in God.

What are the implications of such a declaration? If God is indeed love, then those who say "I love God" and hate others are liars (4:19). Earlier in the same letter John writes, "Whoever hates another believer is in the darkness, walks in the darkness, and does not know the way to go, because the darkness has brought on blindness" (2:11). The result of unlove is darkness in the heart.

II. *Objection: But you don't know my sister-in-law.* You may say, "If you knew what my in-law was like you would agree that it is unreasonable that I should even attempt to love *them!* They don't deserve it."

III. *Objection overruled.*

(a) *Not about the lovability of the object.* Do you see that what the writer is saying here is *not* about your brother or your mother-in-law. It is about your own heart. You and I are not called to "fix" the people in our lives who wound or irritate us; but we are called to allow our own hearts to be fixed. God's command to love has nothing to do with whether the people who wronged us deserve to be forgiven—or have apologized or shown adequate contrition. It is about whether or not you and I have softened our hearts to allow God's love to fill us and flow out from us such that we are abiding in God's love. The love that flowed among the members of the Trinity before the world began is the same love that God waits to pour into us and through us to others. That is our model, and the God who created us in his image created us to function the same way.

(b) *Unlove is not an option for a child of God.* Permitting an unloving heart attitude toward another person to persist is not an acceptable option for a child of God, no matter what the other person has done, because the result is darkness and blindness in the heart of anyone who withholds love, or persists in an unloving heart.

IV. *God's love is characterized by self-sacrifice.* I don't want darkness in my heart, and I don't think you do either. So what is involved in "abiding in love?" What is this love of God like? This passage tells us at least a couple of times about an essential component in this love: God's love is revealed and expressed to humankind in self-sacrifice—in laying down one's life, one's rights, one's preferences, for another. Difficult? Yes, but far better than the alternative of darkness and blindness. [Read 4:9–10.]

Impossible? Yes, if it were up to us to drum up that kind of love on our own. But we haven't been left on our own. Verse 13 assures us that God has given us of his very own Spirit—one of the members of that loving Trinity. Loving another is not about that person's lovableness, nor is it about our human capacity to love. It is all about the God who is by nature love—who chooses to stoop to inhabit my weak heart by his Spirit, to enable and empower me, and you, to be like God.

V. *Challenge and prayer.* In 1 John 5, the next chapter, are words of challenge and encouragement that I invite you to appropriate for yourself as you leave this place and go out into this world—your world—which is so badly in need of the love of God. "And this is the boldness we have in him, that if we ask anything according to his will, he hears us." Is it the will of God that you and I be enabled to love the difficult people in our lives? No question. So are you willing to ask for God's love in your heart? "If we know that he hears us in whatever we ask, we know that we have obtained the requests made of him" (1 John 5: 14–15).

Pray with me:

Holy God, you are the author of love. We ask that this day, this week, you would increase our capacity to live as a people of love—a people who reflect your character and nature in all the places where we live and work. Through your love in us we ask that you break chains and cycles of bitterness and unforgiveness that obstruct the flow of your love from us. Give special grace and help to those who are struggling with painful relationships—enable them to let go of anything that obstructs the flow of your love. You, God, are love, and it is our desire that you would enable us to be like you—to live in your love. Amen.—Martha Berg

ILLUSTRATION

ULTIMATE SHARING.   By causing us to become the brothers and sisters of Christ, the Spirit brings us to share in the love the Son enjoys with the Father. In this manner, we participate in the love that lies at the very heart of the triune God!

Participation in God's eternal love, however, is not ours as individuals in isolation. It is a privilege we share. The Spirit's goal, in fact, is to bring us together into one people who participate together in the love of God and who by their loving relationships show God's great love to all.

Consequently, unlike what TV sitcoms propagate, the Church is not merely a group of friends who happen to share common experiences or even who happen to speak some common language. The Church is a community of believers who because they participate together in the Holy Spirit share in the eternal communion between the Father and the Son. Ultimately this is why God calls us to be a people committed to one another. We are to be a community of divine love, a people bound together by the love present among us through God's Spirit. As a result, we find here true belonging.

Although the words may be a bit archaic, Christians nevertheless still find great meaning in John Fawcett's old hymn:

> Blest be the tie that binds
> Our hearts in Christian love;
> The fellowship of kindred minds
> Is like to that above.
> When we asunder part,
> It gives us inward pain;
> But we shall still be joined in heart,
> And hope to meet again.

—Stanley J. Grenz[4]

SERMON SUGGESTIONS

Topic: The Left Hand of God

TEXT: Ex. 2:11–22

(1) God sometimes permits what he does not direct. (2) God works behind the scenes to overcome and transmute the results of our wrongdoing. (3) God even brings undeserved happiness as a gracious gift of his providence.

Topic: Marks of Our Identity

TEXT: Rom. 8:9–17

We belong to Christ: (1) if we live by the Spirit, rather than by the flesh; (2) if we live as children of the Father, rather than as slaves; (3) if we are willing to suffer with Christ, rather than avoid the claim that love makes upon us.

---

[4]*What Christians Really Believe—and Why* (Louisville: Westminster John Knox Press, 1998), pp. 127–128.

CONGREGATIONAL MUSIC

1. "God Is Love, Let Heaven Adore Him," Timothy Rees (1922)

   ABBOT'S LEIGH, Cyril V. Taylor (1937)

   Based on the Epistle lesson (1 John 4:7–21) and set to an expansive twentieth-century tune, this hymn would be appropriate for the beginning of worship.

2. "All Ye That Fear God's Holy Name," Ps. 22, *Psalter* (1912)

   CANNOCK, Walter K. Stanton (1951), or GERMANY, W. Gardiner's *Sacred Melodies* (1815)

   A free paraphrase of Psalm 22, this hymn could function as a praise expression at the opening of worship or in place of the Psalter reading.

3. "I Am the Holy Vine," John 15:1–5; vers. James Quinn (1969)

   LOVE UNKNOWN, John Ireland (1918)

   The very words have been arranged metrically by the author, thereby offering the opportunity to sing this hymn at the reading of the Gospel lesson (John 15:1–8).

4. "In Water We Grow," Brian Wren (1989)

   HANOVER, William Croft (1708)

   The reading about Philip's conversion and baptism of the Ethiopian eunuch (Acts 8:26–40) could appropriately be accompanied by this contemporary hymn, which explores the myriad implications of water baptism.—Hugh T. McElrath

WORSHIP AIDS

CALL TO WORSHIP.   "I will pay my vows before them that fear him. The meek shall eat and be satisfied; they shall praise the Lord that seek him. Your heart shall live forever" (Ps. 22:25b–26).

INVOCATION.   O God of all the Earth and its peoples—rich and poor, old and young, saints and sinners—we who now worship you in this place seek your favor, that our lives may be what you desire them to be and that we may praise you forever and bring the forgotten and alienated ever more warmly and closely within the circle of your love.

OFFERTORY SENTENCE.   "Offer the right sacrifices to the Lord, and put your trust in him" (Ps. 4:5 TEV).

OFFERTORY PRAYER.   O God, compared with what you have done for us and continue to do, no offering that we bring can hardly be called a sacrifice. Yet we trust that you will receive what we bring in faith and love.

PRAYER.   We thank you, O God, that you tolerate our questions. We come to you with many doubts and fears. We would like to know the absolute truth about Christ before we make a commitment to him. But you have shown us that assurance comes after taking the step of faith and not before. Our Lord has promised that if we are willing to do your will we shall know that truth—whether he speaks merely on his own authority or from and for you. Give us the daring, O God, as well as the willingness, to do your will, and grant that we may discover your truth for ourselves. We pray for all those who spend their days in fruitless efforts to reason out all the puzzles of our human existence. May they see the folly of attempting to surround you with their finite minds. Help them for once to come to you as little children and trust your goodness and your wisdom. Once we have settled the matter of faith and commitment, our Father, lead us on in the quest of knowledge. We would not despise any source of truth. Having found the truth in Christ Jesus, in whom all things hold together, we would go on to new and exciting, even risky, adventures with you. And then, O Lord, open to us ways by which we may humbly share the truth that you have given to us. Help us to be wise, tactful, and patient as we endeavor to teach others. Grant that the strength of our faith may not jeopardize the weak faith of others that hangs by a thread. When we speak of what we believe, let it be with love, and may our words be seasoned with grace.

SERMON
Topic: New Creation
TEXT: 2 Cor. 5:16–21

How does Christian faith intersect with our desire for a new start, for a better and less frustrating and more successful life? Let me begin by saying that Christianity is at the same time the most brutally realistic and the most optimistic of perspectives on the human condition. From the story of our first parents in the Garden of Eden—breaking faith with their Creator, falling out of harmony with the creation, and blaming one another—right on up to the apostle Paul's declaration that "all have sinned and fall short of the glory of God" (Rom. 3:23), the Christian faith teaches that there's a tragic flaw in all of us, that sin is not just an affliction of individuals. It gets perpetuated in institutions and social structures (like racism, for example) so that there really is a sense in which the sins of the parents are visited upon the children to the third and fourth generations (Ex. 34:7). What's more, this sin problem is something we can't take care of ourselves, no matter what a motivational speaker might say. Paul, again, says, "For I do not do the good I want, but the evil I do not want is what I do. . . . Wretched man that I am! Who will rescue me from this body of death?" (Rom. 7:19, 24).

It's precisely at this point that Christian faith shows itself as the most hopeful and optimistic of perspectives on the human condition. What we cannot do for ourselves, what we cannot do by ourselves, God offers us through God's amazing grace. The one who has created us in the first place, the one who has sustained us through all our adventures and misadventures, through all our dreams and quests, has entered into our human condition to transform us from the inside out. So in our text Paul says to the worldly, quarrelsome Corinthians, "From now on, therefore, we regard no one from a human point of view" (2 Cor. 5:16). Our human wisdom sees the limitations in ourselves and others. Too old, too young, too sick, too poor, too addicted. He'll never be any different. She'll always be the same. But the good news of Jesus Christ is, "If anyone is in Christ, there is a *new creation:* everything old has passed away; see, everything has become new" (2 Cor. 5:17).

Wherever people are living in Christ, new creation—God's Kingdom—is breaking out right there. And "All this is from God, who reconciled us to himself through Christ and has given us the ministry of reconciliation" (2 Cor. 5:18). Among the various words that Scripture uses to describe Christ's transforming effect on us, *reconciliation* stands out in this fractured world of ours. We're pulled apart by race, gender, creeds, political loyalties, and the yawning chasm between the rich and the poor that we see right here in Los Angeles and around the world.

Sin separates us from a holy God and makes us lonely and anxious. Sin divides us from one another and fills us with envy, resentment, and blame. Sin even divides us from our own best selves, so we "cannot do what we want" (Rom. 7 again). And we can become poisoned by these divisions.

Biblical pictures of God's new creation—the "peaceable kingdom" of Isaiah 11, where lions and lambs lay down together; and the wedding banquet, where strangers are gathered from the streets and alley ways (Matt. 22)—are pictures of reconciliation.

Wherever God's new creation breaks out, it transforms individuals, groups of people, cultures, and entire environments.

Individuals. I think of Chuck Colson, who was such a cold-blooded political operative in the Nixon administration that he once said he would "run over his own grandmother" if he had to do it to further his political goals. Colson was caught up in the Watergate scandal and sent to prison. He had a dramatic conversion experience in prison, and when he got out, instead of distancing himself from that experience, he founded the Prison Fellowship ministry. And ever since he has spent his time and energy advocating for the most despised and forgotten members of our society—the incarcerated.

Peoples. A hundred years ago, the Naga people of northeast India were fierce head-hunters. They had no written language. They were animists, worshipping spirits of the fields and forests, and living in fear and superstition. Baptist missionaries brought the gospel of Jesus Christ to the Nagas. Tribal warfare gave way to solidarity and mutual respect from village to village.

Environments. We are all aware of the tremendous strain our exploding human population and our technological lifestyles have put on the life systems of planet Earth. When the Gospel of Jesus Christ is understood and lived out in it fullness, entire environments are transformed. As an illustration, let me share another story from India. Many of us have met or at least heard the testimony of Dr. Marian Boehr, American Baptist missionary doctor to India. Over a thirty-five-year period, Dr. Boehr performed more than thirty thousand surgeries. I heard her say she used to operate with one hand on the scalpel and the other holding open the medical textbook, because she encountered diseases and deformities no doctor would ever see in America. And she had to do it all—from delivering babies to removing gall bladders to setting bones to removing cataracts.

Certainly her works of mercy as a medical doctor have blessed thousands of people beyond accounting. But that's only the smallest part of her impact. When she arrived in the village, which was to be her home for thirty-five years, the only land she and the small group of Indian Christians could obtain for a hospital was a barren, rocky hillside with a sunbaked southern exposure. Village leaders made it available to the Christians because it was no good for anything else. The first thing Dr. Boehr and her friends did was to plant dozens of small trees, which they watered every day by hand. Then they built a small clinic building where they hoped someday to have some shade. The trees and the hospital grew together. The trees sank their roots deep into the water table and brought up moisture, which they cast into the air as they respired, creating a humid microclimate in that arid village.

The Christians planted gardens in the new soil to feed themselves and their many guests. Today the hospital compound is the coolest, most beautiful spot for miles around. Since Dr. Boehr's retirement, the entire operation is run by Indian Christians—doctors, nurses, technicians, administrators, and gardeners. And an outpost of the new creation—a transformed human and natural ecosystem—has bloomed on an Indian hillside.

"So if anyone be in Christ, there is a new creation" (2 Cor. 5:17). Its full extent is still out there in the future, but we can begin to see it now. Look around you, look among us, look within—and believe it. This is a new start that's real.—David L. Wheeler

SUNDAY, MAY 25, 2003
Lectionary Message

Topic: When God Breaks Through
Text: Acts 10:44–48
Other Readings: Ps. 98; 1 John 5:1–6; John 15:9–17

During my seminary days, a fellow student with a sense of humor once prepared what he called "The Reader's Digest Condensed Student Sermon." It was an abbreviated parody of what was often heard in preaching classes, and went something like this: "God, God, God, Christ, God, brothers and sisters, God, Godself, should, should, need to, must, must, ought to, justice, love, should, have to, let us, let us, let us, God." Meant in jest, his parody nevertheless pointed out several theological tendencies: the poverty of the language we use about divinity, the overemphasis on human activity, and the absence of enabling grace. Very often our preaching and teaching are heavy on description or analysis of a problem—whether located in the text or the congregation—and then jumps from analysis to prescription—what the congregation must do to resolve the problem. It is as though a ski instructor told a group of students about the hazards of a particular slope and told them what they must do to negotiate it, but neglected to provide them with skis and the other necessary equipment.

The tendency to jump ahead to the application—the "therefore"—is especially tempting with today's text. It seems tailormade for exhortations against prejudice, to favor speaking in tongues as a mark of the Spirit, to support change and openness in the Church. All of these may, in their place, be valid lessons to be drawn from the text. But the good news of the gospel is about what God has done in Jesus Christ, not what we are going to do or should do. And what our Lord is described as doing in the story of Peter's encounter with Cornelius is good news indeed.

I. *God prepares the way.* The baptism of Cornelius and Gentiles receiving the Holy Spirit did not come as a bolt out of the blue. Even before the start of Jesus' ministry, there were signs that the Messiah was to be for *all* people. The prophet Simeon quoted Isaiah in declaring that the Jesus was "a light for revelation to the Gentiles, and for glory to thy people Israel" (Luke 2:32). John the Baptist, who proclaimed Jesus the "Lamb of God who takes away the sin of the world," ministered to tax collectors and soldiers as well as to the children of Abraham (Luke 3:8–14). God's grace was manifested to the outcasts and unexpected throughout Jesus' ministry. In fact, throughout the Bible we're given to understand that God's good purpose is for all people, even though a particular group was called into a covenant relationship. In this morning's reading, too, God prepared the way for the events depicted. An angel spoke to Cornelius and directed him to Simon the tanner's house. The Lord gave Peter the vision that prepared him to rejoice that the good news of salvation through Christ is for all people. We may count on God to prepare *us* in a variety of ways for the mission he has in mind.

II. *God gives himself to those who seek him.* Earlier in the tenth chapter of Acts, Cornelius was described as "a devout man who feared God . . . [who] gave alms liberally . . . and prayed constantly to God." The angel's first words to Cornelius were reassurance that God had made note of his desire. Divine self-giving occurs in several other ways for Cornelius: the proclamation of the Word, the outpouring of the Holy Spirit, the gift of tongues, and the initiation of baptism. The psalmist wrote, "Take delight in the Lord, and he will give you the desires of your heart" (Ps. 37:4); in other words, when we delight in our Maker and desire him, he responds liberally to our desire. The prophet Jeremiah said, "You will seek me and find me when you seek me with all your heart" (Jer. 29:13). We do not know what Cornelius expected in his seeking after God. Nothing is said to suggest he was asking specifically for the gift of tongues, or for fellowship with Peter, or even for baptism. The story of Cornelius suggests that seeking God and being open to divine surprises result in blessings unimaginable, because our Lord is faithful and good.

III. *God confirms the work of the Spirit.* An aspect of this story that is frequently glossed over is the confirmation of the Holy Spirit at work in the situation. We may think of the people's speaking in tongues as a sign of the Spirit's work—and it is—but we stop short if we look no further. At least three things confirm that what has happened is the activity of the Holy Spirit.

(a) *Cornelius and the others spoke in tongues.* We should probably interpret "tongues" in the same way we understand Pentecost, that is, speaking in other human languages rather than in a private prayer language. The reason for this is that the onlookers understood what the speakers were saying, and the speakers were extolling God. Whichever of the gifts of the Spirit (1 Cor. 11:4–11) had been given at that time, we may be sure they would serve the same end.

(b) *They responded to the gospel Peter proclaimed.* We are invited in 1 John 4:2 to "test the spirits to see if they are of God," and the proof is that they bear witness that Jesus Christ, who came in the flesh, is of God.

(c) *They glorified God and bore witness to God's truth.*

These confirming signs can be a gift to the Church today, as we consider new ideas and changes in the life of the community.

Christians in the twenty-first century face many of the "missionary" challenges of the early Church. Discernment of God's leading may not always be easy. However, we may give thanks that God will prepare our way. He will equip us with all we need, according to his riches in glory in Christ Jesus. And our Lord will confirm the ongoing work of the Holy Spirit in ways that bear witness to his unchanging truth.—Carol M. Norén

ILLUSTRATION

PROVIDENTIAL SURPRISE.   The gifts of the Spirit are not always as dramatic as in the scene with Cornelius and Peter, but God nevertheless supplies us with what we need to be in ministry. A few years ago I went with a group on a mission trip to a village in Ecuador. We were to help build an addition on a school. To our surprise, the pastor asked if a few in our group could run an impromptu vacation Bible school for the children. There were very few resources on hand to do this, but three in our group who spoke Spanish said they would try. In the midst of getting ready, one of the teachers came to the rest of us and asked if anyone could draw a lion. She wanted to teach the children about Daniel in the lion's den and have them do a craft project. A few of us tried but without much success. Then I remembered a children's coloring book I'd bought at a dollar store and thrown into the bottom of my suitcase, just in case. Perhaps there was a drawing of a lion in there. I went back to my room, opened the suitcase, and pulled out the book. It fell open to a big picture of a lion; in fact, it turned out to be a Bible coloring book with a whole section on Daniel in the lion's den. God had prepared the way and supplied what we needed before we knew we'd have any use for it. And the Spirit confirmed it through the praise of children singing to God.—Carol M. Norén

SERMON SUGGESTIONS

Topic: The Burial of Moses
TEXT: Deut. 34:1–12
(1) Moses' burial was a secret. (2) On the other hand, Moses' mighty words and deeds have been declared for all to know. (3) Nevertheless, one greater than Moses has come (Heb. 3:1–6).

Topic: A Plea for Peace
TEXT: Phil. 4:9
(1) Peace in the Christian fellowship. (2) Inner peace that passes understanding. (3) Peace with God, the source of all true peace.

CONGREGATIONAL MUSIC

1. "Jesus Is All the World to Me," Will L. Thompson (1904)
   ELIZABETH, Will L. Thompson (1904)
   John 15:15 declares that God in Jesus Christ has called us not servants but friends. This thought is celebrated in this gospel hymn, which could be sung as a response to the Gospel reading.
2. "Sing a New Song to the Lord," Timothy Dudley-Smith (1971)
   ONSLOW SQUARE, David G. Wilson (1971)
   A paraphrase of Psalm 98, "Sing a New Song to the Lord" is appropriate for use as a call to worship. Its folklike tune could be introduced by a choir, which could be joined in the latter stanzas by the congregation.
3. "Spirit of the Living God," Daniel Iverson (1926)
   IVERSON, Daniel Iverson (1926)
   This short hymn could be sung prayerfully as a response to the reading in Acts 10:44–48 about the coming of the Holy Spirit upon the Gentiles.
4. "Rock of Ages, Cleft for Me," Augustus M. Toplady (1776)
   TOPLADY, Thomas Hastings (1830)
   This familiar hymn—particularly its first stanza—is based on 1 John 5:6 and thus would be a natural response to the reading of the Epistle lesson.—Hugh T. McElrath

WORSHIP AIDS

CALL TO WORSHIP.   "Make a joyful noise unto the Lord, all the Earth: make a loud noise and rejoice and sing praise" (Ps. 98:4).

INVOCATION.   As we contemplate the days of our years, with the ups and downs, the joys and sorrows, the good times and the bad, we can always find reasons to sing your praises. Even when we cannot understand your ways—what you do and what you permit—your love in Jesus Christ opens our hearts and tunes our voices to praise you.

OFFERTORY SENTENCE.   "Lay not up for yourselves treasures upon Earth, where moth and rust doth corrupt, and where thieves break in and steal; but lay up for yourselves treasures in heaven, where neither moth nor rust doth corrupt, and where thieves do not break through nor steal. For where your treasure is, there your heart will be also" (Matt. 6:19–21).

OFFERTORY PRAYER.   Gracious Lord, give us hearts that are willing to be drawn more and more toward those things that are lasting, so that when we give we are assured that we are laying up treasures in heaven, not just for our good but for your glory as well.

PRAYER.   God of our Fathers, you watch over the destinies of people and of nations, we rejoice in your presence in the midst of our common lives. We call on you in awesome reverence, for we acknowledge the ground on which we stand to be holy ground hallowed by the blood, sweat, and tears of men and women of previous generations, as well as of our own, who have supremely sacrificed that we might know the heritage that is ours today.

On this occasion, O Father, as we remember in a special way those we have loved dearly and lost awhile, may we enter more fully into the meaning of the "communion of the saints." We thank you for the love, the fidelity, and the aspiration that have been the nobility of these, our loved ones and friends. May we not mourn as those without hope, for you have given us a living hope. Grant us that assurance that "life is ever Lord of death, and love can never lose its own."

To the tasks that these whom we remember today so unselfishly gave of themselves and of their means, may we commit ourselves, that their fondest dreams for this church and its mission in the community and the world will not go unrealized.

We pray for peace. And for those persons seeking to bring reconciliation in the troubled areas of the world, we pray for wisdom and mutual trust of each other, as they probe new solutions to national and international problems, that all peoples may know life and that the kingdoms of this world may become the Kingdom of our Lord and of Christ.

We are sojourners, looking for that Eternal City whose builder and maker you are. Keep us from homesteading at some halfway house, lest we miss our true destiny in you—"our help in ages past and our hope for years to come."—John Thompson

SERMON
Topic: The Man Who Was Too Good to Forgive
TEXT: Luke 7:36–8:3

A Pharisee, an expert in the Law of Moses, invited Jesus to dinner. Jesus had been causing a stir in Galilee, teaching and healing in the name of God, and Simon wanted to check him out. He wanted to see firsthand, without the hysteria of the crowds, just what kind of person this Jesus was.

I can imagine Simon the Pharisee welcoming Jesus to his house the way a doctoral committee would welcome a Ph.D. candidate to her oral exams. He was polite but reserved, watching to see if this person is worthy to be admitted to the rank of the teachers of the Law. Is he really a prophet as some have claimed?

Pharisees make an easy foil for those of us who know how this story ends. Compared to the way Jesus loves and accepts all people, it's easy for us to look with scorn on the Pharisees' self-righteousness and their scrupulous observance of rules and regulations. But remember, Jesus accepted Simon's invitation. He knew exactly what Simon was doing by inviting him to dinner. The Pharisees had been right when they accused Jesus of being a friend of sinners. He was a friend of all sinners, including Simon the Pharisee, whose sin was thinking he was too good to need forgiveness.

While Simon, Jesus, and the rest of the guests were eating, a woman of the streets came into the house and stood weeping at Jesus' feet. She bathed his feet with her tears and dried them with her hair. Then she kissed his feet and anointed them with ointment. As you picture the scene, remember that in that time and place dinner parties were given differently than how they are given today. It wasn't uncommon to see beggars or passersby wandering through the home of a prominent citizen like Simon the Pharisee when he was giving a dinner party. So Simon's reaction to the incident that transpired in front of him wasn't, "Get that tramp out of here immediately," but "If this man were a prophet he would know who and what kind of woman this is." The ironic thing is that Jesus knew exactly what kind of woman she was. She was a woman who knew she needed exactly what Jesus had come to give her—the forgiveness of sins and a completely new life. Simon, on the other hand, was so busy judging, he missed out on forgiveness. He was so concerned with trying to protect God's law, he missed the point of God's law altogether.

Poor Simon. He was so busy worrying about who was in and who was out, he missed the whole point of Jesus' message. So Jesus, always compassionate, always trying to help people understand, told him this parable:

Once there was a man who had two debtors. One owed him 500 denarii, the other owed him 50. (A denarius was worth about one day's wage for a worker.) Neither could pay, so the man canceled the debt for both of them. Jesus asked Simon which man would love the creditor more–the one who had been forgiven 500 denarii or the one who had been forgiven 50? The answer is obvious—the man who had been forgiven more.

That's why the woman had treated Jesus with so much more affection than Simon had. She knew she needed Jesus to free her from her sins and give her a new life. Her soul was parched, and she recognized Jesus as the living water.

What was poor Simon to do? Was he supposed to go out and sin as boldly as that woman of the streets so he could be forgiven more? Romans asks the questions, "Should we sin boldly that grace may abound?" No, Simon didn't have to change his lifestyle. He had to change his heart. None of us can qualify to have our sins forgiven. The more you develop in your faith, the more you realize just how much more forgiveness you need.

Jesus knew that Simon needed to be forgiven just as much as the woman of the streets. In going to the home of the well-educated, well-off Simon, Jesus opened the way for the sinful woman with no education and no resources to minister to the Pharisee and show him what it means to receive the new life in Christ.

How much has Jesus forgiven you? Are you so good that you have nothing to be grateful for? Or has he forgiven you enough that you want to give him your whole life?—Stephens G. Lytch

SUNDAY, JUNE 1, 2003
Lectionary Message

Topic: Witness to the Resurrection

TEXT: Acts 1:15–17, 21–26

Other Readings: Ps. 1; 1 John 5:9–13; John 17:6–19; Ps. 47; Eph. 1:15–23; Luke 24:44–53

During one of the vice-presidential debates several years ago, a candidate was asked why he would want to hold the second highest office in the United States. The candidate, known for his dry wit, responded, "Well, it's indoor work with no heavy lifting." His response drew a laugh. Everyone listening knew that what he said was true. They also knew that those truths were irrelevant to the position he was seeking.

The gifts and qualities we bring to other situations, or our reasons for desiring a particular position, are no joking matter. When a church looks for a new pastor, they naturally want someone who can lead the congregation. A Christian education committee wants Sunday school teachers who are punctual and caring, and who can help with the Christian formation of class members. If we watch preachers on television, we are drawn to those we think have integrity and sincerity, or those who speak in engaging ways. And when candidates for ordination are asked why they seek a vocation in ministry, the interviewing board looks for honesty, poise, Bible knowledge, and other such qualities.

It may surprise us, then, that none of these gifts or qualities is mentioned by the writer of Acts in this account of replacing one of the apostles. To be sure, the office of apostle is not identical to the vocations followed by disciples of Christ today. When the term *apostle* is used in the Gospels, it means one of the twelve closest followers called by Jesus. In the rest of the New Testament, it refers to those twelve plus a few others, such as Matthias, Barnabas, and Paul. In the original Greek, an apostle is one who is "sent out." Nevertheless, disciples of Jesus Christ can look to Acts 1 for guidance as they seek to carry out *apostolic ministry,* that is, as they live out a Christian vocation in light of the Great Commission given to the twelve (Matt. 28:19–20).

I. *Being a witness to the Resurrection is most important.* Whether we call them apostles or disciples, those who gathered in the upper room before Pentecost brought strange credentials for serving Christ. Peter was impulsive, spoke before he thought, and had little education. Matthew had a bad reputation as a tax collector and probable exploiter of the people. Nathaniel was a skeptic. None was noted for being an eloquent speaker, having particular leadership skills, or having other qualities that would make them likely candidates. What they *did* have was a common experience: they were witnesses to the Resurrection. Peter named this as the single most significant qualification as they sought a replacement for Judas Iscariot.

We can understand *witness to the Resurrection* in two ways without doing violence to the text. The first, most obvious sense is that the replacement apostle must be someone who accompanied the other followers of Jesus from the earliest days of our Lord's ministry. He or she must have seen the major events in Jesus' life, been present when he was betrayed and crucified, and been one of those who encountered the Risen Christ face to face. In short, that person must have *witnessed* the life, death, and Resurrection of Jesus Christ. The second way of understanding *witness to the Resurrection* flows from the first: the person must be zealous to give his or her testimony to the events witnessed, and to communicate the urgency of the Gospel.

In the present day, no one has seen Jesus' earthly ministry, watched the Crucifixion, or been approached by the Risen Christ as those first followers were. Nevertheless, our primary calling as witnesses involves the same dynamics. We must be people who have experienced a life-changing encounter with Jesus Christ. We have been invited to know him more intimately, and we have been called to speak and act in ways that bring others to a similar encounter with God.

II. *Witnesses to the Resurrection obey the Holy Spirit's leading.* When Peter called the meeting to order in the upper room, he didn't appoint a search committee or circulate resumes of candidates to fill the vacancy left by Judas. He led the others in prayer for discernment. He trusted the Spirit's leading through the casting of lots that followed the prayer. He and the others trusted that God had spoken, and acted on what had been revealed. Just prior to this section, the chapter notes that the company of apostles plus other followers "with one accord devoted themselves to prayer," seeking the will of God. So also today, the Holy Spirit uses people who are radically open to God's future, seeking the divine will through prayer, searching the Scriptures, worshiping with other believers, and responding to the many ways God's purpose may be made plain.

III. *Witnesses to the Resurrection are connected to one another as well as to God.* Peter did not seek God's will and make a decision unilaterally. Matthias didn't become an apostle and then go off and operate independently. They understood that living out their vocation meant accountability to one another, even when there were tensions or conflicting visions. Today, effective service to God should not be measured only by the size of an individual's following, but by the way a person "equips other saints" for service and thus builds up the body of Christ. Fervent prayer, mutual support, and striving for peace within the household of faith are hallmarks of a witness to the Resurrection.—Carol M. Norén

ILLUSTRATIONS

FUZZY FAITH.   The pastor of a local church was conducting classes for prospective members. He reviewed with them the denomination's statement of beliefs and noted that they would be asked if they confessed them as their own. He added, however, that they need not worry about any doctrinal points with which they did not concur, because "it means whatever it means to you." What would have become of the Christian Church if Peter and the other disciples held the same philosophy in choosing someone to take the place of Judas Iscariot?—Carol M. Norén

DEEP FAITH.   When a jury is selected in the United States, lawyers ask prospective jurors many questions about their background, work, prior experiences within the legal system, and so on. Someone with a vested interest in the plaintiff's or the defendant's point of view is nearly always disqualified from serving on that panel of twelve jurors. A juror is supposed to be impartial. In serving as a disciple, the opposite is true, as Peter's words in Acts 1 demonstrate. A "witness to the Resurrection" has his or her own experience of the Risen Christ and is eager to help others have the same experience.—Carol M. Norén

SERMON SUGGESTIONS

Topic: When Preaching Is Effective

TEXT: Acts 13:26–43

(1) When it interprets history (vv. 26–31). (2) When it interprets the Scriptures (vv. 32–37). (3) When it interprets human need (vv. 38–41).—D. W. Cleverley Ford

Topic: Andrew Inspires Us

TEXT: John 1:35–42

(1) To participate in salvation. (2) To publicize salvation.

CONGREGATIONAL MUSIC

1. "Lord, Keep Us Steadfast in Your Word," Martin Luther (1542); trans. Catherine Winkworth (1863)

ERHALT UNS HERR, J. Klug's *Geistliche Lieder* (1543)

Jesus' poignant prayer that his disciples might be in unity and kept from evil (John 17:6–19) is echoed in this hymn from the great reformer Luther. It could be sung as a prayer preceding the reading of the Gospel lesson.

2. "How Blest Are They Who, Fearing God," Ps. 1; vers. *Psalter* (1912)

ST. ANNE, William Croft (1708)

This metrical version of Psalm 1 could be sung in alternation with the reading of psalm verses as follows: read verse 1, sing stanza 1; read verse 2, sing stanza 2; read verse 3, sing stanza 3; read verses 4–5, sing stanza 4; read verse 6, sing stanza 5.

3. "Because He Lives," Gloria and William J. Gaither (1971)

RESURRECTION, William J. Gaither (1971)

This exuberant popular hymn of assurance reflects the message of today's Epistle lesson (1 John 5:9–13) and could appropriately be sung in connection with it.

4. "If You Will Trust in God to Guide You," Georg Heumark (1641); trans. Catherine Winkworth (1863)

WER NUR DEN LIEBEN GOTT, Georg Heumark (1657)

The reading of the account of Judas' death and the prayerful choice of his successor (Acts 1:21–26) could be followed by the singing of this excellent chorale of trust and assurance.—Hugh T. McElrath

WORSHIP AIDS

CALL TO WORSHIP.   "He that hath an ear, let him hear what the Spirit saith unto the churches" (Rev. 2:29).

INVOCATION.   O God, as you speak to us today through your Spirit in our worship, grant to us open minds and willing hearts, so that we may discern your will for our lives today and have new insights for the days ahead.

OFFERTORY SENTENCE.   "Bring ye all the tithes into the storehouse, that there may be meat in mine house, and prove me now herewith, saith the Lord of Hosts, if I will not open to you the windows of heaven, and pour you out a blessing, that there shall not be room enough to receive it" (Mal. 3:10).

OFFERTORY PRAYER.   Grant us the faith and courage to believe and to give according to your promise, O God, and receive the joy of partnership with you in the work of your Kingdom.

PRAYER.   Here we are on this earthly plain, caught between memory and hope. Save us, O God, from our suicidal ways. Awaken us from our stupor and stupidity before it is too late. Awaken us to see the new thing that you are doing in our day—to the vision of the one family, becoming real in and through the reconciliation that your love in Christ anticipates.

With the dawning of that first Easter morning, the new age was here. Why, then, are we still wrapped in the grave clothes of fear and prejudice and suspicion? You call us to a perennial springtime: "The old is past and done with, behold all things are becoming new."

> Lo the winter is past,
> the rain is over and gone.
> The flowers appear on the Earth,
> the time of singing has come.

Today and every day, may we be open in faith to receive the fullness of your grace in Christ, that we may join all creation in singing the new song of salvation for all.

May we know forgiveness for our every yesterday, that all resources for life entrusted to us may be mobilized to meet the challenge of this new day.

"Today is the day of Salvation. Now is the timely time."

May we live our every day in the faith proclaimed by John from his prison in exile: "We know not what the future holds but we know who holds the future."

New and ever-living God, we praise you for this day with all of its freshness and promise. It is truly the day you have made out of all the creative genius of your amazing grace.

We praise you for your healing grace at work among us: Where there has been brokenness, we have seen wholeness taking shape right before our eyes. There have been transformations among us—where the night has turned to day, where cynicism gives way to hope, where weeping is strangely surprised by joy. Keep the pressure of your Holy Spirit upon us, that the good work you have begun in us may be brought to fruition according to the maturity we have come to know in Christ, who is present in the eternal now of our every day.— John Thompson

SERMON
Topic: Everyone Is Called to Something
TEXT: Eph. 4:1–7; 1 Cor. 15:58

At first this quote may sound so radical that you might want to dismiss it. I beg you not to because it is right on target.

Here is the quote:

"I am convinced that what characterizes people who know Jesus is *not* their lack of sin but the presence of a radical, wild, mysterious calling from God" (Mike Yaconelli).

The mission of the Church in America is not only to save souls; it is also to save people from a life without calling. The Church, through Jesus, must save its people from a life of meaningless, unfulfilling, empty work.

If that sounds radical to you, it may be because we have all too often restricted the concept of call to only one group of persons within the Christian community. We speak often of "the call to ministry," and a part of what a church looks for in the process of "calling" a pastor is that he or she relate the sense of calling to ministry.

My deep conviction is not that we have been wrong in demanding that those in ministry have some sense of calling from God, but that all too often we have been guilty of appearing to limit that sense of calling to roles in ministry.

I. *Everyone has a calling; everyone has a gift.* Here are Paul's words from Ephesians 4, written not to clergy but, as Ephesians 1:1 tell us, to all the saints in Ephesus. This is another good word to reclaim in our faith: Paul always addresses believers (church members) as *saints.* Here is what he writes to *all* the saints at Ephesus and to all of us: "I implore you . . . as God has called you, live up to your calling. . . . Each of us has been given a special gift, a particular share in the bounty of Christ."

If we had time to do an in-depth Bible study, I believe it would not take long to convince you that the calling and gifts for ministry that Paul lists in Ephesians 4:11–12 is not meant to be exhaustive of those who are called and those who are gifted. Paul asserts that every Christian is called and every Christian is gifted.

Too many people think it is a mark of humility to belittle themselves and see themselves as exceptions when God was passing out gifts and callings.

The real message in the parable of the talents is that the man who buried his one talent because it seemed he had so little scorned what the master of the house had given him. He belittled his gift, he belittled his abilities, he belittled his opportunity. And the shocking end of the story is that the master of the house cast him out!

Too many cry, "What can I do with so little? What difference could I possibly make?" Well, I am always encouraged by the words of Rabbi Zusya, who said, a short while before his death, "In the world to come I shall not be asked, 'Why were you not Moses?' I shall be asked, 'Why were you not Zusya?'"[1]

God never asks us to live out someone else's calling or to achieve with someone else's gifts. We are to respond to the calling we have and to invest in life with the gifts we have. It is the old sayings, "Be who you are and use what you have," and "If you can't be yourself, who are you going to be?"

II. Paul uses a phrase that I find most instructive: *Live up to your calling.* We often talk about the downward pull of things. Here is where we can respond to the upward tug of things.

Right after he says, "Live up to your calling," he adds, "Be humble always and gentle, and patient too, putting up with one another's failings in the spirit of love."

I have always maintained that if you have a sense of worth, dignity, and high calling, then you can afford to be gracious and kind. But if your bucket of self-esteem is half empty, you often find yourself putting down other people in order to feel better about yourself (which of course never works).

When believers in the ancient world lapsed into pagan morality, Paul often used the tactic of asking, "Don't you know who you are?"

---

[1]Mandelbau, *Life,* p. 239.

Paul could say of himself, "I press on toward the goal for the prize of the *upward* call of God in Christ Jesus" (Phil. 3:14).

Paul says something in writing to the church at Corinth that I think gives added encouragement to us as we seek to live out who we are and what we are, where we are.

III. *Stand firm and immovable, and work for the Lord always; work without limit, since you know that in the Lord your labor cannot be lost.* Stars come and go and people are quickly forgotten. As you get older you realize how quickly the people and events of your life are hardly recognized by the younger generation.

That is why Paul assures all of us that if God has gifted us and called us, and if we use those gifts and respond to that calling, we can be assured that nothing we do will ever be lost or wasted or forgotten.

That very same theme is echoed in Psalm 90, which talks about the brevity of life and ends with this plea to God, voiced twice: "establish the work of our hands for us—yes, establish the work of our hands."

The message of the psalm is that we can trust God to remember us and our deeds. When someone brings out the old saw as a word of encouragement, it really is the most discouraging thing that can be said: "A hundred years from now, what difference will it make? Who will know? Who will remember?"

A hundred years from now, a thousand years from now, a million years from now, who will know that you lived and struggled and laughed and cried? Who will remember what you tried to do and the calling you tried to fulfill? The answer is, God will! He will never forget you or what you have done. That is the same thing Jesus underscored when he said, "If all you can do is give a cup of cold water in my name, be assured that you will not go unrewarded, your deed will not go unrecorded or unremembered.

What a joy to know that we are living in time but also in the framework of eternity. That the God who knows us and calls us and uses us will never let us lose our identity as the persons we are and what we have done.

Goodspeed translates our verse like this: "You know that through the Lord your labor is not thrown away."—Ronald Higdon

SUNDAY, JUNE 8, 2003
Lectionary Message

Topic: What Does This Mean?
TEXT: Acts 2:1–21
Other Readings: Ezek. 37:1–14; Ps. 104:24–34, 35b; Rom. 8:22–27; John 15:26–27; 16:4b–15

When I was a little boy, letters fascinated me. My father would write the English alphabet on the tiles of our bathroom wall so the children might learn. This was my first introduction to writing. As I grew I wanted to learn more than just the letters. One day I picked up a book from the shelves and asked my dad if he would read me a story out of the book. "What does this mean?" I turned to him and asked, pointing randomly to a sentence and hoping he would explain it to me. To my disappointment he turned down my request and simply said, "Wait until you are old enough so you can read and understand it on your own."

"What does this mean?" The same question was asked by the people who witnessed a remarkable event that took place in Jerusalem nearly two thousand years ago. It was the day of Pentecost, seven weeks after Jesus' Resurrection, when a sound from heaven like the roaring of a mighty windstorm filled the house where the disciples were gathering. Then what looked like flames, or tongues of fire, appeared and settled on each of them. Everyone present was filled with the Holy Spirit and began speaking in other languages, as the Holy Spirit enabled them (Acts 2:1–4). Among those present were godly Jews from many nations. They heard the sound and were utterly amazed to hear their own languages being spoken by the believers. Some of them became suspicious that the disciples might be drinking alcohol.

As Peter stood up and explained what happened, the people began to realize that they were witnessing the dawning of an era of new life, new power, and new mission.

I. *New life.*

(a) *Unity.* Although a situation in which many languages are being spoken in one place might appear chaotic, in this scene there was unity among the believers. Soon after Jesus' Ascension, his twelve disciples regrouped when Matthias was chosen to replace Judas Iscariot (Acts 1:23–26). Also, the dominant usage of the word "all" in this passage suggests unity (vv. 1, 4, 7, 12). For example, we were told that on the day of Pentecost the believers were "all together in one place" (v. 1).

(b) *Diversity.* The "many languages" that believers spoke at Pentecost represent not only linguistic diversity but also ethnic, cultural, and geographic diversity. For the first time, specific names that cover vast regions of the world were mentioned (vv. 9–11). This indicates that the gospel was no longer contained merely in Palestine, but should be preached to the whole world.

II. *New power.*

(a) *New power came in the fulfillment of promises made in both the Old and New Testaments.* In his speech, Peter quoted the Old Testament prophet Joel, that God would pour out his Spirit upon all peoples in order to empower them and their children (v. 17). As the Holy Spirit came upon them at Pentecost, the believers, both slave and free, would soon experience the power to prophesy and see visions, just as the prophet Joel proclaimed. In the New Testament, on the other hand, John the Baptist also predicted the outpouring of the Holy Spirit, that Jesus would baptize the believers "with the Holy Spirit and with fire" (Matt. 3:11). Above all is the promise by Jesus himself, "You will receive the power when the Holy Spirit has come upon you" (Acts 1:8a).

(b) *The outpouring of the Holy Spirit enabled the believers to do mighty works of Jesus.* When the disciples were filled with the Holy Spirit, they began to speak in other languages, "as the Spirit enabled them" (v. 4). This is significant because by this the Holy Spirit symbolically initiated power upon the believers for evangelistic purposes. This power would include driving out demons, healing, prophesying, and performing other miracles.

III. *New mission.* The disciples now had a new mission of carrying the gospel to the rest of the world. Before his Ascension, Jesus told his disciples to stay in Jerusalem until they had received the gift of the Holy Spirit (Acts 1:4). Then, as Jesus foretold, they would be his witnesses "in Jerusalem, in all Judea, and in Samaria, and to the ends of the earth" (Acts 1:8). At Pentecost, the disciples, we are told, were "speaking about God's deeds and power" in foreign languages (v. 11b). The list of foreign languages (vv. 9–11) symbolically prefigures the widely evangelistic activities in which the disciples were about to engage. Jerusalem, therefore, was the pivotal point where Christian faith began to spread outside Palestine. It was also where the disciples received the gift of the Holy Spirit, which enabled them to carry on a new evangelistic mission to the whole world.

What really happened on the day of the Pentecost was a biblical prophecy fulfilled and a crucial event that changed the course of the history of mankind. The outpouring of the Holy Spirit at Pentecost marked the beginning of an era that has enabled all Christians to experience a new life of unity as well as diversity, new power to do mighty works of Jesus, and new mission to bring the gospel to the whole world. This same Spirit continues to be present throughout history in order to empower and sustain all believers.

Today I am still fond of asking the question, "What does this mean?" My father wanted me to experience the joy of acquiring knowledge through reading on my own; this was why he refused to explain the meaning of the words to me when I asked him to. My father saw the value of participating in the experience of reading and learning. Likewise, the outpouring of the Holy Spirit upon early believers at Pentecost was not merely an historical event, but something that we can all relate to. It extends to the present day precisely because Christians today can claim to be witnesses of that event on the basis of the continual presence of the Holy Spirit working in our lives. In other words, we are not bystanders or observers of the outpouring of the Holy Spirit at Pentecost, but we are active participants who witness it firsthand as the event is recorded in the Scriptures.—Liang Kazu Wu

ILLUSTRATION

GOD IS WITH US. Looking back at history helps me keep transition events in perspective, especially when I look for ways and places where God was present.

> God was there in the burning bush
> and in the water of the Red Sea
> and on the mountain of tablets
> and in the disappointment of Moses' staying behind.
> God was there when armies marched behind the shofar
> and in the temple at the shofar's blowing
> and in the loneliness of captivity
> and in the joy of reinventing life in Babylon.
> God was there when Jesus was born in a lowly cave
> and when he talked to the priests
> and when he taught the disciples
> and when he died on the cross.
> God was there in the disciples' disappointment at Jesus' death
> and in the joy of his aliveness
> and in the birth of the Church
> and in the cold room with Paul while Paul was writing.
> God was there last year in our family's marriages and births
> and in the daily smiles and anniversaries
> and in the deaths of family members
> and in the new discoveries about life and death.

God's footprints are solidly planted on the centuries
and in our present-day efforts at reinventing life,
and he has walked in our past year
and runs with us in the future.—Naomi Mitchum[2]

SERMON SUGGESTIONS

Topic: The Gift of the Spirit

TEXT: Acts 2:1–21

(1) The ancient phenomenon: The young Church experienced the presence of God in a new and powerful way. (2) The timeless meaning: God's purpose is to fill the lives of all his people in a creative and unifying experience in Christ. (3) The timely application: All believers are potential witnesses; the Spirit draws us all toward each other at the deepest level; the Spirit gives courage and power to do what we could never do without the Spirit.

Topic: Unity and Variety in the Church

TEXT: 1 Cor. 12:3b–13

The Holy Spirit: (1) leads us to faith in Jesus as Lord, (2) assigns a variety of gifts for the good of the entire church, and (3) gives dignity and importance to each person's task.

CONGREGATIONAL MUSIC

1. "For Your Gift of God the Spirit," Margaret Clarkson (1959)

    BLAENWERN, William P. Rowlands (1905)

    A contemporary expression that gathers up many of the truths about the Spirit of God and is set to a rousing Welsh congregational tune, this hymn is eminently appropriate for the opening of worship on Pentecost Sunday. Part-singing is suggested for the first four stanzas, but broad unison treatment for the final stanzas.

2. "Like the Murmur of the Dove's Song," Carl P. Daw Jr. (1982)

    BRIDEGROOM, Peter Cutts (1969)

    In a different style but fully expressive of the work of the Holy Spirit, this contemporary hymn could effectively be sung antiphonally between choir and congregation, with all joining in the closing petition, "Come, Holy Spirit, Come."

3. "Come, Holy Spirit, Heavenly Dove," Isaac Watts (1767)

    ST. AGNES, John B. Dykes (1866)

    Isaac Watts's great hymn invoking the Holy Spirit has stood the test of time and use. It would be appropriate either sung or quoted as preparation for worship. It would be used most meaningfully as a call to worship.

4. "Holy Spirit, Light Divine," Andrew Reed (1817)

    MERCY, Louis M. Gottschalk (1854)

    This nineteenth-century hymn would be effective as either a call to Scripture for any of the readings set for this day or as a sung response to them.—Hugh T. McElrath

---

[2]*Harps in the Willows* (St. Louis: Chalice Press, 2001), pp. 82–83.

WORSHIP AIDS

CALL TO WORSHIP.   "Since, then, we have a great high priest who has passed through the heavens—Jesus, the Son of God—let us hold fast to our confession. For we do not have a high priest who is unable to sympathize with our weaknesses, but we have one who in every respect has been tested as we are, yet without sin. Let us therefore approach the throne of grace with boldness, so we may receive mercy and find grace to help in time of need" (Heb. 4:14–16 NRSV).

INVOCATION.   Father, as we draw near to you in prayer and song, strengthen our confidence in the power of your grace to satisfy our deepest needs and to equip us to impart your blessings to others.

OFFERTORY SENTENCE.   "Every good gift and every perfect gift is from above, and cometh down from the Father of lights, with whom is no variableness, neither shadow of turning" (James 1:17).

OFFERTORY PRAYER.   Because you are ever the same, O God, we can trust you in good times and bad. Give us, we pray, a greater measure of reliability, so you can depend on us and so that those who need us can count on our trustworthiness. Make us faithful stewards of your blessings.

PRAYER.   O God, we stand in awe of thy marvelous works. The works of men stagger the imagination. How much greater are the creations of thy wisdom and purpose. We do not presume to know all that thou art doing in thy universe; we do not know even half of what thou art doing in the little corner of the world where we live. Yet we are assured that thy works are good. The cross of our Lord Jesus Christ, to some an emblem of injustice, has turned out to be the supreme demonstration of thy wisdom and power. When we are tempted to doubt the goodness of thy doing, help us to look again at the cross from the viewpoint of the Resurrection and in this way find our faith strengthened, so we can begin to make sense of the things that are taking place in our lives. We pray, O God, for those who wander in a maze of meaningless activities, seeking happiness and finding little of it. May they realize that the way of faith and obedience is the way to knowledge and fulfillment. Renew the courage of those who are trying valiantly to wrest meaning from their shattered days and ways. Grant that some sense of thy presence and power may help them to keep on seeking after thee. And grant that they may not demand some spectacular display of thy reality. Satisfy us all with a willingness to be faithful, whatever the difficulties.

SERMON

Topic: Supporting Our Missionaries

TEXT: 3 John 4–8

The book of 3 John was written to a man named Gaius, who was commended by John for his hospitality and support of the traveling missionaries. Missionaries in Gaius's day did not stay in one location. They traveled from city to city and depended on the hospitality and generosity of other Christians for their shelter and support. Word had come to John of Gaius's kindness. John assured Gaius that his action was practical evidence that he was "walk[ing] in the truth" (v. 4). Gaius was doing what he "ought" to do (v. 8). The missionary obligation is part of what being a Christian is all about.

I. *The reasons.* There are many reasons why we should support our missionaries. For one thing, doing so is a faithful work. This is what John said of Gaius's support: "Beloved, it is a fine and faithful work that you are doing when you give any service to the [Christian] brethren, and [especially when they are] strangers" (3 John 5). The meaning is that when you work on behalf of the brethren, you are acting faithfully. Notice the words "when you give any service." When you faithfully support mission, you are performing a fine and noble work. It doesn't matter if you are a five-talent person, a two-talent person, or a one-talent person. If you use what you have in the support of missions, you do "a fine and faithful work."

A second reason why we should support our missionaries is because doing so is a testimony of love. John said of the traveling missionaries, "They have testified before the church of your love and friendship" (v. 6). Wherever the missionaries went, they testified of their support. Wherever our missionaries are today, they testify of the love and friendship of Christians back home who support them and make it possible for them to be on the mission field telling others about Jesus.

A third reason why we should support our missionaries is because we do so for "thy Name's sake" (v. 7). The missionaries on foreign fields are going out in the name of Jesus.

While William Carey was in India, Andrew Fuller was collecting money for his support. When Fuller approached one man about his giving, the man replied, "Seeing it is you, I will give five pounds." Fuller replied, "I cannot take your money if you give it because of me."

The man understood. "Andrew, you are right. Here is ten pounds because they are carrying out the commission of the Lord Jesus Christ."

A fourth reason why we should support the work of our missionaries is because their work constitutes a partnership with us. John said to Gaius, "So we ourselves ought to support such people—to welcome and provide for them—in order that we may be fellow workers in the Truth" (v. 8).

Every time someone on a mission field preaches Christ, we have a part in it. Every time someone gives medicine or a shot to a sick person, we have a part in it. Every time someone teaches the Bible to a student or shows a visual-aid program, we have a part in it. This is what Jesus meant when he said, "I sent you to reap that whereon ye bestowed no labor: other men labored, and ye are entered into their labors."

II. *The resources.* There are several different ways we can support our missionaries. The first and most obvious is with our finances. John says in verse 7 that those traveling missionaries were "accepting nothing from the heathen . . . so we ourselves ought to support such people." These missionaries were not going around with their hands out, asking for money to support themselves. No one could accuse them of soliciting funds. They depended on the kind and generous offerings of people like Gaius. A missionary can always be more effective in his work if he is free from financial worries. The giving of an offering to missions guarantees this freedom to the missionary.

In addition to supporting our missionaries with our finances, we can also support them with our prayers. Jesus commanded us, "Pray ye therefore the Lord of the Harvest, that he will send forth laborers into his harvest" (Matt. 9:38). Not everyone can go to the mission field in person, but all of us can go there in prayer. We are fulfilling the Great Commission when we pray for others who labor there.

We can also support our missionaries by living a consecrated life. All of our giving and all of our praying will be in vain unless they are backed up by dedicated lives. A good report from home or a good headline in newspapers can make their work easier. God demands that each of us, regardless of who we are or where we live, demonstrate a dedicated life.

A fourth way we can support missionaries is by being faithful witnesses where we are. It has been said that we are either missionaries or mission fields. As Christians, it's not a matter of whether or not we are witnesses for Christ, but what kind of witnesses we are!

It is inconsistent to give money to foreign missionaries or to pray for them and never go across the street to tell a lost person about Jesus. We are just as responsible for reaching the people in our own areas as the missionaries are for witnessing to people in the country where they serve.

III. *The results.* Many things will happen as a result of our support of missions. First, *people will be saved.* This is the primary task of all mission work—to tell others about Christ and to bring them to a saving knowledge of the Savior. The late W. O. Carver, professor of missions at the Southern Baptist Theological Seminary in Louisville, Kentucky, used to say, "God is out to save the world—all out to save all the world." Jesus came "to seek and to save that which was lost." He assigned us the same task: "As my Father hath sent me, even so send I you" (John 20:21). A missionary is one who is helping to carry out this commandment.

Not only will people be saved as we bear witness to the saving power of Jesus Christ, but there is also *joy in heaven* when one person repents and accepts Christ as Savior. It thrills the heart of God to see a person receive his Son as his Savior.

Another result will be the privilege of *seeing new Christians growing in their new faith.* The new birth is the first step in the long journey of growing toward Christian maturity. The missionary is responsible for leading the new Christian in this growth process.

One final result will be that *Christ will be glorified.* After all, this is what missions are really all about—whether the work is done on a foreign field or right here in our own homeland. We Christians work for—and missions exist for—one purpose and one purpose only: to glorify Christ.

When any church loses the spirit of the Great Commission, it surrenders the very reason for its existence. Christ's mission is the Church's mission. Missions are not a sideline—they are the lifeline of the Church. We carry on the work of Christ when we support our missionaries in their work.—Allen Reed[3]

SUNDAY, JUNE 15, 2003
Lectionary Message

Topic: Getting to Know You
TEXT: John 3:1–17
Other Readings: Isa. 6:1–8; Ps. 29; Rom. 8:12–17

I. In Christian art it has always been a challenge to depict or even symbolize the Holy Trinity. Triangles, interlocking circles, and even the shamrock have been put to use to convey the concept of one-in-three and three-in-one. Medieval artists tried to be more graphic. They

---

[3]*Award-Winning Sermons,* vol. 1, edited by James C. Barry (Nashville: Broadman Press, 1977), pp. 93–100.

painted and carved images of the Trinity in a composite of an old man with a long, white beard with arms outstretched over the form of Christ on the Cross, with a dove, symbolic of the Holy Spirit, hovering above.

Perhaps the most famous attempt to show the Trinity is that of the Eastern Orthodox Christian tradition, which prefers an Old Testament image of "God in three persons." It is taken from the story of the angels' visit to Abraham beneath the oak of Mamre, when God tells the Patriarch that he is to be the father of many nations. The most beautiful version of this story was painted by Russian iconographer Andrei Rublev in the fifteenth century. It shows a table spread with Abraham's hospitable meal at which sit three angelic figures with identical faces whose clothing, shining with ethereal colors, shows the individuality of each person. This magnificent icon shows the majesty of God revealed in these angelic forms, but it also invites the viewer who meditates on it to become part of the equation. To look at this picture prayerfully is to complete the missing third dimension of the artwork by entering into the life of the Trinity itself and taking into oneself the mystery of God. This can be done only in the act and spirit of prayer.

II. The point, which bears remembering on this Trinity Sunday, is that there is much more to our traditional teaching about the nature of God than can be expressed in a formula, prayer, or doctrine. In fact, the best of our understanding of this teaching is the result not of deep study but of deep prayer, of using not only the mind but also the eyes and the heart to understand the deep things of God.

There are groups that call themselves Christian that have trouble with our time-honored teaching about God being known as Father, Son, and Holy Spirit. They claim that since the term *trinity* doesn't occur in Scripture it is a man-made construct and not truly of divine origin. They interpret the relationship of Father, Son, and Spirit in different ways. In our defense it must be said that any denomination's teaching and life are based not only on specific Gospel texts but also on God-inspired decisions made by our Christian forebears and passed on as part of our tradition. The choice of Sunday, the day of Resurrection, as our "Sabbath," not to mention the establishment of specific houses of worship for Christian use, are nowhere mentioned in the Bible, yet they have become part of almost universal observance. So too with our ancient and central teaching about the Holy Trinity, which although not described as such in Scripture is nevertheless the distillation of biblical truth and inspiration.

Having said that, it must be admitted that the Scriptures make no reference to a clear-cut doctrine or definition of the Trinity. The lectionary readings for this day were chosen because they mention the work of the Father, Son, and Spirit in a single text. Indeed, this becomes a case requiring homework: invoking the help of the Christian fathers and mothers before us who had deep and loving relationships with God and to whom the Lord entrusted by inspiration an insight into who he is and how he works. To read the theological works about the Trinity without recognizing the lives of prayer led by the persons behind them is to miss the vital point: theology is not, or ought not to be, a thing of the mind only, but is also of the heart.

III. What comes from the hearts of the theologians is the insight that the universe should be seen not as a pyramid with a single, all-powerful individual at its apex, but more as a circle in which creation is in a constant state of interaction with its Creator. More than that alone, this Creator is in community even within himself. The love that God shows and that he commends to us in our Lord Jesus Christ is not narcissistic self-love, but always outwardly directed toward "the other."

The insight we get from Scripture in those passages that speak of the three persons whom we traditionally believe to compose the Trinity is a tantalizing glimpse of the inner workings of divinity in which individuals have function but in which unity is paramount. To understand this, perhaps we need to return to the image of the Russian icon and its invitation to enter into the mystery of the Trinity—an image of God's visit to his people in visible form and manifested in the sharing of a meal. To live out this mystery in the context of the Church is to bring our theological speculation down to Earth in the way the Father intended by sending his Son, who shared our human life, died on the cross to provide us with salvation, and assures us of the ongoing presence of the Holy Spirit. We can do this by staying united with Christ and with one another while inviting others into these relationships. This makes the Trinity less an object of theological study and more the practical pattern of all Christian life.

IV. As we celebrate this feast—ancient, venerable, but ultimately mysterious—let us remember that we should not leave it only to the theologians to tell us about God—Father, Son, and Holy Spirit—but we should seek that wisdom and insight ourselves in worship, in prayer, and in fellowship.—Tyler A. Strand

ILLUSTRATIONS

THE TRINITARIAN DANCE.   The triune God is not merely a life of shared particularities. The three persons dwell in unity, held together by the Son, in whom all things are held together, "things in heaven and things on Earth" (Eph. 1:10). The Greek word for this mutual indwelling or holding together is *perichoresis,* which literally means "dancing around." It is not a bad word to describe the Trinitarian life. If you have seen a country dance, you will understand the aptness of the term. At such a dance the participants, while uniquely themselves, dance in harmony not only with the music but also with each other, not being absorbed into each other's roles but playing off of them and coming together in an even deeper and happier unity. Such is God's life—a *koinonia* or communion, neither a collective nor an individual thing but a mutual indwelling, a being in communion.

If human beings are creatures made in the image of this God, then surely we are made for communion with God and one another. Or to put it another way, we become *inhuman* when we forsake this relatedness in the name of a more authoritarian "one" or an indifferent "many." Both subvert our humanity and trivialize our lives.

The human community discovers its true humanity as it is drawn into the life of this Trinitarian dance, a life that celebrates the communion that is ours with God and one another in Jesus Christ. The New Testament name for this life together is "Church," whose reason for being is to teach us to dance. Like the triune God whose life the Church celebrates, the Church can be understood only in terms of its own being in communion—indeed, of its being a body whose members find their lives only in relation to one another.—Thomas W. Currie III[4]

GOD'S EMBRACE.   His call to us is to love our world enough to risk telling it the truth, to love our children enough to teach them the ways of this faithful God, to love our culture enough to embrace it for Jesus' sake.

---

[4]*Searching for Truth* (Louisville: Geneva Press, 2001), p. 50.

There is nothing neutral about such an embrace. Indeed, unless we believe that Jesus Christ is the way God has embraced this world, there is no reason for us to bother anyone else with this story. But if it is the truth that God does embrace us in Jesus Christ, then to embrace this world will always be a costly matter, and will require our reaching out to those who believe differently than we do, who do not believe anything at all, and who may well be offended by our faith—Thomas W. Currie III[5]

SERMON SUGGESTIONS

Topic: A True Vision of God

TEXT: Isa. 6:1–8

Shows God (1) in his completeness, (2) in his compassion, (3) in his commission.

Topic: Leadership of the Spirit

TEXT: Rom. 8:12–17

(1) Gives us life (v. 13). (2) Gives us status (v. 14). (3) Gives us assurance (vv. 15–16). (4) Gives us a glorious inheritance (v. 17).

CONGREGATIONAL MUSIC

1. "Give Glory to God, All You Heavenly Creatures," Ps. 29; vers. Calvin Seerveld (1983)
   ARLES, Charles H. Gabriel (c. 1915)
   The five stanzas of this modern metrical version of Psalm 29 constitute a close paraphrase of the verses of the original psalm. Thus it could be used (possibly alternating reciting and singing the stanzas) at the time of the Psalter lesson.
2. "Come, Thou Almighty King," Anonymous (1757)
   ITALIAN HYMN, Felice de Giardini (1797)
   This most popular of traditional hymns addressed to the triune God is appropriate for the opening of worship on Trinity Sunday.
3. "Holy God, We Praise Your Name," *Te Deum* (4th century); vers. I. Franz (1774); trans. Catherine Winkworth (1853)
   GROSSER GOTT, *Kath. Gesangbuch* (1774)
   This traditional metrication of the *Te Deum laudamus* incorporates the "Thrice Holies" of Isaiah 6:3 in stanza 2 and the "mystery" of the Trinity in stanza 4. Equally effective for the beginning of worship and in connection with the Old Testament lesson (Isa. 6:1–8), the first two stanzas of this venerable hymn could be sung antiphonally between choir and congregation, with all uniting in the reverent singing of the last two stanzas.
4. "I'm New Born Again," African American Spiritual
   NEW BORN AGAIN, words and music arr. J. W. Work and F. J. Work (1907)
   This African American spiritual would be a very effective accompaniment to the Gospel reading about Nicodemus. A choir or soloist could sing the stanzas, with the congregation coming in on the sprightly refrain.—Hugh T. McElrath

---

[5]*Searching for Truth,* p. 65.

WORSHIP AIDS

CALL TO WORSHIP.   "This is how we know what love is: Christ gave his life for us. We too, then, ought to give our lives for our brothers! If a rich person sees his brother in need yet closes his heart against his brother, how can he claim that he loves God? My children, our love should be not just words and talk; it must be true love, which shows itself in action" (1 John 3:16–18).

INVOCATION.   We are here today, O God, because Christ has done for us what we could not do for ourselves. Teach us in what we hear and experience to reflect our Lord's self-giving as we live and move and have our being in this world of deep need.

OFFERTORY SENTENCE.   "For to their power I bear record, yea, and beyond their power they were willing of themselves" (2 Cor. 8:3).

OFFERTORY PRAYER.   Give us, gracious God, the joy of those who know the blessings of being partners with you in what you are doing among us, around us, and even beyond our sight and knowledge. Receive our offerings, we pray, as part of our service in your world.

PRAYER.   Our Father, our God, you have made a place for us where we are safe. You are our refuge and we have put our trust in you. Many forces that threaten us are at work in the world. In many ways they do us harm. Sorrow comes to all. Accidents happen, suffering lays us low, temptation beguiles—yet in your secret place we are safe.

Grant, O God, that we may always depend on you to help us in times of danger and weakness, but may we never presume on your goodness and grace by foolish and willful acts. We need your gift of friends to encourage us, your Spirit to guide us and make us brave, your word to temper our excesses and prod us to daily obedience.

While we receive your good gifts, let us be helpful friends, praying for one another and speaking your words of grace in the precious moment of opportunity or necessity.

SERMON

Topic: The Harp or the Javelin?

TEXT: 1 Sam. 18:10–11

In today's world, two powers are at our disposal. One is the power of the javelin, which typifies violence, force, and physical strength. The other is the power of music, symbolizing love and kindness. Both choices are available. The one we choose determines the kind of world we live in.

The one we choose also determines the kind of persons we become. As Christians, we aim for growth and maturity. We are dissatisfied to stay on the level at which we found Christ. But if we're not careful, we'll transfer the tactics of the world to our own struggle for goodness. We'll get involved in a power struggle for spiritual maturity.

Although the Christian life is one of power, it is not power from the material standpoint. It is the power of submission, the strength of kindness.

Today singing and music are at the heart of our worship. Can you imagine coming to church and not singing? The Bible is filled with examples of the people of God who broke out in song. After Moses had led the children of Israel across the Red Sea, they broke into song. The night Jesus was born, the angels sang. The night Paul and Silas were in prison, after they had been beaten and placed in stocks, they sang praises to God at midnight. In the same situation, I'd likely be complaining or floundering in deep depression.

The last book of the Bible, Revelation says, "And they sung a new song, saying, Thou art worthy to take the book, and to open the seals thereof" (5:9). John added, "I beheld, and I heard the voice of many angels round about the throne and the beasts and the elders: and the number of them was ten thousand times ten thousand, and thousands of thousands" (v. 11). What were they doing around the throne? They were singing, "Worthy is the Lamb that was slain to receive power, and riches, and wisdom, and strength, and honor, and glory, and blessings" (v. 12).

From Genesis to Revelation is a continual song. Music is at the heart of our faith in God.

I. *David held in his hand the power of the harp.* I want us to go back now to the days of Saul, King of Israel. He was a moody person. Of course that's characteristic of all of us. Each of us has periods of depression and elation.

So his advisors said, "We should do something about these periods of depression that come on Saul. Maybe we can employ a musician, someone who can come into his court and, when this evil spirit of depression falls on him, play for him and make him feel better."

So they secured a young man by the name of David, a sheepherder, a poet, and a singer. Then, when King Saul had these periods of depression, David would play and sing for him and the king would feel better.

Music has the ability to change our emotions or to evoke memories that have long laid dormant in our minds. It has tremendous power to touch and move us emotionally. That's why they brought David in to play for Saul. But there came a day when the music stopped, and there's always a risk that a time will come when the music stops for you and me. There's always a chance the music will stop in our churches. I don't mean we'll stop singing hymns, but we'll stop having music and joy in our hearts.

II. *King Saul held in his hand the power of the javelin.* There's also the danger that music will stop in our homes, that it will cease in our communities or in our nation.

There was a day that the music stopped as far as the relationship of Saul and David was concerned, and it did so because of jealousy. Here's how it happened:

A giant, Goliath, in the Philistine army challenged the Israelites by saying, "I'll fight any man you send me." No one volunteered. I don't think I would have volunteered either. Then strangely David volunteered. His father had sent him to visit his brothers who were in the army and take them some food and gifts. He had no armor, sword, javelin, or anything like that. When David volunteered, "I'll fight the giant Goliath," it was a great joke. The other soldiers just laughed and laughed and laughed. It was so funny.

There's a moral here, and Jesus said it in the Gospels, "They that take up the sword shall perish by the sword." Goliath had taken up the sword and he died by the sword. Later, Saul was to do the same thing.

After a great military victory there's a parade. So, as the armies came marching back into the city, the women were singing and dancing in the streets. They made up a new song, which was beautiful to the ears of David but not to Saul. It went like this: "Saul has slain his thousands, and David his ten thousands" (1 Sam. 18:7).

And when word came to the ears of King Saul, it was not music but a threat, for if the women were singing the praises of David in the streets, the time might come when David would take Saul's throne. So Saul decided he must get rid of David. The next time David came into his room to play for him, Saul reached for his javelin, pulled back with all his might, and threw it at David, meaning to pin him to the wall. Fortunately David was fast enough that he sidestepped, and we can hear in our imagination the javelin as it landed with a thud in the wall. That was the day the music stopped. Anytime envy and jealousy and animosity and hatred get the upper hand in your life and mine, that's when the music stops.

If you're like me, you live part of the time by the javelin and part of the time by the music. There are days when we take matters into our own hands and say, "I'm going to get what I want and I don't care who gets in the way and I don't care who gets hurt."

There are also times we use the power of the music, which symbolizes kindness and forgiveness. May God help all of us to depend more on the power of music rather than on the power of the javelin.

Now, at your disposal and at my disposal today is the power of the javelin, which King Saul held in his hand. There's also the power of the harp, which David held in his hand. In our imaginations we see the two at a standoff, there in that room in the palace, as David plays on his harp and Saul fingers the javelin. Somehow the spirit of greed and jealousy got the upper hand and the javelin won and the music stopped.

The music will also stop in your life and mine, in your marriage and mine, in your family and mine, in your church and mine, on your job and mine, whenever we stop to pick up the javelin, because Jesus said, "They that take up the sword shall die by the sword."—Robert J. Hastings[6]

SUNDAY, JUNE 22, 2003
Lectionary Message

Topic: What's the Bottom Line?

TEXT: Mark 4:35–41

Other Readings: 1 Sam. 17:(1a, 4–11, 19–23) 32–49; Ps. 9:9–20, 133; 2 Cor. 6:1–13

It is impossible to have a telephone these days without being harassed by unsolicited calls. Salespeople telephone at all hours (but most often at mealtime), trying to persuade you to subscribe to a local newspaper, have aluminum siding put on the house, support a particular charity, or whatever. One of the most irritating things about these interruptions is how long such callers take to get to the bottom line. They try to come across as your friend, addressing you by your first name and asking how you are. This is followed by a lengthy description of the product, service, or "free" offer, often including tantalizing details to deflect your attention from how much time they're taking. Only if you allow them to give their entire sales pitch do you find out what it will really cost you: what the bottom line is.

I. *A Gospel quick to get to the bottom line.* The author of Mark's Gospel would never make it as a telephone solicitor! Even though the book contains much material in common with Matthew and Luke, the distinctive mind-set and concerns of the author come across vividly.

---

[6]*Award-Winning Sermons,* Vol. 3, edited by James C. Barry (Nashville: Broadman Press, 1979), pp. 49–58.

Here is a narrator who cuts to the chase. From the opening line of this Gospel—"The beginning of the Gospel of Jesus Christ, the Son of God"—we know what the writer's agenda is. He stakes a claim—that Jesus is the Son of God—and lets us know he will be telling us the good news about this assertion. Mark tells us of the early ministry of Jesus in rapid-fire fashion. In the first five chapters, the word *immediately* is used at least fifteen times to describe the action. We may also note that a greater percentage of this book is devoted to the events of Holy Week through Easter than any of the other Gospels. All of Jesus' ministry points toward his Passion, death, and Resurrection. The Passion is foretold the first time just halfway through the book.

II. *The bottom line in the calming of the sea.* The traditional way of dealing with the miracle story recounted in today's Gospel is to focus on storm versus calm. We apply it to our own lives by constructing a typology: Just as Jesus calmed the storm on the Sea of Galilee, so also can the Lord calm the storms in our own lives. We acknowledge the disciples' fear—a reflection of their uncertainty as to whether Jesus cared or would do anything. Then we exhort one another to have faith and trust that Jesus will do for us what he's done for others.

While this interpretation of the text is familiar and comforting, I believe it turns a blind eye to Mark's agenda and the "bottom line" in this Gospel. You see, the framing of this miracle story is similar to the framing of four miracles that precede it; that is, Mark regularly uses a closing statement to focus the listener's attention on his primary purpose, announced at the start of the book. For instance, after Jesus' first miracle, the writer records the crowd saying, "With authority he commands even the unclean spirits, and they obey him." After Jesus healed the paralytic, the crowd glorified God and said, "We never saw anything like this!" After another healing, the Pharisees held counsel as to how to destroy Jesus. And after Jesus healed many (3:7–12), the unclean spirits confessed that he was the Son of God. In other words, Mark does not just tell comforting stories. Nor does he seem to have much interest in the details of the lives of those who were healed. Rather, he demonstrates who Jesus is: Son of God, sovereign over all creation, Savior of the world, worthy of praise and worship. The disciples on that boat were filled with awe, and their amazement was directed toward Jesus, not at the sea, and not at their feelings of relief. They realized that they were face to face with someone more powerful than a storm, mightier than the sea. They were with the Lord of all that is. In the years that followed, they worshiped Jesus, not his miracles.

III. *What's the bottom line for our faith?* The Savior to whom wind and sea are subject is certainly able to calm the storms in our lives. Most Christians can give grateful testimony to times they believe God has intervened in their particular circumstance. Such witness can build up the community of faith. But we would do well to emulate Mark's telling of stories, that is, to say less about ourselves and more that points with urgency to the truth of who Christ is. If it appears we claim discipleship because of what marvelous things Jesus has done for us, we're not that different from the crowds to whom he said, "Truly, you seek me not because you saw signs but because you ate your fill of the loaves" (John 6:26). "The signs" reveal the bottom line: that Jesus Christ is Lord and therefore worthy of our worship.—Carol M. Norén

ILLUSTRATIONS

TRUE PRAISE.   Arthur Gibson, a theologian who analyzed the films of Ingmar Bergman, wrote about *Winter Light,* a film whose central character is a troubled pastor. In one soliloquy the minister confesses, "I became a clergyman and believed in God. An improbably, entirely private, fatherly God. Who loved mankind, of course, but most of all me. . . . A God who guaranteed me every imaginable security. Against fear of death. Against fear of life. . . ."[7] Gibson exhorts the pastor (and his own readers) against such a self-serving, self-absorbed faith with these words: "The only acceptable and redemptive doxology is *gratias agimus tibit propter magnam gloriam Tuam*—we give thee thanks, not for any good thou mayst will to usward but simply because thou art so beautiful."—Arthur Gibson[8]

A MODEL FOR WITNESS AND PRAISE.   A sixteenth-century Latin hymn provides a model for Christian witness and praise. Like the author of Mark's Gospel, the hymn writer acknowledges gratefully what God has done for him, but his bottom line for praise is that it be because of who Jesus Christ is: worthy of our worship.

> My God, I love thee not because I hope for heaven thereby,
> Nor yet because, if I love not, I must forever die.
> Thou, O my Jesus, thou didst me upon the cross embrace;
> For me didst bear the nails and spear and manifold is grace.
> Then why, O blessed Jesus Christ, should I not love thee well?
> Not for the sake of winning heaven nor of escaping hell.
> Not with the hope of gaining aught, not seeking a reward,
> But as thyself hast loved me, O everlasting Lord.
> So would I love thee, dearest Lord, and in thy praise will sing;
> Because thou art my loving God and my eternal King.[9]

SERMON SUGGESTIONS

Topic: When You Least Expect It
TEXT: Gen. 28:10–17
(1) God may visit you. (2) God may change the direction of your life. (3) God may give you a new sense of meaning and purpose for your life.

Topic: The Two Ages
TEXT: Rom. 5:12–19
(1) The reign of death in the age of Adam. (2) The triumph of life in the age of Christ.

CONGREGATIONAL MUSIC

1. "Sing Praise to God, Who Reigns Above," Johann J. Schütz (1675); trans. Frances E. Cox (1864)

    MIT FREUDEN ZART, *Bohemian Brethren Hymnal* (1566)

    This strong old Anabaptist hymn breathes the spirit of Psalm 9 and could well be sung as a response to the Psalter reading.

---

[7]Ingmar Bergman, *A Film Trilogy* (New York: Orion Press, 1967), pp. 84–85.
[8]*The Silence of God: Creative Response to the Films of Ingmar Bergman* (New York: HarperCollins, 1969), p. 102.
[9]Latin, seventeenth century; translated by Edward Caswall, 1849, in Reuben Jon, chair, Hymnal Revision Committee, *The United Methodist Hymnal* (Nashville: United Methodist Publishing House, 1989), no. 470.

2. "The Battle Is the Lord's," Margaret Clarkson (1960)

   LEONE, synagogue melody; arr. M. Lyon (1770)

   David's words of confidence in God as he prepared to fight Goliath are the theme of this modern hymn. Naturally it could either precede or follow the Old Testament reading.

3. "Just as I Am Without One Plea," Charlotte Elliott (1834)

   WOODWORTH, William B. Bradburg (1849)

   This familiar hymn, usually confined to a time of invitation and response to the preached Word, relates specifically to the apostle Paul's rehearsal of his hardships in the Epistle lesson (2 Cor. 6:1–13). This is true especially of stanzas 3 and 4, which could be highlighted by being sung by a soloist, with the congregation singing the other stanzas.

4. "Eternal Father, Strong to Save," William Whiting (1860)

   MELITA, John B. Dykes (1861)

   The story of Jesus calming the storm, recorded in the Gospel lesson (Mark 4:35–41), could be effectively responded to by the quiet singing of this traditional hymn for "those in peril on the sea."—Hugh T. McElrath

WORSHIP AIDS

CALL TO WORSHIP. "How beautiful upon the mountains are the feet of him that bringeth good tidings, that publisheth peace; that bringeth good tidings of good, that publisheth salvation; that saith unto Zion, thy God reigneth" (Isa. 52:7).

INVOCATION. Our Father, all of us here are enjoying in manifold ways the blessing of the good news from the mouth of your Son and from the many who have loved and served him across the ages. Help us in our day to be voices of peace and salvation for the multitudes who need you.

OFFERTORY SENTENCE. "For ye know the grace of our Lord Jesus Christ, that, though he was rich, yet for your sakes he became poor, that ye through his poverty might be rich" (2 Cor. 8:9).

OFFERTORY PRAYER. O God, with the self-giving of Jesus as our example, we bring our offerings to you, realizing that we can never measure up to what he has done, but challenged to give more of our very selves in our stewardship. Receive what we bring, we pray, and use it for your glory.

PRAYER. So often, Father, we find ourselves walking in the dim light of our own misunderstanding, failing to rise to the heights of your purpose for us, and questioning the many circumstances that invade life. We are so driven by emotions that we lose our sense of reason. Pain comes to meet us and we panic. Death invades our bungalow and we are blinded by its searing sorrow. Loss meets us along the way and we feel abandoned. Devious actions come to light and we feel betrayed beyond repair. A child is born and we are filled with exaltation. A promotion comes and we find ourselves rejoicing in our good fortune. Some great gift long-desired is given and we are thrilled. In a thousand ways we are driven by the varied emotions that fill our days and haunt our nights.

Thank you, Father, that we can feel, that we can run the gamut of emotion, and in the wake of its powers make discoveries that will guide us into more usefulness to your purpose in us. This morning give us all the light we need to walk by, so we will not stumble when the stress of emotions dims our senses and clouds our vision. Let what we feel become a stepping stone rather than a stumbling block, as we commit all that we are, feel, and experience to you for your care and keeping and use.

Be especially this morning with those who have had to manage death's visit this week. Comfort them in their loneliness, strengthen them in their sorrow, and kindle hope in their hearts as they rebuild life around an empty place. Then we ask that you be with those who are working hard to make changes in their lives, so they can be better citizens, better family members, and better followers of Jesus. Give them the fortitude and courage to struggle on, even in the face of momentary desires to fall back into old destructive patterns. Make them whole again, Father, that they may glorify your name and power.

Keep us all in the hollow of your hand, we pray, that we may not stray into evil's camp nor become willfully lost in the jungle of demands that are not in keeping with your holy will. Bless us now in this hour with your presence, and call us to you in commitment and service, in Jesus' name.—Henry Fields

SERMON
Topic: The Ministry of Sickness
TEXT: 2 Cor. 12:5–10

Volumes have been written about "the thorn in the flesh." What was it? What was the nature of the sickness to which Paul refers so vividly in this letter? Was it epilepsy? Some are sure that it was, and turn to the seizure that accompanied his conversion for supporting evidence. Others are convinced that it was a nervous disorder, which would now be called a "neurosis." Still others believe that it was some sort of physical disability that may have manifested itself in a slight impediment in his speech. So the scholars continue their guessing game.

The fact is that the question has never been answered, and never will be. We do not know what the nature of his sickness was for the simple reason that St. Paul never saw fit to tell us. All we know is that St. Paul lived a rugged life of travel despite the thorn in the flesh that constantly nagged him; that he had the mind of a giant and often behaved like a boy; that he survived hardship of every conceivable kind; that he was one of the decisive men in human history, the man who "turned the world upside down"; and that he thought the thorn in his flesh helped him do it!

The Bible is full of stories that tell of God's power to heal the sick, and when Jesus came, he came teaching and preaching, but it was his healing power that drew the crowds. As far as I know, this passage from St. Paul's letter is the only place in the Bible where we find a man who uses his sickness to enlarge and intensify his work and understands it to be not a curse but a blessing.

For instance, you may realize for the first time the wonder of the human body—how complicated it is, how delicate it is in its incredible craftsmanship, how its muscles are so deftly put together and how miraculously the nervous system transmits messages to the brain, how mysteriously the different parts are meshed—the mind and the body yoked together, both driven by the yet more mysterious spirit. You may turn to Psalm 139 and say, "I will give thanks unto thee, for I am fearfully and wonderfully made."

Instead of complaining about the present discomfort that may interfere with the operation of your body, you will be grateful for the time it worked so well. If you can't see as well as you once did, you will be thankful that you once had two good eyes.

As you think it may dawn on you that you are not quite so indispensable as you thought you were. You are the mother of three small children; you can't be sick, there is no one to look after them. You *are* sick; someone *does* look after them. You are the head of a business firm; there are decisions to be made and no one can make them without you. You *are* sick; the decisions *are* made and the business goes on.

You suddenly realize that although you are not unimportant, you are not indispensable. The world was here before you came into it, and hopefully it will be here long after you have left it. You may have a decisive role to play in it, but if you are forced to drop out of the cast for a while, the show will go on; and even if you should never return, someone else would take your part.

It may be an important part of the ministry of sickness to cut you down to size.

If you can think this far, you may go on to think about other sick people: how many there are, in and out of hospitals; how many are worse off than you (strange comfort this thought gives us!). You may begin to participate in the largest of all human fellowships: *the fellowship of sufferers.* You may think first of people you know: they are not in any pain that you can observe; they are stricken with no disease; they are well and able-bodied. But you will know that there is more than one kind of sickness, that they are suffering behind a closed door. If this is true of people you know, think of the millions you do not know.

As you begin to wonder why, you may turn instinctively to Jesus, and see perhaps for the first time that he suffered all the way. His family didn't understand him; the people in his hometown didn't want him there; the men he chose to work with him were often incredibly stupid; his critics called him a glutton and a drunkard; his friends deserted him when he needed them most; he was left alone to die between two criminals.

You say, why is life like that? How can it be like that? You turn to him for an answer, but he never answers your question. In fact, he never asked it! That one loud cry from the cross, "My God, why?" is the only time he hinted at the question. But suppose he had not suffered; suppose he had gone along a way as smooth as silk, had an easy time of it all the way. Do you think you would ever hear of him now?

This is all part of the ministry of sickness: to introduce you to the *Wider Fellowship of Creative Sufferers,* to make you more aware of yourself and other people—more sensitive, less self-centered, more tenderhearted, more open on more fronts, more tolerant of weakness, and less tense about the future.

The next time you are sick—whatever the sickness may be—ask yourself this question: Is it possible that this sickness can minister to me? If it can, Lord, don't let me miss it.

O Lord, make me well and strong; but if this be not thy will, help me to use my weakness
to strengthen others; and if this be not thy will, in my weakness let me lean on thee. Amen.
—Theodore Parker Ferris[10]

---

[10]*Selected Sermons* (Boston: Wardens and Vestry of Trinity Church, 1976), pp. 127–132.

SUNDAY, JUNE 29, 2003
Lectionary Message

Topic: New Life?

Text: Mark 5:21–43

Other Readings: 2 Sam. 1:1, 17–27; Ps. 130; 2 Cor. 8:7–15

There is a neighborhood on the south side of Chicago with so many railroad tracks—some at street level—that it is called Grand Crossing. The most direct route from point A to point B may be through Grand Crossing, but many drivers avoid the area. The likelihood of being stopped by a train or encountering a rough pair of tracks is great. Truck traffic in the neighborhood has created more potholes than usual. Yes, it is possible to drive through Grand Crossing without any difficulty; it just isn't easy.

This portion of the 5th chapter of Mark reminds me of Grand Crossing. There's a lot happening here. Like those freight trains, it contains interesting and valuable cargo. But there is so much in these verses that can slow us down or frustrate our understanding that it is tempting to avoid them altogether.

I. *Questions about new life.* If we're going to be honest with the text and with ourselves, we have to acknowledge the difficulties in this story of new life. Two miracles take place in a story within a story: a woman is healed by touching the hem of Jesus' robe, and the dead daughter of Jairus is restored to life. But the account raises all kinds of questions in an attentive reader.

For instance, Jesus tells the woman that her faith has made her well, but there is nothing to suggest that the daughter of Jairus had faith. Did the faith of Jairus make his daughter well, and if so, what are the implications for faith working wonders for a third party?

This is the only healing story that notes Jesus' perception that power had gone forth from him; we might even say it was snatched without his permission. How are we to understand that power?

A third potential difficulty is the resemblance of this account of raising someone to life to other such stories in the Bible, such as Peter raising Tabitha in Acts 9, and Elisha raising the Shunammite's son in 2 Kings 4. If the story follows a formula, is the author framing it intentionally, and how does that shape our understanding?

A lesser issue is the significance, if any, of the number twelve in the story. The woman was ill for twelve years, and the daughter of Jairus was twelve years old. Is there a connection between the two that we have lost?

Preachers with feminist sensitivity may be troubled by the fact that the male characters in the story are named, but the female characters are not, except in connection with a man.

And last but not least, what should we make of the notation in verse 40 that Jesus put everyone out of the room and closed the door? If he did that, how did Mark or anyone else know what happened behind the closed door?

II. *Answers about new life.* A person driving through Grand Crossing *can* reach his or her destination in spite of road hazards and slow-downs. So also can we reach the good news in this story if we keep our focus on what it *does* answer for us.

I believe that there are two primary lessons to be derived from Mark's account. The first is that new life comes in many forms to people who encounter Jesus. For the woman with the issue of blood, new life meant being made whole and being restored to the community that had no doubt shunned her because of her "unclean" illness. New life meant the possibility of financial recovery; after all, the text says she had spent all she had in seeking a cure. What is more, new life meant being given peace by Jesus Christ, who commended her for her faith and addressed her as "daughter"—a term of regard and intimacy.

New life for the daughter of Jairus meant being released from a terrible sickness, and more. Her new life was restoration of the earthly existence she had known before, as was also the case for Lazarus when our Lord raised him from the tomb. This should not be confused with new life in the sense of resurrection of the body (the imperishable body described by Paul in 1 Corinthians 15), which is a qualitatively different thing. We can also imagine new life for that child in the sense that from then on her parents would tell her the story of the wonderful thing the Lord of Life had done for her. Faith in him would be inculcated. His name would be praised.

And there would be new life for all who witnessed the healing of the woman with the issue of blood or heard of the raising of Jairus's daughter. They had known the woman sick; now they knew her clean. They had seen the little girl dead; now she was alive. These actions would naturally evoke amazement and be retold countless times. The witnesses lives would be irrevocably changed by seeing and hearing what Jesus had done for others.

III. *Promises for us about new life.* A second lesson in this text is what it reveals to us about our Savior. His character is revealed in this passage, and it hints at the new life available to us through him. Mark is not suggesting that Jesus will restore any and all of the dead to life as he did the daughter of Jairus. But he does depict a Messiah who does not turn anyone away. We may come to Jesus in faith, whatever our need, and trust him to be merciful and gracious. We may be confident that God's will is ever directed toward his children's good. We may know that even death is subject to him and will not have the last word. No matter what slows us down, causes us to stumble, or threatens to throw us off track, new life through Christ is available here and now, and he can bring us to our heavenly destination.—Carol M. Norén

ILLUSTRATIONS

A SACRED MYSTERY.   Why did Jesus close the door when he healed the daughter of Jairus, when he had done so many other miracles publicly? Why did Simon Peter do the same when he restored Tabitha to life? Perhaps it is an echo—or a foreshadowing—of the mystery of resurrection life described by Paul in 1 Corinthians 15. He says, "Lo! I tell you a mystery. We shall not all sleep, but we shall all be changed." The nature of new life is a sacred mystery, a secret we could not perceive even if it occurred in full view. We understand now in part, but someday we shall know fully, even as we have been known fully.—Carol M. Norén

PRESISTENCE.   Jairus was surrounded by well-meaning people who might have kept him from witnessing the power of Christ. Jairus had made his petition to Jesus and was waiting for our Lord to act when people from his house came and told him it was too late. They even chided Jairus for "troubling" the Teacher any further. Jairus heeded Jesus' words of encouragement—"Do not fear, only believe"—even when a crowd of mourners wailed loudly and laughed at Jesus' promise. Once the miracle occurred, the wailing stopped. We hear no more from these people.

The faith of Jairus is an encouragement to us to be persistent in prayer, keeping our attention fixed on the Savior rather than on those who urge us not to expect too much. Nothing is impossible with God!—Carol M. Norén

SERMON SUGGESTIONS

Topic: An Uneven Match

Text: Gen. 32:22–32

(1) *Situation:* Jacob unwittingly wrestled with God. (2) *Complication:* Though Jacob was strong, he was no match for his opponent. (3) *Resolution:* Jacob lost the bout but won a new name, a high mission, and the blessing of God.

Topic: What Your Baptism Means

Text: Rom. 6:3–11

It signifies and seals (1) your union with Christ, (2) your putting away of a life dominated by sin, (3) your aliveness to God and his will for your life.

CONGREGATIONAL MUSIC

1. "Out of the Depths, I Cry," Ps. 130; vers. *The Psalter* (1912)
   SANDON, Charles H. Purday (1860)
   Use this paraphrase of Psalm 130 instead of reading the original. It could be effectively sung in line-by-line alternation by two singing groups.
2. "Immortal Love, Forever Full," John G. Whittier (1866)
   SERENITY, William V. Wallace (1856)
   This quiet hymn of discipleship and witness could well accompany the Gospel lesson describing instances of Jesus' healing ministry. The stanza that begins with "the healing of his seamless dress" refers specifically to the woman who touched Jesus' garment to be healed.
3. "O Love, How Deep, How Broad," anon. Latin (15th century); trans. Benjamin Webb (1854)
   PUER NOBIS, Trier Mss. (15th century)
   In its grand sweep of his life, death, and Resurrection, this hymn is appropriate for focusing on Jesus' self-sacrificing love, referred to by the apostle Paul in 2 Cor. 8:9. Singing this ancient hymn to its fifteenth-century tune could appropriately follow the Epistle reading.
4. "When Jesus Wept," *New England Psalm Singer* (1770)
   WHEN JESUS WEPT, William Billings (1770)
   A Christian parallel to the lament of David for Saul and Jonathan in the Old Testament reading is expressed in this poignant four-part canon by early American composer William Billings. If a canon performance is not desired, it can be sung straight through in unison.—Hugh T. McElrath

WORSHIP AIDS

CALL TO WORSHIP.   "If we say that we have no sin, we deceive ourselves, and the truth is not in us. If we confess our sins, he is faithful and just to forgive us our sins, and to cleanse us from all unrighteousness" (1 John 1:8–9).

INVOCATION.   Gracious God, cleanse our thoughts and our hearts of anything that would keep us from hearing what you would say to us today through the hymns, the prayers, and the proclamation of your Word. Forgive us our sins, as we confess them to you, and grant to us the peace that you can give us.

OFFERTORY SENTENCE.   "I am not trying to relieve others by putting a burden on you; but since you have plenty at this time, it is only fair that you should help those who are in need. Then, when you are in need and they have plenty, they will help you. In this way both are treated equally" (2 Cor. 8:13–14 CEV).

OFFERTORY PRAYER.   O God, what we are able to give differs from time to time, yet you receive and bless what we bring. Guide us as we learn the ways of responsible stewardship, and guide us as your people in the use of these offerings for the various causes that need our help.

PRAYER.   Our Heavenly Father, Creator and Sustainer of all things, we acknowledge thee as the ultimate source of our lives and of all the good that we know. After the long and painful struggles of our forebears for survival through the ages, we are here. We sometimes wonder why we are here, and what shall be the outcome and contribution of our poor lives. So we look to thee, our Creator and our Father, to speak to the questions for which we shall never know the complete answers. We ask thee only to reply in faith strengthened, hope renewed, and love deepened.

With the passing of the years, we know that what we are outwardly is perishing. Give us, we pray, a continual renewal of what we are or can be inwardly. Grant that the ministry of new friends, new ideas, new challenges, and new experiences may all contribute to this inner renewal, so that each day's living will be a testimony to the truth that old things have passed away and the new has come.

SERMON
Topic: What Is Your Greatest Obstacle?
TEXT: Gen. 4:1–7; Rom. 7:15–25a

What is your greatest obstacle? The one thing that most keeps you from being the person you know you should be and that you would like to be?

Some of us might say that our greatest obstacle is our socioeconomic status; that is, the fact that we were not born wealthy. We may blame our lack of wealth for keeping us from becoming the person we would like to become.

But that's not really an argument, because some of the world's greatest leaders were born poor. Abraham Lincoln is a good example. Lincoln was born as poor as poor could be. Yet he pulled himself up by his own bootstraps, overcame adversity and defeat, and became one of America's greatest presidents.

An even better example is Jesus, who was born into a poor peasant family and spent his early years in a carpenter's shop. More than any other, Jesus is the one who changed the world. So economic status seems not to be viable as our greatest obstacle.

Others of us might cite our lack of good looks as our greatest obstacle in becoming the person we would like to become. But the apostle Paul is said to have not been very pleasant to look at, perhaps because of a debilitating eye disease.

Still others might refer to a physical handicap as the one thing that is keeping them from being the person they would like to be. But numerous persons with handicaps could be cited who lived extraordinary lives—Helen Keller (who was both blind and deaf), Franklin D. Roosevelt (who suffered the effects of polio), and again the apostle Paul, who had some physical problem that he referred to as "a thorn in the flesh."

So the lives of great men and women would seem to indicate that none of the things we might cite—lack of wealth, lack of good looks, physical handicap—is really our *greatest* obstacle in becoming the person we would like to become.

According to the apostle Paul, the one thing that kept him from being the person he really wanted to be was inside him, his own self-will, the carnal nature that led him to do things he really didn't want to do. Listen to what Paul has to say: "I do not understand my own actions. For I do not do what I want, but I do the very thing I hate. . . . I can will what is right, but I cannot do it. . . . The evil I do not want is what I do. . . . When I want to do what is good, evil lies close at hand" (Rom. 7:15, 18, 19, 21).

Can anyone identify with that? You know what you want to do, and you know deep in your heart what you should do, but your own human nature—what psychologists might call "the self"—leads you to do something else. Thus you end up choosing the lesser good, and failing to be or become the person you would like to be.

Paul refers to this inner force that leads us to do contrary to what we would like as the power of sin or evil. How do we overcome this power of sin within us, or the evil inclination to do what we know deep in our hearts we should not do?

In the Scriptures we read we heard two approaches. The first we read in Genesis in the story about Cain and Abel. Abel was a shepherd and Cain was a farmer. The story goes that Abel's offering to God was accepted, whereas Cain's offering to God was rejected. Why? This is one of those passages that have always troubled me. There are a number of explanations. First, back in those days there was tension between shepherds (who tended to be nomadic) and farmers (who tended to be settled). Perhaps the writer of Genesis was shepherd-biased. Second, maybe the offering Cain presented to God was blemished or rotten fruit and that is why it was unacceptable. Or maybe Cain's attitude or motive was wrong.

At any rate, Cain became angry and melancholic. The Lord is credited with saying to Cain, "Why are you angry? If you do well, will you not be accepted? And if you do not do well, sin is lurking at the door; its desire is for you, but you must master it" (Gen. 4:6–7). In other words, Cain had within himself the ability to overcome the temptation and power of sin and do what was right—if he chose to do so. The only thing keeping Cain from doing what was right and becoming the man he was destined to become was himself. Of course we know that Cain failed the test. He misplaced his anger and rose up against his brother, Abel, and in a jealous rage killed him.

The apostle Paul had a much less optimistic view than what we read in Genesis. "Wretched man that I am!" Paul exclaimed. "Who will rescue me from this body" of sin and death? "Thanks be to God through Jesus Christ our Lord!" In other words, Paul felt he needed help to overcome the sinful self within him so he could become the man he knew he should be.

Perhaps a balanced approach to our life is a blending of the two views, in that with the help of God we can overcome the weak or sinful self that would keep us from becoming the persons we know we should be and would like to be. Perhaps the old adage that "God helps those who help themselves" has never been truer.

Our greatest liability, our greatest enemy, our greatest obstacle in becoming the persons we would like to be is not our lack of wealth or good looks, or a physical disability, or some other crutch. It is ourselves. But with the help of God we can change and enable ourselves to become the persons we know deep in our hearts we should become.—Randy Hammer

SUNDAY, JULY 6, 2003
Lectionary Message

Topic: Strength in Weakness
TEXT: 2 Cor. 12:2–10
Other Readings: 2 Sam. 5:1–5, 9–10; Ps. 48; Mark 6:1–13

For years I have remembered the story of a young girl who had been blind from birth. Her blindness caused her to be protected from life to such an extent that she developed a child-like, sentimental picture of the people around her.

One day she underwent surgery. Her eyes were opened and she could see. Two things immediately impressed her. One was that nature was more beautiful than she had ever imagined—the light, the shades, the colors were magnificent. The other was this: the faces of people were sadder than she had expected.

She perceived quickly what an old Scottish preacher frequently reminded his congregation: "Be kind, for everyone you meet is fighting a hard battle." And Virgil, the Roman poet, in an immortal phrase, spoke about "the tears of things."

Pain, suffering, heartache, and disappointment are endemic to the human journey. If one lives long enough, hardship and grief are inevitable. The apostle Paul, in first-century Palestine, wrote of his own dark and difficult journey in his second letter to the Corinthians, but learned one critical lesson through it all: "for whenever I am weak, then I am strong" (v. 10). What could Paul mean by this strange paradox? Chapter 11 and the first ten verses of chapter 12 catalog the pain and suffering the apostle experienced as a minister of the Lord Christ. Because of this suffering and the courage and endurance it took to work through it, Paul had every reason to boast. But Paul's boasting, he insisted, was on behalf of Christ, whose power and grace were the sustaining factors in Paul's risky venture of witness.

One of the most powerful examples of the power and presence of the living Christ in the darkest of times has been Paul's famous personal reference to his thorn (or stake) in the flesh. Though we are unable to identify precisely his great pain (whether eye disease, malaria, epilepsy, severe headaches, sexual temptation, or something else), we do know it was such a distraction for Paul that he begged God simply to remove it. Paul's prayer was not answered in the manner he had hoped it would be, but it was answered nonetheless. God's answer was clear and unmistakable: "My grace is sufficient for you," Paul, "for my power is made perfect in weakness." Here in one succinct sentence is captured the heart of the Christian faith: in the power and presence of the Resurrected Christ, we are gifted with God's grace for the forgiveness of sin, for courage to keep on against all odds, for peace and assurance that all will be well, for love, wonder, and laughter yet to come.

The apostle Paul and believers throughout the centuries, even to this good hour, have discovered that when we reach our limits, when we confess our weakness and our brokenness, God's gifts of *trust, courage,* and *compassion* are released and surface from deep within us. "My grace is sufficient . . . for my power is made perfect in weakness," says the Lord. Among the many gifts of God's power and grace, consider these:

I. There comes to us the power to *trust.* To believe, really believe, that God has released forces for healing and wholeness, love and peace in this universe for all God's creation is difficult to grasp and accept. We have always been taught to take control of our lives, to be aggressive, to seize the day, to be responsible—all of which make it virtually impossible to let go, to trust. Impossible, that is, until we are forced to our knees and made to feel helpless in the face of heartache, pain, and suffering.

Life was pretty routine and free of severe threat for our family until January 1, 1990, when we received a phone call from the Peace Corps in Washington, D.C., that our twenty-five-year-old son had been in a serious automobile accident in his host country, Lesotho (southern Africa). This near-fatal accident called his mother and me to his bedside for five and a half weeks in Bloemfonteine, South Africa, and we were able to do nothing more than talk, sing, and pray with him. We felt absolutely helpless to fix this strong, muscular young man now broken and clinging to life. We did the only thing we could do in our weakness and pain—we let go. We had no control of the situation and we began to place our trust and hope in the Lord to heal him and to heal us in whatever way that might be possible. The reality of the apostle Paul's words rang true for us in the midst of this vigil and in the subsequent healing of this son: "whenever I am weak then I am strong." God's grace was indeed sufficient, a power made perfect in our weakness.

II. In our weakness, God promises the gift of *courage.* Who of us has not been witness to those brave souls who, in the face of tragedy, pain, and loss, have found the will to move forward without becoming broken and embittered spirits? And who of us has not also known the person who through his or her pain and suffering has reached out in service to comfort the grieving, to lift the despairing, to challenge the bored. The temptation to retreat, to withdraw from the fray, to seek the simple life—no pressure to get involved, no psychiatric couches, no great anxieties, no expectations of high potential, just back to the good life—is always there. It is what playwright Eugene O'Neill called "Ah, Wilderness." The lure of the wilderness is strong.

We are learning, however, slowly but surely, that if we do not exercise the moral courage and creative will to address poverty and hunger in this nation and abroad, and if as nations, races, and people of faith we do not join forces against war, disease, and injustice, then this world may self-destruct. God knows we're not very good at this, and in the end we may not succeed. But maybe, just maybe, if enough of us remain faithful and resolve to make a difference where we are, our very courage emerging from the dust of pain and suffering may give God a fresh opening to the world, a new channel to someone's heart. "Give me courage, O Lord, even in my weakness."

III. In weakness, God graces us with *compassion.* Nothing makes us gentler, more tender, more kind and understanding of others than personal heartache and disappointment. Furthermore, few words are more descriptive of God's grace and the life and work of our Lord than compassion. Thornton Wilder has a three-minute drama based on the Gospel story of the Pool of Bethesda called "The Angel That Troubled the Waters." The chief character is a doctor who is himself sick with a wound he cannot heal. In desperation and weariness he goes to the pool for healing, when the water is stirred by an angel. As he starts forward, the angel stops him and says, "It is your very remorse that makes your low voice tremble into the hearts of men. The very angels themselves cannot persuade the wretched . . . children on Earth as can one human being broken on the wheels of living. In Love's service only the wounded soldiers can serve."[1]

The depth of learning that comes to us in our suffering and grief has always amazed me. We discover what's really important in this journey, how to reorder our priorities, the value of loved ones and friends, a receptivity and openness to each new day, and the sustaining power and presence of God when God has seemed most distant and silent. Personal growth and wisdom and empathy become so much more rich when we can identify with our fellow strugglers. Pain and suffering humanize us.

"All sunshine makes a desert," someone wrote. Pain and suffering in partnership with Christ is no desert. It is life, rich and full!—David D. Burhans

ILLUSTRATIONS

THE POWER OF SUFFERING.   Because Jesus was willing to die, a new community could form in his name, one that has redefined its life on the basis of his death. One of the main points in that redefinition has been a new view of suffering. It is no longer something to be avoided at all costs, nor does it mean that God is mad at us. It might in fact mean that God loves us very much, because when someone on a path toward God deliberately chooses the self-offering that goes with that path, then suffering becomes one of God's most powerful tools for transformation. It is how God breaks open hard hearts so they may be made new. It is how God cracks open closed lives so they can get some air into them again.—Barbara Brown Taylor[2]

ON SUFFERING.

> I walked a mile with Pleasure,
> She chattered all the way;
> But left me none the wiser
> For all she had to say.
> I walked a mile with Sorrow
> And ne'er a word said she;
> But oh, the things learned from her
> When sorrow walked with me.

—Robert Browning Hamilton[3]

---

[1]Rex Burbank, *Thornton Wilder* (New York: Twayne, 1961), p. 25.
[2]*God in Pain* (Nashville: Abingdon Press, 1998), p. 64.
[3]Quoted in William Sloan Coffin Jr.'s sermon, *Alex's Death*, January 23, 1983, p. 4.

SERMON SUGGESTIONS

Topic: Hints of a Better Kingdom

TEXT: 2 Sam. 7:1–17

(1) A place of peace. (2) A responsible ruler. (3) A Kingdom forever.

Topic: Is Weakness Anything to Boast About?

TEXT: 2 Cor. 12:1–10

(1) An extraordinary experience (vv. 1–3). (2) An appropriate silence (vv. 4–6). (3) A redeeming weakness (vv. 7–10).

CONGREGATIONAL MUSIC

1. "Sing Praise to the Father," Margaret Clarkson (c. 1964)

    TO GOD BE THE GLORY, William H. Doane (1875)

    This modern Trinitarian hymn would be useful for a worship service in which God's power is magnified in the Scripture readings.

2. "Great Is the Lord Our God," Ps. 48; vers. *Psalter Hymnal* (1987) and *Psalter* (1887)

    TERRA BEATA, trad. Eng. melody; adapt. F. L. Sheppard (1915)

    A fine paraphrase of Psalm 48 that would be appropriate for opening worship, this hymn could be sung by alternately reciting and singing the five stanzas: sing stanza 1, recite stanza 2, sing stanza 3, recite stanza 4, sing stanza 5.

3. "Jesus, Thou Divine Companion," Henry Van Dyke (1909)

    PLEADING SAVIOR, *The Christian Lyre* (1830)

    This early twentieth-century hymn that magnifies Jesus' humanity as a worker at Nazareth would be an admirable introduction to the Gospel lesson (Mark 6:1–13).

4. "How Firm a Foundation," Kim Rippon's *Selection* (1787)

    FOUNDATION, *The Sacred Harp* (1844)

    This sturdy hymn, sung heartily, would be meaningful in connection with the apostle Paul's reference to his hardships and the sufficiency of God's grace (2 Cor. 12:2–10).—Hugh T. McElrath

WORSHIP AIDS

CALL TO WORSHIP.   "Lord, who shall abide in thy tabernacle? Who shall dwell in thy holy hill? He that walketh uprightly, and worketh righteousness, and speaketh the truth in his heart" (Ps. 15:1–2).

INVOCATION.   Lord our maker, accept our gratitude today for the freedom of worship we enjoy in this country and the liberty of soul we enjoy in Christ Jesus. Help us to merge the two in a winsome and brave faith that meets culture with the demands of Scripture and with the love that acknowledges that God was in Christ reconciling the world unto himself.—E. Lee Phillips

OFFERTORY SENTENCE.   "But this I say: he which soweth sparingly shall reap also sparingly; and he which soweth bountifully shall reap also bountifully" (2 Cor. 9:6).

OFFERTORY PRAYER.   Lord, we who have much and share little pray for a reformation in our stewardship that shares much and therefore has even more to share, as does God with those who pray.—E. Lee Phillips

PRAYER.   O loving Father who dost everlastingly stand outside the closed doors of the hearts of men, knocking ever and again, wilt thou now give me grace to throw open all my life's doors? Let every bolt and bar be drawn that has hitherto robbed my life of the air and light of love. Grant to each of us the grace to pray: "Give me an open ear, O God, that I may hear thy voice calling me to higher ground. Too often have I been deaf to the appeals thou hast addressed to me, but now give me courage to answer, "Here am I, send *me.*"

Give me an open mind, O God, a mind ready to receive and to welcome such new light of knowledge as it is thy will to reveal to me. Let not the past ever be so dear to me as to set a limit to the future. Give me courage to change my mind when it is needed, that my Christian experience may be a continual growing and maturing. Give me open eyes, O God—eyes quick to discover thine indwelling in the world which thou hast made. Let all lovely things fill me with gladness and let them lift up my mind to thine everlasting beauty. Forgive all my past blindness to the grandeur and glory of nature, to the charm of little children, to the meanings of relationships, and to all the intimations of thy presence which these things contain.

Give me open hands, O God—hands ready to share with all who are in want the blessings with which thou has enriched my life. Thou whose love goes out to all people, we come now to identify ourselves with thee in thy great love-purpose: we pray for the world, our Father. May our concern be helpfulness and not anxiety. We pray for all the world—the lands we know but also those other lands that stand within our minds as nothing more than names. Each of them is thine, and all the people in them are thy children; and for all of them we pray that life may be their lot and not death, peace and not war.—John Thompson

SERMON
Topic: Cain
TEXT: Gen. 4:1–6

"So Cain was very angry and his countenance fell" (Gen. 4:5 RSV). In the ancient story of Cain and Abel we come face to face with "the mystery of iniquity." It's true that sin has already been introduced into the biblical epoch, in chapter 3 of Genesis, where Adam and Eve have their disastrous encounter with the serpent. We could also say that the first fundamental rupture in the divine-human relationship was far more tragic than Cain's murder of his brother, because it introduced envy, mistrust, and bad faith into our common history and put a curse on all subsequent generations. It set the stage for Cain's homicide, and all the other horrible things that have happened since. Adam and Eve lost their innocence, blamed each other, and became estranged from the natural world, of which we and they are still a part, like it or not. "Cursed is the ground because of you; in toil you shall eat of it all the days of your life; thorns and thistles it shall bring forth for you" (Gen. 3:17–18 NRSV).

So the Genesis 3 narrative portrays the infinitely tragic taproot of sin. But the saga of Cain and Abel in Genesis 4 makes our blood run cold in incomparable fashion. Envy, malice, and bad faith result in this: that we would destroy the very image of God, and our very own mirror image, as it appears in our *brother!* Though human history is scarred with genocides, holocausts, and lynchings, we persist in branding the taking of human life as horrible, and for the most part consider ourselves incapable of it. Anything but that! Large-scale occurrences of murder—whether in irrational genocide or "just" wars—create massive denial or other psychological coping mechanisms, and we are morbidly fascinated when "ordinary" people cross this taboo. How else to explain our fascination with the O.J.s and the Timothy McVeighs among us?

We are shocked and offended when Jesus lumps us all together as murderers in principle as he says, "You have heard it was said to those of ancient times, 'You shall not murder'? And 'whoever murders shall be liable to judgment.' But I say to you that if you are angry with a brother or sister, you will be liable to judgment" (Matt. 5:21–22 NRSV).

Simply and starkly put, the mystery of iniquity—as expressed in this most horrible of acts—begins with an attitude, with a disposition. "Cain was very angry, and his countenance fell" (Gen. 4:5 NRSV).

In spite of the preeminent importance that Western culture has assigned to the individual, we all stand or fall together. Our language, our values, our faith are all a function of our life together. Genesis 1 tells us that we are made in God's own image, and God in our Christian understanding is a triune God, that is, a *social being* to the very core. And so are we. When we acknowledge and accept this truth, then our love for ourselves is positively connected to our love for our neighbors. "You shall love your neighbor as yourself" (Matt. 19:19 NRSV). When we resist this truth, sin breaks out. One way of understanding Adam and Eve's sin is as a refusal to accept any limits on their self-assertion or their self-importance. That same refusal has deadly consequences in Cain's disposition toward Abel. "The Lord had regard for Abel and his offering, but for Cain and his offering he had no regard" (Gen. 4:4–5 NRSV). "How dare he receive any consideration or approval that I haven't," Cain thought.

Every childish sinner is the center of his or her own universe. But if we trust God and regard our connectedness with our neighbor positively, then our neighbor's success or well-being or recognition doesn't diminish us. If we're all in it together, our neighbor's success enriches us. And our diligence at work, faithfulness in friendship, fidelity in marriage, loyalty to our church, and trustworthiness as friends are blessings to all around us. And our *prosperity* should be a blessing for our community, not something we selfishly hoard. That's one thing these offerings that Cain and Abel were making are supposed to signify: sharing multiplies blessing. Much of our economics, much of our competition among businesses, nations, and individuals, is based on the false premise of the "limited pie." There's only so much recognition, so much happiness, so many resources to go around. Cain labored under this tragic illusion, so his response to his brother's approval by God was, "Whatever you get diminishes me."

But when we plug into God's infinite resourcefulness, we experience the multiplier effect of God's grace. After all, God is love—*agape* in the Greek—the sort of love that is overflowing, abounding blessing. When we are the center of our own universe, then we forget that every life is unique and precious before God, including the life of another race, another culture, another faith—even our enemy's life. Many Bible scholars believe that the story of Cain and Abel reflects the age-old struggle between pastoral societies—herdsman, like the Israelites—and agriculturists, like many of the Canaanites. The self-centered person resents and fears difference, and denies the other person's worth. (This happens between cultures and nations as well.) When we deny another person's precious value, we find ourselves manipulating, using, and deceiving that other person for our own pleasure or prosperity. We "objectify" them. "How much can I get from him? How can I use her?" And we have taken the first incremental steps toward wishing that person dead.

The ancient Israelites had no developed doctrine of the afterlife, so wishing somebody dead—explicitly or implicitly, by the way they belittled or disrespected them—meant wishing them *nonexistent* now and forever, even in God's sight. This is *sin*, in its awful, monstrous reality. The wish begets the act, as Jesus reminds us. Cain is all of us to the extent that we let sin have its way. Ironically, to be *free*—as we must be to reflect God's own image—is to be able to sin or, by God's grace, not sin. "Sin is lurking at the door; its desire is for you, but you must master it" (Gen. 4:7 NRSV). The very opposite of sin's death wish is to wish blessing, accomplishment and recognition, importance and value and success for *everyone*— as God our Creator does.

Are we Cain's envy-ridden children? Or are we truly *God's* children? God's love and concern extends even to a murderer!

Cain said to the Lord, "My punishment is greater than I can bear. . . . I shall be a fugitive and a wanderer on the Earth, and anyone who meets me may kill me." Then the Lord said to him, "Not so! Whoever kills Cain will suffer a sevenfold vengeance." And the Lord put a mark on Cain so that no one who came upon him would kill him (Gen. 4:13–15 NRSV).

God's love and concern extend even to a murderer. How about ours? What are the boundaries of our love?—David L. Wheeler

SUNDAY, JULY 13, 2003
Lectionary Message
Topic: Wonder, Laughter, and Thanksgiving
Text: 2 Sam. 6:1–5, 12b–19
Other Readings: Ps. 24; Eph. 1:3–14; Mark 6:14–29

One of my favorite little books over the years has been *Laughing Out Loud and Other Religious Experiences,* by Tom Mullen.[4] It has been a favorite because it captures the essence of a joyful faith and because it serves as a much-needed corrective to anyone who thinks of Christianity as dour, heavy, joyless, and severe. There is no desire here to minimize the awesome demands of Christian discipleship, but there is always a need to let our faith dance and sing and shout.

Three thousand years ago, the spirit of joy and thanksgiving was a vital part of Hebrew life and worship. The Old Testament is full of feast days and celebrations, and the Psalms are a collection of songs and poems that have become a "smoldering volcano of praise." One of the classic events of joy and celebration in Hebrew history is the fascinating account of King David escorting the ark of God to Jerusalem. In ancient Israelite religion, the ark of God was a sacred object (box or chest) that represented the presence of God. The transport of this ark

---

[4]Richmond, Ind.: Friends United Press, 1989.

to Jerusalem was an important event in the life of King David and of great significance in the life of the Hebrew people. David became instrumental in establishing Israel as a nation of power and prestige, and it seemed clear to the Hebrew people that God's hand was at work in all of this. The return of the ark to Jerusalem, therefore, was highly symbolic of God's providence and was cause for great joy and celebration. Regardless of David's motivation (perhaps both political and religious), he was compelled to mark the occasion with music and dancing and shouts of praise. The Hebrew people, King David, and Biblical history invite all of us in succeeding generations to celebrate the high holy moments in our lives and in the life of our churches with *wonder, laughter,* and *thanksgiving.*

I. *The gift of wonder is life giving!* The Israelites were beginning to dream of a new and glorious day—a day when Yahweh would bring Israel to great power and prosperity among all the nations of the Earth, fulfilling God's promise to Abraham, "I will make of you a great nation." The Hebrew people gave evidence of growing awe and wonder at their good fortune and at the renewed promise of a bright future under the leadership of King David and the watchful eye of Yahweh. It is in times like these that we become so much more aware of the many ways God's grace attends us, sustains us daily, carries us through all our days.

The truth is we take the daily wonders of the world for granted until someone or some experience stops us in our tracks and says, "Look! Listen! Stay alert!" Looking into the face of a newborn; putting one's arms around a mate who has been there for you ten, twenty-five, forty, fifty years; catching a sunset; hearing the noise, laughter, and word-making of little children; doing work that is meaningful; having a friend who listens; watching the rain fall after a drought; feeling deep peace in the midst of strife and great joy and excitement, as did David and his people at the prospect of a new day and the hope that the best was yet to be are but a few of those awe-inspiring moments. All of these times remind us that life itself is a miraculous journey and a wonder to behold.

Human exploration and study have probed thousands of secrets and nature's mystery until we humans may be losing our propensity for wonder. Moments of quiet retreat and serious reflection, however, may open the deepest recesses of our hearts and minds and reveal again the glory of life and love and the beauty of all God's creation.

II. *Few things refresh us as laughter does,* and we are impoverished believers if we miss the spirit of joy and laughter reflected in biblical history. Leonard Sweet wrote, "If one does not laugh or at least smile when reading Scripture fairly regularly, . . . one is missing the point."[5] It doesn't take much imagination to reconstruct the scene of joy, even ecstasy, fun, and laughter in the processional parade as the ark of God moved toward Jerusalem. Whether King David led this procession of the ark to Jerusalem as a calculated way to receive the support of Israel's "old guard" and the legitimization of his royal regime, or as an attempt to identify a holy symbol around which the tribes and clans of Israel could become unified, the truth is that this was a time for joy, laughter, and celebration, and David seemed to have been caught up in the moment.

I know of few things that are more heart cleansing, stress reducing, and refreshing than

---

[5]Leonard I. Sweet, *Health and Medicine in the Evangelical Tradition* (Harrisburg, Pa.: Trinity Press International, 1994), p. 69.

laughter. There is even a common understanding that laughter is an effective antidote to illness and disease. Laughter and good humor give us a healthy perspective on life's daily journey and on ourselves. The ability to laugh at ourselves provides protection against all kinds of pompousness and self-righteousness and is valuable in creating intimacy and gratitude in relationships, especially in our families and in the Church.

III. *There is no more appropriate way to respond to the Creator, Redeemer, Sustainer God than with praise and thanksgiving.* This spirit of gratitude is surely part of what inspired David to do his dance of ecstasy before the Lord. The high holy moments in the life of Israel were invariably marked by joy and thanksgiving. And so it is with us.

Someone years ago suggested to me that gratitude may be the acid test of spiritual maturity. The capacity to acknowledge one's dependence on the living God not only as Creator but also as Redeemer and Sustainer reveals a healthy balance of humility, trust, and personal confidence that one is not in this alone but greatly loved and fully accepted as a worthy part of God's creation.

The old Latin proverb, "One person is no person at all," suggests that we are incomplete apart from interaction with others, apart from the socialization that occurs when we respect and appreciate the presence and gifts of others who inform, instruct, stretch, and affirm us as fellow travelers. We are creatures of relatedness, and for that we give thanks.

It was especially fitting for David to worship God with praise, gratitude, and burnt offerings when the ark of God was brought to Jerusalem. This ancient symbol of God's presence no doubt evoked memories of the long, arduous journey of the Hebrew community from exodus to nationhood, from wilderness to Jerusalem, from slave people to free people led and blessed by the hand of God. Hebrew worship was a time of thanksgiving.

We, the people of God, are often compelled to retreat from the world to offer praise and gratitude to God for the blessings of our days, for the gift of healing and health, for daily wonder at the sounds and sights and expressions of love that attend us, for a peace and trust that runs deep within us in the face of all that challenges and threatens, for laughter and good humor, for food and rest and work and play.

I am grateful to God for a faith that sings and dances and knows how to celebrate, for ancestors in the faith who knew wonder, laughter, and thanksgiving.—David D. Burhans

ILLUSTRATIONS

THANKSGIVING.   Many years ago, in a little eastern town in Tennessee, a mother was about to give birth to her first child when the doctor informed her that some complications had developed. The doctor said to the mother, "I don't think I can save the life of the baby and also save your life. The baby may die."

The mother said, "Oh, doctor, if a choice has to be made, please let me die and let my baby live."

The father overheard the conversation and moved in and said, "Doctor, save my wife, and if the baby dies, we'll have to deal with that."

The mother cried and pleaded and finally said, "Take a chance on my life." Finally they decided to take the chance. The baby lived, but the mother died. That week in the county newspaper an editorial was written about the experience. It was entitled, "To What Purpose?" The editor wrote, "This week in our county a mother died so that her unborn son might live. It was a noble gesture of motherhood, but was the sacrifice worth it? The boy may grow to manhood and be a liability to society; certainly he will never appreciate the sacrifice his mother made. It was a noble gesture of motherhood, but was it worth the sacrifice?"

Fifteen years passed and had you been in this county cemetery you would have heard an iron gate open and seen a boy of fifteen walk through that gate, kneel beside a grass-covered mound, reach inside his jacket, and pull out a yellowed newspaper clipping and read the story about himself and his mother. You would have seen tears roll down his face and heard him pray, "O God, make me the kind of man I ought to be so that my mother will not have died in vain."

The young man went to college, attended seminary, and devoted his life to proclaiming the good news of Christ.—Griffin Henderson's story, told by my father, R. S. Burhans

LAUGHTER.   All of us ought to be ready to laugh at ourselves because all of us are a little funny in our foibles, conceits, and pretensions. We are rather insignificant little bundles of energy and vitality in a vast organization of life. But we pretend that we are the very center of this organization. This pretension is ludicrous, and its absurdity increases with our lack of awareness of it. The less we are able to laugh at ourselves, the more it becomes necessary and inevitable that others laugh at us.—Reinhold Niebuhr[6]

SERMON SUGGESTIONS

Topic: The Dream and the Reality
TEXT: 2 Sam. 7:18–29
(1) David dreamed of an everlasting kingdom bearing his name (vv. 18–19). (2) However, only the Kingdom of God is eternal (Rev. 11:15).

Topic: Our Destiny in Christ
TEXT: Eph. 1:1–10
(1) To be holy and blameless before God the Father. (2) To be his children, forgiven by his grace. (3) To share in God's secret plan of the ages.

CONGREGATIONAL MUSIC
1. "Lift Up Your Head, O Gates," Ps. 24:7–10; vers. Bert Polman (1986)
   VINEYARD HAVEN, Richard Dirksen (1974)
   This contemporary version of a part of Psalm 24 set to a fine twentieth-century tune would be an exciting song for the opening of worship. A choir could sing the stanzas, with the congregation responding on the joyous refrain.
2. "To God Be the Glory," Fanny J. Crosby (1875)
   TO GOD BE THE GLORY, William H. Doane (1875); or
   "My Tribute," words and music, Andraé Crouch (1971)
   Either of these songs, both of which incorporate the idea of glorifying God, would be appropriately sung in connection with the Epistle lesson (Eph. 1:3–14), in which the apostle Paul repeats his theme, "to the praise of his glory."

---

[6]*Discerning the Signs of the Times* (New York: Scribner's, 1946), pp. 119f.

3. "The Earth Belongs to the Lord," Ps. 24:1–6; adapt. Hal H. Hapson

  SING, BELIEVERS, Hal H. Hapson (1985)

  The first six verses of Psalm 24 are skillfully paraphrased in this contemporary setting. Again, the refrain could be sung by the congregation, with the stanzas taken by a choir or a group of soloists.

4. "The God of Abraham, Praise," Thomas Olivers (c. 1770)

  LEONI, Synagogue Melody; arr. M. Lyon (c. 1770)

  The rejoicing and singing of David and the people of Israel at the bringing of the ark up to Jerusalem (2 Sam. 6:1–5, 12b–19) can be reflected in the exuberant singing of this great Hebrew hymn.—Hugh T. McElrath

WORSHIP AIDS

CALL TO WORSHIP.   "Delight thyself also in the Lord, and he shall give thee the desires of thine heart" (Ps. 37:4–5).

INVOCATION.   Exalted and gracious Lord, lead us in this hour, that we may respond as never before and find the meaning we have so long sought through the struggles that shape our faith.—E. Lee Phillips

OFFERTORY SENTENCE.   "Every man according as he purposeth in his heart, so let him give; not grudgingly or of necessity: for God loveth a cheerful giver" (2 Cor. 9:7).

OFFERTORY PRAYER.   Lord of life, lead us through Christ Jesus from a sense of self to a state of selflessness that enlarges through giving.—E. Lee Phillips

PRAYER.   O God, you have taught us to pray for one another, to give thanks, to confess, to intercede. You have taught us in the prayers of Scripture and of the saints and in the prayed lives of all faithful people.

Hear us, then, as we turn to you. Where we ask wisely and in faith, grant us our petitions. Where we ask foolish things, be kind. Where we sadly omit, fill in. Where our deepest-felt words Godward are between the lines, listen carefully. For ours is not a praying age and we are not a deeply praying people.

Hear our prayers of thanksgiving: for many good spirits that give us strength; for strong ties of human caring; for families that are very close; for people whose quiet humor clears the air; for persons enthusiastic about life, themselves, and all that is decent and fine; for the rare gift of common sense.

Hear our prayers of supplication, O God. Our best is flawed, incomplete. Only by your light do we see light. In the best of lives there is another side and much to tell. Without your mark of mercy, our burden is more than we can bear. Hear us, then, and help us. We confess, O God, that we are too busy; that we are set in our ways not only of good but of wrong and of half-heartedness; that physical illness troubles us more than spiritual illness; that we say and do awful things to one another and hurt one another deeply and regularly.

Hear, O God, our prayers of intercession. Hear and help us in caring for one another. We pray, O God, for loved ones in nursing homes, for those ravaged by old age, "bare ruined choirs where late the sweet birds did sing"; for persons looking for work; for persons lonely, depressed, and angry; for all undertaking some new thing.—Peter Fribley

SERMON
Topic: The Shadow of the Almighty
TEXT: Ps. 91

In the parched desert lands of the Bible, the adversarial relationship to the sun was a well-understood fact of human life. Shade and water were both friend and colleague in the continuing struggle to defy the elements and survive.

It is not surprising to learn that in this overheated land the psalmist employs beautiful imagery that envisions the protecting God as a sheltering shade. We read such lyrical phrases as "Hide me in the shadow of your wings" (Ps. 17:8). It is variously speculated that this figure of speech may have been suggested by the wings of the symbol of the Egyptian sun god; or by the wings of the cherubim, the creatures mentioned in Isaiah's vision; or more simply by the protecting wings of a mother bird. "In the shadow of your wings I sing for joy" (63:7). This is part of a midnight meditation by the psalmist on his bed, reflecting God's unfailing mercy and help throughout the years, and his joyful hopes for the future. "The Lord is your shade on your right hand. The sun shall not smite you by day, nor the moon by night" (121:5–6). These familiar words are part of a pilgrim song. We have no way to reconstruct the actual situation, but we are helped by the imaginative words of a biblical scholar who reflects on the entire short psalm and reconstructs this picture for us.

The sheltering presence of God in the hearts of the faithful, both then and now, is capable of producing an exuberant faith that bursts forth in song, for ours has long been a singing faith. "You who dwell in the shelter of the Most High, who abide in the shadow of the Almighty, will say to the Lord, 'My refuge and my fortress; my God, in whom I trust'" (1:1–2).

Note that the faithful dwell in the presence of God. They are not occasional visitors but familiar residents. In our time they would love the Church, the community of the faithful, and share regularly in its life, not just at Christmas and Easter. Prayer would be as familiar as breathing. The Bible would be cherished as a treasure for living and becoming. Theirs would be not just the religion of crisis time, when the tornado winds blow or the Earth trembles or the company downscales and the job disappears or death makes its visitation. For all of these times—yes!—for God is always ready to be a very present help in time of trouble. But the eternal presence is also there for the quiet work in the woods, the frantic time of traffic on the freeway, the moment of quiet desperation, the unhappy time when cherished plans go awry, the instant of the knock at the door, and the entrance of the guest who only awaits the hospitality of the expectant heart.

The psalmist notes that they who dwell in the shelter of the Most High will find not only peace and quiet and joy. It will be more than just a safe haven, a place for reflection and meditation. It may become a refuge, a fortress, in preparation for the coming struggle. The life of faith offers no guarantee against adversity; this is the lesson of Job and Jesus, and the testimony of our own experience. The cult that tries to make happiness and feeling good the ultimate objective of faith is guilty of denying the reality of sin, temptation, difficult choices, the straight and narrow way, sacrificial love, and the centrality of the cross in the Christian story.

David Livingstone had every reason in the world to stay quietly at home in Scotland and worship his God in a cultured and dignified manner. But this is what early on he said about himself: "I will place no value on anything I have or may possess except in its relation to the Kingdom of God. Anything I have will be given or kept according as giving or keeping it I shall most promote the Kingdom of my Savior."

List your heroes, the people who have made a difference, and ask yourself how many of them made the list by living the "good life" of ease and privilege, devoid of the call of duty and a sense of personal and public responsibility. Remember the great Polish statesman and musician-composer Ignace Paderewski? He was credited with saying, "It is a gentleman's first duty to put back into the world at least as much as he has received from it." To live with such a lofty sense of duty puts one in the good company of Christian heroes like David Livingstone, Wilfred Grenfell, Toyohiko Kagawa, Albert Schweitzer, and Martin Luther King Jr. All of them, in the language of the psalmist, could be said to "dwell in the shelter of the Most High, and abide in the shadow of the Almighty."

Joseph R. Sizoo, distinguished American clergyman of an earlier generation, wrote of the precious gift of serenity that comes to those who "abide in the shadow of the Almighty," and his words may add to our understanding of the incredible calmness that our Lord displayed in that upper room with his disciples on the night of their last supper together, just before they went to the Garden and he was betrayed into the hands of his enemies. Sizoo has written, "Serenity comes to those who live with unfaltering faith in an unfailing God. Those who live with eternity in their hearts will find a strange calm in their spirits."

Although we are centuries and worlds removed from the psalmists who made their remarkable contributions to the literature of the Old Testament, may we be open to receive the same Spirit as did these pioneers of the faith who were said to "dwell in the shelter of the Most High and bide in the shadow of the Almighty." Amen.—George W. Hill

SUNDAY, JULY 20, 2003
Lectionary Message

Topic: A New and Open Humanity
TEXT: Eph. 2:11–22
Other Readings: 2 Sam. 7:1–14a; Ps. 89:20–37; Mark 6:30–34, 53–56

It is fascinating how throughout biblical history God has worked with the Hebrew people and the followers of Jesus to reveal his redemptive plan of salvation. Perhaps there was something unusual about these people. Apart from the fact that they seemed to be a people of destiny, they often spoke of their love affair with Yahweh and with this Jesus of Nazareth, who captured their imaginations. But there must have been something else at work here, some characteristic that distinguished them from other people.

Among other things one could mention, they may have had an innate ability to trust, or perhaps they were people of unusual courage or people of high sensitivity to spiritual things. In the final analysis, however, this observer wonders if, of all their positive attributes, it wasn't their capacity for adventure, openness, and change that would serve God best in the end. They were, for the most part, people who were able to let God be God and let God's Spirit lead them into new truth and help them find new ways to order their lives.

The letter to the Ephesians is one of those writings that describes a new day for early

Christian believers, a new humanity emerging on the scene—one that would respect and embrace differences among the world's citizens and unite all humanity under the Lordship of Christ. More specifically, the second chapter of Ephesians explains this new humanity as having been shaped by the peace of Christ. In Christ, who is our peace, God has made Jew and Gentile into one and has destroyed forever the dividing wall of hostility between them (vv. 14–16). Unity, respect, and collaboration under the leadership of God's Spirit, rather than nationalism, culture, and religion, would become the defining characteristics of God's people.

I. *To the people of first-century Palestine, the challenge was clear: you are people of intelligence; open your minds to new ideas.* God offered a second covenant to his people based on this great idea: *grace!* This concept was a serious threat to tradition, to the old laws. There are no laws for salvation in this new idea, just the dazzling, unmerited love of God. This dynamic, freewheeling grace in Jesus Christ broke down all kinds of barriers (race, class, gender, age) and proclaimed to every age, to every culture, "Come, everyone who thirsts; come to the waters" (Isa. 55:1).

There is something rather frightening about the closed mind—something that can manifest itself in religious fanaticism, lust for power, and racial purity or white supremacy, which kill and destroy. But there is a perversion that is more subtle still: the businessperson who cuts corners and obsesses on the bottom line; the athlete; the school; the Little League team that must win at any cost; the theologian who thinks that right doctrine will redeem the world; or the religionist who thinks that he or she can explain for all how the Holy Spirit leads and instructs. But grace doesn't seek to control or set narrow limits. Grace is able to let be. Grace respects another's freedom and affirms another's experience and sample of life. Grace is broad and inclusive.

The open-minded person is not someone without fixed points. To the contrary, he or she can say with Paul, "I know whom I believe and I am persuaded that God will keep that which I have committed to him until that day" (2 Tim. 1:12). But the open-minded believer will examine and maybe challenge fixed ideas and established structures whenever there is potential for the gospel to move more freely through the world. The open mind in concert with Christ leads to new truth, to greater possibilities for love and justice and peace. We must be open to new ideas.

II. *In Christ we are flesh and blood creations and must be open to others.* This was precisely God's call to the followers of Jesus, to the apostle Paul, and to the early Church: "Break down the walls that separate, open the doors of the Kingdom; Jesus Christ has created a new humanity and has brought reconciliation to all groups that have been separated."

Division, discord, and animosity increase in our splintered and fractured world. Rather than looking for ways to be open to new friendships and partnerships in our communities, groups of people look for ways to organize and protect their own kind. Somehow we must examine our motives, move beyond our comfort zones, and remember, "The presence of community does not mean the absence of differences."

I continue to be enamored with the diversity of people Jesus gathered around him. Not only women and men, but also the likes of Simon the zealot and Matthew the tax collector. Both were Jews but they couldn't have been more different. Simon was the defender of tradition, the super-patriot of Hebrew ways and zealous for the Jewish nation, while Matthew was the practical man, the compromiser, the collaborator with Rome, the tax collector. Potential for conflict and animosity was always present. But Jesus was first and foremost a uniter, a reconciler. This was his mission: to bring all creation together in harmony and peace, to reconcile all creation with God. Thus, our challenge in families, churches, and neighborhoods is to be open to others, to respect and somehow embrace difference among us in the name of our Lord, for the sake of God's reign of justice, love, and peace.

III. *Finally, we are new creations in Christ and must remain open to the Spirit who will lead us into new paths of service and witness for the Lord Christ, who will help us see the holy all around us.* The public opinion polls in our land continue to suggest that America is a religious nation. Many polls show that in America more than 90 percent of U.S. citizens believe in God. This is a rather staggering figure when one realizes it is difficult for that many people to agree on what day of the week it is. We are a religious people. On the other hand, these polls also show that a dramatically smaller number of people believe that God has any personal connection with them or would ever consider God's will when making a moral or ethical decision.

In contrast, the disciple of Christ who is open to the Spirit is one who is alive to the power and presence of God in daily life, who lives with a clear sense of the sacred. Jesus declared that if you and I love God, this one who is like a father and mother will make a home in us (John 14:23). Amazing! This Creator God of the Universe, this God who could easily get along without us, has not only fashioned a world for us, but has chosen to live in us, to enliven us with the Holy Spirit, to help us see the holy all around us: holding a newborn, seeing your child being baptized or being baptized yourself, crying tears of repentance, attending a high school or college graduation, getting married, having somebody with you when you're sick, sharing a mealtime with people you love, and having a mother and father (my own) who have modeled joyfully and authentically for their sons, daughters-in-law, and grandchildren this simple but profound faith:

> The stars shine over the Earth,
> The stars shine over the sea.
> The stars look up to the Mighty God,
> The stars look down on me.
> The stars will live for a million years,
> For a million years and a day,
> But Christ and I will love and love,
> When the stars have passed away.[7]

Open to ideas, open to others, open to the Spirit—these define the life in Jesus Christ and call us to a holy partnership. Then we are no longer strangers and aliens, but citizens with the saints and members of the household of God (v. 19).—David D. Burhans

ILLUSTRATIONS

OPEN TO THE HOLY.   All religions and philosophies that deny the reality or significance of the material, the fleshly, the Earth-bound are themselves denied. Moses at the burning bush was told to take off his shoes because the ground on which he stood was holy ground

---

[7]Author unknown

(Exod. 3:5), and incarnation means that all ground is holy ground because God not only made it but walked on it, ate and slept and worked and died on it. If we are saved anywhere, we are saved here. And what is saved is not some diaphanous distillation of our bodies and our Earth but our bodies and our Earth themselves. Jerusalem becomes the New Jerusalem coming down out of heaven like a bride adorned for her husband (Rev. 21:2). Our bodies are sown perishable and raised imperishable (1 Cor. 15:42).

One of the blunders religious people are particularly fond of making is the attempt to be more spiritual than God.[8]

OPEN TO OTHERS.   Our presiding bishop was with us and we spent all day Saturday talking with him about the issues confronting the Church and the world: the hamstrung economy, family values, human sexuality, the growing number of poor people, the challenges faced by our youth. We talked honestly and from the heart. We expressed vast differences. We listened carefully to one another. No one booed anyone else, and there was a lot of applause. A sense of mutual respect for one another pervaded our long day of dialogue—perhaps because we prayed together morning, noon, and night—and I think it is fair to say that we all came away with a sense that God was with us, and is with us, in all our differences and struggles.

There is a time-honored saying in the Anglican Church that schism is worse than heresy. What that means is that it is okay for us to disagree and it is even okay for some of us to be way, way out of line as far as orthodox theology is concerned; but what is not okay is for us to let go of one another.—Barbara Brown Taylor[9]

SERMON SUGGESTIONS

Topic: A King Sins
TEXT: 2 Sam. 11:1–15
(1) The temptation (vv. 2–3). (2) The sin (v. 4). (3) The consequences (v. 5). (4) The cover-up (vv. 6–15).

Topic: No Longer Stranger
TEXT: Eph. 2:11–22
(1) Because of peace through Christ's cross. (2) Because of unity through the Spirit. (3) Because of God the Father, the end and goal of life and worship.

CONGREGATIONAL MUSIC
1. "Glorious Things of Thee Are Spoken," John Newton (1779)
   AUSTRIAN HYMN, Franz J. Haydn (1797)
   Newton's great hymn magnifying the trustworthiness of God in all God's promise would be an excellent introduction to the Old Testament reading having to do with God's promise to David (2 Sam. 7:1–14a). It could also function well for the opening of worship.

---

[8]Frederick Buechner, *Wishful Thinking* (New York: HarperCollins, 1973), p. 43.
[9]*God in Pain* (Nashville: Abingdon Press, 1998), p. 79.

2. "My Song Forever Shall Record," based on Ps. 89; vers. *Psalter* (1912)

    WINCHESTER NEW, *Musikalishes Hand-buch,* Hamburg (1690)

    This strong song of praise based on Psalm 89 would be appropriate with the Psalter reading.
3. "Christ Is Made the Sure Foundation," Latin hymn (c. 17th century); trans. J. M. Neale (1851)

    REGENT SQUARE, Henry T. Smart (1867)

    This ancient hymn of affirmation and praise is appropriate with reference to the Epistle reading (Eph. 2:11–22) in which Christ is spoken of as the chief cornerstone of the spiritual dwelling in which all are one.
4. "Your Hands, O Lord, in Days of Old," Edward H. Plumptre (1866)

    ST. MICHAEL'S, W. Gawler's *Hymn and Psalms* (1789)

    Here is a hymn that focuses directly on the healing ministry of Jesus and as such would be suitable to sing in connection with the Gospel lesson (Mark 6:30–34, 53–56).—Hugh T. McElrath

WORSHIP AIDS

CALL TO WORSHIP. "Finally, brethren, whatsoever things are true, whatsoever things are honest, whatsoever things are just, whatsoever things are pure, whatsoever things are lovely, whatsoever things are of good report; if there be any virtue, and if there be any praise, think on these things" (Phil. 4:8).

INVOCATION. Lord of all, renew our minds. Stir our souls. Deal with us justly. Let us listen openly and respond wholeheartedly to the entreaties of the divine.—E. Lee Phillips

OFFERTORY SENTENCE. "And God is able to give you more than you need, so that you will always have all that you need for yourselves and more than enough for every good cause" (2 Cor. 9:8 TEV).

OFFERTORY PRAYER. Eternal God, accept our prayers as tokens of our struggling faith. Show us your grace in the daily beneficence that crowns our existence with ease and comfort. Make our suffering an exercise in doing "unto others as we would have them do unto us" if we lived in their situation and they in ours. Forbid to us either an arrogance that believes we deserve the special favors we enjoy, or the indifference that allows us to turn away from the moment to share a needed gift. In these moments of sharing, make us good stewards of our abundance, and faithful messengers of Christ and his love in our time. We ask in Christ's name, but for all our sakes. Amen.—Paul D. Simmons

PRAYER. Disturb us today, Father, with a disturbing that will drive us to act right, change wrong, and protect holiness in places high and low. We have become comfortable in our lives and need a divine challenge to live worthily even when worthiness leads to discomfort and danger and demands costs of us that we have not been paying.

Disturb us about thousands who are being slaughtered in the name of ethnic cleansing. Remind us of the worth of every human being and give us the gumption to speak against those who would kill innocent women, men, and children because they are different from what is considered to be the norm in parts of the world. Disturb us about the killing fields of our cities and towns, where our children kill children and life is so cheap that to die young, before dreams are even dreamed, is the expectation. Disturb us about the teenage pregnancies and alcohol abuse and the ugliness of child molestation and all the other sins perpetrated by some human beings on others.

Disturb us about the complacency in the Church, where members are more loyal to social demands than to spiritual needs being fulfilled. Disturb us about the laxity of parental example for the young and the teaching of sound values and morals that undergird a strong society and nation. Disturb us about the business-as-usual attitude with which we approach doing church, and lead us to the discovery of an exciting joy in being a part of the family of God in this congregation.

Disturb us about the physical needs of those around us that can easily be met with a little caring on our part as Christian individuals and as a community of Christ's faithful.

Disturb us, Father, by opening our eyes to ourselves, that we may see our flaws, faults, and failures with painful plainness. Help us this morning to truly repent of our laxness and make the commitments that will reverse the tides that seem to sweep us into desperate places in every area of life. Let conviction and cleansing and conversion sweep through this assembled congregation today, that we might truly be disciples through whom Jesus can move powerfully to make a difference in lives and the world. We pray in his name.—Henry Fields

SERMON
Topic: A Matter of Priorities
TEXT: Luke 9:51–62

Jesus can be exasperating. Just when you think you have your life in order and are doing the right thing, he upsets the equilibrium.

That's just what Jesus expects of anybody who wants to follow him—the best. Just when we're ready to settle for what's good and right and completely proper, he confronts us with what's best and offers us a choice.

Jesus had made a choice. He had a successful ministry in Galilee, healing the sick and drawing large crowds when he taught. His work was good. But he chose to do something better. He chose to set his face to Jerusalem and the cross. Along the way he met three men. He offered each of them a choice between what was good and what was best.

One man was ready to follow Jesus, but he said, "Lord, first let me go and bury my father." You'd expect Jesus to say, "Oh, I'm sorry. When did he die? I understand. You have a responsibility to your family. When you're finished there, meet me down in Jericho." But there was not a word of sympathy. In fact, what he said sounds rather cold and harsh: "Leave the dead to bury their own dead; but as for you, go and proclaim the Kingdom of God."

Jesus' response wouldn't be so troubling to me if the man had said, "First let me go close my bank account," or "I've got theater tickets tonight. Let me use them first." But families are entrusted to us by God. The fifth commandment says, "Honor your father and your mother." Families are the cornerstone of society. Nowadays, the term "family values" is almost synonymous with Christianity. Conventional wisdom is that families should be our top priority. Jesus disagrees.

As important as our families are, Jesus asks to take priority over them. It's not that Jesus doesn't appreciate the importance of families. He was moved to compassion when a ruler of the synagogue asked him to heal his sick daughter. The apostle Peter made a special request that Jesus heal his ailing mother-in-law, which Jesus gladly did. As he was dying on the cross, Jesus made sure that his own mother Mary would be well cared for when he commended her to John. He wasn't cavalier about the importance of families or the responsibilities we have for them. But if anyone is going to follow him, Jesus has to come first.

The second man Jesus asked to follow him was concerned about what it would be like along the way. Who can blame him? We need to be sure we're going to be free from physical danger; that we will have food, shelter, and clothing tomorrow and the next day; that the future will be secure. Security is a good thing. It's one of the blessings God gives his people.

But Jesus calls anyone who would follow him to a kind of security that's different from a well-balanced investment portfolio or a warm, comfortable home. The security he offers is the security of knowing that the future is in God's hands. Jesus promises anyone who would follow him an eternal home, but in the meantime the kind of security that worries most of us has to take a back seat.

There was another man who wanted to follow Jesus, but for him the timing was bad. He hadn't had a chance to say goodbye to his friends. You can't blame him. It would be rude to go off for who knows how long to who knows where without even saying goodbye to the folks back home. But that wasn't good enough for Jesus. His reply to that man was, "No one who puts his hand to the plow and looks back is fit for the Kingdom of God."

There are lots of reasons to put off answering Jesus' call to follow him.

But Jesus' call to respond to the good news of the Kingdom isn't something we can put off. There's urgency to it, like the urgency of planting a crop at the right time. When the seeds have to be sown, they have to be sown. A farmer can't wait until he feels like it to sow his crop. There aren't that many days when the season is right and the weather is right and the soil is right. He doesn't have a lot of choice over when he can plant the seed.

When we put Jesus first in our lives, we discover that he doesn't deprive us of any of the basic things we need. He doesn't take away our families; he gives us what we need to love them more. He doesn't take away our security; he gives us a security greater than money can buy. He doesn't take away our goals in life; he makes our goals the same as his: the triumph of God and the glory of his Kingdom. When he calls us, Jesus asks that we give up some very good things—so he can give us something that's even better.—Stephens G. Lytch

SUNDAY, JULY 27, 2003
Lectionary Message

Topic: In Partnership with Christ
TEXT: John 6:1–21
Other Readings: 2 Sam. 11:1–15; Ps. 14; Eph. 3:14–21

This miracle of Jesus is the only one that has been included in all four of the Gospels. It is a critical event in the life of Jesus' Galilean ministry. It reflects something of the Lord's Supper in the early Church and reminds the reader of the countless ways God addresses the needs of his children throughout their earthly journey. So the common thread that runs through these stories is that when we align ourselves with others, we become a force to behold. When we do life with God, make our gifts and resources available to the Creative God of the universe, incredible things happen.

Nevertheless, I have a concern these days with the gnawing, demoralizing sense of inadequacy that threatens to seep into our lives in the course of the daily routine and the many faces of demand and difficulty with which we are confronted. We are savvy enough to know we could easily be overwhelmed by the enormity of our issues and the world's problems. The task of coming to terms with ourselves and our dreams, of learning we cannot run away from our gene pool, from who we are at the hands of parents, siblings, and other's expectations, is a daunting task. And wanting to make a difference in the gnarled and twisted human lives we touch out there tomorrow takes far more than just wishing for it.

Our situation is not all that different from that of the Israelite spies who were sent on a reconnaissance mission into Canaan in the time of Moses (3,200 years ago). You recall that the spies returned not only with tales about a land flowing with milk and honey but also with terror in their hearts because there were giants in the land. The majority report was clear: there was no way to claim this new land. The spies reported that when they saw the situation, "we seemed to ourselves like grasshoppers" (Num. 13:33). But two of the spies, Joshua and Caleb, brought in a minority report. We can possess the land, they said, because God delights in us and God is with us. Divine and human forces joined have an impact!

The disciples of Jesus were in a similar situation when faced with a crowd of people who were gathering around their Master. It was time to eat. "When Jesus looked up and saw a large crowd coming toward him, he said, 'Where are we to buy bread for these people to eat?'" (John 6:5). That's a reasonable enough question, but the disciples were stymied. Philip responded with the suggestion that there was simply no way they could buy that much bread with the resources they had. Andrew said hopelessly that there was a child there with five barley loaves and two fish but that wouldn't do any good. In short, the disciples were faced with a situation that was far beyond their meager resources. That is not unlike where we find ourselves today. Overwhelmed by need out there in the world and feelings of inadequacy within ourselves, we sit before this story and agree with the early disciples that our resources are inadequate.

Jesus then asked the massive crowd to sit down, and he took the loaves and the fish, offered a prayer of thanksgiving, and distributed them to the crowd. Andrew's question was the reasonable one: "What are they [the loaves and fish] among so many people?"

Surely we can identify with the disciples. But Jesus was not perturbed. He gave the bread to the disciples to distribute, and miracle of miracles, the crowd had more than enough to eat, with an abundance left over. Our curiosity is strained and we want to know how Jesus did this. But the Gospel writers wanted us to see what happened to the disciples and to the large mass of people, not what happened to the bread. The crowd was fed when Jesus took these few resources and gave God's blessing upon them. It's that old story again: Abraham, Isaac, and Jacob; David and Goliath; Barnabas and the early Christian Church; Mahatma Gandhi in India; Rosa Parks in Montgomery; Mother Teresa in Calcutta; you and I wherever we live and work. Whenever we offer the Lord Christ our meager resources, there is no end to what God may accomplish. When forces for good coalesce, when we willingly become partners with the Divine, faith may be rekindled, hope restored, and love made more tangible and visible. There seem to be requirements, however, for this energy to be released, for the union of God's power and human resources to become a creative force.

I. One essential condition that must be met is retreat, silence, and perhaps solitude. A recurring message in this story of Jesus feeding the multitudes is the persistent practice of pulling aside, getting away from the daily grind and the pressing crowds for rest, reflection, and communion with God. Before and after this encounter, Jesus' discipline of retreat was strongly intimated (vv. 3, 15). Throughout the Gospels, Jesus found time to pray and to meditate. Prayer was a vital part of his preparation for facing the various crises of his public ministry. How necessary then will it be for us! It is the act of clearing out some space and sitting in it. "If we hope to move beyond the superficialities of our culture—including our religious culture," wrote Richard J. Foster, "we must be willing to go down into the recreating silences, into the inner world of contemplation."[10] The suggestion that prayer, solitude, and silence can become vibrant, constructive, creative forces in this world is precisely the experience that fires our imaginations and leads us to believe we can make a difference for healing, encouragement, hope, and understanding in the lives of others.

II. One other condition or requirement for God's power and our gifts to become creative forces for good are the disciplines of trust and self-confidence, which become antidotes to fear and despair. It may not be a coincidence that this story of Jesus feeding the multitudes is followed by the sudden appearance of Jesus when the disciples are facing a storm (vv. 16–20). How many times in the course of our lives has God's presence sustained us, God's grace forgiven, healed, and strengthened us when we thought we were out there alone?

The trust lesson is a difficult one, for the disciples and for us, but in retrospect we see clearly that God is involved in all the events of our lives and uses these events to bless us and others around us. The vision of God "at work in all things for good" does not mean that all events are directly and solely attributable to God. In fact, we should never tell someone that a given tragedy is the will of God. We simply don't know enough to say that. But we can say that nothing ever happens or touches one's life that does not first pass under his tender and compassionate eye. Our love, compassion, and will to serve others in Jesus' name become a force to be reckoned with when we respond and serve others with trust and confidence, in the knowledge that we are not in this alone. "God is our refuge and strength. A very present help in time of trouble. Therefore, we will not fear" (Ps. 46:1). We can trust God to be there for us and, in turn, to use our meager resources to bless the lives of others.

Retreat, prayer, and reflection, and growing trust and self-confidence that we are not alone, are crucial requirements for becoming agents of God's love and grace. Not only are we ambassadors for Christ, but we are also partners with Christ.—David D. Burhans

ILLUSTRATIONS

ROSA PARKS.   I call this the "Rosa Parks decision" because that remarkable woman is so emblematic of what the undivided life can mean. Most of us know the story of this African American woman who, at the time she made her decision, was a seamstress in her early forties. On December 1, 1955, in Montgomery, Alabama, Rosa Parks did something she was not supposed to do: she sat down at the front of a bus in one of the seats reserved for whites—a dangerous, daring, and provocative act in a racist society.

---

[10]*Celebration of Discipline,* 3rd ed. (San Francisco: HarperCollins, 1988), p. 13.

Legend has it that years later a graduate student came to Rosa Parks and asked, "Why did you sit down at the front of the bus that day?" Rosa Parks did not say that she sat down to launch a movement, because her motives were more elemental than that. She said, "I sat down because I was tired." But she did not mean that her feet were tired. She meant that her soul was tired, her heart was tired, her whole being was tired of playing by racist rules, of denying her soul's claim to selfhood."—Parker J. Palmer[11]

DEALING WITH FEARS.   When I became a minister I was afraid of disappointing the people I preached to. I'm still afraid of that. If I stop to think about it, my mind seizes up and I can't get on with my sermon.

I am even afraid of retirement. What if I don't like being retired? What if I get out there and I'm bored or don't have enough money to live on or my wife doesn't like having me at home all the time? Is it like going on a cruise? If I get out there and don't like it, is it too late to return?

You see what I mean? Life is full of fears, isn't it? Most of us go through our years afraid of more things than we can count—afraid we won't be liked, afraid we won't be successful, afraid we'll be poor parents, afraid we'll get to the end of the way and look back and realize we've taken the wrong road.—John Killinger[12]

SERMON SUGGESTIONS

Topic: A King Repents
TEXT: 2 Sam. 12:1–14
(1) A sleeping conscience. (2) A courageous prophet. (3) A full confession. (4) A gracious pardon. (5) A baffling tragedy.

Topic: When God Is at Work in Us
TEXT: Eph. 3:14–21
(1) We have inner strength through God's Spirit. (2) We experience the presence of the indwelling Christ. (3) We know the full dimensions of Christ's love.

CONGREGATIONAL MUSIC

1. "Eternal Father, Strong to Save," William Whiting (1860)
   MELITA, John B. Dykes (1861)
   This Trinitarian "Navy Hymn" that is always appropriate for either introducing or following the accounts of Jesus walking on water and calming the storm (John 6:16–21) could also be sung at the opening of worship.
2. "O Love, How Deep, How Broad," anon. Latin hymn (15th century); trans. Benj. Webb (1854)
   PUER NOBIS, Trier Mss, 15th century
   This fine hymn echoes the apostle Paul's prayer for the Ephesians (Eph. 3:14–21) that the love of Christ in all its dimensions may be established in their hearts. The six stanzas could be alternately sung and recited by the singing group.

---

[11]*Let Your Life Speak* (San Francisco: Jossey-Bass, 2000), pp. 32–33.
[12]*Preaching the New Millennium* (Nashville: Abingdon Press, 1999), pp. 131–132.

3. "God, Be Merciful to Me," Ps. 51; vers. *Psalter* (1912)

REDHEAD 76, Richard Redhead (1853)

David's sin of adultery was followed by his expression of deep contrition and his plea for mercy and forgiveness, recorded as Psalm 51. Consequently, this paraphrase of his prayer for forgiveness would be appropriate after the Old Testament account of David's sin.

4. "The Foolish in Their Hearts Deny," Ps. 14; vers. Marie J. Post (1983)

MAPLE AVENUE, Richard L. Van Oss (1984)

This excellent modern paraphrase of Psalm 14 could well be sung as a substitute for the psalm reading. If unfamiliar, it could be sung first by a choir before the congregation is invited to join in.—Hugh T. McElrath

WORSHIP AIDS

CALL TO WORSHIP.　　"Know therefore that the Lord thy God is God, the faithful God, which keepeth covenant and mercy with them that love him and keep his commandments to a thousand generations" (Deut. 7:9).

INVOCATION.　　Lord, let this be a community where love is found, where we forgive as we have been forgiven, where we study the Bible, stay sensitive to the Holy Spirit, and serve in Jesus' name.—E. Lee Phillips

OFFERTORY SENTENCE.　　"Now he that ministereth seed to the sower both minister bread for your food, and multiply seed sown, and increase the fruits of your righteousness" (2 Cor. 9:10).

OFFERTORY PRAYER.　　Eternal God, open our eyes until we see your Kingdom more clearly in our midst, and inspire us to seek it more perfectly in our lives. Forbid that we invest so much in getting and spending and so little in seeking the true riches of your Kingdom. Open our ears to the demands of our Lord that we render a faithful stewardship of the abundance entrusted to us.

Open our hands to those devastated by earthquake, wind, and fire; those made homeless and hungry by the vicissitudes of nature; those oppressed and tortured by beasts misnamed men; those in jail through no fault of their own; those who have lost loved ones to hate, avarice, and violence; and the aged and injured who languish in the confines of their homes.

Grant that no one whom Christ would want to have his love escape our notice or our service. We ask in his strong and loving name, but for all our sakes. Amen.—Paul D. Simmons

PRAYER.　　Eternal Father, always more ready to hear than we are to pray, we come into your presence knowing that you know what we need even before we ask. Yet here we are, seeking in a common prayer light for our ways and for strength in our hearts to follow you into the future. Let us have an ear that will hear you today. Bring us some answers to our sincere prayer, we pray.

Some of us here this morning have been misled by evil counsel and wicked practices. Guide us in a straight way through life. Some here have been tempted beyond their ability to resist. We have listened to the cynical voice, the lying tongue, the promising speech, and we have given in to their wrong. Help us to seek not our own will but yours, that we may walk in peace through the valleys of temptation. Let Christ's Spirit become real for us in the everyday walks we must take through the world.

Some here this morning are weighed down with private grief, Father. Some are discouraged, some are lonely, some are disappointed beyond belief, some are weary with life. Come with a new spirit of triumph and hope today, we pray. Send us from this gathering able to say with joy, "Bless the Lord, oh my soul!" Reveal to us resources for power adequate to make us more than conquerors!—Henry Fields

SERMON
Topic: The Story of Stephen
TEXT: Acts 6:1–8:3

Stephen's life was brief not only in the number of pages it takes to tell it but also in the number of years it took to live it. I have divided it into three chapters, and the first is *How he got his start.*

I. This is rather interesting. It all started with a complaint—not a promising place from which to start. And this was the complaint: The widows of the Greek-speaking Jews in Jerusalem, who belonged to a group of Jews who had been brought up abroad and had only recently come back to Jerusalem to live—more highly cultivated, perhaps, and more cosmopolitan than their less-traveled neighbors—complained that they were not getting as much attention as the widows of the native, Jerusalem-born Jews. They sent the complaint to the leaders of the Church. It probably had to do with the distribution of the relief funds that the early Christians always made available for people who needed it.

The Church leaders surveyed the situation and realized that they could not assume any more responsibilities than they already had. They said to themselves something like this: our task is growing every day and we need more people to help us, and particularly some people to help us with the important but secondary part of the work. The preaching and teaching must not be neglected in the interest of these other relatively unimportant matters. So they picked out seven young men and assigned them the particular work of seeing that whatever was to be administered to the widows of the Greek-speaking Jews was administered to them safely and soundly, and that they were not slighted in favor of the home-born Jews. Stephen was one of these young men.

We are sad to see any intrusion of friction, but here it shows its ugly head at the very beginning of the stream of its life, and it never completely disappears thereafter. Two groups with different backgrounds and different interests, each complaining that the other gets more attention than it should, both working not in harmony but in tension—this is something we recognize easily as an all too familiar sight, and we are not proud of it.

Also, when the disciples did the only practical thing they could—namely, divided the responsibility and increased the staff, so to speak—they did a dangerous thing. What they did, you see, was to give the less important part of the work to the young men, assuming that they were keeping in their own hands the most important part. But which is more important, to preach or to wait on tables?

They made it possible right at the beginning for people to assume that one part of Christ's ministry to his people was more important than another part.

However, it was just such a rather unpropitious human situation that gave Stephen his start. What great things in human life often have miserable beginnings! He appeared almost out of the blue, as far as we know, to meet an emergency created by this situation.

And the amazing thing is that if the situation had never arisen, Stephen might never have been heard of. If this particular circumstance had not called out of obscurity a young man named Stephen, "full of grace and spiritual power," that young man might never have been heard of in the history of mankind.

The lesson, therefore, of this first chapter of Stephen's life is simply this: a man is the product of the times he helps to produce. And the moral of the story is, when the times call, don't hang back in the wings.

II. *Why he got into trouble.* Why in the world did this young man with every talent anyone could have for a particular task, with the road open straight ahead of him, why did a man like that get into almost immediate trouble, and finally into the very serious trouble in which he lost his life? Why should this be? Why does it ever happen that way?

There are two good reasons why Stephen got into trouble. This, I suppose, as I often say, is an oversimplification; but remember, this is a great life "in brief." First, he wanted above everything else to see Christianity grow.

There were others who wanted to see it die. It is appalling, as we sit here now and look back quite objectively at the situation, to realize that that was true, and yet it should not surprise us, should it? When you stop to think of it, there has never been a movement forward that has not been resisted by multitudes. And I think we ought to say this: that the Church is not exempt from this weakness, for the Church resisted the movement to know the truth about the stars and the moon and the rocks and the Earth; it resisted the movement for decades. Indeed, in some quarters it is still rigorously resisting it!

Here, you see, were two strong-minded, irresistible bodies—a young, passionate man convinced that in this little seed of life was the life of the world for future ages; and, on the other hand, a group of stubborn, redoubtable, sturdy men and women who refused to let that new movement grow. They were bound to clash, sooner or later, and they did.

Finally, they brought Stephen to the Council Chamber, which we might call the courtroom, to put him on trial, to give him a hearing, so to speak.

It is a dramatic scene and almost impossible for us to reproduce, but there, sitting or probably standing alone, was Stephen. Even his enemies had to admit that there was a kind of radiance about him that the people in their ranks did not have. He shone like crystal, and they were dull, like lead.

Finally, when they asked him to speak, he did speak, and the account in the book of Acts gives a long speech. Now, he said, you are resisting Jesus. Him in whom we see a new life for the world, a new order for society, a new hope for men and women; in whom we find an expression of the love of God such as we have never known before—you are resisting him.

When he finished you can imagine that they were furious. People don't like to be told— you certainly wouldn't like it if I told you—that they are deliberately resisting the Spirit of God; but he didn't even look at them. He was looking up and, without giving them a chance to say anything, he said to them, "Look, the heavens are opened, and I can see the Son of Man standing on the right hand of God." What does it mean? He saw nothing, in one sense, and yet he saw everything, in another sense. Jesus, not dimmed by the mist of confusion into which he had been plunged, but made brighter than ever before, over and above the smallness of humanity, their resistances and obstructions to the life of God; over and above and through that the heavens opened, and there was the greatness of God standing, still calling men on.

III. They quickly led him out of the Sanhedrin and, of course, this action leads to the last chapter, which is very brief because it happened so quickly: *How he died.* They stoned him to death on the spot.

When the passions of people are left undisciplined so that they run down into the lower levels of life, they can be aroused and can perform acts of brutality and cruelty almost beyond our imagining. And that holds for people like us, you know; the most refined ones might be capable of the worst brutality.

While they were stoning him, he prayed. This was the real thing with Stephen. There are people we see all along through life who have what we think is the real thing; but when the actual test comes, they do not. This was the real thing; he followed through. He was saying what was in his heart and what was on his mind and what he believed with all his soul. This rang true and this is what he said: "Lord Jesus, receive my spirit. Lord, lay not this sin to their charge." First it makes you feel mean; then small, when you remember all your little resentments and grudges and desire for revenge. And then, somehow, it makes you feel great, proud to belong to a race that can so emerge from the lower instincts of the animal, which are in every one of us, as to reach from time to time, more often than we sometimes think, heights like this; and as you stand in the presence of that life, you begin to feel the currents of air from other worlds blow through the cramped and crowded ways of your life.

It isn't any wonder, is it, that a young intellectual Jew named Saul, from Tarsus, who was standing there watching Stephen, could never get that face out of his mind? First it haunted him, and then it changed him into the man who turned the world upside down for Christ.—Theodore Parker Ferris

SUNDAY, AUGUST 3, 2003
Lectionary Message

Topic: A Place for Us
TEXT: Eph. 4:1–16
Other Readings: 2 Sam. 11:26–12:13a; Ps. 51:1–12; John 6:24–35

I. The movie *West Side Story* reminds us that there is in all of us a desire to be someplace. There is a longing in the human heart for a kingdom of Camelot where all is kind and wonderful. We are a nation that keeps moving a little further out from the city in order to find a little piece of land where we can create our own paradise. We are all looking for a place for us.

(a) In this morning's passages from Ephesians, Paul is so excited about the thought that the Church is that place for all of us. There is a place for each of us in the unity of the body of Christ, and that unity of the Church is not some dead and artificial unity, but a living, growing, and dynamic unit. God has bestowed upon each of us a vast variety of gifts, all of them demanding their own kinds of expression. All gifts need to be exercised in order to develop and grow. Yet the wonder, the beauty, and the power of the unity of Christ is that our gifts are not developed just for ourselves; they can only be developed, matured, and enlarged as they are merged and united with the other gifts of God's people. The oneness of God's people is a corporate, bodily unity. The more each individual becomes himself or herself and makes a particular contribution to the common life together, the greater the body becomes. The more each person puts first the mission and work of the people of God, the more the Church as a whole will attain the joy, blessing, and ability to demonstrate to the world the power of God for reconciliation. Each individual grows and is blessed as the whole body grows.

(b) Paul urges, invites, pleads, begs, entices, and encourages, all of us to live up to that kind of high-quality living. In Jesus Christ you have been invited and called to this marvelous life of being united into the body of Christ. Look at all the ways we have been given the power of unity. Paul shares this great sevenfold blessing of unity: There is (1) one body animated by (2) one Spirit, cherishing (3) one Hope. There is (4) one Lord, to whom we are united by (5) one faith and in whose name we are welcomed by (6) one baptism. This is all the result of the grace of (7) one God and Father of us all, who is over all, through all, and in all. All the members of the body of Christ are at peace with one another because they are bound together by the love of God.

(c) The gift grows, matures, and develops as it is used in the enrichment of the body, and this one body of the Church is to be the instrument in God's great work of reconciliation, to be the example of how God's love restores creation. There is no reference here to individuals attaining their own Christian maturity. The thought is of the Church as a single organism growing to its full strength, reaching maturity, and so becoming entirely adequate to the purpose for which God intends it.

II. When you start with the biblical text and hold up that blueprint for the body of Christ, the Church, you discover a lot of places where the Word of God creates for us problems we may not have even known we had.

(a) We are impressed with Paul's pleading, begging, and asking us to try to live up to the high calling that we have received. The whole hymn on Christian unity may be an exhortation, but it is not a command. No rules, just what is right. Paul wants us to change, to live out and fulfill the great gift God has given to us, but he is in no position to order, to legislate, to establish requirements, or to demand. Here is the accentuating of the possibilities, the good, and the opportunity. Paul talks about the new reality of living out of the grace and the gift that have been given. Here is our chance to find the place for us if we are willing to live in the unity of Christ's Lordship. If we refuse now, Paul knows God will wait. Because God is love, God is patient; but our delay, our tarrying, is not God's loss but ours. If we will not live up to the high calling that is ours, we will waste more time, as the country song says, "looking for love in all the wrong faces, looking for love in too many places."

The pleading of Paul for each of us to cultivate the meek and lowly mind, the patient forbearance, the charity without which a common life is impossible certainly seems a far cry from what most of the major bodies of the Christian community are doing in their public actions. They preach rules and regulations. The rules grow and expand faster than our membership. The major issue is the requirements and rules. The issue about coming together as part of the body of Christ in unity is argued more as a legal question than as a discussion about the fullness of the body to enrich all gifts. Paul talks about begging us to live up to the high calling that is ours. Nobody is much into begging anymore. We want to pass some rules and require unity.

(b) But that is where this passage is most disturbing. Paul's joy and delight at the sevenfold oneness of faith dramatically shows how much we, in our day, have been affected and diminished by the culture we live in. For Paul sees the perfect Church not as a collection of perfected saints but as one full-grown person, fully expressing the work and ministry of Jesus Christ. We are so caught up in our individualism that we have very little interest in being united with anything. We live in the "just do it" age, where everybody is just supposed to do their own thing. Churches see themselves as the places where individuals go to get help with individual spiritual lives. They teach people how to pray and to read the Bible, tell them what are the things eternal, and send them out. Each person is worried about his own spiritual progress. The fastest growing churches are those that are offering everything to everybody. Paul's view of the unity of the Church is not of so many individuals each pressing on toward individual spiritual maturity, but of a single organism growing to its full strength and becoming fit for the purpose for which God intends it.

The predominant attitude toward church life in our culture today seems to be individual worry about one's own spiritual life, and the job of the Church seems to be to save individuals by conversion and baptism. Whatever unity there may be within the Christian Church at the moment is a result of a common desire for the same ends of special interests. There are those who are united for the advancement of women in ministry. There is a unity of those who are concerned for the advancement of minority rights. There are those united against abortion and those united for choice. There are those united for the recognition of gays and lesbians. But the unity in one Lord, one faith, and one baptism is hard to hear.

(c) And the gifts. Paul's talk about gifts stabbed me as I looked back over my years. How many hours, how much time, have we tried to find people to fill positions, and how little time have I spent trying to find a way to enable somebody to use his gift. Here is a slot, a job, on the organizational chart, and I need to fill it. But over here is a person with a magnificent gift that corresponds to no organizational slot, and we have spent a lot more time trying to fill the slot than we have spent trying to find a way to encourage, permit, and celebrate that person's gift. And how many times have I seen somebody in a position who has been using and enjoying her gift for twenty years and have joined with those who suggested that it might be better to give that person a break. The body has the gift of a heart, but just because the heart has been beating for fifty years does not mean it is time to let the hand try to be the heart. Where did we get the idea that after a long time a gift stops being a gift? The old man had been greeting children at the door to the Sunday school department for thirty-five years. It was his gift. There was no job description for what he did. He loved children, was good with names, and had a great memory for when they were absent. "Where have you been?" He would say to a child returning after a missed Sunday. "I missed you." When he became ill and could no longer greet the children, one of the children said she was so sorry; she missed seeing God each Sunday. Paul says we all have gifts and that they are needed for the good of the unity and enrichment of the whole. It just seems to me that, where I have been, we have spent a lot more time getting people to do jobs than we have spent finding a way for them to contribute their gifts.

There is a place for us in the body of Christ.—Rick Brand

ILLUSTRATION

CHURCH DIVISIONS, ABSURD.   In a New England city a wealthy man gave a beautiful colonial church edifice as a family memorial. The kitchen was modern to the nth degree. After the dedication, however, a group of women in the church wanted to add to the kitchen equipment a newly invented electric automatic potato parer. It was a clever device by which potatoes were washed, scrubbed clean, then moved along a belt to a series of knives that peeled the potatoes and finally dropped them into a kettle for cooking.

But there was another group of women who strenuously objected to this newfangled gadget because it eliminated their happy custom of going early to the kitchen and paring the potatoes by hand while they exchanged in social fellowship the news and gossip of the church.

The two groups of women quickly hardened into partisan groups, one determined to have the new potato parer and the other equally determined that the church should not have this potato parer. The controversy became so heated that the women carried their quarrel home and lined up their husbands as participants in the quarrel. As a result, the entire church membership was divided into the pro-potato parer party and the anti-potato parer party.

One day the pastor of this church, greatly depressed, came to see me, telling me he was resigning. I was astonished and said to him, "How does this happen? You have a beautiful new building, free of debt, a most worshipful sanctuary, and a marvelous modern kitchen."

"That kitchen is just the trouble," he said, and related the story of the quarrel over the potato parer.

"When I get up to preach on Sunday morning, there before me are the two parties—the pro-potato parer party and the anti-potato parer party—bristling with belligerency. Utterly absurd as it seems, their minds are so concentrated on this quarrel that I cannot get through to them with any spiritual message. The potato parer is 'all and in all' to them. It has cut my church sharply in two, and I give up because I can no longer preach the gospel and be heard in such an atmosphere."

Many of our affluent churches are concerned with just such absurdities, while they ignore Christ's mission to the world.—Benjamin P. Browne[1]

SERMON SUGGESTIONS

Topic: Up Toward Home
TEXT: Acts 7:55–60
(1) Our true home is where Jesus is—in the presence of God and with God's authority. (2) Our true vocation is that of Jesus when this Earth was his temporary home—to live and die in the spirit of Jesus (v. 60).

Topic: A Spiritual Odyssey
TEXT: 1 Pet. 2:2–10
(1) What we were—nobodies, rejected. (2) What we are—God's own people, precious. (3) What we can be—witnesses to God's marvelous grace.

CONGREGATIONAL MUSIC
1. "Guide Me, O Thou Great Jehovah," William Williams (1772)
   CWM RHONDDA, John Hughes (1907)
   A grand hymn for the opening of worship, "Guide Me, O Thou Great Jehovah" relates also

---

[1]*Illustrations for Preaching* (Nashville: Broadman Press, 1977), pp. 73–74.

to the Gospel reading. The first stanza recalls Jesus' assertion that he is the bread of life (John 6:35) on which we are to feed.

2. "O for a Closer Walk with God," William Cowper (1772)

BEATITUDO, John B. Dykes (1875)

This venerable hymn of aspiration and resolve echoes the penitent prayer of David for pardon (Ps. 51:1–12) and would be especially suitable sung as a congregational response to the story of David's sin recorded in the Old Testament lesson (2 Sam. 11:26–12:13a).

3. "Christian Hearts in Love United," Nicolaus L. von Zinzendorf (1723)

CASSELL, trad. German melody

The unity of the spirit spoken of by the apostle Paul in the Epistle lesson (Eph. 4:1–16) can find ready expression in this great Moravian hymn. Its regular phrasing and meter would make for effective antiphonal singing between congregation and choir.

4. "Break Thou the Bread of Life," Mary A. Lathbury (1877) and Alexander Groves (1913)

BREAD OF LIFE, William F. Sherwin (1877)

This familiar gospel hymn based on John 6:35 could appropriately and devotionally introduce the reading of any of the Scripture lessons for this day's worship.—Hugh T. McElrath

WORSHIP AIDS

CALL TO WORSHIP.   "And you will know the truth, and the truth will make you free" (John 8:32).

INVOCATION.   Lord, just as we have been kept all week long, we know in this hour of worship that you have something important for us. Help us to find what we most need, that through song and prayer, sermon and fellowship the Holy Spirit might lead us and seal in us mighty hopes.—E. Lee Phillips

OFFERTORY SENTENCE.   "For the rendering of this ministry not only supplies the needs of the saints but also overflows with many thanksgivings to God" (2 Cor. 9:12 NRSV).

OFFERTORY PRAYER.   Add your Holy Spirit's power to our gifts, O Lord, that the mission enterprise of the Church may be enhanced and many souls will proclaim Jesus as Lord.—E. Lee Phillips

PRAYER.   In the brightness of this beautiful morning, we come to you, Father, that we might learn of you and go from this place of worship more determined to live after your fashion and in your likeness. Along the way we have walked in these past days, we have not always made life better and brighter for those among whom we have lived and walked and loved. Pray, this morning, let the healing strength of forgiveness for our failures rain gently upon us, that we may be made clean and experience restoration for the beginning of life anew in this world. We have not spoken always with wisdom and insight born of love, Father. Ours has been speech let loose by anger and bitterness and sometimes frustration and hurt. Pray, this morning, cleanse our speech to others that we may truly learn to speak the truth in love and healing and direction for those who need the truth that we possess and are able to give. We have not always done deeds of helping when opportunity has come to us to lift the fallen and strengthen the weak and encourage the discouraged. Selfishness and fear have hindered our reaching out in Christlike fashion to make the way more bearable for the burdened and the lonely and the lost. Pray, this morning instill in us the desire to meet needs wherever they are and heal hurt wherever it exists and lift burdens wherever they crush the very spirit from those among whom we walk, especially those whom we have come to love deeply and truly in this earthwalk.

Open our eyes this morning, Father, that we may see the grand provision you have made for us in every situation of life. So often we see only the difficult side of life and focus so closely on the impossibilities that we neglect to cultivate what is possible. Expand our vision of what you would have us do and be and become. Open our hearts, we pray, that we might take in those who meet us on the road of life and need our support and companionship, our understanding and our love. So often we exclude them even as they reach out to us and long to be a part of our lives. Open our hands to serve those who cannot at the moment serve themselves. Give us strength and love sufficient to walk with them through their torments until they can stand on their own strength once again.

In so many areas of our existence we need your presence, that we might make the most of life. So, this morning as we wait, come gently and powerfully into our hearts and claim us anew, that we might follow more closely the Lord of life, we pray in Jesus' name.—Henry Fields

SERMON
Topic: Sin and Repentance
TEXT: Ps. 34:11–14; Rom. 3:21–26; 2 Cor. 7:9–11

What do you think is the favorite sermon subject of Protestant Evangelical preachers? Now, I can't document this, of course, but I think the answer is *sin.* That's right. Not God's love. Not God's grace. Not even giving money to the Church! But *sin,* s-i-n.

Of course, many acts that are called sins by certain pulpiteers and others are not sins at all. Too often, cultural norms and personal biases, rather than God's will, are violated by certain acts of ours. Violating cultural norms and someone else's values are not necessarily sinful. But too many of us do not require ourselves to have a keen enough eye to keep the difference in mind. The difference is very important.

Real sin is *conscious rebellion against God.* I want you to remember that definition. Sin is *conscious rebellion against God.* We all make mistakes and err in ways that are not sinful at all. We do things that are, in fact, out of line in some way, but unless we are *intentionally* trying to violate what we know to be the will of God, we are not sinning. (I wonder, do you have more or fewer sins on your list by using this definition?)

You see, both Eve and Adam were told by God not to eat of the fruit from the tree in the middle of the Garden of Eden, and when they did eat of it, they were sinning because they were in clear conflict with a "direct order" from God.

The Lord God took the man and put him in the Garden of Eden to till it and keep it. And the Lord God commanded the man, "You may freely eat of every tree of the garden; but of the tree of the knowledge of good and evil you shall not eat, for in the day that you eat of it you shall die" (Gen. 2:15–17).

If they had not known better, if they had not been warned, then what they did could not have been called sin, and the dire consequences of their acts would not have come. Our sinful acts rob us of the joy and beauty and hope of spiritual life—life in the present and in the hereafter shared with God. And sin is a problem for each and every one of us. The apostle Paul, again, proclaimed that "all have sinned and fallen short of the glory of God" (Rom. 3:23 NRSV).

If serving God and honoring God are the dominant and overriding concerns in our lives, then that is what matters. God knows. And there is no chance, as a college friend of mine constantly feared, that one might die with an unconfessed sin hanging on somewhere—which, he was convinced, would surely send a person to hell. God isn't arbitrary and ridiculous!

God *is* distressed with our bent to sinning, but God never intends the last word to be our refusal to be the people God planned us to be. We have an opportunity, because of God's love and grace and patience, to make things right—again and again and again. But just as sin is no light matter, neither is honest repentance.

The psalmist reduced the idea of repentance to the very simplest way of expressing it in action terms: "Depart from evil and do good" (Ps. 34:17a NRSV).

Our word *repent* comes from a Greek word that means "a complete change, an about face." There is no magic about repentance. There is no formula for repenting. Repentance, rather, is an acknowledgment that God and God's plan may not be taken casually for granted without resultant problems. And that means, as in any human relationship, that when we violate covenant, agreement, protocol, and trust, an apology is called for—especially when this breach has occurred in relationship with someone who cares deeply for us. But when we say we are sorry, we must mean it to the extent that we honestly, sincerely aim not to repeat the behavior. And if both components—authentic regret *and* an honest willingness to try not to repeat the wrong—are not present, then there has been no repentance.

Paul talked to the Corinthians about a kind of grief—what he called "godly grief"—that they felt and that led them to repentance. They were sorry for their wrong to such a degree that they were grieving about it, and as long as we don't get stuck at the grieving stage, this is not inappropriate. He explained to them that "Godly grief produces a repentance that leads to salvation and brings no regret" (2 Cor. 7:10 NRSV).—David Albert Farmer

SUNDAY, AUGUST 10, 2003
Lectionary Message

Topic: Aspects of the Life in Grace
TEXT: Eph. 4:25–5:2
Other Readings: 2 Sam. 18:5–9, 15, 31–33; Ps. 130; John 6:35, 41–51

I. In Jesus Christ we see, hear, and feel the new life that is God's gift and desire for all of us. By our response, by our faith, by our identification with that life, we bring our gifts and our energies into the Kingdom of God, and Paul says that this purpose and will of God flows back into our lives and we see our lives marked by changes. As we put ourselves into the body of Christ, the body of Christ puts itself into us and we begin to see that we are being changed.

(a) Paul says there are lots of dimensions of life where these changes can be seen. We are part of the same body of Christ. Christ becomes part of our bodies, minds, and hearts, and as we become more and more influenced by the Spirit and power of Christ, we find that we stop trying to control and manipulate words and sentences in order to make ourselves look better. Paul says it simply: "We are part of the same body. Stop lying and start telling each other the truth." In the body of Christ we have confessed that we are forgiven sinners; there is no need for us to try to pretend that we are so much better or kinder than we are.

Octavio Paz, the 1990 Nobel Prize winner for literature, wrote about the reasons for lying. "We tell lies for the mere pleasure of it, like all imaginative peoples, but we also tell lies to hide ourselves and to protect ourselves. Lying plays a decisive role in our daily lives, our politics, our love affairs and our friendships, and since we attempt to deceive ourselves as well as others, our lies are brilliant and fertile. . . . Lying is a tragic game in which we risk a part of our very selves" in order to save another part of ourselves. In the grace of Jesus Christ, we have been redeemed. We are saved. All of us are saved so we no longer need to lie. It is no longer our job to save part of ourselves. As the mercy of Christ flows into our lives, we are permitted to speak honestly and openly about ourselves and about our lives and about how others affect us, without trying to save part of ourselves by the lie.

(b) Do you find it surprising that as soon as Paul affirms that we are all one body in Christ, he tells us to stop lying. Does the will and personality of Christ come into our lives and affect our ability to speak honestly about ourselves and our lives because it is the easiest reform to accomplish or because it is the most needed?

II. Certainly the nature and the quality of our speaking, of our language, and of our use of language has dramatically shaped the nature of our community as a people.

(a) There are some who are shocked by the cynicism and sarcasm of the public around them. There are those who are wistful for more patriotism, more idealism, more optimism, and more devotion to values. Nobody believes what anybody says. Everybody is skeptical of everybody else. We seem to be creating people who are willing to believe only themselves, and they don't believe they have to keep the promises they made to anybody else.

But what other kind of community can we expect to have when we have to teach our children, before they are much older than four, that most of what is said on TV is not true? "No, the Jurassic Park figure you buy in the store will not fly like the one you see on TV." "The Chris Webber tennis shoes you buy in the store will not enable you to slam dunk the Washington monument." Sure, some of what we they see on TV is supposed to be a joke, but we still have to speak the truth in love to our children, to tell them that most of what they see advertised on TV is not true.

(b) It is no surprise that most of us are cynical and suspicious about exaggerated language. We have hyped everything so much that now nothing can be wonderful. What kind of trust and confidence can we expect from a people who have had every movie, every book, every CD, and every sporting event promoted and hyped as the event of the century? Garth Brooks in Central Park—the Urban Cowboy revolution? It was a concert in New York for one night, all right?

(c) You are one body. Stop lying. Well, we don't really call it lying. We call it advertising. We don't call it lying. We call it marketing and promotion. But it erodes the very integrity of our language. It creates mistrust, distrust, suspicion, and cynicism. Why is anybody so surprised that so many people have become turned off by the whole political process? Because, as is said over and over by people asked on the street, nothing the politicians say can be trusted. None of the promises they make are kept. All of their speeches are hyperbole. Finally, after twenty years of talking about it, they finally get a bill they claim will balance something, and from the speeches they make about it you would think they had invented water, done something magnificent.

III. When the grace and Spirit of Jesus Christ flows into us as we are united in one body, by one faith and one baptism, our anger becomes an expression of our opposition to evil in life rather than simply an expression that we did not get what we wanted.

(a) Don't become so angry that you sin. Sin is when we separate ourselves from God so we can decide for ourselves what is good and what is evil. Cain became so angry that his sacrifice wasn't received that he decided to eliminate the competition. But God had told Cain that sin was waiting outside his door until the anger gave it a chance to come in. Don't allow your anger to become so great that it separates you from God.

It is a relief to discover in these words the fact that it is not a sin to become angry. Paul does not seem to indicate that just because we get angry in life we have sinned. In fact, there is good evidence in the Scriptures that the more we are filled with the Spirit and power of God, the more we indeed should become angry at the evil and injustices we discover around us. Illegal deaf Mexicans being used as slaves ought to produce in us some legitimate indignation and anger. But as we are united with the body of Christ by his Spirit and by faith, the anger does not provoke us to play God, to take justice into our own hands, to speak or act in some pompous and judgmental way, or to lose our focus on the face of the person before us.

(b) In the body of Christ, under the influence of the works of the Spirit, work becomes different. If you have been a thief, stop. If you have been a taker, stop.

IV. The Spirit of Christ begins to bring us to the place where we see work as the source of obtaining what we can give.

(a) Work so you will have something to give: what a radical transformation that would be for us in our culture. We work so we can acquire. We work so we can have something, to get what we want. We work so we can buy all the things we would like to have. Paul says that as we are part of the same body, the body of Christ, we will discover that our perspective, our desires and our reasons for working, will move from working so we can get—from taking, acquiring, and accumulating—to the working so we will be able to give, to bless others, to help, and to contribute.

(b) The more we merge into the body of Christ, by faith, by hope, by love, the more we are changed. The more we struggle to have integrity about our speech, to stop lying, the more we discipline our anger so that it does not give opportunity to sin. And our work becomes the means of obtaining something to give rather than just the means for us to have whatever we want. These are some of the aspects of a life changed by grace.—Rick Brand

ILLUSTRATIONS

ANGER.   When I am traveling on a freeway and I enter an area where a sign says that a lane is closing two or three miles ahead, I am one of those people who will move into the proper lane early. Then I will rant and rave at all those who speed past me and expect to merge into my lane ahead of me. My anger mounts as we get closer to the merging point and people keep speeding by. My anger gets me to where I begin to wish I had a button to push to destroy them, to consign them to hell, to blow them off the face of the Earth. My anger begins to make me wish I was God and I could destroy them because they were not cooperating with the rules.—Rick Brand

PRETENSE.   A man in a church in Charlotte always pledged a thousand dollars a month during the every-member canvass, but he never paid a penny all year. He just liked to see the look on the elder's face when he gave him the pledge card. He lied because he liked the reputation he had in the church because lots of people heard about the pledge but few heard about how he paid.—Rick Brand

SERMON SUGGESTIONS

Topic: Despising Our Birthright

TEXT: Gen. 25:19–34

(1) The story: Esau, in a moment of weakness, forswore his most precious topic: possession—his birthright, "with all rights and privileges thereunto appertaining." (2) The meaning: A stupid decision made in a time of temptation can begin an entire sequence of dreadful consequences. (3) The application: God offers to us a way of escape from the forces that, at worst, threaten to destroy us, or at least tend to rob us of peace and joy (see 1 Cor. 10:13).

Topic: The Ultimate Remedy

TEXT: Rom. 5:6–11

(1) We, the human race, were weak—sinners all. (2) God nevertheless showed his love for us. (3) Therefore we can here and now enjoy our reconciliation to God by participating in the life of the Risen Christ.

CONGREGATIONAL MUSIC

1. "Out of the Depths I Cry," Ps. 130; vers. *The Psalter* (1912)

   SANDON, Charles H. Purday (1860)

   A close modern paraphrase of Psalm 130, "Out of the Depths, I Cry" could be sung as a replacement of the Psalter reading.
2. "For the Gift of God the Spirit," Margaret Clarkson (1976)

   BLAENWERN, William P. Rowlands (1905)

   One of the prominent exhortations of the apostle Paul in the Epistle reading (Eph. 4:25–5:2) is to avoid grieving the Holy Spirit. This fine contemporary hymn on the Holy Spirit would therefore be an effective response to that reading.
3. "Jesus, Thou Joy of Loving Hearts," Latin (12th century); trans. Ray Palmer (1858)

   QUEBEC, Henry Baker (1845)

   The use of this ancient hymn with its reference to Jesus as "the living bread" (stanza 3) would be effective as a response to the Gospel lesson (John 6:35, 41–51).
4. "Fill My Cup, Lord," Richard Blanchard (1959)

   FILL MY CUP, Richard Blanchard (1959)

   The contemporary chorus, with its prayer "Bread of Heaven, feed me till I want no more," was written in a time of frustration and impatience for its author and composer. It would fit quite well as a congregational response to the Gospel reading.—Hugh T. McElrath

WORSHIP AIDS

CALL TO WORSHIP.   "I give you thanks, O Lord, with my whole heart; before the gods I sing your praise; I bow down toward your holy temple and give thanks to your name for your steadfast love and your faithfulness; for you have exalted your name and your word above everything" (Ps. 138:1–2).

INVOCATION.   Lord of light, shine in the darkness of our rebellion, that we might be drawn by higher urges and deeper thoughts to the cross-won faith that overcomes the world, through Christ our Lord.—E. Lee Phillips

OFFERTORY SENTENCE.   "And my God will fully satisfy every need of yours according to his riches in glory in Christ Jesus" (Phil. 4:19).

OFFERTORY PRAYER.   Lord, let our gifts not come with reluctance or hesitation; rather, let them come with enthusiasm and dedication, lest in any withholding we sabotage the privilege and miss the joy.—E. Lee Phillips

PRAYER.   We come here, O Father, lest we forget the rock from which we are hewn. There are times in life when we need to get back on where we got off. How often your Word is a word that calls to repentance! "Return, return," you say to us as persons, as a people—as a nation, as a world. Frequently the destiny toward which we are intending is not your purpose in creating us. There are those foundations for life—for being and well-being—that you have laid, without which our building is but disaster. As your prophet would remind every generation, "Except the Lord build the house, they labor in vain who build it."

We rejoice in your Word "sure and steadfast," present from the beginning, whenever that was, and now in these last days so fully manifest that we find ourselves exclaiming to one another, "What other foundation can anyone lay than that which is laid in Christ Jesus." "Teach us to build upon the solid rock."

O Father of us all, we would be building community—the community of which Christ is the promise. Where there is any estrangement among us in family or church family, make us courageous to seek forgiveness that we may be open to receive the reconciliation that is already here, present in Christ. As a people, as a nation, may we seize the opportunity that is ours to invest the rich resources entrusted to us in peacemaking. You do call the strong to lift up the weak—not with condescension but in the meaning of your grace. May we so live in relationships with other people and nations that that moral force that can turn the tide from war to peace may be activated and released. As you have ordained from the beginning, it is not by might nor by power but by your Spirit that community is created and sustained.—John M. Thompson

SERMON

Topic: Those Blessed Interruptions!
TEXT: Mark 2:1–12

Have you ever noticed, in reading this familiar story, that Jesus was busy preaching when these men bearing their friend on a stretcher interrupted him? Yet without a word of reproach he gracefully turned aside from what he was doing to honor their presence and heal the poor man they had brought to him.

He was engaged in preaching. I tried to imagine the scene. Here he was, talking about the coming of the Kingdom of God in the lives of the people crowded into the house. He was probably warmed up, and the thoughts and images were pouring out like golden liquid. The crowd was with him, absorbing every word. A little piece of clay fell from the ceiling, then another, and another. People were distracted. "What's going on up there?" they wondered. Suddenly a large blob of clay fell out of the ceiling and they could see four pairs of hands eagerly pulling back the straw and dirt from the opening. Finally, to everyone's amazement, two men let themselves down through the hole and, with the help of two others on the roof, lowered an invalid through the roof on his stretcher.

How do you suppose Jesus felt about this interruption of what he was doing? He was surely interrupted a lot. He didn't have a good executive secretary to divert unworthy callers, or a bodyguard to protect him from unwelcome intrusions. Sometimes the disciples managed to shield him a little. The Gospel of John records an incident when Phillip and Andrew detained some Greeks who wanted to see him (John 12:20–28). But for the most part people seem to have had open access to him wherever he was and whenever they wanted to see him. They even followed him across the lake when he tried to get some privacy in a boat. But there is no record that Jesus ever took offense at people for interrupting him, regardless of what he was doing, and this particular text is no exception. Without a word of reproach— we would be inclined to say, "Here, this is a worship service you are interrupting and you cannot do that"—he turned his full attention to the men who cared so deeply for their friend, and forgave and healed the man so that he got up and walked away with his bed.

It is interesting to note that Jesus *forgave* the bedridden man before he healed him. This indicates the depth of his interest in the man. He didn't merely heal him to be rid of him. He took the time to deal with his inner needs as well as his outer needs. I'm not sure I would have done that in Jesus' place. I think I might have granted what the men wanted merely to be done with them and get on with what I was about when they interrupted. But not Jesus. He gave his complete attention to whoever happened to be in front of him at the moment.

This seems to have been Jesus' way at all times. He dealt freshly and attentively with everyone and everything. He was always fully present in every discussion or confrontation. In fact, he *transformed* every situation in which he found himself.

Maybe we can learn something from this. God is fully present to us in Christ. Perhaps life itself consists of being fully present to everyone and everything we have to deal with—of seeing the life and beauty and mystery of everything. Have you ever thought of that, that you can measure life by your index of attentiveness to everything that comes into your range of vision? If you are always too busy or too engrossed to stop for the interruptions that come along, then you are missing a great deal and aren't living very well. But if your life is open and relaxed, so that interruptions are always the potential bearers of blessing, so you can transform the situations in which you find yourself, then you are living life to its fullest.

This is the way it was with our Lord. His life must have been an unending series of interruptions, one thing after another, and one person after another. Yet his understanding of life itself, his sense of grace underlying everything, gave him in all of it an equanimity that shines positively through the pages of the Gospels. He was always radiant because he saw God's blessing in everything—even in some men tearing up the roof when he was trying to teach a houseful of people about the coming of the Kingdom!

How wonderful it would be if you and I could live with the same sense of grace and the same tolerance for interruptions—if we could embrace the child who interrupts our favorite TV program just at its climax, if we could put aside our paperwork to talk with the colleague who drops by to visit, if we could see the wildflowers beside the road when we have to wait behind a traffic accident, if we could take time to be cordial to the salesperson who stops by to call on us. Life is beautiful and warm and gracious—if we're only the same way.

It can be the same for all of us all the time. We only have to remember that life is a series of interruptions, and that they are all blessings if we will only live with the sense of grace that enables them to be so.—John Killinger

SUNDAY, AUGUST 17, 2003
Lectionary Message

Topic: Seven Habits for a Christian

TEXT: Eph. 5:15–20

Other Readings: 1 Kings 2:10–12; 3:3–14; Ps. 111; John 6:51–58

Author Stephen Covey has created an entire industry with his popular book *The Seven Habits of Highly Effective People.* There are audio versions of his book. There are books with inspirational stories of people who have shared with him how they live the habits. He has written a devotional book of daily readings for highly effective people, and there have been major copycat books: *Seven Silly Eaters, Seven Secrets of Slim People, Seven Habits of Highly Defective People, Seven Habits of Peaceful Parents,* and *The Habits of Seven Highly Annoying People.* And although Covey may not have intentionally stolen the idea from Saint Paul, in this passage from Ephesians, Paul identifies seven characteristics of a dynamic Christian life: (1) Look carefully at how you walk. 2) Make the most of time. 3) Do not be foolish. 4) Do not get drunk. 5) Be filled with the Holy Spirit. 6) Address one another in psalms, hymns, and songs. (7) Always and in all places give thanks.

I. Just as Covey understands that the culture of effectiveness is contrary to the normal activities of life around us, Paul understood that the Christian lifestyle is a very different lifestyle. The Christians of the first century had come from pagan, Jewish, Greek, and Roman backgrounds. Now, in response to God's grace, they had been invited to live as Christians, and that meant they would have different habits, different attitudes, and different standards.

(a) *Watch how you walk.* You will walk funny. You will walk differently. You will not walk the way the world walks. You will watch carefully how you walk.

A teacher sent her top ten students before the faculty in a well-rehearsed "slacking" shuffle, and the faculty wrote that they expected these students to be negative, argumentative, unresponsive, and troublemakers. The teacher dressed up the students, sent them back in with erect postures, strong strides forward, and chests out, and the faculty wrote that they would expect these students to be prompt, courteous, attentive, and productive. It matters how you walk. The way you are treated and the expectations of others are shaped by the way you walk, even as others judge our whole character by the way we live our lives. Take notice how you move, how you act, and how you live, for others will read and interpret how you walk.

(b) *Buy up the critical times.* Make the most of the times around you. Paul was well aware of the stress, pressures, temptations, and opposition to the love and grace of God that were around him. But he urged the young Christians, and urges us today, that as they were involved in the issues and the struggles of the life around them, they needed to be alert to those moments that were most significant. Not all battles are important. The Christian witness is not in peril in all battles. In the culture wars, not every PTA meeting is Normandy. Not every football game or library has to start with prayer or have the Ten Commandments read. Make the most of the times; focus on the critical moments when you must stand fast. "Once to every man and nation comes the moment to decide," but it is not every moment.

(c) *Do not be foolish.* Don't be confused about the value of things. The fool says in his heart, "There is no God," which means that the fool is the one who has no standard by which to determine value. The fool has no concept of what is important and what is without value. If the cross of Jesus Christ is the standard of excellence and love, then from that gift of grace all other acts are measured and evaluated. Do not be foolish and fail to find the true value of experiences in the revelation of God's love in Christ.

(d)(e) *Do not get drunk; be filled with the Holy Spirit.* Do not find your happiness in the bottom of a wine jug. Do not drink to the gods of Bacchus and Zeus. Do not engage in worship services that are built on losing your consciousness or losing control of your mind. Rather, seek your joy in the celebration of life that comes in the Holy Spirit. Christian worship expects all of you to participate—your heart, mind, soul, and strength. It does not try to guide you to waste your gifts in drunken stupors. Do not let the world shape your ideas of vitality, excitement, joy, and blessing. The gift of the goodness of God ought to be able to get your feet moving and fill your heart with joy. How in the world have we ever allowed the beer companies to convince our college students that the only fun thing to do on weekends is to get falling-down drunk? Why do we let Madison Avenue tell us that the only way to know if we are happy is to buy more stuff? So we work to buy stuff, which we never have time to enjoy. We are too exhausted for each other and our children, so the loneliness and isolation haunts us and we call that happiness. Be filled by the Spirit of God, and let that Spirit shape and define your blessings and your joys.

(f) *Address one another in psalms, hymns, and songs.* Always praise God with words and music. Who in the world would want to live in an opera, when all of our speech would be sung words? Addressing one another in hymns would make all of our lives like a Mr. Rogers Neighborhood, with all of our conversations in song. Still, music is so much a part of our lives: whistle while you work; don't worry, be happy; golden oldies. There is something about music, which communicates with us and others, that helps create a bond of community. Zorba the Greek turned to his friends and said, "When the heart is full, what can it do but sing?" Paul wanted Christians to be people who know their blessings and sing in gratitude for all they have received.

(g) *Always and in all places give thanks.* The old Scottish minister had taken these words to heart: If we faced the fact of our lives squarely! We have been created and given life, and as long as we live we should be grateful to have been created. We have been redeemed by grace, and no matter how bad things may seem, we are always forgiven sinners, so we should give thanks for that. The old minister every Sunday gave thanks in the pastoral prayer for all things. Every Sunday was a prayer of thanksgiving. One Sunday the weather was horrible: the rain, the cold, the wind, and the dark cloudy sky. The people of his congregation had been gloomy and quarrelsome all week. They just knew there was nothing the minister could give thanks for. But he began the prayer, "Always and in all places we are to give thanks, so we give thee thanks, O Gracious God, that life in our town isn't always this nasty." No matter where we are or what is in our lives or what is happening to us, we have reasons to be thankful.

Covey knows that seven habits aren't all the habits that effective people have. Paul knows that seven habits of Christian living aren't all that a Christian needs or ought to have, but it's a start; and when the grace begins to move in us and through us, we become new creatures in the Kingdom of God.—Rick Brand

ILLUSTRATION

JESUS' INVOLVEMENT.   No language can do justice to the person Jesus Christ! No description is ever fully adequate when we discuss the truth that "in Christ God was reconciling the world to himself" (2 Cor. 5:19). His involvement with us was voluntary but vital. Jesus entered our human situation at the bottom of the ladder, as it were, so that we might know the one at the top of the ladder. Jesus experienced the world we know so that we can experience the world he knows. Trusting in him and following him will let us learn what he came to show us and gain what he came to give us, with "every rung go[ing] higher, higher."—James Earl Massey[2]

SERMON SUGGESTIONS

Topic: When Faith Breaks Down
TEXT: Ex. 17:1–7
(1) *Situation:* Things go well and faith in God is bright and obedient (v. 1a). (2) *Complication:* Difficulty comes, and questions and doubts arise (vv. 1b–3). (3) *Resolution:* Because God cares for his people, he blesses them despite their unworthiness (vv. 4–7).

Topic: Why Praise God?
TEXT: Rom. 11:33–36 NEB
(1) He is the source of all that is. (2) He is the guide of all that is. (3) He is the goal of all that is.

CONGREGATIONAL MUSIC

1. "Lord, Enthroned in Heavenly Splendor," George Hugh Bourne (1874)
   BRYN CALFARIA, William Owen (1854)
   With its strong Welsh melody and harmony, this hymn is a marvelous one to sing at the beginning of worship. Moreover, its first and last stanzas refer to Jesus as the true and living bread—an appropriate accompaniment to the Gospel lesson (John 6:51–58).
2. "O Give the Lord Wholehearted Praise," Ps. 111; vers. *The Psalter* (1912)
   GERMANY, W. Gardiner's *Sacred Melodies* (1815)
   Also suitable for the opening of worship, this paraphrase of Psalm 111 constitutes a natural substitute for the Psalter reading.
3. "For the Music of Creation," Shirley Erena Murray (1988)
   RUSTINGTON, C. Hubert H. Parry (1897)
   The singing of this fine contemporary hymn written by one of New Zealand's premier hymnists would be a perfect response to the Epistle lesson (Eph. 5:15–20), in which the apostle Paul encourages singing melodies in the heart.

---

[2]*Sundays in the Tuskegee Chapel* (Nashville: Abingdon Press, 2000), p. 124.

4. "I Will Sing of My Redeemer," Philip P. Bliss (1876)

HYFRYDOL, Rowland H. Pritchard (1830)

Fulfilling the same purpose as the previous hymn, this familiar gospel song exalts the place of singing in worship and the ultimate reason for singing—the worshiper's redemption in Christ.—Hugh T. McElrath

WORSHIP AIDS

CALL TO WORSHIP.   "Lord, I have loved the habitation of thy house, and the place where thine honor dwelleth" (Ps. 26:8).

INVOCATION.   Almighty and merciful God, stir in our hearts and renew our minds with truth, that challenged we may act, informed we may be comforted, and prayerful we may be renewed in Jesus' name.—E. Lee Phillips

OFFERTORY SENTENCE.   "Bear ye one another's burdens, and so fulfill the law of Christ" (Gal. 6:2).

OFFERTORY PRAYER.   Lord, we know the prestige that goes with money. Remind us also of the joys of giving, no matter the amount, and of the discipline that stewardship instills. Allow us to catch a glimpse of the way Christ looks at our giving. Whatever our gift, make much of it, we pray.—E. Lee Phillips

PRAYER.   Let thy spirit of wisdom and mercy move this day in the hands and minds of all thy servants, O God our Father: in surgeons who stand at the junctures of life and death; in parents who guard the gates of their children's hearts against fear and build in them a lasting peace; in writers who open the imagination of all ages to visions by which life is glorified or corrupted, that men may see beyond themselves; in social workers who bring clarity to confusion, hope to despair, and counsel to the concerned, that life may not be an impossible burden; in teachers who live at the growing edge of the mind, encouraging, stimulating, revealing truth, and nurturing the abundant life of man; in humble folk who seek to be faithful to thee in every work by which the world is sustained. Amen.—Samuel H. Miller[3]

SERMON

Topic: Taking Time to Smell the Roses, or Relaxing in the Presence of the Holy
Text: Luke 10:38–42

It's a shame about Martha, isn't it? The first known workaholic in history. Here she was with the Lord of the universe in her home and she couldn't stop working long enough to enjoy him. Does it sound like anybody you know? It probably does, because there is at least a little bit of Martha in all of us. There is some Mary, too. But it is the Martha that gives us the most trouble.

The truth is that workaholics don't need much to do in order to keep busy. They *make*

---

[3]*Prayer for Daily Use* (New York: HarperCollins, 1957), p. 30.

things for themselves to do. They are a little like alcoholics. You know, it is said that one test for knowing you are an alcoholic is if you hide your juice in little places around the house or the office. Well, workaholics are the same sort of people. They manage to have a little work tucked away everywhere. If they come home early from the office, they have work in the yard or the garden. If they sit down to read a book in the evening, it is a book related to their work. If they watch television, they do it with a bit of darning or knitting in their hands. If they take a vacation, it is probably a work-related vacation. There is no corner of their lives where there is not some work hidden away that they can do when they are in the vicinity. Martha found work in everything. She wasn't happy with herself when she wasn't working.

Why do you suppose that was? Why wasn't Martha happy with herself when she wasn't working?

Psychologists say there are several things that may account for people being workaholics. For one thing, workaholics are very competitive people. They have a strong need to succeed. Maybe Martha wanted Jesus' visit to her house to be better than any visit he had had anywhere else. There's a lot of that in us, isn't there?

Another possible cause for workaholism is the need to be approved or liked. Perhaps Martha always thought her parents liked Mary better than they liked her. It may not have been true, but she thought it, and that was just as motivating. So she had to work to gain their favor. She had to outdo everybody else in order just to stay even with everybody else.

There's another reason people become workaholics: guilt. That's right: they work to pay off a sense of guilt. Guilt about what? It doesn't matter: guilt about not being liked, guilt about not doing well in school, guilt about not feeling wanted by your parents, guilt about cheating on your wife or your husband. And how do you make up for guilt? You kill yourself by working so hard. Can you see that in Martha? She may have been denying herself the pleasure of sitting at Jesus' feet because she felt guilty about something. Maybe she didn't know she felt guilty, but deep down she did.

Some psychologists mention one more reason for workaholism; they say people work hard to leave behind them a monument of who they were. It's the old mortality-immortality game, isn't it? We don't really trust in the afterlife, so we want to erect a stone for posterity as a witness to our having passed this way. Do you suppose that's the way it was with Martha? She was killing herself with work, and when she died she wanted to be remembered as a good housekeeper or a slavish hostess. That's a lot like the need to be liked and approved, isn't it? Only it doesn't matter whether people like us now; its after we're gone that counts!

Do you see the real problems in Martha's life—and in ours? She hadn't heard about grace, had she? Or if she had heard about it she hadn't internalized it. Everything in her life was work; none of it was gift. Even in the presence of Jesus, she didn't recognize this. She still thought she had to earn everything. She didn't know that God had already given her what she wanted.

Wouldn't that be wonderful, if we could all just learn to be Mary instead of Martha, to say yes to the Mary side of our personalities and banish the Martha side, except as a kind of momentary half-sister when there are unpleasant chores we simply have to do? How much more we would enjoy life! How full of love and tolerance and forgiveness we would be!

We're like Martha fussing about Mary: "Lord, speak to her. She'll listen if you tell her. Remind her of her duties. Tell her to get up and help me with all this work I am so heroically doing."

Wayne E. Oates, in his book *Confessions of a Workaholic,* says that the dyed-in-the-wool workaholic is a perfectionist and has "a vigorous intolerance of incompetence" in fellow workers or other persons he or she lives with. Sound like anybody you know? Yourself, maybe?

Jesus tried to tell Martha the real score in life. "Martha," he said, "you are anxious and troubled about many things, but only one thing is really important in life." What was that? Sitting at Jesus' feet. Recognizing the holy when one is in its presence. Stopping to smell the flowers. Realizing that God has accepted us and affirmed us, and that we can stop knocking ourselves out and enjoy what God is doing in our lives.

God's grace is freely given to all of us. We don't have to work harder than anybody else does in order to receive it. All we have to do is relax and accept the love and affirmation that have come our way, and let it change us into loving, affirming people. How much richer life is when this change takes place!—John Killinger

SUNDAY, AUGUST 24, 2003
Lectionary Message

Topic: Dressing the Part
TEXT: Eph. 6:10–20
Other Readings: 1 Kings 8:(1, 6, 10–11) 22–30, 41–43; Ps. 84; John 6:56–69

I. There have always been those who have thought they could tell others how to fight their battles. Many have been quick to tell those on the low end of the economic scale how, if they would just save their paycheck, not spend it all on beer on Saturday night, buy a little car instead of those secondhand Cadillacs, save and make a few sacrifices, they could work their way up.

(a) But it seems that is advice they would rather give than take, according to the financial aid officers at colleges and universities in the United States. Financial aid officers from all over the country report that the parents of college-age students are spending all they make on second and third homes, on third and fourth cars, and just expecting the colleges to give their children scholarships. The applicants for aid are not even willing to take out second mortgages or make a few sacrifices, such as making their children ride bikes on campus instead of having cars. The parents of children going off to college this year are described as unwilling to make any sacrifices so they can pay for a college education. They just expect the colleges to provide scholarship help.

(b) So you tell me, against whom does this woman struggle? She is a single parent now after nineteen years of marriage. She has always believed in working hard, saving and making sacrifices for her children. She and her ex-husband had accumulated a rather sizeable account to put their children through college. Now she needs a new car, and she reads that article in the paper about how all the other parents have been spending to the hilt. They haven't been saving and they are expecting the colleges to send their children to college. Why should she be such a sap? She has been sacrificing and saving and she discovers in the paper that all the rest of the parents have been having a good time with their money and just expecting the colleges to provide scholarships for "wonderful children." So she is wrestling with whether or not to spend some of that college money for the car she thinks she needs. Who is the enemy she struggles against?

(c) Our lives are a constant struggle. We are engaged in a daily war. The battles and the confrontations are persistent and perpetual, and the struggle is up close and personal all the time. It is hand-to-hand combat, inside our own head, brother against brother, daughter against mother, buyer against seller, store against store, city against city, hope against despair, appropriate against inappropriate, and good against evil. It is more than just ourselves. Against whom does the woman struggle?

II. The words from the New Testament say the evil against which we struggle is more than just our own personal private evil. The evil we struggle against is more than just flesh and blood. Paul describes these struggles we are in as struggles against principalities and powers, against the world rulers of this present darkness, and against a whole spiritual host of wickedness. This struggle is against the evil that is around us, and that is more than just the evil in our own hearts. Everybody else is doing it. Money makes the world go 'round, and it is better to spend somebody else's than your own. Those in debt get more credit than those with a positive balance. Nobody makes sacrifices anymore! The struggle the single parent is engaged in is personal, but it is also against principalities, powers, temptations, attitudes, institutions, and systems, which are all around her.

(a) Hans Küng in his little book on the Apostles Creed, *Credo*, says we must never trivialize the power of evil around us; yet there are two ways in which we constantly trivialize that power. One way is to say that there is no such thing as evil, that nothing is good or evil by itself. There are only evil individuals. There are evil people, but there is no evil power independent of evil people. The other way to trivialize evil is to make the evil powers into a personal, individual, spiritual being. All of the principalities, powers, and forces of evil are condensed into the spiritual being of the Devil or Satan, and all evil people are victims and subjects of the Devil. Paul's language so much more accurately describes the evil as forces, powers, and hosts of spiritual wickedness. Isn't our legal system moving more and more toward basing most of its defenses on the existence of evil forces, powers, and principalities that have made victims of the doers of crime? The lawyers do not claim that the defendant is a victim of Satan, or under the control of the Devil, but they do argue that the evil is a result of evil forces that were beyond the individual's responsibility and control.

(b) Nobody has been denying that we are engaged in a struggle out there, and most of us know we are in a battle with evil even if we haven't spent a lot of time trying to figure out where the evil is or what to call it. The more pressing question is, How can we survive? How can we be equipped to stand firm? There is a struggle; how can we find resources and help to meet the struggle day in and day out?

III. Paul urges us to be strengthened for this battle by our faith and trust in Jesus Christ.

(a) We are to equip ourselves with the weapons and the dress of God's strength. We do not go out in our own strength. We are to be strengthened by the strength and power of God.

Paul says we are to wrap around us the truth that this is God's creation. It is he who has made us, and he is God, and creation and all history are within his ultimate love. For the protection of our heart and chest there is a covering of God's righteousness—not our own being right, but that God by his love and mercy can make us right and redeem our pasts. We walk in the sandals of peace, for we go out in confidence in God's love and mercy for us so we no longer have to go out with the idea that we have to triumph and make a name for ourselves. We no longer go out in the search-and-destroy attitude that if there is to be peace, we have to make it ourselves. For on our heads is the crown of salvation as a gift. We have already received the anointing of baptism. We have a helmet of salvation already upon us. We are not fighting to gain a heaven that has already been given to us in God's mercy and grace.

(b) Paul reminds us that we are not fighting to conquer evil. Jesus Christ has already defeated evil. Death has lost its sting. Evil has lost its enduring quality. One of the features of evil is that it destroys but never builds. But we are seeking by the strength of God simply to stand firm, to hold our place, to defend the ground that has already been given to us, to keep in our control a critical position on a battlefield.

(c) We go out equipped by God's strength not to crush or destroy others but to keep our light shining even in the midst of a storm. The power of evil struggles simply to make us become evil, too. The spiritual hosts of wickedness only want us to become like them. The victory of Jesus Christ was in the fact that, strengthened by the power of God, he looked at those who had crucified him and asked for their forgiveness. He did not stoop to hating them back.

The Emperor only wanted Luke Skywalker to give in to the dark side of the force, to draw his strength from the hatred of evil and thus become a part of and a victim of the evil forces. Paul Hill became so wrapped up in his struggle to save unborn babies that the power of the dark side, the power of evil, won as he killed the doctor at the abortion clinic. And all over the news there was the same question: How can he be any different from the people who have the abortion if he kills a living human being? Paul Hill lost his footing and the Christian faith lost one of its places of witness.

IV. We are in a struggle, and we are not able in our own strength to stand firm; therefore, we must be strengthened by the power of God in us, by the grace given to us in Jesus Christ. We must stand firm in the peace of God so that we do not yield to and allow the evil powers to work through us. Encourage one another, pray for one another, and put on the full armor of God, for we do not contend against flesh and blood.—Rick Brand

ILLUSTRATION

A NEW CENTER.   Children play a game called Follow the Leader. The object is to go where the leader goes and do what the leader does. In that sense Jesus is our Lord. The object of life is to go where he wants and do as he leads. But one main thing that's different from the game is that Jesus gives me the strength to follow him!

When I proclaim Jesus as my Lord, I have a new center for my life. I want to commit all of myself that I know to all of Christ I am coming to know. Paul wrote that it is through Christ as our Lord that we have victory.

Many of us look in all of the wrong places to try to find victory in life. We have possessions, prestige, and power, but deep inside we feel empty and defeated. We are afraid of life and afraid of dying. We have things on the outside, but when we look on the inside of ourselves, we know that we are the losers. Once Paul had all this world could offer, but do you think he would ever go back? Not since he had found that real victory comes "through our Lord Jesus Christ."—Charles B. Bugg[4]

---

[4]*Getting on Top When Life Gets Us Down* (Nashville: Broadman Press, 1990), pp. 86–87.

SERMON SUGGESTIONS

Topic: What Is Real Religion?

TEXT: Amos 5:18–24

(1) Not mere waiting for God to set things right. (2) Not mere rites, ceremonies, and festivals of worship. (3) Rather, a worship of God embodied in genuine efforts to set things right in the world now.

Topic: Dead or Alive—In God's Good Hands

TEXT: 1 Thess. 4:13–18

(1) The Lord will come for all who are united with him. (2) Then we shall always be with the Lord. (3) But now we can comfort one another with this blessed hope.

CONGREGATIONAL MUSIC

1. "How Lovely, Lord, How Lovely," Ps. 84; vers. Arlo D. Duba (1980)
    MERLE'S TUNE, Hal H. Hopson (1983)

    This lovely paraphrase of Psalm 84, suitable to accompany the Psalter reading, would be a good invocation or call to worship at the beginning of the service.
2. "Be Strong in the Lord," Linda Lee Johnson (1979)
    STRENGTH or FETTKE, Tom Fettke (1979)

    Here is a contemporary song that mirrors in its message the words of the Epistle reading about putting on the whole armor of God (Eph. 6:10–20).
3. "Wonderful Word of Life," Philip P. Bliss (1984)
    WORDS OF LIFE, Philip P. Bliss (1974)

    Simon Peter's words, "Lord, to whom shall we go? You have the words of life eternal" (John 6:68) find appropriate echo in this beloved gospel song that exalts God's Word.
4. "God Has Spoken by His Prophets," George W. Briggs (1852)
    HYMN TO JOY, Ludwig van Beethoven (1824)

    "Now the Lord had fulfilled his word which he spoke" (1 Kings 8:20a). This quotation from the Old Testament lesson recounting Solomon's bringing of the Ark of the Covenant to Jerusalem focuses attention on the message of this fine nineteenth-century hymn: God speaks both in the past and in the present.—Hugh T. McElrath

WORSHIP AIDS

CALL TO WORSHIP.   "For we are laborers together with God: ye are God's husbandry, ye are God's building. According to the grace of God which is given unto me, as a wise master-builder, I have laid the foundation, and another buildeth thereon. But let every man take heed how he buildeth thereupon. For other foundation can no man lay than that is laid, which is Jesus Christ" (1 Cor. 3:9–11).

INVOCATION.   Open us, Lord, to all we can be and need to be, through the power of our Lord Jesus Christ, so that in this service of worship we may see ourselves as God does and seek God's will to do.—E. Lee Phillips

OFFERTORY SENTENCE.   "Blessed be the God and Father of our Lord Jesus Christ, who hath blessed us with all spiritual blessings in heavenly places in Christ" (Eph. 1:3).

OFFERTORY PRAYER.   Saving God, if this money we bring can be used to bring many to saving faith in Christ, baptizing them in the name of the triune God and leading them to observe all that Christ commanded, then bless it beyond all we may think or dream.—E. Lee Phillips

PRAYER.   God of the mountains and valleys: trusting the inspired word of the psalmist, who asserts that our help comes from the Lord, we turn to you with a plea for help. Help, please, that student who is so burdened down with work and plagued by a sense of loneliness that she is about to quit school and give up on herself; that young man who is struggling for identity and worrying that he is neither worthy nor capable of relationships; that chairperson of the board for whom work has become a nearly intolerable chore because of the need to give attention to personal problems; that office worker who cannot concentrate on clerical skills because of the threat imposed by medical problems; that friend who is fighting with doubts and seeking a stronger faith; that family member who feels no love, sees no purpose, and experiences no fulfillment in daily life.

As we pray for help for others, we also seek your help for ourselves. It is all we can do to keep from screaming, "Help!" We need your help so badly. None of us has life completely all together. We need you—your love, your guidance, your forgiveness, your grace. O God, yes, most of all we need your grace.

At times we have experienced what the psalmist declared. Our help does come from you. We long to experience that help again. Please, God, help us now.

We ask for help in the name of the perfect helper. Amen.—C. Welton Gaddy[5]

SERMON
Topic: Jesus' First Miracle
TEXT: John 2:1–11

I. Most people, in their youth at least, believe that security and happiness can be found somewhere under the sun. The basic source of these values they look for in love and a home.

(a) How significant that our Lord's first miracle should be performed in the setting of a marriage. In this way, the meaning of the coming of Christ is brought close to the center of human life. The first miracle takes place against the background of the unending quest for solid satisfactions in life.

(b) A wedding among the Jews in those times was a gala occasion. The event in Cana of Galilee was no exception. It is possible that Mary, the mother of Jesus, was in charge of arrangements. It appears that after the festivities were under way, Jesus and his disciples came and joined in.

(c) What a time for the newlyweds! They were treated like royalty for an entire week and, according to the law of Moses, the groom was entitled to exemption from military service for a whole year and was not supposed to have to work for the same period of time.

But that was life. What could be more important to the future of the race than the home? Thus the home, from time immemorial, has snatched serious people from the despair of death.

II. The final answer to the human plight, however, is not to be found in anything that we

---

[5]*Prayers: From Adoration to Zeal* (Valley Forge, Pa.: Judson Press, 1993), p. 47.

do or build. An ominous shadow fell across the hilarity at Cana. Mary summed up the matter when she said, "They have no wine."

(a) Do not people often have to say, "What we have provided is gone"? Enthusiasm dies down. Sickness comes. Disillusionment with one's success or character or religion leaves one wandering in darkness, trying to get to the light without which all other goals have no meaning.

(b) Even the religion of the Jews, to whom the revelation of God was given, was not adequate. Some of them referred to it as "a yoke . . . which neither our fathers nor we were able to bear" (Acts 15:10). Many professed Christians today are under the same handicap. Their personal version of religion is a burden, not a power. It is not true Christianity.

(c) Serious-minded, responsible people like Mary look on and lament, "Our supplies are exhausted. What can we do?"

III. When Jesus Christ takes control of a situation, things really happen. Human limitations become the arena of his triumph.

(a) Jesus' reply to his mother's frantic plaint was courteous, yet firm. He said, in effect, "Dear lady, your authority over me has come to an end. What I do must be at the command of the Father. I now await the time when God's plan will be fulfilled."

(b) Mary agreed and instructed the servants to carry out any orders her Son might give.

In this lies the secret of happiness and purpose in life: to find the proper Master. Thus, it is necessary to cut through all family ties, all national traditions, all personal preferences, and all warm friendships until the supreme object of loyalty and affection is discovered. When that tremendous discovery is made, love, patriotism, ambition, and fellowship have a new, more realistic wealth of meaning.

(c) On order from Jesus, the servants filled purification vessels with water. The total volume of water was over one hundred gallons.

Then Jesus directed the servants to draw out water and take it to the master of ceremonies. Lo, the water was changed into wine. The master of ceremonies declared it good wine, superior to what had been served at first. This is the point: just like the turning of water into wine, the coming of Jesus would turn religion as the world knew it into something of higher quality, which would be adequate and satisfying. In this way, Jesus "manifested forth his glory" (v. 11).

IV. Jesus showed by what he taught and by the way he lived that true religion is not an empty form handed down from parent to child. It is a living relationship with the living God. It is a vital experience of the heart and of the will. In quality, the difference is like water turned into wine.—James W. Cox

ILLUSTRATION

TRUTH IN SIGNS.   These incidents are, so to speak, the pictures he inserts into his book to make the gospel visible; so that at a glance we can take in what would have needed pages to describe.

In some such fashion the episode at the marriage in Cana is the frontispiece to the gospel, summing up pictorially what is to come: how our Lord enters into people's troubles, how unbelievably he suffices in every difficulty, and above all how he enriches things for us. What water is to wine, what that embarrassing insufficiency was to the relief he wrought for his host, so is any other life compared to the fullness, the color, the adventure, the achievement that he gives.

But if that is the main lesson, many other thoughts too leap out and at us arrestingly as we move toward it. There is the fact that Christ was there; that they wanted him to be there;

had no fear that he would be out of his element, or fail to fit in, or make others uncomfortable, as the Baptist, with his asceticism, would have done. And be sure there was no awkward silence at the part of the table where he sat. For Christ did not hold aloof from innocent human happinesses—a fact which many of his followers have forgotten, with tragic enough results, making his religion a more austere thing than he ever did, and by their caricatures of him scaring many from him who are his by natural right.—Arthur John Gossip[6]

SUNDAY, AUGUST 31, 2003
Lectionary Message

Topic: Saying and Doing

TEXT: James 1:17–27

Other Readings: Song of Solomon 2:8–13; Ps. 45:1–2, 6–9; Mark 7:1–8, 14–15, 21–23.

I. "Know this, my beloved brethren: Let every one be quick to hear, slow to speak." More listening than speaking! So often we in the Christian community seem so eager to speak, to bear witness, and to give testimony. James reminds us that we need to be a whole lot quicker to listen than to speak.

There is a need to listen to what is happening in the world around us so that we might be able to know just what to say. Saying the right thing at the right time is the secret of appropriate communications. Let everyone be quick to listen. How can the salesperson know what to offer the customer until she has listened to the customer's needs? So it is important to listen to what is happening around us and to understand what is being said.

The primary message being given to the Christian community by our world around us is that the Christian community is going to be the only one responsible for telling the Christian story. That is a dramatic change. We may feel bad about it, we may lament the loss of support, but society will not be sharing with us the presentation of the Christian faith anymore.

It is no wonder then that Susie and Billy have grown up as they have. Susie and Billy have had nothing but the finest care and attention since birth. They are baby boomer babies; they have worn designer diapers coordinated with their sleepers, and their rooms have been vaporized with cleansing mountain herbal mist. They have had regular well-baby check ups, been read to every night by both parents, and had regular and routine visits to museum, zoo, and library. Susie and Billy have had Ataris, Nintendos, Baby Apples, and now their own power laptop computers. Every social, medical, physical, and intellectual aspect of their lives has been meticulously groomed and cultivated. They have received outstanding parenting—with one small, minor exception.

Not once have they stepped inside a church or synagogue. Their intellectual, psychological, and physical developments are off the charts, but the feeding and nurturing of the dimension of the spirit and the heart—things holy and mysterious, the wonder and awe of life, the mystery and hope of why we are here and where we are going—have never been mentioned. No one has wondered with them, "Little Lamb, who made thee?" Their parents claim they did not want to prejudice them at such an early age. "Let them make up their own minds

---

[6]*The Interpreter's Bible,* Vol. 8 (New York: Abingdon-Cokesbury Press, 1952), p. 491.

about religion when they are grown." Yeah, like they let them make up their own minds about eating vegetables. The folks pretty well settled on the idea that they would let the children choose a faith when they were older. Let them go down to the mall and pick one out like shopping.

Susie and Billy are not alone. Less than 40 percent of the American population now says it has gone to worship in the last month. Susie and Bill have never heard the stories of God's love for them. As Christian people we need to listen to this world to discover once again that there is indeed a hunger and a need for the Christian people to speak the Christian faith to a whole new generation.

If we listen to the world around us we can hear the void and the masses of people who have not had the good fortune of hearing the good news. Then we are ready to speak. As we listen we hear a call to speak the story, and as we listen we hear clearly that nobody else is going to be telling our story. Not the schools, not the city hall at Christmas, not the Ten Commandments in the courthouse, not the stores that now will advertise the Holiday Season. In the words of the old song, "Lonesome Valley," "Oh, nobody else will walk it for us, we have to walk it by ourselves." Nobody else will be speaking the Christian story but Christian people.

II. But how will we be able to speak the Christian story if we have not heard the whole story ourselves? So many of us have been concerned about our individual faith journeys, have been wrestling with our own faith issues, that we have not accepted or received or even bothered to understand the whole Christian story.

Dr. Will Willimon down at Duke Chapel tells about his last year at Yale Divinity School. It was a course in church history and the professor had invited a Greek Orthodox priest. *Newsweek* had a story the other week on the fact that the Greek and Russian Orthodox Churches were having a kind of revival at the moment. Their liturgy and their sense of beauty, mystery, and majesty were evoking from people a hunger for the holy that was not being addressed in other communities of faith. So the Orthodox priest came and gave a rather dry, boring lecture on the development of the Church creeds down through history. At the end of the lecture, one of the students, who was more concerned about his own spiritual development than about the history of the Church, asked, "Father Theodore, what can one do when one finds it impossible to affirm certain tenets of a creed?"

The priest looked confused. "Well, you just say the creed. It is not hard to learn. You can memorize it in a few hours. Most people can learn it quickly by heart and you just say it."

The student said, "No, you don't understand. What am I to do when I have difficulty affirming a part of the creed—say I am not ready to say that Jesus was born of a virgin, or maybe I believe in reincarnation and not the resurrection of the body."

The priest continued to look confused. The question and the answers seemed to be coming from two totally different places. The priest said, "You just say it. Particularly when you have difficulty believing it, you just keep saying it. It will come to you eventually."

The student was getting exasperated. The student was a product of the Protestant church of the 1960s. "How can I with any integrity affirm a creed in which I do not believe?"

The priest was also testy. "It is not *your* creed, young man. It is *our* creed. It is the Church's creed. This is what the people of God believe. You just keep saying it, for heaven's sake. Eventually it may come to you. For some, it takes longer than for others. How old are you, twenty-three? Don't be so hard on yourself. There are lots of things that one doesn't know at twenty-three. Eventually it may come to you. And even if it doesn't ever come, don't worry about it. It is not your creed. It is the creed of the people of God."

III. If we are to be able to speak to Susie and Billy about the nature of our Christian understanding of life and death, then we have to have listened to the whole Christian story. Susie and Billy are going to have lots of questions, and they are going to need more than just our own opinions and our own experiences. If we are going to be faithful sharers of the good news with Susie and Billy, we are going to first have to be good listeners and good participants in Christian education programs, and we are going to have to expect our Sunday school programs to offer solid stuff—classes that expect us to be serious students. As we get ready for Rally Day and a new year of Christian education, we need to prepare ourselves for listening to the whole Christian story so that we will be prepared to speak to a culture that has not often been interested in hearing the full Christian story because it has wanted only the pieces it could exploit.

Be quick to listen and slow to speak. We need to listen to the culture and the world around us. And what it sounds like is that there are many who have not heard a very clear or comprehensive sharing of the full story of the Christian faith. So there is a need for us to speak, but before we speak we need to listen to ourselves and to the whole range and meaning of the Christian creeds. It is not my creed they need to hear, but our faith's creed that we need to speak to them.—Rick Brand

ILLUSTRATION

CONVINCED.   Carlyle Marney was for many years pastor of the Myers Park Baptist Church in Charlotte. He was a powerful man, a man of immense intellectual gifts, a strong social actions champion. He was frequently invited to speak to ministers' gatherings around the country. The U.S. Army invited him to conduct seminars for their chaplains. One time, in Dallas, Texas, he addressed a large gathering of Southern Baptists. He declared to that huge group that he did not believe in the resurrection of the dead. After the presentation, Dr. Albert Outler, professor of theology from Southern Methodist, came up to Marney and said, "Marney, whoever told you that you had to believe the whole creed all the time?" Marney replied, "You are so smart. When do I believe it?" And Dr. Outler said simply, "When you need it." Marney told that story and then said, "I have just come back from two weeks of sitting by the side of my father as he died. We buried him. I now believe in the resurrection of the dead."—Rick Brand

SERMON SUGGESTIONS

Topic: Of Bones and Blessings

TEXT: Ezek. 37:1–14, esp. v. 5

(1) God sometimes faces in his people—individually or collectively—a difficult situation, like the skeleton of a once-thriving life. (2) What is worse, it may be a condition of long standing—"very dry" and entirely unpromising. (3) However, God is resourceful and, as almighty Creator, can give new life and promise.

Topic: What the Christian Life Is Like

TEXT: Rom. 8:6–11

(1) Its outlook is spiritual. (2) Its power is the Spirit of Christ. (3) Its promise is resurrection.

CONGREGATIONAL MUSIC

1. "Come Away to the Skies," Charles Wesley (1735)

   MIDDLEBURY, Ananias Davison (1725)

   The great hymnist Wesley took this day's appointed Old Testament passage (Song of Songs 2:8–13) as a basis for his Christian paean of praise. It could naturally be sung following the Old Testament reading.

2. "I Praise the King with All My Verses," Ps. 45; vers. Marie J. Post (1985)

   O DASS ICH TAUSEND, Johann B. Konig (1738)

   The first three stanzas of this modern paraphrase of Psalm 45 parallel the selected verses of the Psalter lesson. A soloist could sing them as introduction to the reading of the psalm.

3. "As Saints of Old Their First Fruits Brought," Frank von Christierson (1960)

   REGWAL, Leland B. Sateran (1963)

   The readings in James 1, particularly verses 17 and 22, are echoed in this contemporary hymn. Perhaps a soloist, small ensemble, or choir could sing the first stanza (unfamiliar to many) alone before inviting the congregation to join in the other stanzas.

4. "As a Chalice, Cast of Gold," Thomas H. Troegar (1984)

   INWARD LIGHT, Carol Doran (1984)

   The focus of this contemporary hymn is on a worshipful reflection on the message of the Gospel lesson, particularly Mark 7:14–15, 21–23. After the reading of the Gospel, it would be particularly effective to sing or repeat together the words of this hymn.—Hugh T. McElrath

WORSHIP AIDS

CALL TO WORSHIP.   "Create in me a clean heart, O God; and renew a right spirit within me" (Ps. 51:10).

INVOCATION.   As the small dark hours of night await the coming of the dawn, as a daffodil seeks the energy of the sun, as a starving man searches for life-sustaining food, so we come this morning into this sacred place seeking you, Father. May we not be disappointed in our quest. Let this be an hour in which we find you to be sufficient to meet our every need. In the stillness of these moments let us hear the wonder of your call to us, even as you hear our collective voice praying as the Lord taught us to pray: [the Lord's Prayer].—Henry Fields

OFFERTORY SENTENCE.   "Those who are taught the word must share in all good things with their teacher" (Gal. 6:6 NRSV).

OFFERTORY PRAYER.   It is because of your love and provision, Father, that we have means with which to bless others. Don't let us forget how well blessed we are, and lead us to be equal blessings to others as we give our tithes and offerings today, we pray.—Henry Fields

PRAYER.   Without you, Father, we could never have made it through the weeks and days that have led us to this place and these sacred moments. All along the way we have been blessed with your presence, even when we have not felt that you were near and working through the situations with which we were confronted. By your grace we have been presented new opportunities in life that would not have come to us but for your care and guidance. Because of your call to us, we have found new friends who would yet be strangers but for the family of faith that you have given to us. In kindness and gentleness you have called us to view our lives and see our shortcomings and sins. Your assurance of forgiveness upon our confession of sins to you has enabled us to make amends for the wrongs we have done to others. Your strength has enabled us to turn aside from many destructive temptations.

In this sacred moment we ask that you teach us how to live out our gratitude for all the blessings that come from your presence with us. Help us to introduce you to some soul estranged from you, to open the door of encouragement to some discouraged person, to bolster moral courage for that one slipping into a time of desperate testing. Enable us to assure those about us that you truly will and do forgive all manner of spiritual, moral, and physical sin. Empower us to herald your coming with salvation and healing even now.—Henry Fields

SERMON
Topic: Passing Faith Along
TEXT: Isa. 6:1–8; 2 Cor. 2:14–17

Isaiah experienced a dramatic and life-changing moment, not outside but inside the temple. "I saw the Lord," he said, explaining his vision in such a way that readers still feel the thrill of it. "I saw the Lord sitting on a throne, high and lofty, and the hem of his robe filled the temple." Isaiah went on to say that angelic beings surrounded the heavenly throne, their voices calling, "Holy, holy, holy is the Lord of hosts; the whole Earth is full of his glory." The very ground seemed to shake and the room was filled with smoke. Overwhelmed by the power and greatness of it all, the young Isaiah impulsively cried out, "Woe is me! I am lost, for I am a man of unclean lips and I live among a people of unclean lips; yet my eyes have seen the King, the Lord of Hosts!" Intense self-awareness was his as an awesome awareness of God overtook him.

Isaiah's confession of unworthiness was countered by the swift action of one of the angelic beings touching his lips with a heated stone taken from the altar. He was addressed with these words: "Now that this has touched your lips, your guilt has departed and your sin is blotted out." Divine cleansing and forgiveness transformed Isaiah's life in that instant, making him ready for the next and climactic part of his vision. He then heard the voice of the Lord saying, "Whom shall I send, and who will go for us?" No hesitancy was his, no holding back. Isaiah immediately replied, "Here am I; send me!" Thus was the prophet formed and fashioned to become a living and vital witness to the truth of God among the people of his time.

It was this prophet who first anticipated the coming of the Messiah—the saving presence of one who would establish God's justice and righteousness upon the Earth. Significantly, Isaiah helped sustain his people's faith and hope through perilous times. His nation was under constant threat from its enemies, and there were internal problems of spiritual rebellion against God. Isaiah confronted these issues unflinchingly and beckoned his people to higher ground.

Do I hear someone saying, "We certainly could use an Isaiah among us today"? A presence like his might indeed make a difference in public and private affairs, given the spiritual shortcomings of our present age. And who is to know? Maybe such a voice will be heard; maybe such a person will appear. But lacking that, facing, as we do, days of decreasing commitment to traditional religious forms, are there responses that you and I can make? Does Isaiah's experience offer any pattern or guide for us to follow?

Think again of what happened. Isaiah first allowed himself to be exposed to a worship setting; he went to the temple and attended to the practices of meditation and prayer. In the midst of all of that, this man felt the majesty of God, plus the magnitude of his own inadequacy. He felt himself a sinner, unclean, unworthy of such an encounter. But at the very utterance of that confession, forgiveness was granted him, and wholeness of spirit. Isaiah from that point forward was ready, even eager, to go where God would send him, to speak what God would have him say. He became a movingly effective representative of hope and faith, using his talents to serve and bless others for the rest of his days.

The linkages we can make with Isaiah's experience are clear. From personal times of worship and prayer can come the renewing realization that we ourselves are forgiven by God, and when forgiven, we are free to be fulfilled in service to God. The sins, inadequacies, and failures that dog our footsteps are removed. Divine love bestows its healing touch, causing our guilt to depart and our wrongs to be blotted out. Thus cleansed inwardly, we are fortified to share outwardly the goodness and mercy of God.

When individuals like all of us here allow ourselves to confront the holiness of God, when finally we admit that we have stained lips and inhabit a sinful world, when we humbly accept the restoring forgiveness God extends, then, like Isaiah, the good news of God's love flows from our lives, and faith grows strong. We become not peddlers of God's message but persons truly sent from God, passing along the blessings we have known. This is what we are here for! This is the calling every one of us receives. In the unusual analogy of the apostle Paul, "We are the aroma of Christ to God among those who are being saved and among those who are perishing." "Through us," wrote Paul, "spreads in every place the fragrance that comes from knowing God." Paul went on to say, "In Christ we speak as persons of sincerity, as persons sent from God and standing in his presence."

That sort of testimony goes a long way toward encouraging others to consider Christian faith for themselves. Minister James Reid wisely noted that "God is not revealed by argument but by a quality of spirit which creates the capacity to feel and respond, as light awakens the eye to see. Nothing else will reach the heart. . . . Lives which lack serenity or grace have no attractive power." So it is that we who would pass faith along become "the sweet savor of Christ," the aroma of Christ, to draw others to his side.

Our forgiven and surrendered lives may well impart that quality of a perfume that permeates the air, as the apostle Paul described; or they may have about them what can be called a radiance, a brightness. By whatever description, changed lives involve us in ministries to change the world. We take seriously our responsibility for passing Christian faith along.— John H. Townsend

SUNDAY, SEPTEMBER 7, 2003
Lectionary Message

Topic: In Second Place

TEXT: Mark 7:24–37

Other Readings: James 2:1–10 (11–13), 14–17; Prov. 22:1–2, 8–9, 22–23; Ps. 125

We like to be first. First place seems to be the best place: first in line, first in sales, first served in the restaurant, first to answer questions, first to know the "scoop." It feels good; it feels right to be first whenever possible. Life is such that often that's not the position in which we find ourselves. The lesser places or positions tell the story of our lives to a greater degree.

We like for our children to be first. If one has a son who is valedictorian of his graduating class, it's great. If one's son is cited for outstanding humanitarian service in his career, it will be announced. If one's daughter is recognized for dedicated service to oncology patients, how proud the parents will be. To be recognized as first in some way is wonderful, but even more wonderful is if this is true for your children.

I. *Jesus and a "second place" woman.* As we give a nod of recognition to this, can we imagine how it must have felt when the Gentile woman, Syrophoenician by nationality (I wish Mark had given us her name), took her concern for her daughter to Jesus and heard his response? "I'm concerned for the children [of the chosen nation]. The bread is theirs. It's not right to give that to dogs." How would we have handled a slur on our people in the face of such concern for a child of ours?

Why did Jesus answer the woman's request in such a way? He had just been talking to the Jews about what they considered clean and unclean. The bottom line was this: what's in a person's heart is the determining factor. What one speaks from the heart is what defiles. Jesus had entered unclean territory when he entered into the regions of Tyre and Sidon. When the woman, in humility, fell at his feet to make her plea and received such a response, one would suppose that Jesus had fallen back into the ways of his people. Was his answer making a statement about the way his people viewed the Gentiles? Was it for the benefit of someone in the house, unnamed in the story? Was it to test the woman's faith? I wish Jesus had not left us such a puzzle!

The Gentile woman was on a mission. Most of us would have parted company with Jesus at this point. In her time and culture she was probably familiar with begging for her wants and needs. She was perhaps accustomed to being a second-class person. What we do know is that she did not argue with Jesus about the put-down of her people; instead she said, "But even they desire the crumbs that fall from the children's table." She said not a word about who she or her people were, but said, "Even so, we have needs." A concern more important than who she was or what someone called her people was uppermost in her thoughts. We'll take the leftovers.

With rhetorical skill equal to that of Jesus himself in the previous discussions with the Pharisees, the woman turned the saying back to Jesus. Her response was the very thing that Jesus responded to by granting her quest. "Your daughter is healed because of what you have said!"

Oh, to be able to say the appropriate thing in the face of a put-down! One cannot escape the uneasy feeling that there are things in this story that we simply cannot grasp or understand. However, what we can grasp is that this Syrophoenician woman knew where to go for help, that someone else's position or relationship did not change her needs, that Jesus would be able to do what was needful for her child. This was her faith. When she returned to her house, her child was on the couch, "no longer under the control of the evil spirit." God is no respecter of persons but is rich unto all who call upon him.

II. *First and second place in the Church.* It's one thing to speak of discrimination—Jesus versus Gentiles. It is another matter to deal with discrimination within the Christian Church. This was the situation James was addressing. This time the discrimination was rich versus poor. The discrimination against the poor as they came to worship was in relation to their seating. The best, high seats were being given to the well-dressed, those wearing gold rings. The rings, according to the *HarperCollins Study Bible,* may have signified the person's status in the Roman social order. These persons were fawned over, while the poor, in their dirty clothes, were invited to stand in the background or sit at someone's feet. James begins chapter 2 by asking, "My brothers and sisters, do you with your acts of favoritism really believe in our glorious Lord Jesus Christ?" Second place has no place in the Christian family! The Scripture teaches that humans look on the outward appearance, but God looks on the heart.

If we are to be spoken to by the Word of God, we must always ask ourselves what this story or verse is saying to us. What does it say about our position with God? If we have a need or our loved ones are in need, would we search for Jesus, enter into his presence, and kneel in humility and reverence at his feet to bring our need to him? Would we fear there may be others he would be more likely to favor? Other children of the Kingdom who come first? Or would we be determined, by the way we speak to him, that he would hear and our request would be granted? If we persist in asking, will he not respond?

What are our own prejudices? If a person doesn't dress as we do, do we perceive them negatively? A personal story brings this to mind. When my husband was given his first ministerial appointment, we moved from Norfolk, Virginia, to eastern North Carolina. On the day we moved, the van left before us. We were delayed because of signing some leases on our duplex and our realtor was late coming. When our van arrived at the parsonage in Creswell, North Carolina, with boxes marked and stand-up cartons of hanging clothes clearly marked, our welcoming committee decided to hang our clothes in bedroom closets while they awaited our arrival. One person with whom I later became friends confessed that they had looked at the labels in my dresses and thought I would "fit in" there because of my name brands. What they didn't know was that I had been given most of those dresses following the death of a dear friend whose family wished me to have her wardrobe! Whenever I am overly impressed by someone's appearance, I remember Mother Teresa, who was called by God to minister to the poorest of the poor, and in each face saw the image of God.

Second place may become first place if we meet our Lord there. We are children of the Kingdom and he desires that all eat from his table. There is bread for all, and a seat for everyone. Let us ask, receive, and be grateful. Amen.—Bess G. Hunnings

ILLUSTRATION

REVERSAL.   When I was a young pastor, a drunken man stumbled into the sanctuary during worship one rainy, stormy Sunday night. He was unkempt and smelly. In the eyes of some worshipers, the man was despicable. Even some of the church leaders came to me and said, "Pastor, this man is no good, and he's disturbing our service! Shall we escort him outside?"

Thankfully, I heard God's voice speaking to me. I replied, "No. Don't escort him out, but let him come in. God's house is for 'whosoever will'" (Rev. 22:17).

When I extended the invitation to Christian discipleship, this man came to the altar, fell to his knees, and begged God for grace and mercy. He accepted Jesus Christ that night and became a transformed man and a dedicated church member. More than that, he brought his entire family to the Lord; all of them accepted Christ as their Savior and became devoted members.

God's everlasting love and kindness are available to each of us, unconditionally, regardless of how others may judge us.—Donald G. K. Ming[1]

SERMON SUGGESTIONS

Topic: When You Are on Your Own

Text: Josh. 5:9–12

(1) The Lord helps those who cannot help themselves. (2) The Lord then helps them by not helping them when they can help themselves.

Topic: Because of God's Friendship

Text: 2 Cor. 5:16–21 TEV

(1) Something has happened *to* us. (2) Something will happen *through* us.

CONGREGATIONAL MUSIC

1. "I Lift My Eyes to the Quiet Hills," Timothy Dudley-Smith (1968)

   DAVOS, Michael Baughen and Elizabeth Crocker (1970)

   This free paraphrase of Psalm 121 also relates to Psalm 125:2 and it could well accompany the Psalter reading.

2. "Thine Arm, O Lord, in Days of Old," Edward H. Plumptre (1866)

   ST MATTHEW, Tate and Brady (1708)

   The worshippers could appropriately respond to the Gospel lesson (Mark 7:24–37) recounting episodes in Jesus' ministry of healing by singing this classic hymn.

3. "Father, All Loving, Who Rulest in Majesty," Patrick R. N. Appleford (c. 1980)

   WAS LEBET, Johann H. Reinhardt (1754)

   A good musical accompaniment to the reading in James (2:1–13) that deals with the sin of partiality would be the singing of this fine contemporary hymn that focuses on ministry to the poor. (Note stanza 2 in particular.)

4. "Jesus Is Good News to All the Poor," Brian Wren (1981)

   RAILTON ROAD, Peter Cutts (1983)

   The Old Testament readings in Proverbs, which concentrate on the virtue of generosity toward the poor, will find a Christian response in this contemporary hymn by one of the most prolific and thoughtful of twentieth-century hymnists. Because it is unfamiliar, the three short stanzas could be sung by a soloist or small group. Then the entire hymn could be repeated by all in the worshiping congregation.—Hugh T. McElrath

WORSHIP AIDS

CALL TO WORSHIP.   "Worship the Lord in holy splendor; tremble before him, all the Earth" (Ps. 96:9 NRSV).

INVOCATION.   We cannot describe you, Father. We say that you are all-knowing, all-powerful, and everywhere present. But we cannot wrap our finite minds around such infinite

---

[1]*The Upper Room*, ed. by Stephen D. Bryant (Nashville: Upper Room, July 24, 2001).

and majestic concepts. Just knowing that much about you baffles us, whether we dare to invoke your name or invite your presence on any occasion. In our smallness, can we really be trusted with such a prerogative? In honesty, we are not sure. But Father, we do seek your attention. We do desire your presence. We really do want an encounter with you. So we invoke your name this hour. We do long to meet you or be met by you. Pray, hear our invocation. Out of your grace, come to us even as you came to those early followers of Jesus whom he taught to pray: [the Lord's Prayer].—Henry Fields

OFFERTORY SENTENCE.   "On the first day of every week, each of you is to put aside and save whatever extra you earn, so that collections need not be taken when I come" (1 Cor. 16:2).

OFFERTORY PRAYER.   Loving Lord, allow us to give as we are able, that others may receive according to their need; then both giver and recipient may know the blessings of God.—E. Lee Philips

PRAYER.   O you who are the Lord of the Feast, you in whose house there is bread enough and to spare, you who prepare a table before us not just in the presence of our friends but also in the presence of our enemies, you who hand to us a cup that is not only full but also running over—how can we appear before you except in praise and thanksgiving for all of your goodness to us and to all peoples.

As the Divine Host, your gracious hospitality goes out to all. Your sun shines on the evil and the good, and your rain falls on the just and the unjust. What hospitality we enjoy on this planet Earth!

Forgive us our little tea parties—I, myself, and me. Forgive us when our partying is only with like-minded people—no wonder we are so bored, and boring.

Forgive us for being such party-poopers and unwilling to sit at the table with other than our kind of people.

When we are truly at the party, we will want to see the house full. Help us to know the grace of the party—joy in relationship. We pray for the grace that begets both gracefulness and graciousness.

We would celebrate your grace, the healing of your grace, with all of those we have named and all others unnamed who are in need of your wholeness. You pile grace upon grace, and your invitation goes out to Jew and Palestinian, male and female, free and slave. Your love can bridge all troubled waters. We pray for the healing of the nations. We pray for the healing of this nation.

O the grace and graciousness of your invitation in the Sacraments: to be your child, your son, your daughter, and to eat at your table as a family—a feast of grace.

> Love Divine, all loves excelling,
> Joy of heaven, to Earth come down;
> Fix in us thy humble dwelling,
> All thy faithful mercies crown.

Through him who is both host and guest at our every table, and who is among us teaching us to pray and live with all peoples.—John Thompson

SERMON
Topic: The Divine Indicative
TEXT: Ex. 20:1–17; Mark 1:14–15

In his catechism class, Dr. Theo Bovet of Basle raised the question, "What is religion?" Immediately a small boy replied, "Religion shows us the things we must not do."

Such a response is not untypical of popular reactions to this important question. Many people reduce religion to a set of moral maxims, a series of heavy commandments, that must be obeyed. Usually most of the imperatives are negatives—"Thou shalt nots." However, a few of the mandates may be positive—"Thy shalts." Either way, the dominant conception of religion revolves around mandates, imperatives, commandments—do this and don't do that.

To be sure, responsibilities are an integral part of religion. Where the gospel is proclaimed, its truths are understood, and its promises are accepted, duties arise.

Christianity is not heralded by or embodied in imperatives alone. In fact, the very first words of the gospel are not commandments but announcements, not imperatives—declarations of what we must do—but indicatives—statements of what God has done. The fact is that persons are powerless to keep the requirements of the imperatives unless the promise of the indicative has been realized.

Note first the Exodus text, which contains the Ten Commandments. What are the first words in that passage that records God's will for his people? Not imperatives. Not commandments. Listen: "I am the Lord your God who brought you out of Egypt." Do you hear? Prior to any legal precepts to be obeyed comes an announcement of divine activity to be accepted.

Obedience to the Ten Commandments is not a condition for God's love but a response to God's love. People are to live after the pattern of the commandments because they have been accepted by God. God enables us to do that which he expects us to do.

This relationship between the indicative and the imperative persists throughout all of the Old Testament. I know that one demand after another rings out in the prophets. However, every prophetic imperative takes place within and is predicated upon the covenant. God has chosen these people to be his people. God's demands upon them follow God's acceptance of them. Responsibility comes after blessing.

Now look at the teaching of Jesus. Notice particularly how the Lord begins his ministry. Jesus' first sermon in the synagogue at Nazareth consisted of an amazing indicative (Luke 4:18–19). Here is a statement of unmitigated good news. Now hear the words of Jesus' first discourse among the crowds—"The time is fulfilled, and the Kingdom of God is at hand; repent and believe in the gospel" (Mark 1:15). Do you see the pattern?

Only after his initial statement of good news, the divine indicative, did Jesus declare an imperative—"Repent and believe in the gospel."

Do not miss the fundamental truths at stake here: We are loved by God. We are accepted by God. These are statements of fact. Jesus did not declare that we have to live a certain way in order for God to love us. He simply announced God's love. We obey not because we have to in order to know God's love. We obey because we want to, having known God's love.

Apart from the promise of the indicative we would be powerless to carry out the imperatives. As Paul Scherer has pointed out, apart from the indicative of Jesus, even the great commandment of Jesus is an imperative without visible means of support. Our only hope for living like a Christian is living in a relationship with Christ. The indicative must precede the imperative. How we need to hear this truth!

As our belief is shaped by this fundamental truth from Scripture, so is our witness formed. When we tell others of the gospel, we share good news, not bad news. The spirit of our message is one of affirmation. We approach potential disciples with a gift rather than a demand.

No effort is made to escape the demands of the gospel. Where there is blessing, there is responsibility. To ponder the affirmation that every person is loved by God is to be confronted by the most basic requirements of neighbor love. The writer of 1 John understood the proper relationship between the indicative and imperatives and wrote, "We love, because he first loved us" (4:19).

T. W. Mason conveyed the truth graphically: "The loving Christ still has two hands—one to point the way and the other held out to help us along."—C. Welton Gaddy

SUNDAY, SEPTEMBER 14, 2003
Lectionary Message

Topic: Atonement
TEXT: Mark 8:27–38
Other Readings: Prov. 1:20–33; Ps. 19; James 3:1–12

I. In the old calendars the fourteenth day of September is called the Feast of the Exaltation of the Holy Cross. It is a feast that I suspect, though I have never read such a thing, is intended to be a Christian commentary on the Jewish Day of Atonement, which occurs at about this time.

And behold, we have for today's Gospel our Lord's first prophecy of his cross. Let us begin with the great question posed to every one: "Whom say ye that I am?" Peter makes reply: "Thou art the Christ." And our Lord goes on, first, to define what it means to be the Christ: "The Son of man must suffer many things and be rejected of the elders and of the chief priests and scribes, and be killed, and after three days rise again;" and second, to define what it means to be his disciple: "Whosoever will come after me, let him deny himself and take up his cross and follow me." As if that were not enough, then comes a course in philosophy: "Whosoever will save his life shall lose it; but whosoever shall lose his life for my sake, and the Gospel's the same, shall save it."

But I have omitted something: in the midst of this teaching is a moment of verbal violence: Peter's attempt to rebuke the Lord, and the Lord's rebuke of Peter. "Get thee behind me, Satan, for thou savorest not the things that be of God but the things that be of men."

II. As the Lord says, Peter acts for us all when Jesus rebukes him: "You are thinking as men think, not as God thinks." Let me suggest a reason why Peter does what he does: The first half of St. Mark's Gospel is a dream fulfilled—the glorious summer beauty, the incredible healings, the adoring crowds, the easy rebuke of the Pharisees by one who knew the Scriptures backward and forward—and Peter wants that dream to last for ever. So do we.

But the second half of St. Mark's Gospel is filled with foreboding of disaster, then with betrayal, justice perverted, and judicial torture, culminating in an event beyond comprehension. When all of that is foretold by our Lord, Peter quite reasonably—reasonably by the standards of the world's wisdom—rebukes him. So do we. But surely we must confess, if we are going to be Christians in more than word, then the wisdom of God is superior to our own wisdom. And the cross is the wisdom of God—his medicine for a sick world.

Let me show you the wisdom of God by a very ordinary example out of common experience—an example that comes out of the teachings of Scripture, and equally out of the corporate experience of mankind. A woman imitates Christ when she endangers her life to give birth (1 Tim. 2:15). A man, equivalently, imitates Christ when he offers his life to protect his wife and children.

The apparent contradiction—"He who will save his life shall lose it, and he who shall lose his life shall save it"—suddenly makes sense; for does not the mother of children, in preferring their good to hers, experience what it means to be a woman?

And the father who endangers his life in defense of his family, does he not experience what it means to be a man? They who are willing to lose their lives for the sake of others find what it means to be human.

What do we so often see to be the effect of abandonment and mistreatment of children but a wounding that is a kind of death. And if it does that to the abused, what does it do to the abuser? They who prefer their own good over others' are reduced to something that is, in a sense, subhuman. In saving themselves, they lose themselves.

So, on reflection, even though our Lord's words sounded strange when we first heard them, we knew all along what he meant, and that it is the truth.

III. Let us ponder a little further the meaning of the Cross.

Jesus Christ is the image of the invisible God (Col. 1:15), from which we may deduce that what we know of Jesus we know also of the Father. Therefore, the self-sacrifice of Jesus on the cross is a demonstration in time and space of the eternal nature of God, who loves us as a father loves—so greatly that he would give himself for his child.

Jesus is the image of God's righteousness, and he went to the cross because he did what was right and refused to bow the knee before the ruler of this world. The sacrifice of Jesus is a moral sacrifice: he died because he was good.

Jesus, by his willing self-sacrifice for us, has forged a covenant between man and the Father himself. That covenant, sealed in the blood of the cross, makes atonement between man and God. Atonement is at-one-ment. We who are separated from God by sin (though originally united by having been created in his image) are now once more made at one with God, in the blood of Jesus, itself the symbol of his doing what is right.

Faith is accounted to us for righteousness, but that is the beginning, not the end, of salvation. It is not the intention of God that we should only be accounted worthy of being at one with him; we are also called to be transformed into the image of his Son (Rom. 8:29) so that we might (as far as the vagaries of this world—still the subject of Satan, sin, and death—permit) be made worthy of being at one with God.

We become worthy of atonement with God by following Jesus, by taking up our cross and following him.

Where he leads looks initially like death but is revealed to be life.

May we all come, by means of the Holy Cross, to the green fields and blue skies, the summer joy of heaven.—Samuel Logan

ILLUSTRATION

TAKING UP THE CROSS.   During the Second World War, my mother and I, my mother's sister and her two daughters, and my mother's sister-in-law and her infant son lived with my grandmother—sometimes some and sometimes all of us. When the men came home again and the wives and babies went away, my grandmother nursed her mother, a beloved sister-in-law, and my grandfather to their deaths. After my grandfather's death in 1949, my grandmother went to her doctor and said she didn't feel quite right, and he said that perhaps she had had a little nervous breakdown. Why not a big nervous breakdown, I don't know. But she recovered and lived to be eighty-six, dying in 1979. Hers is the greatest personal example I know of someone denying herself and taking up her cross and following Jesus.

I told this story recently to a very wise old minister and then said something about the number of grandmothers I had seen raising their daughters' children in the inner city. He replied that that wasn't happening as much any more because of the destructive effects of drugs, that now it was the great-grandmothers who were raising the children. Then he added, "And thriving, because they have a purpose in life."—Samuel Logan

SERMON SUGGESTIONS

Topic: Untangling Our Obedience

TEXT: Acts 15:1–2, 22–29

(1) *The problem:* Maintaining fidelity to our Lord while pursuing the freedom he gives us. (2) *The solution:* Being guided by the Holy Spirit through wise Christian counsel.

Topic: The Inhabitants of Heaven

TEXT: Rev. 21:10, 22–27

(1) First, the Lord God and the Lamb. (2) Then, those whose names are written in the Lamb's Book of Life.

CONGREGATIONAL MUSIC

1. "Nature with Open Volume Stands," Isaac Watts (1707)

   GERMANY, William Gardiner's *Sacred Melodies* (1815)

   For the opening of worship, this grand hymn is eminently appropriate. Its message relates to both the Psalter reading and the Gospel lesson.
2. "Take Up Thy Cross," Charles W. Everest (1833)

   GERMANY, William Gardiner's *Sacred Melodies* (1815)

   The call of Christ to deny self and take up one's cross to follow him finds urgent expression in this fine nineteenth-century American hymn. It would naturally precede or follow the reading of the Gospel lesson.
3. "The Heavens Declare Your Glory," Ps. 19:1–6, 14; vers. Thomas R. Birks (1874)

   FAITHFUL, J. S. Bach (c. 1730)

   This paraphrase of the first part of Psalm 19 could be sung following the Psalter reading. Its light, airy tune would best be introduced by a soloist before inviting the congregation to join in.
4. "Happy the Man That Finds the Grace," Charles Wesley (1747)

   DUKE STREET, John Hatton (1793)

   The skillful Wesley has based this hymn on verses in Proverbs 1 and a New Testament reading in which the "wisdom" of Proverbs becomes the knowledge that "the Savior died for me." This hymn therefore relates not only to the Old Testament lesson but also to the Gospel reading (Mark 8:27–38).—Hugh T. McElrath

WORSHIP AIDS

CALL TO WORSHIP.   "But thanks be to God, who gives us the victory through our Lord Jesus Christ" (1 Cor. 15:57).

INVOCATION.   In these beginning moments of worship we hear anew your call, Father, to "be still and know that I am God." Break through all the barriers we have erected and meet us with power here this morning, we pray. Let the cleansing presence of your Spirit wash us and make us new. Open our eyes to new visions of mission with purpose that we may be busy about your creation of a new world where Christ is Lord of all.—Henry Fields

OFFERTORY SENTENCE.   "And whatever you do, in word or deed, do everything in the name of the Lord Jesus, giving thanks to God the Father through him" (Col. 3:17).

OFFERTORY PRAYER.   We think that what we give will not do much or go far, Father. Remind us that in your hands miracles are accomplished at unexpected times and through what to us seems small and useless. Here is our offering. Magnify our small gifts for large use, we pray.—Henry Fields

PRAYER.   O Lord Jesus, in whose will is our peace, you have taught us to care for others and to embrace in our concern all your people of whatever sort they are. We lift up to you today the youth of our country—the boys and girls, the young men and women—who stand on varied thresholds leading to either mastery or defeat in life. Give us a renewed sense of responsibility to them, and may we by our example lead them to meet life on your terms rather than their own. Give to this rising generation a fresh enthusiasm for good and helpful living, and a restlessness to recover meaning and direction in fulfilling each common task. Give honest commitment to those who teach, and eagerness for the light of knowledge to those who learn. Give to the Church a clear sense of mission to show both young and old that we are most true to ourselves when we hold on to Christ, and most free when we are held by him. Bless every homemaker in this congregation, especially those with families; may they realize that theirs is a trust from you, and only as they pledge daily loyalty to the Christian way of life will little children sense the claim upon them of something high and someone good. In these times of careless and fruitless living, may we unite the best ideals of church and home, and in the name of him who blessed these gains and died for them, may our fathers and mothers restore to our country families that are brave and strong. Hallow our prayers as we bow before your alter here or in the quiet circle of those we love, and with open hearts may we accept and receive the benediction of your love. Through Jesus Christ, our elder brother and constant friend, we offer our humble prayers.—Donald Macleod[2]

SERMON

Topic: What Really Matters to God? That God Really Matters to You!
TEXT: Matt. 22:34–38

Ninety percent of Americans say that we truly believe in God. Yet for the most part God appears to have little or no real impact on our behavior, our moral choices, and our everyday

---

[2]*Princeton Pulpit Prayers*

lifestyles. A variety of recent polls indicate that most people—even Christians—simply do not turn to God to help them make up their minds about contemporary moral issues. Polls reveal that personal faith in God plays virtually no role in shaping our opinions or our behavior related to ethical business practices; sexuality and marriage; personal integrity and character; the use of alcohol, drugs, tobacco, or other substances; personal and family relationships; financial, political, community, or civic concerns; and the formation and pursuit of personal goals and dreams. For increasing numbers of us, God just does not matter much at all.

A group of the superreligious people of his time came to Jesus and said, "Tell us, Teacher, what do you think matters to God more than anything else?"

Jesus said that the most important thing we can do—out of all the important things we should do—is simply to love God. That is what matters most—more than anything else. That is the heart of it all: that God matters to us!

Love God. It almost sounds too simple. Besides, it's nothing new! It wasn't even new for the Pharisees. Ever since Moses, devout Jews had begun every day by repeating those very words. Maybe that was the trouble. Maybe they had heard the words so often that they could no longer really hear them. Maybe they knew the words so well by heart that they scarcely remembered they were words once spoken by God to the heart. Maybe they had taken the words so much for granted that they hardly ever stopped anymore to think about what the words meant and where the words were trying to take them. God knows, if it was so for them, it is also true of us.

Above everything else, the words say, *you shall love*—not first your neighbor as yourself. That is second and comes later. It is God whom you shall love first—before you love anything else. You are to love him with all that you are and with all that you have within you—whatever that means. The words don't explain it. They simply claim and command it. The point is that God's wholehearted love must not be answered in a halfhearted way, with a mind preoccupied by other loyalties or a strength diluted by other commitments. When God loves, he loves the whole world. When God gives, he gives even his only Son.

This one whom we are expected to love with all our heart, soul, and might is one whom we cannot see at all. Not even Moses could see God when he asked to because humans cannot see God and live. Like Moses, we have seen evidence of him. We have even felt his nearness on occasion. We believe in him. We know he is real. But we haven't seen him—what's more, we *can't* see him. Yet he is the one whom we are commanded to love above all others.

How do we do it? How do we love someone we have never laid our eyes on? I'm talking about wanting to do things for him, because that is the least of what love seems to mean. How do I love him?

Do I love him only when I sense his nearness, only when I have felt his deliverance, only when he has saved me from myself and from some terrible mistake, only when he has answered my prayers, only when he has spared me great pain and grief, only in the course of an inspiring worship experience? When my love for him overwhelms me because of his wonderful and unexpected intervention in the natural course of my life, do I love him the way he expects me to?

I suppose that the truth of it is something like this: The farthest reach of our love for each other is loving our enemies, and the farthest reach of God's love for us is loving us at our most unlovable moments. Just like that, the farthest reaches of our love for God is loving him when, in almost every way that matters, we can neither see him nor hear him, and he simply does not answer us in the ways we want and need him to come to us.

The question the gospel continually holds in front of us is, Who sits on the throne in your life? Who has the preeminent position in your experience? Who sets your values and determines your direction? Who shapes the attitudes and the desires by which you live?

A large city newspaper carried a most unusual advertisement one day. In a very conspicuous place on the front page there appeared a notice asking readers to turn to the back page of section A. The entire back page was empty except for one line of minuscule print in the bottom right-hand corner: "Is this where you have put God in your life?"

That's the question I put to you today: Does God *really* matter to you?—Gary C. Redding

SUNDAY, SEPTEMBER 21, 2003
Lectionary Message

Topic: It Takes a Congregation
TEXT: Mark 9:30–37
Other Readings: Prov. 31:10–31; Ps. 1; James 3:13–4:3, 7–8a

I. Former First Lady Hilary Rodham Clinton wrote a book entitled *It Takes a Village* in which she spoke of the shared responsibility society has for its members. The title was based on an African proverb, "It takes a village to raise a child." Her point, of course, was to emphasize the need for community programs of education and welfare. Yet her title could equally well be used by the Christian Church, if in a slightly altered form: "It takes a *congregation* to raise a Christian." This becomes most clear when we consider how we deal with our children, because not only parents but also local churches help children to develop their ideas of God.

Older norms honored the ancient adage that children should be "seen but not heard." In fact, they were sometimes not even *seen*. Congregations I have encountered deal with their younger members in various ways—and with various degrees of effectiveness. Some banish their youngsters to exile in Sunday school for the length of the Sunday service, allowing them to rejoin their parents only during coffee hour. Others segregate their children for half of the service, either the Liturgy of the Word or the Holy Communion, depending on local preference and denominational practice. Others cultivate the so-called family service, whose length and content are aimed at a golden mean of interest and attention span. There are pros and cons to all three. Of these options, I find the first least attractive because it ignores an important function of the Christian Church: the socialization of its children, and the inspiration in them of a sense that God welcomes them, too, into his house.

II. Like all pastors, I have had my share of services and sermons punctuated not by the "hosannas" and "praise the Lords" of the faithful, but by the cries, shouts, and percussion sessions of the wee ones. Also like all pastors, I have developed my own threshold when it comes to these disturbances—thankfully higher now than at the beginning of my ministry. Part of my development in this regard was due to the realization that, for example, our young people spend increasing amounts of school time in front of a computer screen rather than in a traditional classroom. There are many fewer opportunities in the twenty-first century for young people to learn what it means to be part of a community. The Church has an important task to play in helping its younger members learn church survival skills, etiquette, and plain old good manners. This comes from their picking up cues from those around them as to when they are permitted to speak, when it is OK to walk around, and when they need to curb these natural instincts for the good of the congregation as a whole.

Children are capable of this. My own niece, while a child, was once told that she would probably not wish to accompany her parents to a wake service because it would be "very sad and quiet." "I can be sad and quiet," she protested. Indeed, children do learn social norms early on if they are given a chance. Fear of disturbing the congregation should be a secondary consideration to the value of exposing them to the care, compassion, interest, and example of the Christian congregation at prayer, at praise, and at work.

III. The congregation is involved not only in the issue of behavior in church, but also in the formation of Christian souls. A young mother recently shared with me the theological implications of raising a two-year-old: "I came to realize that my child was developing his idea of God based on his parent's care, love, and discipline. I found myself treating my son the way I imagined God treated me: interested, patient, strict when necessary, but always, always loving. It was a sobering experience, but an incarnational one." Indeed, parents need to be aware of the great potential and great danger that exist in being role models for God in their children's minds. Do they project a God of cruel or even arbitrary punishment for real or imagined faults? Or a God who is a loving, caring parent?

IV. In today's Gospel, when Christ addressed the disciples on how they were to treat one another, he was first speaking about ego and power issues, which are still major challenges to the Church and its ministers. The Lord took a child as his example, and his words were, "If anyone wishes to be first, he must be the last of all and the servant of all." We can easily forget the child in this example while imagining that Christ's teaching is only about behavior among adults. But remember what Scripture says about Jesus and that child: "He put his arms around him and said, 'Whoever welcomes one child like this on my account is welcoming me, and whoever welcomes me, welcomes not me but him who has sent me.'" Jesus knew that the way the child was treated would determine the child's idea of God. The Lord who taught his friends to address God as "Abba" realized that welcoming the child brought the child not only into Christian fellowship but also into fellowship with Christ, and ultimately with God the Father himself.

V. As we consider Jesus' words today, let's look at them from the perspective of the youngest, the most vulnerable, the most impressionable of our members: the children. The responsibility for their nurture in the Christian faith and life belongs not only to their parents, grandparents, and other members of their natural families, but also to the members of their "supernatural" family: the families, couples, and single adults who will be the role models for them in their walk of faith. These are the ones who will show them not only what Christians can be like, but perhaps even more profoundly, what God is like.

"Let your light so shine before men[, women, and children,] that they may see your good works and give glory to your Father who is in heaven."—Tyler A. Strand

ILLUSTRATION

THE URGE TO COMPLETENESS.   One is often surprised to observe, even in shadowed and cramped lives, the will to live and the hope that life will open out and become more worth living. There is in the galled spirit an indomitable dream of some extension of experience, some fulfillment, that will satisfy. This is the urge to completeness, the determination to go on till bigger and more desirable dimensions of life are reached.

It was to this refusal to accept frustration as final that our Lord appealed in his promise of life more abundant. What does he mean by life? He means that human experience becomes life only when it is informed and moved by contact with the Divine. Otherwise it is only a jumble of odds and ends, moods, instincts, and sensations, without any master to harmonize and complete it. To be a vital person, fully alive, brought to the highest and widest stretch of one's being, is to know and serve God, who is the author of life. Anything less than this awakening to the character and purpose of God is not living but merely existing, a poor muddled pretense of the real thing. "By every word of God doth man live." The spirit in touch with God is the only one that reaches the altitude and range of its destiny and enters into "life and life more abundant." This was Christ's teaching.—Arthur A. Cowan[3]

SERMON SUGGESTIONS

Topic: Where Is the Lord, the God of Elijah?
TEXT: 2 Kings 2:1, 6–14

(1) *Then:* God manifested his power in the deeds of Elijah. (2) *Always:* God is resourceful and has shown through the ages that he is infinitely resourceful and can work through whomever he chooses. (3) *Now:* God is active today and can work through one or all of us to "do exceedingly abundantly above all that we ask or think."

Topic: Some Worthy Objects of Prayer
TEXT: Col. 1:1–14 NEB

(1) Wisdom and understanding. (2) A worthy manner of life. (3) Fruit-bearing. (4) Growth in knowledge of God. (5) Spiritual strength. (6) Gratitude.

CONGREGATIONAL MUSIC

1. "Sing Praise to God Who Reigns Above," Johann J. Schutz (1675)
   MIT FREUDEN ZART, Bohemian Brethren Kirchengesaenge (1566)
   This powerful hymn exalting God's love, mercy, and grace is not only appropriate for the beginning of worship but also relates in a tangential, theological way to the Old Testament reading extolling the virtues of a good woman. See especially stanza 3, where a loving God is compared to the tender mother who cares for her children (Prov. 31:15, 26–30).
2. "Savior, Teach Me Day by Day," Jane E. Leeson (1842)
   POSEN, George C. Strattner (1691)
   The Gospel lesson (Mark 9:30–37) focuses on Jesus' teaching about humility and servanthood. This simple children's song would be an appropriate response.
3. "How Blest Are They, Who Fearing God," Ps. 1; vers. *The Psalter* (1912)
   ST. ANNE, William Croft (1708)
   This close paraphrase of the Psalm 1 is suggested to replace the Psalter reading. Its five stanzas could be alternately sung and recited by the worshiping congregation.

---

[3]*Bright Is the Shaken Torch* (Edinburgh, Scotland: Clark, 1950), p. 15.

4. "We Praise You with Our Minds, O Lord," Hugh T. McElrath (1964)
   CLONMEL, arr. William J. Reynolds (1952)

The apostle James commends the "wisdom from above" that is pure, peaceable, gentle, reasonable, and so on (James 3:17). This simple praise hymn that petitions for that wisdom could logically follow the Epistle lesson.—Hugh T. McElrath

WORSHIP AIDS

CALL TO WORSHIP.   "Blessed is the man who trusteth in the Lord and whose hope the Lord is" (Jer. 17:7).

INVOCATION.   O Spirit of the living God, you are savior and friend of all who hear your name. This is our word of greeting as we gather once again to hail and celebrate your wondrous works for the sake of men and women everywhere. We praise you for your sovereign power in the universe you have made, but chiefly we rejoice because you have come close to us in Jesus and formed us into Christian families who take care of the blessings of home in the sure order of our Father's world. We thank you for the story of the Scriptures, where the solitary are set in families; and when this fellowship consists of believing souls, the Church and the nation are abundantly enriched and internally strong. We bless you for the design and support of your Kingdom, which comes to those who commit themselves to its duty and service, and brings the scattered people of each community into bonds of trust and faith.—Donald Macleod[4]

OFFERTORY SENTENCE.   "I will freely sacrifice unto thee; I will praise thy name, O Lord, for it is good" (Ps. 54:6).

OFFERTORY PRAYER.   Father, may your Kingdom be uppermost in our minds, hearts, and lives as we bring our tithes to you this morning. May they represent a rededication of all that we are and have to the greater glory of your Kingdom, we pray.—Henry Fields

PRAYER.   How lovely is your dwelling place, O lord of hosts! For this privilege to be in this place among your people, we worship and adore you. Open our eyes to all the intimations of your presence among us—intimations of your mighty deeds for our salvation in Word and Sacrament. We pray that the seed faithfully sown in this opportunity may fall on good ground and grow to a bountiful harvest of faith, joy, and peace. Praise be to you, Father, Son, and Holy Spirit.—John Thompson

SERMON
Topic: Known by Our Love
TEXT: 1 John 7:7–16

When Jesus began laying the foundation for the Church, he started with three simple questions, found at the close of John's Gospel, where we hear Jesus asking Peter so very simply, "Simon, son of John, do you love me more than these?"

Peter responds, "Yes, Lord, you know that I love you."

---

[4]*Princeton Pulpit Prayers.*

"Then," Jesus says, "feed my lambs."

In the next verse Jesus says again, "Simon, son of John, do you love me?"

"Yes, Lord, you know that I love you."

"Tend my sheep."

Then, for a third and final time, Jesus asks, "Do you love me?" and Peter, not only exasperated but even a little hurt, responds, "Lord, you know everything; you know that I love you."

Jesus says again, "Feed my sheep."

Love: it lies at the heart of the Christian tradition. Whether it be the transforming, forgiving love of God, the reciprocating love of neighbor through Christ, or the simple, joyous love we experience living in the Spirit's presence, love *is* what makes our world of faith go 'round. Christ's questions to Peter remind us all that we're asked again and again to prove our love for God in both word and action. In this final chapter of his Gospel, John tells us, "Forget everything else. It's love that matters most."

It's not just at the conclusion of the fourth Gospel that we get this kind of teaching. In this morning's Epistle, after all, the central theme is, "God is love." In Matthew and Mark, we remember, is the instruction, "Love the Lord your God with all your heart, and with all your soul, and with all your mind" (Matt. 22:37). In John we're reminded, "Just as I have loved you, you also should love one another" (John 13:34–35). Placing love at the center of our tradition, the words of our Gospels and Epistles repeatedly remind us that we are commissioned by Christ to be disciples of love, practicing our faith by living as caring servants, receiving the mercy of God in order to then offer it to others. We're "a people on the move," as author John O'Conner defines the Church—called to love God and one another with genuine devotion and through authentic action. As we see at the close of John's Gospel, we've a tradition formed by saying to Christ repeatedly, "Yes, we love you," then receiving that blessed commission, "Feed my sheep."

It was Mother Teresa, one of the most inspirational Christian lovers of our time, who wrote, "A mission of love can come only from union with God. From that union, love for the family, love for neighbor, love for the poor is natural fruit." That's the point this author's working to get across, not just in his Gospel, but also in the letter we find at hand today. There, with the struggling community in Ephesus near the close of the first century, John tries to keep true Christian faith alive, as disagreements develop over the theology of Christ's person and nature.

John Haynes Holmes writes, "It cannot be emphasized too often that Jesus was not a theologian. He interpreted religion as something not primarily to be believed but to be lived."

That seems to be what the author of John is telling his community as well. "Beloved," he writes, "let us love one another, because love is from God and everyone who loves is born of God."

John is making it perfectly clear, in his words as well as in his ministry of outreach and caring, that the body of Christ is given a new commandment: "that you love one another . . . by this everyone will know that you are my disciples, if you have love for one another" (John 13:34–35).

Here at Old South we know that, like the members of the early Church in Ephesus, we have our own struggles to contend with, named and unnamed, whispered about or openly confronted. We are a church, after all, made up of fallible human beings.

Like the people of Ephesus, we're confronted by the fact that through God's love we're transformed by grace that needs to be shared. Like those men and women of ancient times, we need to ask ourselves, "Just what are we known by? Who is the Lord of our lives? With what convictions and aspirations do we gather together as the Church of Jesus Christ?"

And so we receive Christ's commandment anew today: that as we are loved by God so shall we love one another, for God is love, and to be Christian is to be loving, compassionate, and kind. Beginning a new program year we remember that no matter what we do—in our educational or musical activities, in our times of worship, or in our efforts in outreach and service—we do it in love, sensitive to the Spirit's dwelling in each person and in every place. For today we're given the powerful reminder that the Church is not a creed, not a code, not a physical construction. The church is *us,* the men and women in front of you, beside you, behind you. The Church is our body of people gathering by the grace of God to know and to share the love of Christ. *We* are the Church.—Lael P. Murphy

SUNDAY, SEPTEMBER 28, 2003
Lectionary Message
Topic: Seeking Wholeness in Christian Community
Text: James 5:13–20
Other Readings: Esther 7:1–6, 9–10; 9:20–22; Ps. 124; Mark 9:38–50

I. Several themes contribute to James's forthright message explicating the meaning of faith in Jesus Christ and right relationship with God, among them the love of the neighbor and faith in action. James's message is addressed to Christians living in community, gathered by their common belief and subsequent values, shaped by their faith in Jesus Christ. For James, this Christian community, or *ekklesia,* values the whole, consisting of gathered individuals and basically egalitarian relationships among its members. For James, the *ekklesia* embodies the "royal law" (2:8) to love one's neighbor as one's self. The duality between friendship with the world or friendship with God undergirds James's message that calls to account those who seem to understand theoretically their faith in Jesus Christ, yet need continued formation and admonition in putting their faith into practice.[5]

James's Epistle, and particularly the concluding pericope of 5:13–20, expresses insightful wisdom for the difficult contemporary realities involved with living as Christians in the world. Subtitled the "Prayer of Faith" in the NRSV, the lectionary passage offers guidance to Christians living in community and seeking to embody a witness distinct from the world. In the midst of this prayer, at least two basic activities are described—care for the sick and confession of sins. These practices play a significant role in shaping the Christian community's witness to the world, both then and now.

II. *Care for the sick.* James's instruction to the sick (5:14) to call for the elders of the Church, or *ekklesia,* demonstrates the significance of care for the sick by the Christian community. Such care, in both prayer and anointing, demonstrates the value of the whole as a gathered community of individuals. The practice of caring for the sick seems in stark contrast to the values of the world, which tend to seek the survival of the strongest. This social

---

[5]Luke T. Johnson, "James: Introduction," *New Interpreter's Bible* (Nashville: Abingdon Press, 1998), pp. 177–184.

Darwinism still influences contemporary societal values. The Western and Enlightenment focus on the individual, found especially in outgrowths of North American capitalist and democratic cultures, has in many cases moved beyond an appropriate emphasis on individuals (such as human rights) to an extreme of autonomy that leaves little if any room for communal relationships. James, on the other hand, offers a seemingly timeless message that implores the Christian community to pray over and anoint the weak, frail, and vulnerable within their community rather than ignoring or discarding them.

James also reveals the complexity of caring for the ailing both in the use of oil for anointing and in the prayer of faith, raising up the broken as healed and forgiven (5:15). For James, healing is holistic, addressing the brokenness of both body and spirit. Although James does not understand sickness as a causality of sin, the Epistle writer does acknowledge the common effects of physical and spiritual ailments.[6] The oil used for anointing was used not only for the soothing of spiritual suffering, but also for the healing of physical illness in the Greco-Roman world.[7] Thus, James calls the *ekklesia* to care for broken bodies and spirits.

III. *Confession of sins.* Like care of the sick, the practice of confession is an essential practice for the health of the Christian community. Just as a sensible diet coupled with routine exercise and regular medical exams can help to maintain one's health, similarly the consistent confessing of sins within the *ekklesia* can help maintain the community's spiritual health. Although God's forgiveness extended to us in Jesus Christ through the power of the Holy Spirit is the ultimate cure for our brokenness, the practice of confession is an important aspect of receiving this wholeness. Through the confession of our sins to one another, we build resistance to those ailments that can plague Christian communities—greed, anger, vengeance, and bitterness, to name only a few. Both our individual spiritual well-being and the wholeness of the *ekklesia* depends on our ability to confess our sins consistently to God and one another. Through the practice of confession within the Christian community, spiritual healing is received and the healing of our brokenness is pursued.

IV. *Seeking wholeness.* Jesus' acts of healing often addressed the brokenness of both bodies and souls. Healing in the Gospel texts frequently shared allusions to salvation and the Greek root *sozo,* meaning "wholeness." When we receive initiation into the body of Christ and the covenant to live as Christians in community distinct from the world, one of our first priorities is the practice of prayer. Within the context of a life of prayer, James then instructs the *ekklesia* on the interwovenness of care for the sick among us and the confession of our sins to one another. Through these practices we strengthen the Christian community, and witness to one another and to the world our love for one another and our faith in Jesus Christ. Although care for the broken is a perpetual task of the Christian community, it is an important component of our Christian vocations to fulfill Jesus' commandments to love God and our neighbors.—Laceye C. Warner

ILLUSTRATIONS

LIFE TOGETHER.   The life and witness of Dietrich Bonhoeffer, particularly his text, *Life Together,* explains more fully the practice of confession in an intentional community.

---

[6]Johnson, "James: Introduction," p. 224.
[7]Johnson, "James: Introduction," p. 222.

HABITAT FOR HUMANITY.   Millard Fuller's time with the Koinonia Farm Community—an intentional Christian community known for its pacifism, economic sharing, and racial integration, and organized by Clarence Jordan in 1942—led to Fuller's founding of Habitat for Humanity.

SERMON SUGGESTIONS

Topic: How to Listen to God's Word
TEXT: Neh. 8:1–4a, 5–6, 8–10
(1) With expectation. (2) With reverence. (3) With joy.

Topic: E Pluribus Unum
TEXT: 1 Cor. 12:12–30
(1) The true Church is one body. (2) However, the several parts of this body are a potential threat to the coordinated functioning of the whole. (3) Yet God has given worth and status to each part.

CONGREGATIONAL MUSIC

1. "We Praise You, O God, Our Redeemer," Julia Cady Cory (1902)
   KREMSER, Netherlands folk song (c. 1626)
   Good for the beginning of worship, this hymn reflects the spirit of thanksgiving for deliverance from peril, and the rejoicing that took place at the institution of the Festival of Purim (Esther 9:20–22).
2. "Now Israel May Say," Ps. 124; vers. *The Psalter* (1912)
   OLD 124TH, Genevan Psalter (1551)
   The paraphrase of the psalm for this day's worship could be preformed by alternating the reading and singing, in the following manner: recite vv. 1–3, sing stanza 1; recite vv. 4–5, sing stanza 2; recite vv. 6–8, sing stanza 3.
3. "Where Cross the Crowded Ways of Life," Frank Mason North (1905)
   GERMANY, William Gardiner's *Sacred Melodies* (1815)
   This great hymn on Christian responsibility can constitute a suitable response to the Gospel lesson (Mark 9:38–50). Stanza 3 ("The cup of water given for thee . . .") relates particularly to Mark 9:41.
4. "Prayer Is the Soul's Supreme Desire," James Montgomery (1818)
   BEATITUDO, John B. Dykes (1875)
   The Epistle reading (James 5:13–20) focuses on the power of prayer. This venerable hymn on that theme would naturally accompany that reading.—Hugh T. McElrath

WORSHIP AIDS

CALL TO WORSHIP.   "And the Spirit and the bride say, Come. And let him that heareth say, Come. And let him that is athirst come. And whosoever will, let him take the water of life freely" (Rev. 22:17).

INVOCATION.   In this sacred place, in this holy hour, grant us the power to fix our eyes on the unseen, that we may discover grace sufficient for every need. Show us today how unfailing love really is. Let us discover in your presence this morning how goodness has the resource of the unfilled years, and that behind all the shifting veil and show of things there is a power that cannot be defeated and a love that will not let us go. In the name of him who touched every dusty way with glory, hear us as we pray his prayer for the use of all disciples: [The Lord's Prayer].—Henry Fields

OFFERTORY SENTENCE.   "Verily, Verily, I say unto you: he that believeth on me, the works that I do shall he do also; and greater works than these shall he do, because I go unto my Father. And whatsoever ye shall ask in my name, that I will do, that the Father may be glorified in the Son" (John 14:12–13).

OFFERTORY PRAYER.   We know, O God, that everything we are and have, and everything that we can ever hope to be, ultimately comes from thee. Keep alive in us that sense of dependence upon thee, and give us the grace and the wisdom so to cooperate with thy laws that we may work together with thee to do things which by ourselves we could never accomplish at all.—Theodore Parker Ferris

PRAYER.   How can we appear before you—you who watch over the destiny of men and of nations—except we do come in confession. We have lived by fear rather than by love when we have projected our fears onto others to attempt to justify our wars as holy. What resources we have squandered on the building of bridges to make ourselves "safe" rather than investing in the building of bridges to make the world safe! How often we have sought luxuries for ourselves rather than necessities for others. We have basked in the sunshine of freedom, ignoring those imprisoned by poverty and oppression.

Forgive, O God, the terrible silence of the decent in the face of the injustice and inequities— even persecution—that blight the life of so many of your people, our brothers and sisters. As we must account for every idle word, so we must account for every idle silence. Forgive us for speaking out, too, when that is all we do. Help us fit ourselves to take more than a spectator role in the struggles of these times.

How grateful we are for the Word of this hour. There is a witness of your Spirit bearing witness with our spirit that we have not only heard your Word as it comes in truth—in judgment— but also as it comes in grace—in redemption. Help us to realize that without the truth that judges, there can be no salvation.

Cleanse us, O merciful God, and we shall be clean; heal us and we shall be whole. In our wholeness may we wholly attend to the call to your righteousness, which alone exalts the nation—all nations and peoples.

With the rich heritage that is ours, we do live on hallowed ground. Through the urgencies of these times you call us: "You have been born to the Kingdom for such a time as this." May that vision so imaginatively perceived and so dramatically articulated by the prophet become reality in and through us when "swords shall be beaten into plowshares and spears into pruning hooks."

How can we sing the Lord's song—your song—in this strange land that we find ourselves in this morning? There is "deep speaking unto deep." May we listen in the depths as these times are prodding us to: "He has showed you, O man and woman, what is good: and what does the Lord require of you but to do justice and to love kindness, and to walk humbly with your God?"—John Thompson

SERMON
Topic: Capturing the Quietness
TEXT: Ps. 46:1–11

There is a story that describes the way things are for many of us. It seems that a family moved from the city to the country. Life in the city was high-pressured, stress-filled, and something the family members wanted to escape. The family had been settled for several weeks in their new environment when a neighbor came to call. The neighbor noticed a handsomely printed poem attached to the refrigerator door and asked about it. "Oh that," said the woman of the house. "That's a poem that represents what our moving here was all about. The verse starts out, 'Lord, slow me down,' but I haven't had time to read the rest of it."

Strange, isn't it, how we can feel so harassed and pressured, yet avoid doing those things we know might help to slow us down. Monastic writer Thomas Merton reflected upon such experiences, eventually declaring, "This is no longer a time of obligations." Merton then sought a quiet place where "words cease to resound" (as he said) and where the silence of the afternoon communicated its own renewing blessing. Important for Thomas Merton was his feeling that "this is no longer a time of obligations." Deliberately arranged and adhered to instead was his time for silence. It is the action to which the psalm points when it says, "Be still, and know that I am God!" Isaiah the prophet pronounced this additional word of the Lord: "In returning and rest you shall be saved; in quietness and trust shall be your strength."

An opposite condition prevails for many of us. Instead of finding quiet times in our schedules, we surround ourselves with noise. Unconsciously we may equate quiet with discomfort. Just as music, if it is to be beautiful, must have rests or pauses in its flow, so must our souls. With enormous insight the Scriptures say, "Be still, and know that I am God!"

Curiously, one modern speech translation of that verse reads not, "Be still, and know that I am God," but rather, "Stop fighting . . . and know that I am God." In its context, that particular verse from Psalm 46 follows other verses about how God makes wars to cease and weapons to be destroyed. Probably that context is what led translators to say, "Stop fighting . . . and know that I am God," instead of "Be still." Yet another Scripture version says, "Give in! Admit that I am God!" At first glance, these varied translations seem to say different things. But they really are alike in directing us to interrupt ordinary ways of thinking and behaving. They all are saying—as the Jerusalem Bible does—"Pause a while"; then and only then can you experience the reality of God.

I wonder: do we avoid the quiet because it seems empty, with nothing momentous there? Most of us are results-oriented people. We expect tangible evidence that what we are doing is productive and worth the effort. We want results, and usually within the briefest possible time. But instead of thinking about results, our need is to think about release. Waiting quietly before God has little to do with getting something; it has a great deal to do with letting go. Chief among things to release is our anxiety. "Cast all your anxiety on God, because he cares for you," a familiar Scripture passage says. The verse immediately before that one tells us, "Humble yourselves therefore under the mighty hand of God, so that he may exalt you in due time." "Humble yourselves" suggests being still and letting go of every impediment that blocks our relationship with God. "He will exalt you in due time" suggests leaving results to God, according to God's timetable.

In this respect it is important for us to release all personal agendas as we capture the quietness in coming before God. We often have our own ideas about how the world should run, if we are honest to admit it. Martin Luther's advice deserves to be heeded, however. "Let God be God," he thundered. Presume not to manipulate the Almighty. Offer up every effort that seeks to control life for selfish advantage. Be willing instead to say, "I am thine, O Lord, I have heard thy voice; let me closer be drawn to thee." These are among the ways that the quiet or silence can become meaningful for us.

Capturing the quiet for this kind of knowledge has another implication as well. The value of simple things becomes more evident to us. Plain facts, natural happenings, ordinary events all become means of revealing God. The deeper truths of life are taught by that "still small voice" of which the Bible speaks, a voice not heard in the overriding noises of the world.

We need not expect some dramatic or miraculous event to show us God, in other words. Revelation may become real in simply contemplating the experiences of every day.

What also becomes real is a new sensitivity to our manner of living in the world. We hear and speak frequently about doing God's will. Yet discerning the will of God is easier said than done. Capturing the quiet is one of the best ways we have for learning what God would have us do and how God would have us live.—John H. Townsend

SUNDAY, OCTOBER 5, 2003
Lectionary Message

Topic: Testing One, Two, Three
TEXT: Job 1:1; 2:1–10
Other Readings: Ps. 26; Heb. 1:1–4; 2:5–12; Mark 10:2–16

The sound technician steps up to the podium and taps the microphone, then speaks, "Testing one, two, three." This is not the main event of the evening. Although the speech qualifies for brevity and may indeed be an improvement on the keynote speaker, this is not an attempt to say anything. In fact, this event, repeated in meeting halls, is not intended as a message. No one really stops to listen in expectation of a profound lesson. It is nothing. It's just a test.

It has been a while since I had my radio music interrupted by that annoying tone followed by the explanation, "This has been a test of the emergency broadcast system. If this had been a real emergency, you would have been instructed. . . ." I became so familiar with the test that I sometimes wondered if I would have paid attention to a real emergency. Civil defense was about "crying wolf." Not once at any time in my experience did the radio interruption report a real emergency. If you ask me, the whole thing was a fraud. It was only a test, an irritating, distracting, disarming test.

The first day of any class is devoted to an overview of the course. You get the reading list, a syllabus, and the important dates of the semester, like when the research paper is due and when the mid-term exam and final exam will take place. The week of preparation for the final exam has been lovingly called "Hell Week," and the day of the final, "Judgment Day." I always dreaded the exams. I recall the daily essay we were required to write in freshman English class. Most students began with F's and D's until they began to comprehend the rules of writing. I was shocked with my C–, one of the high grades in class. I can still hear the words of encouragement from Mrs. Constantine, "It's only a test. The grade is not the measure of a man."

On the one hand, testing and measurement are how we get things done around here. If you cannot test it and measure it, you cannot build it. On the other hand, to set the human relationship with God on the plain of testing seems to put us in a category somewhere near the value of a laboratory rat.

Job carried forward an Old Testament, perhaps Oriental, theme that life is a test. Look elsewhere in the Hebrew Scriptures; the rules of the test are set forth in the covenants between God and Israel. The grand judge sits on the bench of the eternal court to measure and evaluate the performance of the pathetic little creatures called humans running the maze called life. It all seems a bit arbitrary, more about power than about grace, and it leaves us wondering, Is this the meaning of life? Is God just tapping the microphone to see if the system is working? Testing one, two, three.

I. *The scene is obscene.* This is the second presentation of the heavenly hosts before God, and the second challenge to the integrity of Job, the good man. In the first deal between God and Satan, Job lost wealth and children. In the second trial, Satan challenged the Almighty to get to the heart (and skin and bone) of the matter, to bring on a life-threatening disease. Afflicted with sores all over his body, Job sits in ashes, mourning his pain while he scratches his sores with a piece of broken pottery.

In 1979, visiting Lima, Peru, I contacted the local missions office and we were given a grand tour of this ancient city by missionary Elbert Smithen. Elbert and I were both Texans, graduates of Baylor, and mutual friends of the preacher-turned-professional-comedian Grady Nutt. Elbert and Grady had been roommates at Baylor. We shared Grady stories most of the day. One of Elbert's stories was something you would remember with a deep shudder. They lived in a converted barracks building affectionately called by the students, "the cardboard jungle." Some of the guys wanted to pull a prank on Grady, so they wired the door to his room with house power between the lock and the doorknob. It was a schoolboy prank fraught with serious implications. Grady could have been electrocuted, or the whole building could have gone up in flames. Elbert said with relief that he never learned what happened that night. He was thankful that it was nothing bad.

The prologue to Job makes the problem of human suffering look like a practical joke gone awry. The story appears to be a Near Eastern folktale patterned after a text known as the *Babylonian Theodicy.* The drama and poetry belong to the ancient world of Uz, wherever that was. To give finality to the setup pictured in the prologue, the Lord God of Israel takes on the appearance of the all-too-human gods of the ancient pagan world. I am far too pious to settle with a god who plays "Let's Make a Deal" with the Satan of our world. This is one of those times when every neuron in my head protests. People like Job cannot be dismissed as test cases to prove a point.

II. *Irreverence toward a god is reverence toward God.* Carol A. Newsom hits the nail on the head in introducing Job: "Why does Job, and by extension any person, reverence God?"[1] I suspect that my sense of outrage was intended by the writer. Paint God in popular strokes and place Job squarely in the middle of the duel between good and evil, and gather around

---

[1]*New Interpreter's Bible,* IV, p. 334ff.

to see how the rat performs. The entire book specifically permits something disallowed by the pious—the questioning of God. The practice is not really new. Read the Psalms. I find more genuine honesty toward God in the prayers and songs of Israel than I have ever allowed myself to express.

Christianity, Judaism, and Islam all flow from the one God of Abraham, but somewhere the three religions took different paths. The Allah of Islam is the god of power and authority who demands blind submission without a hint of compassion or grace. The trial of Abraham in Genesis 22 has stood throughout the ages as a point of controversy in our reverence for God. Would God put any of us to the test by demanding the death of a child? Søren Kierkegaard was haunted by the radical obedience demanded by God in the call to sacrifice Isaac: "It was indeed absurd that God who required it of him should the next instant recall the requirement."[2]

Who among us has not been in a time and place where the challenge to divine justice is the only word that has seemed appropriate? There are times when something inside of me wants to scream at the heavens. As I heard directed to me many times in my passage through the teen years, I want to say to God, "What in the world are you doing?" Rabbi Kushner framed the ancient question of Job in the new dress of his personal journey, *Why Do Bad Things Happen to Good People?*

J. B. Phillips wrote a challenge to popular notions of God, *Your God Is Too Small.* Phillips exposed many of the inadequate pictures of God on the Christian landscape. He touched the issue and opened the door to a sequel that someone could write out of the material provided in trite comments about God in funeral parlors and hospital waiting rooms. Your god may be too small, or just too mean.

Job is better at questions than answers, but question we must. Let the questions roll down like waters until you find God anew in the loving face of Jesus: "He who did not withhold his own Son but gave him up for all of us will he not with him also give us everything else?" (Rom. 8:32). Testing one, two, three—but it is not Job or you hanging there on the cross; it is God's beloved Son.

Lord God of heaven and Earth, God over our victories and trials, you are the refuge of our lives, our haven in a storm, our shelter when all about us spins out of control. When things fall apart, you are the center who secures our lives, assuring us that nothing in all creation can separate us from the love of God in Christ Jesus our Lord. Amen.—Larry K. Dipboye

ILLUSTRATIONS

HONEST WITH GOD. It was October. My wife had died in April. I was a seminary graduate student and pastor of a small congregation near Fort Knox, Kentucky. I put the children to bed and settled into my new routine of staring at the walls, trying to read, listening to music—anything to avoid facing the war going on inside my mind. It was almost 10 P.M. when the doorbell rang. Seminary professor Swan Hayworth was standing at the door. He had been in a conference with military chaplains and decided to make a pastoral call on his way home. He only stayed for a few minutes. I don't recall any euphemisms. That was not his style. He left one abiding word, "Larry, read the Psalms. You will find more honesty with

---

[2]*Fear and Trembling,* p. 46.

God there than anywhere else in the Bible, and you need to be honest with God."—Larry Dipboye

SEARCH FOR MEANING.   Viktor E. Frankl, a Viennese psychiatrist, survived Auschwitz to find a new understanding of the meaning of life and death. In *Man's Search for Meaning*,[3] Frankl wrote, "If there is a meaning in life at all, then there must be a meaning in suffering. Suffering is an ineradicable part of life, even as fate and death. . . . The way in which a man accepts his fate and all the suffering it entails, the way in which he takes up his cross, gives him ample opportunity—even under the most difficult of circumstances—to add a deeper meaning to his life."—Larry Dipboye

SERMON SUGGESTIONS

Topic: Of the Father's Love

TEXT: Luke 15:1–3, 11b–32

Religious leaders criticize Jesus for associating with tax collectors and sinners, and Jesus answers with a parable. The father is the main player in the drama. (1) The father reaches out to a guilt-ridden, down-and-out younger son. (2) The father reaches out to a self-righteous, up-and-out older son. (3) The response of the younger son is clear and full of gratitude. The immediate response of the older son is likewise clear, but it is bitter and resentful. The ultimate response remains in doubt.

Topic: When the Manna Stops

TEXT: Josh. 5:9–12

There come times when we have to live our lives under drastically changed conditions. (1) Matters may get better, and maturity is required to handle our success. (2) Matters might get worse, and faith and courage are required to work through our struggle. (3) In either case, it can be a new and promising beginning with God.

CONGREGATIONAL MUSIC

1. "I Love Thy Kingdom, Lord," Timothy Dwight (1801)

   ST. THOMAS, Aaron Williams (1770)

   This oldest of American hymns in continuous use is a paraphrase of several psalm verses, including Psalm 26:8. It could begin worship or accompany the psalm reading.

2. "Rejoice, the Lord Is King," Charles Wesley (1744)

   DARWELL'S 148TH, John Darwall (1770)

   "He sits at God's right hand," in stanza 3 of this classic Wesleyan hymn, relates to Hebrews 1:3 directly. A good hymn for the opening of worship, "Rejoice, the Lord Is King" could also be sung either to introduce or respond to the Epistle lesson (Heb. 1:1–4; 2:5–13).

3. "Jesus Loves Me, This I Know," Anna B. Warner (1859)

   JESUS LOVES ME, William B. Bradbury (1861)

---

[3]New York: Simon & Schuster, 1984, p. 76.

A universally known and loved children's song, "Jesus Loves Me" could be sung in connection with the Gospel lesson (Mark 10:13–16), which among other things includes Jesus' blessing of the children.

4. "I Would Be True," Howard Arnold Walter (1906)

PEEK, Joseph Yates Peek (1909)

Job, despite terrible adversity, remained true to God. This simple sincere hymn of consecration and dedication would be an apt response to the Old Testament reading (Job 1:1; 2:1–10).—Hugh T. McElrath

WORSHIP AIDS

CALL TO WORSHIP.   "But they that wait upon the Lord shall renew their strength; they shall mount up with wings as eagles, they shall run and not be weary, and they shall walk and not faint" (Isa. 40:31).

INVOCATION.   Lift us in worship, Lord, until the solid instruction of Scripture issues into faithful living that undergirds us in our daily lives and points to Christ, in whose name we dare to pray, in whose example we dare to live.—E. Lee Phillips

OFFERTORY SENTENCE.   "Therefore as ye abound in everything, in faith and utterance and knowledge, in all diligence, and in your love to us, see that ye abound in this grace also" (2 Cor. 8:7).

OFFERTORY PRAYER.   Lord, let love permeate our gifts today—the love of Christ for all of us, our love for God, and the spread of the love of God through Christ Jesus to the ends of the Earth.—E. Lee Phillips

PRAYER.   Open, O God, the eyes of those who have not yet seen the image of the new life. Help those of us who have seen it to keep it fresh, to protect it from all the other images that threaten to put it out of the way, and show us once again in the bread and the wine the image of him who gave himself that we might live.—Theodore Parker Ferris

SERMON
Topic: Communion Meditation
TEXT: John 12:5

It has certainly gone through my mind more than once—that same thought: Why was this beautiful thing put here in the midst of this poverty? Here, in the middle of Mexico, in the central plaza, looking at that huge, magnificent cathedral; gold leaf statues; carved marble tombs; tapestries; and marvelous stained-glass windows. And all around the city are these barrios of poverty. Why was this extravagant luxury built in the midst of all this poverty? Why wasn't the money used to help the poor?

On the fact of it is a very serious question. A magnificent cathedral construction project in New York was stopped because they could not answer that question. How could they continue to build such an extravagant cathedral in the midst of the poverty around them? So they stopped their construction to work on their community.

It is a question that this community faces every day. Over and over again we hear the rumblings from the discontent. Why has all that money been spent on that wonderful new recreational complex when we have all this poverty? Why did we spend all those millions on that fancy new courthouse when we have so many people living in homes without indoor toilets? Why are we raising such a fuss about building a heated and air-conditioned animal shelter when we have children coming to school with no coats? Why in the world is this community thinking about trying to raise 15 million dollars to build a library and a performing arts center when we have no countywide water and sewer system? These are easy questions to raise, but Jesus will not have any part of them. Jesus defends the woman, and we as Christians are invited to share the joy that refutes the hypocrisy of the question.

Jesus knew that Judas was not really interested in the poor. Jesus understood that Judas was using this mask of compassion for his own self-interest, and most of the time the people who raise this question in our area have no interest in the poor, have no desire that 15 million dollars be raised to put a water and sewer system into this county. Those who criticize the new courthouse do not really care about poverty; they are really concerned about their own taxes. The woman in the office supply store who was complaining about the courthouse said she wanted the tax money back so she could spend it on herself. When asked whether she wasn't part of Vance County and so the money was being spent on her, she simply had no reply.

There are always those who will sit around and criticize every spontaneous expression of joy. There are always people like Judas who sound like they have the best motives at heart, and all they ever do is belittle, attack, mock, and sneer at every proposal for fun, every deed of praise, every proposal of expression of love. They never propose anything themselves. They are always against and never for. Dwight L. Moody was one of the early mass evangelists who were constantly being attacked for spreading the joy of Christianity the wrong way. His only reply was, "At least I like my way of doing it a lot better than your way of not doing it."

Jesus said to Judas, "Hush, let her show her affections in this way, for what she is doing is preparing me for my death." This spontaneous display of love and affection, devotion and honor, was Mary's affirmation that she had discovered in Jesus the one who is able to bring life out of death. Her brother Lazarus was there in the room. Mary's anointing was an act that acknowledged that Jesus is the Messiah, the anointed of God, the one in whom she found the love of God at work in the world for her. Jesus was reaffirming that even the poor do not live by bread alone. They too need to find a savior. They too need to worship and honor the King. Jesus was not going to be physically here for long, and worship, recognition, and devotion to the glory of God in Jesus Christ must be acknowledged when it is seen.

Jesus knew that even the poor are touched and changed by the sight of love made visible. The magnificent glory of the cathedral in Mexico was paid for by gifts of the poor because even they know they were blessed by having such a vision of glory in their midst. The black preacher T. D. Jakes in Dallas has a congregation of more than twenty thousand people. He has drawn to his ministry all kinds of people from all walks of life, including a large number of blacks who are economically disadvantaged. He understands that part of his ministry is to teach them how to change what they are doing to break the cycle of poverty in their lives. One demand he makes of his members—of those who live in the ghetto and in the barrios, and in the first and second wards of Dallas—is to put their children in a car and drive them out into the suburbs and the country. Plant a vision in their heart, show them something better, take them out to Preston Hollow and tell them that they will live out there when they grow up.

This is why Jesus told Judas to leave this woman alone. We need the vision of that devotion to inspire our lives. This is why Jesus gave us this table and invited us to come, because as often as we eat this bread and drink this cup, we do show forth the Lord's death until he comes again. As often as we eat and drink, we do set before ourselves and the world the life-changing vision of God's love for us. Let us come then to the joyful feast of the people of God.—Rick Brand

SUNDAY, OCTOBER 12, 2003
Lectionary Message

Topic: A Defiant Faith
TEXT: Job 23:1–9, 16–17
Other Readings: Ps. 22:1–15; Heb. 4:12–16; Mark 10:17–31

Timothy McVey went to his death defying the power of death and the authority of the government that orchestrated his execution. According to attorneys who walked with him in his final months, Timothy never expressed remorse for what he did. He was described as quiet, calculating, intelligent, and defiant to the end. Apart from the horror of his murder of 19 children and 149 adults, Timothy McVey was a living tragedy. I cannot help but wonder, more with compassion than curiosity or vengeance, what was the origin of this destructive emotion? Was his the defiance of a child victimized by the battle between parents, as suggested by the psychoanalysts? Was this the mentality of a decorated soldier trained to kill without remorse? Was he an angry man embittered by the death of the innocents at Ruby Ridge and Waco, as he claimed? Perhaps he died "bloody but unbowed," the boast of his final message from "Invictus" (William Ernest Henley). It appears that he died lonely, friendless, and hated—the victim of his own anger inspired by his act of mindless violence.

I do not have to tell you that anger is a destructive emotion. Angry people tend to be miserable. They drive away friends and companions. They burn up inside with overheated emotions. They become totally unreasonable and blind to acts of kindness and concern of the people around them. They are prone to acts of violence toward others and themselves. Finally, they tend to be so absorbed in the immediate circumstances of their lives that they lose sight of the future and cut themselves off from hope.

You may not be able to keep from visiting it occasionally, but the state of anger is no place to live. Thus, through the ages we have made a virtue of submission. Good children, we have been taught, obey their parents, their God, and their government—right or wrong. We had a mess on our hands when we raised a generation of kids taught to ask questions of all authority. They reacted to the War in Vietnam with "Hell no, we won't go!" The war exposed an element of defiance among the young that we had never seen before. The war was there, and is here, and we are still dealing with the conflict between generations.

Whatever else we may be, we are not a nation of submissive spirits who blindly go into battles defined by our leaders—and we never were. Since the Boston Tea Party, this revolutionary people has defied authority and demanded justice.

There is no defense for the violence or hatred that possessed McVey. However, I would observe that most of us are, at one time or another, companions of Job, defiantly challenging authority and demanding an accounting for injustice in this life. Anger is a terrible master and wonderful servant. When we learn to "be angry and sin not," we find the power of truth and justice that no one can ever touch through blind submission to authority. Clothed in the redemptive grace of God and the righteous indignation of Christ, people of faith are called to heal on the Sabbath, to overturn the tables of money changers in our temples, and to demand from the cross an accounting from God: "My God, why have you forsaken me?"

I. *Faith defies injustice.* If we are companions of Job, we are anything but patient. We are not likely to become good Muslims, blindly submitting to the absolute authority of Allah. Because we believe in a God of mercy, we are confused and hurt when life rolls over us, and with Job we are likely to protest, "My complaint is bitter [and defiant]; his hand is heavy despite my groaning." *Mar* means bitter; *Meri* is defiant. Without the vowels in ancient Hebrew, the words are identical. Perhaps the author wanted us to hear from the soul of Job a play on the words, both bitter and defiant.

This ancient picture of the tension between a man and God may be the most relevant and contemporary book of the Bible. Francois Mauriac tells of meeting the young journalist Elie Wiesel and discovering that he was one of the children seen standing at the Austerlitz station waiting for the death trains to take them away during the Jewish Holocaust. Wiesel had seen his mother, his sister, and all of his family, except for his father, disappear into the Nazi gas chambers and ovens. Mauriac then writes about this child who stood after Auschwitz in the solemn ceremony of Rosh Hashanah (Day of Atonement): "On this day he did not kneel. The human creature, outraged and humiliated beyond all that heart and spirit can conceive of, defied a divinity who was blind and deaf." Wiesel recalled that he did not plea or lament: "I was the accuser, and God the accused. My eyes were open and I was alone—terribly alone in a world without God and without man. Without love or mercy. I had ceased to be anything but ashes, yet I felt myself to be stronger than the Almighty."[4]

We wait for lightening to strike and end Job's tale, but it never happens. Some folks would like to rip this book from their Bibles because of the blasphemy. Job may appear to be a quiet, submissive soul at the beginning of this trial, but he has his moments when he lashes out at the heavens and demands that God give an accounting for the injustice of his suffering. Yet the heavens are silent and God seems absent.

II. *Faith defies the absence of God.* I discovered as a young parent that children will not be ignored. Misbehavior is often a cry for attention more than a desire to be bad. Children would rather have the attention of parental anger and punishment than the isolation of being ignored. If you want to understand Job's or Elie's anger, listen to the silence of God. Job looks for God in all directions: "He is not there. . . . I cannot perceive him. . . . He hides. . . . I cannot behold him. . . . I cannot see him." Nothing is more devastating to the child of God than the sense of God's absence.

Eric Rust suggested that we cannot see God because we have ourselves in the way. When you are self-centered, you shut yourself off from God and from your friends. You become "a lonely, isolated being, full of frustration, concerned only with himself."[5] There is more. Some-

---

[4]Elie Wiesel, *Night Trilogy*, p. 10.
[5]*Professor in the Pulpit* (Broadman, 1963), p. 16.

times we cannot feel beyond our pain or see beyond our own loss. Absorbed by my own grief, I have little or nothing left to give to anyone else. Long before I had ever walked with anyone toward the end of life, I was puzzled by the warning of a teacher that dying is a process of centering on one's self and one's own loss of self.

It is less an act of defiance than an act of faith. Like children awakening in fear in the middle of the night, we cry out in the darkness and plead for God to turn on the lights. The truly tragic child is one who has never known nurture or love and has never learned to expect the comforting presence of a loving parent in the dark. Children without nurture are numb. They seldom cry. We may cry out in anger, but it is the cry of faith that the Heavenly Parent we cannot see is real and present. Anger and defiance are directed at a subject who is real. Only fools lash out at nothing or cry out to a vacuum. The surest sign of an empty life is indifference, not anger.

The German pastor Günther Rutenborn wrote *The Sign of Jonah* to raise questions that plagued humanity after the war. Like Job, every character in the play defends his or her innocence. No one accepts responsibility for the horror of human history. Finally, the Judge must rule. Let God be held responsible for the world. Let God be born as man and be condemned to wander the Earth homeless, thirsty, hungry, born of a woman, a despised Jew. The gavel falls, and God steps down from the bench condemned to the Incarnation. "For our sake he made him to be sin who knew no sin, so that in him we might become the righteousness of God" (2 Cor. 5:21).

Almighty God, we stand in awe of your majesty and in reverence before your mighty power. In this vast universe, we wonder at a God who notices specks of dust like us, yet we bear your image in our lives and we see in the face of Jesus the value beyond measure of every person. Because your love is being perfected in us, we cast aside all fear and dare to raise our heads before you, clothed in the dignity and righteousness of Christ our Lord. Amen.—Larry K. Dipboye

ILLUSTRATIONS

THE SHADOW OF THE HOLOCAUST.   Murray J. Haar wrote of "Job After Auschwitz"[6] as *midrash*. In Judaism, midrash is "a form of biblical interpretation that mediated between tradition and certain unprecedented events that questioned or transformed such tradition." The whole world, Christians as well as Jews, live under the shadow of the Holocaust. We can no longer address the problem of evil or our understanding of anthropology and theology without addressing the suffering of the Jews under Hitler. Job is the exception to tradition that guides a new understanding of God.—Larry Dipboye

THE SILENCE OF GOD.   "When the gods are silent, when existence all around us is not only filled but surrounded by a spectral stillness, this only makes apparent what has always been 'objectively' true. Whether there were always gods, we do not know; but that they never spoke is certain. In our situation . . . we are beginning to see how atheism has always been latent in religion."—Kornelis H. Miskotte[7]

---

[6]*Interpretation*, 1999, *53*(3), 265 ff.
[7]*When the Gods Are Silent*, trans. John W. Doberstein (New York: HarperCollins, 1967), p. 9.

SERMON SUGGESTIONS

Topic: From Madness to Mission

TEXT: Luke 8:26–39

(1) An isolating illness. (2) A healing encounter. (3) A remarkable mission.

Topic: How God Speaks to Us

TEXT: 1 Kings 19:1–4 (5–7), 8–15a NRSV

(1) God speaks to us in a time of need. (2) God speaks in unexpected ways: (a) practically—as with rest, food, and drink; (b) quietly—as in "a sound of sheer silence"; (c) with something specific to do—as in "Go, return on your way."

CONGREGATIONAL MUSIC

1. "With Joy I Heard My Friends Exclaim," Ps. 122; vers. *The Psalter* (1912)
   GONFALON ROYAL, Perry C. Buck (1918)
   Suitable for the opening of worship, this paraphrase of Psalm 122 could also be sung in place of the Psalter reading.
2. "O Jesus, I Have Promised," John Ernest Bode (1866)
   ANGEL'S STORY, Arthur H. Mann (1881)
   This hymn written by and for youth could be meaningfully sung in connection with the Gospel reading about the rich young ruler.
3. "Since Our Great High Priest, Christ Jesus," Heb. 4:14–16; vers. Christopher Idle (1973)
   ALL SAINTS, Darmstadt *Gesangbuch* (1618); adapt. W. H. Monk (1861)
   Here is a contemporary paraphrase of selected excerpts from Hebrews that would be effective as either introduction or response to the reading of the Epistle lesson (Heb. 4:12–16).
4. "Out of the Depths," Martin Luther (1524); trans. Richard Massie (1854)
   AUS TIEFER NOT, Martin Luther (1524)
   This classic Lutheran hymn based on Psalm 130 reflects the lament and longing of the suffering of Job. It would be appropriately sung in connection with the Old Testament reading (Job 23:1–9, 16–17).—Hugh T. McElrath

WORSHIP AIDS

CALL TO WORSHIP.   "Stand fast therefore in the liberty wherewith Christ hath made us free, and be not entangled again with the yoke of bondage" (Gal. 5:1).

INVOCATION.   Sharpen our minds, O Lord; humble our spirits and open our hearts to take the love that once became flesh, that comes among us again and again, that we may not only take him in but also show him to others and let others see him in. We ask it in his name, by his power, and for his sake.—Theodore Parker Ferris

OFFERTORY SENTENCE.   "He that hath a bountiful eye shall be blessed; for he giveth of his bread to the poor" (Prov. 22:9).

OFFERTORY PRAYER.   Holy God, we take from our largesse and give as we have been prospered; thus our prayer of gratitude and our dedication of these gifts are in the ever-giving name of Jesus.—E. Lee Phillips

PRAYER.   Dear Lord, help us to live this week quietly, easily; to lean on thy strength restfully, trustfully; to wait for the unfolding of thy will patiently, serenely; to meet others peacefully, joyously; to face tomorrow courageously, confidently.—Theodore Parker Ferris

SERMON
Topic: The Promise of God's Parenting
TEXT: Rom. 8:14–17

Some have argued that Nicodemus came to Jesus under cover of darkness to warn him of some impending danger from disgruntled Jewish authorities. Others have wondered if the Pharisee wasn't intent on learning more about this itinerant rabbi's teaching, which had become so very popular with the people. Still others have stretched to suggest that Nicodemus actually desired to become a disciple of Jesus. Personally, I doubt that it matters much.

Maybe it was just this simple: Sometimes we are awakened in the dark of the night, haunted by some question for which an answer must be found somewhere, from someone. Perhaps that was also true for the Pharisee named Nicodemus.

Regardless, what we have is a story in which Nicodemus comes to Jesus, and before he can raise either his question or his concern, the rabbi from Nazareth says, "Amen, amen, I say to you, no one can see the Kingdom of God without being born from above." Nicodemus hears the words "born from above" and interprets them to mean "born again" in some physical sense, which is why he reacts in befuddlement, asking, "How can a person once grown old be born again?"

But Jesus presses his point further, and does so because this word of instruction will prove essential to each and every generation of would-be followers. So he says, "Amen, amen, I say to you, no one can enter the Kingdom of God without being born of water and Spirit."

And then you'll recall how on yet another occasion "people were bringing even infants to Jesus that he might touch them, and when the disciples saw this, they rebuked them. Jesus, however, called the children to himself and said, 'Let the children come to me and do not prevent them; for the Kingdom of God belongs to such as these. Amen, I say to you, whoever does not accept the Kingdom of God like a child will not enter it.'"

I sometimes wonder if we haven't become far too sophisticated for our own good. Such sophistication can, and often does, cause a diminishing of our capacity to remain open to mystery.

In his now-famous Epistle to the Romans, the apostle Paul speaks of the Christian life in similar terms. Paul writes, "For those who are led by the Spirit of God are children of God. For you do not receive a spirit of slavery to fall back into fear, but you receive a spirit of adoption, through which we cry, 'Abba, Father!' The Spirit itself bears witness with our spirit that we are children of God, and if children then heirs, heirs of God and joint heirs with Christ."

Without a doubt each of us here could testify to that moment or period in life when we too were "led" astray, seduced by something we thought would fulfill us, or by someone whose charisma caught us off guard. Yet what should trouble us even more is the recognition that being led first required our attachment and commitment to the one leading, or to the thing commanding our unquestioned loyalty. Would that we had been more attentive to the alarm sounded by our Savior: "By their fruits you will know them."

And if we were to ask Paul to tell us, in no uncertain terms, what form and content that same "fruit" would take, I imagine he would have referred us to his letter to the Galatians, chapter 5, verse 22: "The fruit of the Spirit is love, joy, peace, patience, kindness, generosity, faithfulness, gentleness, self-control." You see how this "fruit" is singular—we bear it all, or we bear none!

"For you did not receive a spirit of slavery to fall back into fear" writes Paul, but you received a spirit of adoption, through which we cry, "Abba, Father!" Wonderful, isn't it? Still, I'm troubled by that phrase, "to fall back into fear." And the question pressing itself upon me is this: "Fear of what, or whom?"

Taken into context, Paul's point becomes clear. There are many things we may well fear: the diagnosis, the prognosis, the pain, the failure of a relationship, the loss of a job or a life, the dark, and the unknown. Paul knows that, and elsewhere addresses those apprehensions. But here he's talking about a more particular "fear." He means to say the fear that—in the end—our lives will have proven unpleasant, even unacceptable to God; and to that degree prove to have been pointless.

What if at the conclusion of it all God should scribble across our life, "Brilliant! Entertaining! Marvelous achievements! Pleasant! But you missed the point!"? We have each known that fear. Maybe on the scales of God's judgment our lives will weigh in as having been an abysmal failure!

Paul proclaims that God's love for us is far greater than any form of earthly parental devotion. And it is through God's boundless love that you and I have "received a spirit of adoption" so that whenever we are once more entangled in the tentacles of temptation and sin, whenever we begin to feel as though we have failed him, whenever we begin to fear that our behavior will eventuate in his rejection of us—then, once again, we can cry "Abba, Father!"

And in that one simple cry—spoken aloud or whispered in the silence of the soul's sanctuary—"The Spirit itself bears witness with our spirit that we are children of God."—Albert J. D. Walsh

SUNDAY, OCTOBER 19, 2003
Lectionary Message

Topic: When Questions Answer
TEXT: Job 38:1–7 (34–41)
Other Readings: Ps. 104:1–9, 24, 35c; Heb. 5:1–10; Mark 10:35–45

We gathered on Sunday evenings to discuss the links and conflicts between science and faith. Several local scientists joined us, and I found quickly that I was out of my league in the science side of our subject. One scholar made a presentation of Einstein's Special Theory of Relativity. He took the entire evening mapping the logic of the theory with calculus that consumed the entire board. He left me at the starting gate. I lacked the education and feared that I lacked the intelligence to follow a language that was second nature to him. I was so intimidated by the presentation that at the end I sat in stunned silence, and I was supposed to be leading the conference. I remembered someone's advice: "It is better to sit in silence and be thought a fool than to speak and remove all doubt." I felt better when I read later that in 1915, when Einstein released his General Theory of Relativity, fewer than ten people in the world could follow his explanation.

If science is hard for us to comprehend, how in the world are we to speak of God? Confrontation with the mystery of life and death transcends most of what we think we know. No one has simple equations that explain or defend God in the face of human tragedy. The stages of grief have been identified and catalogued by a multitude of interpreters. The number and explanations vary, but counselors seem to agree on stage one: shock. Shock has been called "a temporary escape from reality."[8] Perhaps shock is the stunned silence of being confronted by an event beyond explanation or an explanation beyond understanding.

In the beginning, Job is the model of piety. In the first round of loss, he suffers in resigned silence before the incomprehensible God: "The Lord gave, and the Lord has taken away; blessed be the name of the Lord." Even in round two, when Job's wife advised, "Curse God and die," he responded with calm reassurance: "Shall we receive the good at the hand of God, and not receive the bad?" The confusion of shock with piety is a common misunderstanding. Eventually the quiet dignity cracks, and Job begins to question God. Ultimately, God breaks silence and raises the questions of Job to a higher level. All the way through this story we are confronted with a mountain of questions, without one single, solitary, simple answer.

I think we all know that we are not going to avoid tragedy. How shall we respond? How shall we pray, and what shall we say to the world? Are we more acceptable to God sitting silently in resignation and defeat, or standing up to life raising our questions and our defiance of injustice? Shall we sit in silence and be thought fools, or speak and remove all doubt?

I. *God transcends our questions.* Last year we received from our son a holiday epistle to friends, with the usual play-by-play description of the latest antics of the children and a rather lengthy journal of family activities for the year. In the opening sentence he noted that busy friends may want to read only the "executive summary." Then he threw in an outline of the letter with half-intelligible sentence fragments. It was intended to be cute, but it also reflects the spirit of our age. We live by shortcuts and executive summaries. In most issues of life, we want to cut to the chase, nutshell the supporting data, get to the bottom line, and move on to the next question. Many of us are content to let the experts wrestle with the big questions, while we rush on with a pocket full of platitudes.

All that Job had left in the world was a cynical wife and three friends, and he did what most of us do. He sat in stunned silence. His three friends approached in reverence; they wept aloud, tore their clothing, and threw dust on their heads. Finally they sat silently on the ground with Job for seven days and nights.

Eventually the shock wears off for all of us. Then come the emotional wave, the depression, the panic attacks, the guilt, and the anger. In my early pastoral experience I thought I had an obligation to rush in with answers before the questions were raised. When I became the victim, I realized that the most perceptive theological construction did not fill the deep vacuum in Job's soul. Job broke the silence with a curse on the day he was born, curses on all of creation, and a barrage of questions and accusations toward God that would have frightened anyone with any thought of the possibility of God. In contrast, Job's friends argued for stock answers and oversimplified explanations, executive summaries of the ways of God.

II. *A questioning faith is bigger than an answering faith.* The catechetical approach to Christian education commits to memory a series of questions and answers about matters of

---

[8]Granger E. Westberg, *Good Grief*, p. 23.

faith. Gathering the best wisdom of the Church through the ages in a collection of answers is not a bad way to educate children in faith. Like hymns, the content of the message does not always sink in when the words are committed to memory. The catechism provides a foundation on which to begin the walk with God, but most of us eventually reach a point where we hit the ceiling. The answers cease to address the real question.

The story of Job is about a community of faith that had simple answers to ultimate questions. Follow the counsel of Job's friends and you will begin to grasp the catechism of conventional wisdom. Question: Why do people suffer? Answer: God punishes the evil and rewards the good. Question: What if you do not believe you deserve the pain that has come upon you? Answer: Too bad; the fact that you are hurting is a sure sign that you are wrong and God is right. Question: Does God care about our suffering? Answer: God cares for the people who humble themselves, repent of their sins, and pray. Thus God rewards submissive silence and punishes defiant questions.

Look again, friends. Job knows all of the stock responses and at one time accepted the simple answers as the way of God; but Job's faith will not stop at the boundaries of tradition. He reminds me of the introduction to the old *Star Trek* TV show. Job goes where no one has dared to go before. His faith will not stop at the boundaries that suggest an unjust and uncaring God. His questions push the boundaries of understanding.

III. *Questions may be a call to worship.* Several years ago Billy Graham responded to the problem of doubt by suggesting that we ought to carry our doubts a step further and doubt our doubts. Perhaps we need to learn to question our questions. The Gospels are loaded with inquiries, many of which are hostile. In his temptations to Christ in the desert, Satan raised basic, important questions about the role of God and the work of the Messiah. The pious interrogated Jesus about the source of his authority and his understanding of the ways of God. Jesus often responded to interrogation by raising better questions than he had been asked. He responded to questions with questions.

That is essentially what happens when Job encounters the voice from the whirlwind. Job is called to a higher level of inquiry: Where were you when the world was created? What is the measure of the universe? What are the foundations that support the creation? Who is in control of this world, and how does nature work?

In our struggle to understand, we need more than understanding. The God who created this vast universe is not likely to be reduced to an executive summary or even to a board full of calculus. We are called to worship in hope of meeting God in the whirlwind of ultimate questions. Paul saw most clearly when he concluded his great anthem on Christian love (1 Cor. 13) with the acceptance of uncertainty. We see through a glass darkly. We live toward the ultimate moment when we will see as we are seen and know as we are known. Knowledge counts for little or nothing. Love, God's love, is eternal.

Eternal God, you alone were present at creation, and you alone are God. We are mortals, created through your grace. Forgive our anxiety and be patient with our cries for understanding. We long to hear your voice, O God, to know as we are known and to love as we are loved. As we wait and wonder, we listen for your Word, in Christ our Lord. Amen.—Larry K. Dipboye

ILLUSTRATIONS
NAMING THE WHIRLWIND.   Langdon Gilkey heard Job's voice from the whirlwind addressing our struggle to speak meaningfully of God in the generation that produced the

death-of-God theology: "Above all, we can know the divine hiddenness in the Void of insecurity, despair, doubt, guilt, and death, which every human faces—even Jesus himself in his cry from the cross. . . . The beginning of faith then appears in the awareness of the sacred in the profane, of joy and wonder in the midst of insecurity, of meaning and truth in the midst of the meaningless, and of life in the face of death, and it culminates with our understanding and affirmation of their ultimate unity in God."[9]

GRIEF BEGINS WITH SHOCK.   Brad's death was tragic for the whole town. He had been an outstanding student and athlete in high school and college. He was everyone's hero. During the receiving of friends, more than a thousand people offered their condolences to the family. Brad's father, a popular physician in town, later commented that he was so numb with shock that he did not remember a single word spoken to him that evening. A colleague later told him, "You were the perfect host, calmly taking care of your patients."

We must be cautious about confusing shock with faith. The calm in the early hours and days of a significant loss is shock. The storm comes later.—Larry Dipboye

SERMON SUGGESTIONS

Topic: Bringing Stubbornness to an End

TEXT: Jer. 18:1–11

(1) God is continuously at work to shape the lives and fortunes of his people. (2) God meets resistance in the stubborn will of his people. (3) God could cast his people aside forever. (4) But God gives his people opportunity to yield to him and be formed into vessels that honor God.

Topic: A Poignant Appeal

TEXT: Philem. 1:21

(1) In gratitude. (2) In love. (3) In confidence.

CONGREGATIONAL MUSIC

1. "Songs of Praise the Angels Sang," James Montgomery (1819)

   MONKLAND, John Antes (1824)

   A fine hymn for the beginning of musical worship, "Songs of Praise the Angel's Sang" starts and ends with a hint of Job 38:7. The singing of this hymn would naturally flow from the Old Testament reading.

2. "God Is Love, Let Heaven Adore Him," Timothy Rees (1922)

   ABBOTS LEIGH, Cyril V. Taylor

   With its reference to Job 38:4 in the first stanza, this modern hymn could also be sung in connection with the Old Testament lesson.

3. "O Worship the King," Robert Grant (1833)

   HANOVER, William Croft (1708) or LYONS, W. Gardiner's *Sacred Melodies* (1815)

   This romantic paraphrase of Psalm 104 by one of the most gifted of hymnic laymen functions

---

[9]Langdon Gilkey, *Naming the Whirlwind: The Renewal of God-Language* (Indianapolis and New York: Bobbs-Merrill, 1969), p. 469.

beautifully when sung as a congregational call to worship. Its use with the Psalter reading is also self-evident.

4. "O Master, Let Me Walk with Thee," Washington Gladden (1879)

MARYTON, H. Percy Smith (1874)

It would be significant to sing this noble hymn of service near the reading of the Gospel lesson on Jesus' teachings about servanthood.—Hugh T. McElrath

WORSHIP AIDS

CALL TO WORSHIP.   "You whom I have taken from the ends of the Earth, and called from its farthest regions, and said to you, 'You are my servant, I have chosen you and have not cast you away: fear not, for I am with you; be not dismayed, for I am your God. I will strengthen you, yes, I will help you, I will uphold you with my righteous right hand'" (Isa. 41:9–10 NKJV).

INVOCATION.   Lord, our Creator, as we withdraw from the world to worship God, acclimate us to the holy, stir in our souls, put us in touch with our faith, that this service of worship will shape us into godly men and women who have walked with God.—E. Lee Phillips

OFFERTORY SENTENCE.   "For all the law is fulfilled in one word, even in this: thou shalt love thy neighbor as thyself" (Gal. 5:14).

OFFERTORY PRAYER.   God of grace, help us to give all we can so that others who do not know the love of God might recognize it in our lives and in this church as we strive to do God's will.—E. Lee Phillips

PRAYER.   Lord, give us grace to hold onto you when all is weariness and when fear and sin abound within, when love itself is tested by the doubt that love is false or dead within the soul—when every act brings new confusion, new distress, new opportunities, new misunderstandings, and every thought new accusation.

Lord, give us grace that we may know that in the darkness pressing round it is the mist of sin that hides your face, that you are there and you do know we love you still, and that our dependence and endurance in your will is still our gift of love.—Fr. Gilbert Shaw[10]

SERMON
Topic: Help in Time of Trouble
TEXT: Job 14:1

There is this that we know about ourselves as human beings: that we constantly get into trouble. All kinds of trouble.

But whatever the nature of the trouble may be, or whatever the cause of it may be, the *fact* of the trouble remains. Job put it in a single sentence that by its very brevity and bluntness is powerful: "Man that is born of woman is full of trouble." Indeed it is so, and we all know it. Amen!

We also know this about ourselves. When we get into trouble we cry for help. Some are more reluctant than others. Some are brought up to believe that they should rely on themselves

---

[10]*The Oxford Book of Prayer*

alone, that they should not be dependent on anyone, nor beholden to anyone. And some are very loath to let anybody know that they need help, that they are faced with something they cannot handle themselves; they wouldn't let anyone know for the world. They are too proud to ask for help. But when the trouble reaches a certain point, only a few are too proud to ask for help. When the trouble reaches the point where it is beyond all the resources that a man has to meet it, then proud or not, self-reliant or not, he reaches out a hand and asks for help.

When we get into trouble we cry for help, and when we cry most of us eventually cry to God. In some cases we do it because we are in almost daily communication with God; we are in the habit of referring everything that happens to us to him, so it is the most natural thing in the world when we are in trouble to turn to him and ask for his help. In other cases we turn to God simply because we are so desperate. There is no one else to turn to.

When trouble comes, trouble that is too much for us, we turn instinctively, almost impulsively, to God and ask him to help us, and we cry with all the people down through the ages, "Lord, hear my prayer, and let my cry come unto thee."

These things we know. We also know (here some of you may not be able to follow me; your experience may not be the same as mine) that when we get into trouble and ask God for help, we get it. Help of one kind or another, that is. Sometimes the help comes directly and immediately, as though God were answering our plea for help at the moment it was uttered.

At other times the help comes indirectly through a person. Another man was facing a rather serious personal problem. He had thought a great deal about it, and the more he thought about it the more insoluble it seemed. Finally he asked God to show him the way. Nothing happened for a long time, but he kept asking God every day to show him the way through the dark woods of this human situation and to give him the wisdom to handle it well. Then one day he was on a train and met a man he knew but didn't see often; he hadn't seen him for several years. The man knew nothing about the problem, never did, never will know anything about it, but in the meeting and in the conversation that took place, the solution of the problem emerged. The help he had asked for came. It did not come directly or immediately; and when it came it came through a person who was not at all aware of being one of God's ministering angels, and probably would not like to have been called that!

At still other times the help we get is not the help we asked for. A child, for instance, is stricken with a serious handicap, and it looks as though all his life would be ruined by this unfair limitation. He turns to God instinctively and asks for God's help. He asks that the handicap be removed. Time goes by and the handicap is not removed, but the child learns almost miraculously to handle his handicap, and to handle it in such a way that it transfigures his life and gives it a nobility and significance that otherwise it might never have had. The help was given, but in this case it was not at all the help that was asked for.

We must reckon, however, with this fact. There are times when no help comes, directly or indirectly, from God himself or from him through another person—not the help we ask for or some other kind of help. No help comes. When, then? Think of it first in terms of the help one man asks from another. A friend of yours is in trouble and he asks you for money. You decide, after looking at all the circumstances in the situation, not to give him the money—not because you do not want to help him but because you know that if you give him the money it will hurt him, for the very thing he has to do is learn how to stand up to the trouble he is in and take responsibility for his own actions. It is one of the hardest decisions, incidentally, that a person ever has to make—that to help someone he loves would hurt that other person.

I am sure there are times when God feels the same way with us—that there are times when God withholds his help from us for the same reason: because to give us his help would ultimately be to hurt us. Later on, years later, we come to see that help did come, even in those times when it seemed not to come, but the help was hidden in the trouble itself!

These are things we know about life, from our own experience. We all get into trouble invariably, sooner or later, some more than others. When we get into trouble, we ask for help; eventually, if not at first, we ask God for it; and when we ask for it, we get it.

These facts of human experience bring certain things into plain view.

(1) There will *never* be a time when you are completely free from trouble—never!

(2) There will *eventually* come a time when you will be in trouble that you cannot handle by yourself.

And may I say this to you? Don't be ashamed to ask God. Even though you have not paid much attention to him when times were better, don't be ashamed to turn to him. Remember that the God who made you makes allowance for all your little weaknesses. He never makes excuses for you, neither will he ever exclude you from his love and care—never. Don't hesitate, don't be ashamed to turn to him. And remember, you will be in good company. You will be in the company of Paul the apostle, who turned to God for help when he wanted to get rid of a physical affliction that he felt was impeding his work preaching the Gospel around the world. He did not get the help he wanted, but he got a greater help—he was given the grace of God, which was more than sufficient for all his weakness. And you will be in the company of Jesus himself, who when he was in the garden asked God to spare him the death he saw waiting for him. He was not spared, but he was given the strength to go through it in such a way that he took the sting out of death forever, for everyone.

(3) You will not get help unless you admit you need it and want it, and ask for it. You know that from your own personal experience. You cannot really give any help to a friend, even though you see that the friend is in a bad way, unless the friend asks for it, wants it.

So God cannot really help us until we are willing to admit that we need the help, and have the humility to ask for it. It is only then that God is able to give us the things he is so ready to give.

(4) Most important of all, if you ask God for help and get it, that experience will be the greatest assurance you will ever have of the reality of God.

Then you will remember this: *When I was in trouble, I called upon the Lord, and he heard me.*

Then you will know.—Theodore Parker Ferris

SUNDAY, OCTOBER 26, 2003
Lectionary Message

Topic: God Is Great; God Is Good

TEXT: Job 42:1–6, 10–17

Other Readings: Ps. 34:1–8 (19–22); Heb. 7:23–28; Mark 10:46–52

The child's prayer, "God is great; God is good," is the most basic and most profound statement we can make about God. The child's prayer is also the philosopher's question. Following clear logic and the abundant evidence of human suffering, E. S. Brightman was among a class of philosophers who declared that you can't have it both ways. God cannot be both great and good, all-powerful and all loving. Either God is able to relieve human suffering but does not care, or God cares but is not able. Given the choice, Brightman concluded that God must be limited in power and knowledge. Rabbi Kushner concluded, "God can't do everything." In *When Bad Things Happen to Good People,* the chapter on God's limits focuses on the teachings of the Talmud about improper prayers, the sort of things we should not ask of God—like changing the rules of nature or doing for us what we are capable of doing for ourselves.

J. B., a "play in verse" by Archibald MacLeish,[11] is a modern version of the Book of Job. Like Job, it is somewhat cynical and irreverent. The setting is a dark corner of a circus tent, a side-show stage. There are times when most of us see life as a three-ring circus. The roles of God and Satan are played by Mr. Zuss and Nickles, two circus vendors, and sometimes the roles seem reversed. After the scene introducing J. B., Mr. Zuss offers a satanic quip, "Well, that's our pigeon" (p. 44). Zuss observes that someone is always playing Job in the world. Nickles seems almost compassionate in his response: "Millions and millions of mankind burned, crushed, broken, mutilated, slaughtered, and for what? For thinking! For walking round the world in the wrong skin, the wrong-shaped noses, eyelids: Sleeping the wrong night wrong city—London, Dresden, Hiroshima" (p. 12). Nickles then chants the little jingle that defines the conflict, the dilemma of a sleepless humanity: "If God is God He is not good; if God is good He is not God."

Job is more than a solitary figure. Job is everyone, a multitude. Although Job is personal and often appears to be like looking in a mirror, he is also global. *J. B.* was first produced in New York in 1958. The world was still emerging from World War II. The full impact of the Jewish Holocaust was just sinking in, and the U.S. civil rights movement was under way. No one really mistook the uneasy truce in Korea for world peace. The cold war and the nuclear arms race were on, and another war in Southeast Asia was about to start up. The hard realities of history raised serious questions about the evolutionary moral progress of the world. Every corner of the globe and every age are involved in meaningless, futile suffering. Our question today is whether we can pray with the children, "God is great, God is good."

I. *God is great.* I am sure you have seen the TV commercial. The guy is watching a video-tape of a football game that has come down to a deciding field goal. The ball is placed and kicked in the air on the way to the goal posts. Suddenly he pauses the action, runs out of the house, drives to the church, kneels at the altar and prays, makes the sign of the cross, then drives back home and hits the play button. The ball goes through the uprights, the game is won, and a celebration ensues.

I confess to getting a chuckle out of the scene, and I have asked myself why I am not offended by the ridiculous and sacrilegious picture of prayer. The whole picture is less about prayer than it is about the way technology has changed our ways of thinking—even about prayer. I have watched ball games on videotape. However, I don't recall ever praying for a change in the outcome of an event that has already been concluded. That is ridiculous. In fact, I do not recall praying for God to change the course of a live ball game. I do not wish to be sacrilegious here but I doubt that God has a favorite in the Super Bowl.

Why, then, do I pray for and with people who are dealing with cancer and plead with

---

[11]Boston: Houghton Mifflin, 1956.

God to change the course of the disease? I assume something about the loving nature of God. I believe that God cares about human suffering. God cares that we are dust. I cannot really separate the goodness from the greatness of God. I have been Job. I have sat with Job in the ashes and I have prayed with Job, and I have sometimes felt, with Job, abandoned to fate by a God who either does not care or cannot help. "If God is God" I assume that God is in control of the universe and the primary cause of all events. Because I believe that God is God, I pray for change in the course of events that I perceive to be in contradiction to the nature of God.

I believe that God is Lord of nature, but I have had to adjust my expectations. I do not attribute everything that happens in the world to God. We have learned from Jesus to pray "Our Father." The role of father means something to me. There was a time with my children when it seemed that I was able to do all things. They looked to me for the basic necessities of life, and sometimes assumed that I possessed powers far beyond my capacity. How often and how painfully I have had to say, "No, we cannot afford that," or "No, I do not believe you need that." Sometimes I have had to say, "I can't fix it. It is broken beyond repair. We will have to do without." The fatherhood of God is a metaphor, an image of God. Certainly God is not limited as I am limited, yet the same kind of exchange goes on between the Father of creation and the children of God. God is great, but we have a child's eye view of the world.

II. *God is good.* The final chapter of Job may be a disconnected addition to the story, a fairytale ending in which they all "lived happily ever after." I see an essential correction to the course of faith. This story began with a capricious deity making deals with Satan to test Job as one would kick the tires on a used car. The God we meet in the whirlwind is the God of creation, who transcends all human understanding, including the crass picture of God in the first two chapters. Finally, it seems that Job bows before the revelation of God and acknowledges that God is great, but translators are not sure whether he resigns to mortality or repents of being dust—defiant to the end.

We almost get a fast rewind to the beginning in the final restoration of Job's wealth, health, and family. Something inside me wants to stop the action and yell, "Foul." This is inconsistent with reality. I know too many Jobs who have lost everything and never recovered. I have seen a few people recover from bankruptcy and from cancer, but I have never seen anyone replace dead children. It is absurd—almost like saying to someone whose child has died, "It's OK. You can get another one." Our families are not like ice cream cones that can be replaced when you drop them on the sidewalk.

In the end, God blesses Job's challenge to the crass idea that God is playing games with humanity. God blesses the angry cries of the tormented soul who believes in justice and mercy. God vindicates Job's questioning faith, and Job sees better days. Interestingly, the friends are sent off to make amends for their wrong-headed ideas about Job and about God. The end is the ultimate. We live toward final things, eschatology.

The man in agony in the garden of Gethsemane prayed, "Abba, Father, for you all things are possible; remove this cup from me; yet not what I want but what you want" (Mark 14:36). Then he went out to face the cross. There he cried out with Job to God, "Why have you abandoned me?" Jesus knew the goodness of God. The jingle of Nickles is cute, but not quite right. If God is God, God must be good.

God of amazing grace, we bow before your mighty power and long to know your redemptive love. We look for your presence in the breathtaking beauty of the sunset, and fear your anger in the raging storms and prowling predators. Somehow, O Lord, we know to look beyond the things we see to the God we cannot grasp. As you have come to us in the sacrificial love of your Son, be known to us in the compassion of your people, and lead us through the valley of shadows as we follow Jesus the Christ. Amen.—Larry Dipboye

ILLUSTRATIONS

HOW DO YOU SEE?   Rachel, age four, climbed into her grandmother's lap and raised a serious issue she had heard from conversations flowing over her head. "Grandmother," she said, "life is tough." Her grandmother smiled and asked, "Why, what is so tough?" Rachel replied, "Well, sometimes I don't finish my dinner, and I don't get dessert."

We respond with a condescending smile at the child's view of life, but we do not ridicule the child for being a child. As we grow, our interpretation of "tough" changes. Would that we could see through the eyes of God!—Larry Dipboye

THEOLOGY IN AUSCHWITZ.   "A 'theology after Auschwitz' may seem an impossibility or blasphemy to those who allowed themselves to be satisfied with theism or their childhood beliefs and then lost them. And there would be no 'theology after Auschwitz' in retrospective sorrow and the recognition of guilt, had there been no 'theology in Auschwitz.' Anyone who later comes up against insoluble problems and despair must remember that the *Shema* of Israel and the Lord's Prayer were prayed in Auschwitz."—Jürgen Moltmann[12]

SERMON SUGGESTIONS

Topic: For a Time of Testing
TEXT: Luke 21:5–19
(1) *Then:* Jesus discussed the signs preceding the destruction of Jerusalem. (2) *Always:* The story of God and his people has always dealt with catastrophic events that call for special courage, wisdom, and faith. (3) *Now:* (a) Expect difficulty. (b) Expect God's intervention.

Topic: While Waiting for the Lord's Return
TEXT: 2 Thess. 3:6–1
(1) Do not coddle people who will not work. (2) Work quietly, responsibly, and untiringly.

CONGREGATIONAL MUSIC

1. "Tell His Praise in Song and Story," Ps. 34; vers. Timothy Dudley-Smith (1976)
   HOLY MANNA, *Columbian Harmony* (1825); attr. William Moore
   Sing this contemporary paraphrase of the psalm of the day to set the tone of the worship. Antiphonal singing by two entities in the congregation would be effective for the two internal stanzas.
2. "Savior of the Nations, Come," attr. Ambrose of Milan (4th century)
   NUN KOMM DER HEIDEN HEILAND, Erfurt *Enchiridia* (1534)
   This grand Lutheran hymn treats the entire Christ event in its five stanzas. Its central thrust

---

[12]*The Crucified God* (New York: HarperCollins, 1974), pp. 277–278.

is Christ's redemption of and intercession for all humankind—the burden of the Epistle lesson in Hebrews 7:23–28. Many a gospel song (for example, "Only Trust Him," "Jesus Saves," and so on) would also relate to this reading.

3. "O for a Thousand Tongues to Sing," Charles Wesley (1739)

AZMON, Carl G. Glaser (1839)

A great Wesleyan hymn, "O for a Thousand Tongues to Sing," could be appropriately sung with the Gospel reading about the healing of the blind Bartemaeus (Mark 10:46–52). If the stanza that begins "Hear him, ye deaf, ye voiceless ones" is omitted (as it is in some hymnals), it should be inserted, for it makes the hymn's message relevant.

4. "God Moves in a Mysterious Way," William Cowper (1774)

DUNDEE, *Scottish Psalter* (1615)

Through travail Job learned respect for the mysterious ways of God, and his confession and repentance led to God's revealing his will and restoring Job's fortunes. This classic hymn celebrates in song these glorious truths and thus would be appropriately used in connection with the Old Testament lesson.—Hugh T. McElrath

WORSHIP AIDS

CALL TO WORSHIP.   "If ye then be risen with Christ, seek those things which are above, where Christ sitteth on the right hand of God" (Col. 3:1).

INVOCATION.   We thank thee, O God, for the doors that thou hast opened into faith; for the new and wide horizons which thou has set before us, leading to ever-increasing lives of usefulness. Give us the courage to go through the door, setting aside our prejudices and our fears, that we may walk the broad highway of thy truth.—Theodore Parker Ferris

OFFERTORY SENTENCE.   "And whatsoever ye do, do it heartily, as to the Lord and not unto men, knowing that of the Lord ye shall receive the reward of the inheritance, for ye serve the Lord Christ" (Col. 3:23–24).

OFFERTORY PRAYER.   Father, may your Kingdom be uppermost in our minds, hearts, and lives as we bring our tithes, gifts, and offerings to you this morning. May they represent a rededication of all that we are and have to the greater glory of your Kingdom, we pray in Jesus' name.—Henry Fields

PRAYER.   O our Savior, of ourselves we cannot love thee, cannot follow thee, cannot cleave to thee; but thou didst come down that we might love thee, didst ascend that we might follow thee, didst bind us round thee as thy girdle that we might be held fast unto thee. Thou who hast loved us, make us to love thee. Thou who hast sought us, make us to seek thee. Thou who, when lost, didst find us, be thou thyself the way, that we may find thee and be found in thee, our only hope, and our everlasting joy.—E. B. Pusey[13]

---

[13]*The Oxford Book of Prayers*

SERMON
Topic: Will Anyone Rob God?
TEXT: Mal. 3:1–12

The anonymous writer who contributed the final collection of oracles in the ancient book of the prophets provides us with the concluding words of our Old Testament. The writings are found in what we call the Book of Malachi, and clearly they came from a very difficult period in the history of Israel.

The writer, whom we call Malachi, addressed the demoralized social situation directly, for the frustrations of the postexilic age had scarred the very soul of Israel.

In a desperate effort to arouse his careless people, the prophet cried out, "Will anyone rob God?" The question itself seemed preposterous.

Malachi held the priests particularly responsible for the moral decline of the people, and wouldn't let them get away with their flimsy arguments. Hear him as he articulates the word of the Lord to them: [Read 2:4–9.]

Strong stuff, indeed. But desperately needed by a nation in moral disarray. Note, however, that neither Malachi nor the one for whom he spoke would let the people off the hook by blaming it all on their shabby priests. Back to the word from on high about the troublesome question. Here is a blending of judgment and mercy, with a challenge to "try it and see for yourself" if God will match your faithfulness with divine favor. [Read 3:8–10.]

For us high-tech moderns who either think we have all the answers or know we can get them in a moment by just flipping a computer switch and roaming the Net, it is easy to smile with a tolerant condescension at the telling of a story out of our ancient past and dismiss it as an interesting bit of folklore with little or no relevance to the modern world. So we've got it made, have we?

Some people maintain that money matters aren't spiritual and therefore shouldn't be discussed in church. We hear this even now, in our profit-driven consumer-oriented society where the bottom line is money and uncounted millions of people are buried in credit card debt aggregating some estimated two hundred billion dollars. Is this a moral and spiritual problem or not? Because Jesus is recorded in the Gospels as teaching more about a person's attitude toward his or her possessions than about repentance, regeneration, and heaven or hell, and as telling us that where our treasure is, there our heart is also, let's take a look at this well-known parable of the talents and recognize three basic truths contained therein.

Jesus reinforced the ancient biblical truth that God is the Creator and Owner of everything, as we learned in Sunday school when we recited from the twenty-fourth Psalm, "The Earth is the Lord's and the fullness thereof, the world and those who dwell therein."

We are God's trustees, from whom is rightly expected a return on the gracious investment he has made in each of us. We are free to recognize or withhold our stewardship indebtedness, but we are not free to choose the consequences of this decision.

The Christian Herald once recorded the comment that "When a man is rich, God either gets a partner or the man loses his soul."

If, while praying "Thy Kingdom come, thy will be done, on Earth as it is in heaven" we withhold a fair portion of the income that by the grace of God we are enabled to earn, we are withholding a significant portion of our life's influence and energy from the work of Christ in the world, and thereby casting some doubt on the sincerity of our prayer. Samuel Colgate's father one day held out a dollar bill before the lad who would one day become a powerful industrialist and distinguished benefactor of the Church and other good causes across America and said, "Son, that dollar represents an Irishman laboring under a blistering sun all day long." The boy grown to prosperous manhood never forgot that lesson, nor should we, and many of us, including myself, a long-ago graduate of the Colgate-Rochester Divinity School, to this day are in his debt.

This is part of a modern miracle. Pack a generous portion of your life's energy and sweat and toil and hope for the future into a coin, wave the wand of Christian stewardship over it, and watch the gleaming metal come alive far beyond the reach of your outstretched hand and your radiant smile. See it bring hope and faith and new life in Christ across the broad spectrum of the Church's Kingdom enterprises at home and abroad. Feel the power of being able to join with others in strengthening the saving ministries of Christ, his good work of reconciliation between God and man, his compassion and healing, his peace with justice—all distinguishing marks of that Kingdom we pray may come on Earth, as it is in heaven. Your generous pledge of renewed love for your Savior and his Church will help the dream become reality.—George W. Hill

SUNDAY, NOVEMBER 2, 2003
Lectionary Message
Topic: If All We Need Is Love, Where Do We Get Some?
TEXT: Mark 12:28–34
Other Readings: Ruth 1:1–18; Ps. 146; Heb. 9:11–14

Whether you are a country music, pop music, or classic rock fan, the song lyrics are always about love. Petula Clark sang, "What the world needs now is love, sweet love . . ." And the Beatles classic is, "All we need is love . . ."

I. Jesus and the disciples have arrived in Jerusalem and the hostility against him so far is verbal. In the holy city of Israel, Jesus is the new kid rabbi on the block and all the religious leaders are lined up to confront him and test his knowledge of the Law. Everyone has gotten in on the act—the chief priests, the scribes, the elders, the Herodians, and the Sadducees. They have challenged his authority and asked him questions that should have tripped Jesus up. In their learned tradition, he has to prove himself worthy of his followers' respect.

Then another scribe walks up. He's heard all the commotion of the confrontation and thinks Jesus has done a pretty good job against these men who have studied Torah all their lives. So this scribe gets down to basics: Which commandment is the first of all?

Jesus answers with the Shema from the book of Deuteronomy. This is both a call to prayer and a prayer for the chosen people because it defines their devotion to one God: "Here, O Israel, the Lord our God is one God. You shall love the Lord your God with all your heart, and with all your soul, and with all your mind, and with all your strength." And though he wasn't asked, Jesus goes ahead and speaks the second commandment: "You shall love your neighbor as yourself."

II. As far as the first commandment is concerned, in the Hebrew tradition there was no split between heart and mind and soul. For Jesus, the heart was the center of the person. By saying we should love God with all our heart, Jesus did not mean a soft, warm, fuzzy feeling. Loving God first with our heart and mind and soul and strength doesn't happen just on impulse. It is a matter of our intention, our decision, our commitment. The Christian life is a life-long process of conversion. Every day we get up and decide whether God comes first in our lives that day or not.

The first commandment is not "Love God if and when you feel like it." The first commandment is not "Love God when you've got some extra time and energy and happen to remember Jesus' commandment." The first commandment is to choose again and again to be committed to seeking God first in our everyday life with Christ.

So how do we do that? The answers are the traditional ones of silence, solitude, prayer, and meditation. We simply can't learn to love God if we never spend time with God. All our relationships with family and friends depend on spending time being devoted to one another. The same is true of our relationship with God. That time spent in silence, solitude, prayer, and meditation keeps us in touch with God. The reason that such devotion is crucial is that God is the source of all love. We can't learn to love well if we spend only a little time connected to the source of love.

III. Most people who have been Christian for a while have the "love your neighbor" part down just fine. We are glad to be called on to offer a helping hand to the poor and the needy. We are glad to cook and deliver a meal to the sick or the grieving. We've discovered the good sense of purpose that comes from caring for others.

So what is the problem with the second commandment for most Christians? It is that "as yourself" part. Pay attention to the commandment. Jesus did not say to love others more than ourselves. He did not say to love ourselves more than others. Rather, we are commanded by Jesus to love others *as* we love ourselves.

And most pastoral counselors can tell you that is exactly what most of us do. We love our spouse, our children, our parents, and our friends just as well as we love ourselves. The problem is that we don't have a healthy, balanced, loving regard for ourselves. So we cannot give other people what we don't have for ourselves. Part of our human limitation is that we don't ever love another person any more or any better than we love ourselves. When we try to love others more than ourselves, or believe that we do, we usually end up expecting a whole lot in return, and feeling disappointed, hurt, and angry.

The kind of self-love that Jesus described is the right proportion of self-respect that keeps us psychologically and spiritually healthy. Self-respect means we trust God's love enough that we can acknowledge our faults to God and to others. It means we don't let other people walk all over us. It means we can appreciate our own loving behavior toward others. Self-respect also means we take good care of our physical, emotional, and spiritual health.

None of these kinds of healthy self-respect is selfish. They are ways of loving ourselves so that our love for our neighbors is free and generous and comes from our connection to God's love. When we live in the knowledge that God loves us, we can then love others with a free and generous heart. We don't love with a hidden agenda that others will love us back just as we want to be loved.

People don't create love. God is the source of love in the world. The more time we spend in prayer, silence, and meditation, the more likely it is that we will believe that God's unconditional love is really meant for us. As long as we look for love in all the wrong places, we'll be disappointed. But when we turn to God, we will be connected to the source of love. We will be able to grow a balanced self-respect, and pass on that love to others.—Mary Zimmer

ILLUSTRATION

GOD'S SPRING OF LOVE.   North of Austin, Texas, there is a nature preserve on the spillway side of Stillhouse Hollow Lake. If you go off the marked trail, you can hike up a lovely canyon where the creek is seldom more than an inch deep. On one hike I decided to go looking for the springs that fed the creek, and I found them. There are about four good-sized ones coming out of caves in the north ridge. I sat and listened to the water pouring from the hidden aquifer after a summer of drought. I thought about John's image of "a spring of water always gushing up to eternal life." God's love is like those springs for us. We may feel as though we are living in a drought, but God's spring of love for each one of us never goes dry; it pours out upon us.—Mary Zimmer

SERMON SUGGESTIONS

Topic: Mass Evangelism
TEXT: Acts 2:14a, 36–41
(1) A convincing message (vv. 36–37). (2) A drastic challenge (vv. 38–40). (3) A clear-cut response (v. 41).

Topic: Guidelines for a Resurrected Life
TEXT: 1 Pet. 1:17–23
(1) Take Christian living seriously (v. 17). (2) Consider the cost of your salvation (vv. 18–21). (3) Let genuine love determine your behavior (v. 22). (4) Thank God for the regeneration that is the source and sustenance of what God wants you to be (v. 23).

CONGREGATIONAL MUSIC

1. "I'll Praise My Maker While I've Breath," Ps. 146; vers. Isaac Watts (1719)
   OLD 113TH, *Strassburger Kirchenamt* (1525); attr. M. Greiter
   This free paraphrase of Psalm 146 by the great Isaac Watts could set the tone of worship when sung at the beginning or in place of the Psalter reading.
2. "Rise Up, Ye Saints of God," William P. Merrill (1911)
   FESTAL SONG
   This hymn of loyalty and courage that reflects the truths of Mark 12:32–33, especially its first stanza, could well be sung as a response to the reading of the Gospel lesson.
3. "Find Us Faithful," Jon Mohr (1987)
   FIND US FAITHFUL, Jon Mohr (1987)
   A contemporary mini-hymn that reflects the spirit of the story of Ruth and Naomi, "Find Us Faithful" could be sung in connection with the Old Testament reading (Ruth 1:1–18).
4. "Come, Thou Fount of Every Blessing," Robert Robinson (1758)
   NETTLETON, John Wyeth's *A Repository of Sacred Music,* Part II (1813)
   Singing this sturdy old folk hymn after the Epistle reading would be meaningful, for it

magnifies the grace of God, whose blood cleanses us from all sin—the focus of Hebrews 9:11–14.—Hugh T. McElrath

WORSHIP AIDS

CALL TO WORSHIP.   "Lift up your hands to the holy place and bless the Lord. May the Lord, maker of heaven and earth, bless you from Zion" (Ps. 134:2b–3).

INVOCATION.   Lord, if in these few moments we can find you, the God who sought us before we sought you, the God who wanted us before we wanted you, the God who loved us before we knew how to love, then we will be whole and complete and filled all over again with praise.—E. Lee Phillips

OFFERTORY SENTENCE.   "From everyone to whom much has been given, much will be required; and from the one to whom much has been entrusted, even more will be demanded" (Luke 12:48b).

OFFERTORY PRAYER.   Gracious Lord, take all that we bring today, bless and use it. Endow all that remains, so that all that is shared and all that we hold might reflect the purposes of God.—E. Lee Phillips

PRAYER.   O God, for your preparation through Israel; for your coming in person in Jesus of Nazareth; for your purpose expressed in and through the Church; for your continuing presence in the person of your Holy Spirit; for lessons from the past and new beginnings; for the heritage—visions, labors, sacrifices—of the many who have gone this way before us; for victories won, healings wrought, difficulties overcome, estrangements gulfed, and faithfulness to the end; for a living hope not limited by time, space, flesh, or any such thing; for the privilege to celebrate on this day, in this place, and with these people your love, mercy, and grace we give you thanks in an offering of praise, adoration, and joy.

In the spirit of your love—you who so loved the world that you gave your only Son—we pray for one another and for all others. In the power of your healing grace we embrace those who are ill, those facing the loneliness of bereavement, those discouraged by failure, those made anxious with difficult decisions.

We pray for the family of faith; we pray, too, for the families in which our lives are most intimately set. To these we bear an urgent responsibility to share the gospel, but often we are hesitant, even reluctant. Increase your love in us, strengthen our faith, empower us with your Spirit to do what we know.

We pray, too, for the family of humankind. How can we worship you except our brother, our sister be with us? We thank you for all who affirm and celebrate your Word, your intention, from the beginning—one world, one people.

We pray for the Palestinians and Israelis, that they may find a way to live together as good neighbors—lest all be lost in mounting tension and widening conflict. We are haunted by our responsibility for the way things are. When frustration to be free and to be treated equally are vented in violent rage, we are there. When we play politics, selfishly seeking our national interest, Lord have mercy.

We pray that we may be more sensitive and courageous to be instruments of your peace and justice.

We pray for those who aspire to lead, and for the electorate, that the franchise may be exercised as privileged responsibility.

Through him who teaches us to pray together as one family.—John Thompson

SERMON
Topic: Present
TEXT: Eph. 1:11–23

When Paul wrote to the little house church in Ephesus he wrote, interestingly enough, "to the saints who are in Ephesus and are faithful in Jesus Christ" (1:1b). In that first chapter, he offered a prayer about what he hoped would happen in their lives and in the lives of their congregation. It is as good a definition of *church* and *Christian* and *sainthood* as I know.

He prayed for four things.

I. "I pray that the God of our Lord Jesus Christ, the Father of glory, may give you the spirit of wisdom and revelation as you come to know him." This wisdom that Paul talks about is not book learning and it is not education or competence. Now of course we know that we cannot leave our brains outside the church door. That's dangerous. And we know that education should open doors and windows to vistas that we have never, ever seen, and we have been touched by that. But we also know that some of the most unwise people are the most educated. Chad Walsh used to say that he never believed in the fall of man until he attended his first faculty meeting. The wisdom that Paul talks about here does not deal with facts or technological expertise. Fred Craddock says that the longest journey that any of us will ever make is from the head to the heart—from "I *know*" to "*I* know." That takes a long time.

Paul said that the saints are the truly wise ones.

II. He also prayed that "the eyes of your heart will be enlightened." Moffatt translates it, "that the eyes of your heart will be flooded with light." The saints are not only wise, but they also see with clarity what other people can't see.

W. O. Carver used to say that with open-hearted clarity we know how significant all God's children are. For all our lives most of us are like the blind man who stumbled around and to whom Jesus gave sight. But remember the story? After Jesus touched him the first time, the man said he could see, but only people like trees—they were blurry. He could see only through a gauzy film. Jesus touched his eyes a second time and he could see clearly. It is our experience that sometimes it takes a third and a fourth and a fifth time before we begin to see clearly. "Oh, I never saw you like that before." It's a gradual seeing, which is really what conversion is. Sometimes we grow discouraged because we keep on breaking resolutions and lapsing into old, destructive patterns of living and thinking. We wonder if we are making any progress whatsoever. And God comes and touches us again. And again. And again. And sometimes we grow in areas in which we never before thought we would grow.

We come here, you and I, and we come here by way of Bethlehem and Jerusalem and all those dusty miles in between. And sometimes after we leave here and walk out the door and go back home, tomorrow we see it differently. For that's what this is all about. It is that we see through different eyes. Saints do that.

III. The third thing Paul prayed for was that "you may know the hope to which you are

called." Saints are the wise ones. They look at things through different eyes. Saints are also the hopeful ones. They believe despite incredible odds. Are you a hoper? Do you see possibilities for this city and for this state?

IV. Paul perhaps saved the best for last when he prayed that "we may know the immeasurable greatness of his power for us who believe, according to the workings of his great might." Saints are wise and insightful and hopeful, and saints are powerful. We could say power-filled. Listen to Paul as he unpacks it: "God put this power to work in Christ when he raised him from the dead and seated him at the right hand in the heavenly places, far above all rule and authority and power and dominion, and above every name that is named and not only in this age but also in the age to come; and he has put all things under his feet and has made him the head of the Church, which is his body, the fullness of him who fills all in all."

F. F. Bruce says, Why all this hyperbole? Why language piled on top of language here? Why all this redundancy when he talks about the greatness of God's power? He answers his own question and says, "Because the text is thinking of the one supreme example of the power of God and he didn't know any other way to do it but to pull out all the stops he had in his vocabulary." He talked about when Jesus was raised from the dead. Everything changed, and that power unleashed by an open tomb and a Pentecost is available to everybody in this room. That's strange. We sell it so short. I don't believe it, and you don't believe it most days. We do not believe in the power of God to turn us inside out. That's what the Resurrection did. And the saints of God are those who come to terms with the power that has touched their lives and changed them forever. They know that if he is Lord and if he is in charge, and if the powers and the principalities really are under his feet, he is present in all of God's children who have stuck out their necks for the cause of goodness, and they are here, too. Present. They are everywhere. We are surrounded. Present. He has dominion over whatever touches and cripples all of us.

Mother Teresa said, "I am nothing. He is all. I do nothing on my own. He does it. This is what I am: I am God's pencil, a tiny bit of a pencil with which he writes what he likes to write."[1]—Roger Lovette

SUNDAY, NOVEMBER 9, 2003
Lectionary Message

Topic: The Glory of a Humble Gift
TEXT: Mark 12:38–44
Other Readings: Ruth 3:1–5; 4:13–17; Ps. 127; Heb. 9:24–28

In Jesus' day, things had not changed much from the days of Ruth and Naomi, when everyone knew a woman's status by her hairstyle and dress, and a widow past childbearing age had no social status at all. She was totally dependent on either her sons' generosity or her husband's family. When food was scarce, widows could be turned out into the streets. That

---

[1]Mother Teresa, *My Life for the Poor*, ed. by Jose Luis Gonzalez-Balado and Janet N. Playfoot (San Francisco: HarperCollins, 1985), p. 95.

would be to a family's shame, but it happened. That's why there are so many commandments and New Testament instructions to take care of widows and orphans. They were completely dependent on the generosity of others.

I. Jesus criticized the scribes because they were proud and because they were hypocrites. The scribes were the class who had enough economic security to devote their lives to the study and interpretation of Torah. They were honored because of their knowledge and wisdom. They held a high rank in the Sanhedrin, the religious court. The scribes took their wealth and status for granted. That's one of the consequences of wealth; you simply forget that the rest of the world is not just as well off and secure as you are.

The pride of the scribes showed in their public dress and manner. They had taken to wearing their religious robes everywhere they went. These robes were originally a sign of humility in prayer and worship and worn only in the synagogue. So when they wore their robes in public, everyone who saw them knew who they were and made the sign of respect—the salaam—to them.

Jesus warned his listeners to beware of people who took their wealth and status for granted. By living at such a level beyond the common folk, they were likely to hurt the innocent. These scribes were the hard-hearted televangelists of their day who used fear and guilt to rob unsuspecting widows until the widows had nothing left. So they were hypocrites because they were officers of the synagogue and the Law says that the community should care for the widows. These scribes didn't really have any compassion for the needy. They were privileged and entitled and they wanted to keep things that way. And Jesus said they would eventually receive the greatest condemnation.

II. Jesus then sat down near the treasury where people came to give their offerings. He watched a widow, dressed in a widow's characteristic dress, put two coins in the offering plate. Because he could tell that she was poor, Jesus told those who would listen that she had actually put more in the offering plate than the wealthy had. They gave out of their plenty; they could easily afford the offerings they made and still have plenty of left over for savings and property. But the widow gave all she could afford—every last penny.

For this widow, God's purposes were more important than her own. She gave to God and trusted that God would provide what she needed. She knew that stewardship is not about money. Stewardship is about what money means to us. It's about what we think about money. It's about how important money is to us. But more important, stewardship is about our trust in God.

Today's Gospel text tells us that God has a different calculator than the ones we use to add up our personal or the church's budget. God's calculator looks not at the amount we give, but at the attitude and spirit with which we give. The amount of our offering is not the issue; the generosity of our heart is what matters to God.

Grady Nutt points out that God loves a cheerful giver, but God also receives the offerings of a scrooge! So God would not turn away the offerings of the scribes and the wealthy in the temple that day. But the widow knew what the scribes might not ever learn. She knew how to live without calculating how to always play it safe. She knew the joy of giving all she possibly could. She had the kind of faith that trusted that God would again provide what she needed the next day. In the most important matters of faith and trust in God, this widow was not poor at all. Instead she was rich and the scribes were the folks who were poor, because they thought that publicly visible status and wealth were what mattered.

We don't all have the kind of faith this widow had. Those of us who have deep faith don't always have such trust in God. But the widow is our example that trust in God is true wealth in our spiritual lives. As stewards of what God has given us, we'll figure out the kind of wealth that is really crucial to us. Then we will be able to extend our trust in God and have faith in God's future for us.

That is the choice for us in the Gospel reading for today. Do we want the wealth of the world? Do we feel compelled to hold on to what we have because that makes us feel secure? Or do we want the wealth of trusting in God that our needs will be met after we are generous givers to God's work in the world?—Mary Zimmer

ILLUSTRATION

A SOCIAL RELIGION.   John Wesley said on one occasion, "The Christian religion is a social religion and if you try to make it a solitary one, you will destroy it. . . . Holiness is only social holiness." Wesley did not have the sophisticated insights into the application of the teachings of Jesus that have come to us in these later years, but he had a simple formula for it all. A man or a woman who has been saved and sanctified must go out and live forth in human society the implications of that divine love that has washed away sin and brought dedication to life. Interestingly enough, John Wesley linked sanctification with social action at every point of the way in his theology. It seems to me unthinkable that Christians would ignore the human tragedies of our world and avoid redemptive involvement in their solutions. Hunger, racism, the bomb, the disintegration of family life, drugs and drink, poverty, housing, the incredible excesses of affluence—these are problems that no child of God dares attempt to escape.—Earl G. Hunt Jr.[2]

SERMON SUGGESTIONS

Topic: Factors in Preparation for Leadership

TEXT: Exod. 1:6–14, 22–2:10

(1) Unpromising beginnings. (2) The discipline of hardship. (3) The mysterious providence of God.

Topic: Our Personal Inner Battle

TEXT: Rom. 7:14–25a

(1) *Situation:* As a believer, I want to do right. (2) *Complications:* As a human being, sin in my nature works against what I want to do. (3) *Resolution:* I find victory over the guilt and power of sin through our Lord Jesus Christ.

CONGREGATIONAL MUSIC

1. "Lord, Enthroned in Heavenly Splendor," George Hugh Bourne (1874)
   BRYN CALFARIA, William Owen (1854)

   This majestic hymn's message relates to the Epistle lesson (Heb. 9:24–28), especially in its reference in stanza 4 to the once-for-all sacrifice of Christ. This hymn, with its exciting Alleluia refrain, would be especially suitable for the opening of this day's worship.

---

[2]*I Have Believed*

2. "Unless the Lord the House Shall Build," Ps. 127; vers. *The Psalter* (1912)

BOURBON, attr. Freeman Lewis (1825)

This paraphrase of Psalm 127, so careful of the original sense, could well be sung in place of the Psalter reading.

3. "Blessed Assurance, Jesus Is Mine," Fanny J. Crosby (1873)

ASSURANCE, Phoebe D. Knapp (1873)

The reference in the Epistle lesson (Heb. 9:28) to the Second Coming of our Lord, for which we watch and wait, is reflected in the third stanza of this classic gospel song by the queen of gospel songwriters—Fanny Crosby.

4. "All Things Are Yours," Bryan Jeffery Leach (1989)

GERMANY, William Gardiner's *Sacred Melodies* (1815)

The Gospel reading about the widow who gave sacrificially (Mark 12:41–44) calls for an expression of Christian stewardship such as is found in this modern hymn emphasizing cheerful, loving giving.—Hugh T. McElrath

WORSHIP AIDS

CALL TO WORSHIP.   "Awake, awake, put on your strength, O Zion! Put on your beautiful garments, O Jerusalem, the holy city; for the uncircumcised and the unclean shall enter you no more" (Isa. 52:1a).

INVOCATION.   Lift us up, Lord, in this hour of worship so we may see beyond the present to the broader redemptive picture of a God who works through history and completes what he begins.—E. Lee Phillips

OFFERTORY SENTENCE.   "Give and it will be given to you—a good measure, pressed down, shaken together, running over, will be put into your lap; for the measure you give will be the measure you get back."

OFFERTORY PRAYER.   Even our best giving is small when compared to what you have given to us, Father. Yet we offer our tithes and gifts today, knowing that you will multiply them as you always have, and through them bless multitudes. So in faith we give in Jesus' name.—Henry Fields

PRAYER.   Immortal, Eternal, Invisible, who hidest thyself in darkness and silence, who veilest thy glory in the lesser beauty of nature, thy form is unknown, thy name we mortals dare not utter; yet thy worship is truth and thy tabernacle is man. Calm our passions, silence our clamorous thoughts, that we may be still and know that thou are God. Put out all lesser lights that we may see the light within. Naked in soul we stand before thy dreaded tribunal, that trembling there we may know no other fear; that gazing upon the face of the Eternal we may not fear the face of man. Lead us through the depths of our own nature, past the gateways of thought, till face to face, heart to heart, thought to thought we are in thy presence.

Break down pride, burn out sin, banish self. May perfect love cast out all fear, perfect sacrifice make an end of sin, and thou, the all in all, smite down the prison house of self and set our spirits free, in tune with the Infinite, at home with the Eternal. Shut us in with thy-self, O God. Amen—W. E. Orchard[3]

SERMON
Topic: Where Do You Draw the Line?
TEXT: Rom. 8:17

Given the choice, none of us would ever choose to suffer, would we? But what do we do with this text—and others throughout the New Testament that echo it? The apostle Paul wrote, "We are heirs—heirs of God and co-heirs with Christ, if indeed we share his sufferings."

It seems to me that there are at least two ways to suffer. We can suffer *from* something or someone, or we can suffer *with* someone. Suffering from something is the pain over which we have no choice. It grabs us, crushes us, and holds us captive and unwilling. It usually comes in the form of physical, mental, or emotional pain; or other people or circumstances may inflict it. In whatever way it comes, it sneaks up on us. We are never ready for it.

Sometimes it slams us in the head just when we think everything is fine and wonderful. There's an accident, a heart attack, a cancerous tumor, or a pinched nerve at the bottom of the spine. Sometimes it just slowly worms its way into our lives—hardly noticeable at first, a growing feeling that something is wrong.

And the mystery of it all is about to kill you. Sometimes we suffer when we're cheated by a crook, betrayed by a friend, or rejected by someone we've grown to love, whom we have believed loves us as well. No matter what hits us, when we suffer from it, it's unwanted, uninvited, and loathed. We would never have chosen it. We bear it—and endure it—the best we can only because we have to. We had no choice about it.

What distinguishes the child of God is the deliberate choice to suffer with other people. Forget about being a victim. Here you decide for yourself whether you will hurt or not. You are free to suffer or to run, free to take on pain or to say no to it. Here you do not suffer because nature wallops you. You hurt only because you have chosen to share the hurt that life has inflicted on someone else. It is not your pain, although you have chosen to suffer with it. What's more, it doesn't hurt any less than suffering from something that is your very own pain.

Jesus suffered both ways. He certainly suffered at the hands of other people. But what was so unique about him—what made him our Savior and gives him the right to also be Lord over our life—was his willingness to suffer with us.

Jesus pointed to suffering people and said, "There, there I am" (Matt. 25:31–46). He said it because he felt their hurt to such an extent that he equated the sufferer with himself. Jesus is your hurting neighbor. He is your hurting child. He is your hurting enemy. He is anyone who is suffering from anything not of his or her own choosing. If you feel the hurts of any person who hurts—I mean if you really feel their pain—you are suffering with Jesus.

When you married your mate, you promised him or her that you would suffer—and no doubt you have somewhere along the way. You have suffered from the temperamental moods,

---

[3]*The Temple: A Book of Prayers*

the selfish thoughtlessness, and even an occasional unkindness. But, mind you, you did not promise to suffer *from* your spouse. If your husband hurts you by knocking you around, physically, emotionally, or spiritually, put a stop to it, now. God never intended for you to be someone else's doormat.

At other times in your marriage you have suffered *with* your spouse. A woman who lives inside her husband's pain while he is slowly, surely devoured by cancer knows what suffering *with* can be like. Maybe it hurts her worse than it hurts him.

She feels the worst of it because she has chosen to feel his hurt with him. She sticks with it in love—real love, the kind of love that suffers long, as long as the one whom she loves suffers!

Sometimes we suffer from our children. They can drive us out of our minds, can't they? They don't always let our dreams for them come true. Sometimes they can shatter a hopeful heart. They can even act like subhuman savages at times. One slightly off-balance teenager can hang the greatest soul out to dry occasionally. Here's a clue: whenever you feel that your son or daughter is a pain in the neck, you are probably suffering *from* and not *with* him or her at the moment.

More often, however, we suffer *with* our children, don't we? We suffer with them when they hide their hurt, when they show only their rage and anger, and when they don't know how to express their fear and confusion. We suffer with them when we know they love us, but all we get is their hatred. We suffer with them when we try to get close but all they want is for us to keep out. We suffer with them when we pray for them in the night—sometimes all night long—and all we get is silence from heaven. Suffering with our kids is some of the most painful hurting we will ever experience.

We can count on being children of God only if we choose to suffer with his hurting children.

As it is, you have your share of problems and hurts. Frankly, you're tired—sometimes so tired under the weight of your own load—that you resent being asked to take on someone else's burden as well—especially someone who's not family, for whom you feel no personal responsibility. You have to be able to draw the line somewhere!

We all need to love more than we do. But God is love—we're not. So we need God. We need him to move us beyond our own weariness and awkwardness—to move us out of our self-pity and into the life of another in order to take his or her pain into ourselves. Never mind that you really don't feel responsible. Never mind that you don't like doing it. Never mind that you're not even good at it. All that really matters is that when you take on the pain of another, you are on the right track, one that will eventually lead you all the way home!—Gary C. Redding

SUNDAY, NOVEMBER 16, 2003

Lectionary Message

Topic: In the Meantime, One More Time

TEXT: Mark 13:1–8

Other Readings: 1 Sam. 1:4–20; Ps. 16; Heb. 10:11–14 (15–18), 19–25

The disciples were looking for reassurance when they walked out of the Temple with Jesus. One of them looked around and said, "Look, Rabbi, at this glorious Temple! Look what we have for worship." His pride in Jerusalem's glory didn't last for long, for Jesus shot him down: "Not one of these stones will be left standing." The disciples spent most of their time with Jesus in a state of confusion, and here they were again. What did he mean? They walked all the way to the Mount of Olives before someone asked the question: What is the sign?

Like all of us, they wanted a sign. They wanted to know ahead of time so they could be prepared for the end of the world. The Temple had stood for hundreds of years; they could see the symbol of their faith. So what sign that the end time had come would they see?

Jesus wanted the disciples to see his truth, so he warned them about false prophets who would seek to lead them away from his true path. Beware of those who tell you with absolute assurance that they have the final, exact truth about God's plan. There will always be gurus setting themselves up as saviors who would rescue us from our fears about what's going on in our world. The problem with gurus is that you don't have to have any faith of your own. All you do is what they tell you.

Then Jesus described what is known as end-time happenings. There will be wars and rumors of wars, earthquakes and famines. Those are supposed to be the signs of the end of the world as we know it.

The only catch to this list of apocalyptic signs is that they have always been happening. There is not an age in the history of the world in which there were not wars, earthquakes, and famines. So it is really hard to see one particular sequence of events as the true sign of the end of the world. Many have tried and predicted, but so far they have all been wrong. We just can't know when the end time will be because we don't control the magma boiling under shifting tectonic plates and erupting earthquakes. We don't control old historical grudges when they erupt into war. We don't control weather conditions that create drought and famine in Africa. Personally, I just don't think any of us are going to get out of the responsibility of continuing to live our witness for the whole of our lives.

That means we are always living in the meantime. We are living in the meantime between the birth of Jesus as Messiah and the return of Christ in glory. And we want signs, too. We want certainty, and leaders who will tell us exactly what is going to happen so we can feel secure. We want somebody to be in charge, so life won't feel so unsettled.

The how of what we do in the meantime is described in our Hebrews reading. We no longer need to make sacrifices in our worship because the sacrifice of Jesus on the cross takes the place of any sacrifice we could make. The Crucifixion was the sacrifice for all of us for all time. In Christ God has come near to us so we don't have to make sacrifices as were once required.

The next verses tell us we are to come to God with true hearts. What is a true heart? I think it means we are supposed to be honest with God. We've all heard the prayers of folks who are mostly praying to be heard by others. A true heart takes us to God with all the mess-ups and mistakes we have made. Our hearts are cleansed by confession. Our bodies are washed in baptism. So we can be honest with God because we know we have been forgiven. We have the assurance of faith that we won't be condemned by God, because God's covenant is already written on our hearts.

In the meantime, one more time, we hold on to hope. We hope for many things. We hope that we will *do* better and that we will *be* better. We hope that our children will follow our faith. We hope that our church will grow together in mutual hope and reach out to those who need to find hope.

Believe it or not, this sermon started with Jesus describing the fall of the Temple, and it will end by making the connection between our keeping the faith and regular worship attendance! How will we ever get there?

The writer of the Hebrews tells us that we are to "provoke one another to love and good deeds." The word *provoke* really means to excite and inspire and motivate. That's why we are Christian community together—because it is so much harder to be a Christian by yourself. By coming together in worship and Sunday school, Bible study and fellowship, we inspire and motivate one another. When we are all together we are reminded that we are here not just for ourselves or for our own family, but for the good of the whole Church.

Sometimes we think it is really other people who make it so hard to be a Christian. It seems like it is other Christians who get on our last nerve most of the time. And here we are told that what being Christian together means is that we inspire, excite, and motivate one another to love and good deeds.

Our good God is a giving God. It is that covenant of God which is written on our hearts that inspires us to inspire others. Just think what your life would be like if you had no one to give to. Think how horrible life would be without a church family to love and do loving deeds for.

We come together as Christian community each week to take turns giving and receiving. We may be in a situation for weeks where we are the needy ones provoking others to love and good deeds. But our turn to be the ones who are giving will come around. This is a kind of glory that far surpasses the glory of the Jerusalem Temple.

It makes a difference every single Sunday that one of us is not here to enjoy community and worship with the rest of use. There is a connection between growing faith, courage, and hope and worshiping together. By worshiping together we are reminded at least once a week that we are not all on our own in this discipleship walk in a hostile world. When we sing together, pass the peace, pray, and check in with one another after worship, we are helping one another to grow faith by the encouragement we receive just from being together in God's presence.

We live in a world that is hostile to Christian community. The rest of the world is always telling us that we can be self-sufficient with the help of all our electronic blessings. But that self-sufficiency is a myth. As Christians, we need one another. We need to be together in worship and fellowship. That is the covenant that God has written on our hearts. That is the way to inspire one another to love and good deeds. That is the way to encourage one another and find hope together.—Mary Zimmer

ILLUSTRATION

THE CHRISTIAN'S WORK.   The New Testament abandons or transforms the cultic terminology so that worship is no longer properly understood as the ritual service of the gods. No longer is it necessary to win their favor by attending to the sacred, sacrificing, or otherwise serving them cultishly. In the process, the New Testament also redefines the idea of service. It chooses the commonplace, quite ordinary, "secular" words *diakoné, diakonia,* and *diakonos* ("serve," "ministry," and "servant," respectively). The root imagery is of waiters at tables, ministering to people's needs. The sense is clear. Because God does not have the same need as the pagan gods, humans are released from cultic functions and are free to serve one another. Such is the importance of the terminological shifts. Because of Jesus' service in the world, the cultic logic for worship has collapsed. Whatever function worship has, it is a response to God's work and is inextricably related to the Christian's work in the world.—John E. Burkhart[4]

SERMON SUGGESTIONS

Topic: The God Who Acts
TEXT: Exod. 3:13–20
(1) He is characterized by his name (vv. 13–14). (2) He is characterized by his relationships (v. 15). (3) He is characterized by his promises (vv. 16–20).

Topic: God at Work for Us
TEXT: Rom. 8:26–30
(1) To help us in particular in our weaknesses as we pray (vv. 26–27). (2) To help us in general in everything as we stage by stage fulfill his purpose (vv. 28–30).

CONGREGATIONAL MUSIC

1. "I Come with Joy," Brian Wren (1968)
   DOVE OF PEACE, trad. Amer. melody; arr. Austin C. Lovelace (1977)
   This fine contemporary hymn that expresses the joy accompanying the presence of the Lord (Ps. 16:11) could set the tone for the entire service if sung at the beginning of musical worship.
2. "When in the Night I Meditate," Ps. 16; vers. *The Psalter* (1912)
   ST. FLAVIAN, Day's *Psalter* (1562)
   This free paraphrase of Psalm 16 offers a good opportunity to sing the psalm to an authentic metrical psalm tune. A pleasant departure from the usual congregational singing would be the lining out of the words in a stanza or two by a precentor.
3. "I Am Thine, O Lord," Fanny J. Crosby (1875)
   I AM THINE, William H. Doane (1875)
   This durable gospel song could be used in connection with the Epistle lesson. It would be an apt response to the readings from Hebrews (10:22).
4. "Lord Christ, When First You Came to Earth," Walter Russell Bowie (1928)
   MIT FREUDEN ZART, *Psalms of David* (1547)
   Jesus' predictions of terrible things to come (Mark 13:1–8) included the destruction of the Temple. Reference to this event is found in this profound twentieth-century hymn, which could form a meaningful response to the reading of the Gospel lesson.—Hugh T. McElrath

WORSHIP AIDS

CALL TO WORSHIP.   "I have set the Lord always before me; because he is at my right hand, I shall not be moved" (Ps. 16:8).

INVOCATION.   Loving Lord, you know our intent in worship, our purpose in seeking, our hope in every prayer, our need we do not always name. Grant that we may have clean hands, pure hearts, and the sight to see God at work.—E. Lee Phillips

---

[4]*Worship: A Searching Examination of the Liturgical Experience* (Louisville, Ky.: Westminster John Knox Press, 1982).

OFFERTORY SENTENCE.   "And walk in love, as Christ also hath loved us, and hath given himself for us as an offering and a sacrifice to God for a sweet-smelling savor" (Eph. 5:2).

OFFERTORY PRAYER.   Now, O Lord, let our prayers of devotion mingle with our gifts of money so that commitment might join with the mighty power of God to save and edify, for Jesus' sake.—E. Lee Phillips

PRAYER.   Most holy and merciful Father, we confess in thy presence the sinfulness of our nature, and our shortcomings and offerings against thee. Thou alone knowest how often we have sinned, in wandering from thy ways, in wasting thy gifts, in forgetting thy love. Have mercy, O Lord, upon us, who are ashamed and sorry for all we have done to displease thee; and forgive our sins, through Jesus Christ thy Son, our Savior. Amen.—*The Book of Common Worship*

SERMON
Topic: Four Great Ways to Cripple a Church
TEXT: Hag. 2:1–9

Do you know the book of Haggai?

Now what kind of question is that? You spend all week long hanging on—up to here in work—hoping that the kids won't completely tear up the inside of the car before you get here. Then you come in and sit down and breath a sigh of relief, and the pastor says, "Do you know the book of Haggai?"

It's only two chapters long. It's one of the books of the minor prophets, but that doesn't mean it isn't important. I think they kept it in the canon because it really speaks to the heart.

You see, in 597 B.C. the Jews were deported from their homeland, much like when the Nazis invaded Poland in 1939 and deported Polish Jews. Ten years later, in 587 B.C., the conquerors ransacked the holy city of Jerusalem, tore down the Temple, and dragged hundreds more off to Babylon. The time of exile lasted about fifty-eight years. They were homeless, living in a strange land that they hated. They were homesick. They were a dislocated people.

There are other exiles. For example, divorce tears at the fabric of your life, and your life is never the same again—ever. You read the newspaper and scan the stories and headlines. Everything seems to have been swept away. Where are the old landmarks like integrity and honor and fidelity and trust? You look out at terrain that is totally strange, and that is the setting in which the exiles prayed that they wanted to go home. We have all prayed this.

So in 539 their prayers were answered. Cyrus, the Persian king, conquered Babylon, and the first edict was to set the captives free. They could go home. So the Hebrew refugees packed up little bundles that they could carry in their hands and started back across the desert yet again—to home.

Eighteen years later, under Zerubbabel, a second group wound their way across the desert until they came to Israel. But the record shows that when they got there, their prayers were not answered exactly as they intended them to be. They never are. Everything was in shambles. Everything—the economy, the government, the schools. The farmlands had lain waste so long that they could grow almost nothing. The temple was no more. It was a time of reconstruction, much like after the Civil War. When they rebuilt homes and replanted farmlands and restored cities, it took enormous energy and enormous effort. When they got there, the first thing they did was begin to rebuild the Temple, which was the centerpiece of their faith. But there was so much opposition from the Samaritans that the Jews said, "We just can't do this any more." So they just stopped at midpoint and left an incomplete Temple. And every Sabbath a little group of faithful Jews would gather around the shell of this Temple and worship God.

Eighteen years went by with the Temple in that state. Then a prophet arose—his name was Haggai. He began as any good prophet does: asking questions. All good leaders ask questions. "Excuse me," he said, "but why is this Temple not finished? I don't understand. You gather out here, even when it rains, under old coverings; and even when it's cold you cover up and try to worship. I don't understand." "Well," they said, "it costs a lot. We've had our homes to rebuild, we've had our families to take care of, and we've had to plow our fields— and you just wouldn't believe the rocks!" Nobody mentioned the opposition of the Samaritans. Not one word. "The cost of building supplies is so high," they said. Haggai responded, "But it's been eighteen years!" And do you know what they said? "Eighteen years is really not a very long time."

It was a parable of their lives—their faith, their lack of commitment, and a crippled institution, just limping along. It was to be the centerpiece of their commitment, and perhaps the half-finished Temple that was there for eighteen years reflected the hearts of the people. That's what Haggai said. They'd had a great groundbreaking ceremony at the beginning. It was a great day. Everyone had stood around with tears in their eyes and laid the foundation, and the scaffolding had gone up—and that was as far as they got. They never completed the project.

Haggai said, "Is it time for you yourselves to live in your paneled houses while the house of God lies in ruins?" (1:4). They just looked at each other. Haggai gave them a challenge: "Get to work! Build a place at the center of your life where God can take up residence. God's house is to be made strong. God's work is to be the heart of your lives." Faith is costly and faith is difficult.

Haggai gives four reasons why the Temple was not completed.

They were discouraged. Now this is understandable. Everything needed attention when they got home. The place was a mess—there was poverty and starvation, and the plans they had drawn up for the Temple looked nothing like the old Temple that Solomon had completed.

They were apathetic. Haggai said, "Well, you can let somebody else do it." For eighteen years they didn't work on the Temple. It was too overwhelming. They looked around at all the stuff that needed to be done and they just didn't know what to do. So they didn't do anything. Apathy can grievously weaken any church.

They felt as though they were on their own. "Now if God was here, if he was really here," they said, "this would never have happened—exiled, burned-out temple. We would have what we used to have when Solomon was here." So they built houses for themselves.

They saw no viable future, and that too can cripple a church.

Haggai spoke to a crippled institution. The people of God gathered on the Sabbath around a broken-down shell of an altar. Eighteen years! And what did the prophet say? He said four things. Three times he said, "Take courage." I am intrigued by the way he put it. He talked first to the king and the priest, and then to the people. The challenge was the same: *courage,*

courage, courage. You can complete the task for the dreams you had. You see, to be courageous is to dare and to dream and to do.

Haggai threw out a little hard word for the second challenge—*work*. He said that the reason we work (even when times are hard) is because of God's great promise. You know what that is? "I am with you."

The prophet said, if you want the Church to grow, "remember the old promise I have given since the beginning of time." What was that? *You don't have to fear.* You don't have to fear. Haggai quoted Yahweh as saying, "My Spirit abides with you—do not be afraid."—Roger Lovette

SUNDAY, NOVEMBER 23, 2003
Lectionary Message

Topic: The Kingdom of Christ
TEXT: John 18:33–37
Other Readings: 2 Sam. 23:1–7; Ps. 132:1–12 (13–18); Rev. 1:4b–8

Did you ever have one of those conversations that seemed to cross paths and go nowhere with every sentence? That's the kind of conversation that Pilate and Jesus seemed to have in the beginning. It was a highly unusual conversation. A Roman prefect didn't have to give a prisoner the time of day, much less provide a hearing. And the story is full of drama because, by Roman law, Pilate held Jesus' life in his hands.

Pilate had a job to do that he didn't really want to do, but his loyalty to Rome and his fears of an uprising at Passover kept him on task. Pilate was willing to use the Jewish religion and its leaders to retain Roman control over the people. Jewish resistance was always just barely under the surface in Palestine, so Pilate really wished that the Sanhedrin would handle this so he could avoid a backlash.

Pilate had returned from a conversation with Caiaphas and the Sanhedrin. He didn't really understand their charges, but they made it clear that they were accusing Jesus not only of religious violation but also of political treason. Pilate was the only one who had the authority to execute criminals, so the religious leaders needed to convince him of the risk this upstart rabbi presented to the peace of Jerusalem.

I. Pilate asked Jesus a direct question: "Are you the King of the Jews?" But he got only an indirect answer, from a man in chains who didn't seem to be afraid of Rome's power. The response Jesus gave indicates that he was not at all intending to threaten the power of Rome. His Kingdom was "not of this world, not from here." Jesus pointed out that if his Kingdom were political, there would already be riots in the streets, and that is not happening.

II. Pilate tried again. "So you are a king?" But Jesus simply turned the question back, because he was not going to incriminate himself for a political charge that was not true. There was something of a battle of wits going on here. Pilate was trying to get Jesus to say what the Sanhedrin believed, but Jesus knew they were not truthful and he would not lie about himself or his Kingdom.

Then the conversation turned toward much more crucial matters than fact. Jesus declared his vocation. He had come into the world to testify to the truth of Jehovah God. Those who listened to him would know the truth, and those who were seeking the truth would listen to him.

Since the conversation had turned religious, Pilate didn't seem to know what to do, so he asked the cynic's question: "What is truth?" Pilate wanted to hedge the issue of the truth of Jesus. He might have wanted to debate the idea of truth or argue about how one knows truth. But Pilate was hardened by his years as a Roman officer. He didn't want to be confused by the offer of the truth of God and a Kingdom that wasn't about power.

III. To say "Jesus Christ is Lord," as we do as part of our baptismal pledges, is to choose to live in and be part of Jesus' Kingdom that is not part of this world. Choosing the Kingdom of Christ means that we choose to always be on the journey of seeking the truth of God about every aspect of our lives. Listening to Jesus for his truth means that we are committed to his truth as the determining factor in our lives and decisions.

Pilate's kingdom was about political and military power over other people. The high priest's and Sanhedrin's kingdom was about the religious status to determine whether a person was clean or unclean and could live in community.

But Jesus' Kingdom is about the eternal truth of God. And that truth has much more to do with the poor, the disenfranchised, the hungry, the prisoner, and the servant. Jesus did not come to command or coerce, but to invite us into the Kingdom of truth. Jesus did not come to lord it over us, but to walk beside us and sometimes even to kneel beside us.

Jesus' Kingdom is not about the safety of power over other people. It is not about the security of status over other people. One clue about whether we are listening to the truth of Jesus' Kingdom is whether our own desires for power and status make us feel as though we are far away from the Kingdom.

In verses in Revelation John writes that Jesus "made us to be a kingdom." So the question of whether we are listening and following the truth of the Kingdom is about whether we know in our hearts that we are part of that Kingdom. We can't think our way into that Kingdom. The only way is to walk the talk of the one who was not of this world but came into this world to teach us and show us the truth of God. We find that truth and we live in that Kingdom when we are doing what Jesus did in his own ministry. We feed the hungry, we visit and pray with the sick and the imprisoned, we seek justice for those who are poor or who have been cast aside by the folks who establish their kingdoms by power and status. That's the Kingdom work of Jesus Christ.—Mary Zimmer

ILLUSTRATION

THE KINGDOM OF GOD AND THE KINGSHIP OF CHRIST.   Subject to the kingship of Christ and his reign, which it confesses and proclaims, the Church does not in itself constitute the Kingdom of God. Up to the end of time it can but announce the latter as its ultimate hope and the hope of the world, and it is only because Jesus Christ acts within the Church and controls it by his Holy Spirit (1 Cor. 4:20) that the Church can here and now, at the heart of this world, raise the standard of the world which is to come. The present sovereignty of Jesus Christ can be apprehended only by faith, while men wait for the day when he will deliver up the Kingdom to God his Father after having destroyed the last enemy, death (1 Cor. 15:24ff.). Until that day the Church possesses no other power than that of its prayer: "Come, Lord Jesus" (1 Cor. 16:22; Rev. 22:17, 20). Such prayerful expectation must remain until the great voice of the book of Revelation trumpets forth: "Now the salvation and the power and the Kingdom of our God and the authority of his Christ have come!" (Rev. 12:10; 11:15).—H. Roux[5]

SERMON SUGGESTIONS

Topic: A Worthy Prayer
TEXT: Ruth 2:1–13, esp. v. 12
(1) Concerning a good deed. (2) Concerning a deserved reward. (3) Concerning a just and loving God.

Topic: In Defense of a Ministry
TEXT: 1 Thess. 2:1–8
(1) Courage in the face of opposition. (2) Desire to please God. (3) Self-giving affection.

CONGREGATIONAL MUSIC
1. "Lo! He Comes with Clouds Descending," Charles Wesley (1758)
   REGENT SQUARE, Henry T. Smart (1867)
   This vibrant Wesleyan hymn takes its initial thrust from Revelation 1:7. Aside from serving well for the opening of musical worship, it could also be used in connection with the reading of the Epistle lesson.
2. "God of Jacob, Please Remember," Ps. 132; vers. Calvin Seerveld (1983)
   BLAENWERN, William P. Rowlands (1915)
   This majestic Welsh hymn carries the sense of Psalm 132 and admirably undergirds the idea of King David, forefather of Christ the King.
3. "Lead On, O King Eternal," Ernest W. Shurtleff (1887)
   LANCASHIRE, Henry T. Smart (1835)
   This familiar hymn that magnifies Christ the Eternal King is based in part on the Gospel lesson (John 18:36) and could appropriately be sung in response to it.
4. "All Praise to Christ," F. Bland Tucker (1938)
   ENGELBERG, Charles V. Stanford (1904)
   The ideal hymn for Christ the King Sunday, "All Praise to Christ" remains one of the finest praise expressions produced in the twentieth century. It could either begin or serve as a triumphant ending to the people's worship.—Hugh T. McElrath

WORSHIP AIDS
CALL TO WORSHIP.   "Speak to yourselves in psalms and hymns and spiritual songs, singing and making melody in your heart to the Lord; give thanks always for all things unto God and the Father in the name of our Lord Jesus Christ" (Eph. 5:19–20).

INVOCATION.   Hear our gratitude this day, O Lord, not only for the harvest of the season, but also for the rewards of seeds of faith sown in souls open to the blessing of God. Deepen

---

[5]In J.-J. von Allmen, *Vocabulary of the Bible.*

us through the physical and spiritual bounty that surrounds our days, and teach us to pray.—E. Lee Phillips

OFFERTORY SENTENCE.   "But my God shall supply all your needs according to his riches in glory by Christ Jesus" (Phil. 4:19).

OFFERTORY PRAYER.   For the yield of harvest and the colors of the season, Lord, we give in gratitude and share with commitment that others may know the power of the grace of God no season can change.—E. Lee Phillips

PRAYER.   Eternal Spirit, in whom is our strength for this world and our hope for that which is to come, we would worship thee with sincere and humble hearts. We find life's problems difficult, its temptations strong, and our own will and wisdom insufficient. We can no more save ourselves than we can save the Earth from winter to springtime by our unaided powers. As we need the sun to bring back the flowers and the leaves, so our hearts need thee, thy forgiveness and cleansing, thy refreshing light, the resource of thy presence, and the guidance of thy continuing fellowship.

With grateful hearts we worship thee. For the wonders of nature; for the heritage of noble sires who left us the wealth of great traditions; for homes that sustain us, friendships that refresh us, and work that gives life meaning and purpose; and for all those secret visitations of the divine whereby we are inwardly made strong, we thank thee. Save us from all self-pity, from vain complaining and idle lamentation of our lot. Thou hast given us resources adequate for our daily needs. Help us to avail ourselves of them, and match us with the challenge of these troubled days.—Harry Emerson Fosdick[6]

SERMON
Topic: A Faith That Surprises: Jesus and the Centurion
TEXT: Matt. 8:5–13

Only two times in the Gospel stories do we find that Jesus was surprised, amazed, or astonished. Interestingly, both times had to do with faith. The first time is found in Mark 6:6, when Jesus returned to his home town of Nazareth following his baptism. We read, "He could not do any miracles there, except lay his hands on a few sick people and heal them. And he was amazed at their lack of faith." Jesus was surprised at their unbelief, and though he would have liked to have done much more, he was prevented by their lack of faith.

The second time we are told that Jesus was surprised is in our Scripture lesson about the centurion from Capernaum, whose approach to Jesus caused Jesus to say, "I have not found anyone in Israel with such great faith."

I. *The centurion and his faith.* The centurions were the backbone of the Roman army. A Roman legion was composed of six thousand men; these were divided into groups of one hundred, called centuries, and the captain over them was called a centurion.

It is noteworthy to observe that every centurion mentioned in the New Testament is mentioned with respect and honor. They were the cream of the crop of professional soldiers.

---

[6]*A Book of Public Prayers*

This centurion, according to Luke, had won favor with the Jews and had even built their synagogue. This means that although he belonged to the conquerors and was a foreigner, he treated Jews with respect and was sensitive to their religious beliefs and scruples.

The thing that really sets him apart is his attitude toward his slave. He is compassionate and concerned about his slave. This was unusual. In the Roman world a slave had no rights. But this centurion was concerned for his slave who "lies at home paralyzed and in terrible suffering."

Matthew tells us that this centurion came to Jesus asking for help (8:6). Why did he come to Jesus? He no doubt had heard that Jesus had the power to heal people. The centurion's faith, however, seems to have been based on more than hearsay. It is likely that he observed Jesus from the edge of the crowd, watched him heal and heard him teach. At any rate, he came to Jesus asking for help.

The response of Jesus was immediate: "I will go and heal him." Many modern scholars think this statement should be translated as a question: "Shall I go and heal him?" Faith, to be effective, must be specific. Blind Bartimaeus called out, "Jesus, Son of David, have mercy on me!" Although Jesus could see he was blind, he asked him, "What do you want me to do for you?" "Rabbi, I want to see" (Mark 10:51). To the man at the pool of Bethesda, Jesus asked, "Do you want to get well?" (John 5:6). So it would not be out of character for Jesus to ask this man, "What are you wanting from me? Shall I go and heal him?"

The centurion's response was quick: "No that's not necessary. I do not deserve to have you come under my roof." That response was probably an indication of the centurion's sensitivity to the Jewish traditional law that forbade a Jew from entering a non-Jew's house; the threat was that such an action would make him unclean. The centurion continued: "Just say the word and my servant will be healed. For I myself am a man under authority, with soldiers under me. I tell this one, 'Go,' and he goes; and that one, 'Come,' and he comes. I say to my servant, 'Do this,' and he does it."

This centurion understood authority. He had authority over his soldiers and he recognized Jesus' authority in the spiritual realm. He knew his authority was derived from something above and greater than himself, and he assumed this was also true of Jesus. The centurion had authority because he was under authority, submissive to and committed to carrying out the orders of Caesar. He recognized that Jesus was in touch with God and that he had authority over sickness and disease.

The centurion's response surprised and astonished Jesus, who turned and said to those around him, "I tell you the truth: I have not found anyone in Israel with such great faith."

II. *What is so amazing about this centurion's faith?* Let's unpack it for a few moments. I want to make five observations:

(a) *The centurion was a Gentile, not a Jew.* One might expect that the Jews, with their whole history of God working mighty deeds through the prophets, would have faith. Yet they were marked by skepticism and unbelief. The centurion knew only that Jesus had a reputation as a healer, and they probably assumed that his authority came from God.

(b) *The centurion recognized Jesus' authority.* Some of the Jews also recognized Jesus' power to heal and attributed it to Beelzebub, the prince of the demons (Matt. 12:24). This centurion, however, simply believed that because Jesus was under authority he could heal the centurion's servant.

(c) *The centurion expected Jesus to heed his request.* He was certain of Jesus' compassion and power, so he expected Jesus to act on behalf of his servant. Faith is more than believing. It must also have an aspect of expectation if it is to be vital.

(d) *The centurion believed that Jesus could heal at a distance.* He believed not only that Jesus' authority was the authority of personal presence but that he had authority to command the spiritual forces that caused disease.

Faith in and of itself does nothing—it is simply a catalyst. In chemistry a catalyst is a substance that enables other substances to interact with one another and even form new substances. But the catalyst itself is unchanged. Faith is the attitude that provides the atmosphere in which things happen that would not occur if faith were not present.

The centurion's faith was placed in the one who had the power to heal. His faith shows in his recognition of Jesus' authority and in his expectation that Jesus would act in response to his request.

(e) *The servant who was healed was not healed because of his own faith but rather because of some else's faith.* Your faith can be effective for someone else! Sometimes a person is too sick to exercise faith. Sometimes a person is too caught up in the syndrome of sin and rebellion to exercise faith. At such times it is good to remember that it is not always the faith of the person that is powerful but the faith of others who believe that God can do the seemingly impossible. Parents, don't quit praying and believing for your children. Your faith can provide the atmosphere in which God will do amazing things.

III. *One more observation.* This passage emphasizes that faith is the currency of the Kingdom of heaven. In verses 11 and 12 Jesus makes the point that Gentiles will come from the east and the west and sit at the feast with Abraham, Isaac, and Jacob, while the natural subjects of the Kingdom will be cast out into darkness.

It is not our heritage or our religiousness or our good works that will get us into the Kingdom. The currency of the Kingdom is the faith that accepts God's promises and trusts the Savior, Jesus Christ.

I read about a man who prayed, "Lord, I want to have faith," and he stopped because he wasn't sure whether that was really true. He wasn't sure he really wanted faith, for that would mean he would have to act on it. So he prayed, "Lord, maybe I really do not want to have faith, but I want to want to have faith."—Carl L. Taylor

SUNDAY, NOVEMBER 30, 2003
Lectionary Message

First Sunday of Advent

Topic: Do We Want Him to Come?

TEXT: Luke 21:25–36

Other Readings: Jer. 33:14–16; Ps. 25:1–10; 1 Thess. 3:9–13

This Gospel text is one of those passages that we rather comfortable Christians in North America find troubling. We were born into a world where our faith does not cause us to be persecuted or shunned. In fact, there are social advantages in regular church attendance. We have been educated that things might change slightly but the world as we know it is quite stable. Even wars have not devastated our surroundings. For most of us, the world has seemed good.

And then we turn to the book of Revelation or to a text like Mark 13 or Luke 21. What do we see in these texts? Most of us see warnings of disaster. The end of the world as we know it would be a calamity. We like this world. We are comfortable here. We do our best to stay here as long as we can. We work hard to keep it pretty much the way it is. Therefore we don't know how to read Bible passages that describe the end of the world.

There are important lessons to be learned from such texts, and they are more than descriptions meant to frighten us into being good. Did you ever wonder how they got into our Bible in the first place? The earliest Christians must have seen something very important—probably very positive—in them, just as the Israelites did in similar texts in the Hebrew Bible. People being persecuted for their faith still read these texts as positive. Their world does not seem so friendly. Their experiences tell them they need somebody to intervene. They welcome the news that the Lord will come again to judge sin and to redeem his people. They—and we—find in passages about the end of the world as we know it several important lessons.

I. *This world is not the Kingdom of God.* In fact, Jesus says that the "ruler of this world" is condemned. In his teaching (John 12, 14, 16) the ruler of this world is Satan.

Perhaps we should not be so easily convinced that the world as we know it is a good place. In fact, it could be that the most effective satanic strategy is to make living here easy for us. Our government, our educations, our health care, our insurance systems, our nice houses, our plentiful food—in short, all the modern amenities—seduce us into thinking that this world *is* our home—we're not just passing through. So we need texts like Luke 21 to remind us that there is a cosmic war going on—that Satan is using all available means to shake our faith, either by shock or by erosion, and God is trying to teach us to follow the divine Lord and not the ruler of this world.

II. *Christ will return and save us from ourselves.* It sounds terribly disruptive, doesn't it? "For there will be great distress on Earth. . . . There will be signs in the sun, the moon, and the stars, and on the Earth distress among nations confused by the roaring of the sea and the waves. People will faint from fear and foreboding of what is coming upon the world, for the powers of the heavens will be shaken." We don't like distress, confusion, fear, and foreboding. We do what we can to escape such calamities. In our case, such comfort with the status quo is precisely what Christ wants to save us from. He knows that we have become comfortable with the reign of the wrong ruler. He knows that we claim allegiance to our heavenly Lord but live allegiance to our worldly ruler. He knows that we have settled for second best, and he has something much better prepared for us. In other words, he knows that we have allowed ourselves to be seduced by Satan, and he intends to deliver us back to our rightful ruler, the Lord of heaven and Earth. He wants to take us to the place called "The Lord is our righteousness."

III. *Such a hope can help us to stand firm in our faith.* As we hear in these strange texts the voice of the Lord calling us back to his future—back to the land we were created to occupy—we begin to recognize that what we are hearing is encouragement.

Texts about the end times are designed not to frighten us but rather to strengthen us for resistance to Satan's strategies. This encouragement is not at all hidden in the text. It is rather clear. Each paragraph culminates in an open exhortation: "Stand up and raise your heads, because your redemption is drawing near. . . . My words will not pass away. . . . Be on guard.

. . . Be alert at all times, praying that you may have the strength to escape all these things that will take place, and to stand before the Son of Man."

You can find the same encouragement in the book of Revelation, where nearly every paragraph uses words of exhortation. We miss this. We miss the very point of the text because we concentrate on the disruption of the world as it is. Instead, if we concentrate on the world as it is meant to be for us who are God's redeemed people, we'll see the great encouragement to hang loose in the world as it is.

IV. *Therefore we can pray, "Come, Lord Jesus."* Because of our attachment to this world, we find it hard to get very excited about its end. We find it odd that the early Church would pray, "Come, Lord Jesus," as we find in Revelation 22:20 and in 1 Corinthians 16:22.

The American way of death, as one writer has called it, is to postpone death as long as possible and then to mask it as well as possible when it comes. This is true even among Christians, and it might indicate that we are so satisfied with life in the here and now that we can't imagine a better life yet to come. It is time that we set our minds on heaven enough that we begin to realize that the world, as it is, is at best an imperfect shadow of the life God has in store for us. "This world is not my home. I'm just a-passin' through. My treasure is laid up somewhere beyond the blue."

Such words come out of painful life experiences, but they should be coming even from those of us who have it good yet yearn to have it perfect. The perfect will come, but only with the Lord. So let us pray, "Come, Lord Jesus."—Bruce E. Shields

ILLUSTRATION

A DIFFERENT ANGLE.   I recently taught a series of Bible school lessons on Revelation. I was struck by the vast difference between how most of my middle-class American students viewed the descriptions and how one quiet member of the class viewed them. He is a refugee from Sudan, where he escaped from violent persecution of Christians and where his wife and children are still living. He sees the end of the world as we know it as ultimate liberation and redemption from a very unfriendly world. The book *The American Way of Death* by Jessica Mitford[7] contains much helpful information to illustrate how we put off and mask the reality of death.—Bruce E. Shields

SERMON SUGGESTIONS

Topic: Who, Me?
Text: 1 Sam. 16:1–13
(1) *The story:* The choice of David to be king. (2) *The meaning:* When God has work to be done, he may choose unlikely people of little promise to do it (see 1 Cor. 1:26–31).

Topic: When Light Begins to Shine
Text: Eph. 5:8–14 NEB
Christians are compared to light. Therefore (1) we have a new and different character (v. 8), (2) we produce wholesome fruits of this character (v. 9), and (3) our lives then stand in a kind of inevitable judgment on deeds of darkness (vv. 10–13).

---

[7]New York: Simon and Schuster, 1963.

CONGREGATIONAL MUSIC

1. "Songs of Thankfulness and Praise," Christopher Wordsworth (1962)

    ST. GEORGE'S WINDSOR, George J. Elvey (1858)

    Relating both to the Old Testament lesson, with its reference to "the Branch of David," and to the Gospel reading on the return of Christ, this noble hymn is a good selection for the beginning of worship on the first Sunday of Advent.

2. "The King Shall Come," Greek hymn (4th century); trans. John Brownlie (1907)

    MORNING SONG, *Kentucky Harmony,* Part II (1813)

    This ancient hymn would be appropriately sung in connection with the Epistle lesson (1 Thess. 3:9–13), with its summons to holy living in preparation for the coming of our Lord.

3. "Lord, to You My Soul Is Lifted," Ps. 2; vers. Stanley Wiersma (1980)

    GENEVAN 25, Louis Bourgeois (1551)

    This modern metrical psalm freely paraphrases Psalm 25. Because it is set to the tune originally used for this psalm in the *Genevan Psalter,* it could be traditionally performed by a precentor lining out the various phrases. Because of its considerable length, the internal stanza could simply be quoted by the congregation.

4. "Long Ago, Prophets Knew," Fred Pratt Green (1970)

    PERSONET HODIE, *Piae Cantiones* (1582)

    A good, relatively new hymn for Advent is this one by the eminent Fred Pratt Green, who died in 2001. It looks forward joyfully to Christ's coming with the haunting question, "Who will make him welcome?"—Hugh T. McElrath

WORSHIP AIDS.

CALL TO WORSHIP.   "Then the seventh angel blew his trumpet and there were loud voices in heaven, saying, 'The power to rule over the world belongs now to our Lord and his Messiah, and he will rule forever and ever' " (Rev. 11:15 TEV).

INVOCATION.   There is a stirring in the air, a movement of expectation, the emergence of a long awaited promise; we are on tiptoe with faith, Lord, as we begin the journey to Bethlehem. Meet us again at the cradle and shine your light into the depths of our souls.—E. Lee Phillips

OFFERTORY SENTENCE.   "Offer unto God thanksgiving, and pay thy vows unto the most High" (Ps. 50:14).

OFFERTORY PRAYER.   Father, help us to understand that what we are is the result of your grace and that what we have is a gift from your hand. This morning we bring back some of the material blessings we have received. Pray, do your gracious work in others through the gifts we bring.—Henry Fields

PRAYER.   All thy works praise thee, O Lord, and thy saints give thanks unto thee. On mountain and field and flower and sky thou hast set thy glory. The hearts of men and women and little children thou hast filled with happiness. "The whole round world is bound with golden chains about thy feet." O give us spirits attuned to the harmonies of thy universe, that this day we may join in the swelling chorus of praise that ever magnifies thy name. Lift us up into thy joy, before which sorrow hides her face, and pain and fear fly away.

We bless thee for thy self-revelation in Jesus Christ, our blessed Lord and Master. We have stood in his presence and have heard him say, "He that hath seen me hath seen the Father." In him thou hast come among us, cleansing our soiled hearts, healing the wounds of body and of mind, giving rest to the troubled conscience, and opening the blind eyes to the beauty and brightness of the world. As we listen to his voice, grief becomes a scorn of ills and the weaknesses of life become our glory. As we look into his face we seek nothing but that we may love him with all our hearts and serve him with all our might. O Christ, thou Son of God, let the cross abide in us! Touch us with the glory of thy sonship, with the power of thy surrendered life, that we, no longer the servants of the world, may become the sons of God!—Samuel McComb[8]

SERMON
Topic: Savior! Who Needs a Savior?
TEXT: Matt. 1:18–25, focus on v. 21

"His name shall be called 'Jesus,' for it is he who shall save his people from their sins." The name *Jesus* has a very potent root. It comes from a Greek word. Its antecedent in Hebrew is translated "Joshua," which literally means "Yahweh saves." In the panorama of the nativity that we find in Luke's Gospel, the heavenly herald proclaims to the frightened shepherds, "Do not be afraid; behold, I bring you good new of great joy, which shall be to all people, for unto you is born this day in the city of David a Savior." From the beginning of Christianity, those who have believed in Jesus Christ have believed in him as their personal savior and as the savior of the world.

This is the good news of Christmas: What we could not do for ourselves, God was willing and able to do for us. But God did not send an angel or a prophet or an evangelist, although all of these are instruments in preparing the way for his coming. He came himself! How beautifully this is expressed in Moffatt's translation of Isaiah 35:4: "Have courage, never fear, here comes your God. He comes himself to save you." So too the apostle Paul wrote to one of the early churches in the first century, "God was in Christ reconciling the world unto himself."

I. *The human predicament: Our sin.* Highly sophisticated scientific and technological achievements have brought us not nearer to salvation but only nearer to our own destruction. At the push of a button there is power available to destroy the human race twelve times over. The theory of inevitable progress that gained such momentum in the early decades of the last century has now been blasted by two world wars and several minor ones (if any war or the killing of one life can be considered minor), in a universe where one sparrow cannot fall to the ground with a broken wing without the concern of the Maker.

Too much of the Church's energy has been dissipated in attacking the sins of man but never getting at the sin. Growing up in a very conservative church and community, I remember the minister, Sunday after Sunday, lashing out against what was considered at that time to be the three cardinal sins. You know what they were: dancing, card-playing, and going to the movies. What about the beastly sins of hate, greed, and lust for power

---

[8]*A Book of Prayers*

that condemn men and women, boys and girls, and youth to a life of degradation and, many of them, to death?

Our predicament is our sin, not our sins. Our sins issue from our sin. Our sin is that we are alienated from our Maker and estranged from ourselves and our fellowman. In a far country—lost! Until we realize our true predicament, we will never seek to find the way back home.

I can hear people saying, "Preacher, you are telling us bad news; Christmas is all about good news." Christmas can never be good news for any of us until we have confronted the bad news it reveals about us. We can never appreciate the light that this season brings unless we comprehend the darkness of this world without God. Isaiah's words are empty rhetoric until we realize that this is our darkness:

> The people who walked in darkness
> have seen a great light;
> those who dwelt in a land of deep darkness,
> on them has light shined.

II. *Sin: self-deluding.* Our darkness, you see, is that we are self-deluded. Just how self-deluded man is about his real predicament is one of the main themes of Charles Schulz's comic strip, *Peanuts.* Lucy often illustrates such self-deception by her pride and self-righteousness. One day she is raving about her ravishing beauty and Charlie Brown is trying to prick her balloon of pride. "Besides, Lucy," he says, "never forget that beauty is only skin deep." Lucy replies, "I deny that! My beauty is not only on the surface; it goes down deep . . . layer after layer after layer! Yes, sir! I have very *thick* beauty!" We chuckle at that, but how do we penetrate such pride and self-righteousness?

"All have sinned and come short of the glory of God" is the verdict of God's Word. To deny our sin, our estrangement from God, our sin-full-ness, our tendency to sin, is to be the worst kind of Pharisee. No one less than the apostle Paul cried out, "Wretched man that I am! . . . For I know that nothing good dwells within me, that is, in my flesh. I can will what is right but I cannot do it. For I do not do the good thing I intend, but the evil I do not want is what I do."

Jesus leveled some of his most scathing remarks at the Pharisees. He caricatured them as "wolves in sheep's clothing." We like to think of ourselves as being the sheep of the fold, but Jesus says, "There is only one way to enter his fold . . . and that is to enter by the door. And I am that door."

III. *Christ as Lord.* God has "highly exalted him and given him a name which is above every name; that at the name of Jesus every knee should bow, in heaven and on Earth and below the Earth, and that every tongue should confess that Jesus Christ is Lord, to the glory of God the Father."

This is our difficulty—to honor Christ as Lord. We want an indulgent Jesus as Savior who will save us in our sins. Until we acclaim and honor Christ as Lord, we are never open in mind and heart to receive God's grace in Christ, that we may know him as Savior. But the good news is that there is a light that penetrates even the blackness we have pictured. This light is the glory of God seen in the face of Jesus Christ.—John Thompson

SUNDAY, DECEMBER 7, 2003
Lectionary Message

Second Sunday of Advent

Topic: Living in the Plan of God

TEXT: Luke 1:68–79; 3:1–6

Other Readings: Mal. 3:1–4; Phil. 1:3–11

This man, John the Baptizer, seems like a strange one to us. His clothes, his diet, his environment, and even his preaching are all foreign to us. In fact, he seems so strange that we tend to fixate on the strangeness and miss the point. That point might be the strangest thing of all: John was announced as an important part of God's plan for the salvation of the world.

We live out our lives wondering about God's will for us, but John's coming was foretold by prophets, his conception was announced by an angel, and his birth was placarded by his father's prophecy. After all that, the adult John came on the scene as an adult confident that he was in the will of God as he preached his message boldly.

Have you ever looked closely at Zechariah's statement after John's birth? First, he insisted that Elizabeth, his wife, was right in naming the baby John as the angel had instructed them. Then he broke his God-given silence with the beautiful statement in our text. The Church came to call it the "Benedictus," because it begins with that word in the Latin translation: "Blessed be the Lord God of Israel." The first eight verses are all praise of God.

I. This statement is praise of God as the merciful Savior, the one who had helped Israel many times before and who promised that he would continue to save them so they could serve him. It is praise of God as the one who was now bringing forth a Savior "in the house of his servant David, as he spoke through the mouth of his holy prophets from of old."

The praise is made up of bits of passages from many parts of the Hebrew Bible. Its primary thrust is that what was happening was in the stream of God's acts of mercy throughout history. What was happening had been promised in ages past. What was happening was in the center of the will of the most high God. What was happening, of course, was the birth of the one we know as John the Baptist, the forerunner of Jesus the Messiah. Baby John, born of older-than-usual parents, was born in the plan of God and in fulfillment of God's promise.

II. The second part of Zechariah's "Benedictus" is directed as a blessing and promise to the baby: "And you, child, will be called the prophet of the Most High." Here we have a summary of the ministry of John. He was to prepare the way of the Lord. He was to lead people to the forgiveness of their sins. He was to introduce the one bringing light to the world—the one bringing "the way of peace."

What a way to begin life—as a reason for his father both to praise God profusely and to prophesy that the baby would grow to be a great spokesman for God! John seemed never to have had a doubt about his place in God's plan. His preaching was clear and forceful. His life and his preaching were so integrated that people of all kinds went to hear him and were deeply moved. Yet John never confused himself with the Messiah. He consistently proclaimed that he was not the Messiah, but rather the one who came to prepare the way. John knew who he was and why he was here. He was living in the plan of God.

III. Wouldn't it be great to have that sort of assurance—to know that you were living in the plan of God? What would it take to have that confidence? Great ability? Outstanding success? Human praise? No, we should not lose sight of the fact that it was God's plan that made the difference in John's life, and God's plan should be the primary focus for us also.

Every Christian is participating in the plan of God. Without great fanfare or applause we are working out God's plan for us. The apostle Paul wrote his letter to the Philippians from prison, and even there he had no doubt that both he and the Philippians were living in the plan of God. In Philippians 1:6 he wrote, "I am confident of this, that the one who began a good work among you will bring it to completion by the day of Jesus Christ."

You see, it is not our circumstances that determine our effectiveness; nor does the visibility of our work measure its importance. The primary factor in the Christian life is the God who has begun a divine work among us and who will bring it to completion. John the Baptist was certainly unusual, but he was not that way just because of the plan of God at work in his life. God works in every believer's life just as far as we will permit it.

We are too rarely conscious of it but we are living in the plan of God, just as truly as John did. God has begun a good work in us and God is at work to bring it to completion. Let us thank God for the divine plan and let us live in the knowledge that we are in the plan of God, so that we too will be able to prepare for the coming of the Lord.—Bruce E. Shields

ILLUSTRATION

EXAMPLES.   Lest the preacher leave a gap between John and us who live in the twenty-first century, biographies of people like Mother Theresa and examples of Christians living under persecution, such as in the Sudan, can help make the transition to every believer's life.—Bruce E. Shields

SERMON SUGGESTIONS

Topic: Results Worth Preaching for
TEXT: Isa. 62:1–5
(1) The coming of justice. (2) The glory of God. (3) The joy of belonging.

Topic: The Work of the Spirit
TEXT: 1 Cor. 12:1–11
(1) *Basically:* The confession of Jesus as Lord (vv. 2–3). (2) *But also:* Varieties of service (vv. 4–11).

CONGREGATIONAL MUSIC

1. "Come Down, O Love Divine!" Bianco da Siena (15th century); trans. Richard Littledale (1867)
    DOWN AMPNEY, Ralph Vaughan Williams (1906)
    The burning, purifying fire that attended the coming of the Lord in the Old Testament lesson (Mal. 3:1–4) is reflected in the beautiful poetry of this venerable hymn. It would be a meaningful response to the reading from Malachi.
2. "Blest Be the God of Israel," *Song of Zecharias;* para. Michael Perry (1973)
    MERLE'S TUNE, Hal H. Hopson (1983)
    This contemporary paraphrase of the *Song of Zecharias* is clearly indicated for singing at the time appointed for the reading of the canticle.

3. "More Love, to Thee, O Christ," Elizabeth P. Prentiss (1856)

MORE LOVE TO THEE, William H. Doane (1870)

The apostle Paul's prayer that the Philippians' love might abound in knowledge and discernment (Phil. 1:9) finds its echo in this familiar gospel hymn. It could form a natural response to the reading of the Epistle lesson.

4. "Comfort, Comfort Ye (Now) My People," Johannes Olearius (1671); trans. C. Winkworth (1813)

GENEVAN 42, Louis Bourgeois (1551)

Sing this hymn as either introduction or response to the Gospel lesson about John the Baptist and his prophetic words from Isaiah (Luke 3:2–6).—Hugh T. McElrath

WORSHIP AIDS

CALL TO WORSHIP.   "And saying, Repent ye: for the Kingdom of Heaven is at hand" (Matt. 3:2).

INVOCATION.   In this sacred hour, on this holy day, we come into your presence, Father, with praise and thanksgiving in our hearts and on our lips. Meet us in the majesty of your power, that we might realize how finite we really are. Open before us the expanse of eternity, that we might come to know the boundaries of Earth time. Show us the depths of your love, that we might see the shallowness of our own. Reveal to us again the wonder of Christ's redemption, that we might find in him our true salvation.—Henry Fields

OFFERTORY SENTENCE.   "Greater love hath no man than this, that he lay down his life for his friends" (John 15:13).

OFFERTORY PRAYER.   Lord of all, please accept out thankfulness for our monetary blessings, that we might remain faithful stewards, ones who give freely and cheerfully in Jesus' name.—E. Lee Phillips

PRAYER.   Accept, O Lord, our thanks and praise for all that you have done for us. We thank you for the splendor of the whole creation, for the beauty of this world, for the wonder of life, and for the mystery of love.

We thank you for the blessing of a family and friends, and for the loving care that surrounds us on every side.

We thank you for setting us at tasks that demand our best efforts, and for leading us to accomplishments that satisfy and delight us.

We thank you also for those disappointments and failures that lead us to acknowledge our dependence on you alone.

Above all, we thank you for your Son Jesus Christ: for the truth of his word and the example of his life; for his steadfast obedience, by which he overcame temptation; for his dying, through which he overcame death; and for his rising to life again, in which we are raised to the life of your Kingdom.

Grant us the gift of your Spirit, that we may know him and make him known; and through him, at all times and in all places, may give thanks to you in all things.—*The Book of Common Prayer*

SERMON
Topic: What Will They Think Up Next?
TEXT: Gen. 18:1–5, 9–15; Luke 1:26–38

A surprise is the unexpected. Amazement is being made speechless, astounded at what you see. Actually, both words are appropriate for the nativity story. The story read this morning is called the Annunciation, the announcement, the angel Gabriel announcing to Mary that she, above all women in the world, is to be the mother of the Messiah.

The story of the Jews begins with Abraham and Sarah, an old man and an old woman who were going to have a baby. It is a wonderful story. They were surprised, to say the least, and acted as you would act, I imagine, if you were their age and had been told that you were going to have a baby. They laughed.

The story says Sarah overheard the angel saying to her husband that she was going to have a baby. She was in the kitchen, her ear pressed to the door. She overheard the angel say to Abraham, "In the springtime Sarah, your wife, is going to have a baby." She laughed.

You have to laugh at the promises of God. Anyone in his right mind is going to laugh at the promises of God, because they are so incredible, so contrary to expectations, so improbable in light of the inevitable realities of this world, the inevitable disappointments that humans experience. In the real world, the world in which you and I live, the promises of God will almost always appear ludicrous. Which is why some theologians point out that from a literary point of view the Bible is really comedy.

If you use the classical distinction between tragedy and comedy, the Bible *is* comedy. Tragedy implies inevitability. It is about fate moving toward a predictable end. That is what tragedy is about. Comedies, conversely, are about the impossible happening. They are about the proud being humbled and the humbled being lifted up and exalted.

There's a tragic dimension in the Bible. I suppose you could say that Job is about tragedy. But essentially the Bible is about comedy, because it's about surprises.

Compared with other histories, Israel's history appears to have been written by Mel Brooks. It records all the foibles, all the mistakes, all the sins of all the people. And it begins, incredibly, with an old man and an old woman being told, you're going to have a baby. And they laughed.

And you can laugh, too, because Israel knows what all nations know but are too proud to admit: that although you can write a history of human achievement and national greatness, there is another history, the real history. The real history in this world is not the history of human greatness. It's the history of God's providence. At the end of every chapter of Israel's story, at the end of every phase of its history, when all rational folk had given up hope, when all things were at their worst, there always came redemption and a new life.

Have you seen any Babylonians lately? The Jews are still here. Their history indicates that they are here against all odds. Nobody could have predicted it. They are here because thousands of years ago God entered into a covenant with them through Abraham that said, "I will always be with you." Because of God's grace alone, God has kept that promise.

Now we as Christians believe that the coming of the Messiah meant that God had opened to all people the promise that he gave to Abraham. God now says to the whole world, "You are my people. You will have a wonderful future, if you believe." That is the promise. So the story of the birth of the Messiah is told the same way as the story of Abraham and Sarah, because it is about the same promise. Once again a promise was being made, only this time the angel said that the glad tidings of a great joy go to all the people, not just to the Jews. Now it goes to all the people.

Gabriel visited Mary. That is when you are supposed to laugh, or gasp in amazement. First, Mary was a woman. Angels appeared only to men in that patriarchal society. This was the first time an angel appeared to a woman. Even Matthew, in his version of the nativity story, says that the angel appeared to Joseph, not to Mary. But in Luke there's a surprise: the angel came to Mary.

And what's more, Mary was not old like the others. She was young. She was also a virgin. This is pointed out not so much to describe her sexual status as to indicate that she was young. It was not until later that the Church became fascinated with her sexual purity. At this point, Luke is interested only in her youth. That's the surprise: she was just a girl. She was an adolescent. Elizabeth, Sarah, Hannah—all of those in the Old Testament who had miraculous births before Mary—were all old women. This was different. This was a surprise. This was something new.

The story is told in that way to get our attention. This was something new, and the something new was that the promise that had been given to Abraham had now been given to us, that God will be with us and will never leave us.

Of course the angel made the announcement the same way he always made it. He had been doing this for a thousand years. He'd memorized it by then. "Hail, O favored one, the Lord is with you!"

Mary answered in the traditional way. She said, "How can this be?" But she doesn't say, "How can this be, because I am old?" She says, "How can this be, because I am too young, and I am too poor, and I am too humble? Besides, I have no husband." The angel said, "With God nothing will be impossible." Which is what he said to Zechariah, and what he said to Abraham. "With God, nothing will be impossible."

That could be called the Bible's philosophy of history: "With God, nothing will be impossible." So don't ever say, "This isn't the right time." Don't ever say, "This isn't the right place." And don't ever say, "I'm not the right person." All of these have been used to dismiss the occasion of God's entering the world. God just loves it when we set things up for him that way. "It's never going to happen." "It hasn't happened here." "It will never happen this way." "It's never happened before." That's when God pulls the rug out, or places the banana peel in the path, or as Mary sang in the *Magnificat,* which we used as the Canticle and anthem this morning, "He knocks the mighty from their thrones and exalts those of low degree."

This is the essence of comedy. Comedy is when what you don't expect to happen, happens. The opposite of what is expected happens, and we laugh. Or when somebody who is exalted or arrogant and struts around is humbled, we laugh. Or when somebody who is humble and stumbles around and can't get anything right all of a sudden is made the prince. Or when the underdog wins the game through a series of unbelievable events that nobody could ever have predicted, but they happen. When they do, everyone laughs, everyone cheers, because it is a happy ending brought about through a series of impossible events. That's what comedy is.

The Bible says that's the way God rules history. It's a happy ending though a series of incredible events that nobody expected. You can see that especially at Christmas.

We give gifts at Christmas for a number of reasons. But the gifts that are most like Christmas are the surprises. That's what happened. Nobody expected it. Not now. Not like this. Not me.

"How can this be?" Mary asked. The angel said, "With God, nothing is impossible."—Mark Trotter

SUNDAY, DECEMBER 14, 2003
Lectionary Message

Third Sunday of Advent

Topic: Good News from John
TEXT: Luke 3:7–18
Other Readings: Zeph. 3:14–20; Isa. 12:2–6; Phil. 4:4–7

We saw last Sunday how confident John was as a person living in the plan of God. Today's text from Luke gives us a glimpse of how that confidence worked out in his life. Our Gospel text today gives us a sample of John's preaching—preaching with confidence to the extreme.

I. No speech teacher today would recommend that a speech begin by addressing the audience as John did here. "You brood of vipers," he began. "You offspring of snakes." Or perhaps to get the emotional flavor of it we might say, "You serpentine bastards." Or maybe not. This is not the way to ingratiate oneself with an audience. An insult as an introduction seems counterproductive, but it appears to have been effective for John.

John went on to tell them to forget their roots and look to their fruits. This was also not designed to make friends and influence people, but it got their attention. The positive results of this negative preaching must have sprung from the deep respect the people had for John. It was obvious that he was not profiting from his prophecy. Both his confidence and his motivation came from God, and this must have shown in his eyes and rung in his voice.

II. John's response to questions from his hearers about what they should do was positive and unflinching. Justice and mercy were the primary characteristics of their God, and justice and mercy were to be the hallmarks of their own relationships. Each group of people got specific instructions, but they all add up to justice and mercy in human relationships.

Can we put ourselves into that audience? Using the criteria of justice and mercy, do we look like children of God or offspring of a snake? How much energy are we misusing that could be used by others in the world? How much food do we waste that could feed the hungry in our cities? How much of our resources are we storing up while people are dying of diseases that are easily cured? Do you have two coats? Do you have extra food in the pantry?

Now, how do you hear this? "Whoever has two coats must share with anyone who has none; and whoever has food must do likewise." To the tax collectors he said, "Be honest." To soldiers he said, "Don't misuse your power, and be satisfied with your wages." We can point to as many societal differences as we like, but we cannot escape John's judging word. When we compare what we have with what most people on Earth have, we look more like a brood of vipers than like children of God.

III. This is prophetic preaching, and John's hearers recognized it as such. He was certainly a prophet. Might he even have been *the* prophet—the Messiah? The third part of his sermon deals with that issue. He told people in no uncertain terms that he was not the Messiah. He said, "One who is more powerful than I is coming; I am not worthy to untie the thong of his sandals." There were no delusions of grandeur in John. He knew he was in the plan of God, and he knew his place in that plan. He was the forerunner of the Messiah. He was the one who came to exhort the people and prepare them for the coming one.

In fact, Luke uses this sermon to introduce the appearance of Jesus as the Messiah. A few verses after our text closes, Luke points out that Jesus came to John and was baptized. The Holy Spirit came upon him in the form of a dove and a voice from heaven said, "You are my Son, the Beloved; with you I am well pleased." From that point on in the Gospels, John's role diminishes, while the fame of Jesus increases.

But before Luke introduces Jesus in this way, he points out that what John was doing was proclaiming "the good news." We have little trouble attaching the term *gospel* or *good news* to the teaching of love and grace by Jesus. However, we find it hard to label judgmental preaching like John's as "good news." But think about it. If the path you are walking on leads to a sudden drop over a cliff, wouldn't you welcome a warning as good news?

That's John's gospel—abrasive but effective. And most important, it led people to Jesus. I wonder at times whether we might take Jesus more seriously if we heard John more personally, especially when he says, "Bear fruits worthy of repentance."—Bruce E. Shields

ILLUSTRATION

RELEVANCE.   Stories and statistics of injustice perpetrated or permitted by otherwise good people are abundant and will well apply John's preaching to the present age.—Bruce E. Shields

SERMON SUGGESTIONS

Topic: The Day Comes
TEXT: Mal. 4:1–6
(1) The plight of evildoers (v. 1). (2) The blessings of those who fear God (vv. 2–3). (3) The attitude toward God's written and prophetic Word that makes the difference (vv. 4–6).

Topic: Maintaining a Christian Work Ethic
TEXT: 2 Thess. 3:6–13
(1) By shunning the company of idlers. (2) By imitating the industrious. (3) By motivating slackers. (4) By doing right even when it is difficult.

CONGREGATIONAL MUSIC

1. "Rejoice, the Lord Is King," Charles Wesley (1744)
   DARWALL, John Darwall (1770)
   With its refrain taken directly from Philippians 4:4, this hymn can effectively begin musical worship as well as relate to the Epistle lesson.
2. "Surely It Is God Who Saves Me," *The First Song of Isaiah* (Isa. 12:2–6); para. Carl P. Daw (1982)
   THOMAS MERTON, Ray W. Urwin (1984)
   This contemporary paraphrase is so close to all the content of Isaiah 12:2–6 that it could be sung at the place of the reading from prophecy. Because of its possible unfamiliarity, a soloist could sing the tune first before inviting the congregation to participate.

3. "Spirit, Working in Creation," John Richards (1978)

    SUNRISE, Luxembourg, *Kyriale* (1768)

This modern hymn contains several hints about John the Baptist and about Jesus during his early earthly ministry. It would logically accompany the reading of the Gospel lesson. Singing the first stanza in unison would familiarize the congregation with the tune. Singing the harmony on stanza 2 would be a good musical as well as devotional challenge to the worshiping congregation.

4. "Come, Thou Long-Expected Jesus," Charles Wesley (1744)

    HYFRYDOL, Rowland H. Prichard (1830)

No Advent season should pass without the congregation at least once singing Charles Wesley's great expectant expression of joy in Christ's coming. It would appropriately open worship as an invocation on this or any other Sunday in the Advent season.—Hugh T. McElrath

WORSHIP AIDS

CALL TO WORSHIP.   "The voice of him that crieth in the wilderness, Prepare ye the way of the Lord, make straight in the desert a highway for our God" (Isa. 40:3).

INVOCATION.   In the sacredness of this hour we come before you, Father, that we may be led to tear down the barriers that separate us from you and in some instances from each other. We follow our own desires and enter into sins that cloud the skies of your presence. We too often forget your mercy because of the blindness of our hearts. This morning we pray that you will cleanse us from all our offenses and deliver us from proud thoughts and vain desires. Teach us the meaning of true meekness and the power of honest confession, that we may experience the wonder of your grace even as we find in you a refuge and strength.—Henry Fields

OFFERTORY SENTENCE.   "So then every one of us shall give an account of himself to God" (Rom. 14:12).

OFFERTORY PRAYER.   O God, as we grope our way out of darkness into light, help us to find that which will release our lives so we can be fully ourselves and fully thine. Help us to gather together the loose ends of life and integrate them into Christ Jesus, so that in us he may live again to save the lives of others.—Theodore Parker Ferris

PRAYER.   "O great forgiving God: our identity as sinners and our need for forgiveness are more than matters of doctrine. They are facts of personal experience. We are sinners who need forgiveness. The depth of that realization inspires the heights of our thanksgiving.

Thanks be to you, O God, for the grace gift of forgiveness. You love us when we are not lovable. You do not give up on us when we give up on ourselves. You provide us strength when our energy is gone. You offer us direction when we wander about in confusion. You affirm our worth when we feel worthless. You assure us of forgiveness when it is certain that we will sin again. You respond with life when our words and actions invite death. Thanks be to you, O God, for the grace gift of forgiveness.

A longing complements our thanksgiving—a desire to be able to extend to others the kind of forgiveness we have received from you. Please help us with our forgiveness as you receive our words of gratitude for your forgiveness.

We speak to you in the name of your Son, who as a perfectly innocent person became sin in order that we, the true sinners, might know forgiveness and have the opportunity to live as new creations. Amen.—C. Welton Gaddy[1]

SERMON
Topic: The Unexpected Christ
Text: No specific text

You say immediately, was anyone ever more expected than Christ? Anybody ever more looked forward to than he was? You know that on February 15, 1564, Michelangelo died and Galileo was born; and that on the 23rd of April in the same year Shakespeare was born. These are three men who shaped our thinking. No one had any reason to expect any one of them. But surely it was not so with Christ; a whole nation was expecting him! They had been waiting for at least two or three hundred years for his arrival. They were looking everywhere for him, and every time they saw someone like John the Baptist they wondered whether he might be the one. The hope of his coming kept them going through the humiliation and the indignity of their exile, and through the coming of the Greeks with their temples, and then of the Romans, with their efficient management of government. So, certainly you can't say they didn't expect him.

And yet the fact is that when he did come, they didn't know it, and they didn't know it because he wasn't the Christ they had expected.

They expected (at least most of them did, and I must warn you that when we say "they" we are not including everyone, because there were always exceptions, then as now) a Christ who would liberate them from Rome. He didn't. He liberated them from Satan—from sin and from guilt. They expected a Christ who would dazzle them by miraculous feats. He didn't. He healed the sick and fed the hungry, but he didn't jump off the Temple just to dazzle them into belief. He refused to do that.

What is more, they expected a Christ who would instill in the young a love of the *Law*— the Law with a capital L because it was the Law of God that Moses had given them, and it covered every aspect of life with rules and regulations, both ceremonial and more. People were neglecting it and were expecting a Christ who would rekindle a love of the Law with a capital L. He didn't. He talked about the law of love, which was quite different. He said that love is the fulfillment of all the laws.

They expected a Christ who would make life easier, reduce taxes, increase employment, bring down prices. He didn't. If anything, he made it harder. He talked about crosses, not crowns.

Above everything else, they expected a Christ who would be a smashing success. He wasn't. He was a dismal failure. They expected a Christ they could keep to themselves as a nation. They couldn't. He was like a river, the current of which is so strong that no bank can contain it. They expected a Christ who would promise a happy ending. Everybody likes happy

---

[1]*Prayers*

endings. He didn't promise the kind of happy ending that all people really long for. He never let them forget about the girls who might have gone to the wedding but didn't because they were too late, and the man who missed the dinner because he was too busy to accept the invitation. He never let people forget the fact that the door can be closed, and that it can be closed forever; that there is the possibility of missing the bus.

They didn't expect anything like that. Only a few of the most perceptive ones could see the possibility of a Christ born in a manger and crucified on a cross. So it is no wonder they hardly recognized him, because he was not the Christ they expected. They weren't ready for the unexpected Christ.

Now we come to another Christmas, the middle of another season of Advent. We know that Christmas will come in the normal course of events. It always has come; the calendar always gets around to the 25th of December, and if we all live we will all have another Christmas. We also know that Christ will come, in one way or another, but instinctively we look for him to come in the way we expect him to, and there is a sense in which he will come in that way. He will break through, here and there, the crust of our fierce, competitive world; he will soften a hard heart, here and there. He will heal an open wound. He will manage to find a small place on the thousands of cards and messages, even the ones that have not a single reference to himself, because the one who sends it expresses his own love and affection on that card. So he will come that way.

But there is also a sense in which he is always the unexpected Christ. We expect him to come in the usual place, which for us is either in the church or in the home or both. For many people he may come in neither of those places. He may come in the streets; he may come on the college campus, where there doesn't seem to be much sign of him at the moment; he may come on a ski slope where a family spends the holidays; or he may come like a shining light in a scientist's laboratory, the flickering of a new idea that will open one of the secrets of the world. We expect him to come in the familiar music of the carols we love and have heard all our lives and will hear again next Sunday and all through the Christmas Season. For many of us he will come in the music. But for thousands he may come in the more primitive rhythm of music that is called rock. I don't understand it, but I am prepared for the fact that that is the way he will come for many people.

We expect him to come in the familiar language of the Bible, especially the King James translation, and in the Book of Common Prayer. He may come in our time in some strange, new tongue that sounds to us so vernacular that it borders on the vulgar. Before you make any judgment about it, remember that the first translation of the Scriptures from Greek into Latin was called the *Vulgate* for that very reason—because people thought it was a vulgar language.

Christ comes as the angel that troubles the water. He says something like this to me, and he may say it to you, but he says it to me this particular year: You can't wrap God up in a proof-sheet of logical, rational reasoning. You can't have me gift-wrapped for a Christmas present. You can't preserve me in your theological formulas or even in your ecclesiastical institutions, because I will always be slipping out for a breath of fresh air. He says, if you want the serenity that I can give you, you must take the restlessness that goes with it, without which the serenity would be nothing but smugness. He says, when I come, I come as I am—like the wind, like a breath of life. If you don't expect me, you will not find me. If you do find me, don't be surprised if I am not the one you expected.—Theodore Parker Ferris

SUNDAY, DECEMBER 21, 2003
Lectionary Message

Fourth Sunday of Advent

Topic: Pray Without Asking

TEXT: Luke 1:39–55

Other Readings: Mic. 5:2–5a; Heb. 10:5–10

Pray without asking! What sort of statement is that? Isn't that precisely what prayer is—asking? Why would anybody pray without asking God for something? Not surprising, these questions. They are very revealing. We assume that people pray in order to get something, or perhaps to escape something, which is the other side of the same coin. In either case we are enlisting God on our side to do something for us—we are asking God for something.

But our text shows Mary offering a prayer in which she never asks for any help, any strength, any guidance, any stuff, either for herself or for anybody else. She prays without asking. In fact, after her opening statement of praise and thanksgiving, she never refers to herself again. As Martin Luther suggested, we can learn a lot about prayer from Mary.[2]

I. *We can learn from her example.* Her opening statement is pure praise: "My soul magnifies the Lord, and my spirit rejoices in God, my Savior." Here Mary refers to God and her attention never wavers from God again throughout the prayer. What worship we see here! What total absorption in God!

Her attitude seems to come not so much from humility as from surprise. "For he has looked with favor on the lowliness of his servant. . . . The Mighty One has done great things for me." Luther wrote, "No one knows less about humility than he who is truly humble."[3] Mary was impressed with two aspects of her reality: her own commonness and God's shocking choice to bring the Messiah through her. What we see as humility in Mary is actually realism. She was just a common woman, and God in grace chose her to bear the Messiah. That kind of humility results from adoration of God.

Mary's surprise is almost palpable when she says, "From now on all generations will call me blessed." Her relative Elizabeth had just greeted her with that word: "Blessed are you among women, and blessed is the fruit of your womb," she cried out. Elizabeth finished her greeting with, "And blessed is she who believed that there would be a fulfillment of what was spoken to her by the Lord." One can almost see young Mary, amazed already by the message from the angel, now trying to get her mind around her older relative's calling her blessed.

What can she say but, "Holy is his name"? Have you ever tried expressing such adoration to God? This is a real discipline—one that Mary displays vividly for us in the Magnificat.

II. *What follows in the prayer is what Luther enumerates as six works of God.*[4] The *first* of

---

[2]See Luther's little book *The Magnificat* in *Luther's Works*, Vol. 21, ed. by Jaroslav Pelikan (St. Louis: Concordia, 1956), pp. 295–358.

[3]p. 313.

[4]pp. 332–349.

these is mercy: "His mercy is for those who fear him from generation to generation." I wonder sometimes why we who lead others in prayer so often begin by concentrating on the great power and wisdom of God. Usually our prayers reveal how impressed we are with the beauty and grandeur of God's creation. We seem at times to be complimenting God on his wisdom in creating us human beings. Is it perhaps because power and knowledge have become so important to us that we recognize them as something deserving praise, even in God? Might it also reveal our devaluing of these "M" words—meekness and mercy? All Mary could see at first was the mercy of God, and that came first, even before the strong arm of God, which is next.

That "strength with his arm," is of course shown in the mercy of his scattering "the proud in the thoughts of their hearts." This is Luther's *second* work of God. Might not "the proud in the thoughts of their hearts" be a good description of us, who are much more impressed with power and wisdom than with mercy? This "scattering" to which Mary refers is a very thorough job. It is something that causes the individual parts to go every which way. That sounds frighteningly like a good description of our society right now. It is going every which way at once. It has no discernable direction. Maybe Mary knew more theology than we give her credit for.

The *third* work of God listed by Luther is, "He has brought down the powerful from their thrones." Luther addressed his little book on the Magnificat to Prince John Frederick, Duke of Saxony, Landgrave of Thuringia, and Margrave of Meissen. The prince happened to be Luther's patron, but that didn't deter Luther from warning him that the God who had given him great authority could also take it away. Mary knew not only her theology but also her history. The stories of her ancestors included many tales about haughty kings who had been brought down. The power of God and the power of humans are often in conflict; and when they conflict, God is not going to be brought down. Mary knew it, and we had better know it, too.

The *fourth* work is the corollary of the third—God has "lifted up the lowly." Mary could see in her own experience how God upsets the normal human patterns. The lift God gives to the lowly is rarely as obvious as the lift Mary got, but God's revelation is consistent in this, that fortunes will be reversed sooner or later. When God's will is done "on Earth as it is in heaven," the lowly will be lifted up, and we believers had better be involved in the process if we hope to be part of the heavenly work.

The *fifth* and *sixth* works of God are similar to three and four, with a different emphasis: "God has filled the hungry with good things, and sent the rich away empty." Again, God turns on its head what appears to us to be the natural order of society. The rich are hungry and the poor are satisfied. The poor wipe the extra food off their lips while the rich go away as beggars. Can't you see the line at the rescue mission? The best-dressed are asking for food and the people in rags are dishing it out. Talk about justice!

III. *Mary concluded her prayer by rooting her worship of God firmly in the history of God's dealings with people.* This was not wishful thinking. This was not human projection. This was faith based on experience. "He has helped his servant Israel, in remembrance of his mercy, according to the promise he made to our ancestors, to Abraham, and to his descendants forever." She knew the kind of God she was dealing with, and she knew not only from her personal experience but also from the experience of her people through their history. That means she knew her Bible as the record of that experience. The testimony of faithful men and women over two millennia lay behind Mary's trust in the God who had chosen her for a special mission.

Thus the end of Mary's prayer is actually its beginning. God had been the Lord of Mary's people for generations, and God had also been Mary's Lord, whom she now magnified both by her prayer and by her submission to the divine mission to which she was called—a mission that would offer salvation from sin to the whole human race.

For this reason Mary has become an announcer of the advent of Christ, a link in the chain of witnesses who bring us the truth about God—the truth on which we can base our own prayers that begin, "My soul magnifies the Lord, and my spirit rejoices in God my Savior." That should be our prayer without asking.—Bruce E. Shields

ILLUSTRATION

ADORATION AND WORSHIP.   I teach courses in worship to seminary students. These men and women have been trained in the rigors of academic research and writing. They are accustomed to spending long hours reading books, translating Greek and Hebrew texts, and contemplating deep theological and philosophical issues. But when I give them a class assignment to spend five minutes a day in prayers of adoration and worship, with no mixture of thanksgiving, petition, or intercession, they discover that they are not prepared for that. They come back talking about how hard adoration is. I send them to the Psalms and to the Magnificat, where they can learn about how to talk with God unselfishly. They learn to say, "Holy is your name," in many different ways. They discipline themselves to concentrate on the reality of God instead of on God as a resource for their own needs and desires.—Bruce E. Shields

SERMON SUGGESTIONS

Topic: A Blessed Sign from God

TEXT: Isa. 7:10–16

(1) The immediate fulfillment in the prophet's time. (2) The ultimate fulfillment in Jesus Christ.

Topic: The Gospel of God

TEXT: Rom. 1:1–7

(1) It was promised beforehand. (2) It was fulfilled in Jesus Christ. (3) It was destined for faith and obedience among all nations.

CONGREGATIONAL MUSIC

1. "Tell Out, My Soul," Timothy Dudley-Smith (1961)
   WOODLANDS, Walter Greatorex (1916)
   This modern setting of the Magnificat of Mary has become well-known and very popular. It should be sung heartily in unison at the place in the worship order for the reading of the Canticle.
2. "Savior of the Nations, Come," Ambrose (4th century) and Martin Luther (1523)
   NUN KOMM DER HEIDEN HEILAND, Erfurt *Enchiridia* (1524)
   One of the classic Advent hymns to come out of the Lutheran tradition, "Savior of the

Nations, Come" would be appropriate for any of the Advent Sundays. Its stanzas 2 and 3 relate particularly to the Virgin Mary.
3. "O Little Town of Bethlehem," Phillips Brooks (1868)
   FOREST GREEN, trad. Eng. melody; arr. R. V. Williams
   Often associated with the prophecy of Micah (5:2–5a), this familiar Christmas hymn could naturally accompany the Old Testament reading.
4. "Lord, Enthroned in Heavenly Splendor," George Hugh Bourne (1874)
   BRYN CALFARIA, William Owen (1852)
   Stanza 3 of this hymn of worship and adoration relates not only to the Micah prophecy but also to the Epistle reading (Heb. 10:5–10). Stanza 4 refers specifically to the sacrifice made once for all by Christ. The broad setting forth of the Christ event makes this hymn a valuable teaching tool when sung often at worship.—Hugh T. McElrath

WORSHIP AIDS

CALL TO WORSHIP.   "And I heard a great voice out of heaven saying, Behold, the tabernacle of God is with men, and he will dwell with them, and they shall be his people, and God himself shall be with them and be their God" (Rev. 21:3).

INVOCATION.   Father, we are thankful for this world in which we live, for its beauty, its vastness, its supportive wealth, and its many challenges. As we view all the demands of life on this Earth, we are made aware of our littleness. Yet through Christ we know the greatness of your love, which gives worth and meaning to our small lives. This morning as we worship may we find sufficient faith to see you more clearly, sufficient confidence to know that we can worship you only, love strong enough to serve you always, and enough wisdom to acknowledge you as Lord in all of our life's situations.—Henry Fields

OFFERTORY SENTENCE.   "As every man hath received the gift, even so minister the same one to another, as good stewards of the manifold grace of God" (1 Pet. 4:10).

OFFERTORY PRAYER.   Here are our gifts and offerings, Father. We give because you have taught us the power of giving. Pray, may these gifts serve as a blessing to others as they are used to magnify your Kingdom on Earth, we pray in Jesus' name.—Henry Fields

PRAYER.   Loving Father, our hearts are moved to gratitude and trust when we look up to thee. We rejoice that through our fleeting days there runs thy gracious purpose. We praise thee that we are not the creatures of chance, nor the victims of iron fate, but that out from thee we have come and into thy bosom we shall return. We would not, even if we could, escape thee. Thou alone art good, and to escape from thee is to fall into infinite evil. Thy hand is upon us, moving us on to some far-off spiritual event, where the meaning and the mystery of life shall be made plain and thy glory shall be revealed. Look in pity upon our ignorance and childishness. Forgive us our small understanding of thy purpose of good concerning us. Be not angry with us, but draw us from the things of this world which cannot satisfy out foolish hearts. Fill us with thyself, that we may no longer be a burden to our-

selves. So glorify the face of goodness that evil shall have no more dominion over us.—
Samuel McComb[5]

SERMON
Topic: Three Thoughts for Christmas
TEXT: Luke 2:7

When you stop to think of it, it was not a very good time to have a baby. The Jews, as a people and as a nation, were just about on their last legs. Things had been going from bad to worse for several generations. Now they were completely under the thumb of Rome. There was a spirit of discontent among the people; they were restless and they rubbed one another the wrong way. Even the Temple was not what it used to be. People who listened for the voice of the prophets heard only the mumbling of the scribes and Pharisees.

So, a young prospective mother might well have asked herself the question, If the baby happens to be a boy, what future can there be for him in a world like this? Among a small despised people, living under rulers from a great empire far away, what future could there be for him?

Can you think of any better time? Our time, perhaps, that shudders under the shadow of atomic and hydrogen bombs that threaten to wipe out the human race? Our time does not seem to offer a new baby much of a future. What about the nineteenth century? We are accustomed, I think, to looking back in a rather sentimental way at the relative calmness of the nineteenth century. Yet Lincoln, when he went to visit Philadelphia in 1861, said, "The heavens were hung with black." And Matthew Arnold, a serious student of literature and a poet, a little earlier in the century complained that "it is no easy task to be a poet in the nineteenth century." And a Frenchman by the name of Musset summed it all up by saying, "We live surrounded by debris as though the end of the world were at hand." So even the relatively quiet and peaceful nineteenth century does not seem to have been too good a time to bring a baby into the world.

The fact of the matter is, of course, that there is never a completely good time to have a baby. The world is never just the kind of world that you would like to bring a child into. We can go further and say that it is never exactly the right time to do anything good and great. The time is always, to varying degrees, out of joint.

In spite of the fact that it was not a very good time to have a baby, Mary went right ahead and had her baby anyway. The story of the Annunciation, while it may be largely legendary, nevertheless indicates the attitude that was the governing spirit of this young Jewish girl in these bad times. When the angel first told her that she was especially chosen by God, she was perplexed, as any young woman would be. And then, when the angel was more explicit and told her that the child she would bear would be Jesus, the Son of the Most High God, she asked, "How can this be?" But when the angel went on and explained to her how the Spirit of God would rest upon her and use her as a channel for his power, Mary said, "Behold

---

[5]*A Book of Prayers*

the handmaid of the Lord; be it unto me according to thy word." In other words, I am ready. The times may not be just right. All the inconveniences I can think of are in my way. The state of the country is a mess. There is no future that I can see for any child that I may bring into the world, but if that is what God wants me to do, I will do it, and I will do it gladly. I will pour into it all my gift of tenderness and motherhood, sacrifice and care, just as if the future were as clear as the sun at midday.

So she went on her way, as the story tells us, and did the best she could. She could not have the baby in her own home, but she might find an inn. The inn was full when they got there, but the innkeeper was a kind and understanding man and let them have a place in the stable. That would do, if that was the best there was. When the child was born, she kept him warm and close. That is what a mother is supposed to do.

A great many of us in these days are making a considerable struggle and effort to live a decent life, and it is not easy. There are too many influences that weaken the foundations of our lives, that invite us to live on lower levels. We are tempted, all of us I think at times, to say—to ourselves, at least, if we do not say it to other people—What's the use?

But there are other people who take the point of view more nearly like that of Mary, and they realize instinctively that in spite of all the threats to civilization and to the life we know, life goes magnificently and irresistibly on. Young people still fall in love, no matter what happens, and babies are born, and families are kept going, and difficulties are met, dared, and defined, with a heroism that appalls you when you see it. Discoveries are still made and appointments with destiny are still kept. When we recall these things, we say to ourselves, The times are not good, to be sure. They are never just the way I should like to have them, but I am made to meet the times and to rise above the times, and to ride them the way a ship rides the waves. To be sure, the times are never quite right, but it's not the times, it's the person that counts.

Yes, Mary went right ahead and had her baby in spite of the times, and her baby was the Savior of the world. Think of it! Just when the Jews were on their last legs, Jesus came. The finest flower of their race, after the garden had been all but given over to the weeds.

If we were not so familiar with that fact, it would startle us, stun us with its intimation of renewal. It implies all sorts of things about the powers and energies and vitalities of God. It is as though we read that just when an old civilization is about to fall, a new one is born. One chapter ends and another begins. That is usually the way things happen to us individually. Not always, but very often.

So, I think we can say, with fair consideration for the facts and with reasonable resistance to the temptation to be sentimental at this time of year, when life looks as though it were ready to break down, it is most likely to bring forth something new. Let the idea open the doors of the future for you. Do not ever talk about the closed chapters of your life. There are no closed chapters, for one chapter as it closes leads into the opening of another. Do not ever talk about the finished symphonies of the world, for there are no finished symphonies. Just when you think the end has come, God has a new idea!

That is why there is a joy about Christmas that is undefeatable and that undergirds all our surface sadness. It is the promise—it is more than a promise—it is the demonstration of the indomitability of the life of God. And its message is, at least one of its messages is, that no matter how near things seem to be to dust and ashes, there are always reserves in God's storehouse, and he will have a new idea and bring forth something new any moment.

These are the three thoughts: The times are never exactly right. It is not the times, it is *you* that counts. When life looks as though it were about to break down, it is most likely to bring forth something new and wonderful. For there is always to be found somewhere some obedient, yielding servant of God who brings forth the new life, and wraps it in swaddling clothes, and lays it tenderly in a manger.—Theodore Parker Ferris

SUNDAY, DECEMBER 28, 2003
Lectionary Message

First Sunday After Christmas

Topic: Where Is Home?

TEXT: Luke 2:41–52

Other Readings: 1 Sam. 2:18–20, 26; Ps. 148; Col. 3:12–17

Luke bridges the information about the birth of Jesus and the reports of the adult Jesus in his ministry with the paragraph that is our text for today. The final summary, "And Jesus increased in wisdom and in years, and in divine and human favor," follows the report that stands as the only specific information in our New Testament about the childhood of Jesus. There are several details in this account on which we can profitably concentrate.

I. *The family of Joseph and Mary were regular attendees at the Temple.* The law of Israel stipulates that whenever possible Jewish men were to worship in the Jerusalem Temple at three festivals each year. The one that became obligatory was the Passover festival. Luke tells us, "Every year his parents went to Jerusalem for the festival of the Passover." Women were not obliged to attend, but they often did, and we are told here that both Joseph and Mary were accustomed to attending.

We can assume that Jesus had made the seventy-mile trip to Jerusalem from Nazareth several times before this time when he was twelve years old. We can also assume that he and his parents were active in the synagogue in Nazareth, where Jesus would have been under instruction by a rabbi to prepare for his *bar mitzvah,* when he would become an adult, responsible for keeping the Law of God.

II. *It would not be surprising that a bright Jewish boy from a strict Jewish family would have questions about his religion when he visited the Temple.* What seems to be surprising in this account is the depth and breadth of the questions that Jesus was asking, and of the wisdom of the answers he was giving to the counterquestions of the teachers in the Temple.

Mary and Joseph had been so confident of Jesus' good behavior that they assumed he was with them in the caravan somewhere and would turn up when they stopped for the night. When he didn't turn up they were understandably upset and returned to the city to search for him. Every parent will understand Mary's strong rebuke of her son when they finally located him in the Temple. The Law, after all, states that children are to be obedient to their parents. And Luke notes at the end of the account that he "was obedient to them."

So Jesus was not just asserting his independence by staying in the Temple. There was something bigger than that going on. It was something that appears to have puzzled both Jesus and his parents. He was surprised that they would need to search for him. They were confused by his statement that he must be in his Father's place, busy with his Father's stuff.

Jesus felt at home in the Temple. He was quite comfortable with the educated leaders of his people. He seemed to belong there.

III. *When John the Baptist preached, people recognized that this world was not their home—that God was at work trying to change things.* When Jesus preached people caught glimpses of what he called "the Kingdom of God." And there in the Temple courts, surrounded by great teachers of God's Word, the boy Jesus felt at home. The one who would become the ultimate revelation of the reality and redemption of God was learning from the teachers and amazing them with his wisdom. I wonder what they thought about this boy.

What might they have said to one another after Jesus was led off by Mary and Joseph? Did they remember the story of the young Samuel brought to the Temple by his mother and left there with Eli, the priest? Did they recall that Samuel's parents also came to the Temple each year? Did they expect to hear from Jesus again when he grew up? Might they have recommended that he study with Gamaliel or some other outstanding teacher in Jerusalem?

Might some of these same teachers have been present later when Jesus drove the merchants and money-changers out of the Temple with the words, "It is written, 'My house shall be a house of prayer,' but you have made it a den of robbers" (Luke 19:46)? In contrast to many of the Temple officials, Jesus seems never to have lost the idealism of his youth about the Jerusalem Temple.

IV. *And what about us?* What do we make of this boy-man who seems to be so intimate with God? How comfortable do we feel around him? Doesn't it seem weird or at least outdated to hear somebody talking about the Kingdom of God all the time? Does it give us the creeps to hear about confrontations with demons? And why does he seem to pick on the religious people so much? If even his parents didn't understand, why are we surprised when we don't understand Jesus?

Could that be the point? We don't understand Jesus because nearly everything that surrounds us is alien to him. We don't understand Jesus because the weight of our culture bends us away from him. We don't understand Jesus because we have been educated to see everything from the point of view of this world. We don't understand Jesus because he was constantly in touch with another world—the world where God rules. Jesus was at home in the Temple; we are at home in the marketplace. Because Jesus was most at home in the Temple, he was comfortable everywhere. Because we are at home in the marketplace, we are rarely completely comfortable anywhere.

Isn't it time that we were at home in our Father's house? Jesus invites us to come home right now.—Bruce E. Shields

ILLUSTRATION

GOD'S PRESENCE.   A study of the Temple in Jerusalem at the time of Jesus will suggest many ways to describe the Temple scene so that people can visualize it. Most important, the consciousness of the presence of God that the Temple elicited is central to this sermon.—Bruce E. Shields

SERMON SUGGESTIONS

Topic: The Ways of a Christlike Life
TEXT: Isa. 50:4–9a
(1) Listening to God. (2) Obeying God. (3) Suffering for God. (4) Trusting in God's vindication.

Topic: A Glory to Sing About

TEXT: Phil. 2:5–11

(1) Glory possessed. (2) Glory relinquished. (3) Glory earned. (4) Glory acclaimed.

CONGREGATIONAL MUSIC

1. "O Come, All Ye Faithful," John F. Wade (c. 1743); trans. Frederick Oakley (1841)

    ADESTE FIDELIS, John F. Wade (1792)

    Christmas hymns and carols are appropriate for use throughout Christmastide. This hymn, one of the most beloved, constitutes a meaningful call to worship for the season.

2. "Joy to the World," Isaac Watts (1719)

    ANTIOCH, G. F. Handel (1741)

    No Christmas celebration would be considered complete without singing this classic hymn by the father of English hymnody. Based on a portion of Psalm 98, "Joy to the World" need not be confined to worship in the Christmas season, however.

3. "Praise the Lord! O Heavens, Adore Him," Ps. 148; vers. *The Foundling Hospital Collection* (1796)

    AUSTRIAN HYMN, Franz J. Haydn (1797)

    The performance of this free paraphrase of Psalm 148 would be a meaningful substitute for the Psalter reading for this day.

4. "O Sing a Song of Bethlehem," Louis F. Benson (1899)

    KINGSFOLD, trad. Eng. melody; arr. R. V. Williams (1906)

    This late nineteenth-century American hymn celebrates the entire Christ event from birth to death and Resurrection. Appropriate for Christmas worship, it also relates to Jesus' boyhood life (stanza 2) and thus could be sung in connection with the Gospel lesson (Luke 2:4–52).

5. This Christmas Sunday is also the best opportunity to sing selections from a great plethora of Christmas carols, such as "Angels We Have Heard on High," "Infant Holy, Infant Lowly," "The First Noel," "Good Christian Friends, Rejoice," and "What Child Is This?" among many others.—Hugh T. McElrath

WORSHIP AIDS

CALL TO WORSHIP.   "Praise ye the Lord. Sing unto the Lord a new song, and his praise in the congregation of the saints" (Ps. 149:1).

INVOCATION.   Lord, get through to us as never before. Turn doubt into faith and struggle into joy. Keep us on the right track. Lead us where we need to go. Fill us in worship for service. In Christ's holy name.—E. Lee Phillips

OFFERTORY SENTENCE.   "And when they were come into the house, they saw the young child with Mary his mother and fell down and worshiped him. And when they had opened their treasures, they presented unto him gifts: gold, frankincense, and myrrh" (Matt. 2:11).

OFFERTORY PRAYER.   Lord, disperse our gifts to proclaim the Messiah's birth so that every human heart may respond to the love that never stops coming to us.—E. Lee Phillips

PRAYER.   God our Father, you see your children growing up in an unsteady and confusing world: Show them that your ways give more life than the ways of the world, and that following you is better than chasing after selfish goals. Help them to take failure not as a measure of their worth but as a chance for a new start. Give them strength to hold their faith in you, and to keep alive their joy in your creation; through Jesus Christ our Lord.—*The Book of Common Prayer*

SERMON
Topic: The Mysterious Fact of Resurrection
TEXT: John 1:4–5

"In him was life, and the life was the light of men. And the light shineth in darkness, and the darkness has never put it out." These are two verses from the grand prologue of St. John's Gospel (1:4, 5). He began his Gospel by setting the background of the story he was about to tell, the story of Jesus of Nazareth. But the setting was not the events that were taking place in Rome and Jerusalem; not the names of emperors, kings, and governors who were in power at the time of the action. The setting was eternity. If it were ever set to music, the direction would be *maestoso,* with majesty.

"In him was life, and the life was the light of men." There are different kinds of light. There is the natural light of the sun, by which the world around us comes back to life every morning, almost miraculously, each object resuming its shape, and the color we thought the darkness had drained out of it once again bright. By it we know where we are, and we can see where we are going. Sometimes the way is beautiful and sometimes it is ugly.

Also, there is the natural light of the moon—not so powerful as the light of the sun, and if clouds come across it we can't see it at all. But when we can see it, we sometimes see a beauty that is almost unearthly, particularly if the moon is full and the night is clear.

Then there is what we might call "artificial light," beginning first with the light of a candle set in the middle of a room to make at least a center of light so that the family could see what they were eating. Then came the gas lamp, and finally the incandescent bulb. Now, with electricity, we can light our cities so that they are sometimes brighter at midnight than they are at midday—alas, too bright for some of us! And by this artificial light signals start and stop the trains and the automobiles, and warn the pilots on their flights.

But there is another kind of light, the light of a life. Picture a room at night, already well lit. Into it steps a person. The minute he enters the room it is brilliant, as it wasn't before. His presence makes it bright. It's the light of a person's life.

This is the kind of light that Jesus is. It was the life that was in his life that was the light of men. He lived simply, but he lived intensely. At times he burned with a white heat. His love overflowed, so to speak; he could not contain it. Everything he touched was more alive. He gave sight to the blind—not only the blind who couldn't see because their eyes were gone, but also the others, many more in number, who couldn't see because they were in the dark.

They were in the dark about so many things. They were in the dark about themselves—they didn't quite know who they were, especially in the presence of God. He said to them, you are servants; you don't need to bow and scrape in the presence of God. You are his friends, his children. Stand up!

They were in the dark about their neighbors. Who were they? He tried to tell them. Your neighbor, he said, is not the one you like the most, not necessarily the one who lives next door to you, or the one who agrees with you. You have a natural affinity with those people, but your neighbor is the one who needs you the most.

They were in the dark about failure. They thought that failure was a disgrace. It is now in the eyes of many of our people. But he was saying to them, don't forget that failure of a certain kind may be the way to let the light through. And suffering—so many people were (and are) in the dark about suffering. They thought it was something sent to them, directed to them personally by God, and usually as punishment for something they had done or not done. By his own suffering Jesus showed them that suffering is the price you pay for being the person you are. If you are any kind of person at all you will suffer, and the way you do it may be something like the light that was in Christ. *In him was life, and the life was the light of men.*

This was not the darkness of ignorance through the long night of barbarian darkness that came down like tidal waves from northern Europe in the fifth, sixth, seventh, eighth, and ninth centuries. That darkness, you would think, would have extinguished any light that Jesus might once have lit; but there were groups of monks here and there who kept it burning. It was dim, but it didn't go out.

This was not the darkness of wealth and power in the thirteenth century. The church of Europe was so drenched with wealth and power that it almost forgot what it was there for. But even that darkness didn't put out the light entirely, because there was a little Italian who went up and down singing about the Lord Jesus. He possessed nothing, yet had all things. Thousands of men and women were drawn to his light.

And in eighteenth-century England, the established Church was almost in total darkness. John Wesley rode up and down the land and wherever he went the light began to shine!

What is more surprising, perhaps, is that even now, in this secular, materialistic, violent, cynical age in which we live, and in which every value that a Christian holds dear has been attacked, challenged, or just ignored, there is a life in Jesus that is light, and the young will not let it go.

This is the key sentence of the sermon: *The Resurrection of Jesus remains the most mysterious fact in human history.* How could it happen? How did it happen? Did it actually happen, or did it take place in the inspired imagination of devout followers? Was it the fulfillment of an extravagant desire?

What is relevant in the New Testament is the men and women who walk through its pages—Peter, Paul, John, Barnabas, Mark, and Luke. A slave like Onesimus—do you know anything about him? A couple like Priscilla and Aquilla. A young girl like Rhoda, so excited that she didn't even let Peter in when he knocked at the door until she had gone to tell her family that he was there, just out of prison. And the prison guards in Rome. Do you remember what happened to them?

One thing they all had in common, different as they were, was that they were all once in the dark and were now in the light. And the light was not a brighter sun or better weather or even a better government or better schools or a more adequately administered welfare system. The light was the light that was in Christ, that not even the darkness of death could put out and now shone across their way.

But you may say, I have never met the Risen Lord on my way to work or in any other place for that matter. Neither have I. If you mean a person walking up the street with pierced hands and feet, I've never met him. Some have, but I never have. But if you mean the life that takes hold of a person and changes him from a self-centered brat into a companionable, loving human being—I've seen him.

I have met that life. In fact, I think if it weren't for him I'd give up. For the darkness of life is deep and powerful. I cannot face it alone. I can face it because I know that in him is life, and that the life is the light of men, and that the light shines in the darkness and the darkness has never yet been able to put it out. In fact, it is shining here now!—Theodore Parker Ferris

MESSAGES FOR COMMUNION SERVICES

SERMON SUGGESTIONS

Topic: Supper of Assurance

TEXT: Mark 14:45; Matt. 26:29

Sometimes, I try to imagine the early Church's participation in the Lord's Supper. I find myself wishing that somehow we could recapture some of the excitement and deep meaning this meal held for Christians living and ministering in a hostile environment. They met to keep this meal because their Lord had commanded that they do so; they met to remember his words and acts, especially those of the night on which he was betrayed and arrested. Further, they met to celebrate his powerful presence in their midst. This shared meal had meaning that one outside the Christian fellowship could not begin to understand.

But I am convinced that the early Christians met and ate the Lord's meal together for another reason: *They met together in order to gain assurance and encouragement for the difficult and dangerous adventure of being Christ's followers.* I can see them as they exhorted one another, as they shared their experiences, and as they gave support by listening in sympathetic friendship. But I think they gained their greatest assurance—a renewed confidence that sent them out to face severe threats with courage—from something Jesus said that night in the upper room before his arrest and death.

The more I think about the scene, the more incredible it becomes. Jesus stood on the edge of the dark chasm of a crisis that would end in his death. Human hounds were dogging his steps, intent on spilling his blood. Jesus had arranged for a final few hours alone with his disciples in order that he might attempt to prepare them for what was coming immediately— and beyond. One thing was certain in his mind: the terrible Roman cross awaited him. Now, unless we make Jesus' humanity a game of "let's pretend," dying at the hands of those who hated him was an experience filled with all the agony and threat imaginable. Indeed, such an experience was even more agonizing for one who was giving himself up voluntarily in order to draw people to God. We can turn over a few pages in the New Testament and read about the Resurrection; we can turn to the last verses of Luke or the first chapter of Acts and read about the Ascension. But to one living the drama of redemption, what loomed ahead for sure was a cross and a tomb.

But let me go back a minute. I said that one thing, death, was certain in Jesus' mind there in the upper room. Actually, two things were certain to him. The other was that *beyond his death, God's purpose would win.* For in talking with his disciples, he said something about drinking no more fruit of the vine until he would drink it fresh in the Kingdom of God. His words betrayed his thoughts; he had no doubt that God's activity in the world on behalf of people would come out as God meant for it to come out. Nothing or nobody could prevent God from realizing his redemptive purpose.

From the tone and content of Jesus' conversation, this meal was no final farewell! A note of sadness was in his words, for the former relationship with his apostles was to end soon. He would no longer walk the dusty trails of Palestine with them; he would no longer teach them, discipline them, and inspire them by his unusual deeds. But instead of a farewell, the time in the upper room was a new beginning. Instead of defeat, what was about to happen on Golgotha would be victory! Beyond the events about to descend so rapidly and with such crushing force, much more was to come.

The disciples were familiar with the Jewish belief in a messianic banquet at the end of the age. The Last Supper was both a foretaste of that kind of fellowship and a pledge that no matter how present circumstances might appear, Jesus' separation from his disciples was only temporary. On the other side of seeming defeat would be glorious triumph. On the far side of death awaited a third day and Resurrection.

Halford Luccock wrote that because of Jesus' confidence in ultimate victory, because of his reassuring words in the darkest of hours, the Lord's Supper was a celebration to the early Christians. It was a joyous occasion—not a look back at tragedy "but a [look] forward to victory and the consummation of a kingdom."[1]

As we come to place ourselves in the context of Christ's suffering and dying for us, his words speak to us. Again, Halford Luccock affirmed that dark hours occur in everybody's experience. Dark hours come in the history of civilization. When these hours come, he wrote, "The only life possible is life with an immanent sense of death at the door."[2] Then people easily drift into a defeatist attitude. In our times of personal doubt and sense of defeat, we need the reassurance of Christ's words, which expressed his own deep, personal confidence.

A touching revelation to me as a parent has been that children sometimes come to their parents wanting nothing more than a reassuring touch or word—proof that the parents are still there and still love them, and that everything is going to be all right. As humbly as children, we come to these sacred moments to experience the reassuring presence of one who said that he would be with his followers to the end of the age. We come reverently into the presence of one who professed and proved his love by every word and act of his life—and by his death.

We come to have our confidence renewed—our confidence that no matter what present indications may seem to be, we are aligned with God's victorious push in history. We who follow Christ are on the winning team because on the other side of difficulties, dangers, threats, and failures is ultimate victory through our capable leader. He is the pioneer of our salvation, the author and finisher of our faith.

Despite all of its problems from without and from within, the Church will be led to triumph. Its strength is not to be traced to human sources but to God, who wills to use it as an instrument of redemption.

And so we come to participate in the Lord's Supper in order to strengthen our confidence in the victory of love over wrong, assured by the God who does not fail. And we come to express our gratitude that our lives have been given that creative assurance.—Eli Landrum Jr.[3]

---

[1]Halford Luccock, *The Interpreter's Bible*, vol. 7, p. 878.
[2]Luccock, p. 878.
[3]*More Than Symbol* (Nashville: Broadman Press, 1983), pp. 40–43.

Topic: Our Mundane Concerns
TEXT: Matt. 6:11; Luke 24:28–35

Bread is seldom just bread. The unleavened bread of the Exodus was a symbol of haste in the flight from Egypt. Leaven thus became a symbol of sin. In the wilderness God provided Israel with manna from heaven, which met the people at the center of two basic needs—hunger for food and hunger for the presence of God. The temptation of Jesus to change stones into bread in the midst of a forty-day fast seems to represent the place of physical appetite in the spiritual nature, while the forty days is a definite reminder of the wilderness experience of Israel. Why not turn straw into gold or some other violation of physics to fill some ravenous human appetite? For Israel, bread had long stood as a symbol of the basic substance of life—to fill both the stomach and the soul. The multiplication of loaves in the feeding of the multitude and the sequential identification of Jesus in John as the "bread which comes down from heaven" reflect on both the physical and the spiritual hungers of life. The unleavened bread of the Passover became the symbol of the body of Christ in the Lord's Supper, and finally the Risen Christ was known to the disciples on the Emmaus Road, "in the breaking of the bread." The symbolism of the Lord's Supper may well be implied in every reference to bread or wine in the New Testament.

When Jesus taught us to pray, "Give us this day our daily bread," he reminded us of the enormous appetites that dominate our existence, at both the physical and the spiritual level. Basic facts of life and rich biblical symbolism stand behind this petition.

I. We need bread. On the surface, the petition for bread identifies a basic human need that everyone can understand and appreciate. Are we not consumed by our need for bread—not just enough to keep us well, but enough for a long and comfortable retirement? I shared an apartment for two years with a business major at Baylor. The difference between us was not as radical as one might assume. Many of our discussions of the Church and the corporation found common ground, and periodically some enthusiastic pastor let our true concern for bread slip out with "The Church is the biggest business in the world." My friend came home one day chuckling about a management class. The personnel officer in a local business had inquired of the business school professor about the anxiety among young job applicants over retirement benefits. He wondered why young people needed to be so burdened about the very distant future. I thought of the commentary of Jesus, "Do not worry about tomorrow, for tomorrow will bring worries of its own. Today's trouble is enough for today." The challenge to our anxiety comes within the same address, in the same chapter as the prayer for daily bread, with the acknowledgment that the Father "knows that you need all these things."

Fasting was an ancient way of worship. Through physical denial one reinforced the importance of the spiritual side of life. Most of us could stand to adopt the practice of the fast for the sake of physical health. We are probably more in need, physically and spiritually, of fasting than we are of food. However, involuntary fasting through famine or war can be a terrible barrier to the deeper hunger of the soul. With James, telling our hungry neighbor to be filled is not the same as sharing our bread. When we pray for daily bread, we must be aware of the tragedy of hunger in this world.

II. We do not live by bread alone. We have needs that far exceed the demands of our stomachs. Scholars tend to agree that the petition for bread may be eschatological—"Give us tomorrow's bread today." Jerome was certain that wanting tomorrow's bread was a reach toward the age of salvation, the bread of life. The bread and water of life had long been associated with paradise, and Jesus looked toward the end when he declared that he would eat and drink with his disciples in the consummation.

I got into a conversation with an associate pastor over the terrible taste of the commercial bread we use at the Lord's Supper. This sent us off into experiments with a common loaf, a Kosher matzo, and finally back to the little boxes of white plaster that threaten your teeth and stick in your throat. I have never gotten enough to eat at the Lord's Supper, but I have been fed in ways that no food could begin to satisfy. Maybe the taste of the bread is not as important as the meaning. Jesus needed to eat as much as we do, but when his disciples expressed concern for his nutritional needs, he said that his food is to do the will of God. In counting the appetites of life, let us remember the deep hunger of the soul for God.

"Pass the bread, please." This casual, almost unconscious request at the family table becomes the primary concern of the Church in the world. God feeds hungry stomachs and hungry spirits through the generosity of the ones who pray for daily bread. Have you met the messengers of God in the answers to prayer? Our bread never floats down from heaven. It comes to us through a community of mutual dependence. There was a time when we could not feed ourselves through either the production of food or the mechanical ingestion of food. We were dependent on our parents and family. They were the messengers of God in our need for daily bread. The day may come when we will be as dependent on our children as they were on us. In the final act of John, Jesus allowed stubborn, independent Peter a glimpse into the future, when he would be dependent on others. We cannot ignore the connection to the repeated request of Peter, "Feed my sheep." Like the child who offered his lunch in response to the call of Christ and the need of the multitude, we are called by God to pass the bread as we pray, "Give us this day our daily bread."—Larry Dipboye

Topic: As One with Authority
TEXT: Matt. 7:28–29

The sermon is finished, the benediction is pronounced—it's time to go home. Matthew became the Arthur Gallup of the Evangelists. He slipped into the skin of the listeners to gather a response. This reading may contain the gathered opinion of all of the reactions Matthew had ever heard about Jesus, or it may be a specific response to the teaching of Jesus about new life in the Kingdom. Actually, it is a direct quotation of Mark about the response of people to the healing ministry of Jesus.

In a word, people were astounded. Jesus was not like the legalists of his time. He spoke with authority. I once heard a cynical evaluation of a popular preacher: "He has never spoken a word he has not read." That evaluation would fit the scribes. The Word of God in the Law was final. Nothing could be added to it. No creativity on the part of an interpreter was even possible. Scribal religion never offered a new insight or a fresh word. Religion was primarily a semantical game, splitting hairs and turning words. Jesus came along and contrasted the standing interpretation of the Law and the spirit of the Law, punctuated with "but I say." When Jesus offered a fresh new word, he would begin with, "Amen, I say to you." He spoke as one who knew the mind of God, and he addressed his audience as people with minds to comprehend and wills to choose. He spoke with authority. Everyone knows that public opinion does not determine truth. The problem of authority is timeless. People tend to respond to authority with either complete cynicism or mindless credulity.

I. *Authority—especially religious authority—has a bad reputation.* All human words and actions are temporal and subject to failure. Lord Acton's maxim, "Power corrupts; absolute power corrupts absolutely," is a familiar warning to people who believe in democracy. Power corrupts because people are fallible. When a political cartoonist draws a negative caricature of the president, he crowns the chief executive and drapes him in royal robes. This nation was founded on the premise that no one person has either the ability or the right to govern the nation. The fallibility of all humankind is basic to our understanding of authority. We tolerate the rule of law and the authority of police because the law of the judge is worse. Order is better than chaos, and the rule of law is better than "might makes right." Yet the rule of law is always imperfect. Makers and officers of the law are subject to seduction by power.

We are in danger of total cynicism. Life is about raising idols to see them topple from the pedestal of our worship. Our age has become a shooting gallery for idols.

II. *The abuse of authority is an opportunity created by the people.* Maybe people worship too easily. How does a despotic ruler like Adolf Hitler manage to gain control of a nation? Hitler's evil would have flickered and died without popular support. A greater wonder than Hitler is the persistent desire of people to be controlled and to be deceived. Tyrants are not born; they are made. They are raised not only by the misdirected worship of the seduced and the exploited but also by the silence of the fearful and the apathetic. Although Matthew's evaluation was positive, not everything about the popular need to follow is good. In the fourth Gospel, Jesus refused the attempt of the people to crown him king. The accounts of his passion agree that the charge "King of the Jews" was attached to the cross.

I find myself in the uncomfortable place of calling the church to worship but having to warn against worshiping too easily. Worship alone is not good. Worship directed toward false deity is corrupt. Christian faith is never gullible. Christ does not call us, as Alice in Wonderland was called, to believe in impossible things. We are called by John to test the spirits to determine whether they are of God. Worship never rises higher than the name of your god.

III. *The authority of Christ is in response.* The authority of Jesus was something more than a powerful delivery or presumptuous manner. It certainly did not rest in the raw power of force or wealth. Listen to the sermon. It is far from a call to blind obedience. Jesus called people to take a deep look at themselves, their neighbors, and the Word of God. He called for response based on motives and understanding. Prohibition may prevent murder, but control of one's anger will control the hatred that produces murder. We are free from the simple rule of law but under the more demanding rule of conscience and principle. We become responsible for our actions. We are responsible to God and neighbor rather than to a collection of words. Jesus moved authority from the external control of institutions and rules to the internal control of principle and decision.

W. D. Davies offered an opinion on the difference between Luke's Sermon on the Plain and Matthew's Sermon on the Mount. More than Matthew, Luke may have been trying to paint a portrait of Jesus as the new Moses coming down from the mountain with the new law. If that is true, I like what Matthew did. He had Jesus take the people to the mountain with him. Jesus came down without tablets of stone, but the people came down filled to the brim with a new responsibility before God and a new understanding of life in the Kingdom. Jeremiah's promise was fulfilled: "I will put my law within them, and I will write it on their hearts."—Larry Dipboye

Topic: Remembered Hope
TEXT: Heb. 11:39–12:2; 1 Cor. 11:23–26

The newspaper feature article was about the first woman Holocaust survivor to be ordained a rabbi. Helga Newmark grew up in the neighborhood where Anne Frank lived. She remembers Anne Frank as a bossy child. Like other Jews, Helga's family was herded into freight trains and transported to the Nazi camps. Her father was soon separated from Helga and her mother. She learned later that he was sent to his death in the gas chambers of Auschwitz. After she and her mother survived the Holocaust, Helga recalls, "I needed to talk about it, but my mother didn't want to hear or ever talk about it again." Following her mother's lead she attempted to bury the past, and along with her memories, she rejected her Jewish roots and her Jewish God. But the memories were too vivid to be suppressed. As she remembered, she began to heal, to seek out the God she had left behind in the death camps, and to allow the question "Where was God?" to arise.

The story of Helga Newmark is about something more than being the first woman Holocaust survivor rabbi. It is about remembered hope. It is about redemption from haunting memories. It is about the move from despair to faith, from deliberate amnesia to decisive faith in God. Helga Newmark had to remember before she could hope. I believe this is a natural sequence for all of us.

I. *The Lord's Supper is a call to remember.* This story is about another rabbi who passed through a personal holocaust. I doubt that any of the Twelve wanted pictures of the Crucifixion to hang on their living room walls, or to participate in groups where the gory details were established and recorded for posterity. We naturally want to shut out horrible memories. It is part of the natural anesthesia in our biological structure. From selective amnesia to a catatonic trance, our minds want to escape from memories that distract us from the duties of daily existence. No healthy person really enjoys pain. Just as we avoid touching a hot stove, we avoid remembering a tragic event in our lives. The last thing any of the witnesses to the cross would have wanted to remember was the horror that began with the arrest of Jesus, and some people are critical of the sadistic violence represented in the Gospels.

Helga Newmark tells of the release of her memories. She was stopped at a railroad crossing watching a freight train pass when suddenly she began to relive the smells and the screams of her childhood journey into hell.

Memories are not so easily suppressed. In 1951, Dr. Wilder Penfield, a neurosurgeon from McGill University in Montreal began a series of experiments that led to the conclusion that the human brain is able to collect in minute detail all of our experiences of life. Dr. Penfield was able to stimulate his patients' memories and emotions about events long lost from their conscious minds. The key is not the capacity to remember; it is the means to recall the memory. Some believe that the mind is loaded with detailed memories of all of our conscious experiences, perhaps even going back to the womb. Tennyson's *Ulysses* declared, "I am a part of all that I have met." All of us are the sum total of our experiences without regard to the good and the evil they represent.

I am sometimes amazed at the advanced understanding represented in the Gospels. Luke and Paul specifically recall the language of the institution of the Lord's Supper as a call to remember. Jesus was opening the door of the memory to let the horror rise to meet the healing grace of God. Go ahead and remember. You cannot shut out real memories. The experiences of our lives play back in our dreams, in our conscious thoughts, and in the acting out of the fears and frustrations emerging from the depths of our souls. Expose the darkness of evil and suffering to the light of God's eternal love. Taste and see that the Lord is good.

II. *The Lord's Supper is a call to hope.* Every time we gather at this table we recover a part of ourselves, the total memory of the people of God through the ages. As a priest, Luther remembered the fear of the Lord's Supper and the awful responsibility for the body and blood of our Lord. I get goose bumps over the distance we span when we repeat the same statement that has dominated the life of the saints through nearly two millennia of shared memory, but that is not the end of it. Every time we break the bread and drink the cup, we proclaim the good news; and we cast our faith toward the future, the coming of the Kingdom of God.

The lines in Hebrews sound sad—"All of these died in faith without having received the promises"—but they are words of hope. "God had provided something better so that they would not, apart from us, be made perfect." The champions of faith paraded out of the Old Testament do not stand alone. If this is just an exercise in nostalgia, forget it. We are reminded that we are rooted in the faithful who have gone before us, and their unfinished business has been passed on to us. They are fulfilled by what we do. All of us together look to Christ as the inspiration to keep on going. Jesus is not buried somewhere in our history. He stands before us as the fulfillment of our hope and of God's dream for the world.

Because God has spoken a final word in Christ, we can allow our memories to rise. Just as we can celebrate what God was doing in Christ, we can celebrate the lives of the saints of God who have gone before us. Even when the memories are too painful to be released, we can face the darkness through the light of God that has been given in Christ.

Jesus gave us the Lord's Supper as a memorial—"Do this in remembrance of me"—but please don't mistake our gathering around this table as a trip to the cemetery or a nostalgic evening with the family picture album. This is a day of celebration of our eternal hope in God.—Larry Dipboye

Topic: The Lord's Presence—in Others
TEXT: Gen. 1:26–31

God is present in other people. He is present not only in the lives of the saints, but in the lives of all kinds of people:

- Brilliant and educated people like the apostle Paul, John Calvin, and E. Y. Mullins
- Uneducated people like William Carey, the cobbler, and William Booth, the pawnbroker's assistant
- Famous people like Billy Graham, and obscure people like the unknown preacher whose sermon touched the heart of Charles Haddon Spurgeon

James Carter contends that God uses all kinds of people. The only requirement is their willingness to be used.

I spoke to the Rotary Club in Kannapolis, North Carolina. The retired superintendent of schools told me this story: There was a preacher at one of the Baptist churches who "couldn't preach a lick," but he dearly loved people. The preacher brought an eighth-grade dropout to the superintendent. The superintendent arranged a two-year course for the young man to graduate. The youth went on to college and seminary, receiving a doctor of philosophy degree. He later taught Christian ethics at Stetson University and the Southern Baptist Theological Seminary. His name? Henlee H. Barnette. God uses all sorts of people. Boris Pasternak reminded us that in the Kingdom of God there are only persons.

We believe that the Lord is in people because human beings were made in the image of God. This means we have freedom of choice, and we have the capacity to know our Maker.

The Incarnation is further proof that God is present in people. "In Christ God was reconciling the world to himself" (2 Cor. 5:19). God was uniquely present, enfleshed in Jesus.

The indwelling of God in believers also speaks of the divine presence: "Christ in you, the hope of glory" (Col. 1:27).

Jesus' priority was people. He placed them above institutions and their observances—even religious institutions such as the Temple, and observances such as the Sabbath. Jesus was always willing to take time with people. He put people first.

Ours is a corporate faith, not simply an individual one. We are members of the family of God and priests to one another. Recall who led you to Christ, baptized you, taught you, encouraged you, and prayed for you.

Yes, God is present—in others.—Alton H. McEachern[4]

Topic: Come, Lord Jesus!
TEXT: Rev. 22:17–21

Did you see the meteorite shower? I was making my final pass through my sermon when Carolyn called me outside at 5:30 A.M. I had forgotten about the cosmic event announced on the news the day before. I moved quickly, with full expectation of finding some great catastrophe. Maybe the dog had died or the house was on fire or the plumbing was broken. The list went on. I hadn't heard the phone ring, and I was certain we did not have a family crisis. If you were out, you saw for yourself: streaks of light were racing across the sky in a cosmic fireworks show like I had never seen before.

Especially in the years immediately following the death and Resurrection of Christ, I think the early Christians must have spent a large part of their time watching the heavens. As I watched the shower, I wondered how the Christians of the first decade would have interpreted this heavenly demonstration. If they had seen what we saw, they probably would have assumed that this was *it*. In Acts the disciples were gazing at the Ascension of Jesus when they were asked by two men in white robes why they were staring at the heavens. Jesus would come again the same way he ascended. They were to go about the daily business of the Kingdom. A watched pot never boils, and watched heavens never move. As you wait for this coming, do the work of the Kingdom. No one knows the hour or the season. They are

---

[4]*The Lord's Presence* (Nashville: Broadman Press, 1986), pp. 25–26.

not important. What is important is to be obedient to the Great Commission and ready for the coming of God.

I recall my grandmother's story about a strange heavenly phenomenon. It was probably Halley's Comet. She said that people in the rural community where she lived were crying, singing hymns, praying out loud, and screaming in terror in the streets. Without a clear warning of the cosmic display, they were left to their own interpretation of the heavenly signs. They assumed the worst: the Day of the Lord—Judgment Day, the end of time—had come.

The destruction of the World Trade Center buildings in New York had a similar effect on many of us. All of the warnings about the end attributed to Christ in the Gospels come to mind as our world experiences earthquakes, storms, floods, wars, and rumors of wars. Folks who have been around a while usually do not panic. They do not interpret every strange event in history to be the end. After a while, most of us learn to take our crises in stride and go about our business.

Well, at least we have the diversion of Christmas. What a nice escape from the troubles of the world! We can hide from the panic and fear of the daily news to reflect on the world of our imagination. The story of a peasant child born in Bethlehem to unmarried parents, the revelation to shepherds in the field, visitations of angels, and the songs of aging prophets allow us to take flight from terrorists, battles, and anthrax. The real is no longer important; only our imaginations or illusions of the real matter. We call it virtual reality; it does not bite or bark or bomb.

Advent is neither escape nor despair at the terrors of the real world. Advent is about the coming of God. The waiting and watching never end. God is not finished. Advent reminds Christians that our hope in Christ is not over and done with. We live by faith in the coming of the Lord.

I. *The end is the beginning.* The Revelation, the final book of our Bible, begins with a salutation from God that grace and peace come from the one "who is and who was and who is to come" (1:4). After a doxology to the Christ, the reader is called to the heavenly vision: "Look! He is coming with the clouds" (1:7). And the identity of God is declared: "'I am the Alpha and the Omega,' says the Lord God, who is and who was and who is to come, the Almighty" (1:8). The book ends with a promise—"Surely I am coming soon"—and the prayer of the early Christians—"Come, Lord Jesus!" (22:20) This final book in the Bible addresses the conclusion of God's salvation and is the message of Advent—the coming of God.

In 1964 Jürgen Moltmann recovered the importance of *eschatology,* the biblical message of Christian hope, in *Theology of Hope.* In 1994, thirty years later, he returned to the same message in *The Coming of God.* Moltmann noted the break in the sequence of terms in the salutation of Revelation. To be consistent, the God of time should have been identified with present, past, and future—the God who was and is and will be. John saw another dimension beyond the prison of time that wraps around our lives. Moltmann noted, "God's future is not that he will be as he was and is, but that he is on the move and coming towards the world." Before Einstein, time and space are related in the Revelation.

Advent is God's nature. Certainly Advent addresses Christmas, the birth of Jesus the Son of God. God has come to us in Christ. But the annual celebration of the coming of Christ leads us beyond the cemetery of time—dwelling on some past event, repeating tradition, or worshiping antiquity. As we celebrate Advent, we worship the coming God.

II. *Our hope is the coming of God.* On the *Today Show* Katie Kouric interviewed the author of a book on the personal lives of upwardly mobile young executives. In general their lives were chaotic and out of control. Marriages were failing, family life was nonexistent, and every hope was sacrificed for the ultimate aim of life—the job. Charles Cousar reminds us of the Latin root of the word *despair*. It literally means "no hope." Nihilism is the philosophy of nothingness. It is the message that we live between birth and death surrounded by a vacuum.

Everyone was talking about Samuel Beckett's play staged at the local playhouse in Louisville in the late '60s. *Waiting for Godot* was first produced in Paris in 1953. It is about two tramps waiting by a tree for someone named Godot to come. The stage requirements are nil and the story is simple—Godot never shows. The play requires only two actors, but they have to hold the attention of the audience with a flow of dialogue that contains very little action. Acting without action is the point. The message—if there is one—is that life is about waiting for a god who never comes. The despair is worse because of the high hopes expressed in the dialogue. You can't miss the suggestion that people who do not hope do not wait and are not disappointed. Despair is born of hope. Disillusionment is the child of our illusions. Beckett's play makes a statement that demands our attention. Do we wait for the God who never comes? Beckett offers no gospel, no alternative to despair, no hope. That's the way it was in 1953. That's the way it is now.

In 1928, Dietrich Bonhoeffer preached on Advent from Revelation 3:20: "Our whole life is Advent—that is, a time of waiting for the ultimate, for the time when there will be a new heaven and a new Earth, when all people will be brothers and sisters; and one rejoices in the words of the angels: 'On Earth peace to those on whom God's favor rests.' Learn to wait, because he has promised to come. . . . 'Yes, come soon, Lord Jesus!' Amen."

God has come to us in Christ. God is coming to us in Christ. We say it at the Communion table: "Christ has died, Christ is risen, Christ will come again!"—Larry Dipboye

SECTION IV

MESSAGES FOR FUNERALS AND BEREAVEMENT

SERMON SUGGESTIONS

Topic: Suffering and God's Grace

TEXT: 2 Cor. 12:7–10

We cannot escape the fact that life involves the extremes of joy and sadness, laughter and tears, pleasure and suffering. As we gather in this setting today, one side of the scale seems most prevalent. Momentarily, the joy is covered by the sadness, tears have washed away the laughter, and this gathering seems to conclude a long journey of suffering. One of the challenges of this moment is to realize that joy, laughter, and pleasure have not been permanently destroyed. In God's grace they will return. As the author of Revelation has stated, "God will wipe away every tear from their eyes; there shall be no more death" (Rev. 21:3–4).

The journey of suffering is not an easy one. This good friend whom we come today to remember knew this experience well. This friend could empathize with Paul, who spoke freely about his own suffering. In the eleventh chapter of 2 Corinthians, Paul listed the five times he received forty stripes minus one from the Jews, and mentioned the occasions when he was beaten (three times with rods), stoned (once), and shipwrecked (three times).

However, the worst of Paul's suffering came from his "thorn in the flesh." We do not know what his thorn was, and it really does not matter. We only know that it caused him great suffering and pain. Scripture indicates that he pleaded three times with the Lord to remove this source of suffering (v. 8). This aspect of his life was not a game to Paul but a very serious matter.

God's response to Paul's pleas has become a source of hope for all who have spent endless night hours in pain. The response of God was and continues to be, "My grace is sufficient for you" (v. 9). Our first impression might be that God had not taken Paul's plea very seriously. Yet even our own experience teaches that God addressed the problem with the only true solution.

Paul understood his circumstances as a way of making him open to Christ's strength. He knew firsthand the meaning of dependence on God, and his experience of suffering actually became an asset to his faith rather than a liability.

For us today, the question that comes from deep within us is, Why did God not heal Paul? Why did God not heal this friend? There certainly was no shortage of prayers offered in his behalf. These are questions that for the present must remain unanswered. No one can speak for God. Yet there is one claim that can be made with all certainty, and it is that God takes no pleasure in the suffering of any of his children. Upon that claim you can rest your faith.

God is no sadist. The God we worship cries with us in our pain. In all circumstances of life he is at work for good. As does any earthly father, God wants his children to be happy and healthy. Then why does God not bring healing immediately? We simply do not have the answers to those questions.

It would appear that the strength of Paul's character came from the weathering of storms. His suffering became for him a source of spiritual strength. I cannot help but think of this aspect of Paul's life when I think of the one we honor today. There was a thorn in his flesh. This friend struggled with that thorn as well as possible, and it would appear on the surface that the struggle ended as a loss. But I remind you that "we see through a glass, darkly" (1 Cor. 13:12 KJV).

This I do know: suffering is not an indication of God's punishment. Once Jesus and his disciples encountered a blind man. The disciples asked who had sinned to bring about the blindness. Jesus refused to point a finger at anyone's sin as an explanation.

Our friend's suffering and death was not the result of anyone's sin. The multitude of questions that arise must simply remain a mystery for now. Someday we will see through a glass that is clear, and we will know in full, not in part. Until then we have no choice but to move on and trust in a God who has all answers and all wisdom. As family and friends today, you are not exempt from suffering. Grief has turned your joy into sadness and your laughter into tears. You know even in this moment the pain that life can offer.

We need security, warmth, and assurance. There is a source available. God's strength is sufficient for our needs now as it will be in all other circumstances of life. Consider the image of comfort offered in Isaiah 40:10–11. The image is a very warm picture of God's love that embraces. "He will feed." "He will gather." "[He will] carry them in his bosom." He will do all of this not just on the good and easy days but on the difficult days as well.

I cannot tell you why good people suffer. I cannot tell you why people become ill and die. For Paul, for our friend, and for Isaiah, God came in strength during moments of weakness.

Isaiah went on to say that all of this is not in vain. God does come to those who wait. Our friend did a full share of waiting, and so have you. At the point of what seems to be failing strength, God gives power to the faint. Because of faithful waiting there has been a great reversal. After a long descent of growing weary, God has kept his promise, and all has been changed. Because of God's presence and power, we will all once again soar like eagles, run and not be weary, walk and not faint (see Isa. 40:31).

For our beloved, that change has taken place. The claiming of Isaiah's promise has taken place even as we gather in this place. That ought to be a source of comfort in the midst of grief for each of us.

As you remember this friend and loved one, let the good memories be a source of warmth for you. There is so much good to be tucked away.

For this friend there is no more pain, no more suffering, only joy and peace. For each of us, God's strength is sufficient.—Al Cadenhead Jr.[1]

Topic: I Am the Resurrection and the Life
Funeral Service for Lucy Walter Miles
February 26, 2002
Conducted by H. Lloyd Storment
Opening Statements: John 11:25; Job 19:25; Job 1:21
TEXT: Rom. 8:31–37; Ps. 46

We meet this morning to show our respect and affection for a unique person. Lucy Miles lived among us with dignity and honor, and although she is now claimed by death, she will con-

---

[1]*The Minister's Manual for Funerals* (Nashville: Broadman Press, 1988), pp. 125–129.

tinue to exist in our minds and in our best thoughts. We knew her as mother, relative, friend, and fellow Christian. Her legacy is a rich one. Her love for life, her devotion to loved ones and friends, her loyalty to Christ, her commitment to organizations to which she belonged, her decision to be an active church person, her interest in family traditions, her willingness to talk about her children and grandchildren, and her interest in a myriad of pursuits are instructive for us today.

She continues beyond this life in a meaningful existence. This was the comfort that Christ brought her, and brings to us in this hour. She was a good and godly woman—not at all unlike the description found in Proverbs 31. Lucy was a woman whose humanity was rich and quiet, and there was a rare goodness about her that fairly radiated in her kindly expressions. Today she has gone home—the home toward which she traveled four score years.

If the good news is anything, it is that we have been found by God with the promise that those who follow him he will lead home. Life as we know it seems incomplete, but the gift of the Christian faith is the persuasion that God does not leave life uncompleted. The apostle Paul said that if God be for us, his love would complete what death could never take from us. He said that three things would remain: faith, hope, and love. Jesus said, "Though you have sorrow now, I will see you again and your hearts will rejoice." You see, he knew something that is unseen. He knew that the end of the story was not the coffin and the grave. He was saying that his love would be waiting *beyond* and *within* this sorrow. In such love there is unspeakable joy that no one can take away from you.

Today we remember Lucy in the background of family and the Christian faith. We remember her always as a Christian lady, for that is who she really was. It was a life of faith in Jesus Christ, who said to her and says to you, "Because I live you shall live also." This great assurance turns despair to hope; it gives us heart to suffer and struggle on, forasmuch as we know that our labor is not in vain in the Lord. On the morning of the Resurrection, Jesus Christ wrote a new last page to the world's life: "And the kingdom of this world has become the Kingdom of our Lord and of his Christ. And he shall reign, King of kings, and Lord of lords, forever and ever, Hallelujah! Amen."

A tribute by Linda Payne: "Attitude is contagious; is yours worth catching?" This is just one of several phrases posted on the refrigerator in Lucy's home, and though they are simple sayings, close examination reveals that they hold the principles on which she founded her well-lived life.

So allow me, if you will in these brief moments, the privilege of reflecting on the attitude of Lucille Sylina Walter Miles.

Born seventy-eight years ago in Frankfort, Kentucky, she was the youngest of seven siblings and is survived by four sisters—Emma, Ella, Catherine, and Virginia—who are here today. It's little wonder that she learned at an early age the importance of doing for others. Lucy was fortunate to have found her life's love at the young age of thirteen, when she and Shirley met and began dating. They married when she was seventeen, and they shared a wonderful life together for nearly forty-six years.

Lucy was a devoted wife and homemaker, setting a beautiful example early on for so many others. Within a day or so after Shirley's funeral, Lucy spent days at the hospital comforting a friend whose husband had undergone heart surgery.

Lucy was—as so many would attest—a wonderful mother to you, Gwen, and you, Cyndi, and you, Mark. So it is not surprising that you would describe your Mom as a "quiet force," "one who always set a good example," "one with a positive nature," "one who was always doing or making," "one who silently urged us on," "a caregiver," "one who everyday—everyday!—did something for someone else."

Another item of wisdom currently posted on the refrigerator says, "You make a living from what you get; you make a life from what you give!"

And give she did! Particularly to eight most special persons here today who had the privilege to affectionately call her "Grandmother Lucy" and "Lama." Lucy had a unique relationship with each of her grandchildren!

And give to others beyond her family, she did! Why, even in her final week—facing a medical consultation and serious surgery—she took time to write thank-you notes and prepare birthday cards with specific instructions for them to be mailed on certain dates so as not to arrive too early or too late for the forthcoming birthdays of friends! For Lucy knew that she would be occupied with recovering from her surgery.

Shortly before that, Lucy was experiencing considerable discomfort, but she tirelessly came to the aid of a dear friend who had been injured in a fall. Lucy ran errands, brought dinner, and served as chauffeur.

Lucy is described by many as a wonderful cook—generous to a fault with her wares! Perhaps you once received a casserole or a cake, or needed items when a situation arose, or maybe you have feasted on her fried chicken, mashed potatoes, and gravy! Were you among the untold numbers to have enjoyed her special braided Christmas sweetbread or cinnamon rolls, left on your doorstep on Christmas Eve or early on Christmas morning?

Or maybe Lucy simply sat with you or listened to you—for friends say she was a "good sitter and listener," "a pal," "an adviser," "one with whom you could disagree but never have a disagreement"—a wonderful and sincere Christian.

This petite, demure, feminine, "quiet force" devoted her life to service. Lucy was a long-time volunteer for the American Red Cross, was active in PEO and an investment club, and since joining this church in 1959 she has given unendingly of her talents to the Broadway family. Many of us knew her as she taught our children in Sunday school; others knew her for her work in the nursery or as a choir member, deacon, trustee, and active member of the WMU. Lucy believed in Missions!

Now I am not certain that this is really true but story has it that Lucy often caused a riot at small Christmas parties or other gatherings where gifts were exchanged—especially when one person could take a gift from another who had previously opened a more desirable one. Friendships were in danger of being dissolved when someone took Lucy's famous caramel candy from the person lucky enough to have drawn it from the pile, and grown men have even stooped to stealing and hiding the precious candies from their rightful owner!

Speaking of parties, this convivial lady loved to plan and give parties, attend parties, and simply have fun!! So, it is interesting to note that most recently she commented on her one regret in life. Lucy said, "I wish I had had more fun!"

Can you imagine what she meant?

Lucy and Shirley traveled a lot, and with some of you! Lucy also devoted a good deal of travel time to being with grandchildren. And when most women might have shied away from traveling without the security of a spouse, that did not deter Lucy at all. She regrouped and found merriment traveling with friends and nieces to faraway places, like the British Isles, Alaska, the Scandinavian countries—just to name a few. Once she even participated in a church-building project in Brazil. Imagine her and three other women—none of whom could speak one word of Italian—traveling all over Italy for five whole days!

Lucy played golf, and like most of us, not exceptionally well, but she laughed and had fun. She learned to water ski at a mature age, and she took a walk almost every evening.

Her family claims that Lucy's physical makeup included the "inherited crying gene." I believe her makeup must also have included the jovial "laughing gene"!

So, as the Scriptures admonish us, this is a time to weep and a time to mourn this one so dear who was unexpectedly taken from her life here on Earth.

The Scriptures also remind us that this is a time to laugh, a time to dance, and a time to rejoice!

The next time you laugh or hear laughter, think of Lucy. The next time you savor the sweetness of a caramel candy, let it remind you of Lucy. On a warm spring evening, as you take a walk, let the beauty of our world make Lucy come to mind. And when I soon see Easter bonnets and Derby hats, I'll think of Mrs. Lucy.

Always remember this one called friend, aunt, cousin, Mom, Grandmother, Lama—for at whatever point in time Lucille Sylina Walter Miles was lovingly received into the hands of the Father, rest assured that she was received with these words: "Well done, my good and faithful servant."

Topic: One Who Feared God
TEXT: Ps. 112

Florence was an amazing person. At nearly eighty-five years old she was willing to do just about anything, and she seemed to fear little. Most of us stood in awe of her seeming tirelessness when it came to helping others, and we were often amazed that she regularly walked "where angels fear to tread." Some might say she lived a charmed life, but she would sum it up this way: "God takes care of fools and old people."

The psalm for this coming Sunday [*Revised Common Lectionary, Fifth Sunday after the Epiphany, Year A*] speaks aptly of her life and legacy. The psalmist describes the righteous as "those who deal generously . . . , who conduct their affairs with justice." Anyone who knew Florence would describe her as a generous person, always concerned with those who were unable to care for themselves. When someone was in need, if Florence could help directly she would. If help was beyond her means or ability, she would try to find a way through some other channel. More people than most of us can imagine have come to rely on her steady, regular ministry to them. In their hearts, her "horn is exalted in honor."

The psalmist characterizes the righteous as those who "rise in the darkness." Over the last few days, many of you have told stories of how Florence would take home projects on which she was working (costumes, quilts, baby clothes, and so on) so they could be completed in a timely fashion. Given the size of some of those projects, no doubt she had to stay up late and rise early. Her faithful care for her sister is yet another example of this.

And finally, the psalmist depicts the righteous as those whose "hearts are steady, [who] will not be afraid." Those of us who knew Florence often winced as she jumped into her car and sped off to do some errand of mercy, retrieve some lost article or soul, or attempt some task that would make younger folks hesitate. If she was worried or concerned, she never showed it.

As fully as Florence matched the psalmist's description of a righteous person, I believe she would never want us to lose sight of the singular aspect of her character that gave rise to all these other characteristics. She was one of "those who fear the Lord, who greatly delight in his commandments." She loved to be in the presence of God. She loved to be with others in the presence of God: in prayer, Bible study, worship, and ministry. From her relationship with God she drew her strength, her joy, her confidence. She lived in the confidence of God's providence—God really does "take care of fools and old people."

Family, friends, and community of faith, the coming days will not be easy. Grief is a hard road to walk. But as we walk it, let's take a lesson from Florence: fear the Lord and delight in his ways. If we do, we will find our hearts steadied. We will learn not to be afraid. And like Florence, we will discover the blessings of God. Let us be "those who fear the Lord, who greatly delight in his commandments." Praise the Lord.—Jim Holladay

Topic: A Man of the Word
TEXT: Isa. 40:1, 6–8, 11, 27–31

The first time I head Herb read the Scripture in worship, I thought, "Oh no! We are going to be here all morning." The lectionary passage was one of those long ones, twenty plus verses, and Herb began reading in an exceedingly sonorous and deliberate (dare I say slow) way. As he read, however, I became less focused on the manner in which he read and more immersed in experiencing the Word he was reading. When he finished I thought, "I really don't need to preach. Herb has drawn us into the presence of the living Word."

It was that way every time he read Scripture. The words of the passage rolled around through his soul, in his mouth, and became for us the Word of God. And though we often smiled knowingly at one another when it was Herb's Sunday to read Scripture and the passage was a long one, none of us would pass up the experience.

Perhaps more than his reading of Scripture, Herb's prayers in worship are something we will miss. Like his reading, his praying was unhurried. He seemed to know that lingering in the presence of God is a crucial part of prayer and worship. Yet his prayers were not those that go on and on. They were meaty and rich, inviting us to consider deeply not only our praise but also our petitions. It was like he wanted us to remember that although God is faithful, God will not be hurried.

Herb's Scripture reading and his praying were reminders of several very important truths—truths that Isaiah speaks to us as well. As we walk through this dark valley of grief, longing for the day when the veil will be lifted and life will get back to some semblance of normality, let us hear these truths. As we seek to reorient our common life, let us absorb these truths.

Backing up through the passage, the first thing Isaiah reminds us is that "those who wait for the Lord shall renew their strength." Herb seldom lost his patience with people or events. Though shaken by his sister's death less than three weeks ago, he was moving toward the next phase of his life with the confidence that with God's help all would be okay. He would want us to live these days with that assurance.

We come next to the words, "He will feed his flock. . . . He will gather the lambs in his arms." By being willing to linger in God's presence in prayer and Bible reading, Herb knew what it meant to experience safety in the arms of God. During these days of grief, let us renew and intensify our conversation with God.

Isaiah reminds us that "all people are grass . . . ; but the word of our God will stand forever." Herb died suddenly and unexpectedly on Sunday morning, after a wonderful day with his family on Saturday. He died as he lived—in the confidence of the permanence of God's presence and promises. As important as family and human support will be in the coming days, Herb would want us to remember that only God is a constant, and only God's Word gives life and hope.

Finally, the passage begins with the words, "Comfort, O comfort my people." Herb knew that God was a God of his word. That is why he was willing to live his life as a man of the Word. By emulating his example, we will find comfort in these days. But beyond these days, we will find joy in living.—Jim Holladay

Topic: The Land Beyond the Stars
TEXT: Heb. 11:40

Shortly before he died in his eighty-ninth year, Robert Frost was talking with Victor Reichart about a recent trip to Russia when suddenly he interrupted himself to ask, "Victor, what do you think are the chances of life after death?" His friend answered with a question, "Robert, what do you think?" Frost bent his head and remained silent for a long time; then lifting his face he replied, "With so many ladders going up everywhere, there must be something for them to lean against."[2]

This conversation between a poet and a rabbi prompts us to wonder, Whatever became of that "invincible surmise" that Christians once called their "blessed hope"? Years ago, the theme of eternal life was a staple of most Protestant pulpits. Every revival series featured climactic sermons on heaven and hell. But now that horizon seems to have receded or even disappeared from the religious landscape. To be sure, every recitation of the Apostle's Creed concludes with "I believe in the life everlasting," but it sounds like little more than a mild palliative designed to mitigate the terrors of death.

Are we really better off to suppress what Wordsworth called our "intimations of immortality"?[3] Does this posture of detachment cause us to become more concerned for the world around us, less addicted to an escapist religion? Or does our indifference to the world beyond result in a shriveling of that dimension of transcendence that should overarch the earthly journey? Let us revisit this neglected agenda in the hope of raising one more ladder to the skies so we might reflect on what it leans against.

I. In seeking a fresh approach to the function of eternity in the life of the believer, I have found fresh guidance from a passage that has had little or no influence on our understanding of the world beyond. As the majestic roll call of faith recorded in Hebrews 11 comes to a climax in verses 39–40 ("And all these, though well attested by their faith, did not receive what was promised, since God had foreseen something better for us, that apart from us they

---

[2]Andrew R. Marks, "The Rabbi and the Poet: Victor Reichart and Robert Frost," cited in Martin E. Marty, *Context,* 1995, *27*(6), 4.

[3]William Wordsworth, "Ode to Intimations of Immortality from Recollections of Early Childhood," reprinted in Helen Gardner (ed.), *New Oxford Book of English Verse, 1250–1950* (New York: Oxford University Press, 1972), pp. 508–513.

should not be made perfect"), the author draws from the pilgrimage of the people of God in the Old Testament a number of conclusions that merit our closest attention:

1. God's promises are not always fulfilled as soon as we prove faithful. Indeed, their bestowal may be deferred longer than our earthly lifetime, even for centuries on end.
2. God's delay is not a matter of divine indifference, as if he were either fickle or forgetful, but is based on his determination to provide "something better," no matter how long that effort may take.
3. Perfection is not automatic or instantaneous even when we go to be with God after death. Rather, it is a dynamic process of development that may progress in stages according to God's providential plan.
4. Reaching the wholeness and maturity of perfection is not simply a matter of either individual achievement or divine provision but is profoundly relational—something that happens in concert with all the people of God. In other words, *each* of us participates in the blessings that come to *all* of us. No matter how early or how late we may have joined the earthly race, each one of us benefits equally from the victory that lies at the finish line.

It is here that we come to the one insight most crucial to our quest for understanding. We know very well from Hebrews that the "something better" that caused God to postpone the fulfillment of his promises to the Old Testament saints was nothing less than Jesus Christ—his better revelation (1:4), better hope (7:19), better covenant (7:22), better priesthood (8:6), better sacrifice (9:23), better possessions (10:34), and better life (11:35). Therefore we would expect our text to say that "apart from *Christ* they should not be made perfect." But no, it says "apart from *us*," which means that we who have benefited from the finished work of Christ will be permitted to share these blessings with those who lived before Christ in time and so waited in hope for the fulfillment of God's promises. Because redemption unfolds throughout history, none of us can capture its fullness in a single earthly lifetime, but eternity will offer the opportunity for each of us to benefit from all that God has ever done for his people, from creation to consummation.

In a word, our test is telling us that God's blessings are *retroactive.* As long as we live in time we can never share with others all of the better things that God is continually doing with our lives. All we can do here below is to live "by faith," which means to live in the creative tension between desire and delay, promise and postponement, wanting and waiting. But when time shall be no more, when all the people of God shall at last be gathered in "that city that hath foundations, whose builder and maker is God" (Heb. 11:10), then we shall be able to bless, and be blessed by, all who were part of the earthly pilgrimage of faith. Then we shall be able to spend as many forevers as our poor minds can imagine building that wholeness of maturity, in both ourselves and others, that is God's agenda for his people throughout all ages.

The cultural event of 1996 in Birmingham was an exhibit at the Museum of Art on the first emperor of China, Qin Shihuangdi (259–210 B.C.). After unifying China between 230 and 220 B.C., Qin moved quickly to become absolute sovereign of a vast domain, rivaling the conquests of Alexander the Great and Julius Caesar. But the one foe he could not defeat was death, despite a frantic quest for the elixir of immortality, which included drinking potions of mercury. So Qin decreed the construction of a vast mausoleum covering twenty-two square miles.

As many as 700,000 laborers were conscripted to work thirty-six years building an elaborate underground fortress containing eight thousand terra cotta warriors with forty thousand bronze weapons. When finished, this artificial mountain was sealed, with all of the Emperor's childless concubines inside, as well as the artisans who could have led grave robbers to its vast treasures; and there it lay undisturbed until accidentally rediscovered in 1974 by farmers digging a well. Now archaeologists are patiently reconstructing this incredible find, representative samples of which were recently displayed in our country for the first time.

Why did Qin surround himself in death with the likeness of an army in battle array? Because he was convinced that in the afterlife he would have to defeat every foe in order to triumph once again. Eternity for him would be but an endless extension of the conquests of Earth. Qin was a brutal tyrant who once had 460 scholars buried alive merely for questioning some of his views, and he would visit the same havoc on heaven if anyone there dared to oppose him. By contrast, the author of Hebrews saw heaven as a place of sharing with others in love the best gifts that have come to us from Christ, whose greatest victory was won on a shameful cross. Here we see how tightly the two worlds are tied together. If this life is one of violence and destruction, then the next life is seen as an opportunity to intensify that chaos. But if this life is an endless quest for growth in the wholeness of maturity, then the next life is seen as the fulfillment of that goal in the perfecting of the saints.

II. What does this breathtaking vision of heaven in Hebrews say to our earthbound souls? Throughout my working lifetime I have always ended a job with the same haunting refrain: "If only I could start over again—not where I was at the beginning but where I was at the end!" In one sense, I never really learned to do a job well until the job was over. But in a deeper sense, what this means is that by the time I finally figured out how to live, my life was almost over! It is not just that I wanted to be forgiven for my immaturities and inexperience, important as such pardon may be. Rather, what I wanted was a chance to share the best gifts of my maturity and experience with those who graciously tolerated my fumbling first efforts. That option is forever denied me by the irreversibility of time—or is it to be "forever"? To be sure, we cannot turn back Earth's calendar; but is there another realm in which time itself will no longer be a threat to our deepest longings for maturity?

Arthur Gordon tells of a wintry afternoon in Manhattan when, frustrated and depressed, "chewing the bitter cud of hindsight," he sought solace from an elderly friend who was also an eminent psychiatrist. The old man took him to his office and insisted that he listen to three tape recordings of patient interviews, then identify the two-word phrase that was their common denominator. After hearing these tales of woe, Gordon was clueless until his counselor pointed out "the two saddest words in any language": *if only*. He explained: "'If only,' they say to me, 'I had done it differently' . . . 'if only I had been wiser.' The trouble with *if only* is that it doesn't change anything. It keeps the person facing the wrong way—backward instead of forward."

Gordon's problem was that he was living in the past tense. His older friend's advice was, "Shift the focus . . . change the key words from *if only* to *next time* . . . push aside the roadblock of regret." As the conversation ended, the psychiatrist reached into his bookcase and pulled out a diary kept by a school teacher in his hometown. Her husband, Jonathan, was an amiable ne'er-do-well whose inadequacies as a provider left her to care for the family and pay most of the bills. The journal was full of angry entries on his many shortcomings and ended when he died, except for one addition written many years later which read, "Today I was made superintendent of schools, and I suppose I should be very proud. But if I knew that Jonathan was out there somewhere beyond the stars and if I knew how to manage it, I would go to him tonight."

The old man closed the book gently and returned it to the shelf with this comment: "What she's saying is, 'if only I had loved him while I could.' That's when those sad words are the saddest of all—when it's too late to retrieve anything."[4] With that the story ends, but our questions are just beginning: Does death mean that there are no more "next times" ever again? When our earthly journey comes to an end, then is it forever "too late to retrieve anything"? Or are our Jonathans whom we never quite learned to love in this life "somewhere out there beyond the stars," and will we manage to go to them when night has fallen for us all?

III. With the ladder of deferred fulfillment rising to the skies, why are we so reluctant to consider what it may lean against? Notice how the insights of our text speak directly to the reasons for our neglect of the life beyond. One reason for that indifference is that our traditional understanding of the future is based on a rather vague and uninviting conception of heaven. Suppose we survive death with our identity intact. Then what do we do? Without fleshly bodies, we are no longer preoccupied with the earthly quest for food, shelter, and clothing. About the only thing that preachers can suggest, particularly from passages in the book of Revelation, is that we will go to church all the time, praising God before his throne. But when we try to imagine what it would be like to do that for an eternity, the nagging possibility of boredom begins to set in. How many verses are there to the "Hallelujah Chorus," and what will we do when we have sung them all? We seem trapped by the timelessness of eternity. Over against these static notions of perfection that tend to imply a life of endless repetition, Hebrews pictures a dynamic heaven in which we will spend eternity learning to become mature by sharing the best gifts of life with all who join us there.

Another reason for our neglect of the life beyond is that we tend to view it only as an answer to the problem of death. The afterlife is seen as guaranteeing survival beyond the grave and thus is of interest primarily to those nearing the end of their earthly sojourn. The problem with this approach is that it makes the life above of no real relevance to the life below. The root cause of this difficulty is that we have related the two worlds *sequentially,* as if Earth comes first and then heaven comes "after" it, rather than relating them *simultaneously,* as if the eternal world above invades and interpenetrates the temporal world below. But Hebrews 11 suggests that we do not live "one world at a time." Rather, we live a bipolar existence according to which both worlds are equally real and present at all times.

A final reason why this world is too much with us is that we absolutize experience—the more momentary the better! We act as if destiny is decided by the latest football victory or presidential election or technological marvel. But our deeper sensibilities know better. The writer of Hebrews knew that only those who live in the disarming awareness of a greater world, with their noses pressed against the windowpane of heaven, find courage to bear a countercultural witness. Only those with an eschatological temperament, whose eyes are fixed on "a land that is fairer than day," are willing to sacrifice themselves as did the martyrs recounted in our Scripture passage (Heb. 11:32–38). Those who believe that this earthly life

---

[4]Arthur Gordon, *A Touch of Wonder* (New York: Jove Books, 1978), pp. 68–72. I thank John Claypool for calling this account to my attention.

ends with a period will finally capitulate to the terrible tyranny of the status quo. But those who believe that it ends with a comma, setting apart what is at best a subordinate clause in the long sentence that is our life, will use their earthly days as an apprenticeship in the kind of perfection that takes an eternity to complete.

As John Bunyan neared the end of *Pilgrim's Progress,* he described the summons by which Mr. Valiant-for-truth was called to leave this world for another. Gathering his friends, he said to them, "I am going to my Father's; and though with great difficulty I am got hither, yet now I do not repent me of all the trouble I have been at to arrive where I am. My sword I give to him that shall succeed me in my pilgrimage, and my courage and skill to him that can get it. My marks and scars I carry with me, to be a witness for me that I have fought His battles who now will be my rewarder." Then Bunyan added, "So he passed over, and all the trumpets sounded for him on the other side."[5]

May all the trumpets sound again when that day is come for you.—William E. Hull

---

[5]John Bunyan, *The Pilgrim's Progress* (New York: Fleming H. Revell, 1903), p. 302.

LENTEN AND EASTER PREACHING

SERMON SUGGESTIONS

Topic: To Triumph Over Temptation

TEXT: Luke 4:1–13

"Jesus, full of the Holy Spirit, returned from the Jordan and was led by the Spirit into the desert, where for forty days he was tempted by the devil."

The Gospels of Matthew, Mark, and Luke each tell the story of the temptation of Jesus with their own unique twist, their own theological objective. Together they cover every dimension of this experience in the life of Christ.

Now, I know how distressed some people become when they hear this kind of thing. The mere suggestion that the individual Gospels were written with theological intent causes some folk to fear that the truth claims of the Gospels are being subverted—which of course just isn't true. In fact, just the opposite is true.

Our Gospels were written to embody all of the richness and depth of a mystery beyond all human description. Each Gospel affords us yet another look, from a slightly different vantage point, at a miracle that is staggering, unique, and completely beyond the capacity of humans to capture in words.

So this morning we have Luke telling us his version of this essential encounter between Christ and the forces of evil. Like the other Gospel writers, Luke wants us to hear that the temptations of Jesus in the desert were fundamentally about how Christ would use his power in this world. Beyond that, like Matthew and Mark, Luke affirms that the messianic mission of Jesus will find its fulfillment in strict obedience to the will and the ways of God.

But Luke has also added some important perspectives that you'll find in neither Matthew nor Mark. For instance, Luke changes the order in which the temptations transpire. That makes it possible to use the temptation at the Temple as the climax to this account.

And if you know anything at all about the Gospel of Luke, then you already know how significant the Temple is in Luke's story of Jesus and the early Church. You'll recall Luke telling us that on the eighth day after Jesus' birth, "Joseph and Mary took him to Jerusalem [to the Temple] to present him to the Lord."

Then there's the famous story about the boy Jesus, who at twelve years of age was found by his parents "in the Temple courts, sitting among the teachers, listening to them and asking them questions."

And when Luke turns his attention to the early Church, in the book of Acts, we find him telling us about the first believers, that "every day they continued to meet together in the Temple courts." He even mentions how "one day, Peter and John were going up to the Temple at the time of prayer."

It's evident that the Temple plays a very important function in Luke's account, and played a very important part in the life of the early Church. But there are some other, perhaps more

330

crucial, differences between the story of the temptations as told by Matthew and Mark, and the story we receive from the pen of Luke. There are three differences in particular that I want to think about this morning, because together they reveal the pervasive presence of evil, and the power of Christ to triumph over temptation and trial.

Have you ever noticed how deep and pervasive evil is in this world? Perhaps you find the question foolish. But the fact is that often we so-called moderns tend to look down our noses at the way the Bible talks about those forces that surround us and threaten to overtake our world by storm. Maybe we no longer think that some malevolent force is responsible for all of the ruthlessness and cruelty and murderousness in our world. But the Bible doesn't blush at all, and it offers absolutely no apology for its vivid portrayal of an underlying wickedness in this world. Like it or not, the Scriptures are frank in demanding that we face the reality of evil forces—present and powerful!

Granted, the images of evil differ throughout the Bible—from Leviathan to the portrayal of evil personified in the character of Satan. Yet the common cry of Scripture is that there are forces in this world in opposition to every form of love, health, wholeness, and peace.

You remember that in his Epistle to the Church in Ephesus Paul wrote, "Our struggle is not against flesh and blood, but against the rulers, against the authorities, against the powers of this dark world and against the spiritual forces of evil in the heavenly realms."

What do you think possesses a person to murder well over one hundred and twenty people? And how do you account for the fact that children throughout the world continue to be victims of violence, starvation, and social neglect?

If this darksome thing we call "evil" isn't part of your perspective on reality, then I don't know how you can read your paper or make sense of the six o'clock news, or understand the shadow side of your own heart for that matter!

Because the Bible also tells us that evil is not simply external to us. It can also find its way into the human heart. From that vantage point, it seeks to spread its terror throughout the world. The classic description of this struggle also comes from the apostle Paul. This time he writes, "I know nothing good lives in me, that is, in my sinful nature. For I have the desire to do what is good, but I cannot carry it out. For what I do is not the good I want to do; no, the evil I do not want to do—this I keep on doing!" Paul is attempting to tell us about the great control that evil can have over the Christian's life.

The story of Christ's temptation makes it quite clear that anyone who seeks to follow God's way can count on those evil forces having a field day with his or her faith! As someone has written somewhere, "If Jesus wrestled with temptation, why should any of his followers think that believing makes them exempt from the battle?"

As a matter of fact, the point made by Paul is similar to the concern of Luke. Both want us to understand how difficult it will always be for those who are called by God and committed to God's will, and who desire to deepen both their total devotion and their daily discipleship. Evil will waste no time in waging all-out war against those who confess faith in God. That's a fact!

Fortunately, it's a fact we needn't face on our own. The truth is that under our own wind we would never succeed in winning one simple skirmish with the forces of evil. We haven't the strength to put a dent in the destructive power of what Paul called "the spiritual forces of evil in the heavenly realms." So, shall we simply resign ourselves to the presence and power of evil? Should we send up the white flag?

Well, before we do let's take another look at Luke's Gospel. Isn't it amazing how frequently

Luke mentions the movement of the Holy Spirit? In fact, the Spirit plays a major role in every single act of redemption. There isn't one scene of salvation in which the Spirit isn't working.

We just celebrated Christmas, right? And in Luke's Gospel, the angel Gabriel is sent to Mary with the message that she will bear the Messiah. Do you recall what he told her? He said, "The Holy Spirit will come upon you, and the power of the Most High will overshadow you. So the holy one to be born will be called the Son of God." That's just the beginning!

After Jesus was baptized, Luke tells us, "as he was praying, heaven was opening and the Holy Spirit descended on him." Then again, in this morning's story of the temptation we heard how "Jesus, full of the Holy Spirit, returned from the Jordan and was led by the Spirit into the desert." And in the synagogue at Nazareth, Jesus, using the prophecy of Isaiah, defined his own ministry as Spirit-empowered. He said, "The Spirit of the Lord is upon me!"

That same Spirit was promised and then present in the early Church, you know? Just turn to the very first chapter in the book of Acts. What do we read? The Risen Christ tells his shaken followers, "You will receive power when the Holy Spirit comes on you." Then, in chapter 2, we're told that on the day the Church was born "all of [the apostles] were filled with the Holy Spirit."

The Heidelberg Catechism confesses that the Holy Spirit "has been given to [us] personally, so that, by true faith, he makes [us] share in Christ and all his blessings."

The Belgic Confession of the Dutch Reformed Church reminds us that, "though great weakness remains in [us], [we] fight against it by the Spirit all the days of [our] lives, appealing constantly to . . . the Lord Jesus, in whom we have forgiveness of [our] sins, through faith in him."

Isn't it apparent by now that we can no more overcome the outrageous power of evil through our own feeble efforts than we can change the course of the planets? Haven't we seen that these malevolent forces of death and destruction are capable of cutting us down at the knees whenever we attempt to confront them on our own? We can't fight these forces alone!

Whenever, wherever we take a stand against evil and seek to serve those who have been victimized by evil's cruel and cunning attacks, we must never rely on willpower or social strategies. Only the presence and power of the Holy Spirit can give us the stamina that such service demands and that such struggles will require. Human effort will always prove inadequate, but God's power will always prove invincible.

Now, take another look at Luke's Jesus out there in the desert. He's "the victor in the time of testing by joining to the presence of the Spirit the appropriate use of Scripture." There's a point worth noting!

Recall Paul's description of our warfare with those "spiritual forces of evil"? Do you know what he recommends we do in order to be amply prepared for a frontal attack from such forces? He encourages us to clothe ourselves in Christ. He calls it "the full armor of God." And as part of that armor we are to wield the "sword of the Spirit, which is the Word of God."

You can also turn to second Timothy, where the apostle writes, "All Scripture is God-breathed and is useful for teaching, rebuking, correcting, and training in righteousness, so that the [saint] of God may be thoroughly equipped for every good work." I wonder if our lives are so saturated with God's Holy Scripture that we can wield it like a sword. I wonder.

Luke's account of the temptation of Christ in the desert forces us to acknowledge that only "the Church armed with the Spirit and with the Scriptures . . . will overcome evil with good."

In every area of life, whenever evil begins to bend in on our lives, we can remember that we belong to Christ. We can call upon his Holy Spirit and find that God is faithful and more forceful than evil could ever hope to be.

Just knowing that can give us the edge we need. Because we know that when anyone from this family must face a "desert," he or she won't ever be deserted. We'll support that person with our prayers and presence. We'll enter that person's pain and share the love of Christ. In fact, we'll walk with one another through those wastelands, won't we?

In fact, that's the really "good news" that Luke's Gospel gives us this morning!

The truth is, none of us need ever face those trials and temptations of the wasteland alone. We always have our Savior with us, and within us, as we walk through this life so riddled with the ravages of evil and temptation.

This Christ, who is in you and in me and in us—this Christ gives each of us and all of us the power to prevail over the tempter's tools and trials. And isn't that really good news!

Now, are you beginning to understand why Luke put the story of Jesus' baptism as a preface to his account of the temptations? If not, then listen to the words of our baptismal service: "In the sacrament of baptism we celebrate the grace and forgiveness of God that we know in Jesus Christ."

Paul put it this way: "Those who receive in far greater measure God's grace, and his gift of righteousness, shall live and reign through the one man, Jesus Christ." Did you hear that? He said, "live and reign!" So, you tell me: Who really has the ultimate power? Satan or our Savior?

The connection between baptism and temptation is this: because we are baptized we belong to Christ, and because we belong to Christ, the devil will use every weapon in his arsenal to destroy us by laying waste to our faith. But it is just because we belong to Christ that we are empowered to overcome some temptations—and that we are forgiven when we falter in the face of others.

Martin Luther once wrote, "For where God built a church, there the Devil would also build a chapel!" I think that's still true today. But Luke is teaching us that Jesus refused to leave the challenge of God's church for the cozy comforts of the devil's chapel.

Christ also empowers us to do the same whenever our very real human needs and desires become the devil's delightful distraction, or whenever our wastelands cause us to wonder if faith in God and God's grace is really worthwhile.

Christ then empowers us to embrace God's grace over the devil's demented deceptions. But we must choose. You and I, and we together as a church, we must choose!

I discovered this lyric tucked away in an old Lutheran hymnal. The words are a translation of the original German. Legend has it they were penned by Luther just after he had come through a particularly trying time in his life. He titled the hymn, "A Mighty Fortress." Listen to this:

> Thus spoke the Son, "Hold fast to me,
> From now on you will make it.
> I gave my very life for you
> And for you I will stake it.
> For I am yours and you are mine,
> And where I and your life entwine,
> The Old Fiend cannot shake it!"

—Albert J. D. Walsh

Topic: Not Dead but Sleeping
TEXT: Mark 5:39

Picture the scene: a distraught father named Jairus raced toward home with a controversial healer named Jesus at his side. The death message that had summoned them seemed confirmed when, upon entering the premises, their ears were assaulted by the jangled discord of despair, "people weeping and wailing loudly" (Mark 5:38). Relatives, neighbors, and friends milled about in anguish, mourning the loss of "an only daughter, about twelve years of age" (Luke 8:42).

No sooner did Jesus encounter the chaos than he confronted their shrieks and sobs with an audacious question: "Why do you make a tumult and weep? The child is not dead but sleeping" (Mark 5:39). So incredible was his claim that their tears turned to ridicule "and they laughed at him" (Mark 5:40). This dramatic clash of irreconcilable perspectives highlights one of the enduring issues of human existence: How may we distinguish between dormancy and death in human affairs?

I. Like the Galilean villagers of old, we seem ready if not eager to declare anything dead that does not meet our expectations of life. "What a dead party!" we exclaim when the conversations or refreshments are not up to par. Many a congregation gets the reputation of being a "dead church" merely because it still meets in a grand old Victorian pile of stones, or because its sermons are a little stodgy and its music a bit languid. Historians such as Oswald Spengler and Arnold Toynbee have taught us to understand that whole nations and civilizations eventually die, ours included. At a more personal level, the plaintive ballads of our folk music lament how easily relationships die when the heart grows cold.

We are a generation haunted if not obsessed by the specter of death. The tumult of our time bears eloquent witness to the pervasive suspicion that much around us is in the process of dying, if not already dead. To be sure, we do not wail loudly like our ancient counterparts, but we pay well to have others do it for us vicariously. Modern art, with its twisted convolutions, testifies to a death that has disfigured our vision of beauty. Modern music, with its clashing dissonances, seeks to shape the sobs of grieving humanity into sound. Modern immorality, with its wild search for forbidden fruit, tries to flaunt the corpse of a dead conscience.

Everywhere we turn we see dead spots. A million marriages die in the divorce courts every year. We actually heard the death rattles of a dominant political system as the Berlin Wall came tumbling down. How many dreams died with the crack of assassin bullets that snuffed out the lives of the Kennedy brothers and Martin Luther King Jr.? How many traditions died as families were uprooted from their rural pasts and thrust into the synthetic culture of our supercities? No wonder nihilism is the dominant philosophy of our age, for it is primarily an intellectual response to the prevalence of decay in our collective experience. This is our deepest instinct: that nothing we cherish is immune to the destructive power of death.

The first gleam of hope from our text is that Jesus was willing to grapple with humanity's ultimate fear. He knew even before reaching Jairus's home that death itself was the issue to be faced (Mark 5:35). His gospel was not limited either to this earthly life, before "the Last Enemy" strikes (1 Cor. 15:26), or to the life beyond, after the Grim Reaper has swung his scythe. Rather, he walked with a grieving father into that dark abyss between two worlds where all seemed hopeless because death had played its trump card. To the shock of every religious opportunist seeking favorable circumstances in which to succeed, Jesus boldly took his ministry to the morgue!

By that decision to help the lifeless daughter of Jairus, our Lord forever demonstrated to his disciples that no human being is too hopeless for them to address in the power of God. We are to go not only to those favorably disposed to religion, but also to those whom the world has given up on as dead. H. A. Williams well described such evangelism as the miracle of impossibility: "It is neither promising people nor lucky people nor deserving people nor likely people who are raised from the dead, but precisely dead people. The background of resurrection is always impossibility. And with impossibility staring us in the face, the prelude to resurrection is invariably doubt, confusion, strife, and the cynical smile, which is our defense against them. Resurrection is always the defiance of the absurd."[1]

Even more shocking, however, was the determination of Jesus to do battle with the diagnosis of those about him. In the face of overwhelming despair, he dared to contradict common sense: "The child is *not* dead." This was not a medical verdict based on a clinical examination of the patient, but a spiritual verdict based on firsthand knowledge of the Creator. To paraphrase, "Not death as you see it, a tragic defeat without any future, but death as I see it, a temporary interlude from which one may awaken rested and refreshed." Jesus was utterly candid in affirming the *reality* of death, but he was equally insistent in denying the *finality* of death (compare John 11:11–14). To him, the *fact* of death was not really the issue; rather, he differed radically from his detractors over the *meaning* of death.

To assert that the child was "not dead" when her body lay lifeless in the next room meant that, for Jesus, outward appearances could be deceiving. Things are not always what they seem to be. Stated more precisely, empiricism as reliance on sensory experience is valid only to a point, for in the spiritual realm realities are operative that are not amenable to controlled observation. The handwriting crow that scorned Jesus was correct as far as it went, but it understood death only in the context of human weakness, whereas Jesus was determined to understand it in the context of divine power. Ultimately, Jesus' defiant "not dead" was based on his conviction that the Creator-Sustainer of the universe "is not God of the dead but of the living" (Mark 12:27); therefore, life is finally mightier than death.

That confidence is crucial to our whole outlook on the human prospect. Everywhere it appears that our world is running down. The law of entropy contends that "the general trend of the universe [is] toward death and disorder."[2] At times it seems that our values and religious commitments are destined for the same fate. But Jesus will not have it so! God does not operate a garbage dump where his precious creation is cast like rubbish into the void. Rather, he is determined that goodness and beauty and purpose shall not only survive but ultimately prevail. In the supreme struggle between life and death, it is finally life that has the upper hand.

If that be so, what are we to make of the malaise that is so easily mistaken for death? How shall we understand the experience of helplessness and emptiness and uselessness that

---

[1] H. A. Williams, *True Resurrection* (New York: Holt, Rinehart and Winston, 1972), p. 57.
[2] J. R. Newman, quoted in Philip B. Gore (ed.), *Webster's Third New International Dictionary* (Springfield, Mass.: G. & C. Merriam, 1965), p. 759.

abounds on every hand? The answer is to be found in the second phrase of our text: "not dead but sleeping."

II. In utilizing the metaphor of sleep, Jesus reached back to recover an Old Testament understanding of death rich with meaning.[3] From the dawn of creation, God had made the day and the night (Gen. 1:4–5), thereby ordaining a rhythm of waking and sleeping. Because humans were created to engage in periodic rather than perpetual activity, interludes of peaceful sleep were seen to serve a divine purpose in overcoming fatigue (Eccles. 5:12; Jer. 31:26). As the daily agent of renewal and refreshment, sleep was welcomed as a gift of life from the hands of God. Moreover, it was viewed as an especially receptive time for God to deal with the inner spirit, both because the outer passivity induced by sleep suggests a lowering of human resistance and because its inner dream world suggests a suprasensual state in touch with the beyond. Thus do we find a remarkable ministry of sleep in such instances as the creation of woman from Adam (Gen. 2:21), the promise to Abraham of deliverance of his descendants (Gen. 15:12–16), the heavenly ladder of Jacob (Gen. 28:11–17), the prophetic visions of Joseph (Gen. 37:5–11), the call of Samuel (1 Sam. 3:2–10), and the prayer of Solomon (1 Kings 3:5–9).

But the Old Testament went one step further and reasoned that if sleep were an inherent part of the divine plan for our daily existence, it might play an essential role in our eternal existence as well. Because a sleeping person seems to have retreated into another world, and because a dead person so closely resembles one who is asleep, it was a simple step to describe life in this world as being awake and to describe death in the next world as being asleep. The historical records in Kings and Chronicles frequently describe a person's demise by saying that "he slept with his fathers." The assumption was that a rhythm of activity and passivity was built into not only our relationship with nature but also our relationship with God.

Nothing that Jesus could have said to Jairus was more hopeful than his use of this biblical imagery of sleep. On the one hand, it acknowledged in traditional Old Testament terminology the reality that the daughter of Jairus was in the grip of death. At the same time it chided the disconsolate crowd for failing to remember that, in God's hands, even death is no more than a gentle respite from the cares of life. But if sleep and death both begin with a lapse into unconsciousness, they do not end alike, because death is the onset of destruction whereas sleep is the prelude to renewed vitality. In other words, Jesus and the crowd both began with the same fact, that of an unresponsive little girl; but they understood this fact in diametrically different ways. What the mourners saw as her worst possible condition, Jesus viewed as her best possible condition.

This grand surmise of the Savior offers us a radically new alternative for interpreting the sleeping sicknesses of our time. His bold option requires us to consider whether a slumbering vitality lurks underneath the dormancy that we have mistaken for death. Perhaps that dead civilization is only sleeping until a true statesman comes forward to challenge its cultural lethargy. Perhaps that dead marriage is only sleeping until the partners learn to love again instead of taking each other for granted. Perhaps that dead church is only sleeping until

---

[3]For a summary of the Biblical theology of sleep, see Albrecht Oepke, *Theological Dictionary of the New Testament*, Vol. III, ed. by Gerhard Kittel (Grand Rapids: Eerdmans, 1965), pp. 431–437; Xavier Leon-Dufour (ed.), *Dictionary of Biblical Theology* (New York: Desclee, 1967), pp. 488–490.

quickened by a prophetic word that mediates the power of Christ. Let us not prematurely send for pallbearers to bury the dead when what we really need is an alarm clock to awaken the sleeping!

Sleep itself is not the problem, even when our torpor is mistaken for tragedy. Nature seems to die each winter, but this fallowing time is really the incubator of a glorious spring lush with growth. So for us, as Shakespeare had Macbeth remark:

> Sleep . . . knits up the ravell'd sleeve of care,
> The death of each day's life, sore labor's bath.
> Balm of hurt minds, great nature's second course,
> Chief nourisher in life's feast.[4]

At a deeper level, Henri Amiel noted in his journal some of the spiritual implications of sleep: "To sleep is to strain and purify the emotions, to deposit the mud of life, to calm the fever of the soul. . . . Sleep is a sort of innocence and purification. Blessed be he who gave it to the poor sons of men as the sure and faithful companion of life, our daily healer and consoler.[5]

Individuals and institutions sometimes hibernate, like the great bears do, as a way to survive "the winter of their discontent," to heal the wounds of a bitter past, and to gather strength for a fresh assault on the future. Sometimes, like Jonah, we sleep because we are afraid of a fresh challenge (Jon. 1:5); or like Elijah, because we are discouraged (1 Kings 19:5); or like the disciples in Gethsemane, because we are confused (Mark 14:37–41). But God is sovereign even in that shadowy domain, Lord both of day and of night, of light and of darkness, of waking and of sleeping. When our spirits sink into what seems to be a coma, we are not beyond God's reach, even at that depth of detachment. Do not despair over the somnolence of soul either in yourself or in others. No matter how sluggish or lethargic or apathetic a heart may seem to be, our ultimate confidence is in the God "who neither slumbers nor sleeps" (Ps. 121:4)!

III. If in place of the tears, grief, and despair over death we put the patience, expectancy, and renewal associated with sleep, then we see that the very hopefulness latent in sleep makes it all the more crucial that we awaken to claim its benefits. Merely to sleep on and on has no value and can lead to the laziness of the sluggard (Prov. 10:5; 19:15). While we do need recurring respite from our toil in order to be refreshed, such sleep is no excuse for indolence and inertia. Indeed, the only way to tell whether someone is dead or only sleeping is to see if they can wake up! The key question, therefore, is, Who can shake our weary spirits from their deepest slumber lest we oversleep and miss the brightness of God's new day? The answer of our text is clear: Christ is the one who can rouse even the dead from their repose.

This summons to Jairus's daughter was so unforgettable that Mark recorded it in the original Galilean Aramaic dialect: "*Talitha cumi*" (Mark 5:41). The tenderness of the words is lost in more prosaic translations. Perhaps the flavor is captured in a paraphrase such as, "Little

---

[4]*Macbeth*, act II, scene II, lines 37–40.
[5]Henri Frédéric Amiel, *Journal*, Mar. 20, 1853. Cited in Carroll E. Simcox, *A Treasury of Quotations on Christian Themes* (New York: Seabury, 1975), p. 58, entry 619.

darling, it's time to get up." The mother may have used some such phrase hundreds of times as she called her sleeping child to awaken: "Sweetheart, it's sunrise!" But on the lips of Jesus this was more than a customary wake-up call to leave the arms of Morpheus and greet the dawn. It was a two-word declaration of the gospel, an invitation to "Come alive!" and throw off the clinging shroud of death. In that simple but unforgettable formula, Jesus announced to a ruler of the synagogue (Mark 5:22) from which he had been excommunicated (Mark 3:6) that the resurrection triumph of life over death was about to take place in his very own home!

Nor was this merely one isolated exception to the rule that death always has the last word. The Roman Church of Mark's day, reeling under the savage fury of a mad Caesar, was driven into the catacombs, persecuted in the Coliseum, ridiculed by the ruling classes, scorned as the scum of the Empire. How easy it would have been to sign the death warrant of early Christianity, for it seemed, like Jairus's daughter, to be "at the point of death" (Mark 5:23). But no, cried the Lord of the Church, "not dead but sleeping"; and back from the brink of despair and destruction came a vital, triumphant movement that dared to write a gospel of good news while its obituary was being read in the streets of the Imperial City. In century after century the Church has awakened to outlive its pallbearers, all because of a Savior who keeps grasping its lifeless hand and crying, *"Talitha cumi"*—Come alive!

How many dead spots lie buried within the human heart! Despite our best intentions, moral commitments are compromised, spiritual disciplines are neglected, the sight of aching need fails to rouse compassion, prayer and worship no longer revive our languid feelings. It is as if the soul has gone to sleep or, worse, is in a coma! "Yes," says Jesus, "there is a sleep like unto death. But your condition is not fatal, for I wake the dead!" And so he comes to us, not when we send for him or recognize him or welcome him, but when somebody cares enough to intercede on our behalf. When others have given us up for dead, when we are viewed as hopeless cases because we have become indifferent, apathetic, and backslidden, he comes to rebuke the hand-wringing mourners and offer us a new lease on life. He whispers in our ear, *"Talitha cumi,"* and invites us to live again in defiance of the spiritual death that seeks to claim another victim.

On May 21, 1967, twenty-year-old Gene Tipps was in an automobile accident near Seymour, Texas, that left him in a permanent, trancelike, semiconscious stupor, utterly unresponsive to any outside influence. Even though he eventually learned to shuffle about with the aid of a walker and could say a few words when prompted, he did not want to do anything. Left to himself he would sleep twenty hours a day. He seemed withdrawn and indifferent, unable or unwilling to see or hear anything. But then on May 16, 1975, shortly after gallbladder surgery, Gene just as suddenly escaped from his dark and terrible dungeon. His first question to his mother was, "How long have I been in the hospital?" to which she guardedly replied, "three days," fearing that he was still confused. Immediately he wanted to rush back to college lest he be suspended for having more than five days of absences. When his mother asked, "Gene, are you awake?" he sat up and responded, "Why sure, Mother. I've never been more awake in my life."

Only slowly could Tipps realize that he hadn't really been awake for eight years. His college mates had graduated, married, and taken jobs. The Vietnam War was over and Lyndon Johnson was no longer president. Neither the attending physician, Dr. Randal, nor the specialists whom he consulted, could explain either his long sleep or his sudden reawakening. But it was all possible because his parents never gave up on him. Day after day they sat by his bed trying to wake him up. They sold their land to pay his hospital bills. His mother's face was now much older than her son remembered it. But the effort was worth it all, for their son was awake at last; he had come back to life as if he had been raised from the dead.[6]

All about us are lifeless individuals and institutions, many of them given up for dead. Some have been utterly unresponsive to the challenges of life for years on end, content just to go through the motions in a sort of spiritual stupor as if they could not or would not hear God's wake-up call. Don't rush out to bury that marriage or that job or that church as hopeless because it appears to be dead. Indeed, don't give up on yourself even if your soul seems to be suffering from a terminal case of sleeping sickness. Perhaps in God's good time you have now slept long enough. Hear the word of the gospel as Christ comes to shout, "*Talitha cumi*"—wake up! Feel his touch as even now he seizes your hand, raises you up, and bids us give you something to eat (Mark 5:43). Take nourishment from God's people and, with our help, learn to live again!—William E. Hull

Topic: Easter People
TEXT: 1 Pet. 1:3–9

Folks who have frequently participated in formal worship tend to know the Doxology from memory, maybe without even thinking: "Praise God from whom all blessings flow." A *doxology* is literally a "word of praise," a short song. It may stand alone in the service, but it is usually sung in response to something else, such as the offering, a prayer, the reading of Scripture, or a final word on the entire event of worship. In planning formal worship, doxologies do not just happen. We collaborate and plot to place doxologies at appropriate turning points in the service. On any given Sunday you may not feel particularly moved to song or overflowing with joy when you are called to your feet to sing, but you stand up with the congregation and join in the chorus anyway. Even if you are still mulling over an argument with your spouse or reeling from the chaos of getting yourself and the kids ready for church; even if you don't feel it deep inside, you sing anyway. Why do we do it? Singing doxology is infectious. Before you get to "Amen" you may begin to praise the God from whom all blessings flow.

There is another kind of doxology. It is that spontaneous sense of overwhelming joy that flows out of the moving experiences of daily life. Most of us have been there. Rufus Ritchie recently sent me the words of an old Louie Armstrong song and observed the element of doxology it contains. It enumerates some of the simple joys of life: "I see trees of green, red roses, too / I see them bloom for me and you." Each experience leads to the refrain: "And I think to myself, what a wonderful world." Have you been there? Have you ever felt like singing in response to a glorious sunset, the birth of a child, a good report after surgery or chemotherapy, or an unexplained epiphany? The best doxology is spontaneous—the song of joy that erupts from the soul in the middle of the day or the darkest moment of night. I think that must be what Luke was thinking in Acts 16:25, in a Philippian prison: "About midnight Paul and Silas were praying and singing hymns to God, and the prisoners were listening to them." Spontaneous doxology from Easter people!

I. *Easter people are reborn into hope.* The metaphor of rebirth tends to get overdone these days. People who have little or no knowledge of the gospel talk about being reborn through

---

[6]Joseph P. Blank, "The Long Sleep of Gene Tipps," *Reader's Digest*, Jan. 1976, pp. 51–54.

hearing a county-western song on the radio, through changing jobs, or by taking a new drug. Jimmy Carter faced ridicule by the secular press when he identified himself as a "born-again Christian." Even in the public square *born-again* has become more a political code word for "right-wing evangelical conservative" than for "transformation through Christ." Perhaps we ought to be jealous of the secular mind that steals language and ideas from the Christian gospel, but I prefer to see this flowing testimonial to the transforming moments in life as the hunger of the human soul for God. Distinct from our religion or our belief in God, all of us pass through portals in life that are turning points and moments of definition. Deep down inside all of us there is a longing for conversion. Maybe that is why "Amazing Grace" speaks to such a large audience. Even secular people long for the kind of experience that proclaims, "I once was lost but now am found, 'twas blind but now I see."

Early Christians came out of the darkness of Good Friday into the light of Easter singing doxologies to God. As Paul did in many of his Epistles, Peter began with a doxology reflecting the new context of life in Christ. Christians are Easter people. The Resurrection of Jesus is more than a memory to be cherished or an anniversary to be observed. Nothing in life was the same after Easter morning. Through the Resurrection of Christ we are born again into a living hope. God's raising Christ from death was the turning point not only for him but for us. Easter became the window through which all of the rest of life is viewed.

Try as I will I cannot remember my birth. It happened through forces totally beyond my control. Christian rebirth is like that. We are born anew through the grace of God, not through a personal reform or the discovery of a new dimension of life. Some believe that this passage was connected to baptism. New Christians were reminded that they were buried with Christ by baptism into death and raised to walk in newness of life.

II. *Easter people find meaning even in suffering.* We visited the Japanese city of Hiroshima in 1995. As we entered the city in the "bullet train," we were impressed by the uniformity and age of the buildings. At the center of town, the steel framework of a public building stands as a reminder of that horrible day—August 6, 1945—when the atomic bomb was dropped on the city. The museum and the Peace Bell are among the many reminders of what happened that day, but the rubble has been removed and a new city has emerged from the ruins.

Not everything in life is good or worth celebrating. That is true for Christians as well as for everyone else. This Epistle to the first-century Christians contains four references to unjust suffering. Peter addresses unjust trials, the unfair suffering of slaves, repercussions for bearing witness in the world, and the "fiery ordeal" of the Christian life. Although no less devastating than any other pain, suffering for a cause in Christ is pictured as the labor of childbirth or the refiner's fire that purifies and refines faith. Life can end in disaster, and it often does. Through the power of God, life can begin anew with the most horrible experience imaginable. How many times have I heard the testimony that following illness, fire, business collapse, unemployment, and death the power of God was at work in bringing life out of ruin? We should not be surprised. Jesus said that we must die to self in order to live, that those who lose their lives for the gospel will save them.

III. *Easter people live by faith rather than by sight.* John proclaimed the word of life that was from the beginning, that witnesses had heard, seen, and touched. But we cannot turn back the clock to the first century and hear the word, see the miracles, or touch Christ for ourselves. We walk by faith, by trust in the God who raised Jesus from the dead, rather than by certainty, proofs, or direct evidence. We are not among the witnesses of the Resurrection or the visitors to the empty tomb. We are totally dependent on the work of God among the Easter people. Yet we are not abandoned here. We meet Christ in his body, the Church, and we experience God's grace in our hearts. Without seeing, we love him. Without the certainty of sight, we believe in him and celebrate with doxologies of indescribable joy.

Branko Lovrec is president of the Baptist Union of Croatia. He told of the days of the Old Soviet Union when the old Communist regime was intent on wiping out the remnants of religion. Some five thousand people were gathered for a lecture by a government representative on the futility of the Christian faith, denying the reality of God and the truth of Christ. As a pretense of fair play, an old priest was brought out of prison to stand before the people and called upon to refute the official party line. Shaken and frightened, he stepped to the microphone. After a pause to gather his thoughts, he declared, "Christ is risen!" and five thousand people responded with the ancient doxology of Easter, "He is risen indeed!" The deep roots of the gospel were still there. We are Easter people.—Larry Dipboye

MESSAGES FOR ADVENT AND CHRISTMAS

SERMON SUGGESTIONS

Topic: Seeing the Light, Reflecting the Light

TEXT: Isa. 60:1–4; John 3:16–21

It all happened at once for Sam. His wife left him. His hours were cut way back at work. Because his income was down, he fell behind on his court-ordered child support. And because he was behind on his child support, his wife started restricting access to their son, who was the one ray of light in his life.

It was at this dark hour that he was invited to church by a friend at work. (He had left his childhood religion behind a long time ago.) His friend was from a different ethnic group than Sam, and Sam wondered just who was at this church anyway. But his friend said, "Don't worry about it; we're all kinds of people at our church. You'll be welcome."

Sam hesitated. The bare walls of his apartment were driving him crazy, but he didn't want to get into a bunch of pushy religious nuts. Yet he was so lonely, and he felt so bitter, toward *her*, toward life. His friend made him feel hopeful. So the question was this: Would he open up to this new ray of light that was coming his way, or would he stay closed up? Would he pass his bitterness and blame on to his son, who was so vulnerable now? Or would he model for his son hope, confidence in the possibilities of the future, a nonjudgmental spirit? Sam wasn't thinking of it in these terms yet, but through his compassionate friend he was having a close encounter with the love of God. How would he respond?

In the dark centuries of Israel's exile, after the Babylonians had conquered Jerusalem and scattered the people of the land, a prophet in the tradition of Isaiah spoke words of hope:

> Arise, shine; for your light has come,
> and the glory of the Lord has risen upon you.
> For darkness shall cover the Earth,
> And thick darkness the peoples;
> but the Lord will arise upon you,
> and his glory will appear over you [Isa. 60:1–2].

Whatever your situation—as individuals, as a family, or as a nation—the love of God is constant and true. God never forgets us or ignores us or ceases to seek our welfare. No matter how dark and hopeless our situation is, God's love is unfailing.

American poet Francis Thompson has characterized our God as "the hound of heaven"— maybe not a positive image if your first association is from old grade-B prison movies, with the hounds baying after some poor unfortunate escaped convict. But if we realize how many of our wounds are self-inflicted, if we acknowledge how often we have shut ourselves off from those who would love us and comfort us, from the one who would heal us and renew us, then perhaps we will see Thompson's image differently. God's love is unrelenting; he never gives up on his own; and at the root, no matter how full of doubt and blame and cynicism we are, we are all God's own. God's love is light in the darkness, hope where there is despair, and the hope of glory—which brings us to our Gospel text.

John 3:16 is probably the most famous and oft-quoted verse in the entire Bible: "For God so loved the world that he gave his only Son, so that everyone who believes in him may not perish but may have eternal life." This is a wonderful summary of God's attitude and intentions toward us and his action on our behalf. But when we are thinking about God's offer of salvation expressed in this text, we usually stop at the end of verse 16. Yet there's more.

John 3:17–21 speaks of two responses to God's love expressed in Christ. Some people are "condemned"—a strong and terrifying word—"because they have not believed in the name of the only Son of God" (3:18). This is not a statement about correct doctrine. Nor is it a teaching about a judgmental, condemning sort of God. For "this is the judgment, that the light [there's that imagery again] has come into the world, and people loved darkness rather than light because their deeds were evil" (John 3:19).

God's love is light. In fact, in the physical cosmos all reality is light. Einstein's famous equation $E = mc^2$ means, in nontechnical terms, that the whole material world is a steady state of radiant energy or congealed light. And the one who said "Let there be light" (Gen. 1:3) at the beginning of creation is continuing to brood over creation in its brokenness, working to heal it and renew it and restore it. Light can encourage us and literally heal us, like the sunlight that lifts our mood after a season of gloom and bathes our skin in vitamin D.

But if we are lying or cheating or going behind someone's back, we prefer the cover of darkness. We are like the *cucarachas* that sprinted under the baseboards every time I turned on the lights in that ground floor bachelor apartment I had years ago in New York City. Untruth and double-dealing hate the light. Some things prefer to be done in the dark. "For all who do evil hate the light and do not come to the light, so that their deeds may not be exposed" (John 3:20). The same divine love that created us in the first place now offers us forgiveness and healing and restoration. But if we cling to our sin, God's light will expose us and undo us.

Popular wisdom says, "What goes around comes around." Jesus said, "Whatever you have said in the dark will be heard in the light, and what you have whispered behind closed doors will be proclaimed from the housetops" (Luke 12:3). So the first stop to our healing is to come clean, to open up to God's love, which must expose our sinfulness and our helplessness in order to heal us. The twelve-step programs that are descendants of Alcoholics Anonymous all begin with the confession that we are in thrall to an alien power and cannot help ourselves. So we must open up to a higher power, which alone can break our bondage.

The light of God's love has broken into our human history in Jesus Christ. How will we see that light? How will we respond to it? When God's love shines into our lives—often in the form of a friend's love, as in the case of Sam—will we open ourselves up? Will we welcome that love and embrace it, even when our initial encounter with it brings the wounding and cauterizing that precedes healing? Or will we close ourselves up to the light? Will we flee and hide? In reality, when we reject the light by failing to trust—God or other people—by hiding behind cynicism, by preferring comfortable lies to challenging truths, we condemn ourselves, as the Scripture says. But when we open ourselves up to the light, we will receive healing and forgiveness and hope and joy. What will be your response?

We've been talking about seeing and responding to the light. But there's one more issue I want to bring up. In John 3:21 we read, "But those who do what is true come to the light, so that it may be clearly seen that their deeds have been done in God." When we accept and embrace the light of God's love, our lives and our deeds become reflections of that light. It is a *reflected* light, not one that we produce ourselves, but it can be a beautiful light, like the sunlight reflected in tones of liquid silver by the moon.

It's been said so often that it's almost a preacher's cliché, but it's still true: you and I may often be the only Christ some particular someone will ever see. A simple invitation to worship by Sam's friend—coming at a dark and discouraging moment in Sam's life—combined with the consistent kindness and friendliness in that friend's life, made that friend become Christ for Sam. He had the light of Christ in his life, and he reflected it onto one who was walking in darkness.

Do you and I consistently reflect the light of the Christ we profess to love? Do we actively express his kindness and his compassion? Do we dare say, alongside the apostle Paul, "Be imitators of me, as I am of Christ" (1 Cor. 11:1)? Are we consistently forgiving, helpful, and eager to seek the best for our neighbor? Do our lives display the "fruit of the Spirit[, which] is love, joy, peace, patience, kindness, generosity, faithfulness, gentleness, and self-control" (Gal. 5:22–23)? And do we display these behaviors with a pure heart, seeking the advent of Christ's reign and not our own glory? Or to put it another way, dare we say, along with John the Baptist, "He must increase, but I must decrease" (John 3:30)?

At our annual Festival of Lights, our great sanctuary will be transformed from darkness into light as our young people process through its length and breadth, both on the ground level and in the balcony, lighting hundreds of candles. Their light represents "the true light, which enlightens everyone, which was coming into the world" at the first Advent (John 1:9). But the candles represent *us*—you and me—who are called upon to reflect the light of the one Savior, each in our own unique way.—David L. Wheeler

Topic: God's Personal Word
TEXT: John 1:1–14

Our God is a God who speaks and a God who, just as truly, demands an answer.

I. (a) The life of God has been manifested as light shining in darkness. The light appeared in the remotest ages of man's history. The light appeared to Abraham, to Moses, to Hosea and Amos, to Isaiah and Jeremiah.

(b) The light appeared to all mankind (Rom. 1:20).

(c) The light shines today. It has penetrated the darkness far more deeply than ever before. Christian missions gird the globe.

II. The light came especially in Jesus Christ, for he was "the true Light" (John 1:9). Besides being called the true Light, Jesus Christ is also designated "the Word" (John 1:14), because he is the expression of the power and activity of God.

A responsible person speaks purposefully and wisely and things happen. God speaks and world is created, a prophet is inspired, history is guided, or man is visited by God in the person of his Son.

III. (a) Human history is one long story of the rejection of light and life. Into the darkness, light has come. But men have tried to extinguish the light. When Jesus Christ, the true

Light, came, men rejected him—but not only the Jews! The message of Jesus was not welcome in many a Gentile city.

(b) Wherever sin has been entrenched and loved in personal life, in society, in business, and in government, men have been less than glad to receive Jesus Christ. Light reveals filth, injustice, dishonesty, and greed. Therefore, when the deeds of men are evil, they love darkness (John 3:19).

IV. The story does not end with the rejection and Crucifixion of Jesus. There were many who welcomed him, loved him, walked with him, and died for him. "To all who received him, who believed in his name, he gave power to become children of God" (John 1:12 RSV).

The story of our Christian experience begins with a conversion experience. At first there may be little emotional evidence that anything remarkable took place when Christ was received. But an intimate friendship with Christ will, sooner or later, make many definite differences. We receive "grace upon grace" (John 1:16 RSV).—James W. Cox

Topic: Christmas Is Coming!
TEXT: Phil. 4:4–13

The apostle Paul takes it on the chin for any number of ethical distortions and apparently unChristian stances that surfaced in the letters he wrote to his churches. He gets it in the neck for insisting that the women in his churches must be quiet and take the back seats. In another letter he urged his friend Philemon to treat a slave like a brother—a kindly gesture, of course—but accepted slavery without a murmur. In most of his letters he took the Hebrew Scriptures and recast their meaning in light of the Messiah criminalized and crucified by the Romans—thus breeding confusion and hostility between Christians and Jews for two thousand years.

But one of his most challenging admonitions, though almost benign, rests in the letter he wrote to the church at Philippi. "Do not worry about anything," he said. James Moffat translates it, "Never be anxious, . . . Do not be anxious." Some of us wonder what Paul is driving at. We take a look at the state of the world and shudder now and again at the terrific changes taking place, wondering about our own capacity to keep up. There is plenty on a global level to be anxious about. The AIDS plague devours southern Africa, wiping out the bulk of the next generation. The rich nations continue to get richer, and of the $1.1 trillion made in foreign investment in a recent year, one half of 1 percent went to the poorest of the Earth's nations. That spells trouble.

The anxieties generated by these global issues only play into more personal issues. We can find ourselves now and again seemingly riding on a roller coaster, and Christmas tends to throw these personal anxieties into bolder relief. Here, for instance, we know a parent who at Christmas is eager for family solidarity and reconciliation, yet he is anxious about how he will communicate with his own children. Or no doubt any number of us worry about how we stack up against others, whether we are liked, or if anyone really cares a whit. Some among us skirt the black hole of loneliness, others discover ourselves afraid of death, and still others are even more fearful of life.

Robert Reich authored a book called "The Future of Success." A reporter asked him, "What's the book about?" Reich answered, "It's about making a living and making a life and why it not only seems to be but actually is getting harder to do both." Most of us are doing better materially in this new economy. Yet we're also working longer hours and under greater stress. The deepest anxieties of this prosperous age are about aspects of our lives that can't be bought—the erosion of family; our own inadequacies as spouses, as parents; the difficulty of sustaining genuine friendships; the brittleness of our communities; and the challenge of keeping intact our own integrity.

And yes, at Christmastime the number of people who take their own lives tends to spike. How come? Well, at least partly because the Christmas light, the Christmas hope, the Christmas promise sharpens our anxieties. Some of us find ourselves giving up, ready to exclaim with Scrooge, "Humbug!" Others of us hang on tentatively to a shard of faith, hoping to scrape through the crisis.

Why, then, are churches all across the world this morning reading an exuberant imperative from Paul's letter to the church at Philippi? Indeed, what was Paul talking about? Why did he urge the congregation in Philippi to rejoice? And especially how dare he insist that they not worry, that they carry no anxiety about anything? Was Paul for real? Did he understand what kind of world this is?

You bet he did. Paul knew as well as or more than most of us what kind of precarious world we live in. The Romans jailed him. He wrote this letter from prison. His life was on the line. His beloved churches in Thessalonica, Corinth, Ephesus, and Philippi appeared on the cusp of the abyss, perhaps faltering to the point of disappearing. Paul battled adversaries who labeled him a liar and a fraud. His closest companion deserted him. He was broke. Nothing went right. And out of it all came this incredible summons, "Rejoice in the Lord always! Again I say, Rejoice. Have no worry; have no anxiety about anything!"

Have no anxiety about anything? Was Paul crazy? Had jail unhinged him? Was this classic denial? No way! Paul told his friends in Philippi—and he tells us—that the most important things in our lives are not necessarily the things triggering our anxiety. He said that we bet our lives on the wrong things—on things that tend to fail and fall apart, on things that disintegrate and lead inevitably to anxiety. He suggested that we tend to invest our lives in what everybody else is doing or saying, on the latest fad or fashion, rather than creating a new reality rooted and grounded in confidence and hope. He told us that through the worst that life can do to us the hand of God holds us, the heart of God bleeds with us. The destiny God promises us resides not so much in how things are today but rather in the courage and hope granted to us to encounter and triumph through tough times and terrible trouble. In short, Paul says that we confuse the transient with the eternal, and anxiety is the baneful consequence.

So what did he do? What was Paul's answer to our problem? What did he recommend for our anxiety? Incredibly, he offered no slick gimmick. He prescribed no therapeutic stunt for the resolution of our anxieties—nothing except offering everything we have to God in prayer and thanksgiving.

My soul! That's it? No counseling? No therapy? No potion, pill, or prescription? Not even perusal of the self-help bibliography at Barnes and Noble that dispenses such profound advice as "How to make people like you in ninety seconds or less," or of that psychiatric masterpiece, *Stress Management for Dummies*. What is this? Prayer and thanksgiving for our anxieties? Yes, by heaven, that's it! Paul knew what gets us off our own hands, out of our binds, and into a new perspective on the things eating us up and doing us in. He knew what finally releases us from thinking that we must carry everything by ourselves. He knew what frees us from taking the blame for life's surprises, brooding over its jagged edges, surrendering to its looming failures. "Come on," he said, "the Lord is at hand! . . . The Lord is at hand!" Do you know what that is shorthand for? "Christmas is coming! . . . *Christmas is coming!*" Your primary security lies in God's hanging onto you through thick and through thin, never letting you go, though all of the props around you seem to collapse, though the things or places or people you trust founder and topple. What the Lord grants is not immunity from life's troubles, not exemption from its breakdowns and trauma. What the Lord provides is strength, courage, forbearance, and patience to brave the troubles, and even, in God's good time, to turn them into good.

Now that is quite a promise. It is a promise borne by Christmas. But I do know that some of us from time to time need not simply big doses of encouragement and faith; we also need little doses. I am a little anxious this morning that some of us are a anxious about Christmas. We worry about expenditures, extravagant use of credit cards, January payments. And some of us worry about what we might give to so and so. We are stumped. We want to offer something but cannot seem to come up with the appropriate item. Well, if you will excuse me for just a few minutes, let me allay some of your anxiety and give you a hint or two. I take my clues from that wonderful Christmas ballad "The Twelve Days of Christmas." We sing it at our Christmas luncheon each year, upstairs in Mary Norton Hall, each table acting out a different gift. Remember? Its first verse goes,

On the first day of Christmas
My true love gave to me a partridge in a pear tree.

And then the carol continues with a whole set of ridiculous and bizarre gifts.

Well, I like the way Halford Lucckock, one of the great preachers, puts it. Are the words of this carol "nonsense?" he asks. "A partridge in a pear tree?" "Not by a júgful of wassail. It is a profound philosophy of giving. It celebrates the high wisdom of completely inappropriate and largely useless gifts. And a good thing to remember just before Christmas."

A partridge in a pear tree? What on Earth could one do with that? That is the beauty of it! That makes it something to sing about! And folks have been singing about it for several hundred years. Would they have sung about a floor mop (highly appropriate for house-cleaning) or a teakettle or a foot warmer? Not likely.

So, to alleviate that gift-giving anxiety I advise you to give to those you love and care about something totally oblique, different, a little off the wall.

Now, of course, if we want precedent for all of this, all we have to do is look at the first Christmas. What kind of gifts were given then? Appropriate ones? Are you kidding? A baby born in poverty in an out-of-the-way rural village, with no pomp, no circumstance, no big celebration except among a couple of folks who could really see—John's mother Elizabeth; an old temple dweller, Simeon; and of course, baby Jesus' mother.

Odd. Unexpected. Stunning! Like a partridge in a pear tree.

So, friends, Christmas is coming! And as we await Christmas with serenity and courage, having surrendered to its promise, Paul urges us, "Whatever is true, whatever is honorable, whatever is just, whatever is pure, whatever is pleasing, whatever is commendable, if there is any excellence and if there is anything worthy of praise, think about these things."

Now there is an ethic for Advent! We live out of our confidence, hope, and security in the love of God. I am told that a wonderful book entitled "Standing on the Promises" says that "hoping for others is hard, but not the hardest. Praying for others is hard, but not the hardest." The hardest part for people who live as if Christmas is coming lies "in living the sort of life that makes people say, 'Ah, so that's how people are going to live when righteousness takes over the world.'"

Indeed. Whatever is true, honorable, just, and pure: how do we sustain that integrity with Christmas coming? Here is a clue. I read the other day of the Connecticut Legislature in session some 220 years ago. They met on a bright day in May and the delegates did their work by the sun's light. But then something happened that no one expected. As they debated, an eclipse hid the sun and the room became shrouded in darkness. Some legislators thought that the day of the Lord was no longer at hand but really bursting in upon them. A clamor arose. Some members urged adjournment. Others called for prayer. Whatever—the legislators sought to prepare for a turbulent Advent.

But the speaker of the house—true, honest, commendable—did not worry. No anxiety there. A Christian, he rose to the occasion with confidence and courage. "This darkness upsets us all," he said. "Some of us are afraid. But the day of the Lord is at hand or it is not. If it is not, there is no cause for adjournment. And if the Lord is returning, I for one choose to be found doing my duty. I therefore ask the candles be brought."

Of course! Is the Lord at hand? Is Christmas coming? Whatever is true, honorable, just, pure, pleasing, commendable—if there is any excellence and if there is anything worthy of praise, think about—and do—these things. Do not be anxious about anything, but in prayer and supplication with thanksgiving let your requests be made known to God. And yes, rejoice in the Lord always. Again, I say, rejoice!—James W. Crawford

Topic: Christmas Hope! Where Does It Begin?
TEXT: Matt. 1:1–17

At Christmastime, why read an arcane, dreary genealogy? Here we gather under a beautiful Annunciation window, with shepherds gazing at angels who announce the coming of peace to our world. We worship in a sanctuary all dressed up for a celebration. We hunger for the radiant story that Luke narrates: Mary's startled and joyful celebration, the holy family and their trip to Bethlehem, the babe in the manger. Or give us Matthew's birth narrative with Joseph's confusion, Herod's threats, the magi's trickery. But please, on the brink of Christmas Day, not an obscure, tedious genealogy. Boring!

Hold it! Don't despair! Don't give up! Don't go home! I have some fantastic news to share with you this morning—news imbedded in this interminable train of names. Like everything else in the New Testament, it comes to us as perceived through the lenses of indomitable hope. It does not necessarily get its genealogical facts straight, but it does get its meanings straight. What appears to us to be an opaque, virtually irrelevant Christmas narrative in fact reveals the radiance of the Christmas hope. And more, it offers clues to where the Christmas story begins; and even better, it tells us who bears the story today.

But let's take just a moment to understand this long string of names. We cannot compare this genealogy to the one gracing our Bibles at home. We find this genealogy cut from entirely different cloth. Our family Bible, for instance, sits on a table in our living room. You can discover bloodlines, genes, and chromosomes pointing right to the clown speaking to you this very moment. It is a conventional genealogical progression. The biology makes sense.

But we find Matthew up to something far different. He could not care less about biology. Bloodlines take the back seat. Genes, chromosomes, DNA—forget them. Matthew tells a story. He tells Israel's messianic story.

If we twenty-first-century types asked where the story of Jesus began, we would no doubt begin searching for a place, date, and time. We would seek information transferable to a birth certificate. You know: "born at 2:37 A.M. at Bethlehem, Judea, the son of Mary and Joseph, December 25, the year zero." Not Matthew. Matthew begins with the telling of a dynamic, redemptive saga. He begins with Abraham. Remember? The one who headed off for a promised land not knowing where he was to go, living only by a promise—a promise that he and his people would serve as a light to the nations. Matthew then tells us about those who bore the promise for literally thousands of years. He includes David, the grandest of Israel's monarchs, who combined religious, political, and economic power—the very definition of messianic hope. Matthew ends by telling us how that promise beginning with Abraham finally culminated in that Bethlehem manger.

Let me give you an analogy. Suppose we tried to tell the story of Martin Luther King Jr. and his beginnings. Where would we start? Perhaps with one grandfather a sharecropper and the other a minister. We would include his birth on January 15, 1929; his marriage to Corretta Scott and the birth of their four children: Bernice, Dexter, Yolanda, and Martin. That is perfect for the New England Genealogical Society over here on Newbury Street. But in Matthew's terms, Martin Luther King's story might look more like this: The story of Martin Luther King Jr. begins with Jesus Christ, and to use the language of the King James Version here, Jesus Christ who begat the apostle Paul who begat John Calvin who begat John Winthrop who begat Crispus Attuks who begat Thomas Jefferson who begat Nat Turner who begat Sojourner Truth who begat Frederick Douglass who begat Abraham Lincoln, president during the great war to abolish slavery and promote human rights. Abraham Lincoln begat Susan B. Anthony who begat W.E.B. Dubois who begat Rosa Parks who begat Martin Luther King Jr.

Bloodlines? No way! Genetics? Forget it. You might call it the bloodlines of freedom, the genetics of justice, the genealogy of hope. These names provide keys to a stunning saga describing the meaning of Americans as a people.

Just so with Matthew: He chooses names beginning with Abraham, telling the story of a people's hope for a new world of justice, grace, and peace. The names that Matthew offers us are not necessarily related to one another by blood. He binds them by a purpose, to bring into our breaking and fragmenting world a new community where, as the prophet says, "The wolf shall lie down with the lamb, the leopard shall lie down with the kid, the calf, the lion and the fatling together . . . and a little child shall lead them." Or in a contemporary vein, a world where the Albanian can live with the Serb, the Muslim with the Hindu, the Israeli with the Palestinian, the Chechnyan with the Russian, the Tutsi with the Hutu, the black with the white—and in that new world joy shall reign among our wild and churning diversity. Matthew marches us through Israel's liberation history right smack up to the Christmas hope for a liberated human community blessed by joy, solidarity, and peace.

Names and stories of hope, you ask? Show us. In spite of the suggestive reading, we see only an eye-glazing, ear-deadening inventory of unpronounceable male monikers. True. But look a little closer and you will see the names, excluding Mary, of four women. See them? Tamar, Rahab, Ruth, and "the wife of Uriah the Hittite," whom we all know to be Bathsheba. Are you looking for some spice in your Christmas punch? Search no further!

Take Tamar, for instance. Absolutely taboo. She connived to bear a son by her father-in-law. Talk about a dysfunctional family! The father-in-law turned out to be a jerk! In short, Tamar's husband, Judah's eldest son, got slain. Judah was supposed to supply additional husbands. His first candidate refused to consummate the marriage, his second candidate turned out to be too young. Judah told Tamar to wait until the boy grew up; then they could marry. But Judah failed in his promise and Tamar was left without children. Yet for Matthew, even more important is that Judah was left without grandchildren. The promise tilted on the edge of disaster. Hope plunged toward a black hole. So Tamar, as Matthew perceives it, for God's sake, for hope's survival, executed a shocking maneuver. She disguised herself as a prostitute and seduced Judah, her father-in-law. Nine months later she bore a child through what the law considered incest! But hear this: by this incestuous seduction, according to Matthew, Tamar kept the Messianic promise alive—a promise and hope arising from her gut. Her courage and desperate daring resulted centuries later in hope's birth in a Bethlehem manger.

Now, friends, would you put Tamar front and center in your family picture album? Hardly. You'd blot her out, prune her from the family tree. But for Matthew, when the future appeared bleak, Tamar and her audacity sustained the Christmas hope. Dump Tamar? Dump Christmas!

Or take Rahab. Now in Rahab we meet no woman disguised as a prostitute. Rahab was the real thing. She ran a brothel. When Joshua, out to conquer the Promised Land, sent two spies to reconnoiter Jericho, they quartered themselves in Rahab's establishment. When the Caananite KGB came to seize the spies, Rahab lied to them. She sent those cops off on a wild goose chase. She concealed the spies and enabled their escape, resulting in her own nation's defeat.

What have we here? A foreigner, a Gentile, an outsider, a tainted woman, a traitor to her own people, another wipeout in the family gallery. But, my soul, there she confronts us in Matthew's family album—a veritable forebear of the Christ. She radically advanced—no! She assured—the promise. Think of it: Ditch Rahab? Ditch Christmas.

Or Ruth. Again we have the astounding story of an irregular union between a man and a woman. Ruth—another despised outsider whose bloodlines carried no status but who, because of her devotion to an alien Jew named Boaz, turned out to be the grandmother of King David. King David, the one who modeled the contours of the Christmas hope. Scrub Ruth? Scrub Christmas!

Or Bathsheba. You know her story. David commanded her to come to his palace, committed adultery with her, and got her pregnant. David plotted her husband's death, they got married, and their love child died. Then she bore Solomon and later, just as a thug tried to usurp David's throne, Bathsheba intervened with David in Solomon's behalf. She saved the Christmas hope. Without Bathsheba, kiss the Christmas hope goodbye.

And folks, if you think the women stretch it, consider the men—totally bad news!—from Jacob, the root of Israel—crafty, shrewd, a master of deceit—through David—conniving, cynical. Talk about giving politics a bad name—David knocked heads to create an empire. These guys—our ancestors in the faith? They are red meat for the *National Enquirer*. Purveyors of hope? Say it isn't so!

What is going on here? What is Matthew doing? He tells us that the Christmas hope made its way through some terrible, narrow scrapes. Hope looked dead and then, in some almost absurd if not perverse fashion, came alive again. The Christmas hope was carried down through the centuries in frail and fragile human hands, in which we see vulnerability to pettiness, corruption, and stupidity. No sentimentality, no fairy tales, no fantasies, no goody-two-shoes characters here. Indeed, the pictures in Matthew's family album look more like some people we have known, maybe some people we *are*. What a parade, this gang that shouldered the promise, salvaged hope, and bore Christmas to consummation. Who was it who said, "God writes straight with crooked lines?"

And after David, a string of names—kings, prophets, monarchs, and hierarchs; the likes of Rehoboam, Asa, and Jehosophat. Some of them were adequate, some were corrupt. Others were incompetent, still others were egregiously wicked or such failures that finally this people bearing the hope of the world was forcibly dragged out of its own land and forced to live in exile under a foreign tyrant. Whatever else that second series of names beginning with Solomon and ending with national disintegration in Babylon means, it is that the promise is held in nations and peoples; it resides in political states and religious institutions. Hear that? Religious institutions like Israel, religious institutions like churches.

That's right: churches. We find Matthew alert to our type in his genealogy, saying simply, "Hey, you churches out there; yes, you Old South in Boston: the Christmas promise can rest even with you; it can come through your slow-moving, inertia-bound, self-interested, myopic, hypocritical operation. Through all your muddle and mess; through your timid witness, your pathetic preaching, your floundering around; yes, through all your good intentions and failures of nerve, you too stand in a long line of nations and peoples who for all their frailty and self-deception, but for the grace of God, feebly bear and attempt to live the kind of world anticipated at Christmastime. Without you—you, in the churches, you in Old South—Christmas, *sayonara*.

But I must tell you that it is that last crowd in Matthew's Gospel that is truly incredible: Abiud, Eliakim, Azor, Achim, Eliud, Eleazar, Matthan and Jacob, the father of Mary's husband, Joseph. Incredible? Here is why: Every other name that Matthew uses in this Christmas genealogy can be found somewhere else in Israel's saga of salvation. But these last names don't appear anywhere else. They are anonymous nobodies. They are the little people in the family album whose names we cannot remember. They are the ones who bear hope day by day—no big deals, no daring, no neon lights, no prominent headlines. Bea Norris, Ione Sykes, Florence Schoennegee, Red Gramlich, Ruby Miller, Roger Anderson—have you ever head their names? Of course not. They were my Sunday school teachers, anonymous bearers of the Christmas promise.

You have a list of those names in your life, too. The ones who told you the Christmas story; the ones who bore the promise, who came to your aid for Christ's sake, when hope sank. Or look to the person on your left, the one on your right, the one in front of you, the one in back. Hey! Look! It's Abiud, Eliakim, Azor, Zadoc, and Eleazar. Right here in church, with you, this morning, celebrating the Christmas story carried by generations of men and women of all sorts, you and me included. We heard the promise from someone who got it from someone who experienced it through someone who saw it through someone who grasped it from someone who knew it through someone who caught it from someone: begat, begat, begat, begat.

So, my friends, where did this Christmas story with all of its promise of hope, its heralding of a new kind of world where peace with justice finally rules, where healing takes place and community flourishes—where did this story of hope begin? Well, according to Matthew it began with Abraham and, astoundingly, it moves through impostors, whores, chiselers, and pretenders. It comes through monarchs, slaves, aliens, outright scoffers, hypocrites, and even churches like this one. We see it borne by the John Does and Mary Roes of the world. With whom you identify in this bedraggled—this *magnificent*—procession I do not know. But I do know this: you have heard the Christmas story; you have been embraced by its grace; you have been restored by its forgiveness; you have been included in its peace; you have been inspired by its promise of new life for the world and for you.

O, friends, the Christmas hope! Where does it begin today? You know where. It begins—it continues—with you!—James W. Crawford

Topic: Getting Down to Earth
TEXT: John 6:37–51

Several years ago an episode of the TV show *Thirtysomething* involved a seasonal religious debate between Hope, a Christian, and her Jewish husband, Michael. Hope wanted to know why Jews bother with Hanukkah. She asked, "Do you really believe a handful of Jews held off a huge army by using a bunch of lamps that miraculously wouldn't run out of oil?"

Of course, that question opened the door for Michael to put his spin on the Christmas story: "Do you really believe that an angel appeared to some teenage girl who got pregnant without a man and traveled to Bethlehem where she spent the night in a barn and had a baby that turned out to be the Savior of the world?"

Actually, Michael's version is a fair summary of the story in Luke. A lot of folks who thoroughly enjoy the music and the lights at Christmas either haven't a clue to what the message is about or they aren't about to swallow the story that Charlie Brown read every year in the *Peanuts Christmas Story.* Evidently Muhammad got the message. The Koran declares, "Those who say that the God has begotten a son preach a monstrous falsehood." C. S. Lewis once wrote about God's plan, "The whole thing narrows and narrows, until at last it comes down to a little point, small as the point of a spear—a Jewish girl at her prayers."

Lewis was right about Luke's Gospel. If we had only Luke's Gospel, we might be limited to that small pinnacle of faith. But the message of the Christ has come to us in four Gospels. William Willimon tells about a student at Duke who came to him confessing problems with the virgin birth of Jesus. Willimon told him tongue-in-cheek to read Mark to avoid having to deal with it. Mark is content to proclaim the gospel without a word of beginning—no virgin, no angels, no shepherds, no Christmas—just Advent.

If the virginal conception of Jesus is a problem, the student might also be advised to avoid reading John. John never mentions the birth of Jesus, but he takes on the big picture and the real issue. John tries the limits of credibility. If Luke speaks for Mary and Matthew speaks for Joseph, John speaks for God. He offers a view from above, of God sitting on the top of time and creation looking down on humanity as if we were dust—as indeed we are, but so was John. John addresses the beginning of beginnings and dares to speak of things known only to the Creator. Without a hint of explanation of how these things can be, John rips right into the soul of the gospel. The power of God in creation was in the Word, and the Word became flesh. Throughout the Fourth Gospel, Jesus is one sent from God, the man who came down from heaven. God in Christ decided to get down to Earth—not just to take a closer look at the struggles of humanity, but to enter into the realm of flesh that God had created. The Creator became creature. That's John's message all the way to Easter.

I. *With all of its mysticism, Advent is an earthy message.* According to Webster, something that is *earthy* is crude, coarse, or unrefined. Someone who uses earthy language is usually given to profanity or to speech about bodily functions that should be reserved for the hospital and the doctor's office. *Incarnation* sounds like lofty theological jargon, but it implies something quite profane. David Lose speaks of the "carnal God." He notes the use of the word from Latin to Spanish, *chili con carne,* "stew with meat." Thus, referring to the Incarnation, to "the God who is enfleshed in the person of Jesus," is like saying God con carne, "God with meat on."

The story in John begins with the only miracle recorded in all four Gospels—the feeding of the multitude. John calls it a "sign," a clue to the origin and identity of Jesus. After the feeding miracle, Jesus walked on water toward his disciples' boat—another sign, evidence of his dominance of nature. The crowd followed him to Capernaum and engaged in conversation on "signs" and "works," John's words for *miracle.* Wanting more, they brought up the Exodus and manna in the wilderness. This provoked one of Jesus' "I am" sayings in John: "I am the bread of life." This was like the voice from the burning bush saying, "I am that I am." The "I am" God of the Exodus sent Jesus into this world like manna from heaven. So John's Jesus made an astounding claim like nothing you can find in the other Gospels: "I have come down from heaven." What audacity!

This was too much for people who had a high view of God. How could any mere human say that he had come down from heaven? Some of the witnesses to this blasphemy knew Joseph and his mother. "Is not this Jesus, the son of Joseph, whose father and mother we know?" These are not secular folks who had no idea of God. They were very religious and thought too highly of God to tolerate anyone who claimed to have come down from heaven. In their minds, the birth of Jesus discredited any claim of his being the Son of God. Knowing the parents is proof positive that Jesus came out of a womb just like the rest of us. He was flesh. That settles. The birth stories in Matthew and Luke that reveal Jesus as the Son of God are just more evidence for Jesus' critics in John that Jesus is a fraud. Birth, incarnation, is beneath God. All of us know that birth is a messy business. Nicodemus had trouble with the demand of Jesus that we must be reborn. He had the same objections as those who protested the claim that Jesus had come down from heaven.

II. *The gospel of Advent reveals a dynamic God.* The message of the Incarnation fits into the physics of our world. All of the matter that we once thought was static and unchanging is really a whirling mass of atoms forming molecules in a constant state of change. If the universe is a massive explosion of matter that never stops moving, the God who set it in motion must be pure energy—the God who never stops, the God who ever escapes our attempts to capture or hold him.

The dynamic God transcends our petty logic. John's Gospel teaches us that the Word of God does not have to make sense in order to be true. An early preacher of the gospel, John Chrysostom, declared that Jesus did not *become* God, for he *was* God. "Wherefore he became flesh so that he whom heaven did not contain a manger would this day receive. He was placed in a manger so that he, by whom all things are nourished, may receive an infant's food from his virgin mother."

Each message in John is a movement. God moved toward us, God came to us in Christ. Thus we need to come to Jesus as obedient followers. The Jesus who in Matthew came to fulfill the revelation of God in the Law and the prophets, to reach sinners, and to stir conflict, in John came down from heaven. If God became flesh in Christ, then people of the flesh must move toward the Spirit. The Incarnation has been called the "perfect paradox"; however, it is far from nonsense. Karl Barth says that it is as natural for God to be humble as it is for him to be great. Dietrich Bonhoeffer spoke of the God who came in weakness, and Moltmann spoke of *The Crucified God.* Yes, this is heavy; but the Word-become-flesh is too essential to the gospel to push it aside.

Søren Kierkegaard attempted to explain the Incarnation in a parable. It seems that a great and good king fell in love with a peasant girl and contemplated how he could win her love. He considered going directly to her or even sending a messenger to ask her to become his wife, but he realized that as a subject she would be compelled to be obedient to a request from her king. He considered disguising himself as a peasant and approaching her as an equal, but eventually the truth would be known and deception and dishonesty violate the essence of love. Finally the king realized that there was only one way left. He must give up all of the power and glory of kingship to become a peasant so that he might be one with his beloved. Kierkegaard concluded, "This is the unfathomable nature of love, that it desires equality with the beloved." Love implies humility. To say with John "God is love" implies the Incarnation.—Larry Dipboye

Topic: New Light for New Journeys
TEXT: 1 Sam. 2:18–20, 26; Matt. 2:1–12

As we remember the Wise Men who traveled by the light of a star, let's think together about our own journey in the new year before us, and about how we might travel in God's light.

The first concept we need to understand today is that God finds a way to get the divine will done. We see that happen in both of the Scripture lessons for today. The Old Testament lesson, from 1 Samuel, is essentially a progress report on how young Samuel was doing as a priest-in-training under the chief priest, Eli. We are told that Samuel was growing in stature and in favor with God and all those around him, those who saw and knew his work. In the first century, sons were supposed to follow their fathers in their calling, whatever it was. But Samuel was not Eli's son. Eli had two sons, but they had rejected the moral life and the priestly role and chosen flamboyant, exhibitionist lifestyles. God therefore blessed Hannah and Elkanah with a son, Samuel, whom they dedicated to God's service. God got God's will done, and in a gracious way for the lives of Hannah and Elkanah. We want to be sure that we are in God's light and traveling in the same direction as God's light is moving.

In the passage from Matthew we have the story of the Wise Men. It is another story that speaks of God's ability to use unusual circumstances to accomplish his will in human life. In a world of darkness, violence, fear, and distrust, God's grace shines forth. A cosmic guide is provided in the light of a star.

We're not exactly sure who these Magi were. They may have been Zoroastrian astrologers from Persia; as such they would have believed in a basic dualism in all creation, a balance between good and bad, light and darkness. They may also have believed that this star was a "fravoshi," the angel of some great person, guiding them on their way. Whoever they were, they were clearly what today we would call "seekers." They were looking for something more than what they had already experienced in life. God had blessed them with the divine gift of the star. They chose to follow this gift of grace, a light from God that illumined the presence of God in their lives. These Wise Men not only studied; they followed as well.

When they got to Jerusalem they asked the question, "Where is the one born King of the Jews?" It's interesting that they could follow the star as far as Jerusalem, but it could not lead them any further. Its precise leading was unclear at that point, so they had to ask questions. They asked for help along the way. They asked the great minds of the Jewish tradition. Those minds went back to their Scripture and said that the Messiah was to be born in Bethlehem. A combination of guidance was provided for these early seekers. It came from the cosmic star, but it also came from the scriptural tradition, which you and I still have.

The Magi's question, "Where is the one born King of the Jews?" is the first human utterance in Matthew's Gospel. The implication is that life is always to be a quest for God's revelation to us. The Magi first followed the star and then followed the Scriptures. They found their way to the Christ child; and when they found the child, they worshiped. The twelve days of Christmas, the period from the birth of Jesus to January 6, is the time that tradition says it took the Magi to arrive in Bethlehem. We symbolically acted that out at the 5:00 P.M. service on Christmas Eve, when the Wise Men got caught behind the children's choir and could not get to the manger scene. Others have said that the reason it took the first Wise Men twelve days to get to Jesus was that they got caught in the after-Christmas mall traffic jams.

The Wise Men are also clearly Gentiles, non-Jews, about as far from the Jewish tradition of that day as one could be. Matthew says to us that the story here is for more than just one people; it's for all people. We're all included in this story. What I ask of you today is to understand that last phrase of the lesson from Matthew in dynamic analogy to our own lives. "And because of a dream they had [another gift from God], they went home by a different way." How do we depart from the birth of Christ by another way? In the words of the sermon title, how do we use the new light from God for the new journey, the journey of a new year?

Our calling from God is to be a disciple of Jesus Christ, to be an apprentice to Christ, to follow his words and his way. Our calling is also to invite others to be disciples. We are to both be and make disciples. Our staff has adopted our own mission statement. Our calling is to be and to make vibrant, thinking, serving disciples of Jesus Christ; to do what we need to grow the church. We who are already a part of the church need to grow in our own spiritual lives. We also need to invite others to come and share in the joy of the life of discipleship to Jesus.

When we join the church we promise to uphold the church with our prayers, our presence, our gifts, and our service. Let me suggest that we get specific about those promises this year. If we do so, we will find that God is shining a new and wonderful light on this new journey we are taking with God and each other. It is those "old" words that I think provide new light for us on our new journey. What I want us to do in the days and weeks to come is to find specific ways in which we can live out those words—prayers, presence, gifts, and service. Let us make five commitments to each other:

1. We will attend worship each week unless sick or out of town. We need to take seriously the need to be together. We come to worship not just for ourselves, not just to receive; but we come also to worship and to witness to others, too, by our presence.
2. We will stretch our faith through, in addition to the worship experience, a Sunday school class, a Bible study, a fellowship group.
3. We will give our time in Christian service to others.

4. We will give proportionately of our financial resources, with a tithe as our minimum goal.

5. We will reach out joyfully to those around us and invite them to join us on this new journey of faith in Christ.

If we do those things, I submit to you that God's light will shine anew in our lives and will guide us on the paths on which God wants us to go in the days to come.

A certain father had a great idea for his children's special Christmas gift one year. He ordered a kit for a tree house from a mail-order catalogue. On Christmas Eve, as he began to assemble the pieces, he discovered to his dismay that although he had received the plans for a treehouse, he had been sent the materials for a sailboat. His letter of complaint to the company brought this apologetic reply: "While we regret the inconvenience this mistake must have caused you, it is nothing compared to that of the person who is out on a lake somewhere trying to sail your treehouse." Ours is a real world full of mix-ups, contradictions, and errors. Let us make sure that we have the directions from God and the raw materials of our own discipleship ready for God's work. Let us use God's light for our new journey of faith.

E. B. White, the essayist, once described an experience he had while shopping one Christmas time in a busy department store. He watched a small boy put his hand hopefully on a cheap plaster Christ Child displayed on a counter. "What is this?" the child asked his harried mother. "C'mon," the mother answered sharply, "you don't want *that thing!*" "And she grimly dragged him away," said White, "her mind dark with other thoughts, following some star of her own devising."

The gospel of Jesus Christ speaks to all, even those following burned-out stars of their own devising. You may be the light that leads them on new journeys of faith. Light from God has brought us to this place, just for this time of ministry.

Friends, God manifests God's self so many times in our lives, in so many different ways, if we will only see it. On this day, let us commit ourselves to seeking anew that light of God, and to follow it on the new journey of this new year. Thanks be to God. Amen.—Jim Standiford

SECTION VII

EVANGELISM AND WORLD MISSIONS

SERMON SUGGESTIONS

Topic: The Possibility of Positive Change

TEXT: Ps. 130; Acts 9:1–20

He was as un-Christian as anyone could ever be. Oh, he was religious; but being religious and being Christian are often two very different things. He was zealous in the faith, well versed in the Law of Moses, and adamant about what he believed, but he was not Christian.

In fact, he *hated* Christians. He broke into peoples' houses, bound them in chains, and dragged them off to prison, for no other reason than that they were followers of Jesus. It is even probable that he had Christians killed. When Stephen, one of the first deacons in the early Church, was stoned to death because of his faith, those who did the stoning took off their coats and laid them at his feet for safekeeping. I repeat: he was as un-Christian as anyone could ever be.

But God is the God of second chances. There is the possibility of positive change. While on his way from Jerusalem to Damascus to search the synagogues for anyone who might be a follower of Jesus, so he might chain them and take them back to Jerusalem for trial, Saul of Tarsus had what has come to be called the Damascus Road Experience. Many of us who struggled with the call to enter the ministry prayed for a similar Damascus Road experience—that is, a sure sign of the call, which would leave no doubt that this was what we were supposed to do. But Saul's Damascus Road experience was unique. It was what it took, no doubt, to get Saul's attention. Saul had been chosen for a special work. He had been given a second chance, and he underwent a life-changing experience.

Such is the nature of God revealed in the Scripture—God is the God of second chances. With God there is the possibility of positive change. This is the message of the psalmist over and over again. I could have selected any number of psalms for this morning's Old Testament reading, but I chose Psalm 130 because it says it so well: "If you, O Lord, should mark iniquities, Lord, who could stand?" (Psalm 130:3). In other words, if God kept a record—or spreadsheet—of our sins and shortcomings, we could not last very long. Our negative balance might soon destroy us. Our loan would be called in. God would get tired of dealing with us.

But the psalmist goes on: "But there is forgiveness with you" (130:4). There is the promise of a fresh start, a clean slate, a new beginning.

How could we talk about the possibility of second chances and positive change without being reminded of Peter? In spite of the warning he received from Jesus, after Jesus' arrest Peter three times denied knowing him. Realizing what he had done, Peter went out and wept bitterly. He had let Jesus down. He had turned his back on his Master. He had folded in cowardly fear. Yet Peter was appointed to feed the Lord's sheep. He became the strongest pillar in the building of the New Testament Church. God is the God of second chances, and he holds out the hope of positive change. Peter was granted a fresh start.

357

Oskar Schindler was a Czechoslovakian businessman, opportunist, and member of the Nazi Party who at the beginning of World War II and the oppression of the Jews by Hitler took advantage of the situation and commandeered about a thousand Jews to work in his factories to produce goods for the German Army. Schindler was a hard, uncaring, insensitive, unbelieving man who cared little for his fellow humans. He was nothing more than a profiteer whose sole motive was to amass great wealth for himself. And that he did.

But a few years later, when Schindler was able to observe firsthand the extreme oppression, injustice, and murder that were being committed against the Jewish people for no other reason than their Jewish heritage, Schindler's heart began to change. When the Jewish laborers who had worked in his factories and made possible his great wealth were in danger of being sent to Auschwitz to be exterminated, Schindler began to use his great wealth to gain their release. By the time all was said and done, he had gone through every dollar of his amassed wealth to buy the freedom of more than a thousand Jewish persons. Oskar Schindler's heart was changed.

It is said that Michelangelo's greatest work, *The David*, was created from a discarded and totally flawed piece of marble. Yet the great artist saw in a flawed piece of marble great possibility, and he carved what is probably the most famous statue ever created by a human hand. Michelangelo has been credited with bringing to life a cold piece of stone. So it is with God. God can take a totally flawed human life—like those of Saul of Tarsus, Simon Peter, and Oskar Schindler—and create something magnificent.

Of all the creatures on our planet, human beings are the only ones who can make a conscious choice to change or let themselves be changed by a higher power. That is one thing that separates us from the beasts of the field—we can choose to improve ourselves, to become better persons today than we were yesterday.

Do you feel that you have let God down? That you have been a failure? Do you feel that, like Peter, you have betrayed God by the things you have done or failed to do? Do you feel that, like Saul of Tarsus, you have been guilty of persecuting Jesus by the way you have lived or the way you have treated others? As you think back over your life do you wish you had done some things differently?

If you have answered yes to any of these questions, there is good news. There is the possibility to begin anew—today. Saul of Tarsus, St. Peter, Oskar Schindler, and countless others have been living proof that positive change is possible and we always have the promise of second chances. We may not have a Damascus Road experience, but we can decide to change.—Randy Hammer

Topic: Let's Run in God's Race
TEXT: Heb. 12:1–3

I believe that if the Bible were being written today we would find in it illustrations from football, basketball, and baseball; golf, tennis, and track and field.

Why? Because when you come to the Bible you discover that the Holy Spirit inspired the authors of Scripture to draw from athletics to illustrate the Christian life. Paul says in 1 Corinthians 9:27 and 2 Corinthians 4:9 that the Christian life is like a boxing match. In Ephesians 6:12 he compares it to a wrestling match. Hebrews 12:1–3 says that the life of the believer is like a race. I believe that the author of Hebrews had in mind a very particular race—the marathon, a 26-mile, 385-yard race. Such a race requires both training and strategy if it is to be run well. What are the particulars to which we must give attention?

I. *We must find encouragement as we run.* Hebrews 12:1 says, "We are surrounded by so great a cloud of witnesses." The author includes himself with those to whom he is writing. I believe that "a cloud of witnesses" refers to the great "hall of faith" of chapter 11. As one surveys the witnesses of the marvelous chapter, two avenues of encouragement are discovered.

(a) *We should be encouraged by the earthly winners.* In Hebrews 11:32–35a, no less than ten incredible feats of faith are catalogued—things like shutting the mouths of lions, becoming mighty in battle, and seeing the dead raised to life again. This is supernatural stuff any way you look at it. We should be encouraged by these champions of the faith.

(b) *We should be encouraged by the heavenly winners.* Paul Harvey reminds us to always hear "the rest of the story," and in Hebrews 11:35b–38 we discover the different groups who ran a very different kind of race. Torture, mockings, prison, and the sword were their lot. Yet in Hebrews 11:39 we discover that "all these obtained a good testimony through faith."

Earthly victors and heavenly victors both serve as a wonderful source of encouragement as we run in the race God has specifically designed for us.

II. *We must focus on the essential as we run.* Again in Hebrews 12:1, three specific guidelines are provided that will enable us to run well in God's race.

(a) *Run cleanly.* The Bible says, "Let us lay aside every weight." Weights are encumbrances, stuff, excess baggage that can slow us down and keep us from running our best for Jesus. Interestingly, weights may not always be bad things. Sometimes a weight can be a good thing, but it is not the best thing. As devoted disciples of Jesus, we must not settle for good. We must strive for the best.

(b) *Run with confidence.* Not only are we to lay aside every weight, but we must also set aside "the sin which so easily ensnares us." I like to refer to this sin as the "octopus" of the Christian life because its tentacles can wrap around us so tightly we can hardly run at all.

Because of the context of this passage (remember, Hebrews 11 precedes Hebrews 12), I believe that the sin God has in mind is the same sin for everyone—the sin of unbelief. Hebrews 11:6 reminds us, "Without faith it is impossible to please God."

Unbelief is an attitude of the heart; it tells me that in order to stay in the race I need God plus fill-in-the-blank. Once we add a plus sign to the equation it does not matter how we fill in the blank. We have stepped into the realm of unbelief. We must run in confidence. We must run in faith.

(c) *Run consistently.* Verse 1 concludes by challenging us to "run with endurance the race that is set before us." The word *endurance* can also be translated as "perseverance." It means to run without throwing in the towel.

God specifically designs a particular race for each of us. What is important is not how *fast* we run, but how *long* we run. You see, it is not enough to begin well; it is crucial that we continue and finish well.

III. *Perhaps most important, we must follow the example as we run.* In Hebrews 12:2–3 we are provided with the ultimate example as we run in God's race—the Lord Jesus. The author of Hebrews challenges us in two ways to follow Jesus.

(a) *Look at him.* "Look unto Jesus" is a challenge to look to Jesus and only Jesus. It means to have eyes for no one or nothing but him. The rationale for this kind of radical devotion is clearly laid out: he is "the author and finisher of faith" ("our" is an interpretive addition). He is faith's pioneer and perfector, its beginning and end. From A to Z it is all about him.

Why should we believe that Jesus is sufficient for us? Again, the text provides the answer. Jesus ran a race. God tailor made a race for his Son, which our Lord gladly embraced. "Who for the joy that was set before him [paralleling the last phrase of 12:1] endured the cross, despising the shame, and has set down at the right hand of the throne of God."

Jesus ran a race that took him to a cross but ended at a throne. He joyfully embraced the Father's will in providing redemption for sinners, counting the shame of it as nothing, and his Father has appropriately honored him with the place of greatest prestige and position. But there is one thing more.

(b) *Think about him.* Verse 3 says, "Consider him." The word means to meditate or reflect. "Consider him who endured [the key word in our text; it appears in all three verses, tying this passage together] such hostility from sinners against himself, lest you become weary and discouraged in your souls." Sometimes the race is tough and the obstacles almost too much to bear. When the thought of quitting or walking away begins to harass us, we need to get our spiritual eyes and minds back on target. We need to bring it all back to Jesus.

When it comes to running in God's race, living faithfully the Christian life, it is imperative that we keep our eyes on Jesus. Indeed, anything in life that gets our eyes off Jesus is, without question, not of God. On this truth we must clearly stand. On this truth we will also run.—Daniel L. Akin

Topic: Grateful for Grace
TEXT: Luke 7:36–50

Luke's story of the woman with the alabaster flask of ointment in Luke 7:36–50 is an excellent example of a biblical narrative that can be preached as such with little elaboration. The story preaches itself.

Jesus must have encountered the woman (not Mary Magdalene, contrary to some interpreters and to *Jesus Christ Superstar*) prior to this incident. The entire point of the narrative is that her act was an expression of her gratitude to Jesus for forgiving her sins.

Simon had invited Jesus for a meal, presumably with some of his friends, probably to sound out this unorthodox new teacher and healer (v. 49). The woman had not been invited, and when she suddenly burst into this august assemblage of religious leaders and rushed to Jesus' couch, her presence was not appreciated.

She took a flask of costly perfume that she had brought with her and began to pour the contents onto Jesus' feet. Sobbing uncontrollably, her tears mingled with the ointment. She undid the long tresses of her hair to wipe Jesus feet with the perfume. Simon was aghast. He had his answer: this man was surely no prophet; no one from God would allow a sinner like this woman to touch him so.

Knowing Simon's thoughts, Jesus introduced a parable at this point. Two men were indebted to a third, he said. One owed a huge amount—500 denarii. Since a denarius was the average day's pay for a Roman foot soldier or a day laborer, it was a debt that could likely have taken his entire earnings for nearly a year and a half. The other man owed less, but nonetheless a significant sum—a couple of months' wages. The lender fully forgave them both.

One should realize at this point that Jesus was not talking about ordinary human circumstances. "Easy cash loan" doesn't forgive debts like that. God does. Jesus was talking about God's forgiveness of our sins, and that is what the woman had received from Jesus.

Jesus then allowed Simon to hang himself, asking him which debtor would love his forgiving benefactor more. Simon had to answer that it would surely be the 500 denarii debtor.

Jesus proceeded to apply the lesson, noting how everything the woman did showed that she was the one with the greatest sense of forgiveness. She loved greatly because she had been forgiven greatly (v. 47). In fact, the woman's act had put Simon to shame. As a host he had failed to carry out any of the social niceties that a gracious host should for a respected guest—no greeting kiss on the cheek, no washing the dust off his guest's feet, no honoring him with a drop or two of olive oil on the head.

In contrast, the woman had done them all in an extravagant fashion, anointing not only his head but his feet as well; not with olive oil but with the most expensive perfume; washing his feet with her tears and kissing them constantly as she wiped them with the tresses of her hair.

The woman was the forgiven 500-denarii debtor. But what about the 50-denarii debtor? Jesus hardly needed to apply the lesson. Simon was the "forgiven little, loves little" debtor—not because he was any less in need of forgiveness than the woman. No, Simon was the self-righteous Pharisee. He had little sense of the need for forgiveness, either the woman's or his own. He was incapable of experiencing forgiveness because of his own self-righteousness. In that sense he knew neither forgiveness nor love.

This story is the story of each of us, for we all stand as this woman stood—as sinners in need of God's forgiveness. And what is the natural response to God's forgiveness? Is it not gratitude, as so amply demonstrated in this woman's response?

Her act is a model of gratitude. It was *extravagant*. She was a poor woman of the streets, a sinner, in Simon's words. Quite possibly the expensive ointment was the most valuable thing she possessed. She wanted only the best for Jesus. How do you thank the one who has accepted you in all your unloveliness, forgiven you and set you on a new path? You give him your very best.

The woman was also totally *transparent* in her expression of grateful love for Jesus. She had no agenda, no hang-ups. She actually broke a number of social codes. Probably no woman was welcome in that group of men.

And this wasn't just any woman at that. She was a sinner—one who would never be welcome in the "righteous" Pharisee's home. Her emotional outburst was unseemly, and she did the unthinkable in the presence of those men: she let down her hair. In her culture, only one sort of woman would let her hair down in the presence of male strangers, and that was the sort of woman she had been before meeting Jesus.

She acted in total innocence, and Jesus accepted her expression of gratitude. This, of course, is no warrant for us to go around offending people by flaunting social codes. It *is* a challenge for us to look at people's hearts when they express their faith and love for Jesus, especially those who may come from different backgrounds and express themselves in fashions that may not be altogether acceptable in our social circles.

A final lesson taught by this woman is that gratitude is often best expressed in deed rather than in words. So often we think of gratitude in terms of words—the spoken thank you. This woman spoke not a single word in the entire narrative. Jesus and Simon did all the talking. But the woman was totally eloquent with her deed, her lavish expression of gratitude.

We ministers, often by professional hazard, are too word oriented. In our ministries, we can often serve the Lord more effectively through our deeds than through our words. Like this woman, we are all sinners saved by the grace of God. How does one respond to grace? By gratitude, as she did. Linguistically, grace and gratitude are related, in Greek as well as in English. Gratitude is the natural response to grace—gratitude that is pure and transparent, extravagant, expressed in concrete deeds through a life of service to Jesus.—John B. Polhill

Topic: On Receiving Little Children
TEXT: Mark 9:33–37

One great difficulty in grasping the deepest import of Jesus' message is caused by our unwillingness to let it shock us.

Today we consider a text that is doubly difficult to treat as controversial because it deals with little children. Surely nothing in the Gospel story has been sentimentalized more than the way in which the gentle Jesus welcomed little ones into his arms and blessed them. So let me give fair warning: *prepare to be shocked by what you are about to hear* as we stand and read together Mark 9:33–37.

I. *The human drive for greatness.* As Jesus reached the turning point of his ministry in Galilee, he began to excite the ambitions of his disciples by predicting that some of them would soon see the Kingdom of God coming with power (Mark 9:1). Shortly thereafter, on the Mount of Transfiguration (Mark 9:2–8), three of the twelve were indeed permitted to glimpse that eagerly awaited glory. As they turned toward Jerusalem, Jesus spoke repeatedly of rising from the dead (Mark 8:31; 9:31; 10:34) which would surely confirm his messianic credentials. No wonder his closest followers began to consider seriously what their status might be in such a time of triumph.

It is little wonder that the disciples were too embarrassed to recount for Jesus this jockeying for position, which had quickly degenerated into petty bickering over status; the very question of who is greatest is inherently competitive.

Regardless of how the greatness is determined, there is no way for someone to become greater without everyone else becoming lesser. In the greatness game, if you're not at the top, you're nowhere. There is only one winner, but there are many losers.

Like the disciples of old, we seem to have an insatiable desire to determine the "greatness" in every field. This is especially true in sports. Elaborate statistics are kept over many years to determine not only the greatest teams but the greatest players and coaches as well.

Our arguments over greatness extend to every area of life, even to who might be the twelve best preachers in America. The debate intensified as we approached the end of a century and millennium. In every field of human endeavor, all that seems to matter is who is on top. Like the disciples of old, we too should be embarrassed to tell Jesus just how obsessed we are with the question of greatness.

II. *The divine paradox of greatness.* The aching silence of the disciples in response to Jesus' question was mute testimony to their realization that arguing over greatness was in flagrant contradiction to his teachings. Jesus had linked his own destiny to a cross and had called them to the same kind of self-denial: to save their lives by losing them (Mark 8:34–35). Here he not only repeated the paradox of becoming first by being "last of all and servant of all" (Mark 9:35), but in an effort to overcome their continuing confusion (Mark 9:32), he added a simple object lesson by setting a little child in their midst. Before providing any additional explanation, Jesus acted out his message by taking the child into his arms and clasping it to his bosom. Everything he was about to teach them would be reinforced by that living picture.

In a remarkably perceptive analysis of this passage, Judith Gundry-Volf has pointed out that in the Greco-Roman world of Jesus' day, children were the least valued members of society.[1] Being considered not yet fully human, they had no legal rights. A father was entitled to punish, pawn, sell, expose, or even kill his own child. Baby girls were especially vulnerable to rejection because of their limited economic potential. Typically it was only women who cradled the young in their arms; men thought it beneath their dignity to show such attention to a mere child, as the disciples would soon demonstrate (Mark 10:13). Remember how baby Jesus is always depicted in the arms of Mary, never in the arms of Joseph? By this parabolic action, Jesus assumed a stereotypically female role to show his shocked disciples what it means to be "greatest." Imagine, the Messiah of God's glorious Kingdom more interested in showing tender concern to a helpless little child than in passing out political patronage to his loyal but impatient followers! Surely they thought to themselves, hugging kids is no way to rule a kingdom.

They wanted a hierarchical community characterized by supremacy from above by whomever among them could be designated as greatest. But Jesus wanted an egalitarian community characterized by solidarity from below, based on a discipleship of equals, a community in which the kind of "grunt work" done by women in caring for little children constitutes true greatness. This is how one attains Kingdom status—not through power conferred but through love shared. Can you begin to see it now? Jesus was turning the pecking order of his day upside down and creating "a new kind of community in which service of the least counts the most."[2]

III. *The claim of the child on the disciples.* On the basis of this breathtaking object lesson, Jesus went on to shock his disciples even further by spelling out two truths implicit in what they had just seen.

First, he taught that "whoever receives such a child in my name receives me" (v. 37a). That is, Jesus not only embraced little children as the object of his affection but he bonded with them so deeply that their destiny became his destiny.

After all, it would not be long until he became as vulnerable as an abandoned child when they nailed him to a cross. If the disciples were too squeamish to embrace a nameless child, they would hardly relish embracing a crucified messiah.

Second, Jesus compounded the shock even further by teaching that "whoever receives me receives not only me but him who sent me." "Look at me," Jesus said, still holding the little child in his arms, "God is like that! He is not playing the greatness game of command and control. You will find him not at the top of the power structure but at the bottom. He is not in the business of competing and winning but of loving and serving. If you want to receive God, then wrap your arms around a little child." We may infer from the vivid picture in John's prologue that the early Christians soon adopted the revolutionary understanding of God

---

[1]Judith M. Gundry-Volf, "Between Text and Sermon: Mark 9:33–37," *Interpretation*, 1991, *53*(1), 57–61.
[2]Gundry-Volf, 1991, p. 59.

taught here by Jesus, daring to picture the Sovereign of the universe in a maternal pose of filial embrace.

Today we have made great strides in lifting the status of children. Grateful for these advances, and for the crucial role that Christianity has played in transforming the attitude of society toward its most defenseless members, we still have far to go before every child feels the warm embrace of Christ.

Many churches still consider their children's ministry as little more than a baby-sitting service staffed by hourly workers so that the members will not be bothered. Many politicians still refuse to make children's needs a legislative mandate, favoring instead those special interest groups that can reward them handsomely before the next election.

Beyond these sins in high society, there is a creeping "child crisis" of alarming proportions among the lower classes. At the World Summit for Children held in 1990, leaders gathered to grapple with "the plight of 150 million children under the age of five suffering from malnutrition, 30 million living in the streets, 7 million driven from their homes by war and famine."[3] Where, we cry, are those who will throw the loving arms of Jesus around the neglected children of America, the orphaned children of Kosovo, the starving children of Rwanda?

IV. *How shall we respond?* Mark's account of this incident focuses on the radical demands of Jesus, while the parallel account in Matthew 18:1–5 emphasizes how we as disciples should respond. To "receive" children as Jesus did requires nothing less than a complete about-face—a literal conversion on the part of his followers (v. 3a). This redirection of attitude means that we no longer seek greatness as the world understands it, but we ourselves "become as little children" (v. 3b).

Again, imagine how doubly shocking it must have been for the disciples—caught in the act of trying, behind Jesus' back, to grab places of glory, and being told not only that they would have to *receive* little children but also that they would have to *become* little children! What Jesus was teaching is that we will never fully understand and accept little children until we realize that there is a child inside every one of us. Only as we get in touch with our own childlikeness will we learn not only how to care deeply for children but also how to be sensitive and compassionate toward the hidden weaknesses of others.

Our journey ends where it began: with a paradox. The gospel is forever telling us to grow up (1 Cor. 3:1–3; Heb. 5:11–6:2), to put away childish things and become adults (1 Cor. 13:11; Eph. 4:13–15). But it also tells us to be born all over again (John 1:13; 3:3, 5, 7) and become as little children (Matt. 18:3; Mark 10:15). Somehow it is as important to become a child as it is to become an adult, but how can both be equally true? The answer lies in Jesus' teaching about children. When we try to find life in our quest for greatness, we will lose it in the competitive struggle with others seeking to snatch the same prize. But when we are willing to love and serve the least by becoming the least ourselves, we will gain everything, because that is precisely where we find our Savior and our God.

Amazing, isn't it, that the crucial test of whether we have experienced the kind of conversion that will open the door to the Kingdom is determined by what we think and do about the children?—William E. Hull

---

[3]"Suffer the Little Children," *Time*, Oct. 8, 1990, p. 41.

Topic: Will the Real God Please Stand Up?
TEXT: 1 Kings 18:17–39

In the 1960s and 1970s, and again just recently, there was a television game show called *To Tell the Truth*. Three contestants, each claiming to have the same identity, appeared before a panel of judges and a TV audience. It was the job of the panel (and the at-home audience) to question the contestants and then determine which person was telling the truth about his or her identity. At the end of the show the host called for the real person to stand up. And that is what Elijah is doing in our text: he is calling for the real God to please stand up. Why is he doing this? Why is he playing TV game show trivia with the people of Israel? Why is he calling for the real God to reveal his identity? And why is it necessary for a similar call to resonate in our day and time? The answer is found in the passage of Scripture before us.

As the scene begins and the curtain opens, the prophet of God emerges after a prolonged absence to confront the wicked, hen-pecked husband of Jezebel—Ahab, King of Israel. Their last meeting was an unpleasant encounter. The prophet had informed Ahab that because of his idolatry and because he had led the people away from worship of the one true God, no rain would fall over Israel for a three-year period. With the promise of a drought, God whisked the prophet away and protected him from the drought by providing nourishment for him, through the odd combination of a raven and a poor widow. I submit that when you do as God desires, he will provide for you, using the wings, claws, and beak of an insignificant animal or the cupboard of an insignificant person.

Now, in the third year of the drought, Elijah was commanded to return to face the furious king. When Ahab saw the prophet he addressed him as the "troubler of Israel." "Your finger is pointing in the wrong direction," the prophet responded. "You, with your attempts to sway and confuse the people about who the real God is; you, O King, with your pantheon of divine wanna-bes; you who succumbed to Jezebel's bamboozling and hoodwinking—you are the real troubler of Israel. Because you are playing out this TV game show by forsaking the commandments of God, and because you have followed the Baals, I have a proposition to settle the issue once and for all, to determine who the real God is and who the people should pay homage to." The proposition involved a call to observe their condition, a contest of clarification, and a consequence of either concession of defeat or confirmation of deliverance.

In verses 19–20 Elijah called on the king to use his governmental influence to sponsor a mock TV game show. Ahab responded by requiring all the Israelites and the prophets of Baal and Asherah to assemble at Mount Carmel. In verse 21 Elijah came near to all the people and said to them, "How long will you go limping with two different opinions?"[4] The call of the prophet is a call of observation, a call for the people to evaluate their relationship with God. It is a call that begins with a question for self-reflection and self-analysis. It is a call for the people to evaluate their own actions. How long will you go limping with two different opinions? How much longer are you going to hobble about on two crutches?

The picture is one of a people hobbling between two forks at a crossroads. The Hebrew

---

[4]All Scripture references in this sermon are quoted from the New Revised Standard Version of the Bible.

verb here means to limp as in the case of injury. That is to say, this back and forth between God and the Baals or the divine wanna-bes had a crippling effect. Their ambivalence was injurious to their welfare. It stifled their growth, capped their spirituality, and slowly sapped their ability to recognize the difference between good and bad, right and wrong. It distorted their comprehension of the difference between what was real and what was false. "Enough is enough!" the prophet exclaimed. "You have limped through life long enough. The time for decision has come. The decisive moment has arrived. If the Lord be God, follow him; but if Baal be God, follow him." The back and forth between the two gods demonstrated a lack of faith in either one. It is equivalent to the ambivalence of the church at Laodicea in Revelation 3:14–22. Jesus said to the church, "I know your works; you are neither cold nor hot. I wish you were either cold or hot. So because you are lukewarm, I am about to spit you out of my mouth." In the Sermon on the Mount Jesus cautioned his disciples that no one can serve two masters (Matt. 6:24). The question that beckoned from the prophet's mouth was a call for Israel to see that lack of faith is the same as living life without a central core of hope that makes it meaningful.

This back and forth leads to nothing but weariness and confusion. It is symbolic of the person who wants to have his or her cake and eat it, too. But I submit that you can't both keep it and eat it, you can't both have it and sell it, and you can't both give it and take it. It's an either-or concept. The prophet's question calls the people's attention to their confused and weary state, a state that leads to the depletion of one's spiritual discernment.

This back and forth between the two beliefs gives one a false sense of security, causing one to believe that one has the best of both worlds when one has nothing at all. How many times have we experienced it in our own lives—moderating between the two and ending up with nothing at all? Rhythm and blues singer William Bell stated it so well, that trying to love two ain't easy to do. This lack of focus blinds us to our need to set our sights on a main object. That is to say, we cannot please both God and everybody else. The line must be drawn. Sides must be taken. Moses asked the people, in Exodus 32:26, "Who is on the Lord's side?" The call to follow God or Baal is the call to choose sides. Joshua told the people "Choose you this day whom you will serve" (Josh. 24:15). It is the call to see where you are, to take notice of your activities, and to evaluate your relationship with the Lord God. I asked you to consider where you are in this life. What are you doing? Who are you serving? What is the extent of your relationship with God?

But not only did the prophet call upon the people to take notice of their flip-flopping ways, of their interest in TV game show masquerading, but he also promoted the game show imagery even further by invoking a contest to determine divine authenticity. Notice verses 22–24 of the text. Elijah suggested that he was a one-man group and that the 950 prophets of Baal and Asherah made up the other group. Each group, according to Elijah, would be given an animal to sacrifice, along with the necessary ingredients to make a burnt offering, except the fire. Each group would be allotted enough time to appeal to their own divine figure to respond, and the one that responded by fire would be declared the real God, God Almighty. It was the contest to end all contests—the contest to determine the object of their worship, trust, and service. The once silent audience signified its approval, and the contest to end all contests began in earnest the search for the real God, the one true God. Jezebel's prophets chose their animal to sacrifice and prepared it, and the show commenced. Verse 26 tells us they called on the name of Baal.

Be sure, my friends, that the time will come when your God, your religion, your spirituality will be put to the test. At some point in your existence you will be called upon to demonstrate, and your God will be called upon to act, and to act decisively. The prophets of Baal experienced just such a situation. In 1 Kings 18:26, they cried, "O Baal, answer us?" But only silence and inactivity followed. Oh, how bad it is to have put your all in the gods of this life and when you need them to help you they are not there. You know how it is! You put all of your hope, all of your trust, all of your faith in someone. When they needed you, you were there. When they called you for help, before they could hang up the phone you were there. When they needed money, you dipped into your billfold to help them out. When they were having relationship troubles, you listened until you were blue in the face. In short, when they needed a friend, you were there. But when the tables turned, when it was their time to step up to the plate, they were nowhere to be found. The prodigal son, as told in Luke 15:11–30, left the complete love of his father, moved to a faraway country, forsook his upbringing, and did anything he was big and bad enough to do. But when the going got tough, when he had no more to give, then the pretty girls who fancied him, the so-called friends who shadowed him, the acquaintances who adored him all left him, and he found himself in the "pigpen of life." The gods of this life deceive us into believing they are for us, but their only goal is to lead us to the pigpen of life. The Bible says he would have eaten the husks, the slop, the pods the pigs ate, but no one gave him any (Luke 15:16).

The prophet called for this contest for the people to see how foolish it was for them to trust in self-serving people and to follow a god or gods that could not be trusted. The second chorus of this story shows us where we will end up if we give our allegiance blindly to the Baals of life. Only the pigpen can be our home when we trust in conniving and untrustworthy gods. Whatever the god is, if it does not challenge us to be more than we are, if it does not seek and compel us to better ourselves and others, if it does not focus our attention on accomplishing something viable and worthwhile, if it does not provide an example and standard to live by, and the power to meet it, then we need to be cautious and discerning.

The gods of drugs, of gloom and doom, of vengeance and retaliation, of disregard for human suffering and the plight of others, of blaming others for our failures, of procrastination, of letting opportunities pass by will not be able to pull you out of the pigpens and defeats of life once they get you there. Notice again the words of the text: they cried, "O Baal, answer us" (1 Kings 18:26). But there was no voice and no answer. They limped around. The verb *limped* here means they were helplessly crippled as they moved around the altar they had made.

Elijah mocked them, "Cry louder." In others words, "Surely your god is all you thought he was. Maybe he's trying to figure out what to do." The contest for them ended in the concession that their god was no god at all. And remember today, if you serve a god that can't show up, then he can't put up, and if he can't put up, then he can't live up to supplying your needs. The psalmist said of such gods, "They have mouths, but do not speak; eyes, but do not see. They have ears, but do not hear; noses, but do not smell. They have hands, but do not feel; feet, but do not walk. They make no sound in their throats. Those who make them are like them; so are all who trust in them" (Ps. 115:5–8). The contest led to the consequence of concession and defeat for the prophets of Baal and Asherah.

The scene now shifts from the prophets of Baal and Asherah to the lone prophet of God. All eyes were on Elijah. What would he do? The prophets of Baal had gone down conceding defeat and despair, the consequence of their failure to evaluate adequately their god and themselves. How would the next prophet fair? Look at his activities. He called the people to come closer, and then he did four things.

First, he repaired the altar, which was symbolic of the proper attitude of worship. Elijah placed the worship of the most-high God as the first order of the day. The New Testament reminds us to strive for the Kingdom of God and his righteousness (Matt. 6:33).

Second, he prepared the sacrifice. The prophet of God set the tone for worship by delicately preparing the offering unto the Lord. It is the equivalent of preparing our hearts to receive God's holiness.

Third, in 1 Kings 18:33–34, he commanded them to fill four jars with water and pour them on the burnt offering three times. Notice the four and the three. These numbers are important, for two reasons. First, if you add the four and three you get seven, which signifies and represents the perfect presence of God in worship. Second, if you multiply four times three you get twelve, the number that represents completion. So, in preparing the altar and the sacrifice, the prophet was aiming for the perfect and complete presence of God in worship.

This aim is supported in the fourth activity of the prophet, noted in verses 36–37: Elijah prayed. Notice his prayer: "O Lord God of Abraham, Isaac, and Jacob: let it be known this day that you are God in Israel, that I am your servant, and that I have done these things at your bidding. Answer me, O Lord, so that this people may know that you, O Lord, are God, and that you have turned their hearts back." The action of the prophet reminds us of the importance of worshiping God in spirit and in truth.

The first contest ended in the contestants of Baal conceding defeat because Baal did not answer. What will be the consequences of the contest for Elijah? To make matters worse it appears that the prophet is aiding in his own demise. He prepared the altar and the sacrifice, and amazingly drenched it with water—not once, not twice, but a total of twelve times. Now we both know that water is important for many things. It is essential for life. A baby is born in a bag of water. The body is made up of a very high percentage of water. When one is thirsty, Coca Cola, which claims to be the "real thing," just won't do. One must have water. But here water is used out of its natural context. The prophets of Baal knew that Elijah was cutting his own throat by drenching the sacrifice with water. But there was one thing they did not know that the prophet did know. He knew that God was a God who gloried in reversals. This God had made or created something out of nothing. This God had made time stand still. This God had turned a river into a thoroughfare. This God magnified himself when the odds demonstrated humanity's impossibilities. Elijah drenched the sacrifice in water and called upon the name of the Lord. In other words, instead of using water to put out a fire, he used water to start a fire. The text says that he called upon the name of the Lord. For the better part of the day the prophets of Baal had called on their gods, but nothing had happened. Now Elijah called on the God of history. Somehow, between the pouring of the water on the sacrifice and the ending of the prayer, I surmise, the chemical makeup of the water underwent a turbolic transformation and acted like kerosene. God sent the fire that licked up the water and the burnt offering. God's immediate response left no doubt about it! The "real God" had shown up. The text says that the people shouted in great acclamation, "The Lord indeed is God; the Lord indeed is God" (1 Kings 18:39). I declare that as the prophet received confirmation from heaven, likewise the consequences of your decision to hold to the worship of the one true God means that he will confirm you.

The prophet wanted to clear up the misunderstanding. He wanted to straighten out Ahab's error and lead the people back to God. What started out as a game show, "To Tell the Truth," where the divine wanna-bes and impostors were paraded before the people as the real God was not a game show at all. I hear the prophet Isaiah asking, in Isaiah 40:18, "To whom then will you liken God, or what likeness compare with him?" Isaiah concluded, like Elijah, that God is God all by himself. "Have you not known? Have you not heard? The Lord is the ever-lasting God, the creator of the ends of the Earth" (Isa. 40:28). So, in essence, what seemed like a game show was not a game show at all, for God is God all by himself. He is the one who will be there when you need him most. In other words, when you need him he will show up; and not only will he show up, but when he shows up, he will put up, and when he puts up, he will shut others up.

I am glad that he is my God and yours. This passage of Scripture calls us to observe our relationship with God. Often we must discern by way of contest who the real God is. But if we hold to what we know in our hearts is true then we will be confirmed and affirmed by his power. God calls us out of our ambivalence to him. To trust in another god results in concessions and defeat. But to trust in the God of Elijah, the one true God of heaven and Earth results in your vindication and deliverance. God may not always answer by fire, but the truth is, he always answers. The story is not a story about the real God standing up. God created you and gave himself for you in his Son Jesus Christ. He is always there for you and you can trust him. No! The story is not about the real God showing up; it is about our commitment to hold on to God's unchanging hand in the midst of the temptation to do otherwise. It is about being true to God. The question is not whether you can count on God. The question is, can God count on you?—David Groves

Topic: God's Agenda for Mission
Text: Micah 6:6–8; Luke 4:18–19

Thank you for inviting us to share with you the exciting and challenging opportunities of ministry at the United Nations. We are reminded daily of the extensive network of persons in the CBF family who pray for us and support the missionary enterprise in a world without borders.

Justice, mercy, and humility are the high stakes that believers in Jesus Christ, in their quest, continually strive to reach. These qualities remain abstract, however, until we put a face, a body, a person as their object.

Sometimes on my way to the United Nations headquarters a few blocks from our apartment I prepare myself for the heavy agenda of issues being discussed in the precincts of this world organization. Many debates relate to justice, mercy, and humility on the world scene.

I ponder mercy and justice. Can I with a good conscience pass by a homeless person asking for a coin on my way to a briefing in which the World Bank will determine how to help restructure the economic woes of some African country?

Can I rally the U.S. government to seriously consider accepting the notion of an international criminal court to prosecute dictators and leaders who practice ethnic cleansing after watching a flower vendor from Central America, exploited by an Asian merchant, tremble in the cold while working on an uncovered sidewalk for twelve hours for a pittance?

When Micah expressed God's agenda for mission in the eighth century before Christ, the people of God were enjoying economic prosperity and religious indifference. His exhortation is as appropriate for us as it was for them.

If we read carefully verses 6–7, we observe that the people of Israel were defending their "virtues" regarding religion. They catalogued their burnt offerings and asked God if he would be pleased by human sacrifice. The prophet's answer proved that God is more interested in the attitude, the heart, and the essence of true religion than in all its practices.

In our day the same argument could be used regarding missions. Some people may say, "I give my missions offering, I pray for the missionaries; what else is God requiring of me?" In the spirit of Micah, God would answer with the same threefold admonition that is at the heart of the agenda for mission.

I. *To act justly.* When we consider the implications of the phrase "to act justly," we may let our minds and hearts wander. As we look at the firmament, many clouds darken the horizon. If we look with the lenses of our emotions and feelings, we may burst into tears as we see so many injustices around us. If we look with the lenses of our biblical grounding, we may despair because we know that all around us are victims of injustice, and that we, though sincere Christians and active church members, may be perpetuating injustices even in the circle of our own influence. If we look with the lenses of world affairs, then we are really in for some shaking of the foundations of all our easy assumptions about what so and so nation ought to do, and what so and so political leader ought to do, and about how so and so people of some country ought to behave.

This clouding of the vision came to me recently as I heard Dr. Robert Seiple, Ambassador at Large for International Religious Freedom of the U.S. State Department. Congress has approved Seiple to direct the office that functions as a watchdog of religious freedom around the world. His office has prepared the first annual report on international religious freedom. This is an eleven-hundred-page report documenting violations of human rights of about one hundred countries. Seiple, an evangelical Christian and former president of World Vision, shared his commitment to the cause of religious freedom and tried to personalize the abuses of human rights that governments practice against many religious groups.

Foreign ministers of countries being surveyed for violations asked him such questions as, What right does the United States have to police the rest of the world? and Have you set your own country in order about human rights? These pointed questions may bring us to a reality check. We know we are walking on eggshells when we try to explain the NATO bombing of Serbia, and the continuous bombing of Iraq by the United States. In our own country we are haunted by such recent events as youth carrying guns to school, the murder of a gay student in Wyoming, and the dragging of an African American man to his death in East Texas.

What I am trying to say is that it is difficult, if not impossible, to act justly, unless we allow a supernatural force, a supernatural being, a supernatural cause, and a supernatural commitment to fulfill God's agenda for mission.

Consider the contradictions that Jesus had to endure. He returned to Nazareth, his hometown. The former carpenter was now a rabbi. He read the Isaiah scroll instead of building cabinets. He announced that a prophecy was fulfilled in his person. He invited his people to join him in proclaiming the acceptable year of the Lord to bring liberty to the captives. What did he get in return? An assassination attempt by hardhearted people who got inflamed when they heard the word *Gentile.*

I am inspired by Jesus and his desire to fulfill God's agenda for mission and his practice of justice. I am moved by Jesus' attitude toward women. He acted justly, loved mercy, and walked humbly with God.

When the woman at the well discussed religion with Jesus, he reached out and confronted her with her immorality, but he did not outrightly condemn her. Instead, he offered her the refreshing water of eternal life. When the disciples were amazed that he was speaking to a woman, Jesus tried to exhort them to look beyond appearances and search for opportunities for mission.

When the woman caught in adultery by self-righteous religious leaders was brought to him for judgment, he paused, probably moved by the injustice of the men who did not bring the man who was also caught in adultery. When the accusers were gone, he forgave the woman and sent her onto a new path of salvation.

Women's issues are an integral part of our ministry to the United Nations. Ana is active in planning forums related to the Commission to Eliminate Discrimination Against Women. She has organized and hosted luncheons with UNICEF for the betterment of women around the world. She has been blessed by the endorsement of Kofi Annan and Hillary Rodham Clinton in compassionate projects of education, development, medical improvement, and empowerment of women and children.

A few weeks ago we were privileged to entertain in our apartment a Nigerian business-woman who is actively promoting the cause of women in Africa. She is dreaming of women who can become independent in starting their own businesses and she is willing to commit financial resources to that cause. What a privilege to hear a sister in Christ dream great dreams of justice in the economy of nations!

Once at the weekly UN briefing it was a privilege to hear the First Lady of Venezuela, Marisable Rodriquez de Chavez, speak with eloquence of what her country is doing to improve the lot of families who are being affected by urbanization, poverty, unemployment, and the lure of greed. She exhorted the UN community to work in harmony for the improvement of family life around the world. After she had finished and was greeting those who waited for her, I shook her hand and gladly told her, "Dios le bendiga"—"God bless you" in Spanish. She thanked me for my wish.

II. *To love mercy.* Other translations render this phrase "to love kindness." God requires us to practice faithful love, love that is not necessarily deserved, love that is not regulated by law. It is the covenant love that was shown supremely in Christ's sacrifice on the cross.

Jesus said, "Blessed are the merciful, for they shall receive mercy." Many of his parables are saturated with stories of mercy. The most poignant story is the one about the love and mercy shown by the waiting father to his prodigal son when the son returned home; the father rejoiced that his son who had been lost was now found.

When Jesus invited himself to dine with Zacchaeus he became vulnerable to the gossip of the religious elite, but in his mercy he rescued a crooked tax collector from greed and enrolled him in the school of the faith of Abraham.

In our ministry at the United Nations we are associates of merciful works of love around the world. Because of our place of ministry, we come across possibilities to practice mercy at the personal level. Others are the instruments of mercy; we facilitate the process and rejoice when God's people exert their gifts and improve the living conditions of others.

It was a joy to host in our apartment the first councilor of the Uganda Mission to the UN. He, his wife, and a friend had dinner with us and our colleague Dwight Jackson from St. Louis, who was directing a development project in a village close to the Ugandan capitol city of Kampala. They discussed the details of the trip of volunteers from the United States and England. They planned to determine how the Ugandan government could assist in the projects of economic development.

All of us were moved when Dwight related that their main goal in the next trip would be to build a home for a grandmother of eight who was caring for her grandchildren because their parents had died of AIDS. She was living in a hut with limited resources and the local people of the village were willing to cooperate because they saw that the volunteers had come on an errand of mercy.

We were also privileged to see the smiles on the faces of refugees from Kosovo who came to New York. We networked with our colleagues Rick and Martha Shaw, who ministered with refugees in Macedonia. They made us aware that a man named Skender was bringing his family to the Bronx. With the help of Ronnie Adams and the Metro Baptist Church we tried to help them settle. After the first encounter, father, mother, and four children embraced me and kissed me for the little effort of help I had secured for them. I was deeply moved.

In international affairs the movement known as Jubilee 2000 is an attempt toward economic mercy. Western nations have generally provided assistance to developing countries when disaster has struck. The recent floods in Mozambique have moved countries to send relief, food, supplies, and medical assistance. However, what many of these countries need now is to restructure their debt to the World Bank so they may have better economic prospects. Many religious nongovernmental organizations are advocating for forgiveness of this debt through the Jubilee 2000 movement. We are glad that the U.S. government has acted to forgive the debts of some of these countries in Africa and Latin America. Recently the U.S. government forgave the debt of Mozambique.

Mercy is needed at the personal level, as illustrated by the Publican who said, "God be merciful to me a sinner." It is also crucial at the collective, community level. At Pentecost the crowd asked Peter, "What must we do to be saved?" I wonder, what mercy deeds can we do this week?

III. *To walk humbly with your God.* To walk humbly means to be teachable. It is an attitude of joyous, willing submission to God's will that proves our dependence on him.

I am forced to practice humility weekly as I go through security checks to enter the UN headquarters. It seems easy, but on occasion the beep of the metal detector has kept me humble as I've poured all my coins, keys, and pens into the tray. Talk about walking humbly!

I am inspired by the humble attitude of deacon Philip as he evangelized the region of Samaria. He, a layperson, was the only one trying to fulfill the Great Commission by being a witness to Samaria. His ministry was blessed by great multitudes of converts. Then, in a turnabout way, the Holy Spirit impelled him to go to the desert and witness to a diplomat in transit, to follow him back to his home. Philip humbly obeyed. He instructed the Ethiopian about Christ and baptized him, then allowed the diplomat "to go happily on his way." Philip walked humbly, and God used him as a spiritual guide for the eunuch.

When we walk in New York City we try to walk as representatives of Christ. The verse that has often inspired me in ministry is Paul's quote in Romans 10:15 based on Isaiah 52:7, "How lovely on the mountains are the feet of him who brings good news, who announces peace and brings good news of happiness, who announces salvation and says to Zion, 'your God reigns.'"

Our walks in the city can be exciting and humbling. Our walks during September reminded us of the security precautions. During the opening of the UN General Assembly, we watched from our apartment window all the barricades set up by the police to provide security to presidents, kings, queens, prime ministers, foreign ministers—all who came to address the General Assembly. Walking humbly takes into account persons with personality, faces, and accents. It is a daily occurrence as I walk the streets of midtown Manhattan. Recently, in a three-block walk of my daily routine, I engaged in casual talk with some individuals. I was walking with Jesus by my side as I spoke with these urban pilgrims:

- A young Mexican florist working for a Korean-owned flower shop told me that he was sending funds to his family in Mexico while he tried to obtain his green card.

- A Russian owner of a photo shop shared with me our common love for soccer, reliving her husband's enthusiasm for the sport as a coach of young people in his country.

- A Dominican porter took off his gloves to shake my hand when I handed him a Spanish Bible he had requested when he learned from other porters that I had Bibles in different languages.

From mid-June to mid-September, Manhattan is the home of the parade. Every Sunday there is a parade. A parade is a symbol of walking for a cause. In a parade people walk proudly, not humbly. They want to show off. This is how it is for all of the national parades: St. Patrick this last Friday; Dominican, Puerto Rican, Italian. The parades also portray different religions: Muslim, Hindu, Asian religions. The city without borders allows diversity for all to see and experience.

During these days of Lent I am reminded of the most merciful parade. Jesus' entrance into the city was a parade of joy and crowning. He entered the city mounted on a donkey and the people threw palms and vestments on his path. "Hosanna, blessed be the Son of David." The next Friday it was a parade of disgrace. Simon of Cyrene helped Jesus carry the cross, and people spat in his face. "And they crucified him." In his Via Dolorosa, our Lord incarnated God's agenda for mission: "to act justly, to love mercy, and to walk humbly with your God."

When many people hear about God's agenda for mission they begin to concoct ideas of mission boards, budgets, buildings, and personnel. The exhortation of the prophet and the sacrifice of Jesus dealt with an inner attitude of the heart.

- If our heart does not hurt for the things that hurt the heart of God, all the sacrifices of mission offerings will not make a difference.

- If our minds are not devoted to the courageous struggle for human rights and justice, for religious liberty for everybody, all the conventions and treaties of the 188 nation states of the United Nations will be of no avail.

- If our feet do not desire to walk humbly with our God, then we will let the allurements of a media-crazed society deceive us that glitz, fame, and an attitude of being number one is all that counts in life.

Can we hear the master call us and plead with us? "The harvest is plentiful but the laborers are few; therefore ask the Lord of the harvest to send out laborers into the harvest." Are we speculating as the disciples did? "Lord, will you restore the Kingdom of Israel?" Jesus responded, "It is not for you to know the times and the seasons . . . but you will receive power when the Holy Spirit has come upon you, and you will be my witnesses in Jerusalem, Judea, Samaria, and to the ends of the Earth." Let us rededicate ourselves to God's agenda for mission! Amen.—David F. D'Amico, Missionary to UN Diplomats

SECTION VIII

RESOURCES FOR PREACHING FROM ACTS

BY JOHN B. POLHILL

Acts offers a variety of materials for preaching. It is especially suitable for narrative preaching, because it consists primarily of narrative. One can often simply let the story preach itself. The following sermons have been selected to illustrate the different types of approaches to which Acts lends itself.

Topic: Waiting
TEXT: Acts 1:6–14

It isn't easy to wait. It never has been for me. I remember how as a child I waited for what seemed forever for that special Lone Ranger silver-bullet ring to arrive in the mail. As a young adult I wondered if I would ever receive word about whether or not I had been accepted into graduate school. My real lesson on waiting, however, came as a parent, waiting for my teenaged daughter to get ready for church.

Just think how intolerable the waiting must have been for the disciples in the period covered in the first chapter of Acts, the interval between Jesus' Resurrection and the coming of the Spirit at Pentecost. The first forty days were not so bad. Jesus was still with them. Then he ascended, having commissioned them to a worldwide mission. But he told them, "Not yet; wait for the Spirit." So, after his Ascension they waited. For ten days they waited, packed into a crowded upper room.

Still, their waiting was necessary. Waiting is often necessary. Sometimes we need to wait before we go about the Lord's business. What the early Christians did in their period of waiting can be instructive for us when we too must wait.

I. *They waited for instruction.* Acts 1:2–5 relates a period of forty days in which the Risen Lord was with the disciples. This was primarily a period of learning for them, during which the Lord applied the Old Testament Scriptures to himself. His interpretation of the Scriptures would serve as the basis for the disciples' own witness to Jesus. Jesus knew that if they were to be effective witnesses, they needed to be firmly anchored in the Word of God.

Instruction is just as important for today's disciples. As a teacher at a seminary, I am particularly aware of this. Some of my students are what might be called "activists." They would rather be out serving the Lord than sitting in Bible class. Sometimes activist students do stupid things. I learned this during my own seminary days when I served as a student chaplain in a ward filled with alcoholics. I thought I was being the truly caring minister. The senior chaplain pointed out that I was showing total ignorance about the problems of alcoholics. Instead of helping them, I was serving as a substitute "bottle," thus contributing to their dependency. I needed to learn something about alcoholics first before attempting to minister

375

to them. This rule applies to any Christian ministry. Instruction comes first, whether it be witness to Christ or something as seemingly mundane as gathering relevant data for a building project.

II. *They got their priorities straight.* The disciples' priorities weren't straight at first. Their question to Jesus in verse 6 shows this: "Lord, will you at this time restore the Kingdom to Israel?" Jesus pointed out to them that other things had to be done before the Kingdom would come. A whole world lay before them, for which they needed the gospel (v. 8).

Before we rush off to do some ministry, we need to wait a moment to make sure our priorities are in order. Churches have a way of developing too many ministries, of spreading their physical, financial, and human resources too thin. It is often necessary to sit down as a church body and draw up a list of priorities.

III. *They determined their leadership.* Judas was dead, having abandoned his place of leadership among the twelve. It was symbolically important in this initial period of the Church that the twelfth position be filled, to align the new covenant people of God with the twelve Israelite tribes of the old covenant. The gathered community proceeded to lay down the qualifications for this apostolic replacement, to determine the two candidates who met these qualifications, and then to lay the matter before God for his selection.

Their procedure is still valid. A church can make serious errors if it fails at any point. First, it can fail to consider the qualifications for a particular task—that is, a job description. Some people are simply not qualified for some tasks. To put persons in roles for which they are unsuited is fair neither to them nor to the church. Second, the selection of leadership should be turned over to God.

Having determined the two qualifying candidates, the whole church in Acts 1 prayed that God would lead them to make the right choice. In this instance, they resorted to the Old Testament precedent of casting lots, asking God to show his choice through the outcome of the lot. This is the only time they used such a method. Thereafter they seem to have made their decisions through the consensus of the body. They always included God, however, committing each decision to prayer. In fact, prayer is probably the most important ingredient of all in any waiting period of the church. The *primary* activity of the Christian community between the Ascension and Pentecost was prayer (vv. 12–14).

Waiting—we resist it. Our culture tells us that it is wasted time. On the contrary, time spent in instruction, in formulating priorities, in selecting qualified leadership, and in prayer with God is never wasted time. For the Christian community, waiting is essential to any successful ministry.

Topic: Barnabas, Son of Encouragement
TEXT: Acts 4:36–37; 11:19–26

Barnabas is at best a minor character in Acts. Acts has only two major characters—Peter, to whom nine chapters are devoted, and Paul, whose story is told in sixteen chapters. Stephen occupies two chapters, and Philip, one. Many others play lesser roles in Acts. Of them, Barnabas is perhaps the most prominent. He appears in fairly regular snippets from chapters four through fifteen. His prominence is due not so much to the regularity of his appearance but to the portrait of his character. In this regard, Barnabas wins the Oscar for best supporting actor hands down. Nothing negative is said about him in all of Acts. He alone is called "good"

(11:24). Most of us would like to be considered good. What does Barnabas teach us about being good?

For one thing, Barnabas was *generous.* His first appearance in Acts (4:36–37) emphasizes this trait. The early Church in Jerusalem had a practice of voluntary contributions in which those of means would sell their goods and bring the proceeds to the apostles, who would distribute them to the needy. Barnabas is singled out for his generosity in giving the receipts from the sale of a parcel of land.

A generous person is usually liberal in more than material gifts. Generosity marks total liberality of spirit. This is what Jesus meant when he spoke of the "evil eye" making the whole body dark and the "sound" (or "single") eye making the whole body light (Matt. 6:22–23). The evil eye is a Semitic idiom for stinginess; the single or sound eye is idiomatic for generosity. Barnabas was a single-eyed person, full of light and generous not only with his goods but also with himself.

Barnabas's willingness to share himself is evident in the manner in which he regularly stood in the background, giving the limelight to others and faithfully playing a supporting role. This trait emerges in chapter eleven (vv. 19–26) when the Antioch church began to witness to Gentiles. Up to this point the Church as a whole had confined its outreach to the Jewish community. The mother church in Jerusalem thought it best to check out this new ministry in Antioch and sent Barnabas as its official representative. In this role Barnabas had considerable prestige and power. He did not pull rank, however. When he saw that God was blessing the Gentile mission, he joined the witness and even went to Tarsus to find Paul and bring him back to assist. Barnabas knew that as a Greek-speaking Diaspora Jew Paul was particularly suited for the Gentile outreach. He probably was also aware that Paul would take the lead now and Barnabas himself would have to play a less visible, supporting role. That is precisely what he wanted—whatever would be best for the Lord's work.

Barnabas believed in bringing out the best in others; he was an *encourager.* According to Acts 4:36 his nickname was "Son of Encouragement." It was an apt designation. Every time we meet Barnabas in Acts he is encouraging someone. He was the first in the Jerusalem church to support Paul's ministry after his conversion, and he introduced Paul to the apostolic circle (Acts 9:27). As we have seen, he encouraged Antioch in its Gentile outreach and brought Paul to assist, yielding the leadership to Paul. Above all, Barnabas appears as an encourager in the incident involving John Mark (Acts 15:36–40). Paul and Barnabas had taken Mark as helper on their first missionary journey, but for some unknown reason Mark abandoned them midway in the work and returned home (Acts 13:13). When Paul asked Barnabas to accompany him on his second mission, Barnabas wanted to take Mark along, to give him a second chance. Paul would have none of this, and the two parted ways. Two missions resulted, with Paul taking Silas as his partner and Barnabas taking Mark to work in Cyprus. The future of the Christian mission lay with Paul, and Barnabas surely knew it. He also knew that for John Mark there might be no future at all if he abandoned him to Paul's rejection. Mark was most likely at that vulnerable late-teens age when young people are often insecure to begin with.

Barnabas's encouragement evidently rescued Mark. After his Cyprus mission with Barnabas, Mark went on to become Peter's trusted coworker (1 Pet. 5:13). The Gospel that bears Mark's name was probably the first to be written, and tradition holds that Mark based it on Peter's memoirs. Most ironical of all, however, Mark became Paul's coworker as well, and he is mentioned fondly in several of Paul's letters (Col. 4:10; Philem. 24; 2 Tim. 4:11). One might almost say that Barnabas rescued Mark from Paul ultimately to serve Paul.

In Acts 4:36 we are told that Barnabas was a Levite. Perhaps this is a key to his personality. Levites were the servants of the Temple. They opened and closed the heavy gates, furnished the music, and cleaned up the mess from the sacrifices. They were never in the limelight like the priests were, but they were absolutely essential to the Temple worship.

The Church in every age has depended on servant types like Barnabas—people who give generously of their resources and selves; those who are usually standing in the background and rarely in the foreground; those who are always supporting, encouraging, and bringing out the best in others. The Church may never have gotten off the ground without strong personalities like Peter and Paul. It would not, however, have survived long without "good" people, "sons and daughters of encouragement," like Barnabas.

Topic: The Unhindered Gospel
TEXT: Acts 10

In his commentary on Acts, Frank Stagg described the main theme of the book as the early Church's struggle for an "unhindered" gospel. He observed that the last word of the book is an adverb. This almost never occurs in Greek literature. He concluded that this rare construction was probably deliberate on Luke's part and employed for emphasis. The adverb can be translated "without hindrance; unhinderedly." Tracing the root word (hinder, forbid) throughout Acts, Stagg discovered that it occurs at key points where the gospel overcame barriers of human discrimination and prejudice. Stagg was my doctoral supervisor and colleague for many years. He recently passed away. I would like to dedicate this sermon to his memory.

No narrative in Acts illustrates the unhindered gospel better than Peter's encounter with the Roman centurion Cornelius (Acts 10). Cornelius was a "God-fearer," that is, a Gentile believer who had embraced Jewish monotheism, who was a faithful supporter of the synagogue, but who had not become a full convert (proselyte) to Judaism. Up to this point in the narrative of Acts, the Christian witness had primarily targeted Jews and not Gentiles—not even Gentiles like Cornelius who worshiped God. Peter's witness to the centurion was an entirely new experience for him.

The story rotates around two interlocking visions, each repeated three times in Acts 10:1–11:18. The repetition underlines the significance of the event. The first vision came to Cornelius, who was instructed by an angel to send for Peter at Joppa. The second and central vision came to Peter at Joppa. Waiting for his lunch on a rooftop at Joppa, Peter saw a sheet descend from heaven filled with all sorts of animals. Some were clean, others were unclean according to the Old Testament food laws, rendering the whole collection unclean. A heavenly voice instructed Peter to satisfy his appetite from among the animals. The instruction was repeated three times, thoroughly perplexing Peter. He had been taught from childhood that God forbade the consumption of unclean food. Now God seemed to be contradicting his law. Jesus had already taught that "all foods" are clean, as Mark observed in his Gospel (Mark 7:19). Perhaps Peter had not yet drawn this conclusion from his recollection of Jesus' teachings. His understanding, and especially this vision of the sheet, may well lie behind Mark's comment.

In any event, with the arrival of the emissaries from Cornelius, it soon became apparent to Peter that his vision was not so much about food as it was about people (10:27–28). Arriving at Cornelius's home, Peter gladly shared his testimony. He set the theme in his opening words, which stated that God accepts all people equally, showing no partiality (vv. 34–35). He then proceeded to outline the ministry of Jesus: his preaching and teaching, his death and Resurrection, and the apostolic witness to the Resurrection (vv. 36–41). He moved to an implicit call to commitment by alluding to the need for repentance in light of the coming judgment (vv. 42–43).

Peter was unable to complete his sermon. He was interrupted by the inspired utterances of the members of his Gentile audience, who had all been filled with the Holy Spirit (vv. 44–45). Their ecstatic praise served to demonstrate that the conversion of these Gentiles was God's doing, not man's. Stagg's key word *forbid/hinder* occurs in verse 47. A major barrier had been overcome. Gentiles were baptized into the fellowship. The gospel progressed "without hindrance." Verse 48 is also significant. While staying for several days with the Gentiles, Peter was surely exposed to unclean food. He did not let his former understandings about food laws get in the way of his fellowship with his new brothers and sisters in Christ.

Acts has many examples of the gospel overcoming barriers erected by humans against other humans: the conversion of the Samaritans, so often despised by their Jewish cousins (8:4–13); the baptism of the Ethiopian eunuch, whose physical condition would have limited his access to worship in the Jerusalem Temple (8:26–40); the conversion of Lydia, who was herself probably a God-fearer, not to mention a woman who was not only accepted into the Christian community but also assumed a leading role, providing her own home for the gatherings of the church (16:14–15, 40).

Barriers to the gospel still appear, often within the church itself. Most American congregations remain largely segregated along racial lines. True, this is often by preference of all parties and due to different worship styles. Still, churches would profit by more congregational interaction and cooperative ministries. Even among racially homogeneous congregations one finds barriers. Churches are often socially and economically divergent. Their theologies and attitudes tend to become stratified, with each congregation showing little acceptance and understanding of the other's differences. Barriers are erected within denominations and even within individual congregations over such things as worship style and gender in positions of leadership.

How do we overcome barriers? Peter's experience gives us a couple of pointers. First, we need to be open to God's leading us in new directions and to new understandings. A century and a half ago, slave owners in the United States were convinced that the New Testament condoned slavery, until the real meaning of "neither slave nor free" was driven home for them (Gal. 3:28). Second, we must learn to be more accepting of one another, to stop erecting barriers by insisting that our way is the only way. Like Peter, we would profit by sitting at table in fellowship with our Christian brothers and sisters whose views and customs may differ significantly from our own.

Topic: Full of Idols
TEXT: Acts 17:22–31

Acts is full of sermons. Approximately 30 percent of its text consists of speeches. Paul's speech delivered from the Areopagus ("Mars Hill") in Athens is the prime example of a sermon to pagans. In this instance, the audience consisted primarily of the Athenian intelligentsia.

The main theme of Paul's Areopagus address is *the ignorance of idol worship*. The scene was set when Paul arrived in Athens, where he found the city literally loaded with idols (17:16). His sermon probably began to form in his mind at that very instant. His opportunity to deliver it came later when some of the Athenian philosophers led him to the Areopagus to hear more of this new teaching he was bringing to their town. The term Areopagus could refer either to a court that met in Paul's day in a building in the marketplace or to a hill below the Acropolis where the court had formerly met. Either location furnished an appropriate setting for Paul's sermon: both were surrounded by idols.

Paul took as his point of departure a statue he had observed in the city dedicated "to an unknown god." Archaeologists have not yet discovered a statue with such an inscription. It is plausible that one existed, with the pious Athenians providing it lest they offend some god whom they had failed to include in their pantheon. Paul played on the word *unknown*. The Athenians knew many gods. The only one they didn't know was the only one that counts, the one true God. Their religion was thus grounded in ignorance.

Paul's sermon was directed mainly to the philosophers. Most of them would have rejected the crass idolatry of the common folk. The Stoics were exemplary of these philosophers, being pantheists who believed that a divine principle is to be found in all animate beings. For them, to find God was to look within oneself. Paul thus began with the Biblical view of God: God is not found *within* creation; God is *Creator* (vv. 24–27). Paul even took his text from the philosophers: "We are his offspring" (v. 28) is from the Stoic poet Aratus. For the Stoics the phrase meant that humans are all children of divinity and thus are themselves divine. Paul applied the quote quite differently, stating that humans are a part of God's creation, children of the one true God.

Paul then moved to the error of idolatry (v. 29). Idolatry is exchanging the creation for the Creator, worshiping creation rather than its Maker. Worse still, it is the perversion of the image of God. As God's offspring, we are created in his own image. When we make idols, we get matters upside down. We fashion God in our image instead of allowing him to make us in his image. The idolater ultimately makes himself creator, fashioning his gods after his own likeness.

Paul concluded with a call to repentance (vv. 30–31). He stated that God would no longer tolerate our ignorance; he would no longer put up with human idolatry. He had revealed himself in Christ and shown his power in Christ's Resurrection. The time was approaching when all would face divine judgment. The idea of a final judgment and resurrection was completely alien to the Athenian philosophers. Most laughed Paul off the podium, but a few believed (vv. 32–34).

Most contemporary Christians would probably see little relevance in Paul's Areopagus speech. Most of us are not idolaters in the literal sense. In our society, even among non-Christians, few would bow down to an idol. Perhaps the occasional Buddhist would, but not many in America. However, idolatry is rampant in our culture. An idol is any object of devotion that serves as a substitute for God. Most of the sophisticated Athenian philosophers would have rejected the naive veneration of graven images. They instead worshiped the divinity within themselves. They fashioned their god in the likeness of themselves, thus making God after their own image. Paul condemned them for this blatant idolatry and called them to repentance.

Every person has an object of worship. If it isn't their Creator, it is bound to be some aspect of creation. Whatever people look to for personal fulfillment, whatever they turn to for ultimate security, becomes their god. It may be a political system. It may be the acquisition of personal wealth. It may be physical health or attractiveness, or a hedonistic devotion to pleasure. Almost anything can serve as one's god, one's idol.

Even the Church can get caught up in idolatry. It can idolize its leadership or its programs; its forms, its worship, or its creeds—anything that becomes a substitute for a living relationship with God. Worse still, the Church can easily become a mere reflection of society. God is then fashioned after the values of society. God is made in the image of humans and humans become their own God. Such gods are easy to manipulate; such gods are dead.

Whether in the secular realm or in the Church, all idolatry has the same basic problem: idols are always creatures and never God. They offer a false security. When they crash, as they generally do, those who worship them have no place to turn; they are left with no God.

Topic: The Storms of Life
TEXT: Acts 27:21–16, 33–36

As a frequent traveler in a day when journey by sea was fraught with peril, Paul often faced the prospect of shipwreck. In 2 Corinthians 11:25 he tells how he was shipwrecked three times and once was adrift at sea for a day and a night. We know nothing more of those incidents, but a subsequent shipwreck is told in great detail in Acts 27. It is an exciting story, written in Luke's consummate style. The prisoner Paul was being transferred to Rome in order to appear for trial before Caesar when his ship encountered a violent Mediterranean storm. It would have been destroyed but for the grace of God.

Most of us will never experience as dangerous a storm of this literal variety. We all, however, face our storms in life—storms of threatened health, failing securities, broken relationships. They can be just as shattering and usually more enduring in their effects than nature's storms. Perhaps one reason Luke devoted so much space to Paul's shipwreck is because it serves as a model for each of us in riding out life's storms.

I. *We can feel totally desperate and lost when life hurls its storms at us.* This was true for the crew on Paul's ship. Already caught in adverse weather well past the safe season for sailing, they made a quick dash for a safe harbor where they could spend the winter. The maneuver failed and they found themselves trapped in a violent Mediterranean "northeaster." The sailors did everything they could to secure the ship: they tied up the lifeboat, undergirded the ship with cables, let out drift anchors, threw most of the cargo overboard, and even jettisoned much of the sailing equipment. It was all to no avail. The storm continued unabated. With neither sun nor stars, because of the clouds, by which to take their bearing they didn't even know where they were. For two weeks they were tossed by the storm. All hope of deliverance was abandoned (v. 20).

Life's storms have a way of treating us like that. We exhaust our best resources, doing everything we can, but to no avail. We find ourselves in situations we cannot handle.

II. *God does not abandon us to our despair.* It is at times like this that we turn to God. When we trust in him, he does not abandon us to our despair. This is what happened to Paul. In a night-time vision, almost surely in the context of prayer, an angel of God appeared to Paul, assuring him that everyone on board would be rescued and that Paul would surely give his testimony before the Emperor. God often assured Paul in the night. He did so in night visions at Troas (16:9–10), at Corinth (18:9), and at Jerusalem (23:11). There is a certain symbolism in this. In the darkness of the night, in our hour of deepest despair, God brings assurance. It may have to be that way: when we hit bottom and get our own egos out of the way, we open up and allow God to come through to us.

Like Paul's traveling group, God does not abandon us to the storms of our lives. He does not always deliver us, but he is always with us, to help us through the night, to guide us through the storm. It was so with Paul. God did not always deliver him, but he was always with Paul, even in his darkest hour. Paul's words in 2 Timothy 4:6–8 were probably written in anticipation of his impending death. They are words of triumph and assurance, that no storm could blow away the certainty of God's presence in his life. It was that way with my colleague Frank. He lost his wife to cancer at an early age, leaving him with two small children. God did not deliver Frank's from the tragedy of his wife's death, but he did give him the grace to rear those children as a single parent. God also brought a blessing out of the experience, leading Frank to write a powerful book on God's assuring presence, a book that the storm of his own life's experience particularly qualified him to write.

III. *Encouragement is contagious.* After fourteen days of storms, everyone was thoroughly beat, even after Paul's promise of their rescue, even after the sailors sensed they were nearing land. The shore was rocky, the ship could have foundered on the rocks, and some sailors even attempted to abandon ship by stealing the lifeboat. At this point, Paul once again rose to his feet to assure everyone aboard that God would certainly deliver them. He urged them to take some food for strength. He set an example by eating before them. Everyone was then encouraged and took sustenance. Eventually all made it safely to land, just as Paul had promised.

A cheerful, confident spirit can be contagious. We have all witnessed this. When I was a ninth grader, one of the best athletes in my school chose me and several other nonathletic types to be on his football team. We couldn't believe it. He knew what he was doing, however. He pointed out to me that I was heavier than most of the other kids and would make an excellent center. He showed nothing but confidence in all of us. He was sure we could win the intramurals that year. His encouragement knew no bounds and his confidence was contagious. In spite of all odds, we did indeed win the tournament.

Like individuals, churches often experience storms in their corporate lives. A fellowship can go through the same cycle as Paul's ship—facing stormy times, lost in despair and hopelessness. Those nighttimes of a church's soul can be turning points, periods when God's assuring presence can come in a special way. God had a job for Paul to do and he brought Paul through the storm to do it. He has a task for every congregation. Sometimes it takes just one voice of encouragement in a fellowship to awaken the confidence of all and bring them through the storm to embrace the work that God has for them to do.

RESOURCES FOR PREACHING ON SELF-DISCOVERY

BY WILLIAM POWELL TUCK

Topic: Seeking Divine Guidance
Text: Prov. 3:5–6

Most Christians have indicated at one time or another that they want to feel they have a sense of direction from God in their lives. Few persons who are Christians really want to say, "I am living in opposition to what I think God wants me to do."

The writer of the Book of Proverbs asserted, "Trust in the Lord with all your heart and he will direct your paths." An ancient rabbi has stated that this text is the "hinge" on which all the essential principles of Judaism rest. Trust in God is the hinge on which most of our life really does depend. This call to trust is for those who already believe in God. It is addressed not to those outside the faith but to those who are within.

I. *"Trust in the Lord with all of your heart, but lean not on your own understanding."* Some of us do lean too much on our own understanding. The injunction to "trust in the Lord" would not be necessary if everyone did.

(a) The idolatry of self arises from those who puff themselves up and feel they have enough insights to make all the necessary decisions regarding life without any divine guidance. They feel no sense of dependence on God or on others. They feel sufficient in their own abilities.

(b) Others say that the vastness of the universe makes it impossible for us to be known. "How could there be a God who is concerned about us on this tiny speck in the universe?" they ask. Others point to the accidents, suffering, and pain in our world and declare that these enigmas deny the love and providence of God.

(c) Still others declare that even if there is a God, we can't really communicate with him. "Why," they laughingly declare, "we can't even talk to each other." One of our biggest problems is understanding each other. How can we talk about communicating with God?

(d) The words *acknowledge* and *trust* come from a rich Hebrew word whose root meaning is "to see" or "to know." This word involves much more than just physical vision or intellectual knowledge, though that is a part of it. This knowledge encompasses the heart, will, and mind. When you and I acknowledge God with all our capacity, then his direction will be clear.

The ancient wisdom writer uses the word *all*. "In all of your ways acknowledge him." The emphasis on *all* acknowledges our absolute dependence on God.

The ancient writer reminds us that we are to trust God with all of our heart. With the word *trust,* the ancient writer of wisdom often links two related nouns, security and confidence. Trust in God enables us to go through life not relying on our own strength alone but living in quiet confidence in the resource of God's presence.

II. *The wisdom writer has assured us that if we acknowledge God with all our heart, he will direct or make straight our paths.* This is the promise we have from God if we love him with all of our being. How do we determine the guidance of God? Let me offer some brief suggestions.

(a) *Follow the light you have.* We sometimes do not perceive clearly what God wants us to do because we have not followed the light God has already given us. We are not able to go any further in understanding what God wants us to do until we have been willing to step into the light we already have.

Walking daily in the light of his presence, we are enlightened by the knowledge of his way. God sometimes works slowly in the inner consciousness of our mind to guide us.

(b) *Use the reasoning powers you have.* I don't know why we think that to use our mind is to go counter to what God might want us to do. Why do we think that God is always going to guide us by imparting something from outside of ourselves? Sometimes God may be saying to us, "You have a mind; use it." God has given us a mind so we can think.

(c) *Study the Scriptures.* The Bible is not some book of magic that we thumb through for quick answers. When you search the Scriptures you find the eternal principles and teachings about how God has worked in the lives of other people in the past. Then you seek to understand how you can relate these principles and teachings to your own life. The Ten Commandments, the Old Testament prophets, the Beatitudes and other teachings of Jesus, and the insights of Paul and others are all principles and guides for our lives. Seek to discern how God worked in the lives of ancient biblical persons and be open to the divine presence through prayer.

(d) *Wait patiently for God.* God is much more patient than we are. Most of the time God moves very slowly to accomplish his will. On the other hand, we usually want everything right now, but God waits patiently to realize the goals he intends to reach. The Scriptures advise us to "wait patiently for the Lord." "Be still and know that I am God."

(e) *Draw on the resources of the Church.* The spiritual heritage of those who have gone before us in the faith and of some who are living today can give us guidance for discovering God's will. We can look to the Christian saints in the past and present, to how they have understood God's will. Their experiences might offer us guidelines for our own.

Even the apostle Paul, later in his life, struggled to discern God's guidance. He had wanted to preach the gospel in Spain, but he ended up in jail in Rome. He may have never understood why the door to Spain didn't opened for him, but his detour to a Roman prison was the place God enabled him to write letters that we are still reading today for spiritual guidance.

(f) *Remember how mysteriously and unexpectedly God moves.* We never know for certain how God works in people's lives. Because each person is different, God's guidance may be varied. God may work through your reasoning ability, your inner resources, your friends and acquaintances, or through delays and obstacles. Who knows? But the one thing about which I am firmly convinced is this: God does guide our lives. When we trust God completely we will discover his leading. As Dante has said, "In his will is my peace."

Topic: Learning to See

TEXT: 2 Kings 6:15–17; Mark 8:22–26

A blind man was brought to Jesus, who was asked to help this man. Jesus led the man outside the village of Bethsaida, then took clay and put spittle upon it and placed it on the man's eyes. Jesus asked the blind man if he could see anything. The man responded by saying, "I can see men moving as though they were trees walking." Then Jesus placed his hands on the man's eyes again. After the second touch, the man was able to see.

This story was inserted in Mark's Gospel right after the discussion with the disciples about their being unable to perceive who Jesus was. Immediately following this healing, Peter made the dramatic confession that Jesus is the Christ. Mark used this story like a parable to stress that we are often blind to Jesus' identity.

Jesus said to the man, "Can you see anything?" That is my question, too: Can you see? How blind many of us really are! Animals and insects often have much better sight than we do. How blind we human beings often are, to so much of life. We seem to miss so much.

I. There are many people who at one time had a strong sense of vision but who, because of circumstances in life, may have lost that vision. It may have faded to delusion, and they have given up hope.

A lot of people lose all sense of perspective when they experience failure. When life becomes difficult and their vision fades, delusion sets in. They simply cannot see.

(a) Jesus said to the blind man, "Do you see anything?" The blind man said, "I see men as trees walking." A lot of us have blurred vision, don't we? If you wear glasses and take them off, you know about seeing blurred images in front of you. But distorted vision is not limited to persons who wear glasses. Many of us go through life with an inability to focus. We cannot really see very well. We need to receive a clearer vision.

(b) How often we simply cannot see or hear at all. There is so much around us to see and hear but we are unable to perceive it. Yet there are others who seem to have eyes that see everything.

Some see so much while others are blind. If we could only see as some of the poets and artists have seen! The world around us is laced with beauty, mystery, and majesty, and how often we are blind to this wonder and mystery. We simply do not see it; therefore we do not take time to marvel at it.

II. And Jesus said to the blind man, "Are you able to see?" "I see men as trees walking." Jesus touched his eyes again and the man was able to see. Have you ever imagined the resources that are hidden to you?

Think of the spiritual, physical, and mental resources that are untapped by us. Elisha awakened one morning to find himself surrounded by the Syrian Army. His servant came out and saw this mighty army and was petrified. "What will we do?" Elisha prays that the Lord would open his eyes. His servant's eyes were opened and he saw the army of the Lord encircling the mountains on horses of fire.

The presence of God is available to us if we will only open our eyes and ears to see and hear. We cannot begin to perceive what is available to us from God!

III. Then Jesus touched the blind man's eyes a second time. We are not sure who this man was. He seemed to be a Gentile. He was brought to Jesus, probably without any real expectation of anything happening. But Jesus touched his eyes again and he was able to see.

(a) Some of you may have lost your sense of vision. Through the years your faith has become dampened and you have become cool. You have lost some of your excitement in following Jesus Christ. You need to feel the second touch of Christ upon your life.

(b) O Lord, we need to pray, open my eyes that I might see you. We do not want to be blind. Moses was tending sheep on a mountainside when he saw God. Isaiah went to the Temple to worship and saw the Lord high and lifted up. Their eyes were opened and they were able to see.

(c) Have you ever wondered what eyes Jesus must have had? Why, he saw as no other person was able to see. He could see into the ordinary things of life—a woman baking bread, sparrows in flight, wheat blowing in the breeze, a coin on the floor—and all of these common experiences provided parables and truths about the mystery and majesty of God and life. Jesus saw God everywhere.

Jesus saw a woman drop a mite in the Temple offering plate and recognized the extent of her sacrificial gift. He looked into the face of Mary of Magdalene and saw a potential disciple. He saw in the face of denying Peter one who could become a foundation stone in his Church. He saw in doubting Thomas a faithful disciple. He saw in Zacchaeus one who could minister in his name. He saw in Saul a great apostle and missionary.

God sees potential in our lives that you and I have never dreamed of before. Pray that we will let God touch our eyes so we can see that God is all around us and within us. Could this sight give us the power to be his servants in the world and to be assured of his support and grace? Could this sight make us aware of the inner resources that God gives us? God is present now and can enable us to see. "Do you see?" "Lord, I see men as trees walking." Jesus touched the blind man's eyes again and he was able to see. Are you able to see now?

Topic: Who Do You Think You Are?
TEXT: Ps. 8; Eph. 4:9

In Washington, D.C., a place often noted for confusion, a man was seen one day wandering through one of the public office buildings. He was pulling drawers open, looking into filing cabinets, and even checking the trashcans. A police detective came into the office where the man was and arrested him. "What are you looking for?" he asked him. "I'm looking for myself," he replied. And so are we all.

We live our lives in pilgrimage to discover who we are. Unfortunately, some people live their whole lives and never really discover who they are. Who are you? Who are you really, deep down inside with your mask ripped off; beneath the veneer, the makeup, and the pretense? Who are you really?

I. *Who are you? How do you discover who you are?* The question of the psalmist then is the question of the ages: "When I look at the heavens which you have made, O God, and all of your handiwork in the world, what are man and woman that you should consider them?"

(a) Some have not given a very positive reply to that question. They have taken a very negative attitude toward humanity and life. Some of our modern novelists have given us some rather negative images of life. One writer described human life as "a small but boisterous bit of organic scum, which for the time being coats part of the surface of one small planet." Another depicts man as "an ingenious assembly of portable plumbing." Ernest Hemingway described human beings as "a colony of ants in a burning log."

(b) Not only do we have a dim view of humanity, but our perspective is also partial. Who has the full view of man or woman? We all have such an imperfect and partial view of life. None of us seems to be able to see man or woman in their totality.

II. *Here enters the contrast of the biblical message about who man and woman are.* Listen to the Bible's elevated concept of who humanity really is. The psalmist declares that man and woman are the crown of God's creation. They are kin to God and kin to the Earth.

(a) "When I consider all of your creation and I see man or woman," the psalmist asks, "why do you value them?" What is God's declaration in response to such an inquiry? Why, man and woman are the crown of God's creation. Mere man and woman are encircled with the glory and honor of God. This denotes their high sense of worth.

(b) The psalmist continues in his declaration that humanity is not only the crown of God's creation but has also been created "a little less than God." This is a better translation than "a little less than angels." The reference to man and woman being crowned with glory and honor denotes attributes ascribed to God and makes that rendering better. Humanity has been given dominion over the rest of creation.

(c) The psalmist has a high view of humanity as God's creation. To humankind God has given rule over the rest of nature. To give God's children such power indicates the love and care God has for human creation. Those who would depict life in images of negativity and futility have not really heard the biblical declaration that creation in God's sight is good, and that God has crowned man and woman with honor and glory. Human beings are his instruments of service in the world.

III. *In Ephesians, we find an even greater declaration about who man and woman really are.* In Ephesians Paul points to the lofty height that you and I are challenged to reach toward to be like our Lord.

(a) Paul writes that Christians are to reach toward "maturity"—a mature personhood. The world *maturity* is a better translation than *perfect*. We have seen what God is like in Jesus Christ. Christ is the ideal human being. He has set an example of the heights we can reach in our human nature. Christ pulls our fragmented selves together. Christ is our model, our example, and the goal toward which we strive.

(b) Paul also reminds us that all persons are important in Christ's Kingdom. Every single individual has some gift, and these gifts are significant in Christ's ministry. The unity of Christ's Church is not uniformity but recognizing and affirming the diversity of all these gifts.

Each person is an important part of the total unity. No person is seen as being of lesser value than another, no matter who that individual might be. Color, race, sex, and status are not important in the sight of God. God has created and redeemed all of us.

Our Lord never perceived persons as having no worth or value. Jesus could see the potential in all persons and sought to get them to commit their gifts unto God's service. He recognized every person as a child of God. If we reject anyone because of color, race, or sex, we are rejecting God's children. God loves all persons and seeks to draw them unto himself.

(c) Paul has challenged his readers to reach toward mature personhood, which Jesus Christ offers. Christ is the head and we seek to model ourselves after him. As we move toward that goal, we reach toward "the measure of the stature of the fullness of Christ."

Christ is our goal, ideal, and standard for personhood. We are to strive to be like him. This will not be easy. It is a goal always beyond our reach. We struggle to reach it but realize that we never fully will. Nevertheless, we aim to be like our Lord himself.

Remember who you are. You are a child of God. As Paul wrote, "You have been bought with a price." Christ laid down his life that you might have life. None of us has ever realized the potential within us. No one has ever arrived spiritually. None of us is ever full-grown. We are always in process, forever reaching, and seeking to measure up to the fullness of Christ. As Paul wrote, "We shall become mature persons, reaching to the very height of Christ's full stature."

Topic: Moving Beyond Failure

TEXT: Matt. 26:69–75

The story of Peter's denial is surprising. It is amazing that it is in the New Testament. After all, Peter was a hero and leader in the early Church. This story records Peter's absolute failure in the face of his first real test in following his Lord. Look at what his story tells us about Peter and ourselves.

I. *The story begins by acknowledging Peter's weakness.* This story could be in the New Testament for only one reason: Peter had told it to others. There was no other disciple present that night. Peter was the only disciple who went into the courtyard to see what would happen to Jesus. He had enough courage to risk his own life. Peter boldly shared his own failure in the moment of his temptation. But what a testimony it must have been to the early Church. If Christ had forgiven him, how much opportunity would there be for others to know forgiveness and experience a new beginning?

(a) *Peter failed, I believe, because he was overconfident.* He thought he could withstand whatever came his way. When Jesus predicted the suffering and difficulties that lay before him, Peter stood up and with a ringing cry said, "Lord, if everybody else forsakes you, I never will." He did not recognize his own weakness. We cannot act as though we have no weaknesses. There are temptations, and we cannot master them with our own resources.

(b) Some of our most devastating temptations, however, confront us in what we think is our greatest strength. Peter did what he thought he would not do. When he realized his failure, he fled and wept bitterly. But he did not give way to despair. His weeping led to repentance and a changed life.

(c) Peter denied his Lord, but who among us has not denied our Lord? We were ashamed of the best that we have ever experienced and we gave in to the lowest dominion in our lives. But the realization that this is possible for us is the first step toward combating the temptations that can drag us down and destroy us.

The good news for each of us is that we can find forgiveness and the possibility of beginning anew in Jesus Christ. Peter was willing to acknowledge his weakness. By acknowledging his failure, he experienced forgiveness.

II. *Notice that Peter accepted the challenge that Jesus gave him.* In the twenty-first chapter of the Gospel of John, the writer recorded the experience in which Peter and six other disciples met the resurrected Christ on the shore of the Sea of Tiberius.

(a) Jesus forgave Peter for his denial, and then gave him a challenge and responsibility to go and minister in Jesus' name. He had denied his Lord, but that was not the end of his life. Later Peter became one of the great heroes and ministers in the early Christian Church. He felt that he had turned his back on his Lord and he hated the action he took. Like many of us who have sinned, he wished he could undo what he had done, but it was too late. It was finished.

(b) Sometimes pride can be the factor in our life that pulls us down and destroys us. Other times, however, our concept of our self-worth is too low, and this prohibits us from serving in the name of Christ.

Many of us struggle with lack of self-worth. We do not think we are important enough. But Christ comes into our lives to tell us that no matter who we are or what we have done, we are worthy people in his sight. He loves us and wants us to become the best people we can be. He asks each of us to use the gifts we have to minister for him.

In Jesus Christ we find the restoration of real personhood. We can take pride in what we are because we have the assurance of God's creative and redeeming love. No matter what we may have been or done, Christ can change our lives and give us a new beginning. Like Peter, we too can know forgiveness and the summons to serve our Lord again.

(c) Peter also found that his vision was restored. When he started following Jesus Christ, he was among the first of the disciples to commit his life to the Lord. When Jesus was nailed to the cross, Peter thought his dream was over. But the resurrected Christ restored his dream. Christ forgave Peter for denying him and gave him a new commission.

(d) Sometimes I see people in church who gave their lives to Christ a long time ago but whose vision has become dull and faded. Their involvement in the work of Christ and his church has become lean. These persons need to recapture their dreams and have their vision restored.

III. *Notice finally that Peter affirmed his faith by his life.* He denied Christ in the courtyard of the High Priest. Can you not imagine the fear that leaped in Peter's heart the first time the question was asked: "Are you one of his followers?" He probably wanted to slip into a dark corner or run away. Would you have stayed?

(a) Before you condemn Peter for denying Christ, ask yourself whether you would have stayed nearby after Jesus was arrested. You would have to fear not only the Crucifixion of Jesus but likely your own death as well. When he was asked, "Are you not one of his disciples?" Peter denied it. But he did not run. He stayed nearby in the courtyard.

(b) Later, after Peter was forgiven and was commissioned again, he served his Lord through his words, his teachings, and even his death. Tradition states that Peter was crucified later in Rome. Through his words and life he later demonstrated his faith.

Christ has called us not to flee from the world but to live out our faith in the world. It will not always be easy, but we have the assurance of his presence with us.

SECTION X

CHILDREN'S SERMONS

January 5: How Do You Fit?
Text: Col. 1:15–20
Object: Tinkertoys

Inside the bag today I have a long cardboard container shaped like a Quaker Oats box, but I think that what is inside the container is even more fun than oatmeal. It looks like some of you don't think oatmeal is fun. As I take this box out of the *Time for Children* canvas bag, I wonder if anyone recognizes what it is?

Some of you said "Tinkertoys" and you are exactly right. Perhaps some of you could read the label on the container. Does anyone know what Tinkertoys are? That's right. You build things with them. Did someone say they are old-time Legos? Well, I'll accept that. I'm glad you know what they are, because when I was your age I really had a good time playing with them.

Let's take a closer look at what is inside. What do you see in my hand? That's right, sticks of different colors and lengths. You can't really build anything with them or join them together. They are loose and they stay loose. See? But let's take this one wooden circle out of the box and put it beside the other pieces of wood you see in front of you. Now watch as I put the loose sticks into the larger wooden circle. Now they hold together. They do not fly apart or roll in different directions.

Sometimes in a family or even in a church we do not seem to belong together. We can all be going in different ways. The same can be true inside a person. We do a lot of things—take music lessons, play sports, go to school, attend Sunday school. How does it all fit together?

Our Scripture today says that in Christ all things hold together (v. 17). It also says he is above all things. When he is at the center of our lives, everything else takes its rightful place. Our Tinkertoys have been a reminder of that this morning.—Gary D. Stratman

January 12: Center Your Life in God
Text: Ps. 100:3 (NIV)
Object: Apple
Song: "Now I Belong to Jesus"

Children, watch closely as I show you a hidden surprise in this apple. [*Using a knife, cut the apple crossways through the center to reveal a star. Hold the apple so all of the children can see the center.*] Say, did you know this apple has a surprise inside? Did you know about the star? Look in the center and you will see apple seeds. This is the most important part of an apple. Apples are also good to eat. If we plant these seeds and they receive water and sun, they will produce an apple tree. If these seeds were not present, the apple could not bear other fruit.

When we belong to Jesus he becomes the center of our lives. If we are to grow in a Christ-like way, we must follow his will for our lives. Just like the apple seed must have water and

390

sun to grow, we must make Jesus our personal friend. Pray daily. Read the Bible or listen as your parents read it to you. Attend church and Sunday school. All of these things will help make Jesus the center of your lives.

God made you, and you, and you. [*Point to each child as you speak.*] He made me. Psalm 100:3 says, "Know that the Lord is God. It is he who made us and we are his; we are his people, the sheep of his pasture."

Let's invite the congregation to join us in singing one verse of "Now I Belong to Jesus." Make that your prayer today. [*Continue playing softly as the children return to their seats.*]—Carolyn Tomlin

January 19: God's Wonderful Treasures

TEXT: Eccles. 3:11 (NIV)
Object: Seashell
Song: "All Things Bright and Beautiful"

Boys and girls, I'm holding a gift from the sea. It's called a seashell. It's something that people could not make. Only God could create something of this beauty. Now, I want you to think with me for a minute. Name something beautiful that is found in nature. [*Wait for response.*] Let's see. There is the golden sunshine, the fluffy white clouds, the sweet-smelling flowers, the birds that sing, a winter's snow—we could go on and on and never name everything, right? God has given us so many wonderful treasures that are free for everyone. And he has given us eyes to see, ears to hear, a nose to smell, hands to touch, and a mouth to taste delicious food. God certainly had a plan for this Earth, and he had a plan for making us capable of enjoying the treasures he created.

The Bible speaks many times of the beauty that God created. Ecclesiastes 3:11 says, "He has made everything beautiful in its time." Everything God created has beauty.

Today we are singing "All Things Bright and Beautiful." This is an old song, written in the 1800s, and it describes the beauty of things both great and small. God is such a loving God to give us all these wonderful treasures to enjoy in life.

[*Lead prayer that these children will use their senses to learn more about God through his creation.*]—Carolyn Tomlin

January 26: Night—A Time for Rest

TEXT: Gen. 1:16; Ps. 104:19 (NIV)
Object: Drawing or picture of the moon and stars
Song: "All Praise to You, My God, This Night"

Boys and girls, these pictures you see represent an important part of God's plan for us. When the moon and stars are visible, we call that time *night.* The sun shines in the day to give us light. Without light, plants cannot grow. But the night is just as important. Who can tell me why? [*Wait for response.*] Yes, night provides a time for rest. For example, how do you feel when you don't get enough sleep? Can you do your best at school and play when you are tired? Do you remember a time when you didn't go to bed on time and you didn't want to get up the next day? [*Give two or three children an opportunity to relate this feeling.*] I've felt the same way on some occasions.

God gives us the nighttime to let our bodies rest. Sleep is so important for staying healthy. Listen as I read about the night from God's Word. God made two great lights—the brighter light to govern the day and the lesser light to govern the night. He also made the stars (Gen. 1:16). The moon marks the seasons, and the sun knows when to go down (Ps. 104:19).

Please bow your heads and pray with me, thanking God for the moon, the stars, and the nighttime that helps our bodies rest.

[*Ask the pianist to play as a soloist sings "All Praise to You, My God, This Night." Have the pianist continue playing as the children return to their seats.*]—Carolyn Tomlin

February 2: Prayer
TEXT: Jer. 33:3
Object: An old rotary telephone (This sermon can also be adapted to use a cellular or other phone.)

What do you think is in the bag today? A clue? Okay. When we shake the bag we hear a rattle and a bell sound. Let's bring it out of the backpack. Wait, you still don't know? If I had buttons on this and not a dial you would know what it is. That's right, it is a telephone. I know some of you don't believe me. Trust me.

Before you call somebody you need to know what? Yes, what you want to say. What else? That's right: the person's telephone number. Very good. I remember phone numbers of my childhood that sounded like this: Wabash 2–500; and today we have calling cards with special numbers. Now even with all these helps, you can still get a wrong number or a busy signal.

That is why I like the verse we just read from the Bible. It is a very important reminder that although we can't always reach who we want to on the telephone, we can always reach God through prayer. He has promised that we can call on him day or night, sunny weather or stormy. The connection is always made, the time is always right, no matter how many other people are calling him at the same time. God is able to do more than our best inventions.

It might help you to remember the address of this verse as a telephone number: Jeremiah 33:3.

Let us pray together: God, we thank you that we can call on you at any time and you will hear us and lead us in the ways of love and truth through Jesus. Amen.—Gary D. Stratman

February 9: God Interrupts Our Plans
TEXT: Job 17:11
Object: A cell phone

Good morning. I have the best object lesson for you today. [*Cell phone rings.*] Just a moment. "Hello? Yes, blah, blah, blah. Goodbye." Please excuse the interruption.

We all make plans for the future. Our plans may be as simple as going swimming with a friend or as complex as running for president of the United States in the year 2040. Our plans may be interrupted by God, just like we were interrupted by the call on my cell phone. When our plans are disturbed we may become very irritated or sad. It is frustrating to intend to do something and have our designs ruined. A man named Job felt like that. Listen to this verse.

We should leave some room for God to change our plans. When God intervenes in our lives it is always for a good reason. David, the great King of Israel, made plans to build a majestic temple for worshiping the Lord. He accumulated gold, silver, and building materials to complete the construction. God interrupted David's plans and told him that one of David's sons would build the temple instead of David.

God interrupted David for a special reason. Through the changed plans God revealed the coming of Jesus into the world. David was grateful after he understood the Lord's intentions.

Whenever we are kept from completing our intended projects we should not become frustrated. God is working to complete his master plan of salvation for our world. Sometimes we must put aside our cherished projects to cooperate with the Lord's work. Most of the time God blesses our good intentions with his power and presence (Ps. 20:4). When the Lord must redirect our efforts we shouldn't get angry; we should simply be thankful that we are a part of God's plan for the ages.—Kenneth Cox

February 16: The Unwrapped Gifts

TEXT: Rom. 12:6–16a

Object: Items that people tend to save rather than use, wrapped in gift paper.

Good morning, boys and girls. How many of you received a gift that you really liked last Christmas? Do you remember the gift you liked the most? [*Let them answer.*] How many of you have some gifts that you have not opened yet? [*Wait for an answer.*] I wonder what it would be like to keep our gifts wrapped and open them just once in a while rather than opening them all on Christmas? How many of you would do that if I asked you to do it? I know some people would keep their gifts wrapped for years and never use them. Can you imagine receiving a gift and just putting it away in a drawer? I can't imagine doing that either, but I know some who do exactly that sort of thing.

Let me show you some of the things I have found put away and never used. [*Unwrap the packages to reveal, for example, sheets and pillowcases, a shirt, a billfold.*] What would you think if you gave someone a gift like one of these and found it months or years later wrapped the same way it was when you gave it? [*Let them answer.*] I know how I would feel. I would think that the people didn't like the gift I gave them, or that they didn't need it, or they had so many gifts that they couldn't use my gift. That's the way all of us would feel.

I have told you all this because God is the giver of magnificent gifts and many of the things that he gives to us are never used. I wonder how God feels about the person who is given a beautiful voice and never sings, or a great mind and never uses it for anything that helps others. Some people are given great gifts of healing and teaching, and when they are not used or shared it is like the person who takes the gifts that I have shown you and puts them away in a closet or drawer. God gives the gift so it can be used, not saved. What good is a voice that isn't used, or an idea that isn't shared? It is like a sheet or pillowcase kept in a drawer, or a billfold that is never opened. God gives gifts so we will use them, and the wonderful thing about gifts is that as we use and share them, God gives us so much more. Now, you must think about the talent or gift that God has given you and how you can use it. Just think how much fun it will be to share with others what you have, and know that a lot more will be given when you use what you've already received.—Wesley T. Runk[1]

---

[1]*Pass It On* (Lima, Ohio: CSS, 1977), pp. 7–8.

February 23: Jesus Makes a Good Yoke

TEXT: Matt. 11:28–30

Object: Picture of a yoke

This is a picture of a wooden yoke. A yoke was used before tractors were invented. The yoke would fit over the heads of a team of oxen, mules, or donkeys. This curved part would rest on their shoulders as they pulled the plow through the fields. A good yoke was important for keeping the animals from being injured. A yoke also helped the animals to work efficiently.

Yokes were used when Jesus was on Earth. Jesus was trained as a carpenter by his father, Joseph. Tradition holds that Jesus made the best yokes in Israel. The yokes that Jesus made reputedly never irritated the shoulders of the oxen and helped them with their tremendous burdens.

Jesus talked about yokes for human beings, too. He compared our life's work and trials to the burdens that were shouldered by the farm animals. Jesus told his disciples that if they would follow his commandments and trust his words, these truths would be like a yoke helping them shoulder life's burdens. Listen to this verse.

Jesus still makes the best yokes in the world. God doesn't intend for our lives to be full of anxiety and worry. The Lord will give us tasks to accomplish, but he will also grant us the power to complete what he has challenged us to do. If our jobs and chores are discouraging and awful, we need to stop and ask Jesus to help us with his yoke. As we learn to follow Jesus we will discover that our life's work and trials will be manageable and rewarding.— Kenneth Cox

March 2: What You Are Worth

TEXT: Luke 15:1–3, 8–10

Objects: A handful of coins. (The Chucky Cheese token I found in my change added interest to this rendition.)

You can see in my hand objects that you see everyday. They are so common that you are already saying what they are before I can ask the question. Raise your hands if you know the answer. That's right: pennies. Yes, dimes. All kinds of coins. This one is a little larger than the others. No, it's not a quarter. Wait until I hold it up so you all may see. Wow! What a response. It is a Chucky Cheese token. Imagine that you could claim the prize you really want, but you had all the tokens except one. To find that one token you would turn your whole house upside down. You would look in the dumpster with a flashlight. You would do everything you could to get a prize such as a plastic cup with Chucky Cheese's picture on it.

Think how much more God would do to get back those he loves who are lost. That's why Jesus told this story in the Gospel of Luke. Jesus always used things that people recognized, like coins or sheep, to tell them about something greater and longer lasting than the objects he used in his stories.

We are reminded here just how valuable we are to God. When we are confused, alone, or lost, or have just forgotten our true worth, God will go a long, long way to bring us back and remind us who we are. We are so precious in God's sight that Jesus, God's Son, died for us. Coins (or tokens) are also useful, and when we know who we are we are able to be used for God's purposes. That brings joy to us and to God.

Let us pray. Dear God, thank you for using the stories of Jesus and this part of our Sunday worship to remind us who we are and whose we are, in Christ. Amen.—Gary D. Stratman

March 9: We Can Make Special Memories
TEXT: Mark 14:9
Object: A keepsake

I keep this plastic coffee cup on my bookshelf because it reminds me of Boyd Williams. Boyd was the custodian of a church I served in Beaumont, Texas. One day while I was out of town Boyd was cleaning my office and knocked my coffee cup off the desk and broke it. The next day I came to church this mysterious cup was sitting on my desk. Boyd soon came in to explain the accident and his purchase of this cup.

The cup that was broken was not special to me at all. However, I have always treasured this very plain replacement cup because Boyd bought it for me. Boyd didn't have to buy the cup. I think he knew I wouldn't get upset about the accident. That was just the way Boyd acted. Boyd was a quiet, gentle man who enjoyed laughing and talking to the members of the staff. He wasn't a large man, but he was a very hard worker. He had eight children and it was easy to tell he loved people very much. Boyd touched my life in ways he is not aware of. [*Adapt by using your own memory story.*]

Memories like this are special to us. One day a woman poured a bottle of very expensive perfume on Jesus' feet. Others who were present said the woman had just wasted a lot of money that could have been used to help the poor. Jesus didn't see it that way. Listen to this verse.

We can make memories in other people's lives, too. The secret to Boyd's memories was his kindness. People long remember acts of kindness. For Jesus, the memory consisted of the woman honoring him with her very best. Jesus' prediction about people remembering the woman's act came true. The action of the woman is recorded in the Bible, and songs are sung about her pouring out her life in honor of Jesus. When we demonstrate acts of kindness and honor Jesus with our best, we will make memories, too.—Kenneth Cox

March 16: An Open Door
TEXT: Col. 4:2–6, 12
Object: A doorknob or handle

It is so good to see all of you this morning. What I brought with me just for you to see is not going to appear to be a great treasure. As a matter of fact, you are most likely to find this object in what some people call a construction surplus center, or maybe in a place you have heard of—a junkyard. Do I have your interest? I can tell I have yours, Ben. You can find some neat stuff in a junkyard.

We will change the rules this morning. You don't have to raise your hands. As soon as you know what it is, you can say it out loud. Okay, I'm taking out of the bag . . . it is . . . that's right—a doorknob. You recognized it right away because you see doorknobs and handles all the time, but they are usually on doors so we don't think of them as valuable. They don't cost as much as the door to which a set of doorknobs might be attached, but they make it possible for that door to be opened and for you to have the freedom to go through that doorway to someplace you want to go.

In our story from the Bible today, Paul is in a place where you could really understand praying to God that the door would be opened. Where was he? He was in jail. He had no handle to use to open the door and get out. But he didn't pray to get out. He didn't deserve to be there, but he didn't ask God to get him out. He prayed and asked his friends to pray that a door would be opened for the Word of God to be preached. Wherever he was, in jail or out, the door he wanted to be opened was a chance to say a good word about Jesus Christ, the one who opened to him a way of being with God and serving God in this life and beyond.

God is the one who can open the door to help someone who is lonely, such as someone who is in a place he doesn't want to be, like a new city; or someone who doesn't want to be the only child in her family anymore. God can open a door for us to speak a word or show a sign of love even if we are in a strange or new place. God can open for us a door to the Word. Now that is good news!—Gary D. Stratman

March 23: Praise God for Springtime

TEXT: Gen. 1:11; Song of Sol. 2:12 (NIV)
Object: Fresh flowers or green plant
Song: "This Is My Father's World," no. 43, *The Baptist Hymnal*

Boys and girls, I'm going to give you some clues about the topic of our children's sermon today. Listen carefully. This is a season that comes between winter and summer. Trees and plants put on new leaves. Growing plants turn green. Flowers bloom. Many animals have new babies during this season. Now, can anyone guess the season? [*Allow time for response.*] If you guessed springtime, you are correct.

Spring has always been my favorite time of the year. We enjoy being outside in the beautiful world God created. During warmer weather, we can play outdoors with our friends, eat outdoors with our families, or take long walks. Yes, spring is a wonderful season.

This plant I'm holding represents springtime. God made the plant grow and bloom. The writers of the Bible must have enjoyed the spring also. Listen as I read: Then God said, "Let the land produce vegetation: seed-bearing plants and trees on the land that bear fruit with seed in it, according to their various kinds. And it was so" (Gen. 1:11). "Flowers appear on the Earth; the season of singing has come, the cooing of doves is heard in our land" (Song of Sol. 2:12). Aren't these beautiful thoughts?

During this week I want you to look for at least three things that God created that remind you of spring. Let us pray that we will be reminded of God's goodness to us during this season.

[*Lead the children in one stanza of "This Is My Father's World." Have pianist continue to play as the children return to their seats.*]—Carolyn Tomlin

March 30: Be Yourself

TEXT: Ps. 100:3 (NIV)
Object: Packet of seeds
Song: "Jesus Loves the Little Children"

Boys and girls, today let's think about this packet of seeds. What a miracle! [*Hold up the packet of seeds for the children to see.*] These small seeds have no brain, yet they knows exactly what to do. They know what they will become when they grow up. For example, I've never seen a corn plant strain to become a tomato, have you? And I've never seen a petunia huff and puff trying to grow sunflowers on its branches. Instead, these miniature seeds know God's purpose and plan exactly—right down to their roots.

Contained in these seeds is all the information needed to produce stems, leaves, blossoms, stamens, sepals, and pistils. Another important point is that much of the work takes place underground. Therefore, only the stems and blooms receive our compliments.

The next time you see a packet of seeds, remember that God has a plan for each of you. Your life already has a blueprint or design of how you can please God.

God is the giver and sustainer of life. In Psalm 100:3 we are given a way to give thanks. "Know that the Lord is God. It is he who made us and we are his. We are his people, the sheep of his pasture."

Remember that Jesus loves all children everywhere.

[*Lead the children in singing "Jesus Loves the Little Children of the World." Lead the children in prayer that each child will follow God's will for his or her life. Have the pianist continue to play as the children return to their seats.*]—Carolyn Tomlin

April 6: Steps to Heaven
TEXT: John 3:16 (NIV)
Object: Small stepladder
Song: "Only Trust Him," no. 317, *The Baptist Hymnal*

Boys and girls, I know you are wondering why I brought a ladder into church this morning, right? Can someone tell me the purpose of using a ladder? [*Allow time for response.*] Yes, I hear you saying that a ladder is used to reach something higher. To climb. And it's used for construction or building. Yes, a ladder is useful for many things. But think with me a minute. Could we use a ladder to climb into heaven? [*Wait for response. Begin to climb the ladder as you talk.*] What do you think? No, of course not. A ladder will not get us into heaven.

The only way we can get into heaven is to trust Jesus as our Savior and turn our entire lives over to him. We have to believe that Jesus will save us and forgive our sins.

One of my favorite Scriptures in the Bible tells us how to be saved. It's one you need to memorize. It is found in John 3:16. Can you say this Scripture with me? "For God so loved the world that he gave his one and only Son, that whoever believes in him shall not perish but have eternal life."

The hymn "Only Trust Him" is appropriate to end our children's sermon. I ask the congregation to join with us in singing this great hymn as the children return to their seats.—Carolyn Tomlin

April 13: If You Believe
TEXT: Mark 9:23
Object: Peach pit
Song: "Only Believe"

Boys and girls, I'm holding something in my hand that you may not recognize. [*Hold up the peach pit; wait for response.*] This object is called a peach pit. It is located in the center of the peach and is a very important part of the peach. As you know, peaches grow on trees. This pit is the seed of the fruit. If a peach didn't have a seed, we wouldn't have peaches. Let me ask you a question. If you planted a peach pit, would a peach tree grow from the seed? [*Allow time for response.*] Yes, of course. Just like if you planted a pecan, a pecan tree would grow. Or if you planted beans, a bean vine would grow. Whatever you plant, you believe that it will produce it's own kind.

But there is something else that must go along with this planting. God sends the rain and sunshine to make the plant grow. The plant depends on God for life.

As boys and girls who love Jesus, we place our trust and belief in him. Then we ask God to help us grow strong in faith. We ask him to show us how to help others. We pray and ask him to forgive our sins. And just like the plant needs rain and sun, people need God's care to help us grow more Christlike every day.

The Bible has much to say about belief. Matthew 9:28–29 says, "According to your faith will it be done to you." God wants his children to believe that with him all things are possible.

Let us invite the congregation to join with us in singing "Only Believe." [*The children may return to their places as the pianist continues to play.*]—Carolyn Tomlin

April 20: Jesus Gave Up His Crown
TEXT: Phil. 2:5–8
Object: A crown

This is a crown. Crowns are worn by kings and queens. Monarchs become royalty at birth, but they must often wait to become king or queen.

History records an interesting story about one king. In 1936 a man named Edward became King of England. His official title was King Edward VIII. Edward didn't stay king for very long. He was in love with an American woman, Wallis Simpson, and wanted to marry her. There was one problem: If Edward were to marry this particular American woman, he would have to give up his crown. In an emotional announcement, he abdicated the throne, giving up his crown so he could marry the woman he loved. Marrying Wallis was more important to Edward than being king.

That is an amazing story, but there is another story that is even more magnificent. The Bible proclaims that Jesus lived in heaven before he was born on Earth, that he is the King of heaven and Earth. Jesus loved you and me so much that he left heaven, giving up the throne and crown of the royal Son of God, and came to Earth and lived with us. Listen to these verses.

We follow the example of Jesus by giving of our time, money, and skills for special projects. If we hoard our gifts and abilities and never share them with others, our lives cannot become amazing and magnificent. Think how wonderful the world would be if everyone gave of themselves as Jesus did. There would be no poverty or hunger. There would be no loneliness or fear. The more we keep to ourselves, the more the world withers in want. The more we give, the wealthier we and our world become. Remember what Jesus did and give of yourselves to others.—Kenneth Cox

April 27: Gifts
TEXT: 1 Cor. 12:4–11
Object: Small cross to be held in the palm of your hand

The Scripture we just read tells us that all Christians have special gifts that God has given them. What do we mean when we say *gifts*? That's right. Gifts are something we buy or make that tells the people we gave them to that we care about them.

When Jesus was born, lived, and died for us, it was so we might come to new life through him. A part of that new life is the gifts Jesus places in each one of us. Now, we are not talking about toys or clothes or other presents that don't last forever. The gifts we're talking about are ourselves (gifts from the Lord) and the parts of ourselves we use to worship God and help other people. How do people use the gifts that God has given them in the church? [*To lead singing, give money, preach a sermon, teach Sunday school, plan a building.*] These are all good examples, but sometimes we think only of the gifts that adults have. But your gifts are just as important. Don't ever think that you don't have big gifts from God or that you are not big enough to have gifts from God. The song we sang this morning—"if you can't preach like Peter, if you cannot pray the Paul . . . you can tell the love of Jesus and say he died for all"— that is why I have this cross in my hand, to remind us that one of the greatest gifts God has given us, no matter what age we are, is to tell the love of Jesus in the words we use and the way we treat people, and to tell the story.—Gary D. Stratman

May 4: Home—A Happy Place
TEXT: Col. 2:6–7
Object: Picture of a house
Song: "Happy the Home When God Is There"

Children, please look at this picture I'm holding. Now, we all know that this is a house, but it's so much more. Who can tell me what it is? [*Wait for response.*] Yes, you're right. It's a home. How is a home more than a house? What takes place in a home? Let's name a few things. [*Allow time for response.*]

In a Christian home, boys and girls have parents who take good care of them. God provides parents for children. A home gives shelter from the weather. Children feel safe in this place. Nutritious food is provided for you to eat. Home is a place where your friends and relatives enjoy visiting. Families who love Jesus take time for learning more about his Word, the Bible. Wouldn't you say that a home is a special place God created for families to live in together?

As you grow older you must remember the biblical teachings you learned in your home. Colossians 2:6–7 speaks of this: "So, then, just as you received Christ Jesus as Lord, continue to live in him, rooted and built up in him, strengthened in the faith as you were taught, and overflowing with thankfulness."

"Happy the Home When God Is There" is a special song about the Christian home. Let us sing this song together. Bow your heads as I ask God to bless our homes. [*The children return to their seats as the pianist continues to play.*]—Carolyn Tomlin

May 11: Special Persons
TEXT: 2 Tim. 1:4–7
Object: Brightly colored gift bag (sold in all greeting card shops). It also helps to have something like a Mother's Day card or token. In this rendition it is a refrigerator magnet that proclaims "Mom is special."

Today is not just the Lord's Day, the day we come to church to worship God. It is also a day on which we give thanks for our mothers. What do we call this day? Yes, you are all so right. This is Mother's Day. There are lots of reminders of why we celebrate this day. Inside this gift bag I have one of them. When I bring it out of the bag, raise your hand if you know what it is. Yes, you have told me what it says: *Mom is special.* But what is the object I hold in my hand? It is a magnet with a message that you might find in your kitchen. Why is the kitchen a good place to have a reminder that moms are special? You are right: because it reminds you of the ways your mom helps provide you with good and healthy things to eat.

Our Scripture reminds us of another way in which mothers and grandmothers can be very special. Paul says of his younger co-minister, Timothy, "I am reminded of your sincere faith, a faith that lived first in your grandmother, Lois, and in your mother, Eunice, and now, I am sure, in you" (v. 5). How special it is to have a mother and grandmother who tell you about and show you faith in Jesus Christ by the way they live and love.

Faith is a gift from God, but people in our lives help us to know and receive that gift. Timothy had people like that in his life. I have had a mother and a grandmother show me what it means to know Jesus and serve others with joy. Maybe today would be a good day to give thanks for mothers and grandmothers who have helped you to keep that gift you have in you alive and bright (v. 6). Thank you for being here on this special day.—Gary D. Stratman

May 18: God Gives Us Wisdom
TEXT: James 1:5 (NIV)
Object: A piece of real and a piece of artificial fruit
Song: "Savior, Teach Me Day by Day," no. 461, *The Baptist Hymnal*

Boys and girls, I'm holding two objects in my hand. Who can tell me what they are? How are they alike? How are they different? If you were going to eat one of these, which one would it be? The real piece of fruit, or the artificial piece? [*Allow time for several children to respond.*]

I think we would all agree that the real piece of fruit is the one we would eat, right? [*Hold up the artificial fruit.*] This one is constructed from a man-made material. Its function is to resemble the real thing, but we know there is no comparison. Why, you can even smell the difference! We have the wisdom to know the difference.

Now, boys and girls, please remember what I say today. When we put our faith and trust in Jesus, he is the real thing. Some people may think they are worshiping, but they bow and worship idols. Idols are images made of stone, metal, or other materials. They can do nothing for you. These images cannot help you when you are lonely or afraid. But when you believe in Jesus and ask him to help you, he hears your prayers. God will give us wisdom to know what is real and what is artificial in life. Isn't it great to have a friend like Jesus?

The Bible speaks of wisdom. In James 1:5 I read, "If any of you lacks wisdom, he should ask God, who gives generously to all without finding fault, and it will be given to him" (NIV). [*Lead congregation in prayer asking God to give the children wisdom to know what is real and what is not. Then ask a soloist to sing "Savior, Teach Me Day by Day" as the children return to their seats.*]—Carolyn Tomlin

May 25: The Right Way
TEXT: Ps. 9
Object: An illustrated map or a map and brochure for a vacation destination

How many of you are looking forward to the summer? It looks as if you all are looking forward to the summer. So is the whole church family. Vacation Bible school, church camp, and trips to *Six Flags* and a Cardinals baseball game are all a part of the summer months. It will be fun, won't it? Now, what would happen if you all had cars, with adult drivers, and I told the drivers to drive about three and a half hours and we would all meet at the ballpark. Would that be enough information? You are right. It is not enough. What city? Which ballpark? What direction should we go? You have all made good suggestions that would help us find our way.

You have helped me to see what the writer of this song or poem that we call Psalm 19 had in mind. It describes two important ways we can find God. Earlier some of you said that our drivers going to St. Louis could use a map. How did you know that a map is exactly what I brought with me this morning? What does this map have on the outside? [*Hold up the travel brochure or illustrated map.*] Yes, there are pictures of the Gateway Arch and other attractions in St. Louis. The first part of Psalm 19 gives us pictures of the ways God speaks through nature, God's creation. The psalmist says that the skies tell of the work of God's hands. What is in the sky that God made? Yes, yes, the sun, moon, and stars. You are all right. Who else could make such wonderful things?

Then this psalm tells us that if we are to know this wonderful God, we are to know God's Word. God speaks to us through the law, statutes, precepts, and commands (Ps. 19:1–11). This is all a way of saying that the teachings from God help us to know God and how to live and enjoy God forever. The psalm says that the precepts of the Lord are right, giving joy to the heart. Jesus, the living Word, gave us himself so we could be with God forever and know how to live now. His commands included "love your neighbor." That's our map. [*Show the other side of the map with the route to your destination marked.*] It shows us the way to move through life. The commands of the Lord point us in the right way and bring us joy.—Gary D. Stratman

June 1: Praise God for Summer

TEXT: Ps. 74:17 (NIV)
Object: Large picture of a family having fun, a map, and baseball, and a sand bucket
Song: "Jesus Loves Me"

Children, isn't summer a wonderful time? What's so special about this season? [*Allow time for response.*] Is summer wonderful because school is out? Or because you can sleep late in the morning? Or because you have more time to spend with family and friends? It's also a time to read more books. Summer is all these things—and more.

Look at this picture of a family having fun together. [*Talk about what the family is doing.*] Look at their faces. How can you tell they are enjoying being together? [*Allow for response.*] Many families go on a vacation during the summer. They might use a map to locate the right highway. Some might watch a baseball game. Some of you may play baseball. Or you might take a sand bucket and go to the beach. All of these are good activities for family time.

When we have fun this summer, let us thank God for providing the seasons in the year. We want to remember that it was God who made the water, the sand, and the warm summer days for us to enjoy. Jesus loves us so much that he wants us to enjoy his creations. The writer of the psalm says in chapter 74, verse 17, "It was you who set all the boundaries of the Earth, you made both summer and winter."

[*Ask the children to offer one-sentence prayers with you, thanking God for one specific family activity this summer. Afterwards, lead the children in singing "Jesus Loves Me." Ask the pianist to continue to play as the children return to their seats.*]—Carolyn Tomlin

June 8: What Is Spiritual Renewal?

TEXT: Ps. 80:18–19

Object: Tarnished brass candleholder, jar of Brasso, cleaning cloth

Our spiritual lives can resemble this candleholder. When we first accept the Lord as our Savior, we are excited and responsive to God. We may recall a time of spiritual insight when our Bible reading and prayer time were very important to us. However, exposure to the world and its disappointments can tarnish our spiritual lives. Sickness, money problems, or the bad behavior of other believers may cause us to lose our spiritual luster.

Brass is easy to take care of. Let me show you how to shine it. We apply some Brasso with a cloth and then rub it off. See how the brass shines again. It is just like new.

Our spiritual lives can be renewed and revived, too. Revival services are useful for repairing the wear and tear on our spiritual lives. The joy of salvation may be recaptured just by remembering the bright points in our spiritual pilgrimage. When we return to the pattern of reading our Bibles, praying, and simply trusting in a loving God, we are renewed. Listen to these verses.

I love to see old homes restored. When the process starts, the roof might be leaking and the paint might be peeling. There is little to desire in an old abandoned house. However, with new paint and wood, and much loving care, a dilapidated house can be made beautiful again. Everyone who drives by a restored mansion feels like dropping by for a visit. That's how it is with our spiritual lives. What appears beyond repair is remedied by turning to God. The Lord renews us as we turn to him. The renewal of our spiritual lives is a blessing to those around us. Turning to the Lord wherever we are, no matter how dark the times, is always rewarded.—Kenneth Cox

June 15: Our Daily Bread

TEXT: Matt. 6:7–13

Object: Pewter bread tray (A grain of wheat or a loaf of bread can be used instead; they will change the narrative but not the flow and goal of the sermon.)

What do you think this is that I am holding in my hands this morning? You think it looks like a tray of ice. Well, you are warm, or should I say cold? Well, you are right. It is a kind of tray. Now I am going to tilt it toward you so that those who read can tell us what is stamped on this tray. *Give us this day our daily bread.* That is exactly right. Those words are found in our Scripture lesson for this morning and they are part of what has been called the Lord's Prayer. This is a tray for serving bread and it is made out of pewter, a material that was used long before our modern plastics were available.

How many of you have been to Mt. Vernon? That's right, there is a Mt. Vernon just thirty minutes from here, but I am thinking of the home of George Washington, our first president. In his home that is more than two hundred years old, many of the cups and bowls are made of pewter. Needing daily bread is not new.

Do we really believe that the food we need to stay alive comes from God? If I were to ask you where your bread comes from, you would say, "From the store." But let's look again at the plate used for serving bread. The design on it is not a loaf of bread but stalks or shafts of wheat. You see, we have to look at what happens before the bread is on our table or even in the store. It is made from wheat. Who provides rain and sunshine for the wheat the farmer plants? That's right: God does. Who gave the farmers two hundred years ago, two thousand years ago, and today the strength and learning to plant the wheat? That's right: God did. Who gave us everything that goes into providing the food that keeps us alive and helps us grow? Yes, you are right again.

When we ask God for our daily bread, we are remembering how we start our prayer: "Our Father who is in heaven." God is the one who gives us every good and perfect gift. The most perfect gift is his own son, Jesus Christ. We know that the God, who gave us Jesus, will give us the things we need each day to serve and honor him. Even when we are asking for these things we need each day, we are praising God for being the source of all good things, "Our Father, who art in heaven. . . ."—Gary D. Stratman

June 22: Idols and God
TEXT: 1 Thess. 1:1–10

[*Sometimes the most effective children's sermon comes not from an object or image opening the door to the gospel, but from a movement that catches the participants by surprise. The following time for children is a living memorial to a teenager who was one of those participants several years ago. It is based on the fact that children's sermons are presented pretty much in the same physical setting each Sunday. I have noted this as I have visited churches of various denominations.*

The tradition well established in our church is that I would take my place in front of the children and begin by greeting them and telling them how glad I was that they had come to the front of the church. As I spoke, I would slowly move from in front of them to in back of where they were seated. They would turn their bodies around and face me in my new position.]

There are many words that you hear mostly in church, yet we don't usually take the time to explain to you what they mean. Take the word *conversion:* anybody know what that word means? You may not be sure what it means, yet you just demonstrated or acted out what it means. You may not realize it but you all just turned around so you would be facing me.

In our Scripture this morning, the apostle Paul described what had happened to his friends who had turned away from idols and toward God, to serve a living and true God. What a clear picture: they used to worship human-made objects like statues of gold or silver, and now, by the power of God, they were turned around and facing a new direction. They now had hope in the future, because God had raised Jesus from the dead. They worshiped a living God, and so do we. We are able to turn our backs on idols that can be the thing we try to build our lives on even though they are not gold or silver statues. Our idols can be the need to be most popular or to have the most toys or to be the winner in every game. Whatever we are facing, God is greater than all our fears and the giver of all that will not pass away.
—Gary D. Stratman

June 29: Jesus Is the Way to Heaven

TEXT: Luke 23:40–43

Object: A ticket

This is an enlarged copy of a ticket. Recently we bought some tickets like this at the carnival, to ride the carousel. The horses and big rabbits on the merry-go-round are fun to ride because they go up and down as the carousel spins in a circle. After buying the ticket at the booth we must give it to the operator at the entrance to the ride. If you don't have a ticket the operator will not let you ride the carousel.

People wonder how to get into heaven. Some approach life like they need to purchase a ticket to heaven by acting a certain way or by making sure their name is on the membership role of a church. But the way to heaven is through faith in Jesus. It is a decision we make in our hearts by believing and trusting in God. There are no tickets to buy or contests to win.

On the day Jesus was crucified, two other men were put on crosses with him. Both of these men were thieves and were being punished for their crimes. Before Jesus and the other two men died that afternoon, one of the thieves asked Jesus to save him. Listen to these verses.

Did you notice how simple that was? The man asked Jesus to "remember" him. The criminal's regret and desire for forgiveness are evident in his request for mercy. Jesus freely granted the man's petition and said they would soon be in heaven together. God loves us so much he is willing to accept all who come to him in the name of Jesus, like that thief.

At carnivals some kids can only look at the carousel and wish they had money to buy a ticket and ride. Without Jesus no one goes to heaven. However, the way to heaven is not purchased; it is obtained by asking God for forgiveness through simple faith. All who call upon the name of the Lord are saved (Rom. 10:13). That's the good news of Jesus Christ.—Kenneth Cox

July 6: God Made the Animals

TEXT: Gen. 1:25 (NIV)

Object: Several small toy animals

Song: "All Creatures of Our God and King"

Boys and girls, these objects are part of a group that God created. What is the name of this group? [*Wait for response.*] Yes, they are called *animals.* How many of you have a pet at your house? Would someone like to tell us about your pet? [*Give several children the opportunity to tell something about their pets.*] Yes, pets are wonderful to own. However, when we have a pet, there are responsibilities. Can someone tell me how we must care for our pets? [*Wait for response.*] Yes, we must feed, water, exercise, and take them to the vet to keep them healthy. With ownership comes responsibility.

God made many animals for us to enjoy. Let's name some other animals. Some are wild animals that must provide for their own food. Some are livestock that are raised on a farm. And some crawl along the ground.

In Genesis 1:25 the writer tells us about the different types of animals God created. "God made the wild animals according to their kinds, the livestock according to their kinds, and all the creatures that move along the ground according to their kinds. And God saw that it was good." Aren't you glad that God made animals for us to have as pets, and others that provide resources we need?

[*Lead the congregation in prayer that God will bless these children and that their pets will be a comfort to them. Ask the pianist to play "All Creatures of Our God and King" as the children return to their seats.*]—Carolyn Tomlin

July 13: Jeremiah Needed God's Security
TEXT: Jer. 1:6, 8
Object: A security blanket

This is a security blanket. Linus, a little boy in the *Peanuts* cartoon strip, has a blanket like this to hold onto when he is frightened. Having something familiar to hold makes us feel safe.

It is easy to think that Jeremiah the prophet was a spiritual superman. Jeremiah had a Bible book named after him that is fifty-two chapters long. However, Jeremiah got scared just like we do. When God first spoke to Jeremiah about becoming a prophet, the first thing Jeremiah said was that he was scared. Listen to this verse.

Some experts did a survey some time ago and found that one of the most frightening things that anybody ever does is get up in front of a group and give a talk. Jeremiah was afraid like that. If God commanded you to get up in front of church next Sunday and preach a sermon, you'd probably be afraid, too. That's okay; it's perfectly normal.

Other things that God commands us to do may be frightening. We may be afraid to pray publicly. We might be terrified of telling our closest friends about Jesus, even though we talk to them about everything else in the world. But we must not let fear keep us from doing the things God commands us to do. God knows we need his help. Listen to what he told Jeremiah (v. 8a).

We discover that God is with us by taking the first step that God has instructed us to take. Even though we are afraid, if we just take one step of obedience we will discover that our task isn't impossible after all. Then we can take the next step, and so on. By doing this we learn that fear needn't keep us from being obedient and victorious in Jesus.

Don't let fear stop you from doing good things for Jesus. Stand up for Jesus, do the right thing, and tell you friends about him. You'll discover something very exciting when you do: God is with you and will be your security blanket.—Kenneth Cox

July 20: Listening When God Speaks
TEXT: Prov. 20:12 (NIV)
Object: Radio
Song: "Jesus Calls Us," no. 293, *The Baptist Hymnal*

Boys and girls, who can tell me what I'm holding? Yes, this is a radio. [*Plug into an outlet and find a station. Allow a few seconds of listening, then turn off.*] Before television, your grandparents would sit around the radio and listen to programs and music. Most families had only one radio in the house. Therefore everyone came into a central room to listen, and they enjoyed being together. There is something about a radio that is different from a television. Who can tell me what is different? [*Allow several children to respond.*] We can't see what is happening. And with both radio and TV, we can hear their conversation but they can't hear us. We can laugh, whisper, yell, or even stand on our head—and those talking on the radio or TV have no idea what is going on in our homes.

But there is a personal friend we all have who can hear us when we speak, and he can talk to us, too. Who is this person? [*Wait for response.*] Yes, his name is Jesus. He is our best friend.

So the next time you listen to the radio, let it remind you about our friend, Jesus. He hears us when we pray, and he talks to us in our hearts and minds.

Listen as I read from Proverbs 20:12: "Ears that hear and eyes that see—the Lord has made them both" (NIV).

[*Lead the children and congregation in singing one verse of "Jesus Calls Us." Ask an adult to pray that these boys and girls will listen when God speaks and will talk to him daily. Ask the pianist to continue to play as the children return to their seats.*]—Carolyn Tomlin

July 27: What Is Your Gift?
TEXT: 1 Cor. 12:17
Object: A gift-wrapped box

When we hear the word *gift* we may think of this—a present. Actually, this is an empty box covered with wrapping paper. The word *gift* is also used to describe a special ability.

Nolan Ryan's pitching career spanned twenty-seven seasons. He holds a couple of league records: 714 strikeouts and seven no-hitters. In one game in 1974 he struck out nineteen batters! When Nolan Ryan was elected to the National Baseball Hall of Fame in 1999, he called his pitching ability a gift. That means this very successful baseball player believed his pitching ability was given to him by God.

In God's Kingdom each of us is given a gift or ability to serve God. Listen to these verses.

All of our gifts are different. According to the Bible, a person may be given the gift of healing, prophecy, administration, or giving. We can also add the gifts of missionary service, teaching, singing, or playing a musical instrument. The gifts that God gives each of us are very different because the Church is called upon to be and do many things for people. God gives the Church all the gifts it needs to serve Jesus Christ effectively.

As you continue to be faithful in your attendance at and devotion to church, you will be able to discover what your gift is. It is not too early to ask God to help you identify your ability. Just as every part of our bodies has a special function, so every member of the Church has a gift to serve the others.

After you discover what your gift is, it will be very important to develop and use your gift. Nolan Ryan practiced hard to develop his gift for pitching. We must do the same with our abilities. If we fail to use our gifts to serve Jesus and his people, we will loose the powerful potential that God has given us.

When we use our gifts we are happy. Nolan Ryan always seemed to have a smile on his face. He enjoyed playing baseball. When we are serving God with our gifts, we will discover our lives to be full of joy. Do something kind for someone today. After completing that good deed, you will probably have a big smile on your face. When we use the gifts that God has provided for us, our lives will be full of joy.—Kenneth Cox

August 3: Water—A Gift from God
TEXT: Ps. 23:1–2 (NIV)
Object: Jar of water
Song: "How Great Thou Art"

Children, I'm holding something that is necessary for all living things. Without this precious liquid we could not survive. [*Hold up the jar of water for all to see.*] Can you tell me how you use water? [*Allow time for response.*]

I hear you say that water is used for keeping our bodies clean. For example, when we wash our hands we protect ourselves and others from germs. The major organs of the body, such as the heart, lungs, kidneys, liver, and brain, and all the veins and arteries, must have water to function properly. Water is used to wash our clothes. Water that falls as rain makes the plants that produce food grow. Animals must have water to live. So you see, God has provided us with this most wonderful gift. We should praise him for this resource.

When I think of praising God I always remember Psalm 23. I hope you will commit this Scripture to memory. In verses 1 and 2 this psalm of David says, "The Lord is my shepherd; I shall lack nothing. He makes me lie down in green pastures; he leads me beside quiet waters." Imagine the boy David watching his sheep and praising God for the green pastures and a place to rest beside the quiet waters.

A song that helps us praise God is "How Great Thou Art." Let's ask the congregation to join with us in singing this song. [*Pray that the boys and girls will praise God for his wonderful gifts. Ask the pianist to continue to play as the children return to their places.*]— Carolyn Tomlin

August 10: Escape from Temptation

TEXT: 1 Cor. 10:13

Object: A piece of fruit

The Lord generously gave Adam and Eve the privilege to eat fruit from all the trees in the Garden of Eden except one. God told Adam and Eve that they would die if they ate from the tree of the knowledge of good and evil. Satan tempted Adam and Eve by making them doubt what God had clearly said. Satan lied and said that God would not punish them. Satan made the forbidden fruit look so good that Adam and Eve fell into his trap. When Adam and Eve ate the forbidden fruit, sin entered the human race and Adam and Eve were cast out of Eden.

The devil still uses temptation to make us do wrong things. Temptation is the lure of Satan to entice us to break God's laws. Like a fisherman baiting a hook with a worm, the devil conceals his purposes and makes doing the wrong thing look attractive. Satan outsmarted Adam and Eve, but he doesn't have to get the best of us. God is more powerful than the devil (1 John 4:4) and provides a way of escape when we are tempted. Listen to this verse.

Everyone is tempted. It's kind of scary to think about it. When the evil one sets a trap for us we can suffer harm by getting diverted from God's perfect will for our lives. However, since we know we will be tempted, we can be on the lookout and avoid ruining our lives with sin.

Temptations are common. The devil seems to use the same traps over and over again. Whenever we know something is wrong, we shouldn't do it, no matter how sugarcoated someone makes the wrong action seem. Our way of escape is assured when we make a decision to obey God's Word in every situation.

Someone may try to trick you into stealing a candy bar from a store. We know that stealing is wrong—no question there. Temptation comes when someone says, "Everyone is going to do it," and "We won't get caught; I did it last week and got away with it, and that candy bar tasted so good." That person may be popular and good at school or sports. But if what we are asked to do is wrong, it is always wrong, no matter who tries to convince us otherwise.

Once we escape temptation there is a sense of relief. Temptation is like a weight that is pulling us in the wrong direction. We have to throw that weight off or we will fall. When we do escape, and we can every time, we have the sense that we were obedient to God. If we give into temptation we always have regrets. After we give into temptation we will wish we hadn't said or done that evil deed. It is always too late to take the action back. So we must escape before getting caught in the trap of temptation. God has promised that he will always provide a way out. If we look for it we will see it.—Kenneth Cox

August 17: Sharing with Others
TEXT: John 15:17 (NIV)
Object: Bag of small individually wrapped candies
Song: "Jesus Loves Me"

Boys and girls, I'm holding something that most children like. [*Display bag of candy.*] Now, what do you think I'm going to do with this candy today? I could eat it all myself. I could throw it away in the garbage. I could keep it. Or is there something else I could do with the candy? [*Wait for response.*] Yes, that is what I thought you would say: I could share the candy with every one of you. How many think that is a good solution? [*Wait for response.*] I'm going to give each of you a piece, but wait until later to eat it, OK?

You know, when we love someone we want to share what we have. Jesus talked many times about sharing with those in need. Remember the boy who came to see Jesus and shared the loaves of bread and small fishes his mother packed for his lunch? After Jesus blessed the food, it was enough to feed many people, and there was plenty left over.

Jesus wanted his followers to obey his words. He said in John 15:17, "This is my command: Love each other." This means to love all people—regardless of the color of their skin, where they live, or how much money their family has. Jesus gave us many examples of his unselfish love throughout the New Testament.

One of the favorite hymns sung by children is "Jesus Loves Me." Let's sing this special song and remember how much Jesus loves each boy and girl here today. [*Ask the pianist to continue playing as the children return to their places.*]—Carolyn Tomlin

August 24: Our Words Guide Our Lives
TEXT: James 3:4–5a
Object: Sailboat model or drawing

This is a sailboat. This part in the back is called the rudder. The rudder determines the direction of the sailboat. It is small in comparison to the boat. However, if this little rudder is pulled sharply to one side, the whole boat will abruptly change course. Even though the rudder is small, a turn of the rudder makes a big difference.

The Bible compares the words of our mouths to the rudder of a boat. Although our mouths are small in comparison to the size of the rest of our bodies, what we say determines the way our lives go. Listen to this verse.

What a person says reveals much about a person. Someone who is not sure of himself may brag a lot. A person who is afraid may talk quickly and use a lot of words. If we say cruel words, our tongue reveals that we are a vicious person. And the more we speak a certain way, the more we become that way. For instance, if we use profanity, those foul words begin to slip into every conversation.

Our lives are directed by what we say. If we tell lies, then our lives are directed into the murky waters of untruthful living. When we tell lies our lives become very complicated. It is hard for liars to remember what they have made up. The truth is not hard to remember. Most liars eventually get confused about all the stories they have told and are embarrassed when they finally get caught in their fibs.

When we believe in our hearts and say "Jesus, my Savior," our lives are directed in God's way. Also, when we pray our mouths direct our lives in the right direction and help others to find God's healing, grace, and strength.

What we say is most important. Though a rudder is small, it directs a whole ship. Our mouths are small, too, but even a whisper can put our lives on the wrong track. Let's always say what God wants us to say.—Kenneth Cox

August 31: You're Part of a Jigsaw Puzzle

TEXT: 1 Cor. 12:27–31a
Object: A jigsaw puzzle

Good morning, boys and girls. How important are you? [*Let them answer.*] You may not feel very important because you don't have a job or make lots of money, but I want to tell you that I think you are very important, and so does Jesus. Let me show you what I mean.

A long time ago St. Paul wrote a letter to the people in the town of Corinth. He told them about their importance in the Church. Not everybody felt very important, so he explained it to them this way. He said they were just like different parts of the body. Some of them were like fingers and others were like arms and legs. There were a few who were like eyes and some who were like ears. He said that they were all important. Well, I guess Paul knew what people would think, so he went even further. To make a whole body you need all of the parts, and that means the little finger is as important to the whole body as the thumb is.

Here is another way to help you understand. How many of you work puzzles? Everybody likes a puzzle. A puzzle has a lot of parts and you have to work hard to put them all together. If one piece is missing you will search and search until you find it. [*Show the puzzle with one piece missing, then two and then three.*] With each missing piece the puzzle is less and less complete. You need all of the pieces to make the puzzle whole. [*Put the pieces back until the whole puzzle is put together.*]

That's the way it is with God's Church. You may think that the only person God needs is the pastor. You are wrong. Maybe the organist and the choir director? You are still wrong. The ushers, the choir, and the Sunday church school teachers? You are still wrong. God says that if his Church is going to be whole he needs each one of us because there is something important for every boy and girl and mother and father to do. Without all of us, the Church is like a body or a puzzle with something missing. You don't know how important a finger is until you don't have one of them, or you don't know how important each piece of the puzzle is until you're missing one of them. They are all important, and so are you to God. Remember how much God is counting on you to do your job; then you will know what a very important person you are in this world.—Wesley T. Runk[2]

---

[2]*Pass It On* (Lima, Ohio: CSS, 1977), pp. 73–74.

September 7: Praise God for Fall

TEXT: Gen. 1:14 (NIV)
Object: Colored leaves (one per child)
Song: "For the Beauty of the Earth"

Boys and girls, I'm going to give each of you something special this morning. [*Give each child a colorful fall leaf.*] Look at the front and back of the leaf. On the back you can see the veins that resemble lines running through the leaf. We know that leaves grow on trees. God sends the rain that reaches the roots of the trees. From there the moisture goes up through the leaves.

During this season, ask you family to go for a walk in the woods or in a park. Look for yellow, red, orange, and rust-colored leaves as you walk. Notice other signs of fall. You might see squirrels collecting nuts for winter, or wild geese migrating to warmer climates. Look for nuts that have fallen onto the ground. Notice the beautiful fall pumpkins and gourds at roadside markets. Yes, fall is one of the most colorful seasons God made for us to enjoy.

When God created the Earth, he divided it into day and night, and into seasons. In Genesis 1:14 we read, "And God said, 'Let there be lights in the expanse of the sky to separate the day from the night, and let them serve as signs to mark seasons and days and years.'" God had a plan. The four seasons of the year were part of God's plan.

[*Ask the children to think about the words from the song "For the Beauty of the Earth" as they sing. Ask an adult to lead in prayer, thanking God for the fall season. Have the children return to their seats as the pianist continues to play.*]—Carolyn Tomlin

September 14: I Don't Want to Hear

TEXT: Exod. 20:12
Object: Cotton balls

Never put anything in your ears. I am being very careful today, but don't even do this without mom or dad's help, OK? When I put these cotton balls in my ears I can't hear. What did you say? Huh? I better take these cotton balls out so I can hear you.

We honor our mothers and fathers by being obedient to them and respecting them. When our parents tell us to do something, the oldest trick in the world is to say, "I didn't hear you." We say, "I didn't know" and act dumb. Pretending not to hear is one form of disobedience to parents. Most of the time we do hear and understand our parents' directions.

Exodus 20 contains the Ten Commandments. The fifth commandment addresses obedience to parents. Listen to this verse.

There is a promise in this commandment. As we honor our parents and are obedient to them, our lives are happier and longer. Isn't that strange? We think we will be happier by acting like we didn't hear and by doing what we are determined to do. When we are obedient we feel good inside. When we are obedient our family is happier because everyone fits into the home pattern and enjoys a nicer place to live.

After we are grown we must be careful to listen to God. We may not want to listen or we may pretend that we know better. However, when we are obedient to God we are the happiest people we can possibly be. By discovering the joy that comes from being obedient to our parents, we learn how to love and follow God.—Kenneth Cox

September 21: God's Little Beggars
TEXT: John 4:46b–53
Object: A tin cup

Good morning, little beggars. Oh, I mean good morning, boys and girls. Is it all right if I call you "little beggars"? Does anyone else ever call you a beggar? Do you ever just beg and beg your mom for a new dress or a candy bar or to go to a drive-in movie? Do you know what I mean by that kind of a beggar? [*Wait for several answers.*] This kind of a beggar is someone who keeps asking for something over and over again. I have seen beggars on the street corner with a cup like this and they beg people for money to buy food and clothing. It is not an easy way to live and people do this when there is nothing else they can do. Maybe they have lost their sight or some other part of their body and they do not know how to do any other work. A beggar is someone who must depend on others to support him or help him with whatever problem he has.

Now, I am going to show you how I beg. [*Take the cup around and ask the children for things such as hair ribbons, money, and so on. Try to show how dependent you are on them by the tone of your voice and walk.*] It is not easy to be a beggar because it is not easy to show people how much you must depend on them.

Once a very important person heard that Jesus was coming to Galilee. He began to look all over for the one they called Lord. This man was a government official and he had a very sick son who was going to die. He had tried all of the doctors and no one could help his son, whom he loved very much. When he found Jesus, he begged and begged him to heal his son. This was very hard for the important man to do because he was not used to begging anyone for anything. But the official needed Jesus because he believed that Jesus was the only one who could help him, so he begged and begged and begged Jesus to come to his house to see his son. Jesus listened to the man and then told him to go home where he would find his son well. The man believed that what Jesus said would really happen and he left for home. When he got home he found that what Jesus had promised was true.

The official was very glad that he had begged Jesus because he knew he himself could do nothing for his son to make him well, and neither could anyone else. We are like beggars with God a lot of times. There are all sorts of things that we cannot do without God's help. We need God and we ask him time and time again to forgive us our sins, to heal our sicknesses, and to grow our food. We need God and we need to understand how much we count on him doing the things that he does.

The next time you see a tin cup, maybe you will remember the story of the important person who came to Jesus and begged to have his son made well. Then you will also remember how we are like beggars with God.—Wesley T. Runk[3]

September 28: Picture Frame Support
TEXT: John 15:26–16:4a
Object: A picture frame with foldout support

Good morning, boys and girls, and how are you today? Did you come to church today all by yourself or did you come with someone else? [*Let them answer.*] Who did you come to church

---

[3]*God's Little Beggars* (Lima, Ohio: CSS, 1976), pp. 81–82.

with today? Your parents and your brothers and sisters came with you to church. Do you think you would have come to church today if you had to come all by yourself? It would be a pretty long walk, wouldn't it? None of you drives a car, do you? I didn't think so. Do you think that you could have gotten up all by yourself, dressed yourself, fixed your breakfast, and come to church if someone would have brought you? Some of you think that you may have done it. It is kind of nice to have your mothers' and fathers' support, isn't it? I mean, you are glad they help you, aren't you? I knew you were.

I have something else that needs support and I want to show it to you. What is this object I have in my hand? [*Let them answer.*] That's right, a picture frame. And the picture in it, of my son, is one of my very favorite pictures. We keep this picture in our living room on the table by the couch. Whenever someone comes into the living room, he sees this picture just sitting there and smiling at him. Don't you think that a picture like this makes us happy? You're right, of course.

This picture frame couldn't just sit there all by itself without some help. Do you know what holds the frame up so you can see the picture whenever you come into the room? [*See if they can answer.*] That's right; there is a little piece behind the frame that kind of sits at an angle and holds up the picture. That little piece supports the whole frame and holds it up. Otherwise, it would just fall over on its face or back.

This little piece keeps my picture frame from falling down, just as our parents keep us from missing church. We call that support. Jesus is also a form of support. It is his teaching that keeps us from falling away from God. Jesus told us a lot of things about the way God is and feels, so we would know we can trust God to care for us. It would be easy to give up and go to the devil if it weren't for the things Jesus taught us. He told his disciples and he teaches us that we should always know that God is on our side and we should never fall away from God. Jesus supports us just like the little piece on the back of the picture frame holds up my son's smiling face and just like your parents support you when they bring you to church.

So, don't forget why we listen to what Jesus teaches us. He supports us and keeps us from falling away from God. The next time you see a picture frame, look on the back and see if you see one of these supporters; then tell others how Jesus supports you.—Wesley T. Runk[4]

October 5: The Strength of Partners

TEXT: Luke 10:1

Object: Picture of workers

This is a picture of two men working on a race car. There is an old saying, "Two heads are better than one." The Bible says that if one man falls, "his friend can help him up" (Eccles. 4:10). These truths teach the importance of the buddy system.

You may have noticed the necessity of partnerships. On school field trips each person is told to select a partner. When the group gets off the bus each person must stay with his partner so it is noticeable if someone falls behind. At summer camp, swimming is made safe by the buddy system. The lifeguard blows the whistle and each person has to grab and raise the hand of his

---

[4]*God's Little Beggars* (Lima, Ohio: CSS, 1976), pp. 35–36.

or her buddy. When the lifeguard sees that everyone is safe with their buddy, the whistle is blown and everyone can swim again.

Jesus believed in the buddy system, too. When Jesus sent his followers out to spread the gospel, he sent them in pairs. Listen to this verse.

When we serve the Lord it is good to remember the power of the buddy system. If you want to invite a friend to come to Sunday school, get one of your church friends to go with you. When we take a buddy we feel more confident, and when we discover something that is especially challenging, our partner can help.

Having a buddy is also good for praying. When a friend is asked to help in a prayer, they are called a prayer partner. When two persons pray together, Jesus has promised that their prayer is powerful (Matt. 18:20).

Remember the importance of the buddy system. When we are alone we tend to be weak. When we have a partner we are strong.—Kenneth Cox

October 12: Follow Me
TEXT: Mark 1:14–20
Object: Fishing equipment

Good morning, boys and girls. When Jesus was looking for disciples, he chose some men who would not only be good followers of him but who would also be leaders of other people. All of us need to follow a leader, but when the leader tells us what to do and how to do it, then we must be ready. Jesus needed good people who would help other people find Jesus and follow him.

Some of the people Jesus asked to follow him were fishermen. These men worked every day at catching fish. That was their job. What kind of a job does your father or mother have? [*Let them answer.*] If your dad is a doctor, then he goes to work every day to help people feel better. If your dad works in a store, then he goes to work every day to sell the things that are in the store. If your mother works in an office, she goes to work every day to type letters. The disciples had jobs like your father and mother have jobs, only their job was to catch fish so that people could have them to eat. It was a hard job, but it was the kind of a job they liked doing.

Jesus told the disciples that he wanted them to be a different kind of fishermen. When they fished for fish, they had to catch the little things or big things that swam around in the water. How many of you have ever gone fishing? [*Let them answer.*] If you went fishing you took a pole, some worms, a stringer, a box like this one with all sorts of little things in it, a net, and maybe some other parts that I don't even have.

Jesus told his new friends, the disciples, that he did not want them only to catch fish out of the lake. Jesus also wanted his fishermen to catch men. He wanted the disciples to find people and tell them what he had taught them and make them followers just like they were followers. That is why Jesus called them fishers of men.

You can be a fisher of people just like Peter, John, James, and Andrew were. You can be a disciple of Jesus. You must look for boys and girls like yourselves and bring them to Jesus. Jesus will love them like he loves you and teach them all of the good things they should know about God.

The next time you go fishing, or you see someone fishing, I want you to think about the time that Jesus invited some men who were fishermen to come to work for him and help him teach others about his Father in heaven. Amen.—Wesley T. Runk[5]

October 19: A Prayer a Day Keeps the Lions Away
TEXT: Dan. 6:10
Object: A toothbrush

This is a toothbrush. Dentists instruct us to brush each day after every meal. That would mean brushing our teeth three times a day. If we skip brushing our teeth, bacteria build up on our teeth, which can lead to cavities and gum disease. So it is very important to brush regularly.

Praying and reading the Bible should be done every day, too. Without regularly seeing and listening to the voice of God we tend to go astray. When a sheep goes astray, predators like wolves and lions are likely to attack them. Our lives can be endangered, too. If we go a day without asking God for strength, we will end up like a toy whose battery has gone dead. We may stop dead in our tracks.

A man named Daniel is famous for being in the lions' den and escaping without being harmed by the lions. The key to Daniel's spiritual strength was his daily devotion to God. Daniel prayed three times a day. Listen to this verse.

After we have learned to brush our teeth after every meal, we feel like our teeth are dirty if we miss a brushing. We feel the same way when we don't read our Bibles and pray every day. We learn that our spiritual discipline gives us strength in the Lord (Eph. 6:10) and this power is something we begin to value. I know you won't forget to brush your teeth. Don't overlook your daily devotions and prayer either.—Kenneth Cox

October 26: Helping Others
TEXT: Rom. 8:38
Object: Mirror
Song: "Because I Have Been Given Much," no. 605, *The Baptist Hymnal*

Boys and girls, I want you to line up in a row and pass this mirror to each person. As you look at your reflection and see your face, think about how you can help others. God has made each of you special. You have individual talents that belong only to you. You have special gifts that only you can give. God wants us to use our talents and gifts to help others. Do you think God is happy when we have unique talents and keep them to ourselves? Do you think he is pleased when we don't give our time to help people? What can we do to please God? [*Wait for response.*]

Can you think of people who have helped you? [*Pause for response.*] They may be your Sunday school teacher, your music teacher, your Little League coach, a kind neighbor, a grandparent, or a classmate. People who are happy help others.

Acts 20:35 speaks of helping others: "In everything I did I showed you that by this kind

---

[5]*Let's Share Jesus Together* (Lima, Ohio: CSS, 1982), pp. 4–5.

of hard work we must help the weak, remembering the words the Lord Jesus himself said: 'It is more blessed to give than to receive.'" Jesus expects us to help others. This is written many times in the Scriptures.

[*Ask a soloist to sing "Because I Have Been Given Much." Say a prayer asking God to help each child become a person who is concerned about the needs of people. Have the pianist continue to play as the children return to their places.*]—Carolyn Tomlin

November 2: Giving Should Be from the Heart
TEXT: Mark 12:42–44
Object: A penny

The penny is the smallest denomination of U.S. currency. It takes one hundred pennies to equal a dollar. Because of its small value some people will not bend over to pick up a penny that is lying on the street. In Mexico it takes several pesos to equal one penny.

One day Jesus and his followers were in the Temple, near the gathering place for offerings. As they watched, some individuals contributed large amounts to the offering receptacles. A widow came by and put two mites, worth less than a penny, in the offering chest. Being a widow means the woman's husband had died. Without a husband her family would not have been able to earn a large income and she would have been poor. Listen to this verse to learn what Jesus said about her offering.

To Jesus the amount of our offerings is not as important as what is in our hearts. The people who gave large amounts were very wealthy and could do without their tithes and offerings. The widow gave all the money she possessed. She would have been completely broke after that offering. In so doing she was putting her hope and trust in God. To Jesus the woman gave much more than all the rest.

We may not think we have much to offer God. As we look at others with more talent or wealth, we might feel small. When we give to God our very best, he values it highly. God can take our offerings and multiply them to meet special needs. There is an old saying, "Little becomes much when placed in the Master's hands."

We should never give to the church out of pride, demanding recognition. Furthermore, we should never look down on what someone else gives. Because of their situation they may be giving much more than we have given.

We give God the most when we give our time, our best efforts, and our material things from loving hearts. The next time you see a penny, remember the widow who was praised by Jesus when she gave all she had.—Kenneth Cox

November 9: Peace
TEXT: Col. 3:12–17
Object: A referee's striped shirt

This morning we all heard these words read from the Bible: "Let the peace of God rule in your hearts." What do you think the word *peace* means? Think about it for a moment and raise your hand if you think you have an idea of what *peace* would be like. Not fighting, no more wars. These are all good answers.

We hear the word *peace* on the television news, we hear it at church, and we hear it at home. I remember my dad saying, "All I want around here is a little peace—" When I paused after *peace,* some of you were able to finish what my dad used to say—"and quiet." I'll bet you've heard it before in your house—every one talking at once with your outside voices, lots of confusion and noise. Let there be peace!

Well, we use the word *peace* in lots of ways. In Jesus' time and tradition, the word *heart* was often used to describe the spiritual place in us where we made decisions and felt things deeply. Things can get pretty noisy and confusing in that place, too. It's not a physical place, like a room or a part of your body, but it is real. It is the place where you have thoughts like "That really hurt when she said that; I'm going to push her when no one is looking." Or "Maybe she said that because she is so lonely. I need to forgive her." See what I mean? So many feelings and decisions. Which one is right?

Our verse said, "Let the peace of God rule in your heart." The word that the apostle Paul uses for *rule* meant what a referee does in a sports contest. We have referees today. [*Show the shirt.*] Who would wear this? That is right, a referee at a basketball game or a football game. To referee is to keep things flowing in the right direction and to rule over disputes to bring order out of confusion. The word *peace* in Hebrew is *shalom.* Some of you have learned that word in vacation Bible school. God's peace, shalom, or completeness helps rule over the questions that come up in our hearts, like "Should I push her when no one is looking?" We know the answer. Jesus Christ said, "Do not return evil for evil." He gave himself for us, and our Scripture lesson says that. We are to let the Word of Christ be in us. Then peace will rule, or referee, in our hearts. Go in peace.—Gary D. Stratman

November 16: The Bible Is Our Guide

TEXT: 2 Tim. 3:16 (NIV)

Object: Bible, cookbook, map, and directions for playing a game

Song: "Holy Bible, Book Divine," no. 260, *The Baptist Hymnal*

[*Hold up each book or object. Ask the children to tell the purpose of each item or what it teaches.*] What if we wanted to travel to a new location? What would we use? A map, of course. What is the purpose of a cookbook? To help us follow a recipe and prepare food. Why do we need to understand the directions when playing a new game? So we will know the rules and so everyone can have a turn.

[*Hold up the Bible.*] What does this book teach? [*Allow time for the children to respond.*] There is something I want all of you boys and girls to remember about the Bible. All that the Bible says is from God. God inspired the Bible. This book gives us rules for living a happy, joyful life.

Listen as I read from 2 Timothy 3:16. "All Scripture is God-breathed and is useful for teaching, rebuking, correcting, and training in righteousness, so that the man of God may be thoroughly equipped for every good work" (NIV).

Yes, all these other books and objects are useful, too; but they may change or soon be out of date. The Bible is always the same, now and forever. God's laws never change.

[*Invite the congregation to join the children in singing "Holy Bible, Book Divine." Say a prayer that the children and their families will seek answers about living from the Bible. Ask the pianist to continue to play as the children return to their seats.*]—Carolyn Tomlin

November 23: Father, We Thank You
Text: Ps. 100:4 (NIV)
Object: Horn of plenty, filled with fruit
Song: "Come, Ye Thankful People, Come," no. 637, *The Baptist Hymnal*

Boys and girls, I'm holding an object that many of you may not know. Would anyone like to guess what this object is called? [*Allow time for response.*] It looks a little like a basket that is large at one end and goes to a point at the other. This object is called a *cornucopia*, or a *horn of plenty*. It symbolizes peace and prosperity. Your family may place one on the dining room table during the Thanksgiving season. It represents the fruits of the harvest that God has provided for us to enjoy.

At Thanksgiving we praise God for all he has given us. We want to thank him for giving us our families, our health, our food, and our homes that protect us from the rain and cold weather. God gives people the knowledge and strength to grow our food. Then he sends the sun to make the plants grow. The rain waters the Earth and helps the plants to make fruits, grains, and vegetables. God is so good to us. He provides for our needs.

The book of Psalms is filled with words of praise and thanksgiving. In Psalm 100:4 we read, "Enter his gates with thanksgiving and his courts with praise; give thanks to him and praise his name."

Would you each say a sentence prayer to God for one thing in your life for which you are thankful? I'll close the prayer.

[*Have the pianist play "Come, Ye Thankful People, Come" as the children return to their seats.*]—Carolyn Tomlin

November 30: What's Your Prize?
Text: John 6:24–35
Object: A bag of garbage

Good morning, boys and girls. Today I want to share with you a prize that I know you are going to love. The prize I have is in this bag and it will go to the person who wins the big race. Some people may want to know what's in the bag, so I think I should tell you ahead of time. It's a bag of garbage. How many of you would like to win a prize like this? A great big bag of garbage. [*Let them answer.*] None of you want to win the prize? I don't understand. I thought everybody liked prizes. Why don't you want to win this big prize? [*Let them answer.*] You don't like garbage, not even if it's in a beautiful bag like the one I have it in? You probably don't even want to be in the race if you are going to have a chance at this prize then.

Your life and my life are like a race. We are all in it, and the only difference between the way some people run their lives and the way other people run their lives is in the prize they get. Some people run the race of life for a prize that is just like my bag of garbage. Their prize is worthless. It doesn't mean anything. These people have lived only for themselves and for what is bad. They have lived badly and done bad things to other people. They either do not know God or they hate him. Their prize at the end of their life will be worse than a bag of garbage. What they will get will be just plain rotten. They have lived their whole life and when it is over, like the end of a race, the prize will be just rotten.

But God says there is another way to live our lives, another way to run the race, for a different kind of prize. If in this race you fill your life with love, share yourself and the things you have with others, and try to be helpful, the prize you will get at the end of life is something that never rots but goes on forever. The prize is eternal life. It is living with God in a wonderful world that he makes for us.

The prize for living with God and according to God's ways is something that never breaks or wears out or rots. It is something that will last forever. You have a choice as to which way you live or which race you run in. I hope you end up not with a bag of garbage but instead with a wonderful life that goes on forever with God. In Jesus' name, amen.—Wesley T. Runk[6]

December 7: Praise God for Winter

TEXT: Ps. 147:1, 16
Object: Mittens
Song: "Everything Was Made by God," no. 45, *The Baptist Hymnal*

Boys and girls, I'm holding something that is worn in cold weather. Can you name this object? [*Allow time for response.*] Do any of you wear mittens or gloves when you play outdoors in cold weather? Tell me, why do you wear mittens? [*Wait for response.*] Yes, you wear mittens to protect your hands from the cold. You may wear them when you play in snow or go for a sleigh ride. Mittens are associated with cold weather. They represent this time of year.

Winter is a time when nature slows down. The trees and plants have lost their leaves. Many animals are hibernating, or sleeping. They must eat extra food during the other months to carry them through the cold period. Sometimes families do different things during the winter than they do in the warmer months. Who can share one thing your family enjoys during winter? [*Allow several children to respond.*] Perhaps you play games together, sing favorite songs, enjoy popcorn around a fireplace, or take a walk in the snow.

This winter, as you think of family activities, remember to praise God for all seasons. Psalm 147:1, 16 says, "Praise the Lord. How good it is to sing praises to our God; how pleasant and fitting to praise him! He spreads the snow like wool and scatters the frost like ashes."

"Cold wind in the winter, pleasant summer sun, ripe fruits in the garden; he made them every one. He gave us eyes to see them, lips that we might tell; how good is God our Father, who doeth all things well." [*Ask the pianist to play as the children return to their places.*]— Carolyn Tomlin

December 14: You Are Special

TEXT: Luke 2:8–14
Setting: Advent—Christmas
Objects: Three toy sheep (These may be stuffed toys or sheep from a nativity scene. Make sure that one of the sheep is fancier than the others. The description that follows gives one way of doing this; putting a bright, bold ribbon on only one sheep will also do the trick.)

Today in my back pack I have an animal that I believe was present at the very first Christmas. No, not a reindeer; that's another story. That's right Rachel. I have a sheep. Why do you say

---

[6]*Let's Share Jesus Together* (Lima, Ohio: CSS, 1982), pp. 65–66.

sheep? Well, that is right. I do have a collection of sheep in the pastor's study. You have seen some of these sheep [*show the sheep in the pack*].

But why do we think of sheep at the first Christmas? That's right: because shepherds, those who take care of sheep, came to see the baby Jesus who had been born in a manger. We read of that night in the Bible and we have sung of it in our Christmas carols. What we can imagine is that there might have been some young lambs the shepherds couldn't leave. The sheep we have this morning are not real sheep; if they were, we would not keep them in a back pack. They also wouldn't have clothes on. Well, only one has fancy clothes on. Maybe she has a sense of the glory that shone around the shepherds and this place, and that to dress up sometimes signals a special day, like Sunday. But the lambs without the fancy dresses are just as special in the sight of the baby who is asleep on the straw. Their wool (black or white) shines brightly before the one to whom the angels sing. Even our little pretend animals can help us prepare for Jesus' coming to Earth, by reminding us that we can come to him just as we are.—Gary D. Stratman

December 21: Worshiping the Christ Child
TEXT: Matt. 2:9–10 (NIV)
Object: Large star cut from poster board, covered with a cloth
Song: "Away in a Manger"

Boys and girls, I want you to please close your eyes. Wait until I tell you to look at what I'm holding. [*Uncover the star.*] With your eyes still closed, I want one of you to run your fingers around the outside of this object. Can you guess the shape? Now, everyone open their eyes. Yes, this is a star. Stars have been used throughout history to show people how to travel at night. They point the way. They lead to where you are going.

Many years ago a star led the shepherds—and later the magi, who were know as the Wise Men—to where the baby Jesus had been born. The account of this discovery is found in the book of Matthew. We know that this writer was inspired by God to tell this story.

In Matthew 2:9–10 we read, "After they had heard the king, they went on their way, and the star they had seen in the east went ahead of them until it stopped over the place where the child was. When they saw the star, they were overjoyed." Can you imagine the wonderful feeling of finding the young child? If you had been searching for the baby Jesus, how would you feel when you discovered him? [*Wait for response.*]

Boys and girls, today you can find Jesus. All you have to do is invite him into your heart and accept him as your personal savior.

[*Lead the children in singing "Away in a Manger." Have the pianist continue to play as the children return to their seats.*]—Carolyn Tomlin

December 28: A Name of Hope
TEXT: Gen. 3:20
Object: A nametag

I am wearing a nametag. Nametags are used when there is a large group of people who have not been introduced to one another. If I am wearing a nametag, a complete stranger could walk up to me, look at my nametag, and say, "Hello, Ken, how are you?" Nametags promote friendship. People like being called by their names; it makes them feel comfortable and accepted.

In the Bible, names indicate what a person was or did. For example, when someone sees me and says, "Hello, preacher," they are using my occupation as my name. That is the function that names served during some phases of Bible history. A name might be given to indicate a person's destiny. A person's destiny is what they are intended by God to be in the future.

The first mother's name was Eve, which means "giver of life." Listen to this verse. Adam called the first mother Eve because she would be the mother of all who would live. Eve is a name of great hope. Adam and Eve had broken God's commandment and eaten the forbidden fruit. Because of their sin, Adam and Even realized that they were going to die. However, through the motherhood of Eve, life would continue. Thus they had hope.

Adam and Eve hoped that their children and grandchildren would populate the world. Also, Eve was promised that the savior of the world would come through her children's children. Thousands of years later, Jesus was born, miraculously, to Mary. Jesus was the fulfillment of Adam and Eve's hope.

Having babies is painful. Taking care of babies is not easy. Mothers have to be full of love and hope to have children and take care of them. Every time a child is born there is great hope.

Don't forget to say thanks to your mothers today. Nothing gives moms greater joy than to have their children say, "Thank you for being my mom."—Kenneth Cox

SECTION XI

A LITTLE TREASURY
OF ILLUSTRATIONS

THE GIFT OF LIFE.   During her first term in office, British prime minister Margaret Thatcher went to Brighton for government meetings. She checked into her hotel and was going about her business when a bomb exploded that was meant to end her life. She lived, but four of her closest friends died. In a way that we have come to associate with the British, the prime minister carried on and did what needed to be done. But two days later was Sunday and the prime minister was in church. It was a situation familiar to her, as it is to us. That particular day there seemed to be a special light shining in the candles, and when the sun streamed through the stained-glass windows she began to weep. For at last it hit her that this was a day that she was not meant to see. There were those who wanted her dead, and they had very nearly succeeded. But this day was a gift, a gift that she has not been intended to receive. With sadness at the death of her four friends, but with gratitude that she was alive, the tears streamed down her cheeks.—David J. Randolph

TOWARD THE PROMISED LAND.   My friend Sara felt stymied in her journey toward the Promised Land. For weeks she had seemed to travel in circles in her private wilderness of isolation and fear. She struggled with the depressing feeling that her woundedness was all she had for companionship on her life's journey. But then God came to her through her wound. God came to her in a dream. Sara dreamed that she was frolicking in the snow atop a mountain, and as she awoke from her dream her head was filled with that well-known melody from Dvorak's *New World Symphony* popularly known as "Going Home." Later Sara would see through the dream that this surrender to her dark side, to her fear that she was so vulnerable, was precisely the point when God could say to her, as he did to Moses, "My presence will go with you and I will give you fullness." It was now time to frolic to the music of a new world. Sara was on her way to the Promised Land. And so with you. And so with us all.—Donald M. Wardlaw

THE THREATENING CROWD.   Too many Christians are not free because they submit to the domination of other people's ideas. They submit passively to the opinions of the crowd. For self-protection they hide in the crowd and run along with it. They are afraid of the aloneness, the moral nakedness that they would feel apart from the crowd.—Thomas Merton

LOVE IS BEING FOR.   It is helpful to recall that, for John, love is not a feeling; rather, it is being *for* the other person and acting accordingly. To love is to be for another and to act for another, even at cost to oneself. The way in which love for one another is measured is God's love for the world, and Christ's love, which carried out in full and final obedience is that love of God.—Bishop Charlene Payne Kammerer

RESOURCES OF COURAGE. The necessary courage comes only with the trial itself. There are people who constantly worry over whether they will have the courage to face this or that deprivation—old age, a painful illness, infirmity, or the death of husband or wife. I have always tried to reassure them, for as long as the trial they fear is not there, the courage cannot be there either. And they are probably the ones who will bear it most courageously if it does come. Over and over again I have marveled at the resources of courage these worrying people reveal themselves to have when they have to face the real thing and not the phantom of their imagination!—Paul Tournier, *Creative Suffering*

BOUGHT AND PAID FOR. When I became a Christian, I thought I'd surrendered myself to Christ, but in reality I was giving him little pieces, a part of myself at a time, like poker chips or something of value. Every time I'd give a little bit more of myself to God, I'd wait for him to be impressed, to brag on me for surrendering a little bit more. I remember how scary it was when I came to the realization that he wasn't going to brag on me for those little pieces of myself. He wanted everything there was. He was treating me as if I were bought and paid for. He was treating me as if his name were written across me. The God who would not withhold his only Son but gave him up to die for us on the cross while we were yet sinners will never apologize for using us to the utmost.—William H. Hinson

THE SHARING OF LOVE. For many years there was a wall between one of my sons and me. Finally he was able to express his dislike of me, his doubts and fears. I did not reject him or criticize him. A real friendship developed between us and I could begin to share the depth of my caring for him. I could love him as he was, not expecting him to be what I wanted him to be. Sometime later I was with him in my own need and he could share his love freely and deeply with me.

Exactly the same truth applies to our relationship with God. He cannot give me the love I desire until I trust him enough to bring all of myself and so realize that he can love all of me. I never know the depth of God's love until I bring all of me again and again and again. God cannot by his very nature give me the love he desires to give me until I approach him as the loving Father that he is. Only in relationship to him can I begin to grow into that loving being I am capable of becoming.—Morton T. Kelsey, *Adventure Inward*

REBUILDING AROUND THE CROSS. There's a great story about the artist Rodin, who one day saw a huge carved crucifix beside a road. He arranged to have the crucifix carted back to his house, but unfortunately it was too big for the building. So, of all things, he knocked out the walls, raised the roof, and rebuilt his home around the cross. The calling of the American church! How can we let go of ourselves and, renewed by Jesus Christ, rebuild ourselves into the larger Church, the one Church that dares to follow Jesus Christ? Bluntly, we must be willing to die as denominations so that a new, freer, braver, united Christian word may be spoken.—David G. Buttrick

THE MEANING OF LIFE. I doubt whether a doctor can answer this question in general terms, for the meaning of life differs from man to man, from day to day, and from hour to hour. What matters, therefore, is not the meaning of life in general but rather the specific meaning of a person's life at a given moment. To put the question in general terms would be comparable to the question posed to a chess champion, "Tell me, Master, what is the best move in the world?" There simply is no such thing as the best or even a good move apart from a particular situation in a game and the particular personality of one's opponent. The same holds for human existence. One should not search for an abstract meaning of life. Everyone has his own specific vocation or mission in life to carry out a concrete assignment that demands fulfillment. Therein he cannot be replaced, nor can his life be repeated. Thus, everyone's task is as unique as is his specific opportunity to implement it.—Viktor E. Frankl, *Man's Search for Meaning*

JESUS' WORK METHOD.   It is true that, when Jesus of Nazareth went about Galilee and Judea, he was sometimes surrounded by a flurry of excitement, but he himself never made any noise or shouted out. Only once was it said of him that he cried out with a loud voice, and that was when he died on the cross. When he went about his work of preaching, healing the sick, and forgiving sins, he did so quietly and inconspicuously. We know that we can achieve many things by making a noise and shouting in the street. But not healing a person in body and soul. Every doctor will tell you that he cannot treat people in the hubbub of the streets, that people need quiet if they are to be cured. And the words of forgiveness cannot be shouted through loudspeakers. Our Lord was gentle and humble of heart. He chose to use this method. To some people it may seem to be too slow. But try to remember, each one of you, how it was with you. How did this Lord of ours call you and attract you? How did he awaken your trust and faith? Was it by shouting or through his quietness and love?—Pavel Filipi

PLEASING GOD.   Let all, therefore, who desire to please God condescend to be taught of God, and take care to walk in that path which God himself has appointed. Beware of taking half of this religion for the whole, but take both parts of it together. And see that you begin where God himself begins: "Thou shalt have no other gods before me." Is not this the first, our Lord himself being the Judge, as well as the great, commandment? First, therefore, see that you love God; next, your neighbor—every child of man. From this fountain let every temper, every affection, every passion flow. So shall that "mind be in you which was also in Christ Jesus." Let all your thoughts, words, and actions spring from this! So shall you "inherit the Kingdom prepared for you from the beginning of the world."—John Wesley

JESUS—TRADITIONALIST AND IMPROVISOR.   My musical tastes do not run particularly to jazz, but I do admire the ability of a good jazz group to improvise without getting completely lost. If a jazz group is to be free to do what it is intended to do (that is, improvise), it must first understand and internalize the basics, the tradition. And somebody—the bassist or drummer—must hold the line and keep the improvisation rooted in musical reality. Otherwise, we have not music but chaos. Jesus the Improvisor was first Jesus the Traditionalist.—Allan M. Parrent

PROVIDENCE AND FAITH.   It is not the case that the man who believes in providence may easily or by means of any art read the book of history and see there the ways of providence. It is the case, however, that the word of God in which he believes, and which he believes, can as such cause him to see something of God's rule, not his universal plan or total view, but God himself at work at various points, and always in every respect enough to give the man's faith in him the character of a knowledge in which he may genuinely and rightly live by his faith.—Karl Barth

DEFINING LOVE.   Genuine love is tough to squeeze into a definition. But if you want to test genuine love against its counterfeits, ask yourself time and again, Where is my focus? On myself or on another? On my satisfaction or the other's advantage? Am I only a consumer, a taker, a sponger, a leech? Or is my mind-set, How can I help? How much can I give?—Walter J. Burghardt

RELIGION OF LOVE.   I wanted to be a doctor that I might be able to work without having to talk. For years I had been giving myself out in words, and it was with joy that I had followed the calling of theological teacher and of preacher. But this new form of activity I could not represent to myself as being talking about the religion of love, but only as an actual putting it into practice. Medical knowledge made it possible for me to carry out my intention in the best and most complete way, wherever the path of service might lead me.—Albert Schweitzer

LOVE THAT MAKES OR MARS.   Next to the love of God comes the love of man or woman, as a factor in the education of a human spirit. Each one of us is capable of giving out a vast wealth of love; we must love and be loved, and almost everything depends on the twin spirit whom we choose as the object of our affection, and on the hearth at whose fires we may warm ourselves when called and repelled by an unfriendly world. That love may make or mar us, may transfigure or degrade us—and which it shall be is settled by the objects we choose, and the way in which we treat them.—F. B. Meyer

WATCH AND PRAY.   Holy Scripture does indeed tell us something about the future, that is to say, about the plan of God for the world and for ourselves. It tells us indeed something about the future course of events—but no more than we already know—that we must be watchful so as not to be surprised and crumple up like an army which has set no sentry posts or whose sentries have fallen asleep. Hence the ever-repeated warning: *watch and pray.*—Emil Brunner

HUMAN DIGNITY IN THE IMAGE OF GOD.   I would like to lift up a verse from Psalm 103. "For God knows our frame. God remembers that we are dust." I love that verse. It is so liberating. God knows. There is no shame in being weak and mortal. Weakness is not sin. Weakness does not conjure up guilt, or should not. One of the difficult things with Western Christianity is that it cultivated a kind of introspective conscience which somehow thought that one gave honor to God by describing oneself in utter depravity. Men and women are created in the image of God. In a world full of many tensions, we need to reach back to our common humanity. Remember that the dignity of human beings lies in the fact that we are created in the image of God. The rabbis asked, "Why did God create only one human being, Adam?" "So that nobody should be able to say, 'My father is better than your father.'" To be created in the image of God, there lies our dignity.—Krister Stendahl

GOD IN OUR MIDST.   Because he is the *living* God, who is near and who is one, he really walks among us, in our midst, whether we take notice or not, whether we like it or not. He walks among the old and the young, among the sick and the healthy, among the extroverts and the introverts, among the good and the evil. Because he is God *almighty,* he never grows weary. And let no one imagine he might succeed in delaying or hindering God! Because he is the *holy* God, he cannot be deceived. He cannot be snubbed as we are likely to snub other people, nor can he be mastered as we think we master certain people or opinions and situations, if not our destiny itself. And because he is the *merciful* God, he will not take offense. He will not grow bitter, nor will he be confounded in his love.

> Like a father from his children
> Never takes his love away,
> Though they often turn against him
> And deceive him day by day,
> Even my most grievous failure
> Does my faithful Lord forgive,
> Chastening me with wrath and mercy,
> Not the sword, that I may live.

This, then, is how the holy God, walking in our midst, deals with us, whether we work or rest, whether we are glad or sad, whether we wake or sleep—in this year of 1956 and certainly also in the years thereafter—in time and even more in eternity when we shall see him face to face, the living God who is near and who is one.—Karl Barth

GOD AND THE BIBLE.   During the ceremony of the coronation of a British monarch, the moderator of the Church of Scotland presents a Bible to the new sovereign and says, "We present you with this book, the most valuable thing that this world affords." This statement is followed by words that set forth the value ascribed to the Bible: "Here is Wisdom. This is the royal Law. These are the lively oracles of God." This explanation indicates that the authority attributed to the Bible is ultimately the authority belonging to God. It is, therefore, not an authority intrinsic to the book as a piece of typography, but is linked with the conviction that the book emanates from God. Because God is held to be holy, the Bible, too, is described as "holy," as we speak of the "holy Scriptures" or "sacred writings."—Bruce M. Metzger

TWO KINDS OF PEOPLE.   I really believe there are just two kinds of folk: those who work to make the world a better place for everyone and those who work to make a better place for themselves in the world as it is. Moses was of the former stripe. He could have taken for granted the enormous good fortune that had befallen him and forgotten all about his downtrodden kinspersons, *but he did not!* What was happening to them made a difference to him. He could not rest in luxury while they were languishing under oppression, and so he chose the way of true morality: he voluntarily took on problems he could have avoided on behalf of his brothers and sisters. And let it be said that this is the only way progress can be made in the area of social justice—when those who are not involved as victims are willing to become involved on behalf of victims.—John Claypool

GOD'S PRESENCE IN US.   God is indeed a living God and is not simply present in Jesus like a piece of jewelry that we can place in a strongbox, that will stay put until we want to take it out. It is much more like a child that grows in its mother's body, and that of course must be constantly nourished and breathed for, in order that it may grow. If the mother poisons herself with anything, then she also poisons the child. She may notice nothing at all for some time, though the child is long since dead. That is how it is with God's presence in us: it lives, but it is not simply to be taken for granted; rather, it must be nourished and cared for, be resuscitated.—Eduard Schweizer

GOD IN ACTION.   But when all is said, the healing ministry of Jesus runs back to this, that *in him the power of God was present in the Earth,* and present in an absolutely unimpeded form at last. Everything turns on that. This was nothing less than the Spirit of God, the living God, in action. To the disciples, as they came to share something of that Spirit, something of the same power was given. But in the great words of the fourth Gospel—"God gives him the Spirit in no sparing measure" (John 3:34, Moffatt). The story of Jesus, who went about continually doing good to men, is the story of immeasurable energy in contact with measurable need. Here the eternal love of heaven was meeting the transient tragedies of Earth. Nothing else could have happened on that battlefield but what did happen: need and tragedy had to own themselves defeated, and love and life were victors. For the work of Jesus was the work of the everlasting God.—James S. Stewart

THE HIDDEN ONE.   At Mount Rushmore, South Dakota, are the carved figures of four U.S. presidents—Washington, Jefferson, Lincoln, and Theodore Roosevelt. The sculptor was Gutzon Borglum. Asked how he did it, he replied whimsically, "Well, those figures were there for forty million years. All I had to do was dynamite 40,000 tons of granite to bring them into view." Isn't this what Christ is seeking to do: to bring into view the real person he knows us to be?—John N. Gladstone

DISCOURAGEMENT.   The devil decided to have a garage sale. On the day of the sale his tools were placed on display for public inspection, each being marked with its sale price. There were a treacherous lot of implements: hatred, envy, jealousy, deceit, lust, lying, pride, and so on.

Set apart from the rest was a harmless-looking tool. It was quite worn and yet priced very high.

"What is the name of this tool?" asked one of the customers, pointing to it.

"That is discouragement," Satan replied.

"Why have you priced it so high?"

"Because it is more useful to me than the others. With that tool I can pry open a man's heart and get inside—even when I cannot get near him with the other tools. It is badly worn because I use it on almost everyone, since so few people know it belongs to me."

The devil's price for discouragement was high because it is still his favorite tool, and he is still using it on God's people.—Glen Martin and Diane Ginter, *Drawing Closer*

WITNESS TO GOD.   When Adolf Hitler sold his program to the German people, he didn't sell prisons and ovens and genocide. You know what he sold? He spoke of a way to peace and joy, of every home a quiet place, of children happy and well. Did Germany want that? Of course! Then came the means, the painful, necessary steps. Holocaust! I do not seek to excuse anyone, but rather to say the German people didn't vote for holocaust. They voted for something for which people everywhere search, search, search.

When Karl Marx sold the Russian people on a system of communism, he didn't sell them on the idea "Let's get rid of forty million Ukrainians; let's put microphones in every public building; let's suspect, watch, imprison, exile." He didn't sell that. What he sold was, "From each according to ability, to each according to need, so that all may. . . ." "So that all may"— what a wonderful thing! The most terrible systems of the human race are distortions of a longing for peace, quiet, love. The depths to which people sink are but another register of the heights to which they are capable of rising, because God has never been without witness in the world. Never. Anywhere. That is why upon hearing the gospel for the first time, listeners experience déjà vu: they have a sense of familiarity when offered a new experience.— Fred B. Craddock

ORDEAL AND THE COURAGE TO FACE IT.   By November 1961 I had come to know for a year the four black six-year-old girls who initiated school desegregation in New Orleans at the behest of Federal Judge J. Skelly Wright. I have many times described the ordeal of Ruby Bridges, who had to fight her way through angry, threatening mobs every day for months. Federal marshals escorted her to and from the Frantz School because the city police and the state police were unwilling to protect her. Obscenities were her everyday fare, and often she heard grown men and women, mothers and fathers, tell her she was going to die one day soon. She withstood this ordeal with remarkable resilience and even managed to find time occasionally to pray for her tormentors.—Robert Coles, *The Call of Service: A Witness to Idealism*

CHURCH DEFINED.   You may know the song, "I am the church, you are the church, we are the church together." The church is people. I heard Willard Heckel speak a couple of years ago. He was dean of the Rutgers Law School and a former moderator of our national church. He said he was complaining about the problems in the world and the church, and his whole life was changed when a woman challenged him with this question: "What are you doing about it?" God wants to use us, his people, to change the world.—Kathleen J. Crane

ACCEPTING COMPLIMENTS.   Accept a compliment for what it is: someone letting you know that you have done something good, you have been successful. Let it end there. Don't pursue the negative thoughts that might erupt. Catch yourself if you start musing, "Now, I'll have too much to live up to next time," or "I wonder what she wants from me," or "What a fool he must be! He didn't even realize that I forgot to cite the two most obvious precedents." Stop those thoughts! Compliments should give you some added reassurance. They should help dispel self-doubts, not add to them. Replace the negative thoughts with positive ones.— Joan C. Harvey with Cynthia Katz, *If I'm So Successful, Why Do I Feel Like a Fake?*

QUESTIONS AND ANSWERS.   All of us walk, sooner or later, along the avenues of life where the "lights go out." Tragedy comes uninvited, and suddenly. Sorrow invades. Failure comes. Relationships crumble. Bad news enters the picture. Despair and disappointment hang their drapes of darkness. Who speaks to life in these moments with the words that ignite hope and give promise? Who takes the ugly threads of ruin and begins weaving meaning back into life? Who comes in the midst of darkness and shares light? No one but Jesus.

I like the little girl who asked the question, "What was God doing last night during the storm?" Then she answered her own question by saying, "Oh, I know, he was making the morning!"— C. Neil Strait

TALK, TALK, TALK.   If someone were to ask you, "What are the three most important words in any marriage?" you might give one of these answers:

> "I love you."
> "You are beautiful."
> "Please forgive me."

All are excellent choices. But from our workshops, out of letters we receive, in counseling sessions, too, we've concluded that the three most important words are "Talk! Talk! Talk!"

Why? Because without talk, talk, talk, "I love you" won't get through. Neither will that all-important "You are beautiful," or the magic eraser, "Please forgive me."

Any way we come to it, "I want to know you and I want you to know me—no reservations." Any couple willing to make this statement, and live by it, has arrived at the wellspring of true love.—Charlie W. Shedd, *Remember, I Love You*

REDEEMING PUZZLES.   There's Peter crucified upside down on a cross. There's Joan of Arc hearing heaven's voices, burned at the stake as a witch. There's Bonhoeffer about to die in Hitler's prison writing prayers, singing psalms. There's Sojourner Truth, black woman converted and called by Christ in Civil War times to fight for the freedom of blacks and the rights of women. There's Abraham who hung onto faith through years of unfulfilled promises and through those moments of terror as he led his son up that hill to an unthinkable death. There's Ruth, who lived out steadfast love in her mother-in-law's country and taught the Jews what their God was like. There's Luther hurling inkpots at devils, searching for faith, standing on God's word and splitting a church he was trying to purify. There's Martin Luther King Jr., announcing God's dream that God's people were not ready for, unveiling the violence of our ways, and dying at the hands of that exposed and terrified violence.—H. Stephen Shoemaker

SEVEN DEADLY SINS.   No one who has looked at Abbey's noble painting of the Seven Deadly Sins in the Boston Public Library will ever forget the power of the painter's conception and the way in which it symbolizes the terrific reality of the moral struggle. The seven deadly sins of classic tradition portrayed there are pride, envy, anger, covetousness, gluttony, lust, and sloth. These sins are individualistic. They all have widespread and dire social consequences, but as is natural in any list drawn up in the Middle Ages, they are sins of the individual, personal life.

Canon Frederic Lewis Donaldson of Westminster Abbey has set forth a list of seven deadly sins of a more social character. It is a list of arresting significance to an age of complex social forces and relationships. The seven deadly social sins, according to Canon Donaldson, are these:

> Policies without principles
> Wealth without work
> Pleasure without conscience

Knowledge without character
Commerce and industry without morality
Science without humanity
Worship without sacrifice

—Halford E. Luccock, *Living a Thousand Lives*

WAY THE CROSS DRAWS US.   The cross draws us because it is the way in which Christ moved beyond all the tensions of his ministry to triumph. We should not judge the disciples' despair at the cross, for we look at the cross through the perspective of the empty tomb, through the reality of the Resurrection. Ordinary vision would stand at the foot of the cross and say, "This is the end." Only the eyes of faith could take in that scene and say, "This is the beginning."—Kenneth L. Chafin

FORGIVENESS.   My Christian friends, let me remind you of what you already know, that God knows your sins and forgives them. God knows the wickedness of your heart and still finds you lovely. God knows us to be a people with a victim mentality but says get up and walk—our sins are not remembered. God knows we are a community of backbiting and defensive gossips but says that is forgiven—tell the truth now. God knows our sinful society oppresses and abuses but says those iniquities are forgiven—from now on live justly. God knows that many suffer from illness, poverty, oppression, and abuse and says that is the essence of the divine life lived with joy and grace—after Crucifixion comes Resurrection.— Robert Cummings Neville, *The God Who Beckons*

HEART OF THE GOSPEL.   I once attended a prayer service where those present were invited to express their praise in three-word sentences. One person said, "God answers prayers." Another said, "God is love." And another, "I love Jesus." Finally, an elderly man whose speech had been seriously impaired by a stroke stood and haltingly spoke these words: "Jesus—loves—*me!*"

Not that we love Jesus but that *he loves us*—this is the heart of the gospel.—Page H. Kelley

RESURRECTION NOW.   The message of the living Lord is simply this: We do not have to die to live, and to live that truth is to realize that death can no longer intimidate life. To know that truth is to know an incredible freedom in a world that is held hostage daily to doubt, to fear, and to death. And the key to all of that is to remember that's what the angel said, to remember what Jesus said: "Remember how he told you while he was still in Galilee that the son of man must be delivered into the hands of sinful men and be crucified and on the third day rise." His resurrection *then* enables our resurrection *now:* that's incredible freedom.— Peter J. Gomes

DIFFICULTIES.   We must never suppose that the difficulties that confront us indicate that we are not on God's path and doing his work. Indeed, the contrary is generally the case. If we are willing to walk with God he will test the sincerity and temper of our soul; he will cause men to ride over our heads; he will bring us through fire and through water. But out of all he will bring us into a large room and give us the very thing on which we have been taught to set our hearts. The further banks of the Red Sea with their song of victory will wipe out the memory of those bitter disappointments, those sharp speeches, those hours of lonely anguish.—F. B. Meyer

THE REALITY OF JESUS.   "Who do you say that I am?" Ronald H. Bainton, a former professor of church history at Yale Divinity School, felt that to end in skepticism about Christ because of the diversity of pictures of him is not warranted. He found a symbol of this struggle to know who Jesus is in a mosaic of Christ in a church in Constantinople. When the Turks invaded the city, they plastered over the picture of Christ on the wall so it could not be seen. But centuries later the plaster has cracked and one can see features of the face of Jesus Christ showing through the broken plaster. Maybe, maybe these various images that people have given of Jesus Christ have some dimension of truth about him in each. Each separate image might contain some fragment of the reality of Jesus to which people have responded.— William Powell Tuck

REGRETS.   Happy, however, is that man who, when he weeps for his departed, has not to reproach himself with unkindnesses and bitter words. We cannot always understand what makes people weep when we stand with them on the loose earth beside the open grave. In many cases their sorrow is due to pure affection; in some cases, however, there is an additional saltiness in their tears, because of unspoken regret. "I wish that I had not acted so; that I could recall those words; that I had had another opportunity to express the love I really felt but hid; that I had taken more pains to curb myself to be gentle, loving, endearing, and endeared. Oh for one hour of explanation and confession and forgiveness!" Let us see to it that we may never have to drink such bitter ingredients in the cup of our bereavement; and so that we may not, let us not fail to give expression to those nobler feelings which often strive within our breasts but which we too often repress.—F. B. Meyer

WHY WE ARE HERE.   I've always wanted to get up and tell people that I believe I was put on the *Today Show* for a purpose. I think the good Lord placed me there, because there are so many things that shouldn't have worked that did. And nothing that I've ever done in connection with that program—whether to stay on the show or to get around and do the things that I've been able to do, to appear at various functions and affairs and to represent what I believe in around this country—none of those things could have been done without some superhuman power. And that supernatural, superhuman power is the love of Christ that put me there. I am convinced of that, with all my heart and soul.—Willard Scott

SENSE OF ABSENCE.   One thing is for sure: there is no sense of absence where there has been no sense of presence. What makes absence hurt, what makes it ache, is the memory of what used to be there but is no longer. Absence is the arm flung across the bed in the middle of the night, the empty space where a beloved sleeper once lay. Absence is the child's room now empty and hung with silence and dust. Absence is the overgrown lot where the old house once stood, the house in which people laughed and thought their happiness would last forever.

You cannot miss what you have never known, which makes our sense of absence—and especially our sense of God's absence—the very best proof that we knew God once, and that we may know God again. There is a loss in absence, but there is also hope, because what happened once can happen again and only an empty cup can be filled. It is only when we pull that cup out of hiding, when we own up to the emptiness, the absence, the longing inside—it is only then that things can begin to change.—Barbara Brown Taylor, *Gospel Medicine*

SEPARATION FROM GOD.   What happens when there is no God is that men and women do one of two things. Blaise Pascal, a great philosopher and theologian of three centuries ago, once said that when a man is separated from God he either seeks to be God himself—and that's what's happening in a lot of the world—or he seeks the gratification of his senses—and that's exactly what's happening in our society today.—Charles Colson

ACKNOWLEDGMENTS

All of the following are used by permission:

Excerpts from Chevis F. Horne, *Preaching the Great Themes of the Bible* (Nashville: Broadman Press, 1986), pp. 65–75.

Excerpts from C. E. Autrey in *Southwestern Sermons,* ed. by H. C. Brown, Jr. (Nashville: Broadman Press, 1960), pp. 1–6.

Excerpts from Ralph L. Murray, *Plumblines and Fruit Baskets* (Nashville: Broadman Press, 1966), pp. 78–81.

Excerpts from Ralph L. Murray, *Christ and the City* (Nashville: Broadman Press, 1970), pp. 87–95.

Excerpts from Herschel H. Hobbs, *Basic Bible Sermons on John* (Nashville: Broadman Press, 1990), pp. 103–111.

Excerpts from J. Alfred Smith, Sr., *The Overflowing Heart* (Nashville: Broadman Press, 1987), pp. 58–60.

Excerpts from Robert W. Bailey, *Award Winning Sermons,* Vol. 2, ed. by James C. Barry (Nashville: Broadman Press, 1978), pp. 107–111.

Excerpts from W. Le Ray Fowler, *Award Winning Sermons,* Vol. 4, ed. by James C. Barry (Nashville: Broadman Press, 1980), pp. 82–87.

Excerpts from Allen Reed, *Award Winning Sermons,* Vol. 1, ed. by James C. Barry (Nashville: Broadman Press, 1997), pp. 93–100.

Excerpts from Robert J. Hastings, *Award Winning Sermons,* Vol. 3, ed. by James C. Barry (Nashville: Broadman Press, 1979), pp. 49–58.

Excerpts from Eli Landrum Jr., *More Than Symbol* (Nashville: Broadman Press, 1983), pp. 40–43.

Excerpts from Alton H. McEachern, *The Lord's Presence* (Nashville: Broadman Press, 1986), pp. 25–26.

Excerpts from Al Cadenheand Jr., *The Minister's Manual for Funerals* (Nashville: Broadman Press, 1988), pp. 125–129.

INDEX OF CONTRIBUTORS

SERMON TITLE INDEX

Children's stories and sermons are marked as (cs); sermon suggestions as (ss).

436

SCRIPTURAL INDEX

INDEX OF PRAYERS

INDEX OF MATERIALS
USEFUL AS CHILDREN'S STORIES
AND SERMONS NOT INCLUDED IN SECTION X

INDEX OF MATERIALS USEFUL
FOR SMALL GROUPS

TOPICAL INDEX